MW01627330

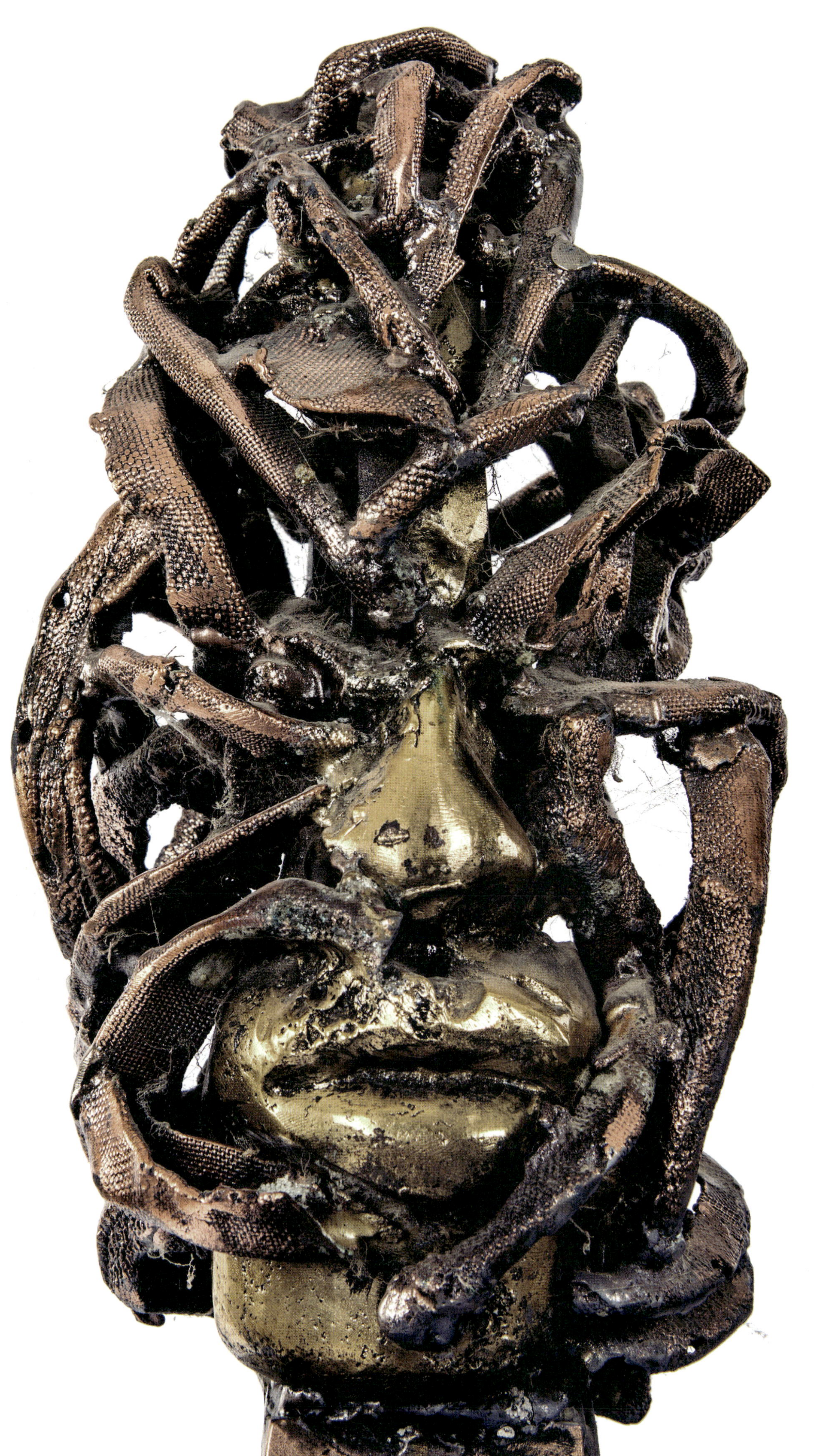

The Conversation, 2016. Detail. Photo by Humayun Memon

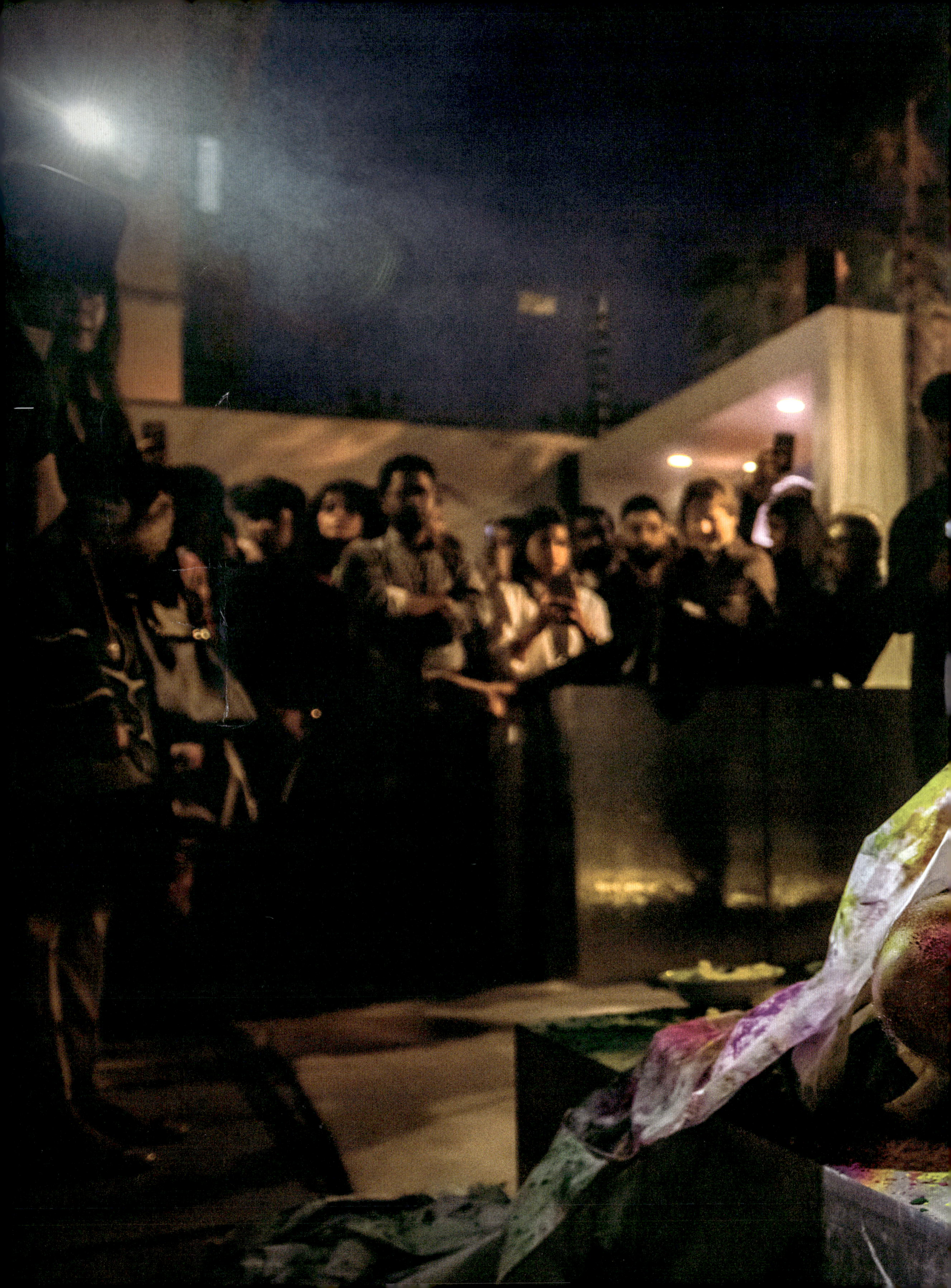

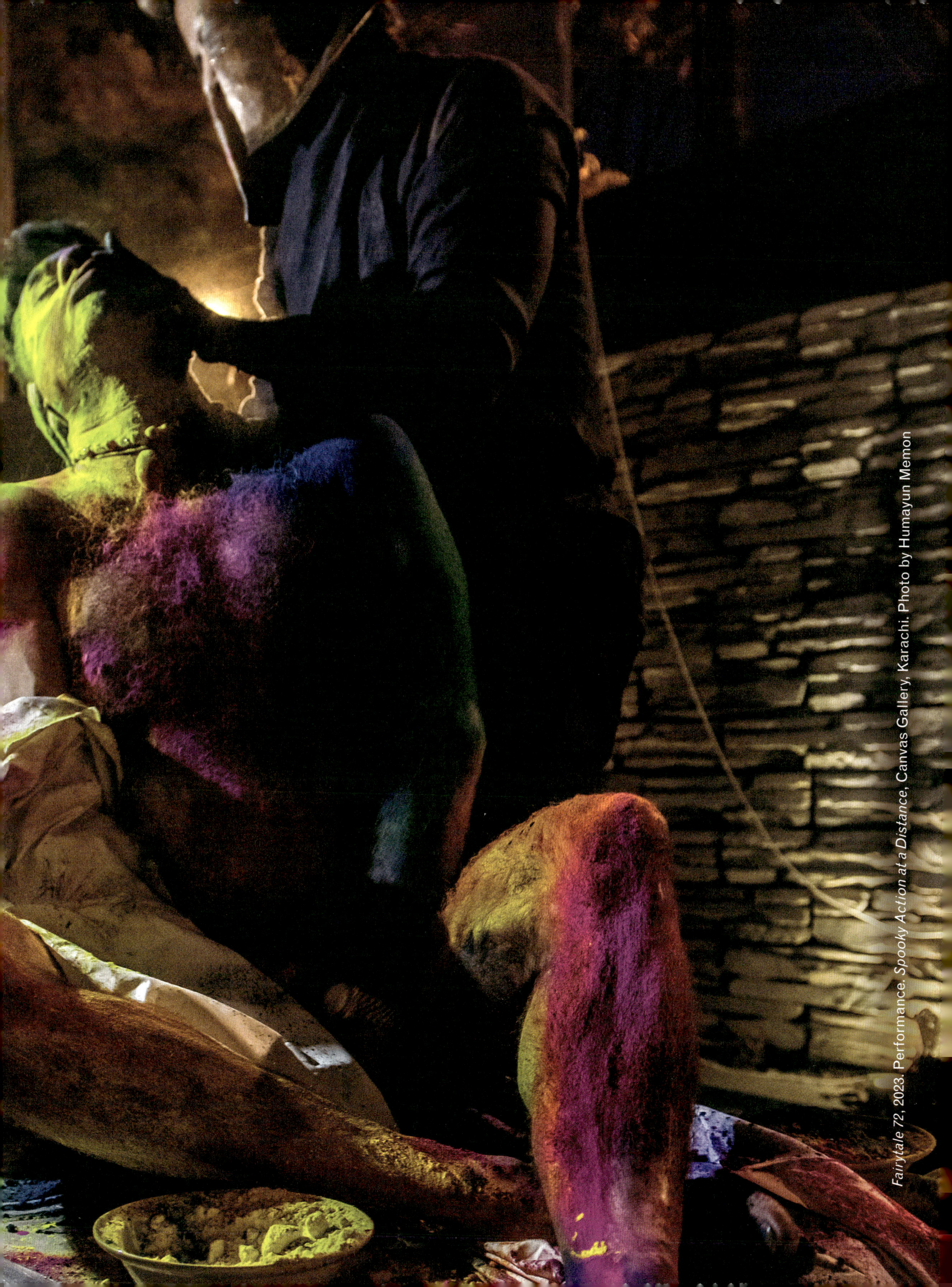

Fairytale 72, 2023. Performance. *Spooky Action at a Distance*, Canvas Gallery, Karachi. Photo by Humayun Memon

AMIN GULGEE
NO MAN'S LAND

SKIRA

Contents

Invitation to New Works of Art

Oleg Grabar

As a longtime historian of the arts of Muslim lands, I tend to feel more at home with works made many centuries ago than with those of my own time. I feel at home with them, because I myself and other historians like me have created that past and have always lived in it and with it. We have identified the forms which characterize every period and every region and we have decided what constitutes that past tradition. Within the rich history of art in Islamic lands, it is calligraphy, geometry, the arabesque, sources of luxurious pleasure, and it avoids a direct confrontation with living beings, human or animal. And we automatically seek, find, and occasionally praise the appearance of these traditional forms in the works of contemporary artists from the Muslim world, because, for reasons which have something to do with old "orientalist" positions, we expect artists from that world to be closely connected to their tradition, while Western artists are praised for their innovative originality.

But things have changed now, as a global awareness of the arts restricts the pressures of local or historical traditions. We must now begin by looking at the works of art themselves without cultural or ethnic prejudice and preconceptions. Thus, works like the recent ones by Amin Gulgee bewilder us by the variety of their expressions, by an apparent freedom in technique and design, by the range of pleasures they offer. In almost automatic and thoughtless fashion, we start by seeking reflections and memories of the past and we find them in seeing letters of the Arabic alphabet with their connotations of piety and faith, even when these letters may not have been meant to be there, or in being impressed by a geometry implying an orderly control of the universe. There are occasional leaves reflecting the nature which surrounds us and then there are fragments of bodily parts, hands or feet, occasionally a face, which are sometimes like Near Eastern arabesques and other times like Romanesque columns or capitals. These subconscious memories or willed reflections have been transformed into powerful and exciting modern forms, but their original features, although not their meanings, were always present.

But Gulgee's most recent work exhibited here has left most of these memories behind or has willfully escaped from them, as it points to three different directions that are partly in playful or thoughtful contradiction with each other.

One direction is the simplification of lines to the point of creating exciting skeletons of possible "things". In some cases, possibly most of them, these lines are themselves bare of any design, but at times they are partly covered with ornament, as they could, in the past, have been covered with writing. A second direction is, on the contrary, to make masses which can be geometrically structured or simply wild mixes of concrete items like hands or leaves. And the third, and possibly most original, direction is the creation of a sculpture which fully expresses a tension inherent to the medium itself. It is a tension between the vertical pull of constructing forms at will that dominate their surroundings by rising upward and the horizontal pull of filling spaces with patterns or representations taken from a wide body of sources – human, animal, vegetal – but without any one source predominating.

These are all formal considerations and observations from which one can deduce, albeit hypothetically, that, like many artists before him, Gulgee is seeking the most striking and the purest ways of making his chosen medium accessible to the viewers. This direction finds a most spectacular example in the stunning assemblage of concentric circles creating something which can be an object of practical use as well as an arbitrary work of art. It is clear that Gulgee is trying to find the limits of a sculptor's art. But these works also possess a human or psychological dimension. As their titles show so vividly, they are a new and original attempt at understanding the universe and man's role in it, or, more specifically, man's control over matter and man's construction of something which may even be more beautiful than matter, than what we see and know directly. This is the great gamble of all art since time immemorial and it is because of that possibility that since Plato moralists and religious leaders have been afraid of the power of art. Gulgee's new work is a step in his development as an artist; he gives pleasure to the senses and excites the mind.

This essay first appeared in the exhibition catalogue *Amin Gulgee: Drawing the Line*, Galeri Petronas, Kuala Lumpur, 2007.

Amin Gulgee's Optimism

Alexi Worth

Even before he "discovered" performance, Amin Gulgee was a performer. In college he was already famous as the most outrageous talker in any dining hall. I remember new acquaintances looking faintly shell-shocked as they adjusted to the spectacle of his loud, laughing, saliva-showering presence. Smiling nervously, we asked ourselves, "Is he crazy?" In an appreciative sense, he was. Disinhibited, impulsive, at war with decorum, young Amin was already a typhoon of endearments and insults, ideas and provocations. Maybe he waited till he was in his thirties because performance seemed too natural, too obvious a way of mining his own outrageousness.

For American audiences, who have not had opportunities to see the last twenty years of his performance work, documentation provides only a teasing glimpse. And yet, the photographs and videos do provide a sense of Gulgee's range, ambition, and something of the spirit of his work: an omnivorous, freewheeling optimism that calls to mind Robert Rauschenberg. Working literally around the world—in Karachi, Paris, Rome, Kuala Lumpur, New Delhi, Dubai, and London—Gulgee might be a South Asian reincarnation of ROCI, the Rauschenberg Overseas Cultural Initiative. Everywhere he goes, Gulgee absorbs and repurposes materials, ideas, stories, and other artists. Increasingly, he is a curator/impresario, whose willfully inclusive and heterogeneous productions grow out of a cosmopolitan vision so sweet and pure that it might, like Rauschenberg's, almost be mistaken for naïveté. "In this seeming chaos, I hoped," he wrote for *One Night Stand*, his 2019 opus composed of 32 concurrent 70-minute performances, "to claim a temporary territory where the dreams and visions of people across the globe could unite—if only for a one-night stand."

That final phrase is pure Gulgee: an acknowledgement of the unlikeliness of multicultural utopias, and at the same time, a bawdy, affectionate invitation to smile, to join in. Optimism, cosmopolitanism, bawdiness: within the larger contemporary art world, these are hardly surprising attributes, but for a Pakistani artist living in Pakistan, they are not reflexively available in quite the same way. Optimism, for example, has a different valence when you have walked into your parents' home, as Gulgee did, to find their bound, murdered bodies. Optimism has a different valence when you consider the gap between today's Pakistan and its not-so-distant past, about which Gulgee, along with John McCarry and Niilofur Farrukh, edited a fascinating book, *Pakistan's Radioactive Decade: An Informal Cultural History of the 1970s*. The point is that Gulgee's projects embody a complicated lightness of spirit that is itself an achievement, and that grows out of conditions more challenging than anything in recent US history, however dismal.

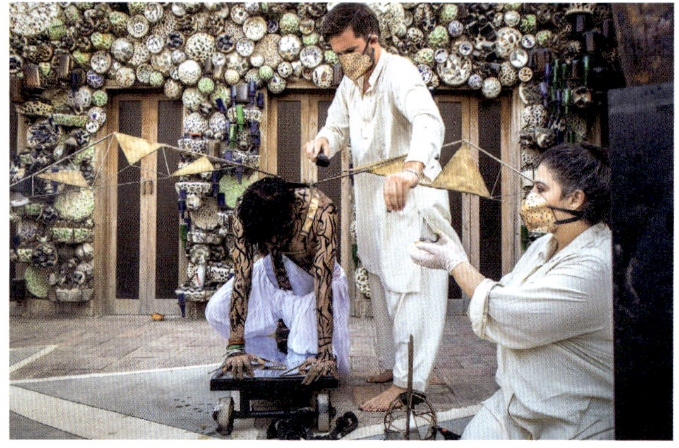

Fig. 1. *Healing II*, 2020. Performance. Amin Gulgee Gallery, Karachi. Photo by Humayun Memon

But perhaps "lightness of spirit" is too casual a phrase. In a performance called *Love Letters*, Gulgee asked audience members to write a declaration of love "to a person, place, or thing, past present or future." Eventually, at the end of the show, these declarations were neither recited nor sealed away, but destroyed, unread. Commentators have praised the piece as a celebration of privacy, but it seems to me typical of Gulgee's work in being equally lyrical and somber, shadowed by the suggestions of futility and muteness. Still more somber are performances like *Healing II*, from 2020, in which Gulgee offered an outdoor meditation on COVID-19 that expanded to become a ritualistic memento mori, accompanied at one point by a reading from Albert Camus' *The Plague*. The central performer was Gulgee himself, adorned in armor and calligraphy, looking like a doomed earth-bound Icarus.

It is clear enough, from stills and videos, that the drama of *Healing II* (fig. 1) came from more than just the performances. Equally important was the set, a soaring openwork structure in glass, copper, terra-cotta and bronze that served as a reminder of Gulgee's other artistic identity, as a sculptor. "Other identity," in fact, is something of an understatement. While performance and curation have taken up an increasing fraction of his energy, sculpture may still be the mainstay, the center of Gulgee's art. So it makes sense, in introducing Gulgee to American audiences, to say something about his sculptural practice as a whole.

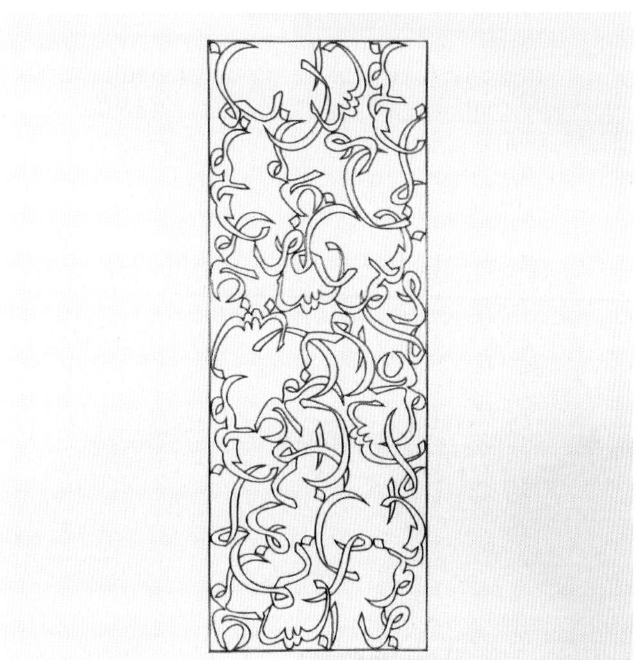

Fig. 2. *Salt Screen III*, 2018. Copper and steel. 244 × 89 × 11 cm. Photo by Humayun Memon

The most obvious thing about Gulgee's sculptures—generally composed of Arabic letterforms handmade by the artist in copper and steel—is that they are objects of extreme elegance. In the "Perforated Scroll" series for example, the design of each tall panel has a dazzling, restrained irregularity, its scimitar curves bunching and releasing, tapering and swelling, with the hypnotizing intricacy of musical polyrhythms. The slender copper piping of the *Salt Screens* (fig. 2) is even more seductive, each one a maze of intersecting, twisting, doubled patterns.

But how, beyond elegance, do we understand them? The familiarity of Quranic calligraphy is akin to the familiarity of the Roman alphabet. And yet, it's hard to imagine Gulgee's sculptures as directly analogous to, for instance, Jasper Johns' various "Letter" paintings and sculptures—as a form of ironic abstraction. Should we "read" them in light of their textual meaning, primarily as religious art? Should we understand them more generally, as affirmations of cultural identity? At the very least, we recognize their striking double-sidedness. They belong to a centuries-old tradition of Islamic screen-forms, while also engaging with the planar modernism of artists like David Smith and Jasper Johns.

What is disconcerting is that Gulgee's sculptures do both these things so equally, so fully. In the West, we are used to thinking of religious and avant-garde traditions as antithetical, but Gulgee's occupy a strange sweet spot where these frictions vanish. The pioneer of this sweet spot was Gulgee's father, Ismail Gulgee, long celebrated in Pakistan (and somewhat confusingly remembered there by the single name "Gulgee"). With their color-braided painterly impasto, the elder Gulgee's paintings adapted the language of American Action painting to Muslim textual motifs. I wonder, however, if they ever quite lost the sense of ingenuity, of being a marvelous, willful hybrid. By contrast, one of Amin's basic formats—the screen—belongs naturally to both traditions. The younger Gulgee makes being Muslim and being Modern seem not just reconcileable, but synonymous.

That in itself is a provocation, isn't it? Or at least a reminder of Gulgee's optimism, his belief that the "Clash of Civilizations" was always nonsense. In their own decorous way, Gulgee's screens are another kind of *One Night Stand*, a silent proposition. The artist trusts his audience, Muslim and non-Muslim, sectarian and cosmopolitan, to be seduced by beauty.

Through These Years, A Thousand Adventures

Zarmeene Shah

I first met Amin Gulgee in the early 2000s, when he was one of the jurors on the panel judging my BFA painting thesis. Even then, I remember being struck by his incredible energy, and the way in which he talked about my paintings as objects, completely turning all the popular intellectual concerns that had occupied me as a young art school student on their head, and providing me with a different lens through which to view my own work and practice. In those years, I would come to meet him again a couple of times, in social settings, but it was not until 2013, when I went over to see him, to speak about his then-recent solo exhibition in New Delhi, that our connection was truly formed, and the relationship that we have today would begin to manifest. Today, I know Amin closely, in varied capacities: as an artist whose work I have curated and written about several times; as a curator with whom I have worked closely and often; as one of the pioneering artists and curators engaged with performance art in Pakistan; as the creator of some of the most exquisite and unique pieces of jewelry I have seen produced in the country; and of course, as a dearly beloved friend.

As a friend, Amin is perhaps one of the most generous individuals that I have ever known—both with his love, and with the time he takes out to make sure that love is felt in the routine functions of one's life. Often, this translates into small but ever-meaningful gestures, one of my favorites of which is the fact that he regularly gives me books. Sometimes, these are books he picks up especially for me, but more importantly, and more often, these are books that he himself has just read, and which he thinks I should too. Amin is a voracious reader, and I find the word "devour" to be fitting of the way in which he encounters, and moves through each book he picks up. This means that by the time the book reaches me, it is marked by Amin's encounter with it—pages are turned over, marked, covers are bent, spines are creased, and water marks sometimes flow through the text. The book is changed into an object with a story and a journey, one that continues as it changes hands, and for a sculptor, what could be more fitting?

Reading, in essence, then becomes central to many of the ways in which I have come to see Amin's practice, and to be involved in it. Unsurprisingly, in that first real conversation that we had in 2013, talking about his work as a sculptor and the exhibition titled *Through the Looking Glass*, we came to speak about Lewis Carroll, and about one of my favorite essays by Gilles Deleuze on his seminal texts on the adventures of Alice. We talked for some time about the amazing and complex metaphor that Carroll had woven into the story of Alice in Wonderland, through the bizarre and seemingly nonsensical events that take place once Alice has moved through the surface of the looking glass—or down the rabbit hole.

I remember telling Amin excitedly about Deleuze's essay in which he speaks of Alice's conquering of surfaces: how, as she moves through the looking glass, she comes to create and pass in between other surfaces, sites that do not occupy a real world but are worlds that are real nonetheless. In the mirror, an event occurs, one that is not an act of mere imitation, but of reflection and alteration. It represents, but it draws the thing that it represents into its own space, a space in which nothing is as it seems. Things are turned upside down, inside out; characters stand on their heads and she is never quite "right"—too big, too small, not "like herself", Alice who is not quite Alice.[1]

In turn, and with equal enthusiasm, Amin would liken this to the experience of going into his own workshop; a space of madness and order, where things are never quite as they seem to be and one never knows how one will eventually navigate through its space: "an endless journey where questions have no answers but only lead to more questions."[2] This is the place where acts of creation occur and reality is challenged, configured and reconfigured again and again in a consistently evolving practice that submerges itself, through a continuous exploration of persisting concerns, in an act of difference and repetition through which new events are allowed to transpire and alternate spaces come to exist. In this process the artist himself is formed and re-formed time and time again, his face made whole, broken, reassembled, turned on its axis, flipped on its head (*Me in the Matrix I & II*).[3]

Faces, hands, leaves, calligraphic texts, geometric forms that fuse with the organic in an unrelenting exploration of form and space—these are all recurring motifs in Amin's work, the repetition of which has often solicited one of the most common (and superficial) criticisms of his work. While Western philosophy ceaselessly defends this position, from Nietzsche's concept of infinite return to Deleuze's difference and repetition, and Derrida's *différance*, it would be perhaps more apt to turn towards a philosophy closer to home, that of the spirituality inherent in the repetition of Islamic Art. Where complex geometric patterns come together to create a seemingly unending repetition that alludes to the infinite nature of Allah, they also indicate the importance of the small, singular element, through the repetition of which one is able to aspire towards an infinite whole.

The Islamic tradition is in fact the one from which Amin's practice has consistently drawn, whether in the iconic calligraphic works, or in the exploration of the *Chahar Bagh*, the Persian style of Islamic gardens that takes the form of a four-garden layout centrally intersected by axial pathways and stands as a powerful metaphor for man's need to organize and impose order/control onto nature. In the Mughal tradition, this layout is also seen as symbolic of the Garden of Eden, the exploration of which one saw clearly in a later collaborative, dance-based performance work titled *Where's the Apple, Joshinder?*, telling the stories of five individuals, including Amin himself. A different iteration of this would also be present in *Through the Looking Glass*, in the form of the *Garden Triptych* (2015) (fig. 1), composed of three free-standing panels, and alluding to Bosch's iconic 15th century painting, *The Garden of Earthly Delights*, an exquisite triptych of paintings most often interpreted as Paradise, earthly sin and Hell.

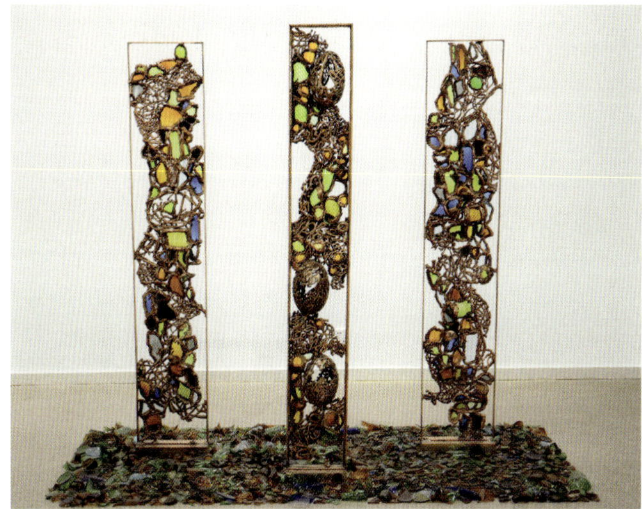

Fig. 1. *Garden Triptych: Fecund Landscape*, 2015. Copper and glass. 188 × 165 × 25.4 cm. Photo by Humayun Memon

In Amin's work, of course the most recognizable Islamic motif arises out of the calligraphic works, which unendingly seek to construct, deconstruct and construct again anew verses from the Quran, fashioning them into tall, delicately balanced forms, or as in an exploration which was on view at his exhibition (*7*, 2018, Rome), here taking the form of tall vertically configured screens that Gulgee refers to as "scrolls", conducting simultaneously a play of light and shadow, form and space, visible and invisible, at other times as zoomorphic calligraphic letters that seem to twist and turn, to spin in the air, like dancers that come to precariously balance themselves on the delicate points of evidently fragile, almost spindly legs.[4] It was also here, in the process of writing about *7* that I would discover a key into Amin's work: that of a verse recurring continuously as a motif, through the years, and perhaps also our deepest and most powerful turn again towards the act of reading:

Iqra wa rab bukal akram
Al lazee 'allama bil qalam
'Al lamal insaana ma lam y'alam

Read!
And your Lord is the Most Generous
Who has taught by the pen
Taught man that which he knew not.

[Quran, 96: 3-5]

The 96th chapter of the Holy Quran, the Surah al Alaq ("The Clot", also referred to as "al Iqra") is widely believed to be the first revelation sent to the Prophet Muhammad (PBUH) in the cave at Hira, in the city of Mecca. Composed of 19 verses, it is said that verses one to five were the very first to be revealed to Muhammad on that day, with the rest to follow later. The first two verses are translated as follows: "Read! In the Name of your Lord who created / Created man from a clinging substance (clot)" [Quran, 96:1-2].

This initial encounter between the angel Jibrael (Gabriel) and the Prophet Muhammad is one marked by the significance of creation, of discovery, and of enlightenment, both in its content and in its account, where the Angel appears to Muhammad and repeatedly asks him to read, to which he replies that he does not know how. Grasping him forcefully, the Angel repeats his command, with the same response, whereupon, on the third instant, seizing him up once again, Jibrael delivers to Muhammad the first revelation of the Quran: "Read! In the Name of your Lord who created."[5] In the significance given to knowledge, to learning, to the infinite possibility within the unknown, this first gift is momentous and profound. So much that Muhammad is overwhelmed by it, his body almost unable to contain it, shaking, as he narrates the story to his wife, Khadija. It is in this, in the fifth verse of al-Alaq, where we are told that God "taught man that which he did not know," that Amin's calligraphic structures/sculptures are rooted.

In Gulgee's work, this fifth verse recurs continuously as a motif, in the early years perhaps more legible, however progressively deconstructed in the last decade, taken apart, thrown over to chance, and constructed again into assemblages that explore a myriad formal, conceptual, and often metaphysical concerns. In this deconstruction, he enacts a kind of Foucauldian gesture, an act of forgetting, to let go of the knowledge that one has, in order to discover the thing again anew. For Gulgee, the verse is now "personal,"[6] internalized, absorbed, its legibility no longer important. In this becoming, in the process of internalization, a becoming-private, where the verse becomes "spirit" versus subject, deconstructed into seven parts, made unreadable, illegible, *unknown*, Gulgee is perhaps closest to that of which the verse itself speaks: the power and possibility within that which is not known.[7]

Indeed Amin's practice is nothing if not spiritual, inward looking, deconstructive, unendingly breaking open the familiar in order to reveal the new, rethinking, reimagining, reassembling. This is evidenced also by his choice of material, bronze and copper, elemental, almost alchemical in their very essence. And while works such as the "Chapati" series may make easily recognizable political allusions to hunger, poverty and games of power and control, they are also, and perhaps more importantly, testament to a deeper, personal endeavor where the tightly coiled and flattened copper discs become a means of exerting order and control over a chaotic and madly unraveling world. Simultaneously, these golden discs are equally transcendental, moving across cultures and symbologies, evoking images of the moon, of sun-discs and of the golden halos of Early Christian art.[8]

The moon would in fact become an important motif in the layers of the relationship that Amin and I would come to cultivate. In 2015, I curated Amin Gulgee's solo exhibition *Washed Upon the Shore*, presented at the Canvas Gallery in Karachi, and once again marked by the act of reading, one which would find its initial inspiration in a book by Haruki Murakami. In the many conversations that ensued in the months preceding the exhibition, I remember Amin not only handing over to me his copy of the book, marked with his presence, but also fervently explaining to me the complex narratives contained within the layers of Murakami's bizarre and epic romance originally presented as three books and then later contained into two volumes within a singular cult novel.

As *1Q84* begins, the central character Aomame is in a taxi in Tokyo, late for a work assignment (an assassination). At the driver's suggestion, she decides to exit the taxi and take an emergency staircase down the side of the highway to street level, although he warns her of the consequences before she does so. "Please remember, things are not what they seem," he says. "After you do something like that, the everyday look of things might seem to change a little."[9] And change they do, though at first only subtly: in the guns carried by policemen, and more importantly (for our purposes), in the appearance of the two moons, one pale and natural, the other green—like Amin Gulgee's.[10] In the exhibition, Amin's two moons—one fashioned from amber glass held by an intricate copper webbing, the other green—would become the resplendent focus of the show, suspended from the ceiling, facing each other as if in conversation, their seeming weightlessness defying their immense weight (each at over 100 kilograms) (fig. 2).

In Amin's world however (unlike Murakami's), a third element would manifest, a third moon, a darker moon representing a darker side, one apart from the other two, not within their dialogue but instead acting almost as witness to them; its solid metal surface corroded and oxidized, older and impenetrable, a mysterious sentient presence within an otherwise porous and translucent world. The inclusion of this third moon would in fact

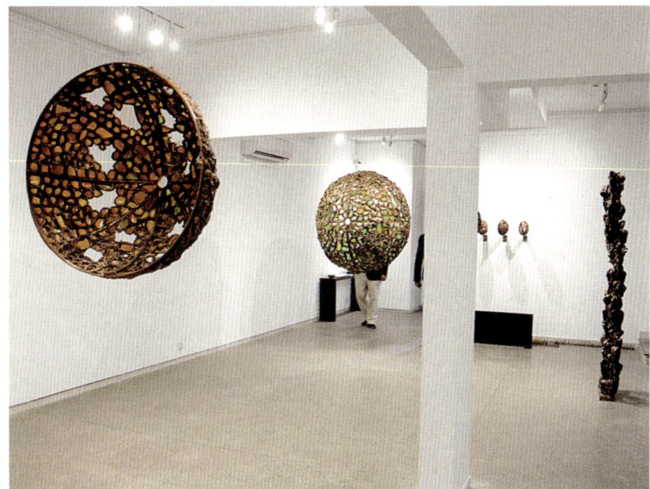

Fig. 2. *Amber Moon* and *Green Moon*, 2015. Installation view. Canvas Gallery, Karachi. Photo by Humayun Memon

give me another insight into Amin Gulgee, the artist, the collaborator, the individual, and this was of his openness, not simply in giving, but also in receiving.

One day, during the time that the work for *Washed Upon the Shore* was being produced, I visited Amin's workshop. After a while of observing the space and his process, as I turned to leave, I spotted the dark moon (fig. 3), installed high up on one of the walls of the workshop, close to the entrance. I remember being struck by it—standing there staring at it for several minutes. In the contrast that it provided to the resplendent glass and copper moons, it was poignant, poetic, powerful, and oh so achingly beautiful. By this time Amin and I had developed a synergy, a mode of understanding each other that required little conversation. I remember pointing to it, and looking at him and saying "Amin..." "Yes!!" he replied, and understood.

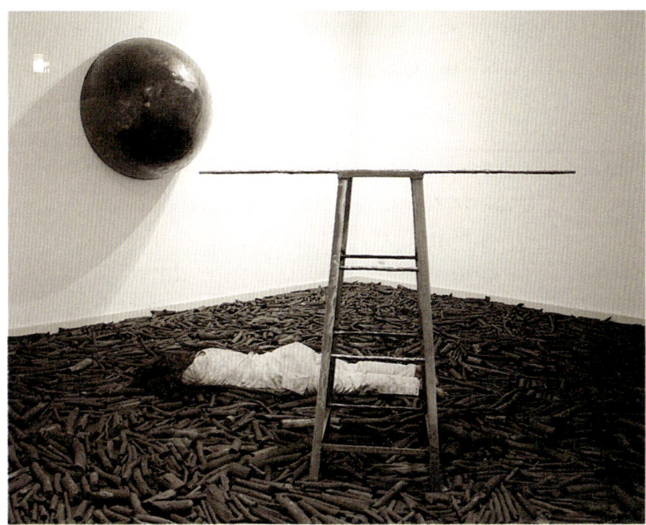

Fig. 3. *Third Moon*, 2015. Installation view. Canvas Gallery, Karachi. Photo by Humayun Memon

This connection arose out of the work that Amin and I did together as co-curators on *Dreamscape* (2014), an exhibition showcasing over 50 contemporary performance and installation-based works. In fact, on that day in 2013, as we spoke about Alice's adventures, about surrealist metaphors, and of Yoko Ono's famous line about collective dreams, Amin invited me to curate a show with him. Later, I would come to recognize this act as one that is continuous in Amin's varied practices, that of a movement between the private and the public, the contained isolation of the studio and the outward reaching nature of collaboration and performance, characteristic of Amin's approach towards his practice, perhaps from the very beginning. This proclivity for reaching outward, for an inclusiveness and generosity of spirit, whether in dealings with people or in the approach to his own practice, has also led to Amin being one of few artists who have successfully navigated between the art and fashion worlds, acting almost as a bridge between the two.

In 2001, arising out of the "Egg Series", a 30-minute fashion and performance show titled *Sola Singhar* was hosted at the Sheraton Hotel, exploring ideas of conception, birth and creation, viewing pregnancy almost as a magical, alchemical practice. The year before, *Alchemy* followed much the same pattern of operating as a site where performance and fashion converge. Amin speaks of this as a time in Pakistan's art and fashion history that was much more fluid, a time when the boundaries between disciplines were less defined and the taking of risks much easier, perhaps subject to a lesser critique and scrutiny, allowing for freer collaborations across the board and the possibility of new and exciting modes of practice. During these years, Amin's jewelry pieces, crafted of pure copper and plated with 24-carat gold, often including the use of precious or semi-precious stones, each one of a kind, became internationally known and appreciated, his clients including the iconic designer Carolina Herrera as well as Mrs. Boutros Boutros Ghali, to name a few.

To Amin, these were simply an extension of his practice, a new mode of exploration within a larger framework, acting almost as preliminary works to larger sculptural pieces: "I do not sketch out my sculptures before making them. I work out my ideas through jewelry." In so doing, and in the fact of his success in this, Amin (perhaps unknowingly) subverts the grounding principles of both fashion and art, and evokes Baudrillard in his commentary on fashion: "Potlatch, religion, indeed the ritual enchantment of expression, like that of costume and animal dances: everything is good for exalting fashion against the

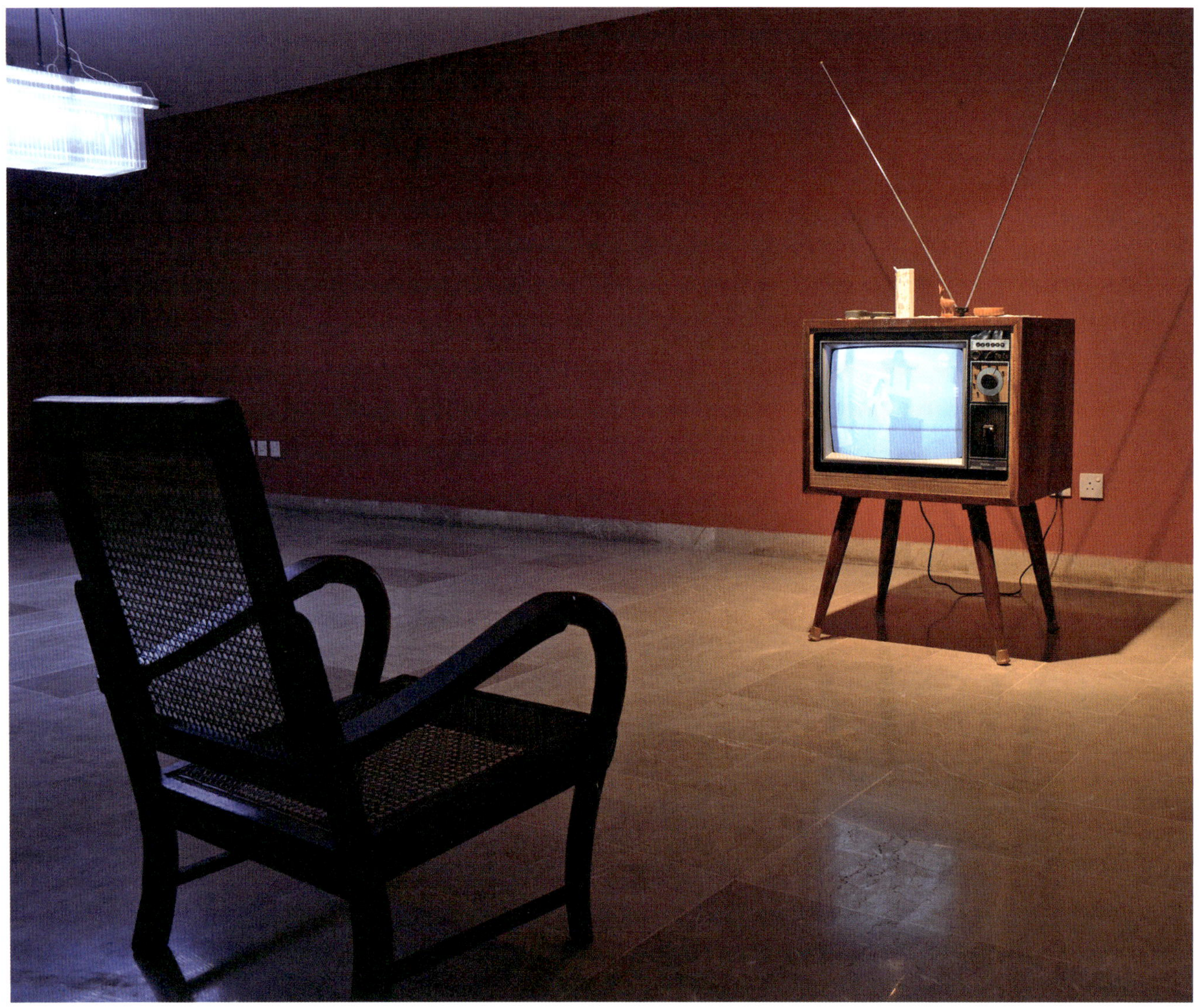

Fig. 4. *Dreamscape*, 2014. Installation view.
Amin Gulgee Gallery, Karachi. Photo by JY Photo

economic, like a transgression into a play-act sociality: [...] We would like to see a functional squandering everywhere so as to bring about symbolic destruction."[11]

Where the connection with fashion is often overlooked in the context of Amin Gulgee's involvement in performance art in recent years, an organic line of growth can be traced back to these shows in the early 2000s, its links visible in later performance works such as *Love Marriage*, part of the exhibition *Band Baja Baraat* hosted by IVS Gallery in 2012, which saw Amin and fellow sculptor Saba Iqbal, their faces an identical Kabuki white, wearing a copper helmet and a body armor/bustier studded with nails respectively, silently breaking eggs into each other's hands, while audience members posed and took photographs with them as would be regular practice at a wedding. Where Amin's own performative work has often addressed issues of gender and identity, his engagement with the practice of performance has been at a much larger level. Earlier in 2013, Amin curated and hosted *Riwhyti: One Night Stand* at the Amin Gulgee Gallery, where 30 Karachi-based artists simultaneously performed individual works over the two-hour period of the show.[12]

Our very first collaboration as co-curators, and arising partly out of our mutual interest in the conceptual framework of Carroll's story while simultaneously taking inspiration from the quote by Yoko Ono ("A dream you dream alone is only a dream. A dream you dream together is reality."), *Dreamscape* (fig. 4) indiscriminatingly brought together about 50 visual, performance and theater artists, fashion designers and musicians in a museum-sized exhibition of installation and performance art. Fostered through regular individual and group meetings with the core group of about 35 Karachi-based artists over a seven-month period, with the curatorial agenda finding its basis in enacting a kind of "collective dream," artists were encouraged to form visible connections and collaborations alongside the production of individual works created specifically for this show. More than a dozen artists from out of station were also invited to send a "dreamscape object" that represented their individual interpretation of our collective reverie.

Where Amin and I were often viewed as unlikely collaborators, we found our (sometimes contradictory) energies to work in perfect sync, finding our grounding in our unequivocally inclusive stance as practitioners within the field of art—an expansionist view that did not discriminate between the creative potential of individuals.[13] And while Amin and I would go on to curate a number of shows together, perhaps nowhere was this more apparent than in the inaugural Karachi Biennale in 2017, which was led by Amin as its Chief Curator, and to which I was invited to serve as Curator at Large.

The first Karachi Biennale (KB17) held its opening ceremony on the evening of November 21, 2017 at the sprawling premises of the 152-year-old Narayan Jagannath Vaidya (NJV) High School—the central site of the biennale—and opened to the public the following day at 12 locations across the city, with works by over 180 local and international artists responding to the curatorial premise: "Witness." This large roster of participating artists represented a diverse mix of practitioners across fields of art, architecture, dance, theater, music and film.

In the spatial configuration of the city, the sites could be divided into four clusters, with the one forming in and around Saddar, the old city center and business district of Karachi, representing what could be viewed as the central node.[14] The diversity of the sites then, the historical significance of many of these to the city, and their spread across Karachi became a critical point of departure in our many considerations of Karachi Biennale 2017. For those wanting to see all 12 sites, the two weeks would come to signify a kind of expedition around the city that would likely not be routinely attempted, particularly considering the chaotic frenzy of traffic across the main arteries of the city that would need to be traversed to reach a majority of locations.

Eventually, the curatorial framework came to rest on viewing each site as a nucleus, a kind of pivot, in and of itself, each one functioning as a totality, a singular (but smaller) whole that was able to encompass the concerns embedded within the premise of "witness," while maintaining its connection to the larger complex of the biennale. Set against each other, both these complexes (the site and the biennale, and thus the site and the city) form the micro- and macrocosmic lenses through which to perceive the ideas disseminated through the works. In doing so, the sites then became integral to the narrative of the exhibits that they housed; each space, unique in its character, architecture and history (and yet unmitigatedly distinctive also of the city of Karachi), becoming definitive of the ways in which medium, content and message would be perceived and received. This was of course apt, as at its heart KB17 was a deeply localized project, rooted in the city it took place in, the city of Karachi.[15]

Earlier, I talked about how Amin and I have often been viewed as unlikely collaborators, sometimes (I would venture to say) even by ourselves. There is no doubt that our approaches are different, as are our energies, however it is exactly the energy that Amin Gulgee brings to each project that is remarkable, and that first caught my attention all those years ago, in the early 2000s. It is also this energy that has allowed us to push past differences, to engage openly and transparently with each other, and with the hundreds of artists we have worked with, and to see projects through in the manner that we have. While in some ways difference may define our relationship, this may be apt, as our largest project, KB17, also aimed to celebrate and showcase Karachi as a city of differences, where no one voice could ever come to represent the multitudinous views, approaches and dialogues that it holds and fosters.

Years ago, when I first came to deeply investigate, and to write on Amin Gulgee's work, I found that it was a challenging task for someone whose lens had most often been geared towards a kind of specialist critical discourse, that most of contemporary work is easily viewed through. Amin's work, I soon discovered, was able to partake in these discourses but did not confine itself to them; in fact, it moved through these and into much more diverse realms: through ideas of the contemporary, the historical, the Islamic, the political, gender, sexuality, and a kind of esoteric knowledge that was based on the materials, mediums, and spaces that he had been engaging with for a long time.

From then to now, I have found new ways of seeing and understanding, of approaching and navigating, of making links and connections that extend beyond a restrictive, codified lens, and it is perhaps this that has allowed me to see beyond and to understand that at the heart of Amin's practice, beyond all other "external" discourses, lies the fact that his is a practice entrenched in the studio.

This is the core of the work, the artist within his own space of creation, from the chaos of which he is able to derive order.

Those years ago, in the beginning, I was reminded of what Gilles Deleuze says in his book on Francis Bacon, that I had been first struck by while researching for my postgraduate thesis; that we must learn to listen more carefully to artists for it is in what they say that we will find most clearly the concepts disseminated in their work. In listening to Amin Gulgee, I was able to discover new modes of understanding, to see his connection with the varied and rich sources of which he speaks and to realize that the connection exists perhaps simply in the layers—in the complexity that each brings and which forms their common linkage, and yet allows them to remain unrestrained and open.[16]

It is this openness, this sense of curiosity and of wonder that allows Amin Gulgee to be who he is, and to do the things he does. Amin Gulgee is a force of nature, and if you can hold on and move with him at the fervent pace he consistently maintains, he is a man who will lead you on a thousand adventures, through a thousand different lands. It is perhaps apt then, in summing up this text, and perhaps specifically the ways in which I have experienced Amin Gulgee, my longtime collaborator and friend, to return to the act of reading, and to our shared love of the book, and to end with the words most often attributed to Sheherezade in the epic of the Arabian Nights: "A funny thing happened on the way to my potential..."[17]

Notes:

1. Gilles Deleuze, 'Lewis Carroll', *Essays Critical and Clinical* (Verso: London, 1998).
2. Amin Gulgee, in conversation with the author, Karachi, November 2013.
3. Zarmeene Shah, 'Matrix of Possibilities: The Work of Amin Gulgee', *Herald Magazine*, Dawn media group, Pakistan, December 2013.
4. Ibid.
5. Summarized from the account as narrated in the Sahih Bukhari: Muhammad M. Khan (trans.), *The Translation of the Meanings of Summarized Sahih Al-Bukhari: Arabic-English* (Chicago: Kazi Publications Inc, 1995).
6. Amin Gulgee, in conversation with the author, Karachi, January 2017.
7. Zarmeene Shah, Into Seven (x / ÷), catalogue essay accompanying the traveling exhibition *7* presenting new works by Amin Gulgee, Amin Gulgee Gallery, Karachi and Galleria d'Arte Moderna, Rome (April 2018).
8. Shah, 'Matric of Possibilities', 2013.
9. Haruki Murakami, *1Q84*, translated by Jay Rubin (New York: Vintage, 2013, reprint edition).
10. Zarmeene Shah, 'The Glimmer of Copper on the Moon', curatorial essay accompanying the exhibition *Washed Upon the Shore* (Karachi, Canvas Gallery, 2015).
11. Jean Baudrillard (1976), *Symbolic Exchange and Death* (London: Sage, 1993).
12. Zarmeene Shah, 'An Expansionist View: on Amin Gulgee's Practice', *ArtNow* Pakistan, 2015.
13. Ibid.
14. Zarmeene Shah, 'The Inconceivable: On the First Karachi Biennale', *Critical Collective* (online academic journal based in India), November 2017.
15. Zarmeene Shah, 'The City as Witness: Ways of Speaking, Seeing and Being Seen', *KB17*, exhibition catalogue (Karachi: Markings Publishing, 2019).
16. Shah, 'The Glimmer of Copper', 2015.
17. Anonymous, *The Arabian Nights: Tales from a Thousand and One Nights*, translated by Richard Francis Burton (New York: Modern Library Edition, 2004).

Performing the Cosmic Loop

Dominique Malaquais

You are not a country boy. Cities, aggressive, loud, electric, are your bailiwick. Yet, here I am, seated among trees in a garden, hours from the bustle of urban streets, imagining an installation of your chapati sculptures. I see dozens of them and, moving among their copper grace, you, performing.

The idea is not so farfetched...

Allow me to explain.

Many moons ago—we were barely out of our teens—on an Ivy League campus, you were studying economics. Determined not to follow in the footsteps of your illustrious artist father, Gulgee, you were planning a career in banking. Then as now a dyed-in-the-wool romantic, I, on my end, was determined you would study art—or, in any event, its history. Amused, you agreed to accompany me to a class on Baroque architecture, sculpture and painting. Thirty-five years on, we both remember the darkened space where the class was taught, shuttered to keep out the afternoon light, and on the screen, Sant' Andrea della Valle, Gian Lorenzo Bernini, Caravaggio. Most importantly, we remember the gardens: Versailles, the Villa Castellazzo...

You went on to take many other courses on art (I had succeeded: you graduated with a double major in economics and art history) and, for your senior thesis, moving far beyond the European Baroque, you wrote a magnificent paper on 17th century Moghul gardens. Recently, with delight, I reread that paper. In its pages, alight with joy and eyes simultaneously trained on the details of rich and complex politics, you tell a tale of intricate links between nature, the body and the soul, power and claims to divine right.[1]

In the mid 1990s, after several years of research in Central Africa, I defended a Ph.D. thesis on related (if historically and formally radically different) concerns in the chieftaincy of Bandjoun, in the grasslands of West Cameroon[2].

In both your work on Moghul gardens and mine on the chiefly domains of grasslands rulers, performance—bodies moving through space, sitting, standing, dancing, posing ritually and otherwise—plays a critical role. Decades later, we continue to share a fascination for performance as both practice and form. You were known, for many years, principally as a sculptor; you are now, as well, a renowned performance artist. For many years, my principal focus as an art historian was the intersection between architecture and power; now, too, I write, teach and have started to make films about performance as politics. Next September, we will be collaborating, in Paris, on a project linking our shared interest in performance art.

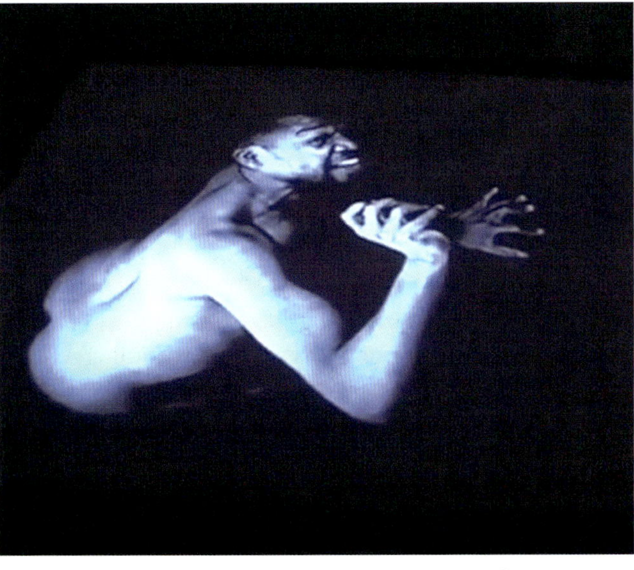

Fig. 1. *The Beautiful Beast*, 2009. Still courtesy Goddy Leye

Undergirding this interest for us both is the influence of a teacher from whom we learned a great deal on that Ivy League campus so long ago: the late Sylvia Ardyn Boone. The focus of her work was the Sande women's initiation association in Mende communities of Sierra Leone. There, in the 1970s, she was exposed to a metaphysics of poise, bodily and spiritual alike, of which she spoke and wrote as "the good made visible." Of particular interest to her were notions of healing through beauty.[3]

As you were writing about Moghul gardens, under Sylvia Boone's guidance, after a summer spent studying in Northern Côte d'Ivoire, I was writing about the art of forging metal—an art that would shortly become a mainstay of your art. If I remember correctly, we finished our papers the very same day. As I reread us, I see our words, both yours and mine, shot through with our professor's deep and abiding conviction that the quest for beauty is one also for healing—for care in the making of a world more just.

At the same time, fascinated by the Baroque, you and I were intimately aware of connections between beauty and violence. This too we have carried with us. Your performances, my publications on performance, the exhibitions and events around performative practice we have curated, each on our own, together and with others, engage all with a double-edged aesthetics of beauty as healing and violence.

By violence, here, I do not mean physical confrontation so much as confrontation with a world radically unjust and thus in need of radical healing. Around this very idea, in the larger context of a project titled *Imag(IN)ing Cities*,[4] ten years ago in your Karachi gallery, we staged an installation of *The Beautiful Beast*, a 2009 work by the late Cameroonian artist Goddy Leye (fig. 1). Goddy had passed away a day earlier. In his piece, a filmed performance projected from the ceiling onto a bed of sesame seeds, we found both solace—healing for a death come decades too soon—and the means to cry out in anger (Goddy had succumbed to a simple illness, which basic medical care, denied to millions the world over by a vastly inequitable world order, could have easily cured).

In 2020, as COVID-19 was carving swaths of death planetwide, you staged *Healing II*, in echo of *The Healing*, an earlier performance work in honor of your parents, lost to a most violent death. Confined a continent away, I followed at a distance. Of *Healing II*, you write as follows:

> There is a tenuous zone of belief one enters when doing a performance. It is a submission to the energy of the moment. A metamorphosis occurs and there is a oneness with the objects your wear; there is no separation and they become a part of your body. *Healing II* was my very personal ritual with all the participants connecting within a cosmic spider's web.[5]

Though—you know this well—I am not particularly spiritually inclined, the image of a cosmic spider's web resonates strongly with me. On my living room mantle is one of your early works, *Pain* (fig. 2), a self-portrait in bronze. It has been with me since you first showed it to me in Washington, D.C. It is a piece both terrifying and powerfully centering. As you have portrayed yourself, you appear to be screaming; there is sheer terror on your face. And yet, in this baring of what I read as an expression of inner turmoil, there is simultaneously immense strength. You claim your fear. On many an occasion, I have found myself going back to this claim, to this admission of pain, and making it mine, finding in it strength—spiritual strength, I suppose—for my own journeys.

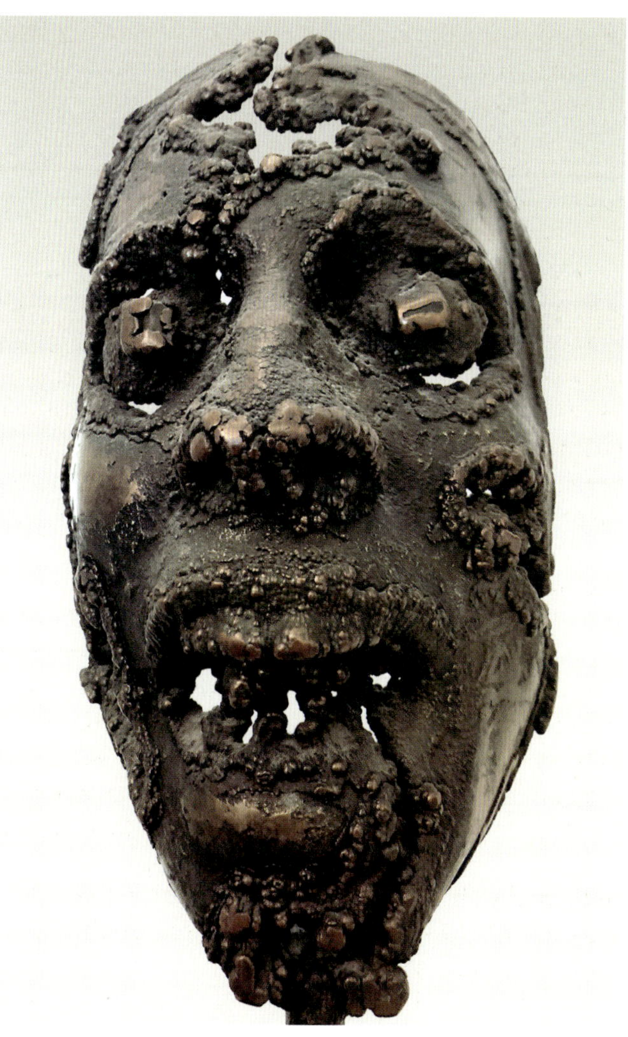

Fig. 2. *Pain*, 1991. Copper, bronze and rock crystals. 33 × 15 × 10 cm. Photo by Dominique Malaquais

This very same piece became an integral part of a performance work you staged two years ago in Paris, the city where I make my home these days. To me, this felt very much like a cosmic time warp. Three decades on, through a practice you and I both have come to embrace as fundamental to the way we see the world, the young man you were in the 1980s was warp-speeding into the middle age we now share. As I handed over to you the self-portrait you had handed over to me thirty-three years earlier, we were kids in that dark classroom again, lost in the delight of Baroque gardens. At that moment, performance—your moves, my words—felt like the most powerful medium of them all. Like magic, really.

Which brings me back to the garden in which I began writing these words. And to the hope that, city boy though you are, you will meet me there. That we may speak of chapatis, performance and cosmic loops.

Notes:

1. Amin Gulgee, "A Walk through Shalimar: A Char-Bagh Garden of 17th Century Mughal India Seen as a Manifestation of Imperial Divine Right", unpublished Bachelor's thesis (New Haven: Yale University, 1986).
2. Dominique Malaquais, "Architecture, Power and Resistance in the Bamileke Highlands of West Cameroon", Ph.D. thesis (New York City: Columbia University, 1997). Published as *Architecture, pouvoir et dissidence au Cameroun* (Paris: Karthala, 2002).
3. Sylvia Ardyn Boone, *Radiance from the Waters: Ideals of Feminine Beauty in Mende Art* (New Haven and London: Yale University Press, 1986).
4. https://www.gulgeeamin.com/portfolio/imagining-cities-digital-guide-catalogue/.
5. Amin Gulgee, "A Performative Life", in John McCarry (ed.), *Healing II*, exhibition catalogue, (Karachi: Amin Gulgee Gallery, 2020), 14.

Collaborative Praxis: The Life and Art of Amin Gulgee in the Time of Coronavirus

Atteqa Ali

Like a potential novel waiting to be written, Amin Gulgee's experiences during the coronavirus pandemic chronicle an extended moment of time that shifted all our fundamental actions and thoughts. His trials and tribulations mirrored the unpredictability of life for us as a global community undergoing a radically new mode of existence. It may have seemed too early to respond to the condition; however, there is validity and significance in commenting on a dark age in real time. This is, in fact, what one of his collaborators Sara Vaqar Paganwala emphasized during a webinar on the project *If These Walls Could Talk*. Apparently, it was on Gulgee's insistence that the initiatives should be documented and archived immediately, thereby indicating the urgency for the artist and curator of understanding conditions as they occur.

The year 2020 provoked Gulgee into action to produce events that offered insights into what the spread of coronavirus meant, as well as to improvise and initiate undertakings that the contagion directly impacted. Our systematic accounting of this terrible year in due time will certainly reveal the profound changes that have now become commonplace. Gulgee was knee-deep in these transformed circumstances while they were happening, and his archiving of the period was evolving as the situation evolved, reflective of the moment within the moment. In the past, he has utilized the medium of performance art in his practice, and parallels could be drawn between his approach to events in 2020 and typical features of performance art, including how it is often enacted and documented within a moment in order to make sense of the age or point out to others its conditions. It can be argued that all art has that potential; however, performance art has a particular zeitgeist air to it because it often only occurs within a certain timeframe and usually has an immediacy to an audience.

Performance art's typical encroachment of the space of the viewer envelops bystanders to become part of the narrative, the problem, and the solution. It reaches out beyond the conventional scope of art to touch the viewer. It challenges the sacred divide of life and art, and what art can constitute. Some may argue that art cannot be everything because then art is nothing. However, respected artists in history have attempted to achieve "nothing" through producing art. Eva Hesse and Parviz Tanavoli come to mind but many other practitioners struggled to achieve a nothingness, recalling the actions of the devout to strip themselves of the objective, materialistic world. Performance art moves away from thingness to a realm beyond. Perhaps it is a spiritual zone that is detached from a world full of objects.

The history of performance art has a rich connection to ritualistic practices and otherworldly matters. Think of the work of Ana Mendieta who connected with the earth in an ephemeral way, or Joseph Beuys and the myth of the shaman that he espoused in art and life. The spiritual dimension was perhaps needed in 2020, a year of death and pain. Gulgee felt the need for healing—so much so that he revived an old work of his to create an updated version. *Healing II* has ritualistic and religious elements that plead for a higher realm of existence during the days when life on Earth seemed tragic and doomed. Even though the performance art piece did not have an audience, it was shared almost immediately to express to others the spirit of the age.

Despite the darkness and uncertainty of the times, as expressed in the performance, the artist could not help but be hopeful and optimistic, as exuded in the accompanying webinars organized alongside different events that took place during the pandemic. This is indeed how he experiences life. Perhaps it is because he is often surrounded by others, be it friends or collaborators. This need and desire to be and work with others is also a key feature of a multidimensional approach to making art that is sometimes labeled collaborative art praxis. A relatively recent mode of practice, collaborative art has become significant in global contemporary art since the 1990s. For some, it is the defining feature of art today. Collaborative art praxis is a discursive approach in which artists forge collaborations with individuals and groups to make art. It is often an act that is more experiential than object based. There are some obvious parallels to be drawn between collaborative praxis that is often socially engaged and performance art. The history of performance art, notably happenings, has certainly prompted the rise of social practice art, another term used to describe art that engages varied communities in the production and presentation of art. This is dialogical art through which artists connect with the world around them through forging relationships.

Amin Gulgee's life and art reflect similar ideals as collaborative art praxis. This is true not only in his works of performance art, but also, and even more so in his curatorial endeavors. In fact, collaborative art seems to blur the divide between art and curating. Artists often take on the role of a curator as they produce a collaborative art project, typically manifesting in several aspects ranging from events and meetings to temporary displays of art, food, and a whole host of other tangible and nontangible elements. Gulgee's curatorial endeavors could be considered

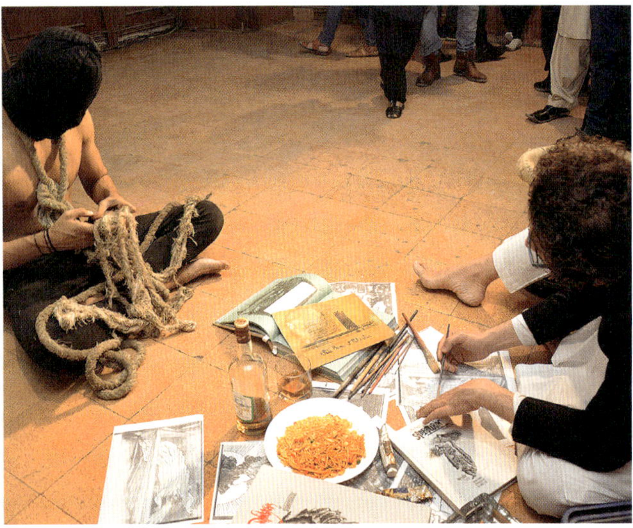

Fig. 1. *LAL JADOO/RED MAGIC*, 2020. Karachi House, Karachi. Photo by JY Photo

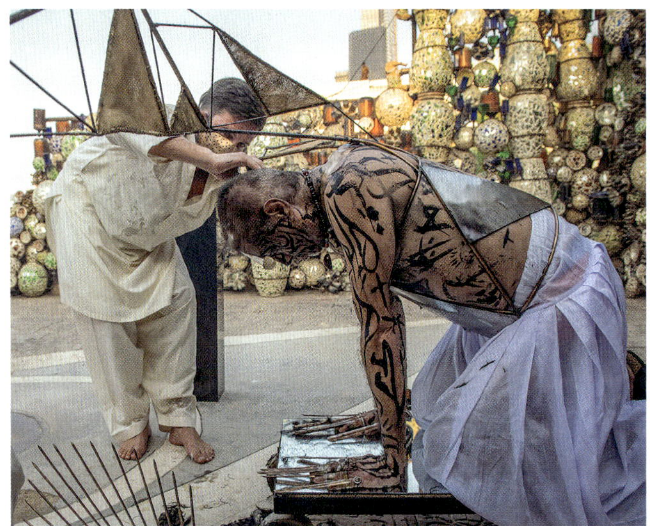

Fig. 2. *Healing II*, 2020. Performance. Amin Gulgee Gallery, Karachi. Photo by Humayun Memon

another form of artistic expression, one that enlists others in its execution. To be sure, he involved no less than hundreds of individuals to come together in interventions and happenings organized during a most dangerous year when we were forced to separate.

Initiating *The Corona Chronicles* with *LAL JADOO/RED MAGIC* (fig. 1), Gulgee put on his "curatorial" hat to produce an event that he may have organized in any given time, and, at first, it was like any other year. Of course, when it was to be staged, the production could not continue as planned. Instead of performances enacted in front of a live audience, they were broadcast on Facebook during a fixed period. The online intervention was a direct response to the official lockdown imposed on the city of Karachi and beyond that was announced just hours before the event was to take place. Rather than cancel the extensive undertaking, Gulgee and his co-curator carried forth with the major cyber-display of performance. Later labeling it a happening, the scheduled online presentation and ongoing presence on the social media site allowed for a much larger audience than would have ever been possible if it was only held as an in-person event. As it was, the large-scale production involved more than sixty people, both artists and curators.

Gulgee's collaborative praxis continued next with *The Trojan Donkey* that increased the number of collaborators by thirty percent. The second chronicle of the no-good year expanded the selection of performance art to an international scope, whereas *LAL JADOO/RED MAGIC* was limited to Pakistani practitioners. Involving so many people to come together is no small challenge at any time, but during a pandemic, it was decidedly problematic. Of course, the union of multiple bodies could only be possible virtually. And so, another online happening took place to bring the physical across the walls that have divided us over the past year and more. Rather than corporeal forms that could be touched, cyber-bodies performed for virtual audiences. The topic was the pandemic.

With curatorial platforms it may be expected to include numerous participants, yet even Gulgee's performance art practice compels the support and involvement of several individuals to enact it. In July 2020, a handful of collaborators joined the artist to perform *Healing II* (fig. 2), one that would be shared with others only through a video format. As mentioned above, the work was the second time in which Gulgee addressed the need to nurse wounds. The first *Healing* happened after the tragic murder of his parents. *Healing II* reflected the new tragedy of so many deaths around not just him, but all of us. As such, it provided a tool for a global community with which to experience and make sense of an incomprehensible destruction.

Our collective situation across the world has united us, but it has divided us as well when we were forced into safety behind closed doors away from others. This dynamic was explored in the final undertaking of *The Corona Chronicles*. *If These Walls Could Talk* (fig. 3) was screened at the Village Restaurant in the heart of Karachi. It was a drive-in cinema projecting performance art pieces in silence while the audience sat in their cars (i.e., their safe bubbles) and enjoyed a visual feast, together but apart.

For collaborative art praxis, it has been a difficult year to carry forth with the typical modes of engagement and coming together that practitioners associated with this type of work desire. As we have adjusted to the situation, perhaps the most significant outcome is the realization that we do need each other on some level. Connecting with people and sharing ideas and concerns, having dialogues, and seeing faces virtually have sustained us for many months. We will soon be able to meet again in person; however, the availability of online platforms and our increased awareness of them will mean that we will not need to be in the same room physically to collaborate. In the expansive possibilities, new modes of cooperation will arise. Amin Gulgee has already taken substantial steps to ensure that artists, arts professionals, and audiences continue to co-exist and thrive under any circumstances, and via any mode of connection, be it simulated or somatic. His collaborative approach to endeavors grew at a time when it was supposed to shrink and be eliminated. Now a greater potential to collaborate exists in the life and art of Amin Gulgee.

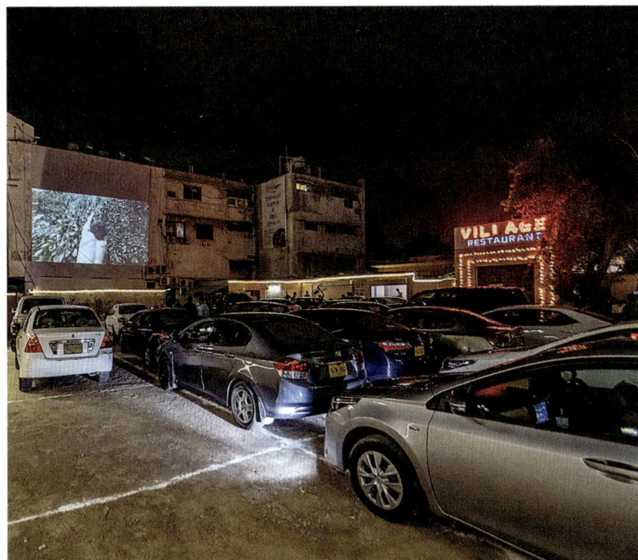

Fig. 3. *If These Walls Could Talk*, 2021. Village Restaurant, Karachi. Photo by Humayun Memon

Amin Gulgee Demands Attention

H.M. Naqvi

Amin Gulgee demands attention: when he enters, his laughter, a throaty staccato, fills the room. When he speaks, he speaks energetically, emphatically, gesticulating with lanky limbs, waving a lit cigarette—he will make his point whether you like it or not. He has been this way since I have known him, for two decades, larger than life.

Amin's sculptures are dramatic, his visual vocabulary distinctive: you can never mistake his work for somebody else's, somebody else's for his. I remember attending his *Char Bagh* exhibition at his gallery in 2003, possibly my first, to behold massive graven geometric copper, bronze and steel structures, feats of technical rigor, feats of stamina, and conceptual depth. In recent history, I remember attending a preview of *7*, also at his gallery, an exhibition that featured large copper frames sometimes hung vertically like scrolls, sometimes standing like doors, perforated by calligraphy in arabesque configurations. When *7* travelled to Rome in 2018, the structures cast shadows in the courtyard of the Galleria d'Arte Moderna that changed through the course of the day, inviting light, interpretation.

The conceptual framework that informs Amin's material oeuvre has been, in a way, consistent throughout his practice: an engagement with Islamic intellectual discourse and aesthetics. The Persianate concept of "charbagh," for instance, is derived from the four gardens of Paradise mentioned in the Quran in Chapter 55, Verse 46 and Verse 62: "And for him, who fears to stand before his Lord, are two gardens." "And beside them are two other gardens." In *7*, Amin draws from the dramatic verse in the Holy Book in which the Angel Jibreel descends from the heavens upon the Prophet, famously ensconced in the darkness at the Ghar-e-Hira. The Angel demands of the Prophet, "Read! In the name of your Lord!" The Prophet initially, understandably responds with bewilderment. But the Angel persists. God is intent on "teaching man that which he does not know." It's such a powerful verse, such a compelling point of departure.

Amin's undergraduate thesis is titled "A Walk through Shalimar: A Char-Bagh Garden of 17th Century Mughal India Seen as a Manifestation of Imperial Divine Right." In it, he walks us through early Mughal history—a fairly straightforward amble through familiar territory, terra cognita. According to the historian John Lehrman, the "Islamic garden" is "The achievement of a universal order that symbolized the unity of God...based on abstract principles." Amin, however, differs with the historiographical orthodoxy: he emphasizes that the vision is mediated by man, indeed that it is fundamentally a manifestation of imperial power. He invites discourse to see the construct of the Char Bagh in a different light.

In a thoughtful review of a show dating back to the 1990s, Zehra Javeri wrote: "Religion is a powerful symbol in Amin's work. In Islam, where there is no symbol for God, geometric calligraphy encapsulates the vision of the divine. It is [in] the precision of the Kufic script that Amin finds inspiration." This is a defensible observation, one that I might share with Zehra. But Amin, God bless him, subverts a mere literal reading. "Yet, as he claims," she continues, "he is not interested in *khatati*. In fact, Amin has altogether liberated calligraphy from its traditional two-dimensional realm. For him words become a pattern that acquire meaning through shape and texture, rather than text."

I must agree. I don't believe Amin is only moved by grand questions such as the relationship of

God and Man, interpretations of history in our present sociocultural context. As a novelist, I suspect there is more to it. The literary theorist, Stanley Fish, begins his treatise *How to Write* with the following telling anecdote:

> Annie Dillard tells the story of a fellow writer who was asked by a student, 'Do you think I could be a writer?' 'Well,' the writer said, 'do you like sentences?' The student is surprised by the question, but Dillard knows exactly what was meant. He was being told, she explains, that 'if he likes sentences he could begin,' and she remembers a similar conversation with a painter friend. 'I asked him how he came to be a painter. He said, I like the smell of paint.' The point, made implicitly...is that you don't begin with a grand conception...You begin with a feel for the nitty-gritty material of the medium, paint in one case, sentences in the other.

I suspect Amin enjoys the smell of copper smelting in the morning.

o

Amin demands attention: when you witness Amin's performance pieces, you cannot look away. I remember strolling onto the grounds of Frere Hall one night in 2014 on the occasion of Sindh Art Festival, curated by Adeela Suleman and Sameera Raja, standing amongst others, gawking at Amin and his collaborator Joshinder Chaggar conduct *Paradise Lost* (fig. 1), a coordinated pantomime within a large steel scaffolding. I remember copper leaves twisting on strings, a bed of marigolds, torches alight. At some juncture, I remember the scaffolding burning down. It was dramatic, unsetting—quite literally, a house on fire.

Over the years, I have witnessed many such spectacles, from *Love Marriage* (fig. 2), at the Indus Valley School, a dystopic wedding ceremony featuring Saba Iqbal as a stone-faced bride and Amin as a helmeted groom ritually exchanging eggs with each other and the audience, to *Dreamscape* (fig. 3), a show co-curated with Zarmeene Shah at the Amin Gulgee Gallery that you entered through a tea party in a tent, a conscious evocation of Lewis Carroll's *Alice in Wonderland.* Falling through the rabbit hole, you happened upon Sara Vaqar Pagganwala, another frequent partner-in-crime, "offering plaster casts of her own body" as cake set upon a buffet or refractory table; "audience members," according to the artist statement, were "encouraged to eat and become part of the artist's body and mind." Upstairs, I remember Shalalae Jamil lying alone in a full-sized bed, gazing at projections on the ceiling. The audience was invited to lie beside her, watching what she watched without interacting with her—a meditation on the relationship between the public and private.

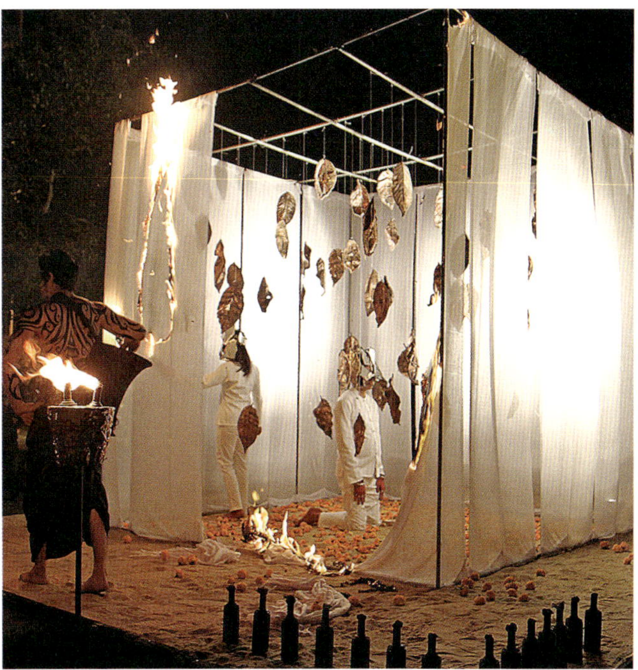

Fig. 1. *Paradise Lost*, 2014. Performance. Sindh Art Festival, Frere Hall, Karachi. Photo by Jamal Ashiqain

Standing among the passers-by, lookers-on, I wondered about the resonance of the medium in Pakistan, in Karachi—a city that often verges on the surreal. It's not just the routine political posturing

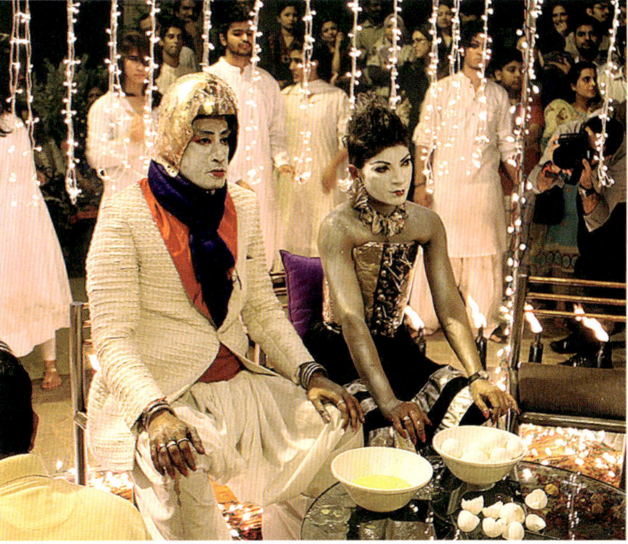

Fig. 2. *Love Marriage*, 2012. Performance. Indus Valley School of Art and Architecture, Karachi. Photo by Jamal Ashiqain

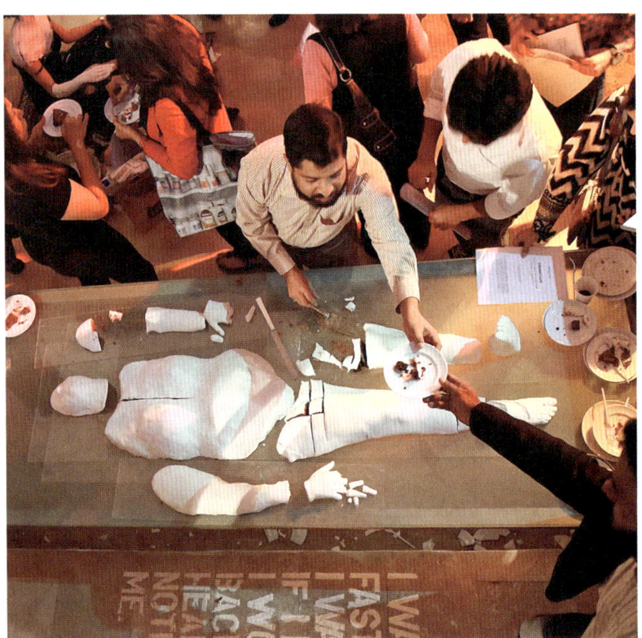

Fig. 3. *Dreamscape*, 2014. Amin Gulgee Gallery, Karachi. Photo by Humayun Memon

and posing for control of the city, the choreographed protests of religious parties, shutdowns and sit-ins by mercantile mafias—it's witnessing a naked man happily driving a motorcycle down Drigh Road late at night or your car drifting in knee-deep water during the monsoon (and when you push your car to the side of the road, wading to a refuge for the night, you almost fall into a manhole). A dwarf playing carom in the courtyard of the Amin Gulgee Gallery at *Dreamscape* is not particularly remarkable then.

The catalogue for *One Night Stand / Coup d'un soir*, a 2019 performance art exhibition curated by Amin at the Cité internationale des arts, might provide explication. Amin writes, "The idea was to create an immersive experience through the close juxtaposition of simultaneous performance works...in which all five senses were accessed." He continues: "This was reminiscent, for me, of the sensation of navigating...the mazaar of Karachi's patron saint Abdullah Shah Ghazi. I remember 27 years ago, when my father, John McCarry and I visited the shrine, we were overwhelmed by smells, colors and sounds... the cacophony of the devotees' voices mixed with devotional music, the pungent smells of rose petals and incense and the vibrant hues of the clothing and the offering to the saint enveloped us in a mystical spell. In these shrines people of all economic classes, ethnicities and religions brush against each other..."

There is no doubt that Amin has shaped the topography of performance art in Pakistan, a mode of art practice that emerged from American counterculture in the late 1960s. It is experiential, ephemeral, defies commodification, the market: you cannot buy it, possess it, hang it on the wall to match your drapes. In the *Dreamscape* catalogue, Zarmeene invokes the work of critics including Walter Benjamin, Claire Bishop and Jacques Rancière, a cohort I am not familiar with. But Rancière's observation about the need for performance art makes eminent sense to me: "a theater where spectators will be participants...instead of being passive viewers."

This is what I understand: as is often the case with Amin's performance art extravaganzas, the distance between artist and audience becomes a hair's breadth—everybody is sucked into the rabbit hole; everybody becomes part of the spectacle. I have been there—I know.

o

Amin demands attention: curated by Amin, KB17, Karachi's inaugural biennale, could not be ignored by denizens of the city or discourse. A milestone in the cultural life of the city, the Herculean logistical feat brought the works of some 182 artists to a dozen venues stretching from the old city to the suburbs. Walking into the stately hundred-and-fifty-year-old Narayan Jagannath Vaidya Government Higher Secondary School Building on Bandar Road on the inaugural night, ambling from room to room, floor to floor, I was struck by the quality and quantity of work, struck like everybody else—it was chock-a-block. I wondered where next?

Over the course of the next fortnight, I made my way to nearly every site, sometimes brushing shoulders with schoolchildren, sometimes with artists and critics from abroad, sometimes by car, sometime on foot. The sites were arranged in four geographical "clusters": Cluster A, spanning the middle-class cantons of Gulshan Iqbal and Bahadurabad, comprised the Karachi School of Art, the oldest in the city, and VM Art Gallery, one of the finest in the city. Cluster B stretched up and down Bandar Road, old Karachi: Capri Cinema, 63 Commissiriat Lines, NJV, Pioneer Bookhouse and Jamshed Memorial Hall—once the headquarters of the Karachi Theosophists (and where once I taught a creative writing seminar.) Cluster C was familiar territory—the erstwhile colonial town hall, Frere Hall, a city landmark, Claremont House down the street, and the Alliance Française; Cluster D extended into the suburbs: the Indus Valley School of Art and Architecture and the tiny FOMMA gallery tucked into that park in Defense. Logistically, it was an uncannily thoughtful arrangement.

There was, however, more to KB17 than feats of logistics. On display was clarity of vision. Each site was individually curated under the conceptual umbrella of "Witness," a word that is both noun and verb, both transitive and intransitive. As a noun, the word is variously defined as "attestation of a fact or event: testimony;" "one that gives evidence;" "something serving as evidence of proof." As a verb, it is defined as "to testify to;" "to take note of;" and "to constitute the scene or time of." "Witness" is an imperative. Amin and his team urged us to do so.

Amin's curatorial statement was cogent, succinct:

> The curatorial aim of KB17 is to ponder not only our times but also the narratives surrounding them. I do not have answers, only questions: Do we want to reinforce stereotypes of earlier centuries? Does art have to be global to be relevant in the 21st century? Can a bruised city like Karachi enter into an international discussion on art today?

As a novelist, a Karachi-based novelist, these questions have particular resonance: when embarking on *The Selected Works of Abdullah the Cossack* I also had to think about how to come at the city, the sixth largest in the world depending on how you cut the numbers, but one that was insufficiently imagined in literary discourse. Growing up, I can recall only a single novel set in Karachi (Adam Zameenzad's *The Thirteenth House*). Now, there are so many that I have lost count. And now Karachi hosts several animate literary festivals that attract writers and audiences from Nazimabad and New York alike.

Growing up in the 1980s, I also remember there was only one gallery in the city (not including the then moribund Arts Council and Bashir Mirza's salon in Sindhi Muslim Society): Ali Imam's Indus Gallery. There were a couple of critics, a handful of artists, a discrete audience. Amin cut his teeth in the Karachi of that time. The topography of the art world has changed dramatically since—I, for instance, have lost track of the galleries that dot the city. And Karachi has become the canvas for a biennale.

KB17 was the culmination of an organic process that spanned almost half a century. It was not simply a matter of artwork or infrastructure but also a matter of culture and community that support and appreciate artistic endeavor, from sculpture to performance art. KB17 contributed to our understanding of ourselves as denizens of Karachi—indeed, many if not most saw the city in a different light. By demanding attention, Amin has contributed to this evolution. He has mine.

In Conversation with Amin Gulgee

Maryam Ekhtiar

Maryam Ekhtiar: Describe your persistent focus on the art of sculpture. You have always worked with this medium. What drew you to this medium and what makes you stay with it?

Amin Gulgee: I am not legacy. My parents' wish was that I would not be an artist even though my father was one. I wholeheartedly agreed with this sentiment and was looking forward to living in America after attending Yale with a steady job. I majored in economics, and it was only after going to my first art history class, which I was literally dragged to by my classmate Dominique Malaquais, that I decided to pursue a second major in that subject.

I wrote my senior thesis on Mughal gardens. I have always been fascinated by how space is handled in architecture. The form of the structure delineates and creates areas that have specific functions. I am drawn to form. An object, unlike a two-dimensional image, has a myriad of viewing perspectives. An object, especially in the mediums I have chosen (copper/bronze), can be touched. This tangibility is extremely important for me.

I began my career in object making by creating what I then called "jewelry" in gold-plated copper. These initial works were heavy and unwearable. I showed them at the PACC (Pakistan-American Cultural Center) in Karachi. Jewelry gave me distance between me and my father since he had engaged with many art forms, but never that one. For my show in 1990 at the Indus Gallery, owned and curated by Ali Iman, I made jewelry that could actually be worn. I also made free-standing sculpture. Jewelry was exciting because the audience could physically engage with it, unlike my sculpture, which people were reluctant to touch. I remember mentioning this to Dr. Annemarie Schimmel, who had come to see my father at our home at the time. She told me that the word *begreifen* was the most "Sufi" word in the German language. She defined it "as learning through touch."

That is what is so wonderful about my process. It truly is understanding though touch. My ideas emanate from the act of hammering, welding, and grinding. It is physical. For me, it is exhilarating to create form that occupies space. The three-dimensional realm is a rabbit hole that I am happy to fall into. The possibilities of form remain various and seductive for me.

ME: Your work has evolved through the years. My first encounter with your sculptural works was back in 1996 when I was drawn to your work entitled *Nur*. I was mesmerized by its movement and materiality. Although purely calligraphic, it reminded me of the Sufi celestial dance, the *sama*. Can you comment on this? The materiality was unique as well. You integrated rock crystals into the metal alloy. Can you say a few words about the mixed media approach you were using at that time?

AG: In the mid-1990s, I extensively incorporated rock crystals into my objects. I discovered them when I was taken as a child by my father to Peshawar, the city of his birth, to buy lapis lazuli for his mosaics in the pietra dura technique. I thought that it was magical that the seemingly random forces of nature could produce these linear, six-sided prism stones, which were as clear as glass. For me, they seemed to embody a divine geometric pattern. The Fatimid Caliphate, an early Islamic dynasty (909-1171 AD) in Egypt and North

Africa, produced ewers and other objects carved from these crystals. I did not want to carve upon these structured stones, so I enmeshed them into copper in their entirety. For me, copper was warm, organic and fluid. The crystals were cold-structured and absolute. I wanted to synthesize these opposites. I also wanted light to flow through my work.

My first works incorporating quartz crystals were in the form of the double helix, the dancing, intertwining strands of the DNA molecule. This led to *Nur* (light) in which the sculpture, balanced upon a point, turns onto itself in a genetic swirl. The text I have used in this work is *Al-Hamdullilah* (Praise be to God) in the square *kufic* script of Arabic. I was interested in the tension between the geometric nature of the writing and the curvilinear form of the object.

ME: Your early works seemed to be rooted in your faith and background. Since then, you have moved into different directions—installations, performance, etc. Can you comment on that?

AG: I was born and bred in South Asia. My parents were avid collectors of antiquity, and I was surrounded by images of Krishna, Buddha and Ganesh growing up. As a child, I spent hours talking, touching, and playing with these statues and they became part of my personal mythology. Coming back to Karachi after almost seven years in America, I had this great need to appropriate this imagery and to remember.

My interest in Islamic art stems from conversations I had with the late Professor Oleg Grabar. It was a challenge at Yale to convince the art history department to allow me to write about Mughal Gardens since at that time Islamic art history was not taught there. Professor Grabar very kindly agreed to be my secondary advisor although he was then teaching at Harvard. This is ironic because my father had been very engaged with Islamic calligraphy, but at that point in my life the idea of being an artist was completely blocked from my mind.

My performance trajectory began with my engagement with the fashion scene in Pakistan. During the restrictive dictatorship of General Zia-ul-Haq in the 1980s, fashion shows were not encouraged due to his official policy of "Islamization." In the early 1990s, fashion exploded; shows were extremely experimental. There was also a great dialogue emerging among visual arts. Female models strutted bravely down the catwalk with their heads uncovered, creating larger-than-life, theatrical personas. Initially, I included my gold-plated copper jewelry onto various designers' clothes. In 1999, I had the opportunity to conceive and present a show of my own that I titled *Alchemy*. Having worked closely with the country's top models over the years, I was extremely familiar with the way they moved. I created individual, large metal objects for each of these women that they could wear and walk on the runway. *Alchemy* was divided into three acts: Bronze, Silver and Gold. Each was introduced by a performance work. Before the first section, I covered my body in clay and clamped a double-sided bronze self-portrait mask weighing three kilos, seventy grams onto my head and danced to a morning raga. I can still remember the weight of the headgear and hearing myself breathe beneath it. It was a transportive experience.

In 2004, a year after the American invasion of Iraq, I stepped away from the catwalk format. In *Other Works*, my solo show of sculpture and installation at Canvas Gallery in Karachi, I included my performance *Calculate*. In this work, I asked Seema Nusrat, who had recently graduated from the IVS (Indus Valley School of Art and Architecture), to calculate a horizontal abacus made up of dolls' heads from the colonial era. Set in a room with flashing lights and dressed as a dystopian moppet, she broke the heads as she violently shifted them from left to right. In my practice, I feel the need to physically activate objects that I have created, blurring the line between my sculpture, installation, and performance.

Performance is ephemeral: It becomes a medium to express ideas that challenge and question societal norms. In the context of Pakistan, performance is new and that allows many an idea to be publicly explored and digested.

ME: What is the role of calligraphy and the written word in your work?

AG: I have never claimed to be a calligrapher. My father was an accomplished one, who taught himself how to write in many of the Arabic scripts. In my work, I am obsessed by repetition. Over the years, I have used only two lines from the Quran in a particular script. One of these lines is from the *Iqra Ayat*, which states, "God taught man what he did not know," in *naskhi*. The other line is from the *Surah-e-Rehman*, which asks, "Which of the favors of God can one deny?" in new style *kufic*. Initially, these lines could be read in my objects, but later they became deconstructed and unreadable. For me to remain within these parameters is challenging. Form in my work becomes as important as content. I have also used the phrase *Al-Hamdulillah* (Praise be to God) in square *kufic*, that is derived mathematically. Initially I started using this script upon curvilinear organic forms, for example, in *Nur*. However, later, utilizing just the geometric letters themselves, the sculptures developed into linear, architectonic structures. The division of spaces in these works was done numerically and the text remained readable. The phrase *Al-Hamdulillah* appealed to me because it is often used in our vernacular, escaping the confines of the mosque. For instance, it is uttered after a sneeze, or if something good happens to you.

ME: Also, I see that you have a fascination with scale. Your works have become larger and even public in the past decade. Why is that?

AG: Commissioned work scares me. Even at the beginning of my career, I always thought that I would much rather make a small pendant that I have complete control over rather than a large sculpture envisioned by a client. My first commissioned work was in the mid-1990s for IBM, which was opening an office in Karachi at the time. They wanted a work reflecting the future of technology. The company gave me access to their warehouses in which discarded computers were stored, which I ravaged. For me to understand this new material, I smashed these machines and, from their entrails, excavated motherboards. These captivated me. The grid of these boards reminded me of the square *kufic* script that I had been using. I ended up creating for IBM a 274-cm-high work in the shape of a DNA molecule. The work was entitled *The Neuron Chip*.

In 2002, I was asked by a group of national and multinational companies to suggest a public sculpture that could be placed upon Bilawal Roundabout in Karachi. Since I don't sketch my objects before making them, I proceeded to make several models. Because of my interest in text, I used hieroglyphics from Mohenjo-daro, an ancient city of the Indus River civilization. My clients, who approved the project, were ideal: After giving me all the money upfront, they ignored me for two years. The sculpture I had proposed to them was supposed to be 610 cm high. However, both committed to and inspired by the project, I increased the scale of the work to twelve meters although I had to pay the remaining balance from my savings. I figured: Why not? When will I ever get another chance to create a public work for my hometown? Megalomania set in.

The form of *Forgotten Text* was comprised of three Indus River hieroglyphics, a writing system that is yet to be deciphered. The body of the object was covered in computer motherboards worked upon with copper wire and embellished with round mirrors, which are often embroidered into traditional Sindhi clothing. The grid of the motherboards was like an aerial view of my city, ordered yet chaotic. I wanted *Forgotten Text* to be a charioteer referencing the roundabout as a traditional starting point for donkey cart races. Back in the day, on weekends, these donkey chariots would fly across the streets of Karachi, navigating hazardous traffic. The donkey, for me, was my metropolis, which has seen years of bloodshed and violence. It is an animal that is overworked, stubborn and yet incredibly resilient.

After its placement, I was thrilled that the city had appropriated it. It was festooned with the flags of the PPP (Pakistan People's Party) for the birthday of our former prime minister, Benazir Bhutto. For the Prophet's birthday (PBUH), it was illuminated by green lights. In January 2008, some weeks after the murder of my parents, as I drove around the roundabout where *Forgotten Text* had been placed, my partner, John, and I could not help but notice that this monumental public work had literally disappeared overnight.

My other public sculptures, for example, in front of the Parliament building in Islamabad and at the United Nations in New York, were not commissioned and they were installed after I had made them for myself. There is always a challenge in scale. As soon as I could afford more copper and bronze, which are expensive mediums, I started increasing the size of my work. Since most of my work is assemblage and not done in a single casting, there are structural and aesthetic concerns that arise when enlarging it. Usually, when a series of work begins, it is relatively small. I do not sketch my sculpture before construction. Gradually, when I am more comfortable with the form, I start increasing the size of the work to better understand it.

As an artist in my context, it is a joy and a privilege to have one's work on public view. In Pakistan, there are almost no museums with permanent collections of modern or contemporary art. If a work is bought, it usually goes into an inaccessible private collection. Art belongs to everyone. I was honored to be appointed the Chief Curator for the inaugural Karachi Biennale in 2017 (KB17). Despite having a modest budget, my team and I, which included Zarmeene Shah, Sara Vaqar Pagganwala, Humayun Memon, Zeerak Ahmed and Adam Fahy-Majeed, were ambitious. We had a dozen sites across the city in which to install the works. In the end, KB17 included 182 national and international artists. The idea was to bring challenging works not only to the elite, but to people at large.

ME: I have always enjoyed the playfulness and idiosyncrasy of your works. I am referring to your *Spider* and your *Cosmic Chapati* series. It seems that they straddle commentary and playfulness. Can you elaborate?

AG: I am beholden to my process. One idea leads to the next and I submit to the flow. It is my web and I precariously try to discover and generate the threads. When I came across Louise Bourgeois' 1996 sculpture *Spider* in person it affected me, and I wanted to create spiders of my own. There is a tradition in Islam of zoomorphic calligraphy, and I used letters from the line of the *Iqra Ayat*, one I have repeatedly engaged with, to create my own arachnids. The text in the *Spider* series is unreadable. I was also aware that Louise Bourgeois had said, when talking about her sculpture, that it was: "An ode to my mother. She was my best friend. Like a spider, my mother was a weaver...Spiders are helpful and protective just like my mother."

The *Cosmic Chapati* body of work arose after my parents' murder. My life was in turmoil and my work went in two separate directions. In my *Ripping the Bird's Nest* series, hands reappeared in my work tearing holes into the copper nest. The making of these organic objects was cathartic for me. *The Cosmic Chapati* series, on the other hand, is linear and plays with the precise division of space as well as attempting to reconcile the circle with the square. Since my mind and life at that point were turned upside down, I perhaps felt the need to exert structure and control over the only thing that was left for me, my process. I escaped into my comfort zone of a universe defined by numbers. Within the parameters of a cube, my *chapatis* both create and divide the space. I ended the series by leaving this geometric construct with a work titled *Cosmic Chapati 48: The Hunger Game*. In this, *chapatis* are placed upon a rectangular board made of a grid composed of mirrors. Here, the chapati, a round flatbread that is a staple food of South Asia, could be moved and played anyway one wanted in a potentially performative act.

ME: Tell me about your *Char Bagh* installation. What inspired it? It is based on the Indo-Persian four quadrant garden, the *Chahar Bagh*. This garden form is ubiquitous in Iran, Central Asia, and the Subcontinent. It finds expression in paintings, carpets, and other art forms. Can you elaborate on your fascination with this form? What does it mean to you?

AG: My interest in form has gravitated both to the geometric and the organic. In geometric form, I have engaged separately with the circle/sphere and the square/cube since the start of my trajectory. In 2003, I held an open studio in my gallery which I titled *Char Bagh*. The *Chahar Bagh* is a four-garden quadrant in which two lines intersect at a perpendicular. One can draw a circle or a square around its edges. In these sculptures, I attempted to reconcile the cube with the sphere in quarters. For me, these geometric forms are diametrically opposed. I felt the cube to be finite and temporal and the sphere infinite and eternal. There is an inherent tension in their juxtaposition.

Before the Mughal conquest of South Asia, the gardens that existed were organic and unstructured. The first Mughal emperor, Babur, introduced the *Chahar Bagh* grid into garden design in an attempt to organize nature. What I found fascinating was how curvilinear motifs, like the lotus, which were inherently local to South Asia, were incorporated within the geometric grid of these gardens. The stylized lotus was the throne of many deities of Hinduism. Undulating lotus blossoms appear on the outline of the rectangular reflecting pools in the Shalimar Garden in Lahore, for example, rhythmically softening its linear parameters.

The liminal space of the *Chahar Bagh* between the organic and geometric led to my installation. I wanted it to be experiential, referencing an infinity within an eternal garden.

ME: Your work seems to have hidden meaning that resonates with today's concerns within your own country and globally. How does your *Chahar Bagh* articulate these meanings and concerns?

AG: In my early sculptures, I engaged with leaves which, for me, were magical elements. My father spoke to me of how the early calligraphers were inspired by the movement of foliage in the wind to formulate their script. These leaves surrounded my heads of Krishna and Buddha, as well as entering my calligraphic sculptures. Later, in works like *Plant that Can Grow Without Water*, they became fantastical. In *Looking for the Magic Center* and *In the Garden I* and *II*, they explored the geometric realm of the cube.

In my installation, I freed the leaf. Each leaf became a personality that could exist alone. I relished in their bends and folds. I wanted them to dance independently. The cold, mirrored sheets I used echo the reflecting pools of Mughal design. These smooth surfaces capture not only the imagery of the fluid leaves, but of the viewer in my garden.

ME: What materials did you use in the *Char Bagh* installation? What was the vision behind using the copper leaves and the mirrors?

AG: This potent symbol of two perpendicular lines meeting at the center has been appropriated by many religions and cultures throughout time. In Hinduism, it appears as the *mandala*, reflecting a view of the universe, and is a symbol of life. In ancient Central Asian myths, it represented the four rivers from whose intersection a cosmic tree would grow to the heavens. And later in Christianity, it appears as the Greek cross. The repeated use of this symbol by many different people of various cultures through time perhaps is an indication of how we as humans can share a mythical consciousness.

Mirrors echo the reflective pools set in the roofless enclosures of Mughal gardens. The rectangular structures capture imagery of both the foliage and the sky, connecting heaven and earth. Their water bodies appear in all three categories of Mughal gardens: the palace/fort garden, the autonomous garden, and the funerary garden. In the funerary garden, the tomb is in the center of the *Char Bagh*. The only exception to this rule is in the funerary garden of the Taj Mahal. At this site, the tomb is located at one end. A water body is at the center of the space, reflecting within it the marble structure. My personal theory is that the Taj Mahal, a tomb the emperor Shah Jahan commissioned for his beloved wife Mumtaz Mahal, originally had another tomb for the emperor himself planned on the other side of the garden. If it had been built, the tombs' reflections would have united at the center of the comic *Char Bagh*.

The English word "garden" comes from the Old English "geard", meaning enclosure. Gardens were then about cultivation of the earth by humankind. It was man's attempt to enclose and utilize the soil. The transition from hunter gatherers to agrarian societies did not initially benefit early Homo Sapiens. Life expectancy fell; one had to work longer hours on farming and one's diet was restricted to grains. However, human beings were able to reproduce rapidly and spread their DNA. The astounding success of our species to proliferate has also raised questions about our balance with nature.

ME: Is there a thread that runs through your sculpture?

AG: I have always submitted to my process. It is an act of letting go. I have to make what I make. The forms in my head demand to be bought physically into space. I am terrified of looking back because I fear that my threads might disappear.

When I came out to myself as artist as a young man in New York City, I buried myself in the energy of production. I realized that I think by making. I returned to Karachi in the early 1990s with John because my parents had a backyard, and I needed a free space to create my objects. It was a challenging homecoming because of the career path that I had chosen. My father was calm as always, but neither encouraged nor discouraged me. Initially, I was hurt because he refused to see things in process and would only comment on work once it was done. Later, I realized that I was extremely grateful to him because he gave me freedom and allowed me to find my own voice. My mother, on the other hand, was dead set against me being an artist and told me, "*Beta* (son), I have spent my life with one artist, and I don't need another in my life." She also asked, "Do you want to live off your father's money the rest of your life?" This was of concern to me because both my parents were self-made and I had always told myself that after attending college in America, which they generously paid for, I would support myself.

The climate of the time in Karachi was also not conducive to showing objects. Ali Iman, the owner of the Indus Gallery, which was then the preeminent gallery in the city, told me that sculpture does not sell and can be controversial. I begged and pleaded with him for months before he agreed to give me a solo show.

At that point, I had very little money for equipment, and I used to go to Jamshed Road and work with the metal workers from 12 am to 4 am, the cheapest time to use their expertise and tools. It was on the streets of Karachi that I started expanding my technique. It was an incredible learning process and an eye-opening experience for me as well. I saw another Karachi late at night. Heroin was smoked openly, and a surreal, medieval atmosphere prevailed where *malang* (dervishes) would appear, covered in chains. Pakistanis are not shy. As I worked and learned, small groups of street urchins and passersby would congregate around me, peppering me with questions: Who are you? What are you doing? Why are you doing this? All good questions, which I am still trying to answer. Those eleven months on Jamshed Road were a stark contrast to how I had grown up. I attended the Karachi American School for the first twelve years of my school life. The classes were small and there were about ten foreigners (mostly American) and ten Pakistanis in each class. All of our teachers were American, and the ethos was conservative and extremely Norman Rockwell. I escaped into books, both fiction and non-fiction. My idea of a fun weekend was going to the library and taking stories home with me.

During this time on the road, so to speak, I not only learnt about the city of my birth, but also that the process of object making is truly necessary for me. The thread that runs in my work is the thread itself, which I tenuously hold onto, and leads me where it chooses.

ME: What are some of your most recent immersive installations? What concerns do they express?

AG: One could argue that the Mughal Shalimar Garden in Lahore, the focus of my undergraduate thesis, is an installation on an imperial scale. The Shalimar, unlike the gardens of Versailles, does not have a palace anchoring it. It is an autonomous enclosed space. The space is divided into public, semi-public, and private space via its elevated terraces. As I argued in my paper, this separation allowed the garden to not only serve as a "pleasure garden," but to express the divine and secular power of the Mughal emperor.

Bernini's *Ecstasy of Saint Teresa* can also be perhaps viewed as an installation, in which sculpture, architecture and paint become a cohesive whole surrounding the viewer in a sensory, narrative experience. Bernini was not only a sculptor but also a great architect. The only time I came close to being an architect was in the design of my gallery space. I worked on it closely with Kishwar Rizvi, who now teaches Islamic art and architecture at Yale. Completed in 2000, my space was severe yet designed to be flexible. I wanted my roof, however, to explode with a permanent installation. Before I began working on this project, I constructed an installation I called *Purdah* for my roof. The word *purdah* literally means curtain in English. *Purdah* was a veil for my roof created out of lunettes sourced from junkyards that I hung from iron beams. A lot of architecture from the 19th century is being demolished in the interior of Sindh and the remnants of these homes find their way to backstreet shops in Karachi. I covered these retrieved wooden structures with a skin of copper, replacing some of the broken colored glass and adding bells. This curtain afforded me privacy.

It took 17 months to complete the mosaic on my roof. I titled it *Salaam Gaudi*. Gaudi's garden in Barcelona, Park Guell, had a profound effect upon me and I wanted to pay homage to this incredible artist/architect. My *Salaam* is an amalgam of traditional earthenware vessels in a skin of white concrete with mirrors and glass and bottles held together by a web of iron. The earthenware was made in villages in Sindh. I constrained myself to using their shapes, a few harking back to the Indus River civilization, and didn't commission any new ones. Some of the green bottles I used for the mosaic were ones that my friends and I had drunk out of. Most of the amber bottles, however, had once contained highly concentrated sulfuric acid, which I use for my copper work. I also bought recycled bottles from Bottle Gali, a fairytale-like, winding lane in Karachi whose shops were once lined with glistening, recovered objects of glass. Today Bottle Gali has been reduced to only a few shops. Similarly, one can no longer find traditional earthenware on every corner of my city. My fascination with bottles began at a class I took at Yale, taught by Robert Farris Thompson, a professor known on campus as "Mambo Bob." He introduced me to the bottle trees of the American South. This Congo-derived tradition was brought to America as a consequence of the trans-Atlantic slave trade. African-Americans would hang bottles from the limbs of trees as talismans against evil spirits. I was entranced by the visuals of these magical trees and the idea of empty bottles becoming a source of protection. The talisman-like space of *Salaam Gaudi* is also an ode to *mina-kari* (enamel) of traditional South Asian jewelry; the encrustations of the ocean; and the colors of my province of Sindh, an arid land of light and mirror.

In 2018 I was invited to show my installations *7* and *7.7* at GAM (Galleria d'Arte Moderna) and Mattatoio in Rome simultaneously. Paolo De Grandis and Claudio Crescentini were the curators of the shows. I previewed this work at my gallery in Karachi before taking it to Italy. "Seven" refers to the number of parts of the line from the *Iqra Ayat* that I had divided and reassembled to create the objects for my installation. The text in *naskhi*, which I had often repeated in the past, now become unreadable. At GAM, I occupied the central courtyard of this 17th century Discaled (barefoot) Carmelite monastery, which is an order founded by Saint Teresa. I installed my geometric *Char-Bagh* garden in this bright, open enclosure wanting my eight *Salt Screens* and *Perforated Scrolls* and four *Ascensions* to pay tribute to the passage of the blazing Roman sun casting shadows upon the ground. A long carpet created out of gravel and *Iqra* copper letters ran across its breadth, uniting the space. Gravel was used for Roman roads that webbed the empire, facilitating communication. For me, it also reflected the austerity of this barefoot order. It was important for me to have a gentle intrusion upon this monastery reacting to its past to create a contemplative, liminal garden.

In stark contrast to the naturally lit courtyard of GAM, Mattatoio was dark and brooding. It was originally the old slaughterhouse of Rome built between 1888 and 1891. The hall for my installation was immense, divided into two parts by a partial glass wall. Entering, the viewer was confronted by my 1999 × 610 × 6 cm coal carpet, which had tarnished copper letters set within it. At the far end of the carpet *Zero Gravity* floated upwards, escaping the stygian river of coal. Coal is literally carbon, a core element of life. Yet its emissions today threaten our survival on Earth: It both gives life but also threatens it. On the other side of the glazed partition, I hung a plastic screen upon which was projected an algorithm that could be viewed from both sides. *Algorithm* was composed of black letters from the *Iqra Ayat* appearing on a white screen until the entire surface turned black. White letters then randomly appeared on this now black screen until it turned white. The cycle continued endlessly. Each time a letter appeared, a note of a *rubab*, a string instrument originating in Afghanistan, was heard. Algorithms intrigue me because they deal with numbers. Also, the word algorithm is derived from the name of the 9th century Persian mathematician Muhammad ibn Musa al-Khwarizmi, who was widely read in Medieval Europe. In front of and behind this projected screen, 77 letters of copper with nickel plate and mesh were delicately suspended within a dimly lit area. For me, there was a call and response, a dialogue, between *7*, installed in the sunny courtyard of GAM, and *7.7*, which lay in the shadowy and cavernous abattoir of Mattatoio.

In 2022, I had the opportunity to participate in *If There is a Paradise on Earth*, a group exhibition at the Lahore Fort curated by Sabah Hussain, whose concept note included a quote by Amīr Khusrau (1253–1325 AD), the Indo-Persian Sufi singer, musician, poet and scholar: "If there is paradise on earth it is this, it is this, it is this." Being allowed to intrude upon this Mughal site was a spiritual homecoming for me. I installed my installation *Spice* in its subterranean Summer Palace. Eighteen trays, 91 × 91 cm, created a grid upon the floor. Half of these trays contained cayenne pepper and the other half turmeric. The smell of spice was overwhelming as one entered this enclosed cellar whose walls were covered with crumbling frescoes, the ceiling above it occasionally dropping pieces of white plaster like tears. I drew inspiration not only from the curator's reference, but from *Dune*, Frank Herbert's epic science fiction saga, in which the pursuit of "spice," an essential natural resource in his tale, causes inter-planetary warfare.

Later that year, I presented three installations —*Spice Tray*, *Char Bagh: The Spice Garden*, and *Liminal Letters*—for my solo show, *The Spider Speaketh in Tongues*, at the South Asia Institute in Chicago curated by Adam Fahy-Majeed. This landmark building dating from 1911 was originally a tire showroom. The repurposed gallery had two protruding walls dividing one side of it into three niches, which became altars for my installations. *Spice Tray* and *Char Bagh*, both measuring 335 × 335 cm. In *Spice Tray*, abstracted Arabic letters in warm-colored copper were embedded within 99 kilos of turmeric and cayenne pepper. In *Char Bagh: The Spice Garden*, a cross-section of turmeric paths divided four quadrants into a garden of twisting, gleaming copper leaves rising from mirror. These polychromatic, aromatic installations were placed on the floor. They were positioned on either side of *Liminal Letters*, my third installation, in which steely, abstracted calligraphy floated in an infinity space of mirrors, coldly reflecting both the letters and the viewer in an endless repetition.

My installations have usually been in dialogue with the architecture that envelops them. They respond to, and are determined by, the space into which they flow. The exception to this is my interest in juxtaposing two objects to explore the in-between. In my work *Reflection*, which I installed at *OPEN* in Venice in 1998, two copper and rock crystal constructions confronted one another. At one end, the calligraphy (which at that time was readable) appeared in the negative space; at the other, the text was in the positive. This was not a mirror reflection but a reflection of space. In 2015, I hung two facing moons created out of broken bottles and copper for my solo show *Washed Upon the Shore* in Karachi. These amber and green moons were inspired by the world Haruki Murakami created in his novel *1Q84*. *Horn I* and *Horn II* celebrate that essential domesticated animal in South Asia, the water buffalo. Placed adjacent to one another, the sculptures gravitated towards one another, referencing a buffalo submerged in water with only its horns visible.

In 2022, I installed *Memory Room 305* in one of the 7.62-by-9.14-meter classrooms of the NJV for the Karachi Biennale. On one side of the room was an arrangement of my parents' furniture; above it was a wall mosaic of objects, personal photographs, and paintings, including my father's work from my home. On the other side of the room were 15 steel racks protruding from the wall containing spice, creating an intense odor in this relatively small space. In the center of the room was an early 20th century wooden bed on which was projected a short video of my face covered in turmeric, gasping. On the celling I had stretched 38 saris of my late mother. An algorithm randomly changed the light in the room from red to blue to green. It also arbitrarily and loudly played seven guttural sounds that I had pre-recorded. This confrontational room was a way for me to deal with my history.

ME: How has the COVID-19 pandemic effected your work? Has it added a new layer of meaning to your practice?

AG: I don't keep a diary. On March 15, 2020, I entered a mirror and, like Alice, the world around me felt "curiouser and curiouser." As the Mad Hatter in Lewis Carroll's *Through the Looking Glass* states, "If I had a world of my own, everything would be nonsense.

Nothing would be what it is because everything would be what it isn't. And contrary wise, what is, it wouldn't be. And what it wouldn't be, it would. You see?" The absurdist reality of the Mad Hatter's world became mine during the pandemic of COVID-19. It was the catalyst for three shows I co-curated over the course of 2020: *LAL JADOO/RED MAGIC*, *The Trojan Donkey*, *If These Walls Could Talk*, as well as a performance work of my own, *Healing II*. Each exhibition organically led to the other and bore witness to the times. The first show in this trilogy had to adjust to the new reality; the second capitalized on the lockdown; and the third allowed limited human interaction in the "new normal." These series of events were not preplanned, and one surrealistically led to the other. The four catalogues that document these events form my *Corona Chronicles*, becoming my journal of this plague.

On March 15, 2020, my co-curator, Sara Vaqar Pagganwala, and I had scheduled our one-night performance art happening, *LAL JADOO/RED MAGIC*, in Karachi. Our venue was a semi-abandoned office building on I.I. Chundrigar Road, the Wall Street of Pakistan. The focus of *LAL JADOO/RED MAGIC* was this emerging art form in Pakistan and its history. We not only included 22 archival works from the past, but also featured 43 live performances. This happening was envisioned as an experiential event in which the audience would be required to traverse a labyrinth of rooms and stairs engaging their senses of sight, sound, smell, and touch. However, on March 13, a lockdown was announced in Karachi. Sara and I decided that *LAL JADOO/RED MAGIC* should be accessible only on live feed. For the first time in my life, I went on social media to demand that people not attend in person. I remember this being extremely frustrating for me, as we had worked for months on the project. Karachi went under extreme lockdown and a curfew was announced.

During this quarantine, Sara, Adam Fahy-Majeed and I agreed over the course of extensive phone conversations to curate another performance show, which we titled *The Trojan Donkey*. Given the pandemic, the exhibition had to be virtual. This meant our scope could expand beyond Pakistan. My curatorial interest has always been cross-disciplinary. We reached out to artists, actors, directors, architects, critics, poets, curators, and students across the globe to either go live on April 25, 2020, or send us a video which we would upload on that date to our Facebook page. *The Trojan Donkey* was broadcast between 9:18 pm and 11:13 pm (Pakistan Standard Time) on a Saturday with 85 works infiltrating walls in an attempt to record our globally shared experience and our reactions to it. For me it was a postcard of these times. This endeavor was an attempt to bypass barriers and document our shared human experience of isolation and plague.

The lockdown continued for months in Karachi. Restaurants and health clubs remained closed and large public gatherings were banned. During this isolation, I was fortunate to have the catalogues for the past two shows to work upon. Perhaps the energy of the performative works I was documenting seeped into my bones, and I felt the great need to create a new work of my own. I called it *Healing II*. A decade ago, in 2010, my performance, *The Healing*, was presented for a public event at the Beach Luxury Hotel in Karachi honoring the late Ali Imam. One of the first and most pivotal gallerists of Pakistan, Imam was a very close friend of both my mother's and father's. *The Healing* took place three years after the murder of my parents and their maid by their recently hired driver and his accomplice. The specter of death looming large during this pandemic, it felt imperative to have a second iteration of the work. As in *The Healing*, I had my head shaved. The participants in both works were close to me. *Healing II*, however, did not have an audience and I did not live stream it. It occurred on the roof of my gallery on June 31, 2020, and was documented for video.

In the middle of May, I reconnected with an old friend from high school, Ayesha Baigmohamed, who had recently moved back to Karachi from Washington, D.C. and was in charge of the Village Restaurant, which has been owned by her family for decades. It is well known for serving Pakistani barbeque, and, in its heyday in the 1970s, was the place to be. In 2002, in the post-9/11 world, it became infamous as the site of the kidnapping of the American journalist Daniel Pearl, who was later beheaded by terrorists. The restaurant is located smack in the heart of the metropolis at the starting point of Shahrah-e-Faisal, a boulevard that runs across Karachi and is one of its busiest. It has large parking lots and, because of Ayesha's enthusiasm and support, was ideal for our next curatorial venture, *If These Walls Could Talk*. My co-curator, Sara, and I envisioned a public art event in which the audience would remain in their cars and witness over 77 minutes of art videos silently projected upon a large outside wall of the restaurant. Although the videos were soundless, they spoke to the audience through visuals, removing the barrier of language that can sometimes divide us. This was also exciting for us because the large projection would be visible from the street outside and could therefore access a wider public. Our show was scheduled for August 18, 2020. On August 10, all lockdown restrictions were removed in Pakistan. I was extremely concerned, however, that this deadly virus was still very much among us, and I was happy about the social distancing measures that we had taken. *If These Walls Could Talk* featured 34 video/film works from 21 countries. Each of the works was around three minutes or less in duration giving the audience a fast-paced visual kaleidoscope. The idea was to bring forth a myriad of perspectives. We hoped to form a narrative through their juxtaposition.

Each of these three shows—*LAL JADOO/ RED MAGIC*, *The Trojan Donkey* and *If These Walls Could Talk*—was followed by a webinar. The format of these webinars was loose. My co-curators and I asked around seven to eight participating artists to present around a five-to-seven-minute presentation. We then had an open forum to discuss ideas. Perhaps it was the plague that brought forth a raw and vulnerable exchange among us.

ME: How did the Amin Gulgee Gallery come into being and why did you establish it?

AG: When John and I arrived in Karachi, my parents constructed a living room and a bedroom on the roof of their house for us to live in. I did a mosaic on the outside walls, and we had many a party up there. After a few years of carefree habitation, my mother decided that we, being in our mid-20s, were both too old to live with them and that we needed to move out. She shifted us to an empty 1829-square-meter plot across town which my parents owned. On the far end of this site were six rooms each with a separate entrance. Three of the rooms became my workshop and the other three is where we lived. The land was covered by thorny bushes and a myriad of birds would flock there. After a few years, my parents decided to build my father's museum on this plot. They generously gave me 549 square meters to build my gallery and home.

My gallery and my father's museum were completed in 2000, each with a separate front gate, but connected at the back through a courtyard. I had an exhibition space on the bottom floor, and we lived on top. It was exciting for both John and me to finally have a gallery space to utilize, as this is something we had long dreamed of. We decided that this was going to be a non-commercial space for new ideas and experimentation. It was to be a kind of laboratory to incubate different perspectives. Around once a year, we would remove all my sculpture and host shows which would be documented. Karachi is where most of the commercial galleries are located in Pakistan. However, there are few areas for non-art market activity. John thought that the gallery should be named after me, although I had many other poetic names for it. I thought that he should be the coordinator of the space, facilitating the guest curators and artists and helping with the cataloging of the shows.

Our first show was for Vasl, an international artist residency, of which I was a founding member. For this, the works that had been created in the workshop in Gadani on the Baloch coast were brought to Karachi. The second show was *Dish Dhamaka* (dish explosion) in which I asked artists to work upon a satellite dish. This was one of the first object-based exhibitions in my city. Although the exhibitions at the gallery attracted large crowds and received a lot of press attention, both in print and on TV, John and I never managed to get funding. One reason is that there is very little money in Pakistan for art sponsorship and the other was perhaps the controversial nature of some of the work that was shown. We had to rely upon the generosity of the artists, who created incredible work without receiving any money as commission. Largescale shows were put together by love and Scotch tape. The process of setting up these exhibitions was exhilarating and there was many a discussion and argument about art. This space also gave me an opportunity to explore my interest in performance art.

I feel eternally grateful to my parents, who provided this space to us, which we could open up to my city. For seven years John and I lived side to side with them. Through the activities of my gallery, my father and mother could meet a new generation of artists, and they could meet them.

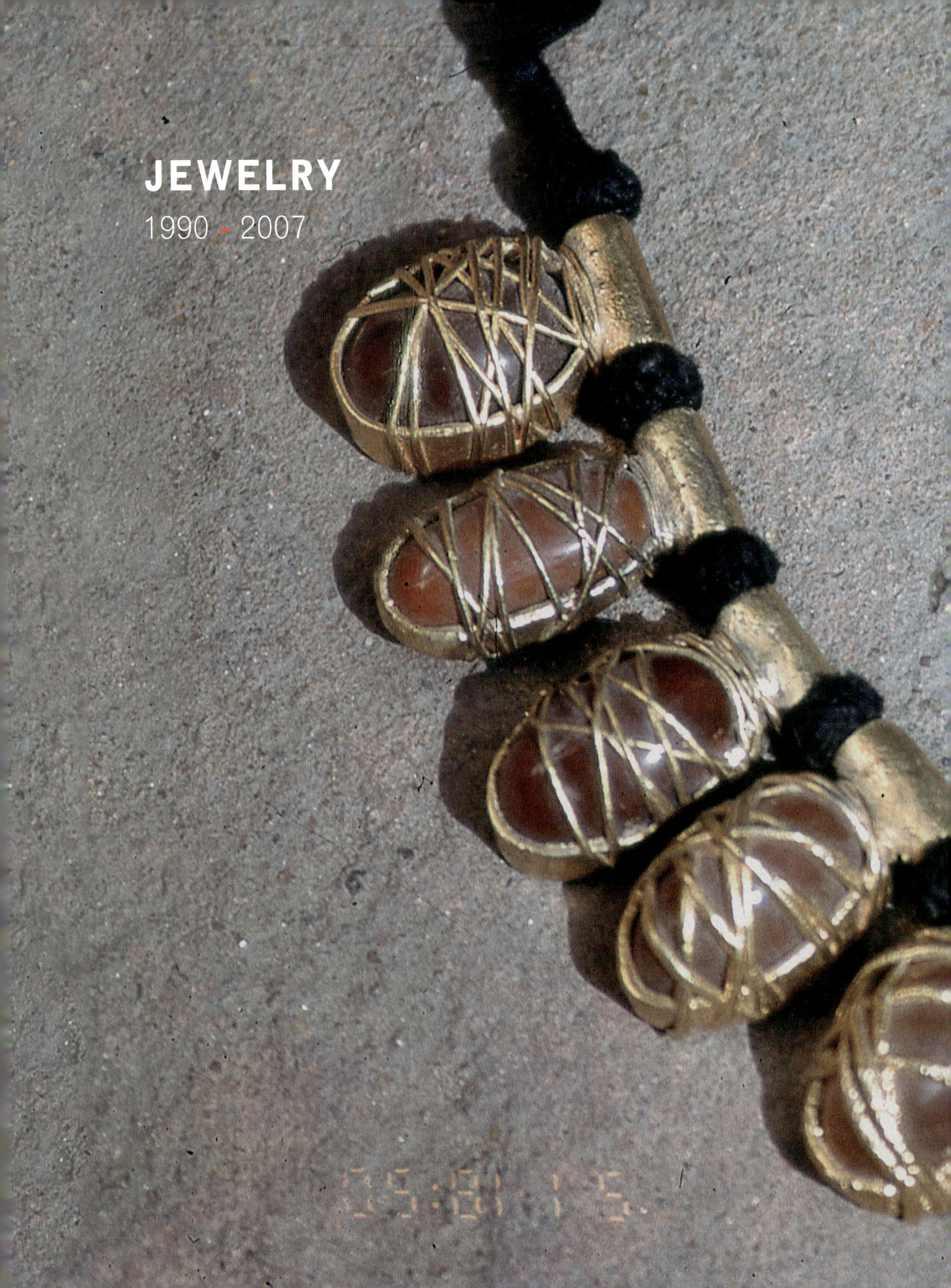

JEWELRY

1990 - 2007

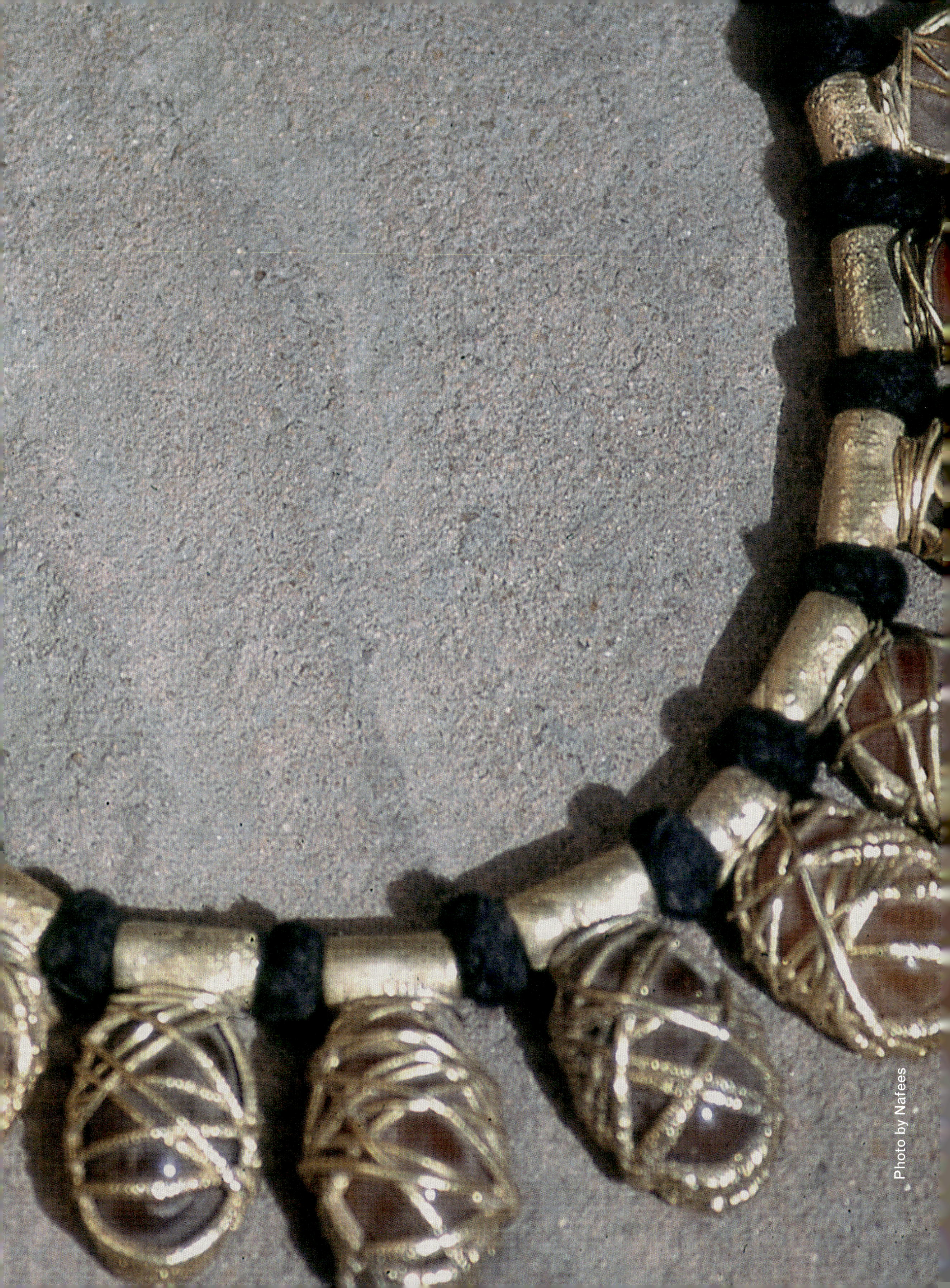

Photo by Nafees

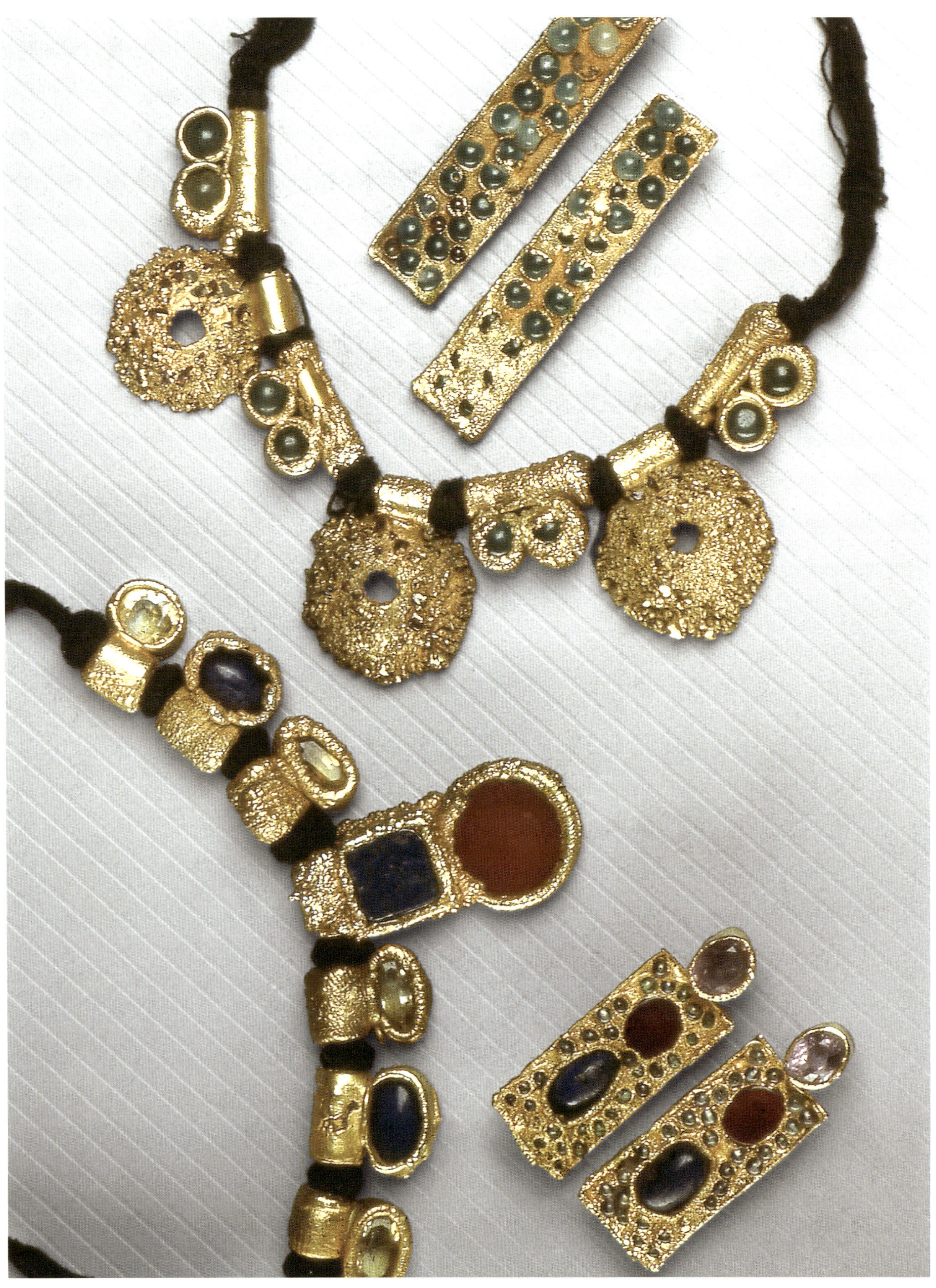

Untitled, 1989. Gold-plated copper, lapis, amethyst, agate, and golden citrine. Photo by Tapu Javeri

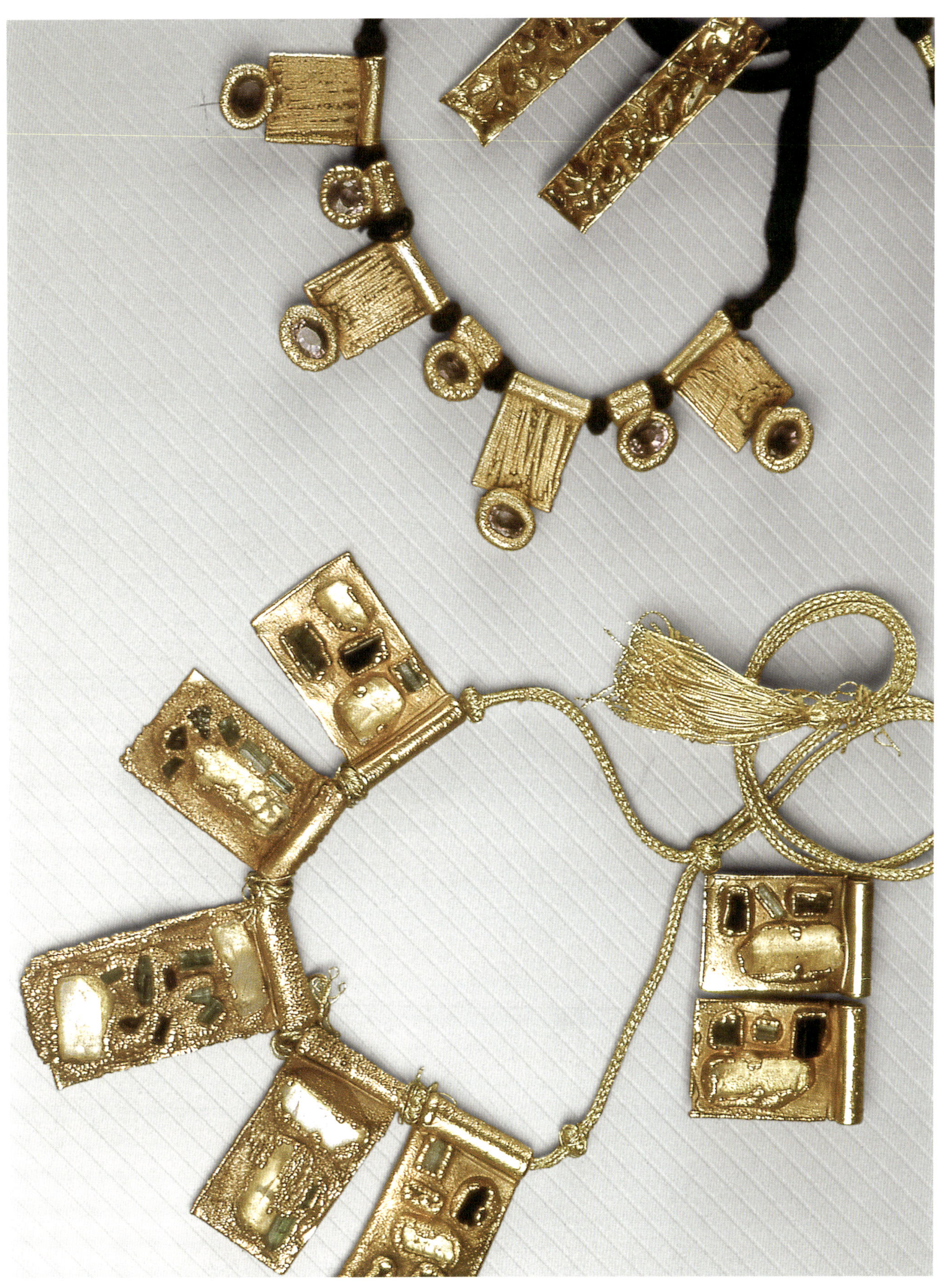

Untitled, 1989. Gold-plated copper, rock crystal, amethyst, green and black tourmaline.
Photo by Tapu Javeri

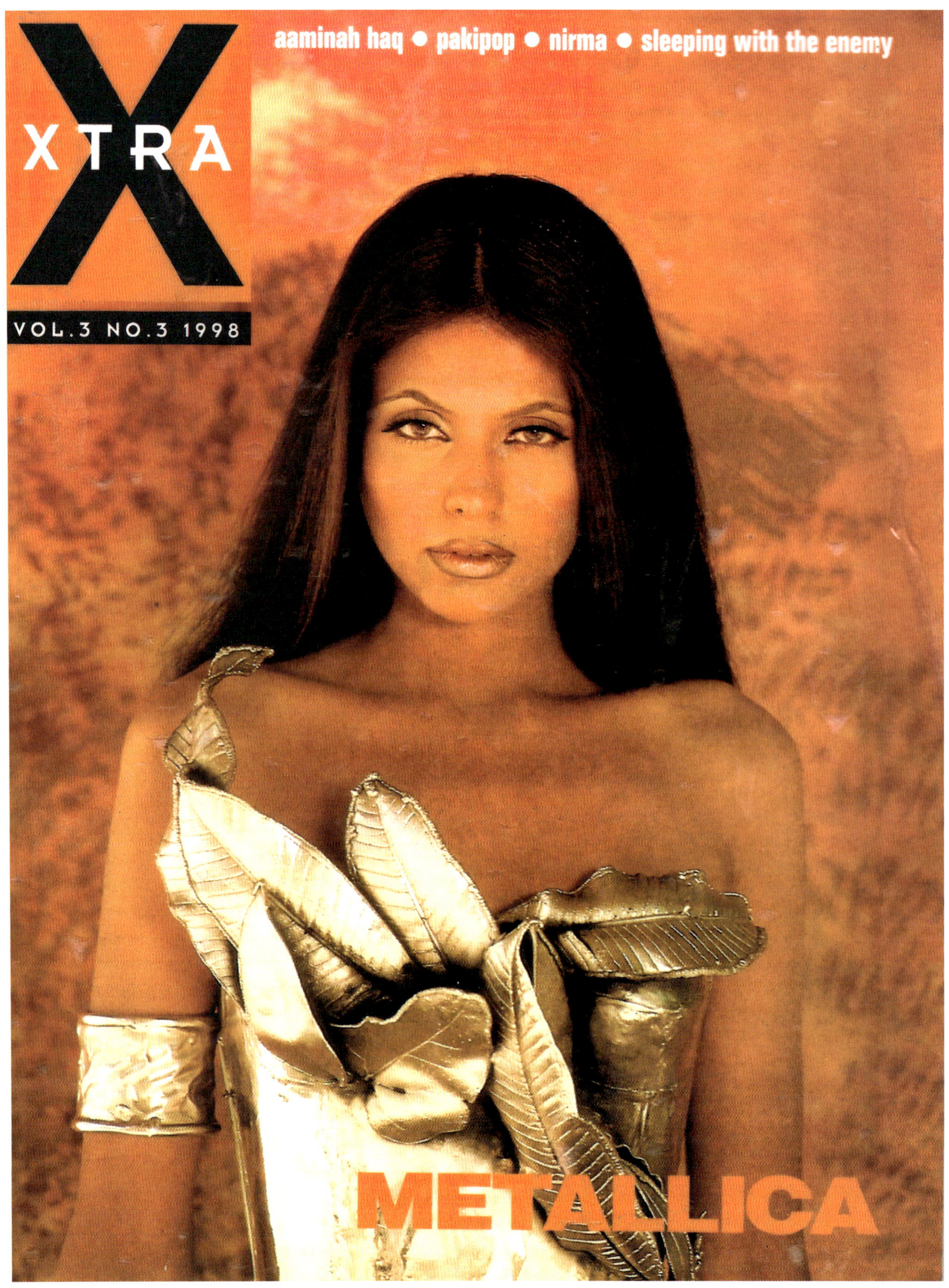

Xtra magazine, Volume 3, No. 3, 1998. Photo by Tapu Javeri

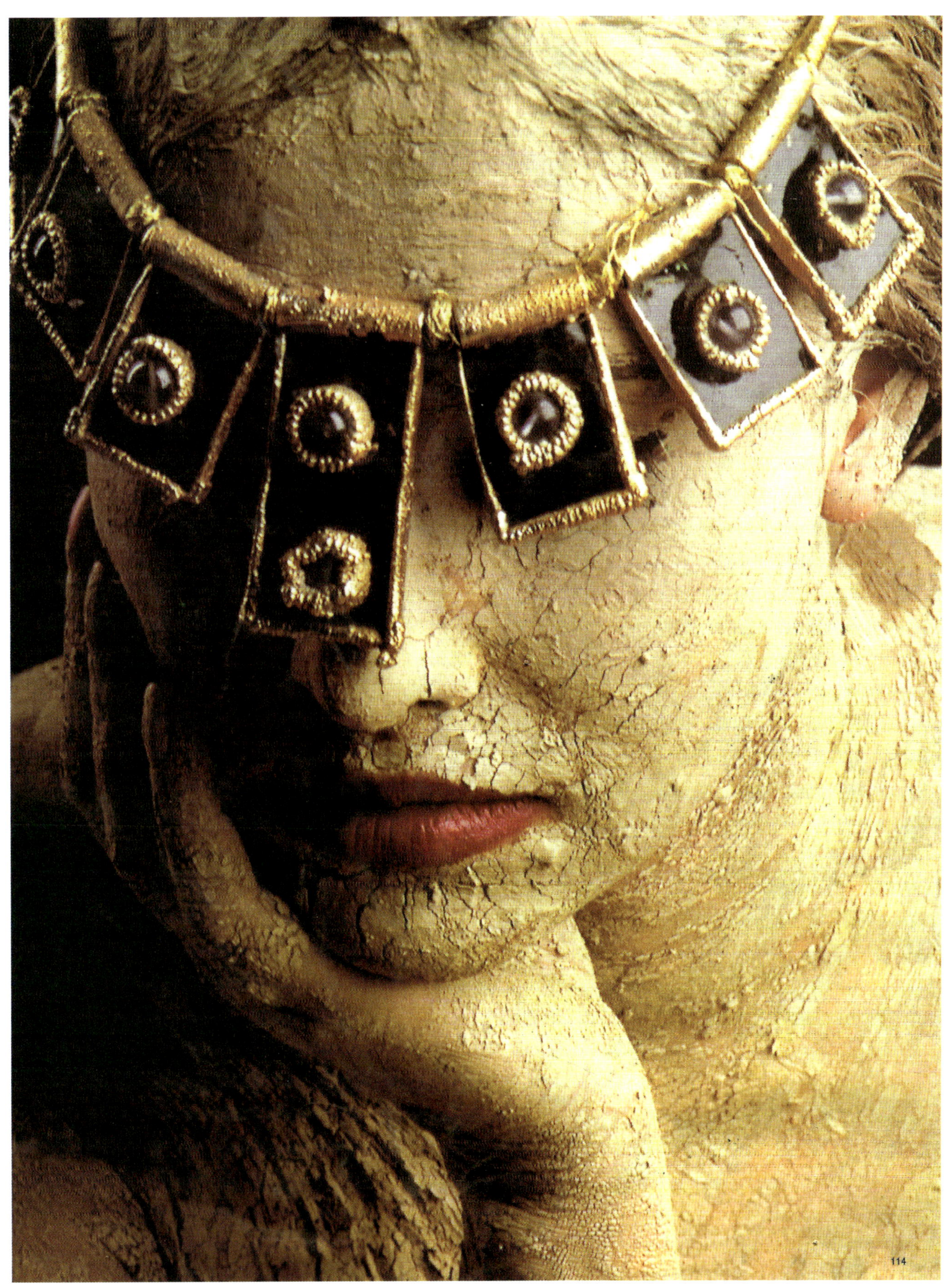

Visage magazine, December 1991. Photo by Asif Raza

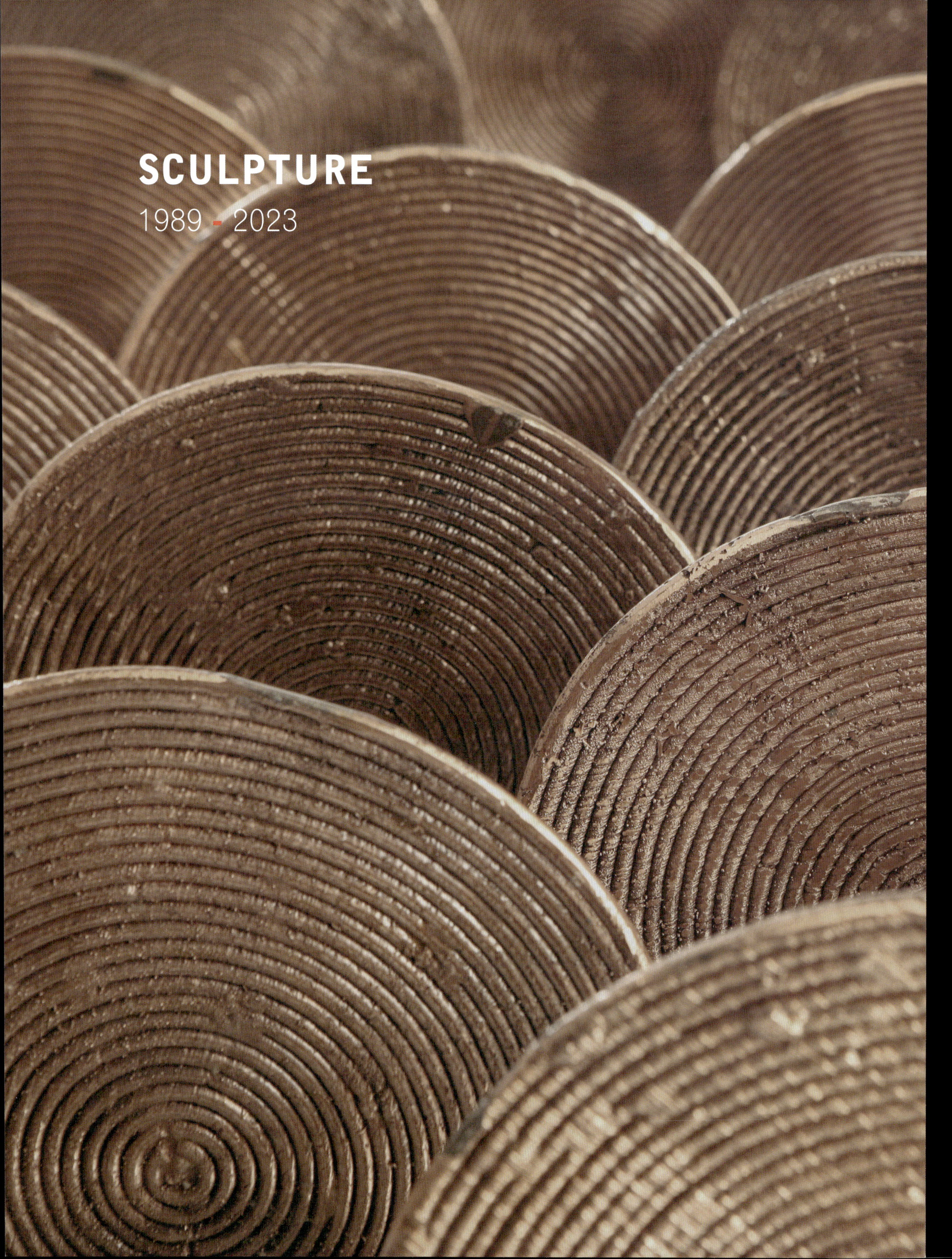

SCULPTURE

1989 - 2023

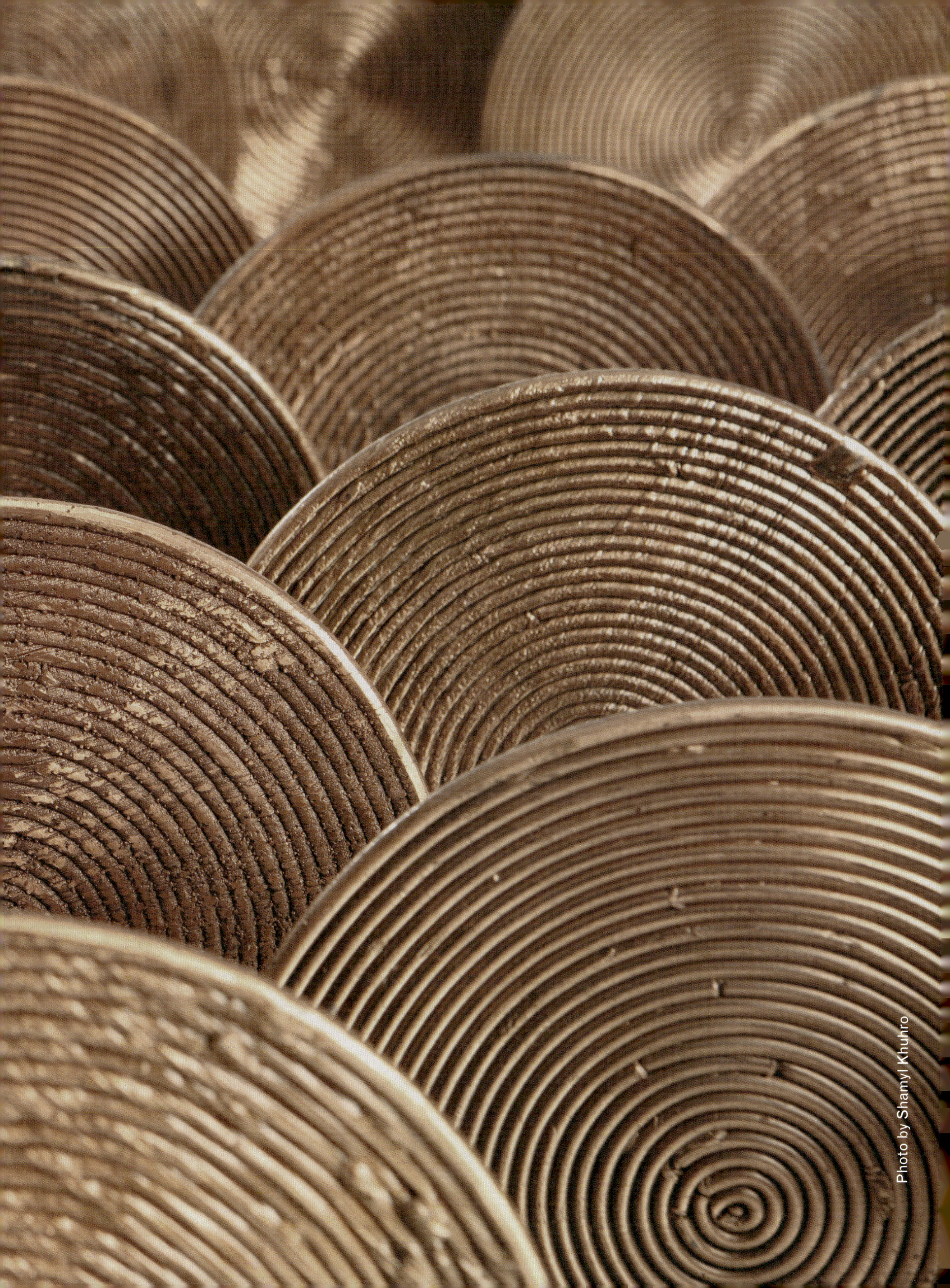

Photo by Shamyl Khuhro

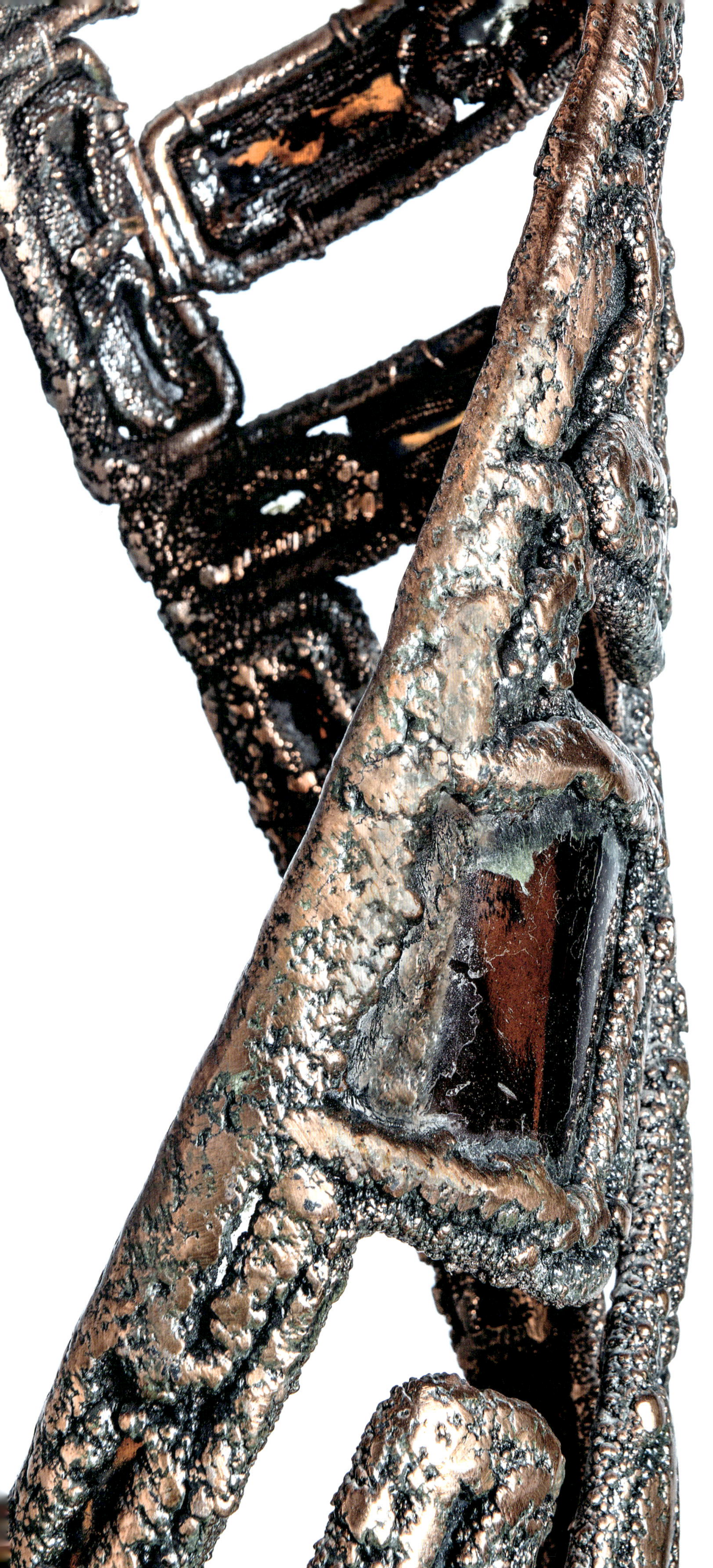

Sufi | Helix

1991 - 2001

Photo by Humayun Memon

Sufi II, 1995. Copper. 61 × 10 × 5 cm. Photo by Nafees

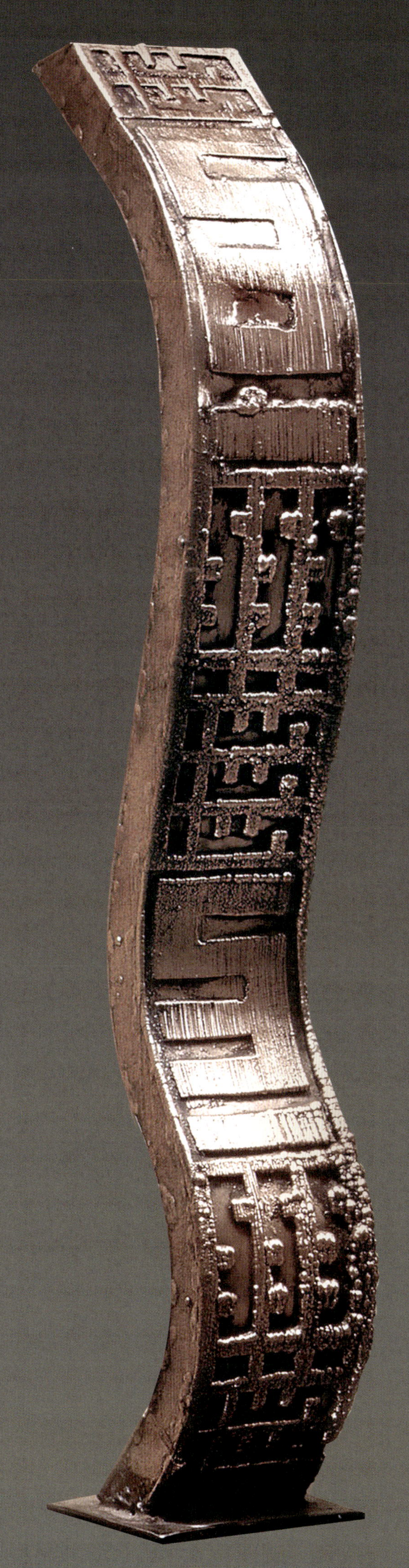

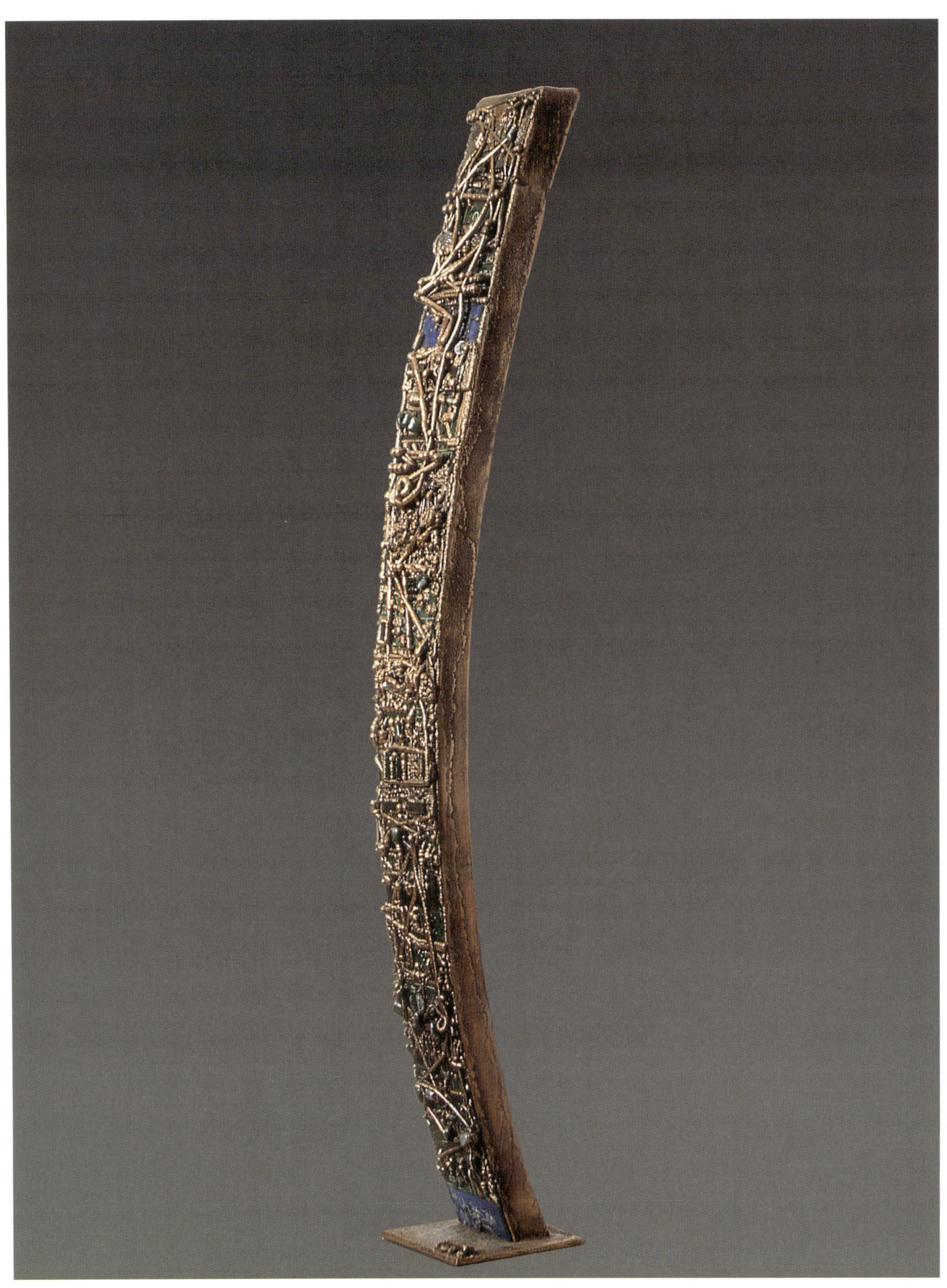

Sufi III, 1996. Copper and computer motherboard. 63.5 × 5 × 10 cm. Photo by Nafees

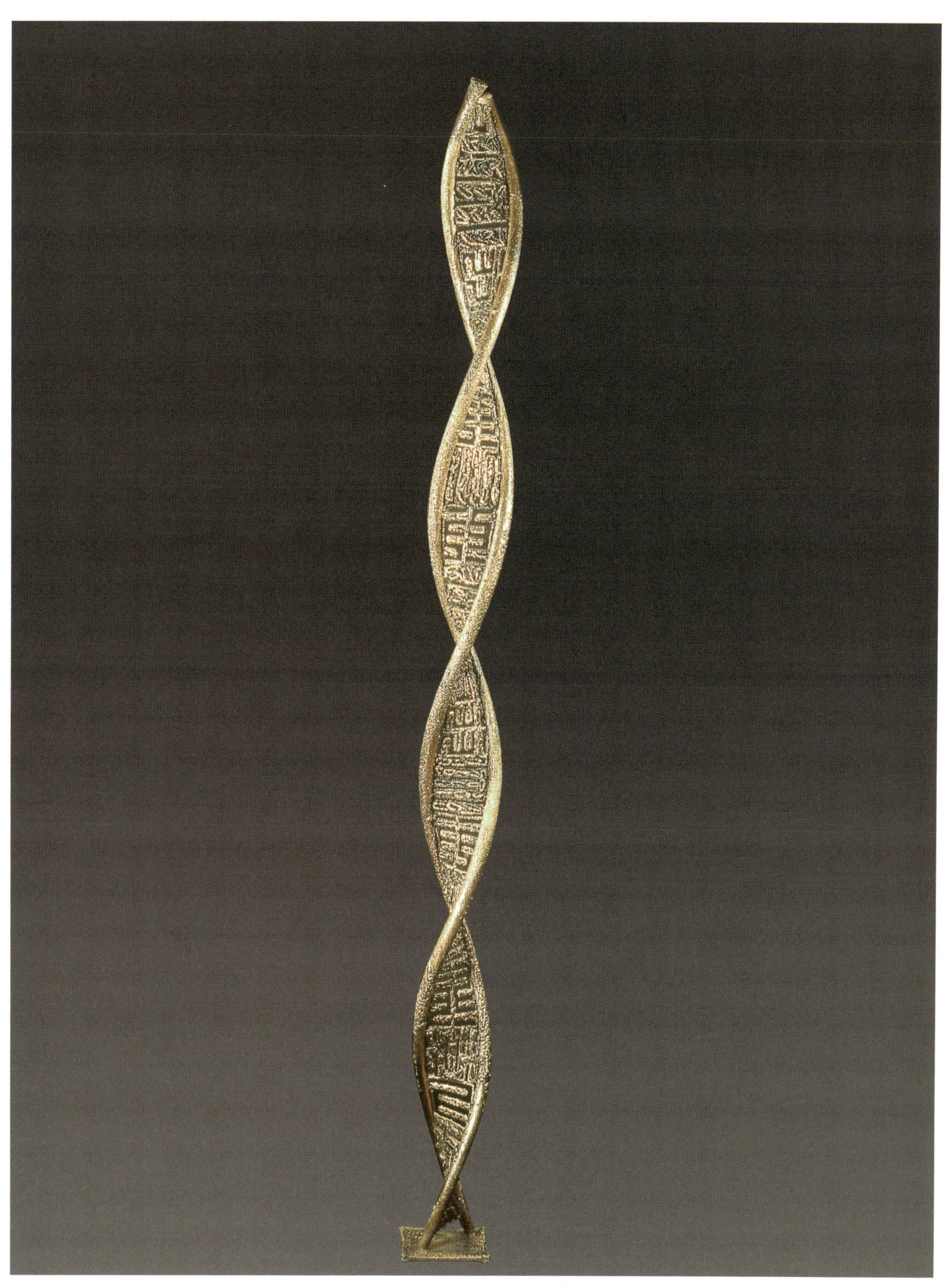

Chance, 1999. Copper and rock crystals. 152.4 × 10 × 10 cm. Photo by Nafees

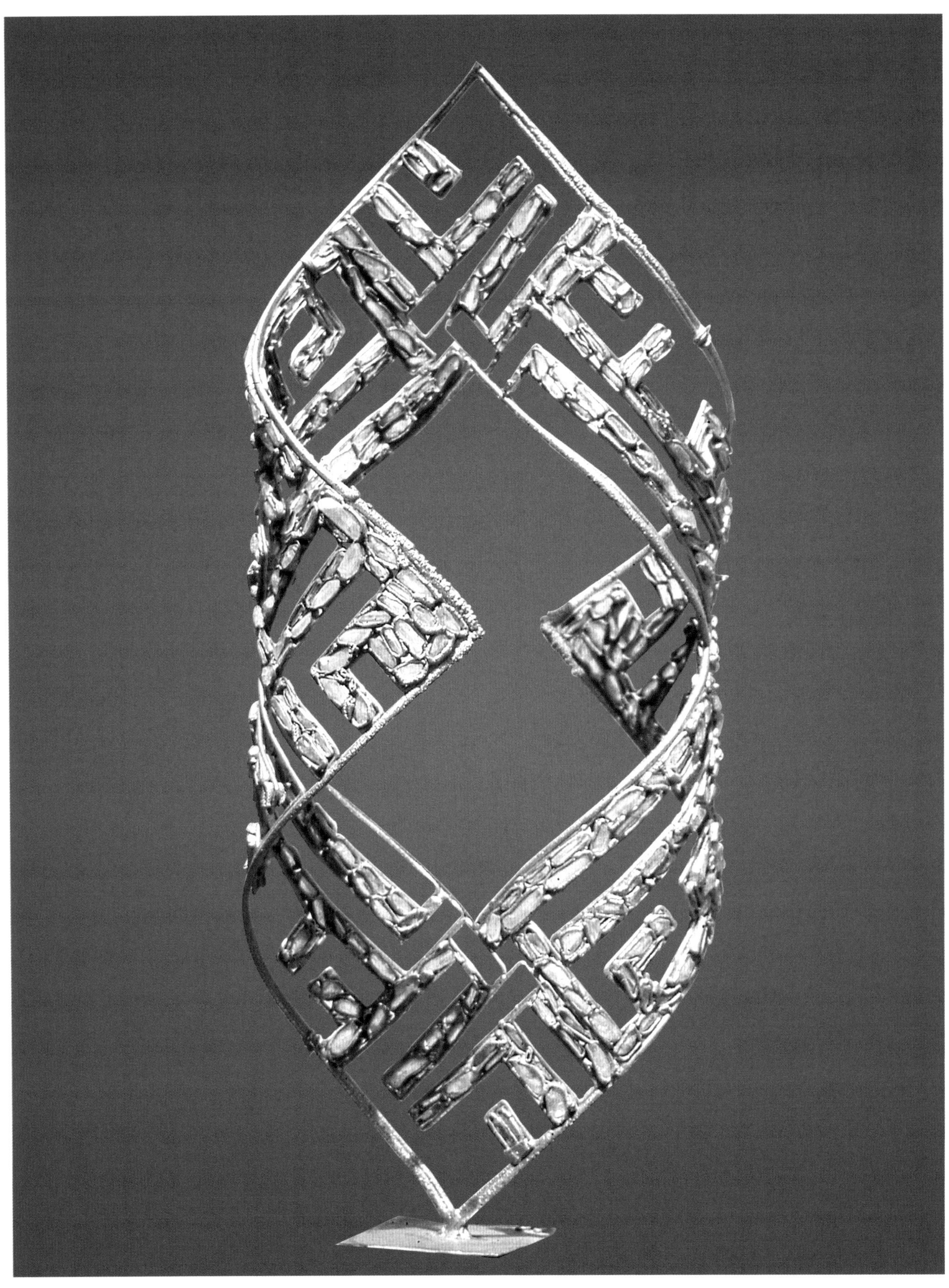

Nur, 2000. Copper, nickel plate and rock crystal. 61 × 35.5 × 17.7 cm. Photo by Nafees

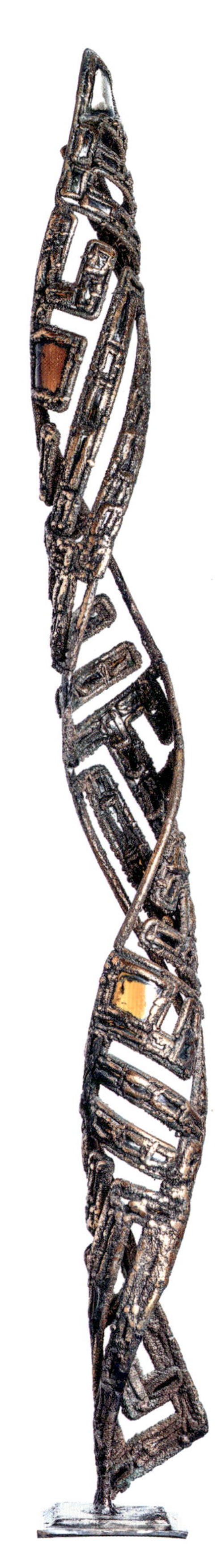

Helix III, 2001. Copper and glass. 127 × 18 × 18 cm. Photo by Humayun Memon

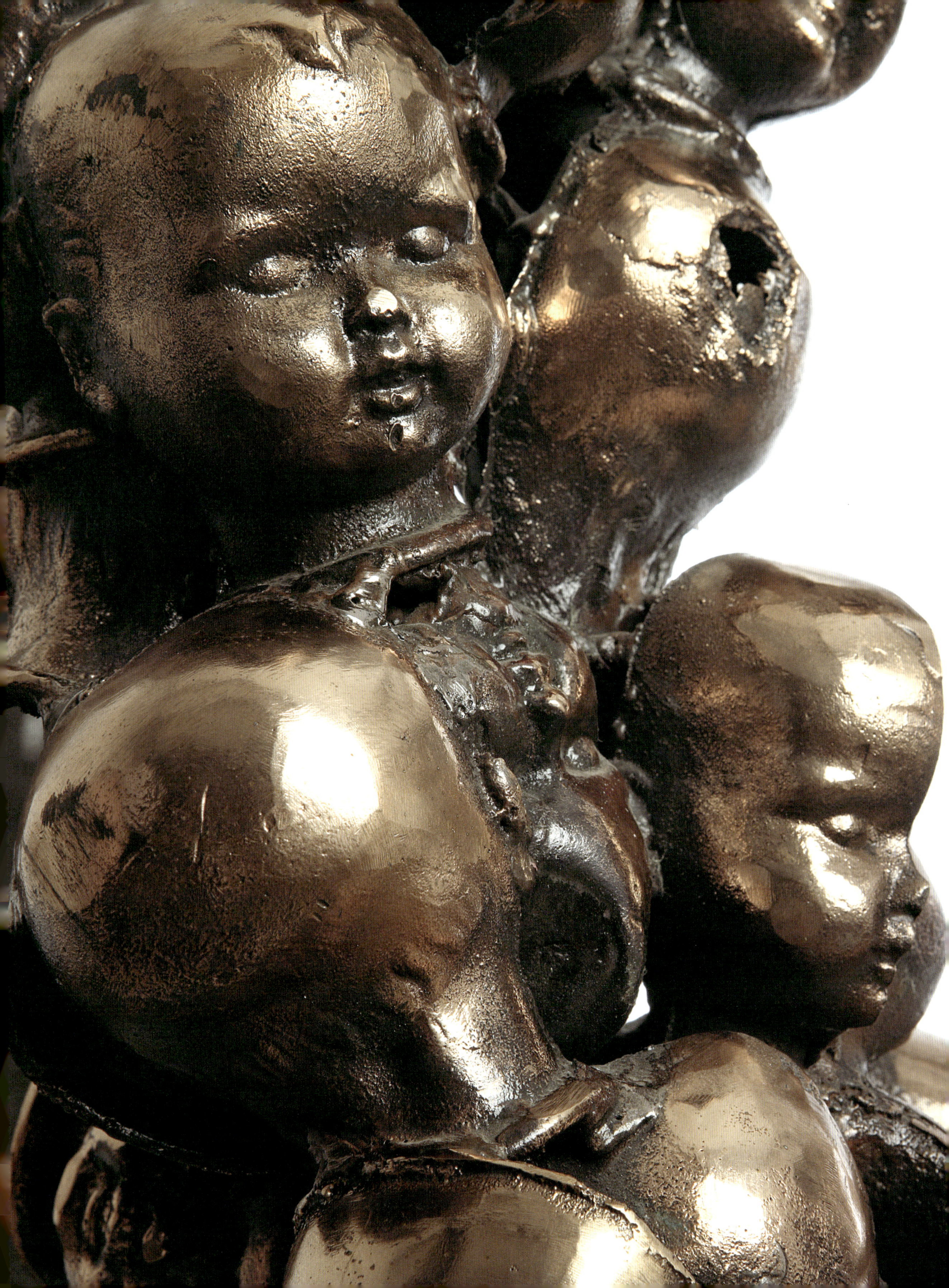

Appropriation

1989 - 2011

Photo by Shamyl Khuhro

Atomic Buddha, 1989. Copper and bronze. 81 × 68.5 × 68.5 cm. Photo by Nafees

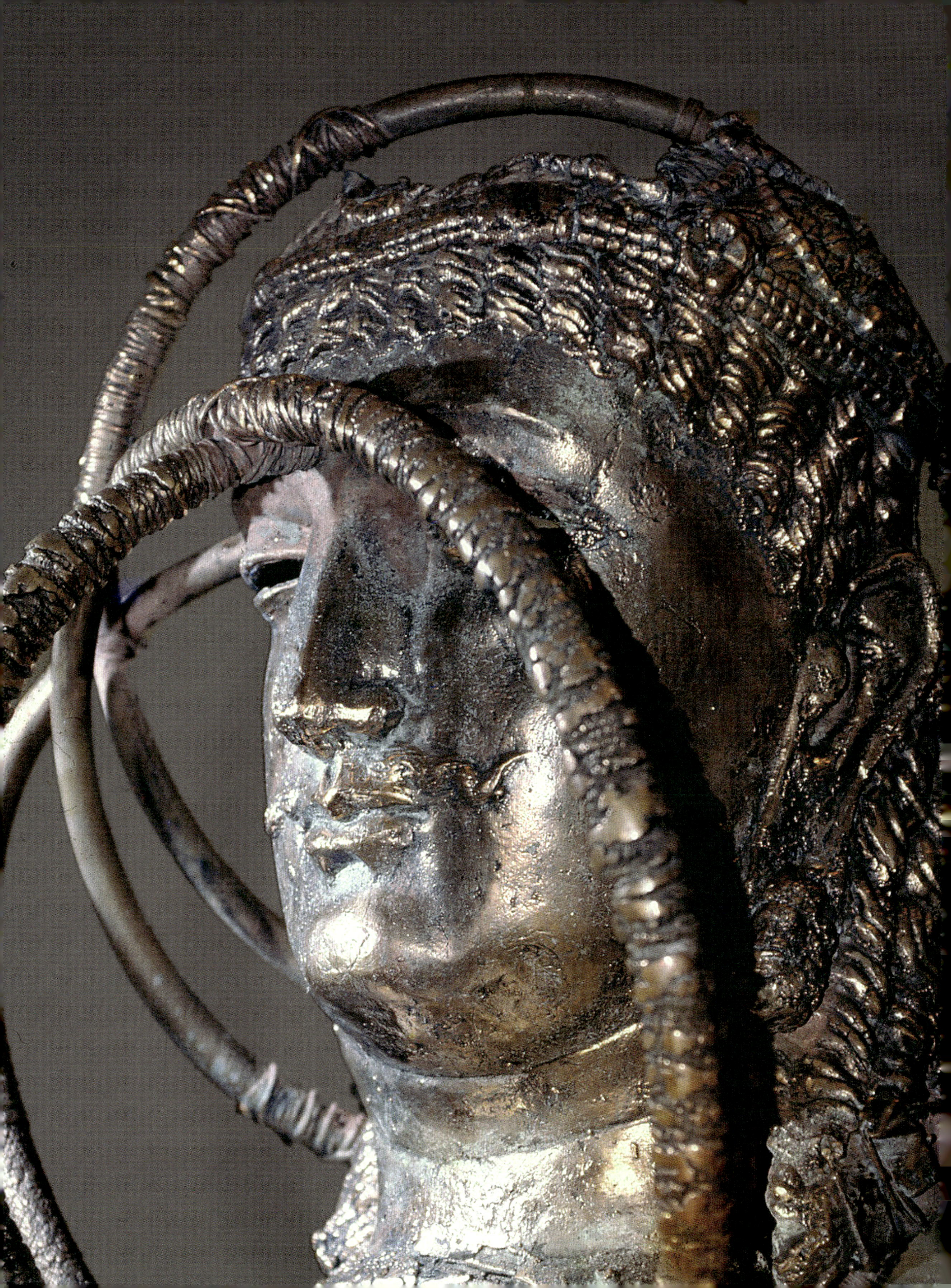

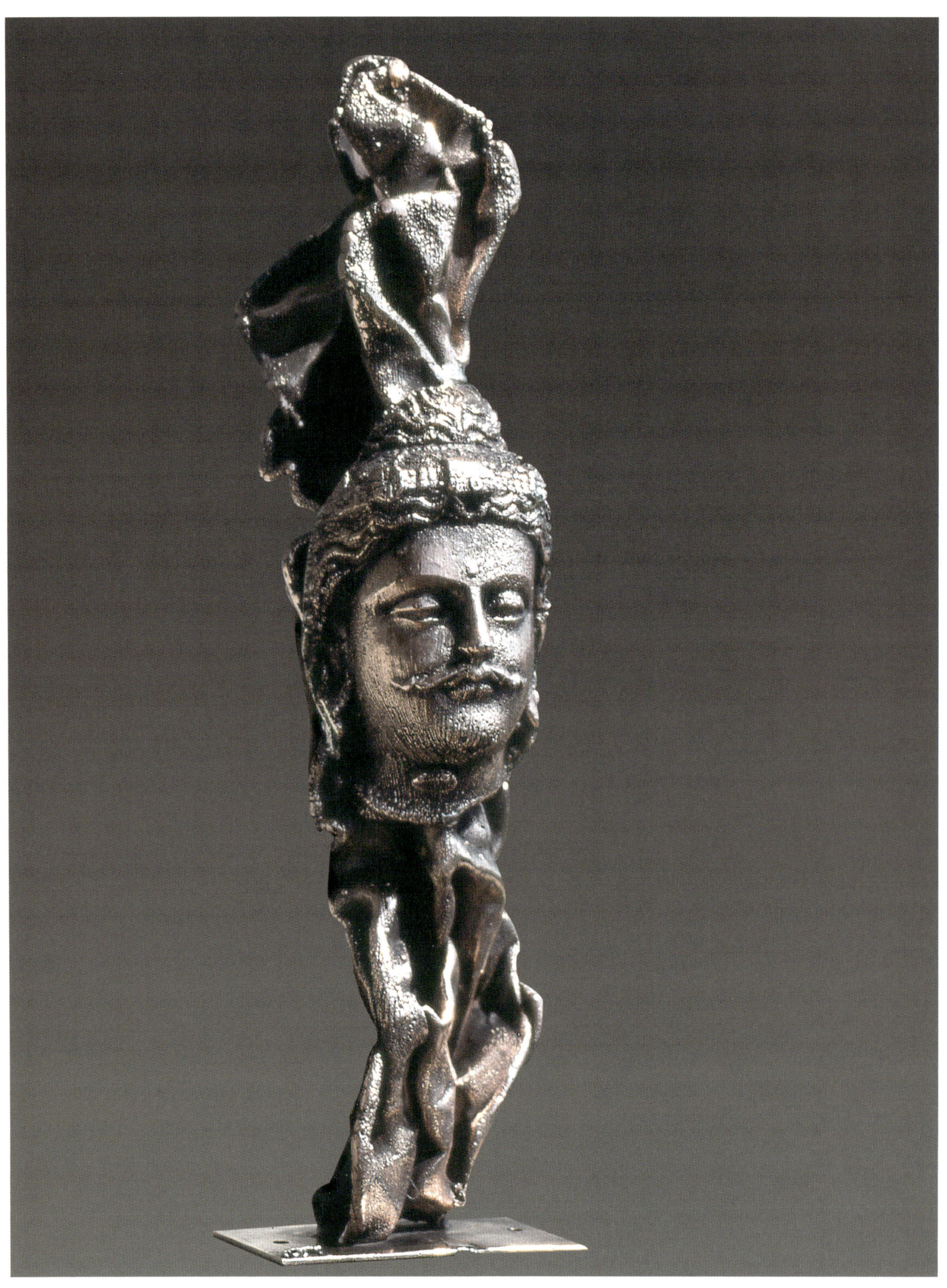

Flying Buddha, 1992. Copper and bronze. 63.5 × 12.7 × 17.7 cm. Photo by Nafees

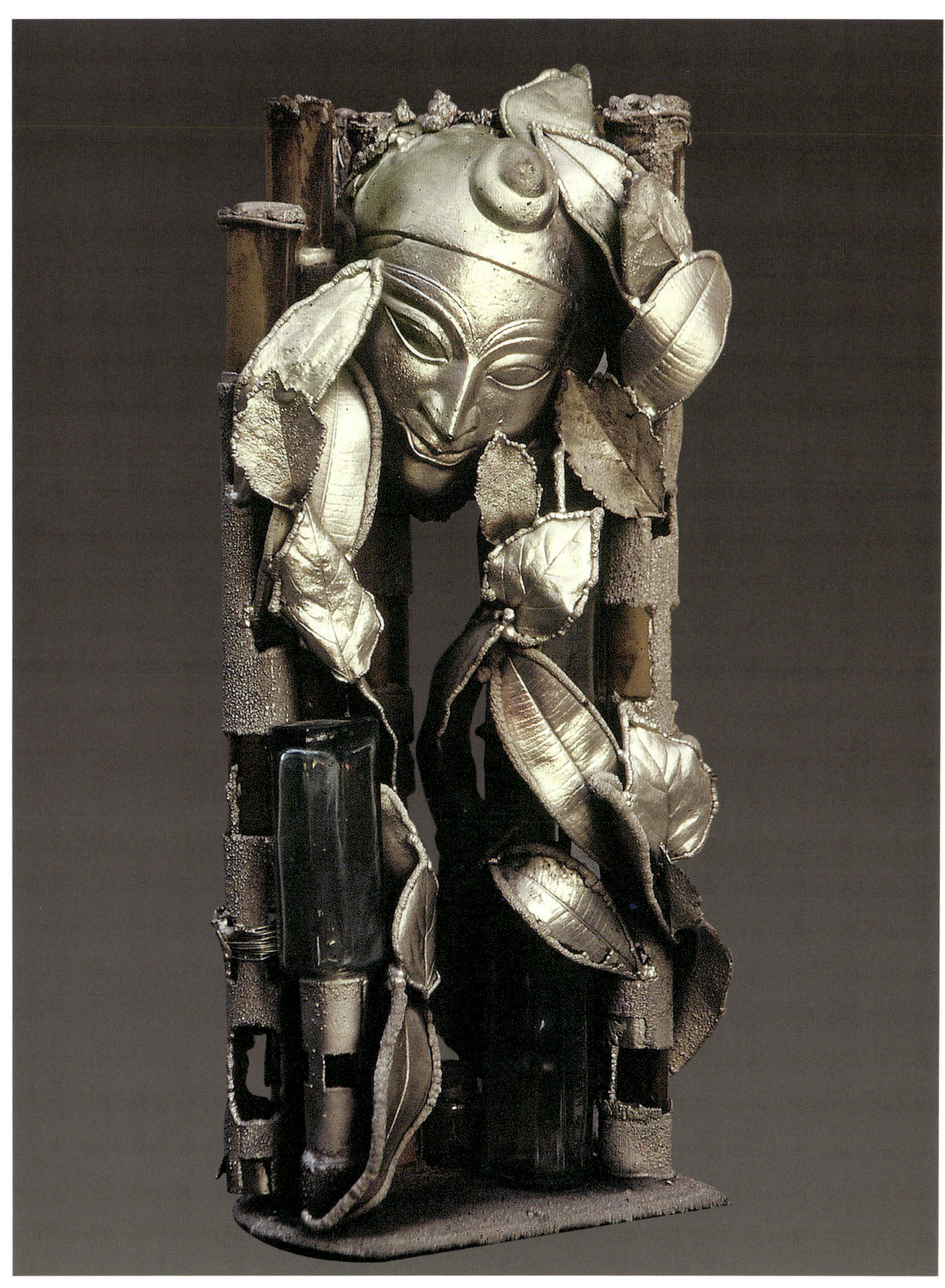

Krishna in Time, 1993. Copper, bronze, nickel plate and glass. 40.6 × 35.5 × 35.5 cm. Photo by Nafees

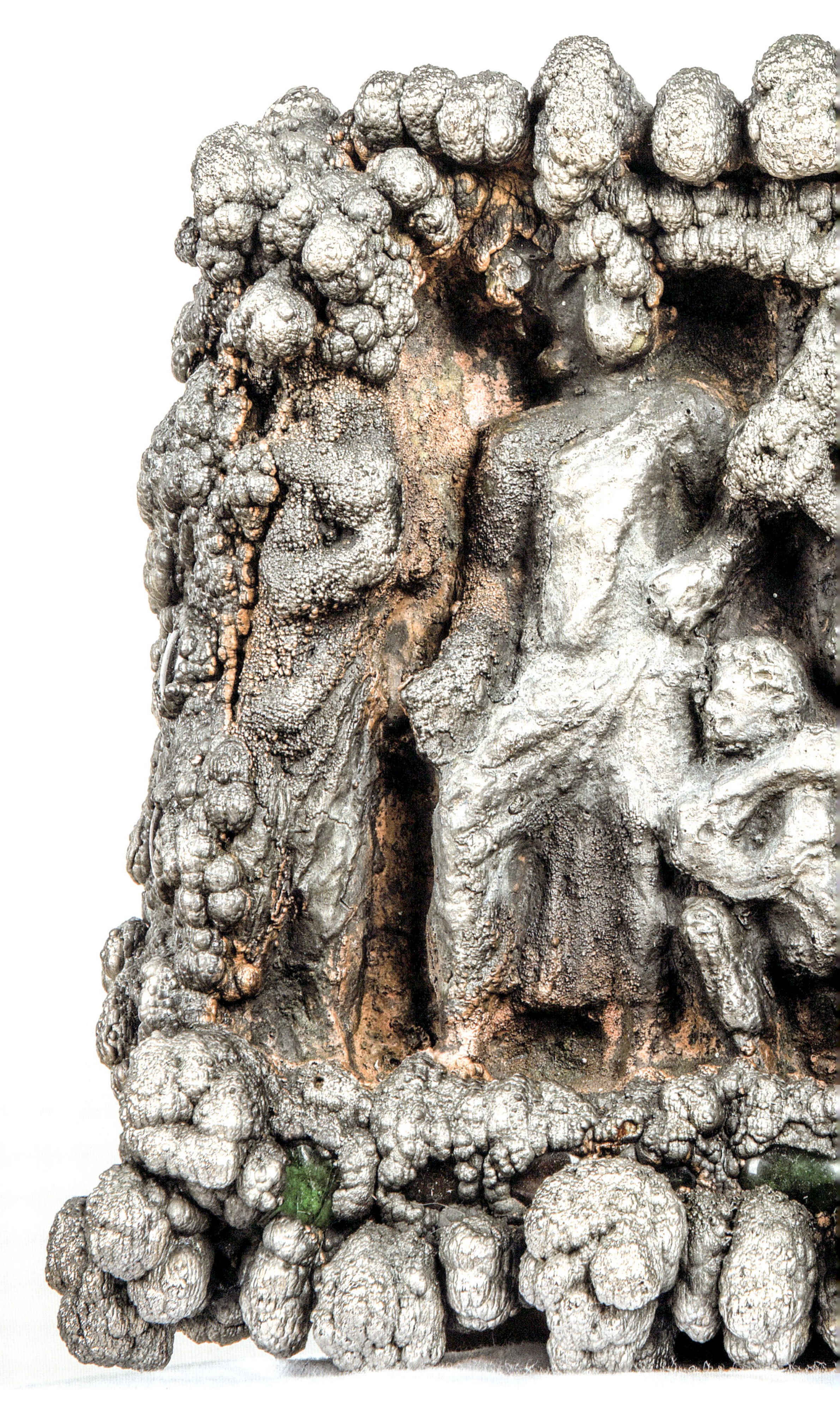

Buddha Departed, 1993. Copper, bronze and enamel. 22.8 × 30.4 × 10 cm. Photo by Humayun Memon

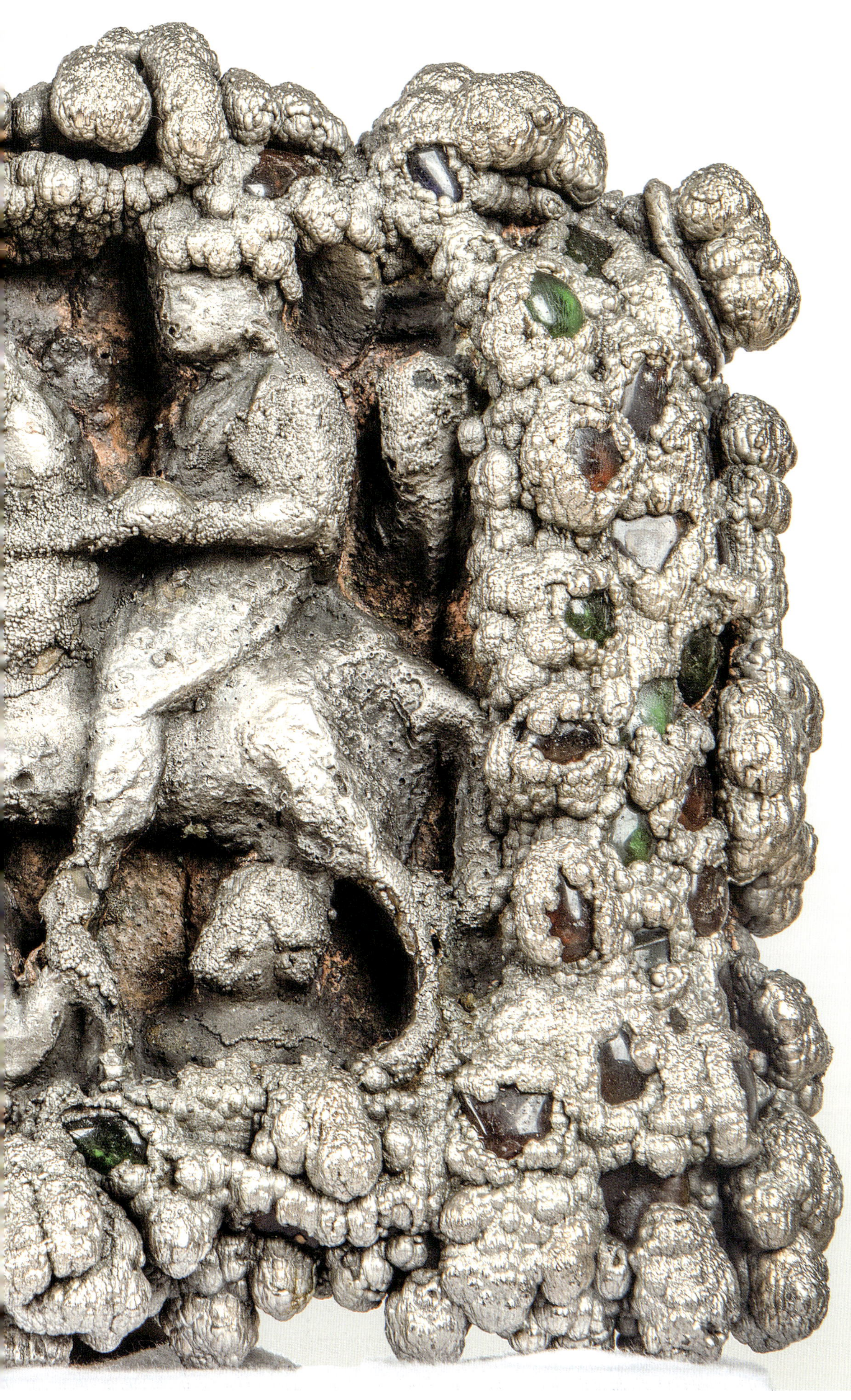

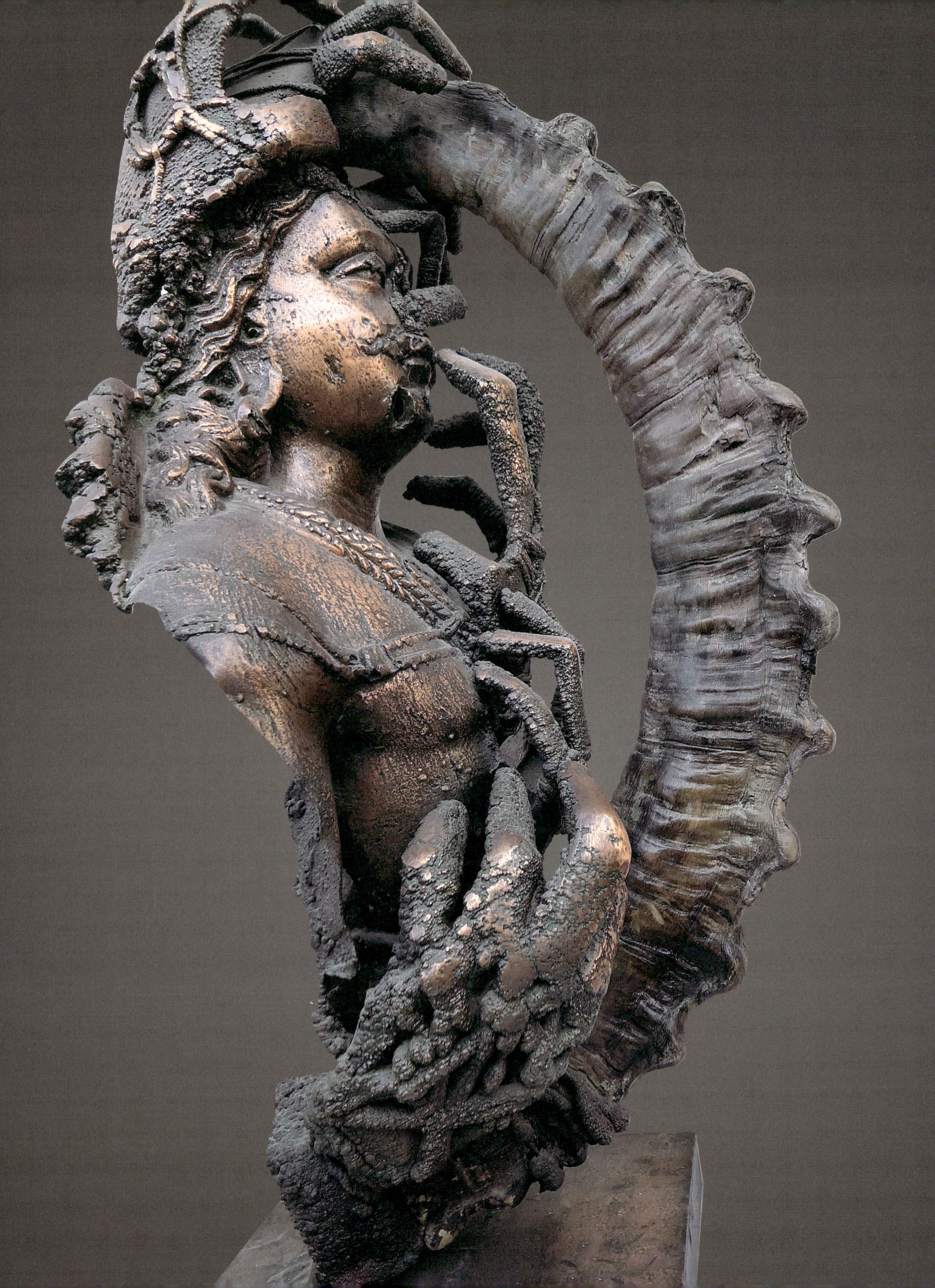

Horn Buddha, 1994. Copper, bronze and horn. 59 × 39 × 28 cm. Photo by Michele Ranieri

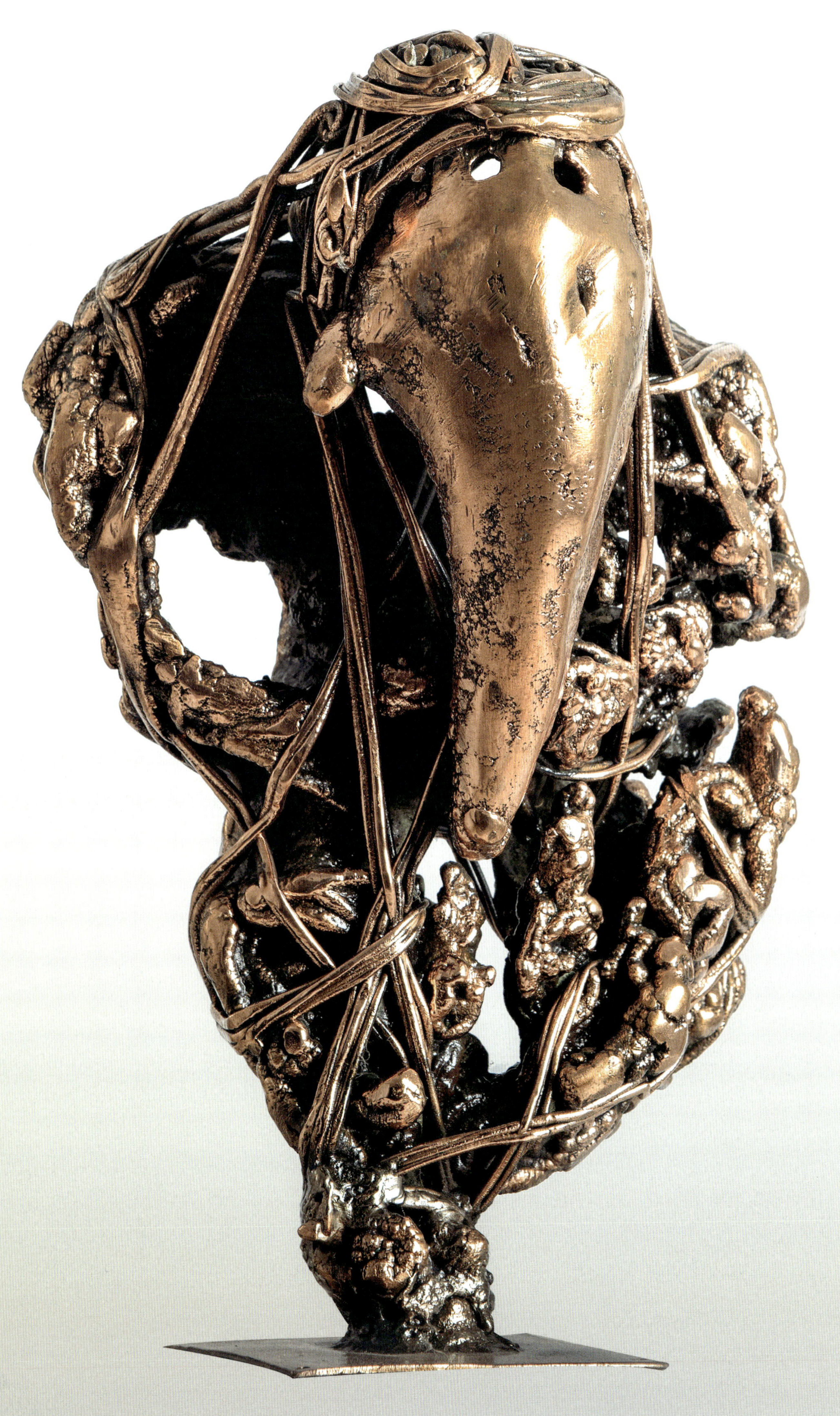

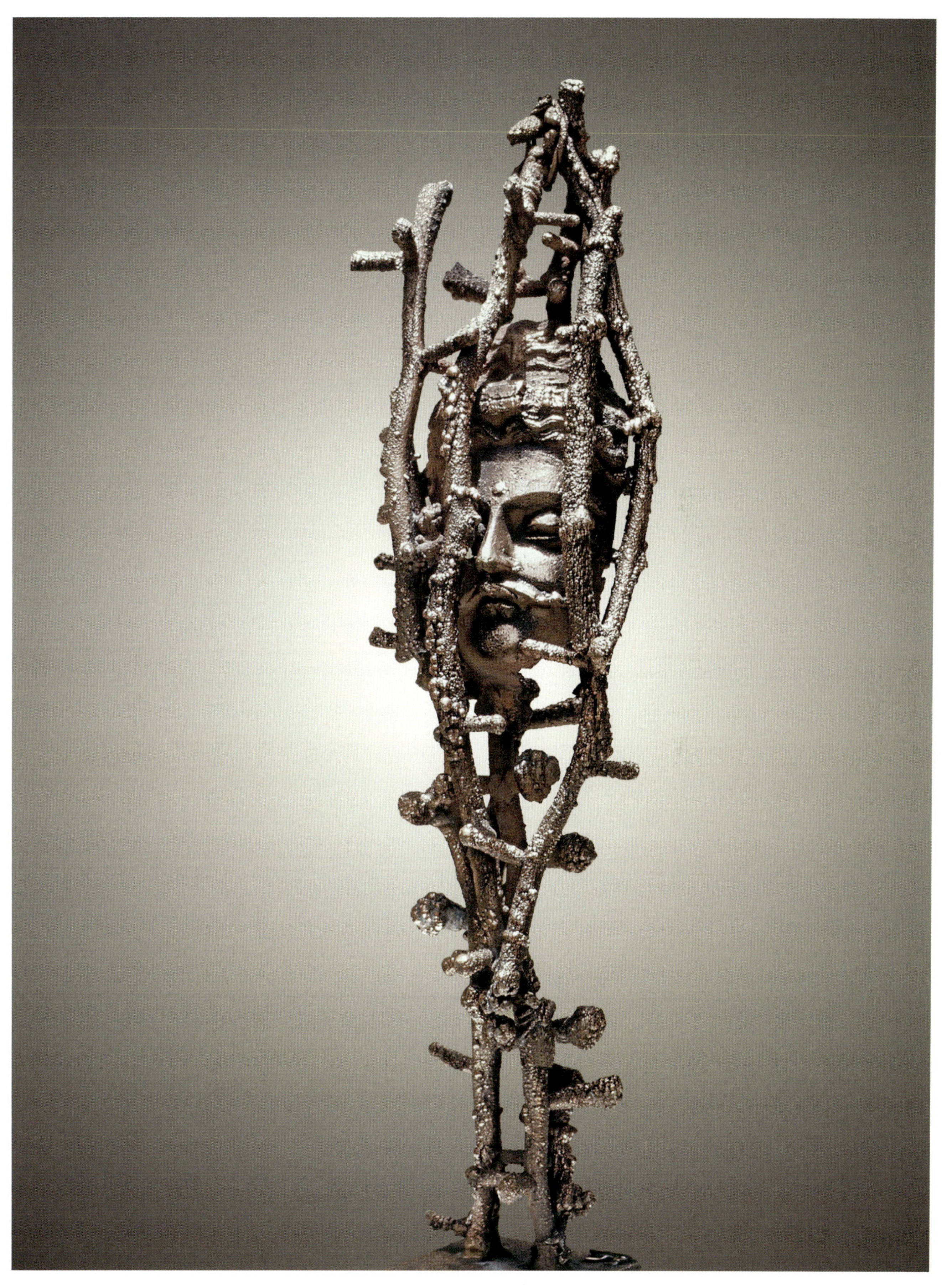

Buddah in the Kikar Jungle, 1998. Copper and bronze. 62 × 15 × 17 cm. Photo by Nafees

Opposite page
Ganesh, 1996. Copper and bronze. 33 × 25 × 18 cm. Photo by Humayun Memon

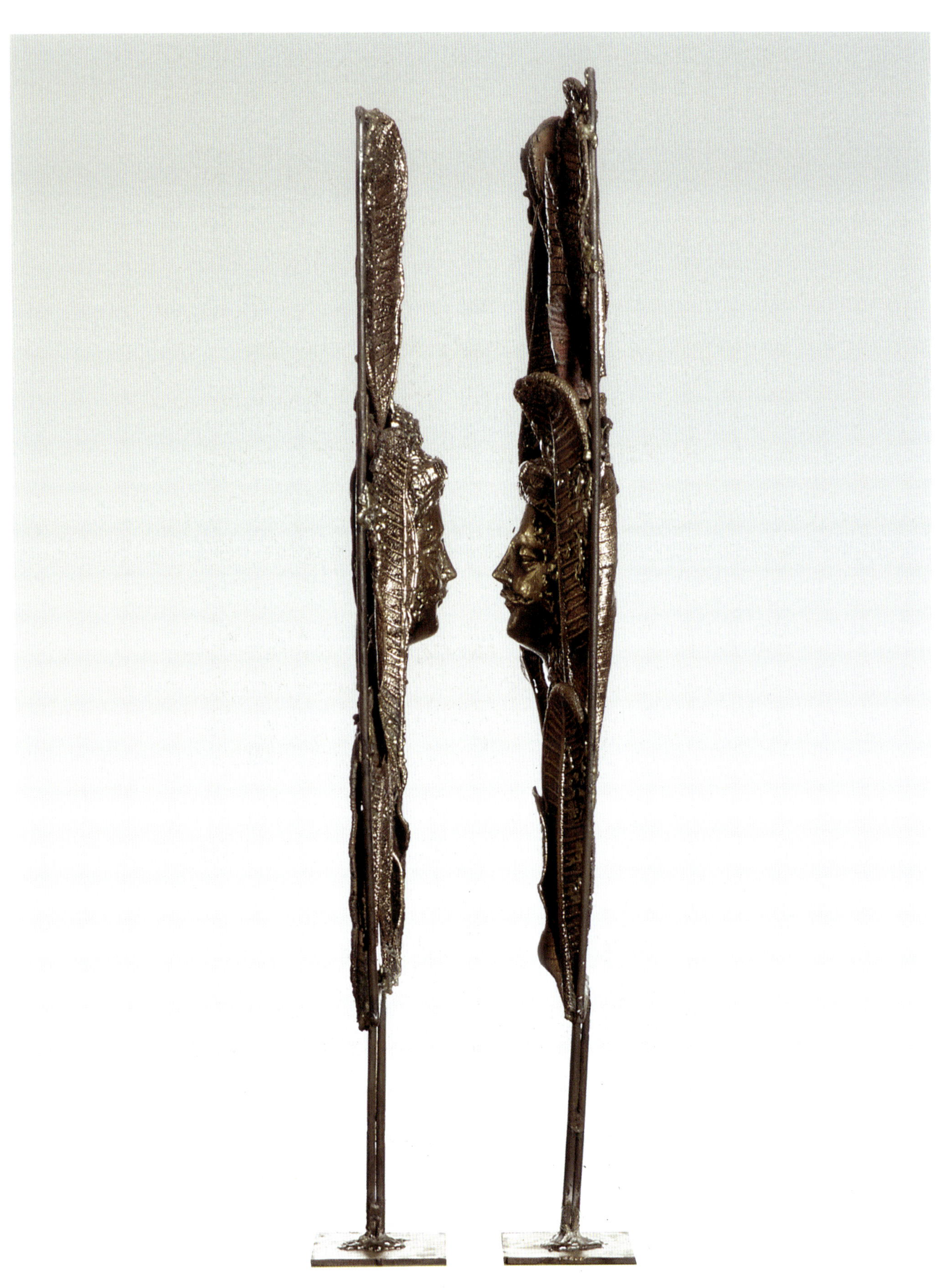

Talisman, 2003. Copper and bronze. 132 × 63.5 × 10 cm (each work). Photo by Nafees

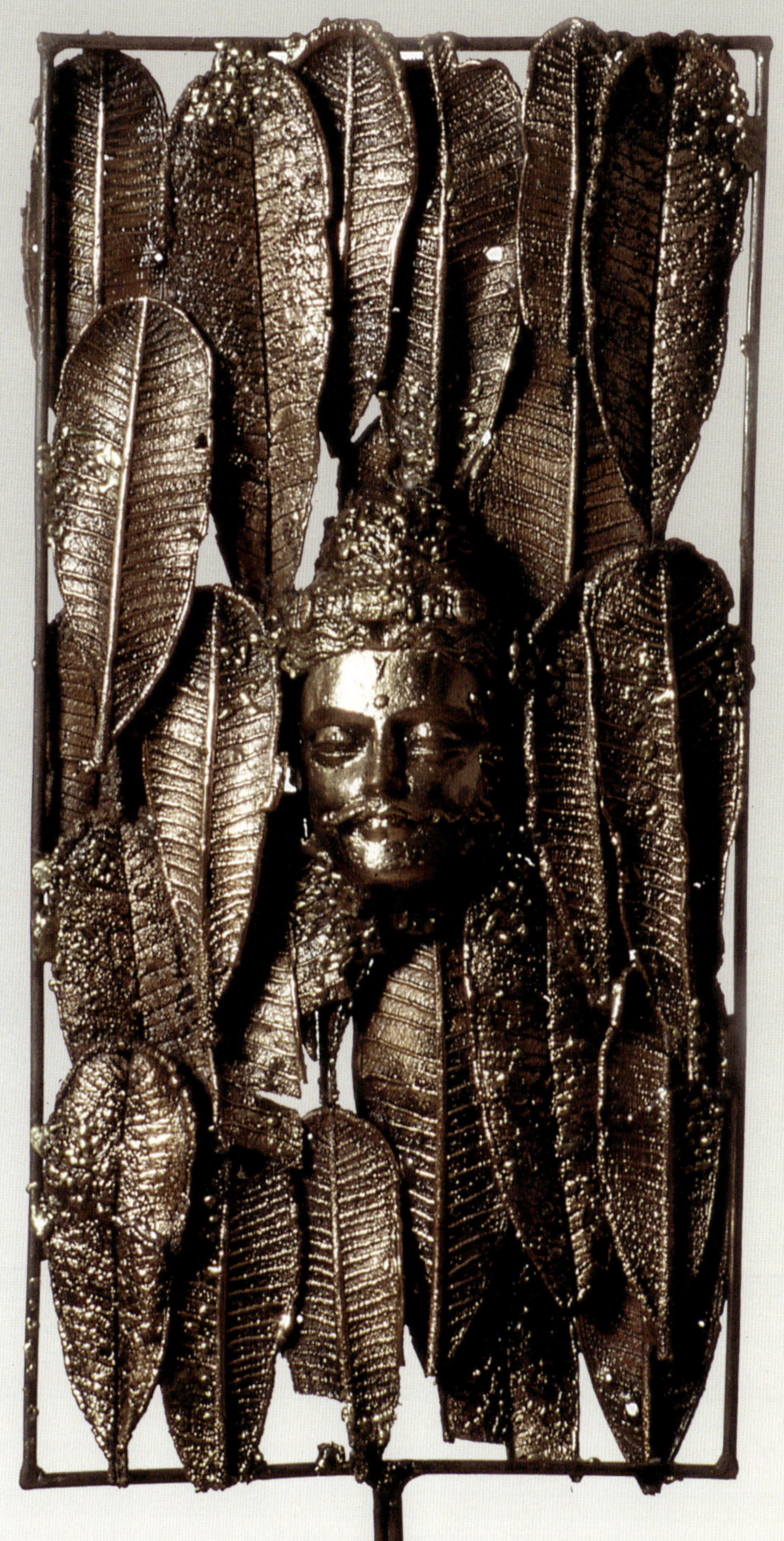

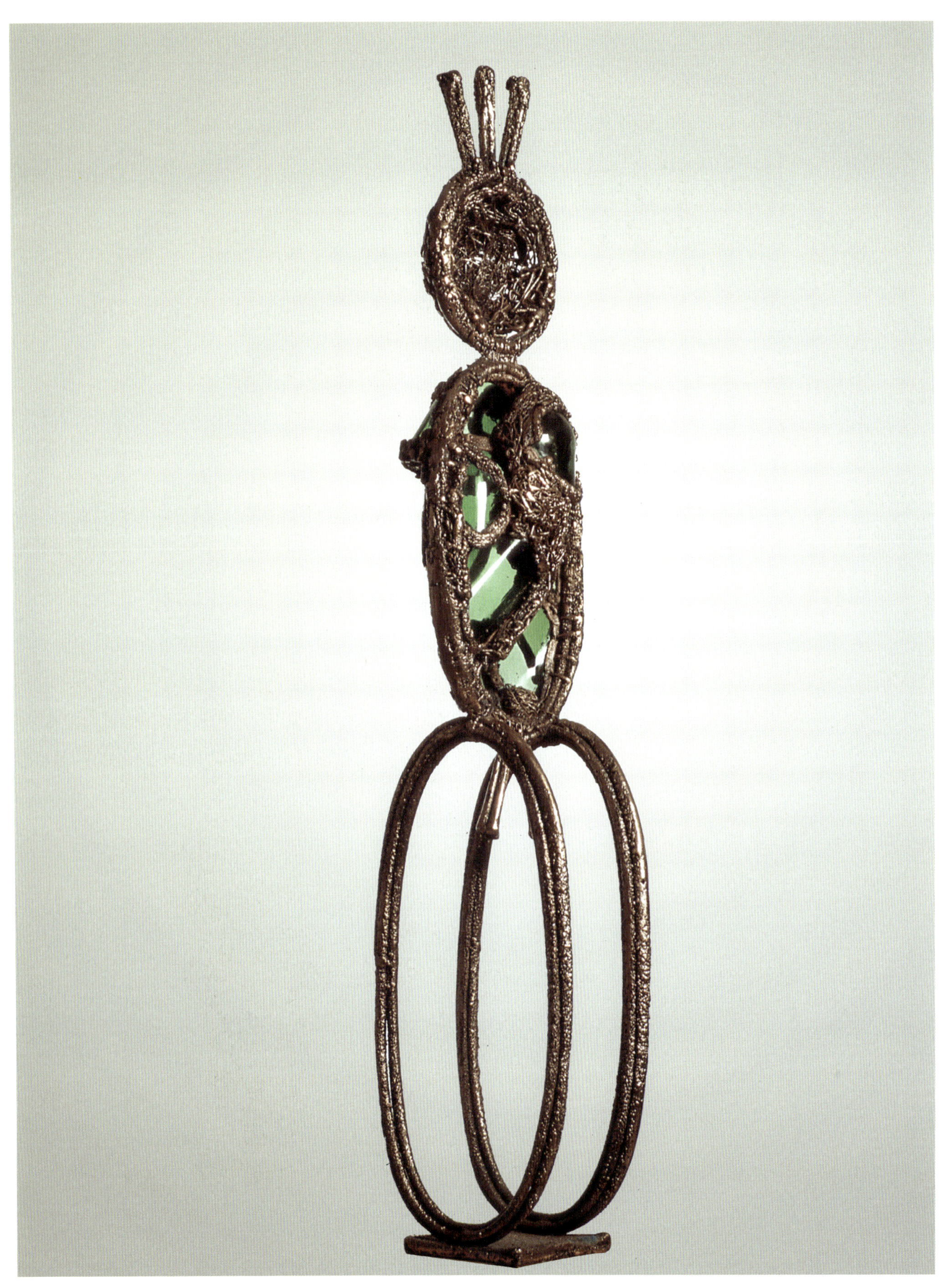

Hieroglyphics II, 2003. Copper with glass. 78.7 × 25.4 × 17.7 cm. Photo by Nafees

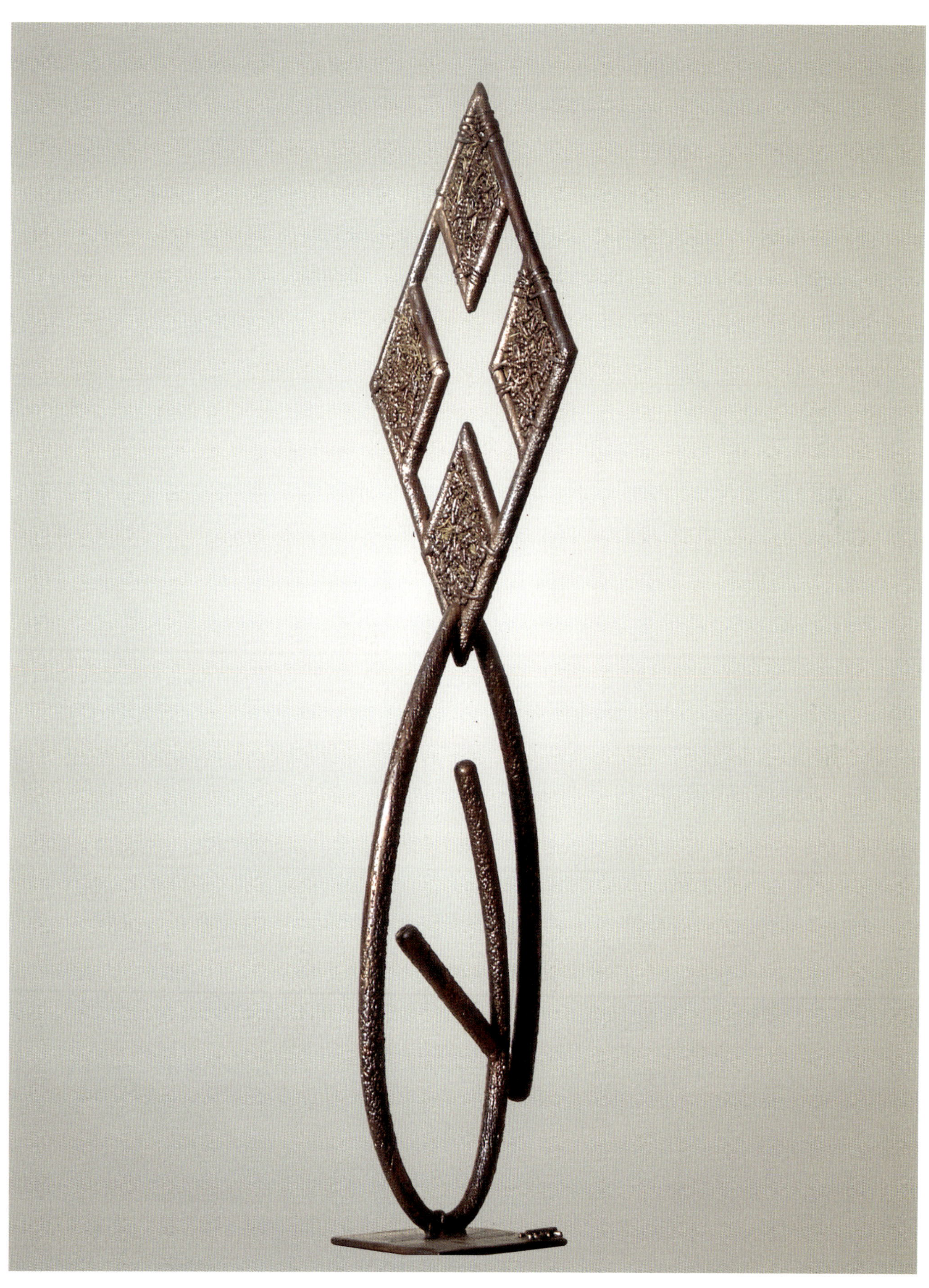

Hieroglyphics III, 2003. Copper and computer motherboard. 68.5 × 17.7 × 15.2 cm. Photo by Nafees

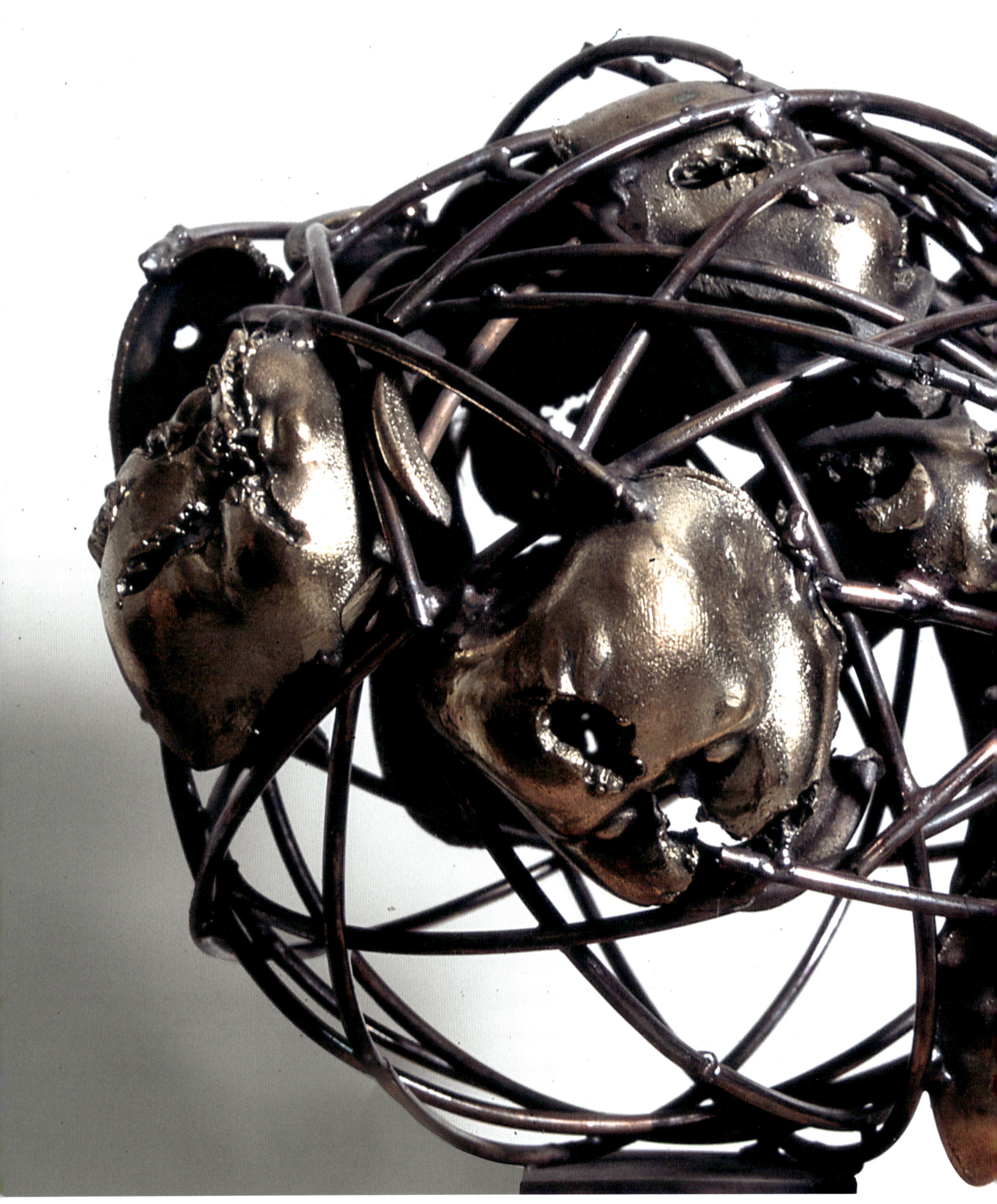

Calculated Head VII, 2004. Copper and bronze. 35.5 × 30.4 × 33 cm. Photo by Shamyl Khuhro

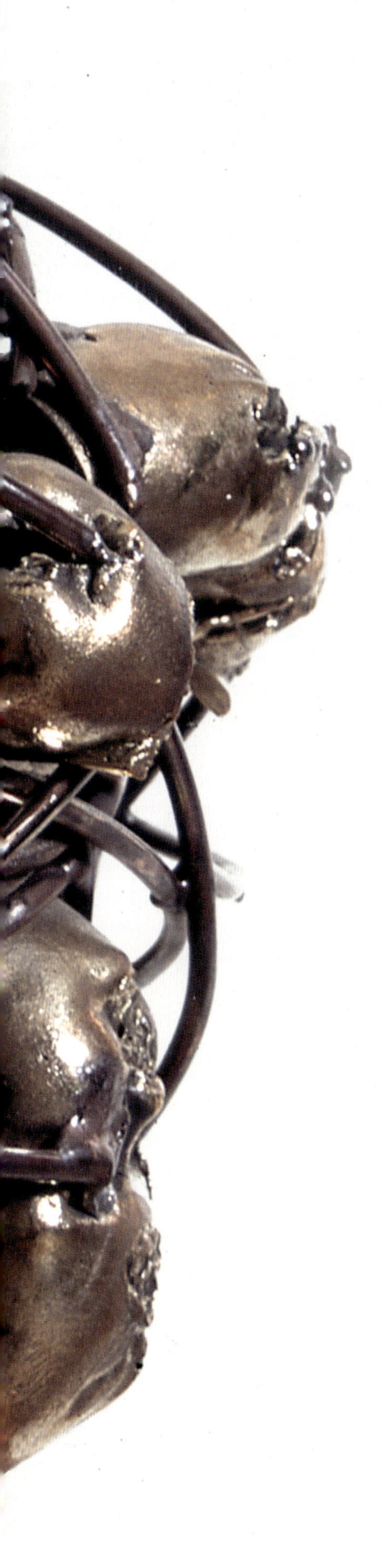

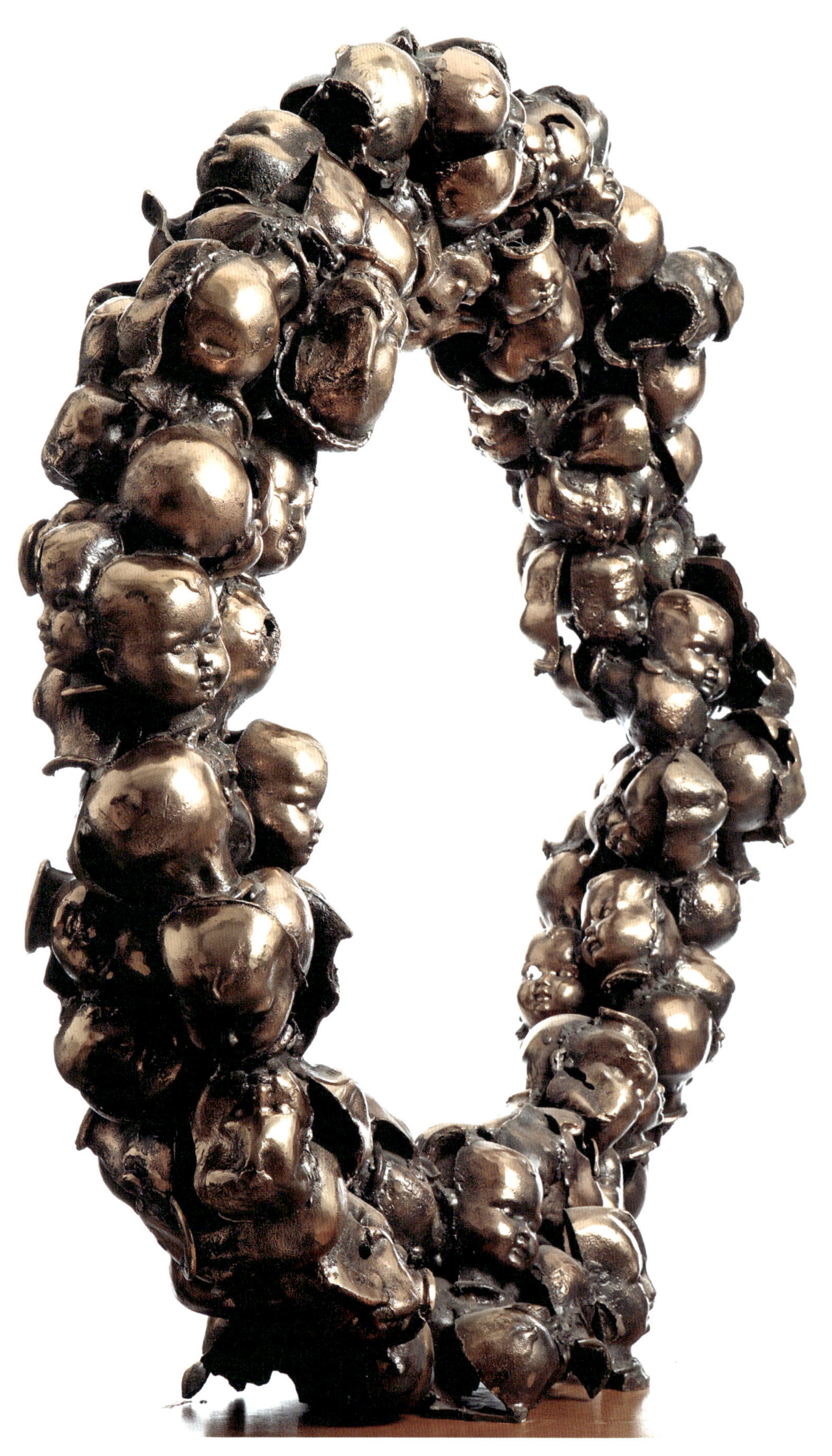

Sundried Heads: The Wreath, 2011. Bronze. 86.3 × 86.3 × 25.4 cm. Photo by Shamyl Khuhro

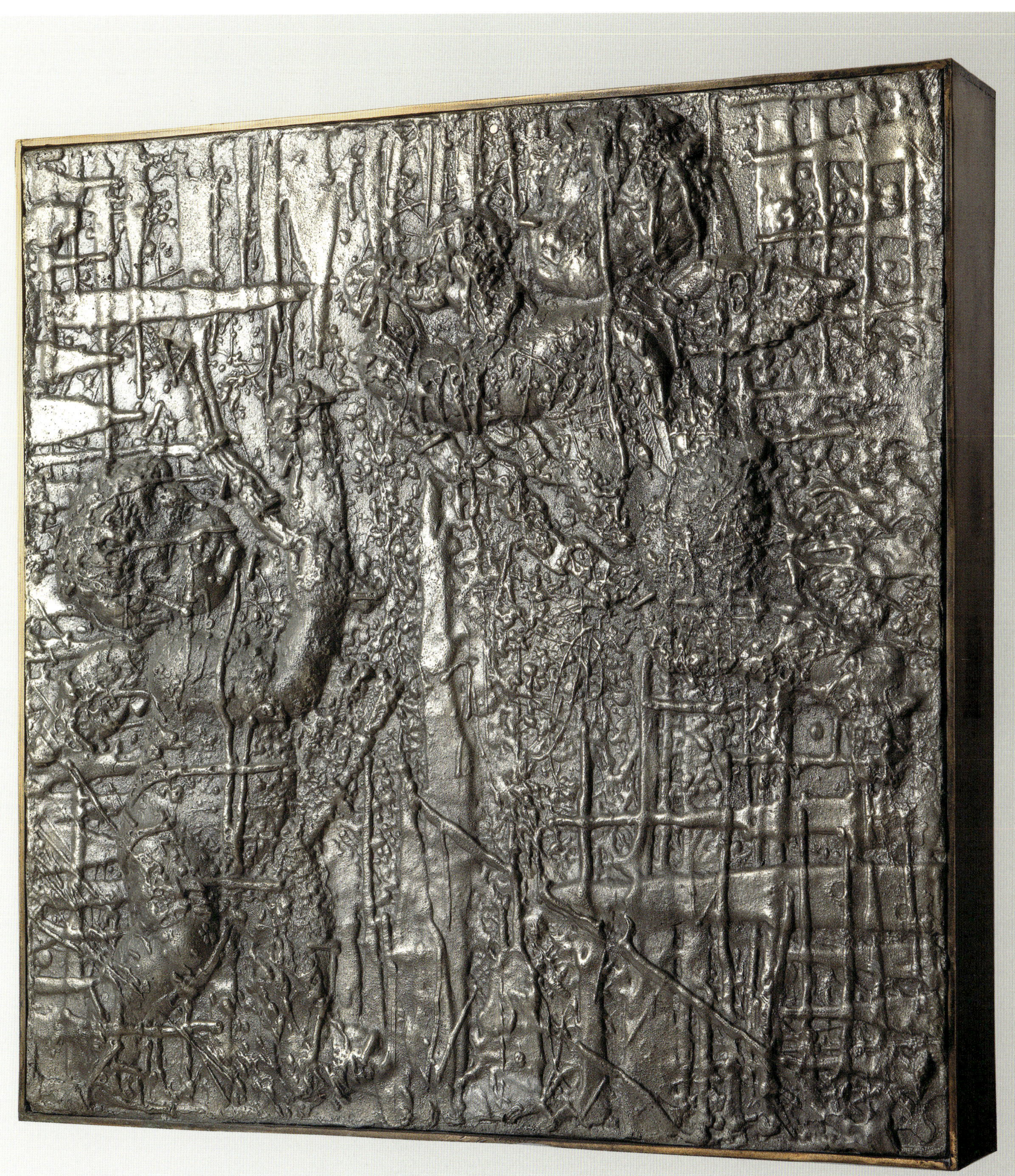

Better Angels, 2010. Cast aluminum and copper. 61 × 61 × 10 cm. Photo by Humayun Memon

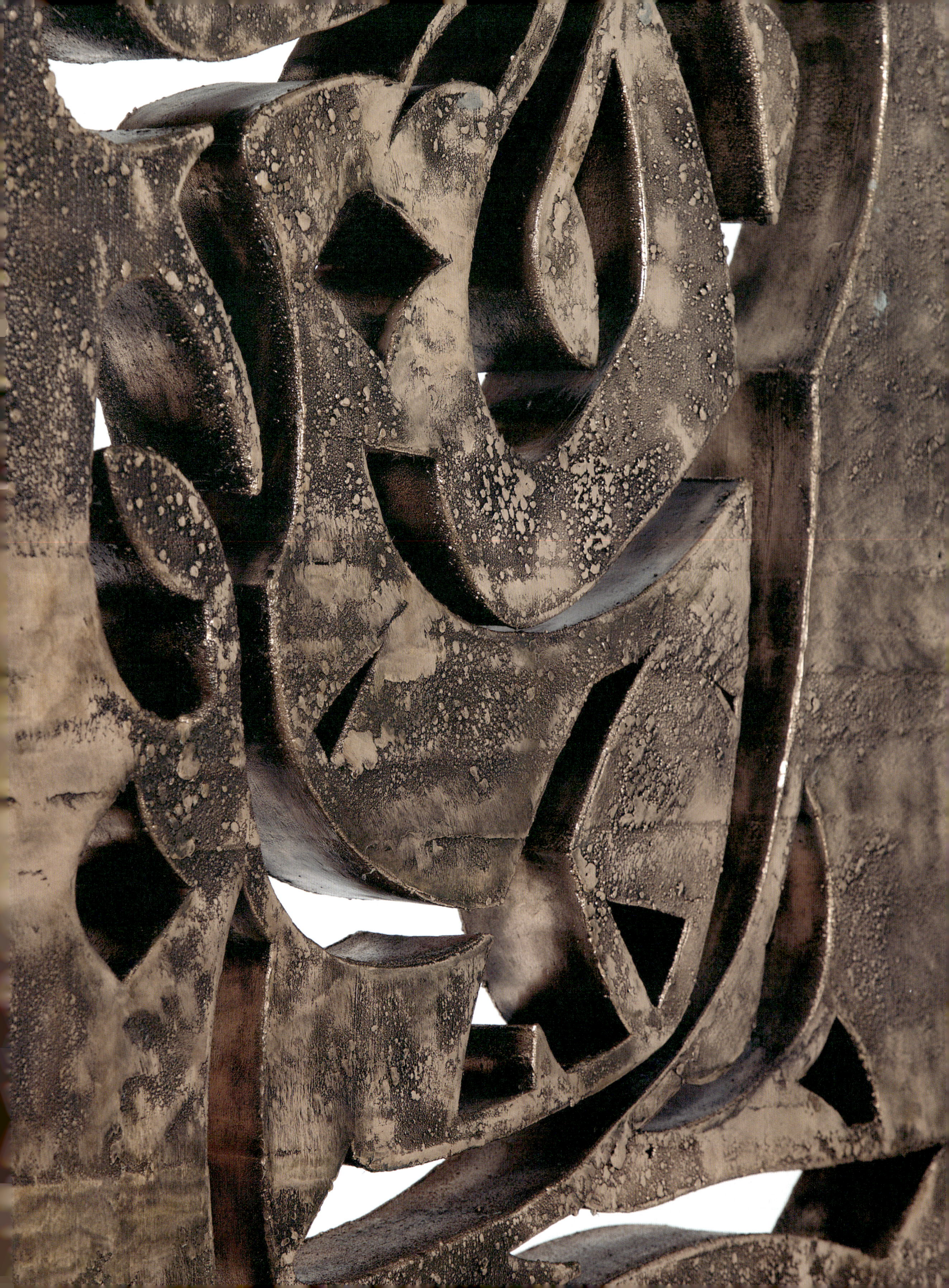

Architectonic

1990 - 2016

Photo by Shamyl Khuhro

Golden Column, 1992. Copper, rock crystals and gold leaf. 39 × 10 × 10 cm. Photo by Nafees

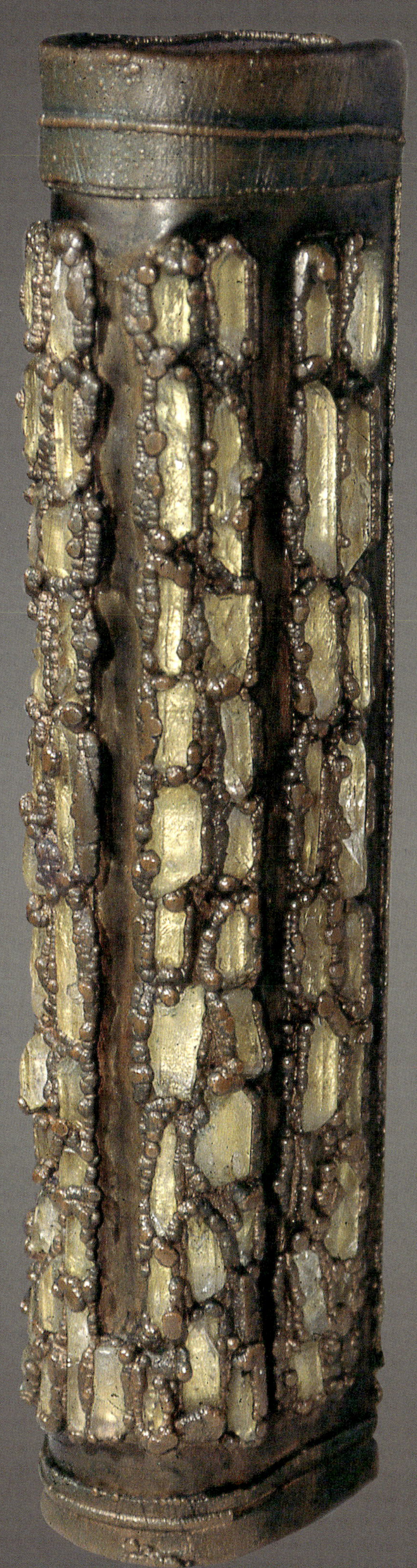

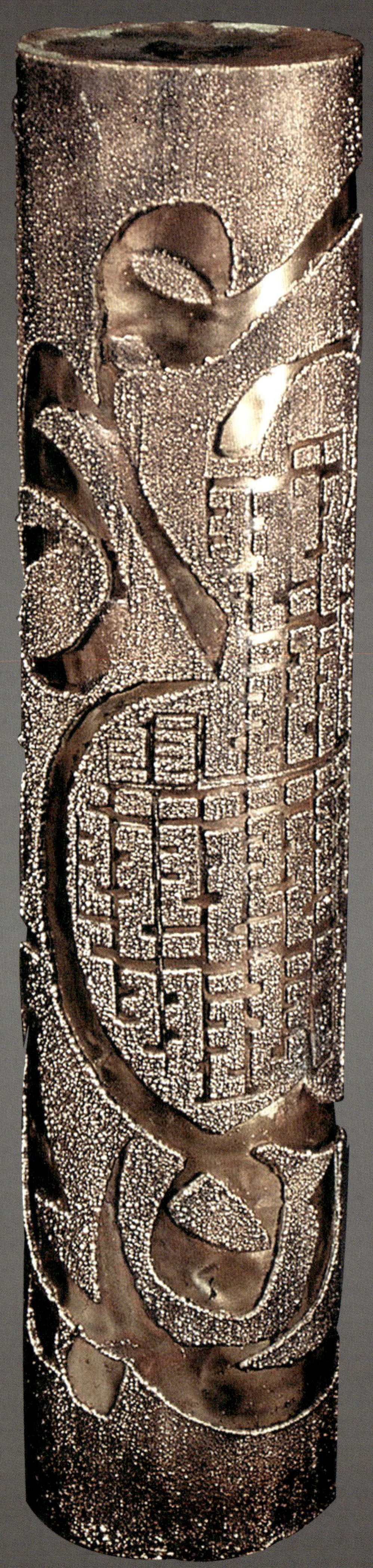

Column, 1995. Copper. 78 × 17 × 17 cm. Photo by Sebastian Bachem

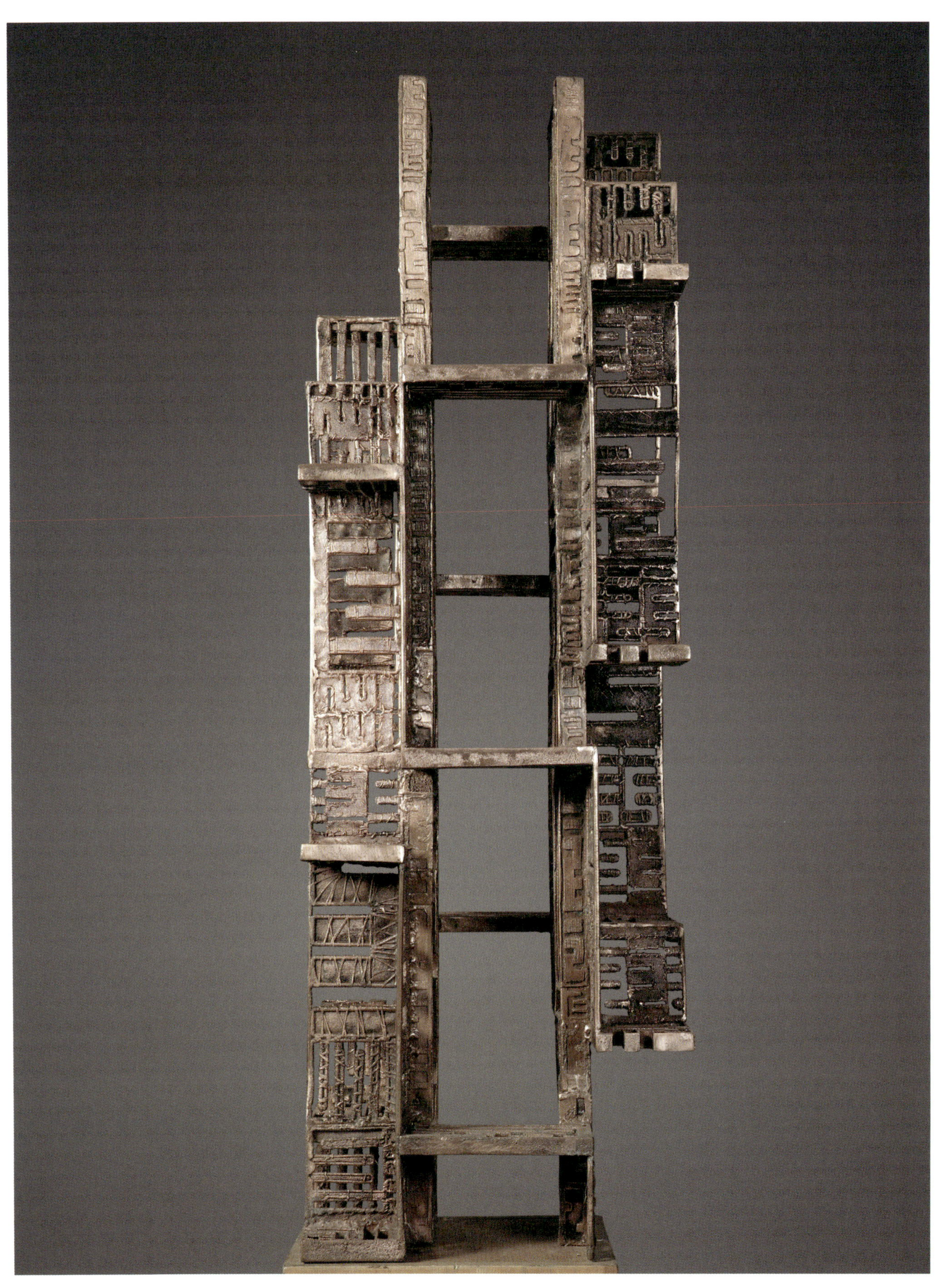

One on Three, 2006. Copper. 106.6 × 35.5 × 35.5 cm. Photo by Tapu Javeri

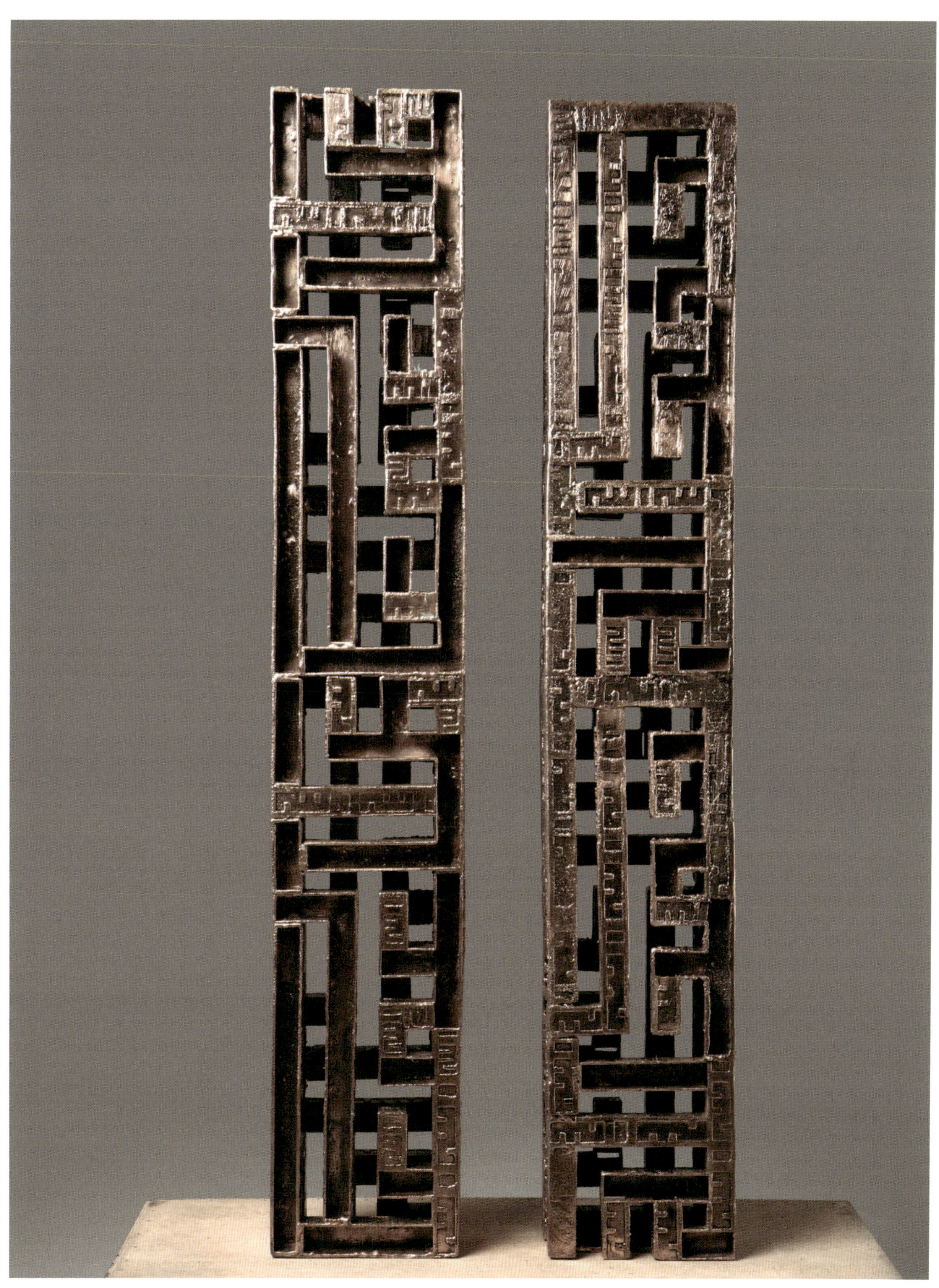

Towers II, 2008. Copper. 109.2 × 20.3 × 12.7 cm (each work). Photo by Tapu Javeri

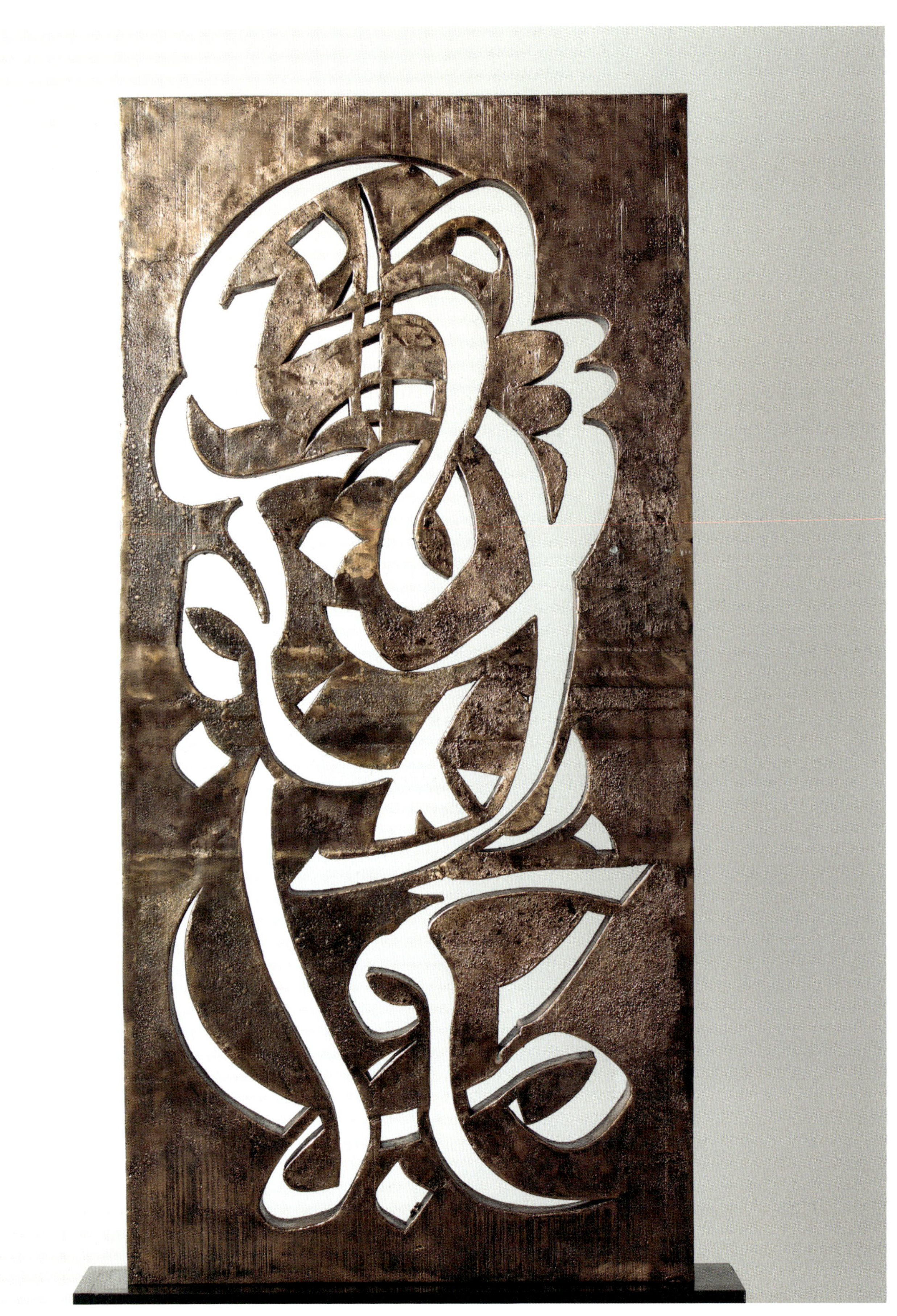

Perforated Wall I: Love Letter, 2014. Copper. 153.6 × 77.4 × 8.8 cm. Photo by Shamyl Khuhro

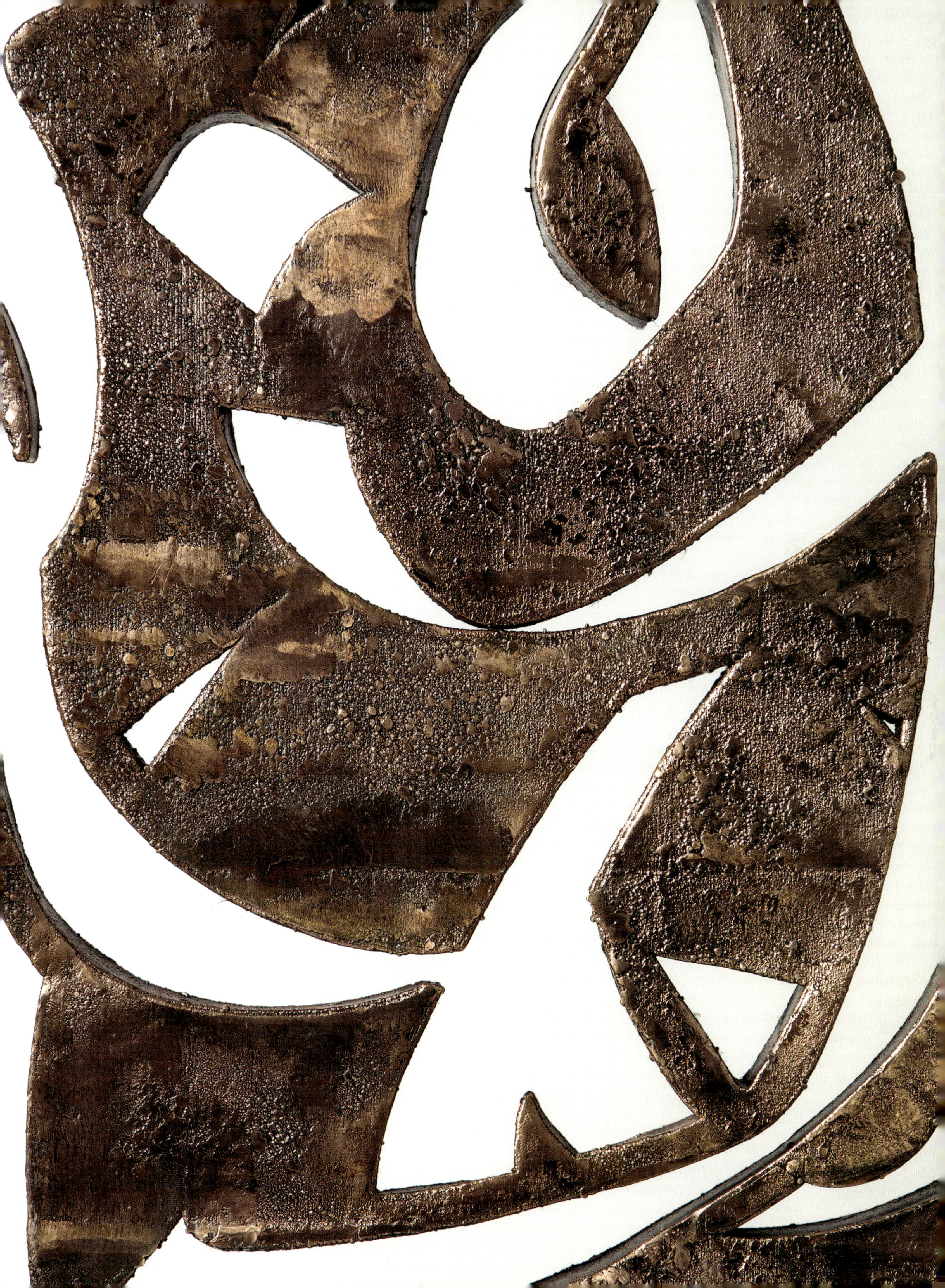

Perforated Wall II: Rosetta Stone, 2014. Copper. 153.6 × 76 × 8.8 cm. Photo by Shamyl Khuhro

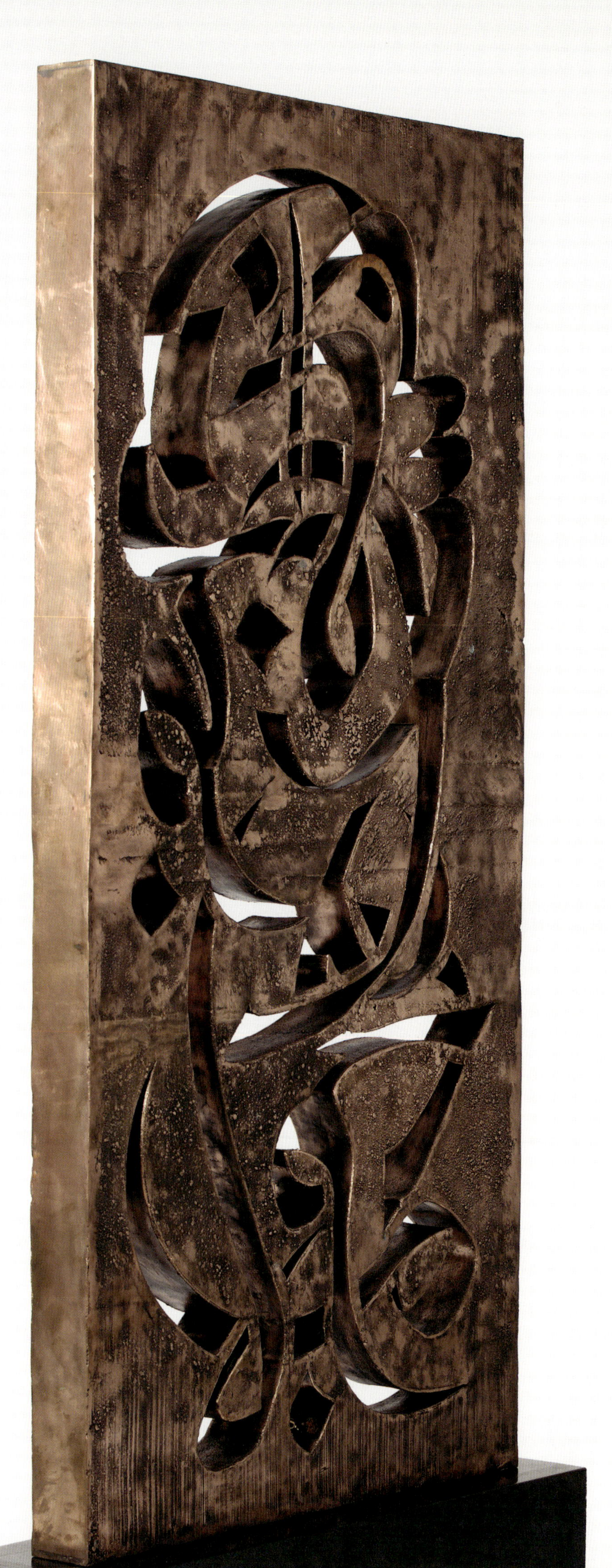

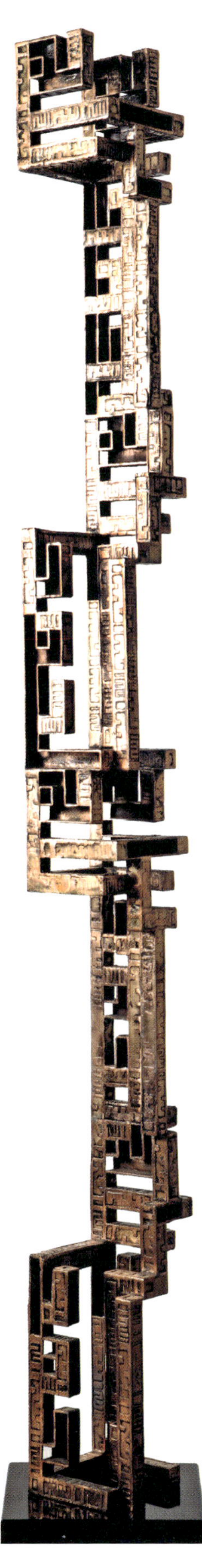

Algorithm I, 2015, Copper. 213 × 17.7 × 17.7 cm. Photo by Shamyl Khuhro

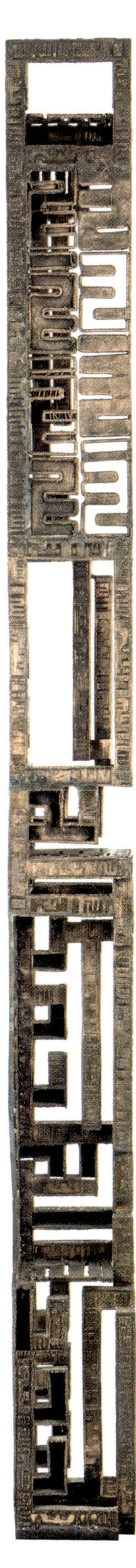

Algorithm III, 2016. Copper. 213 × 17.7 × 17.7 cm. Photo by Humayun Memon

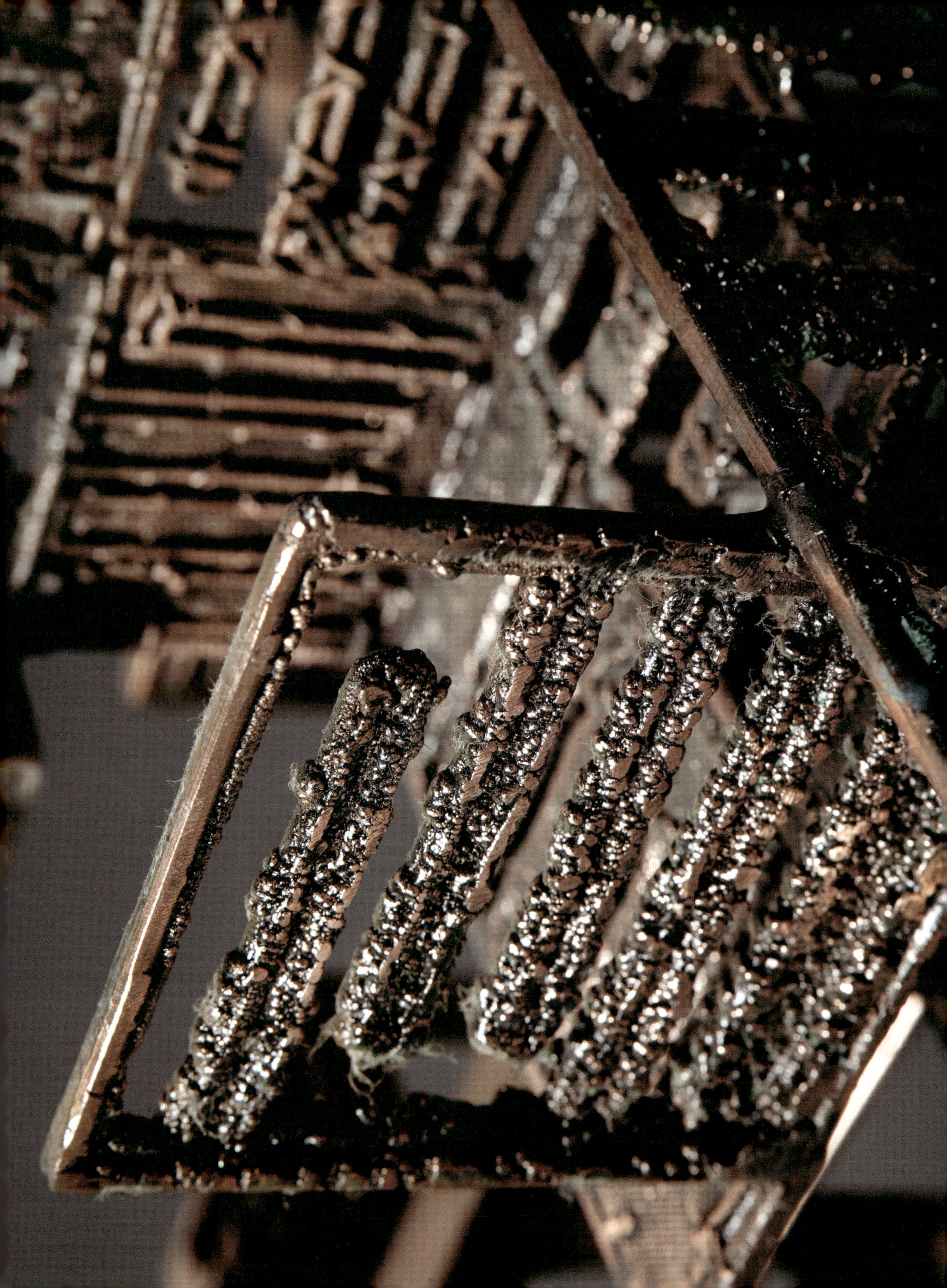

Cube | Square

1991 - 2022

Photo by Tapu Javeri

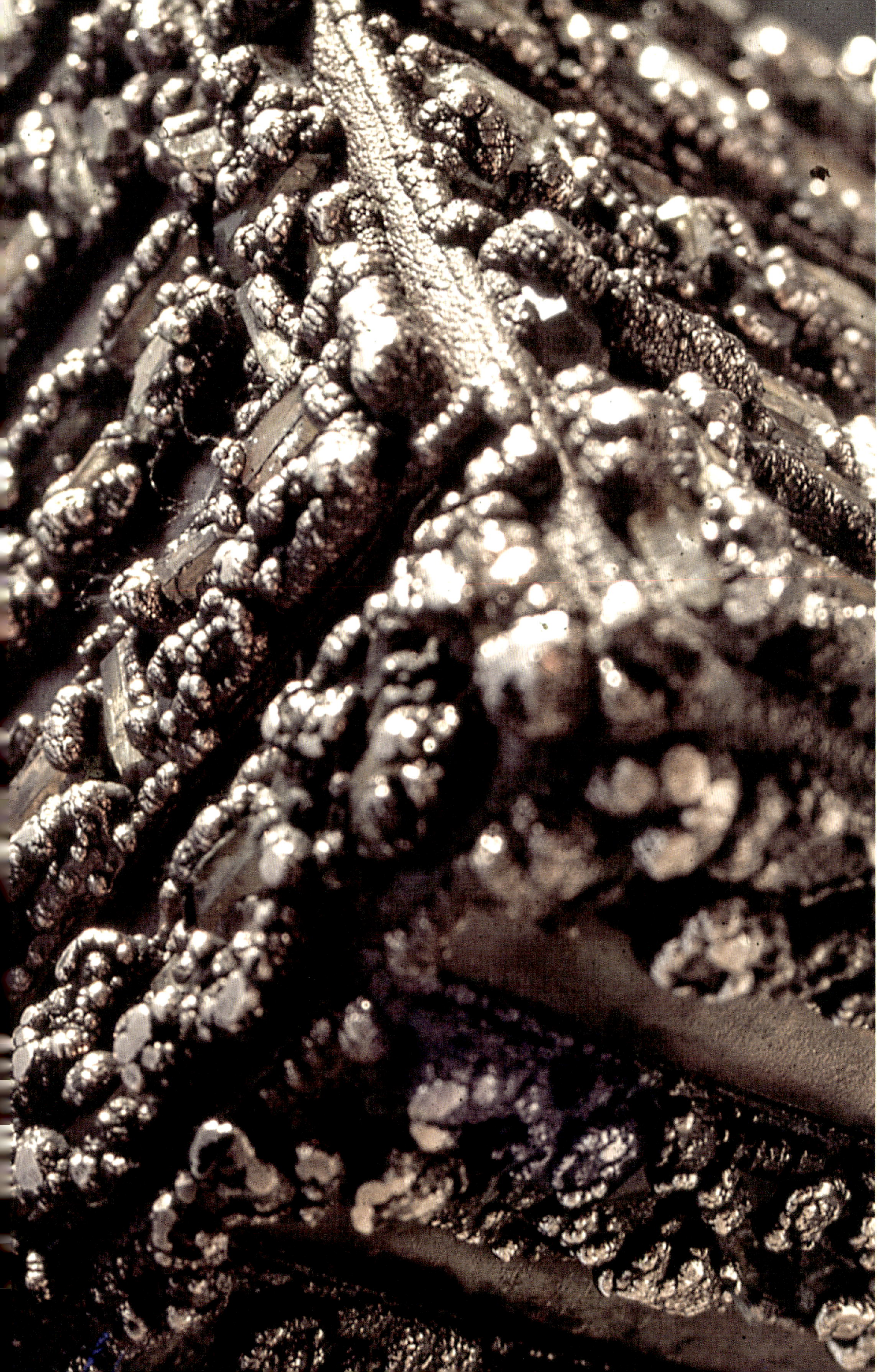

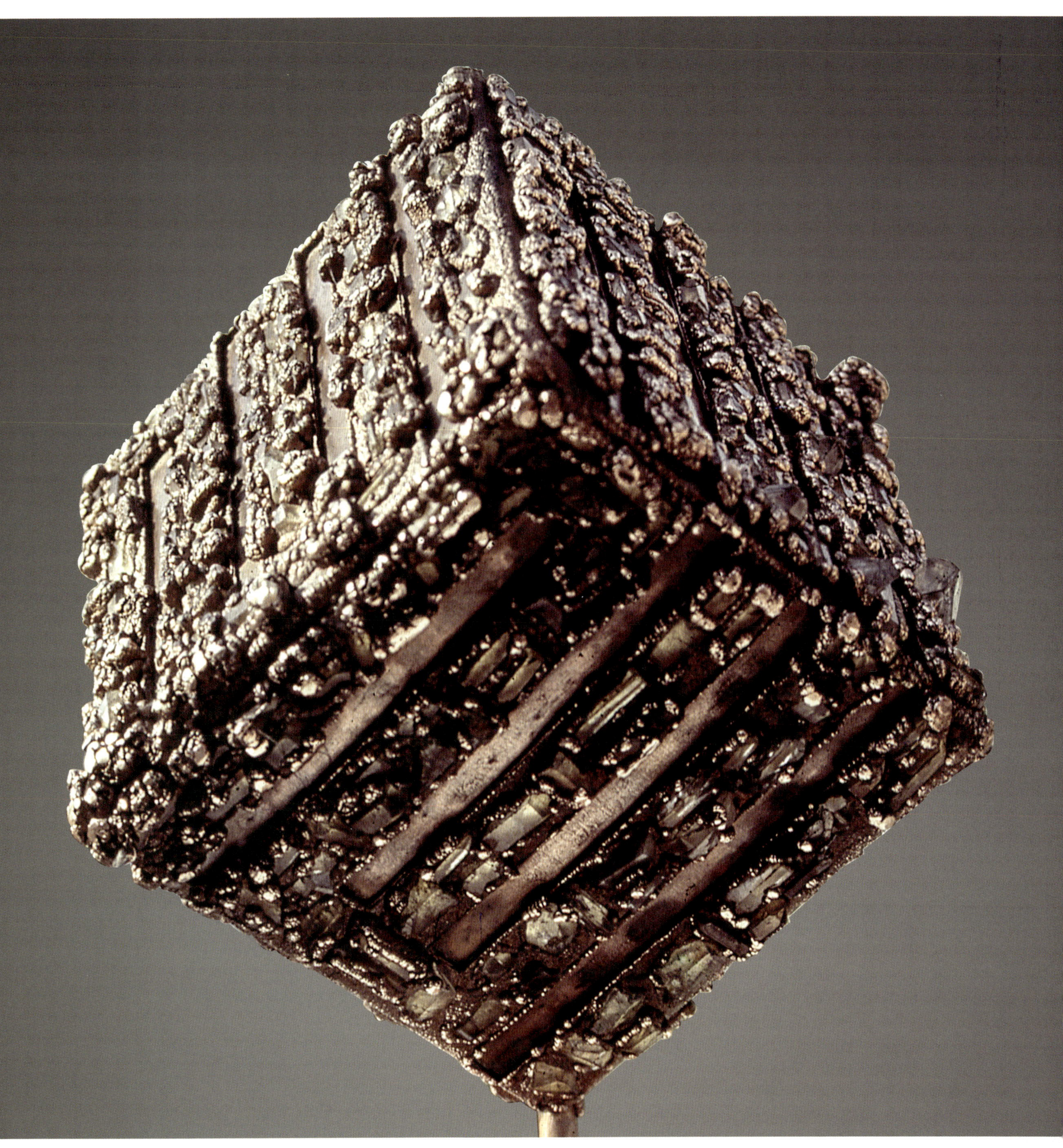

Cube I, 1991. Copper, rock crystals and gold leaf. 48 × 38 × 38 cm. Photo by Nafees

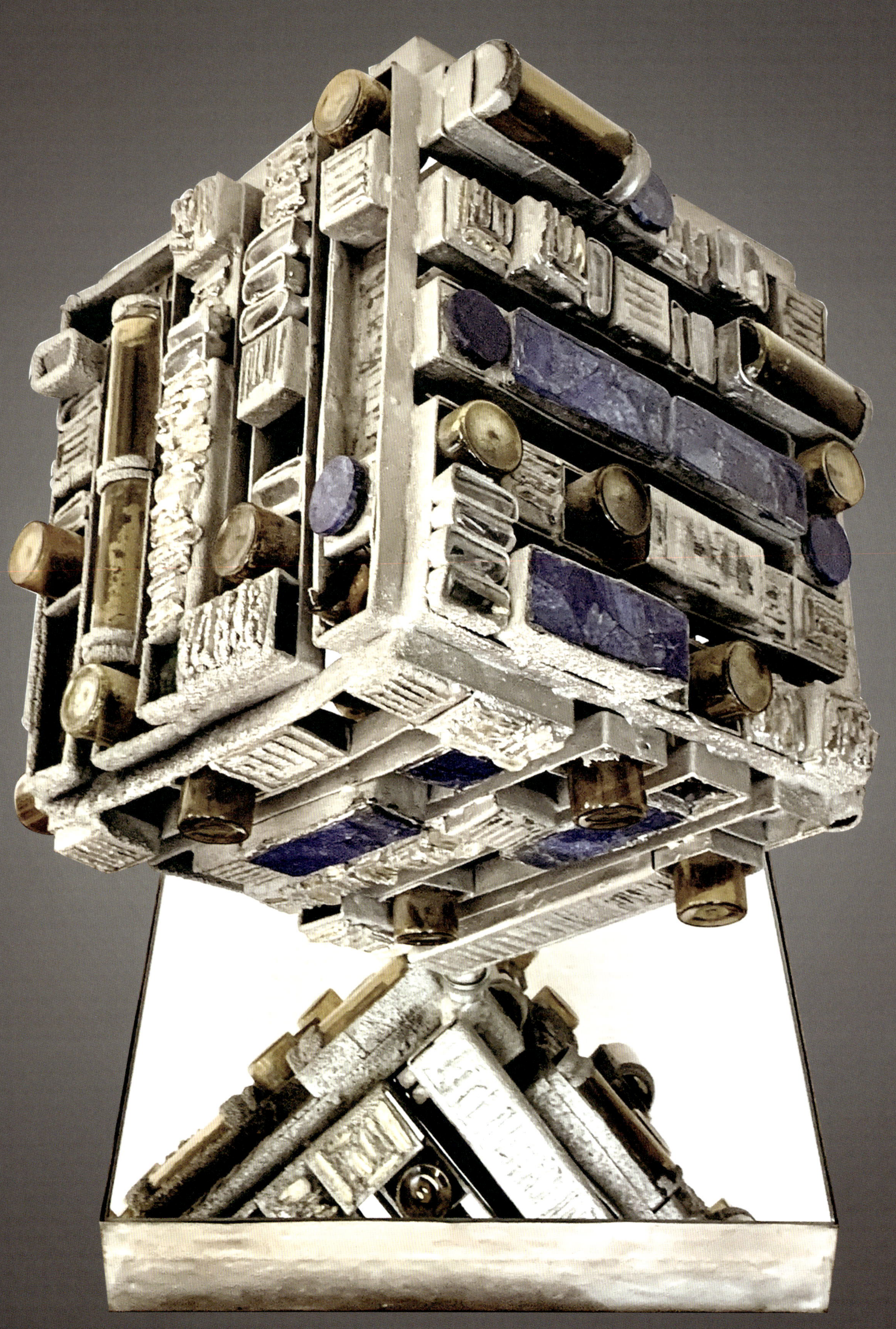

Cube VII, 1993. Copper, nickel plate, rock crystals, gold leaf, lapis lazuli and glass. 48 × 38 × 38 cm. Photo by Sebastian Bachem

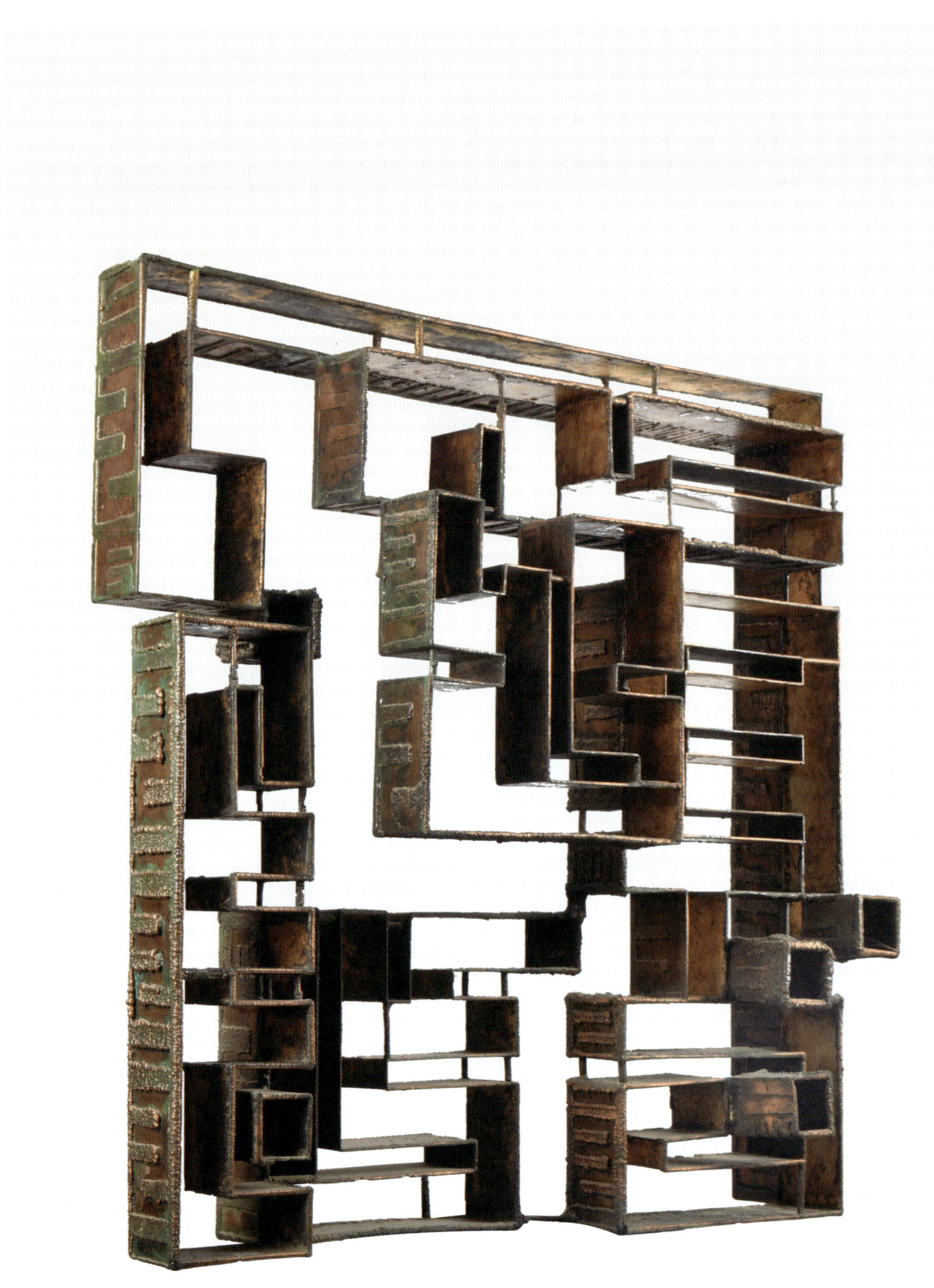

Square I, 1994. Copper. 81 × 81 × 25.4 cm. Photo by Nafees

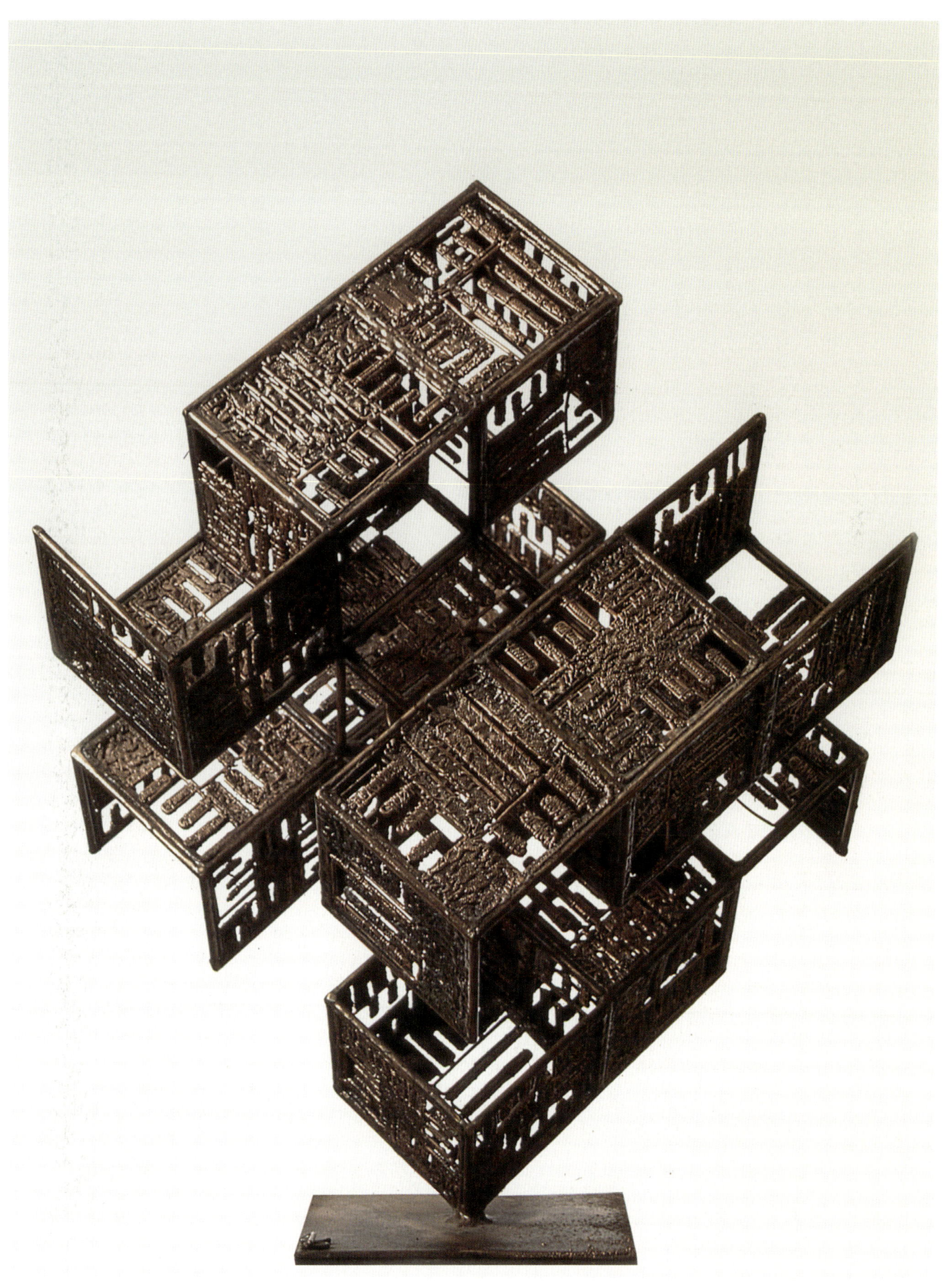

Deconstruction, 2003. Copper and gold leaf. 64 × 64 × 64 cm. Photo by Nafees

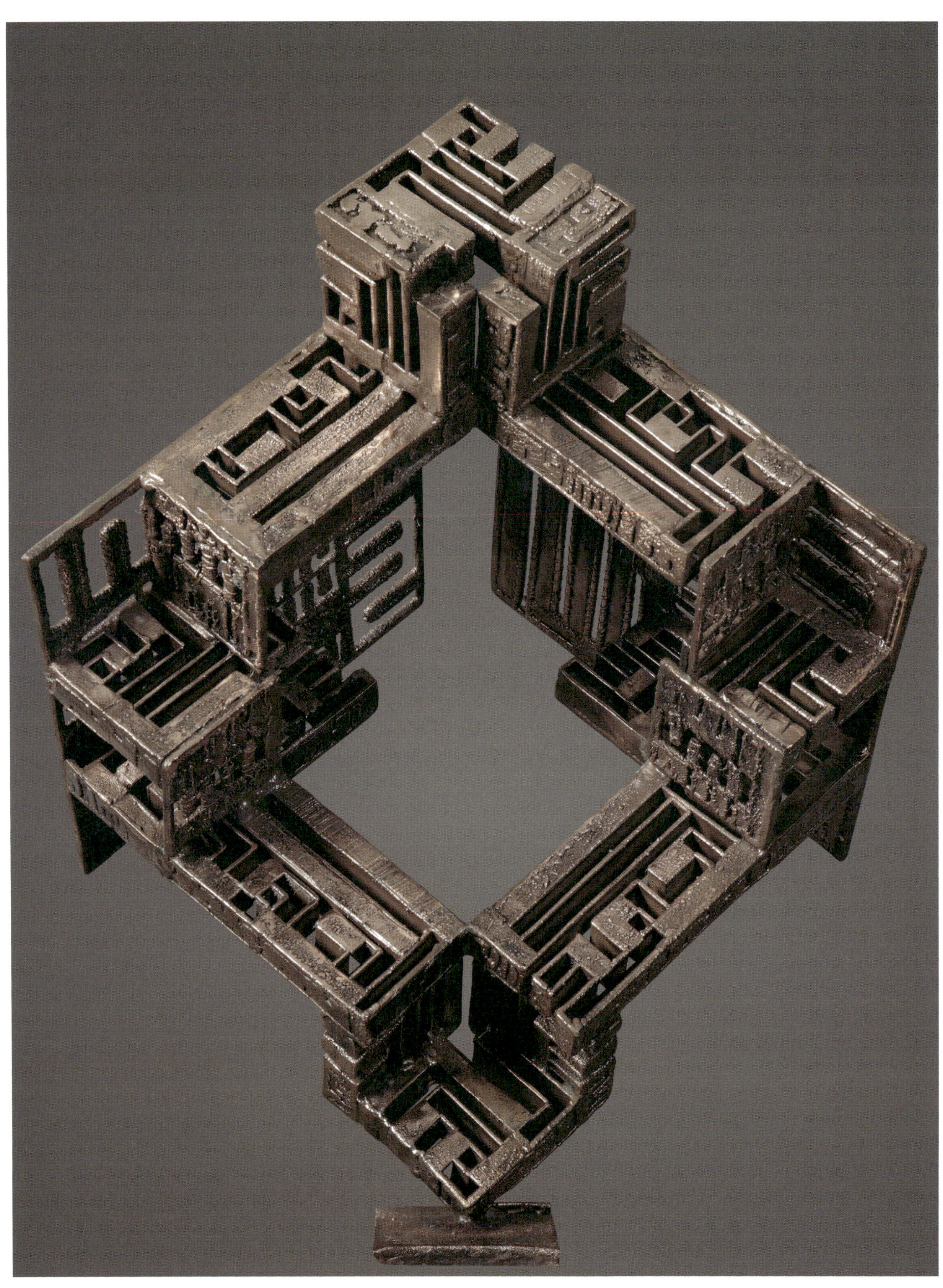

Steps Enclosed, 2007. Copper. 63 × 51 × 51 cm. Photo by Tapu Javeri

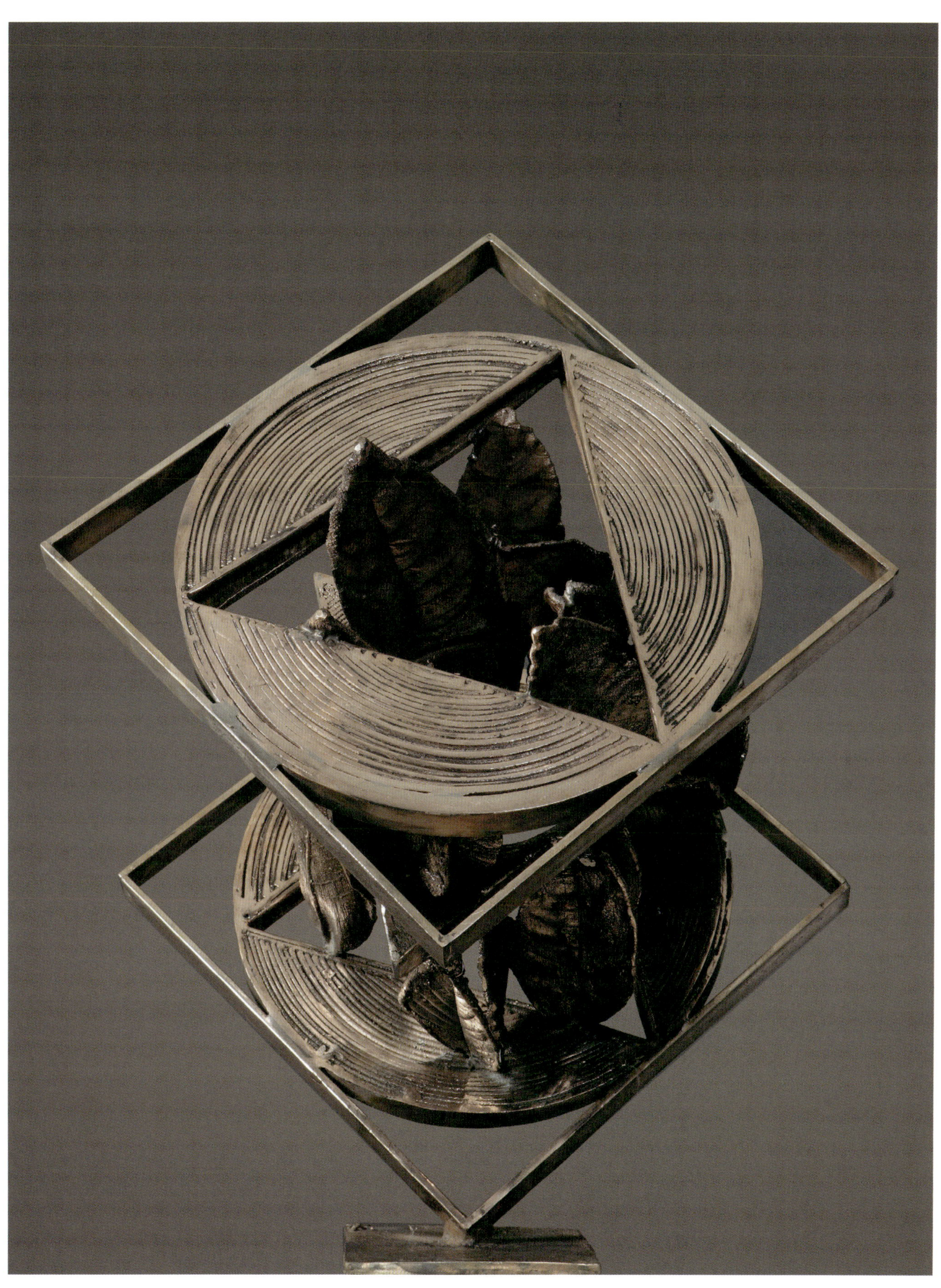

Looking for the Magic Center in the Garden II, 2007. Copper. 78.7 × 63.5 × 53 cm. Photo by Tapu Javeri

Habitat III, 2007. Copper. 76.2 × 76.2 × 55.8 cm. Photo by Tapu Javeri

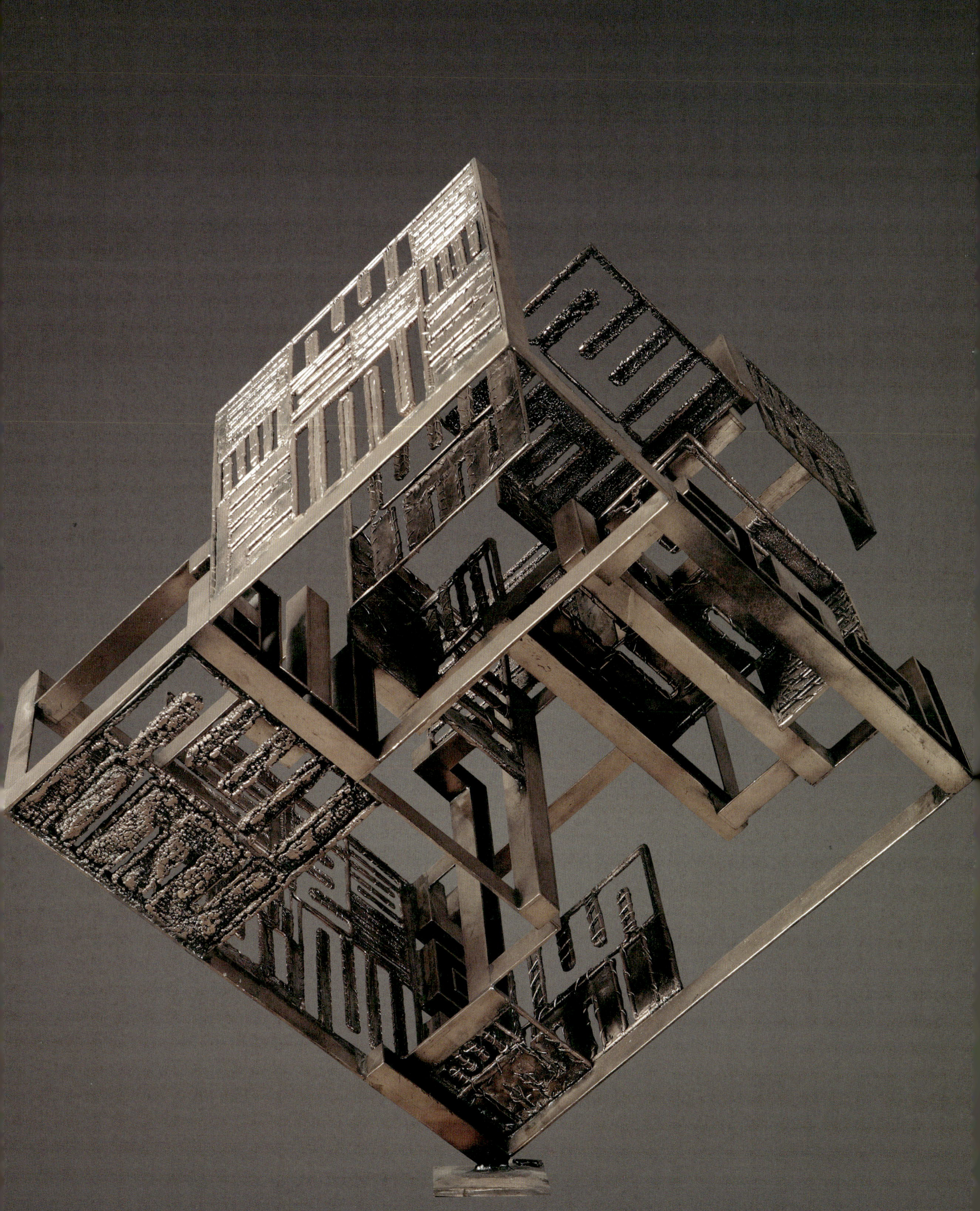

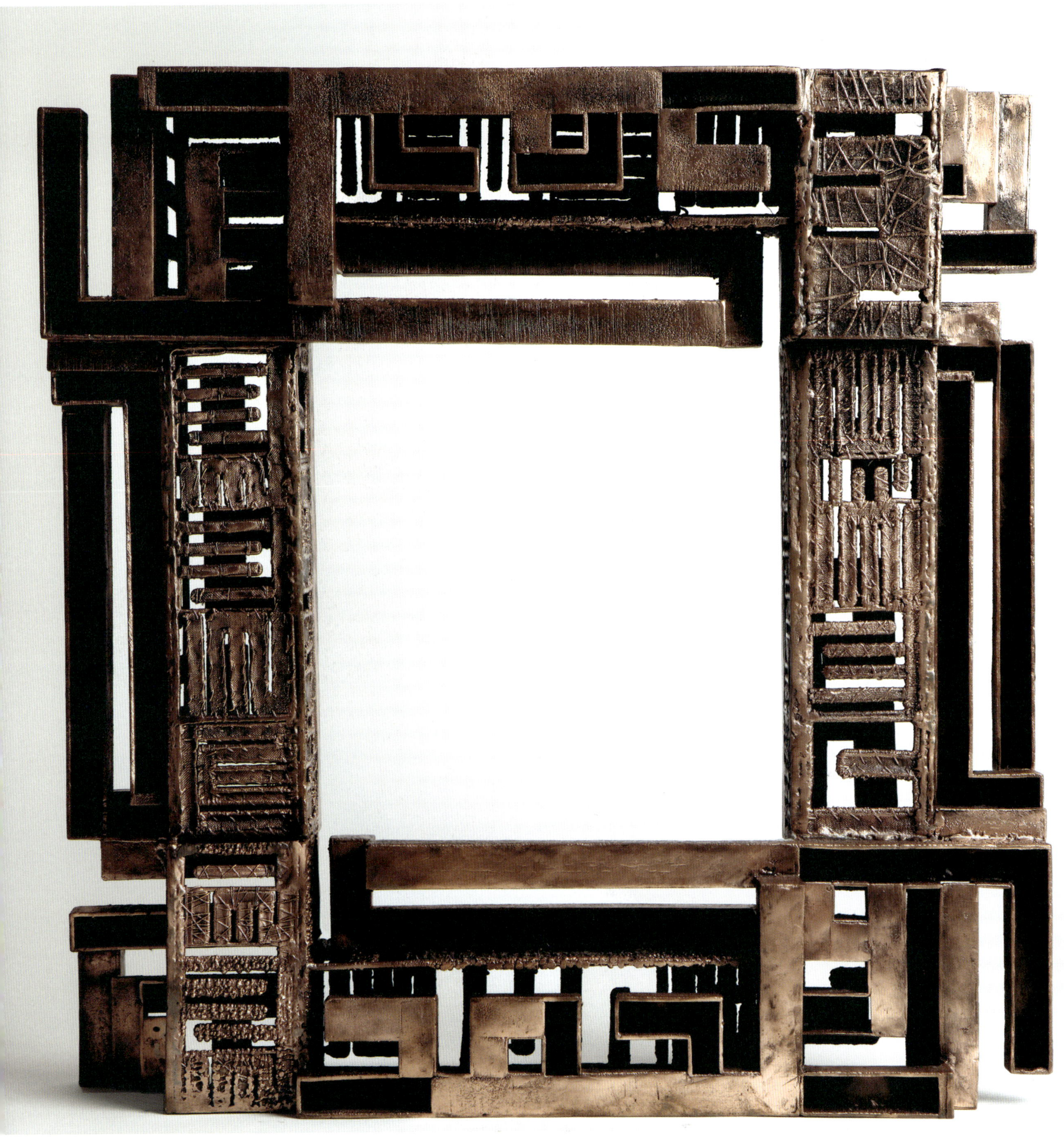

Entrance, 2011. Copper. 71 × 71 × 17.7 cm. Photo by Shamyl Khuhro

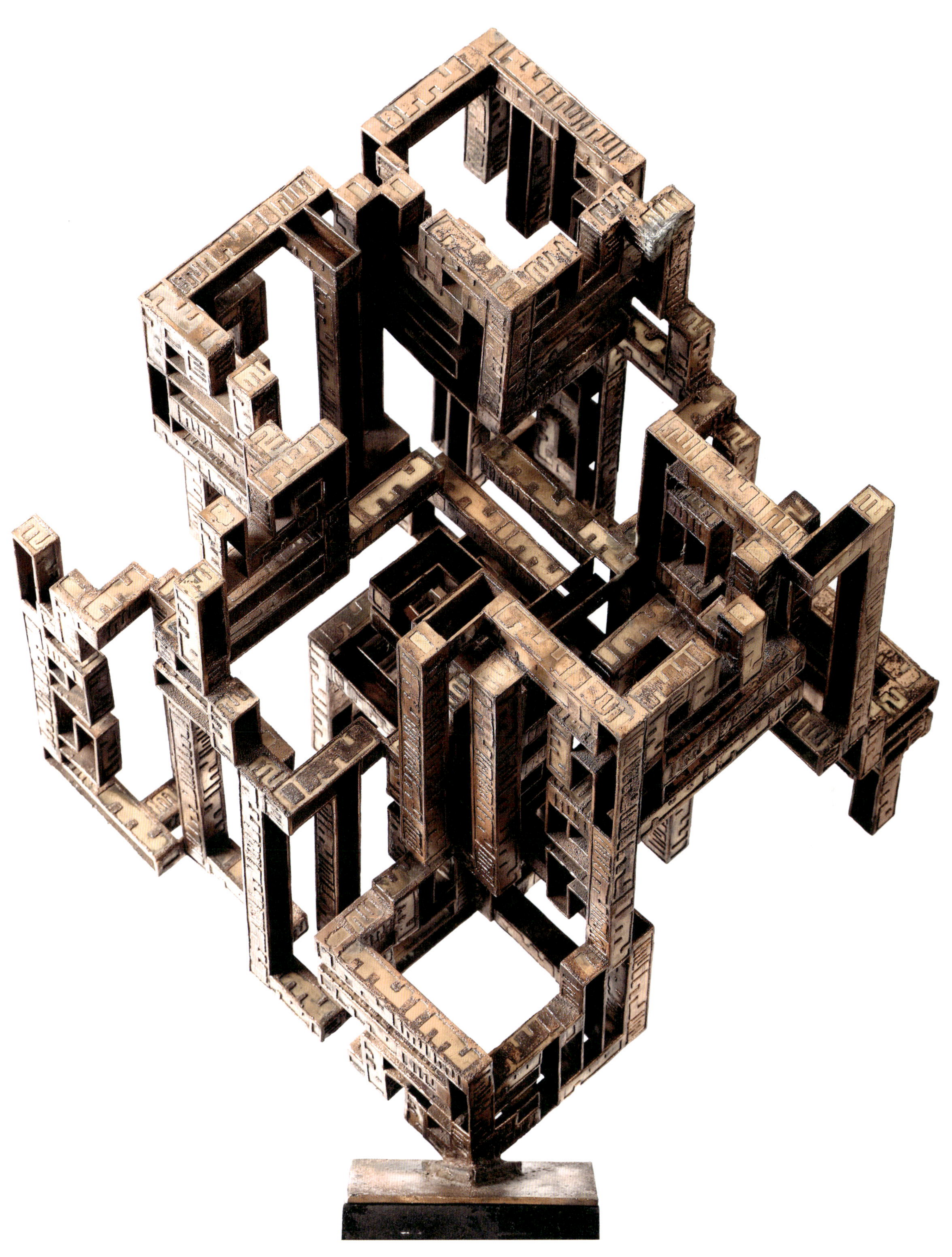

Algorithm II, 2015. Copper. 96 × 74 × 78.7 cm. Photo by Shamyl Khuhro

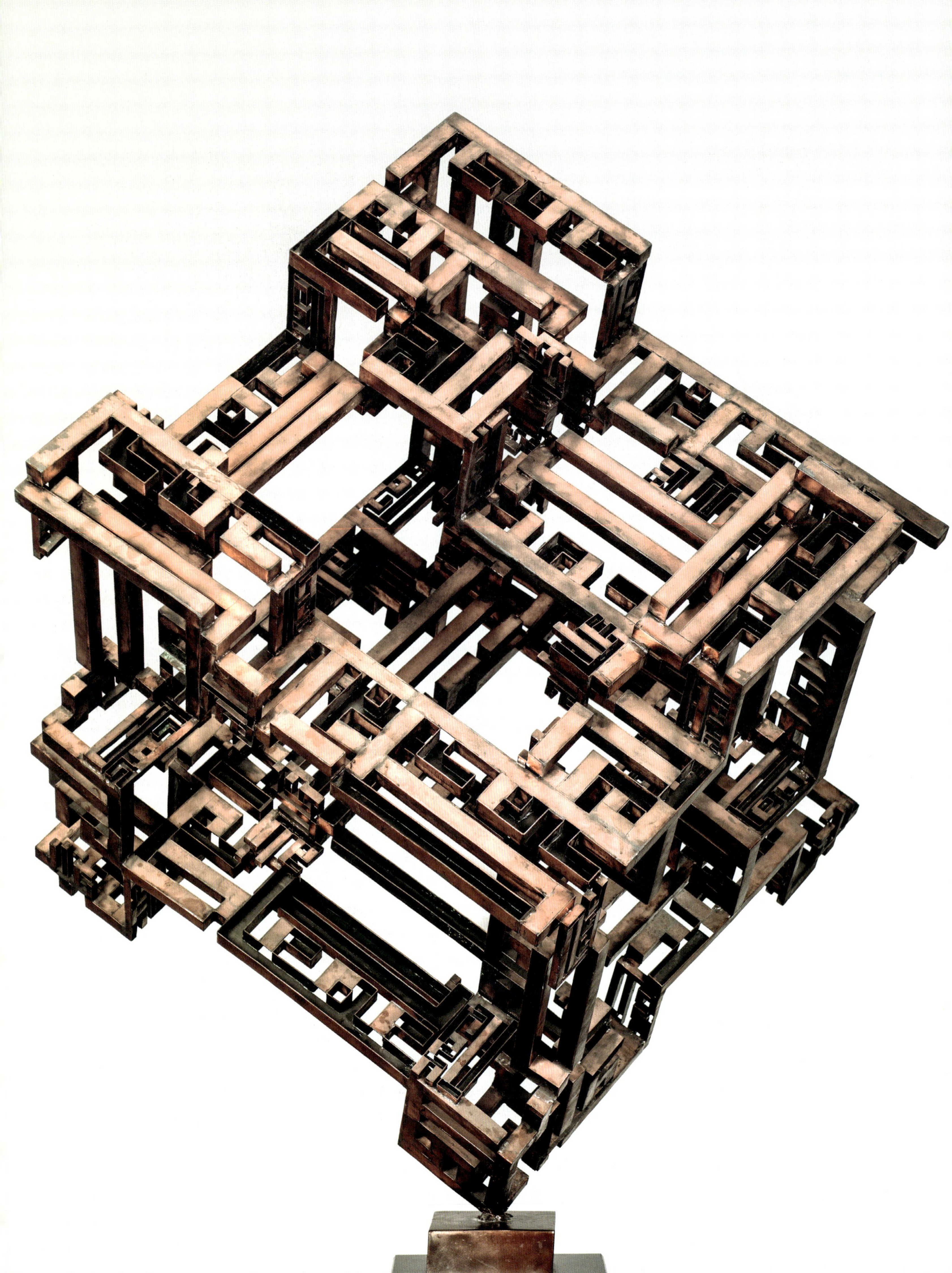

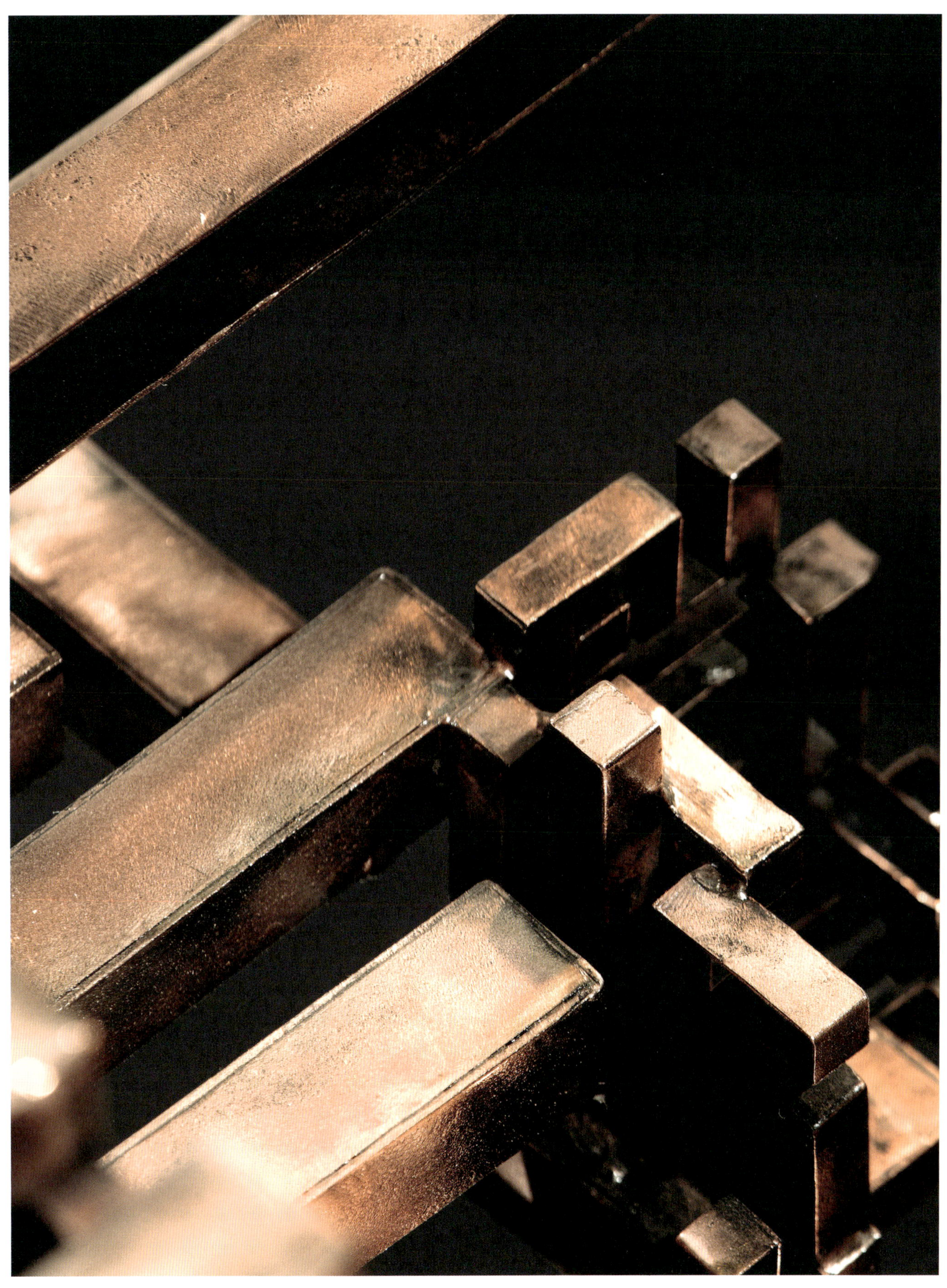

Non-Binary Cube, 2022. Copper and steel. 162.5 × 124.4 × 89 cm. Photo by Humayun Memon

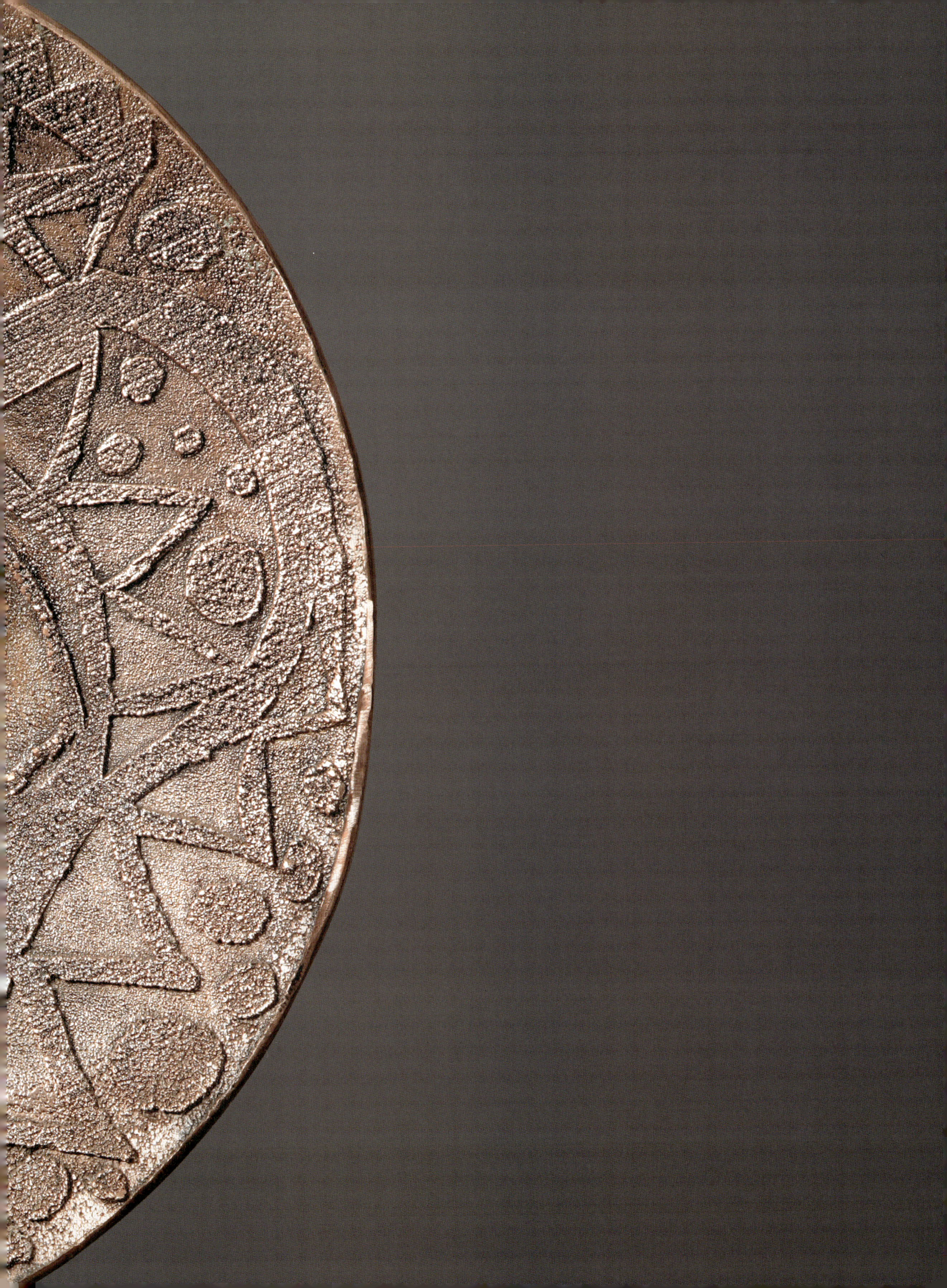

Circle | Sphere

1994 - 2007

Photo by Tapu Javeri

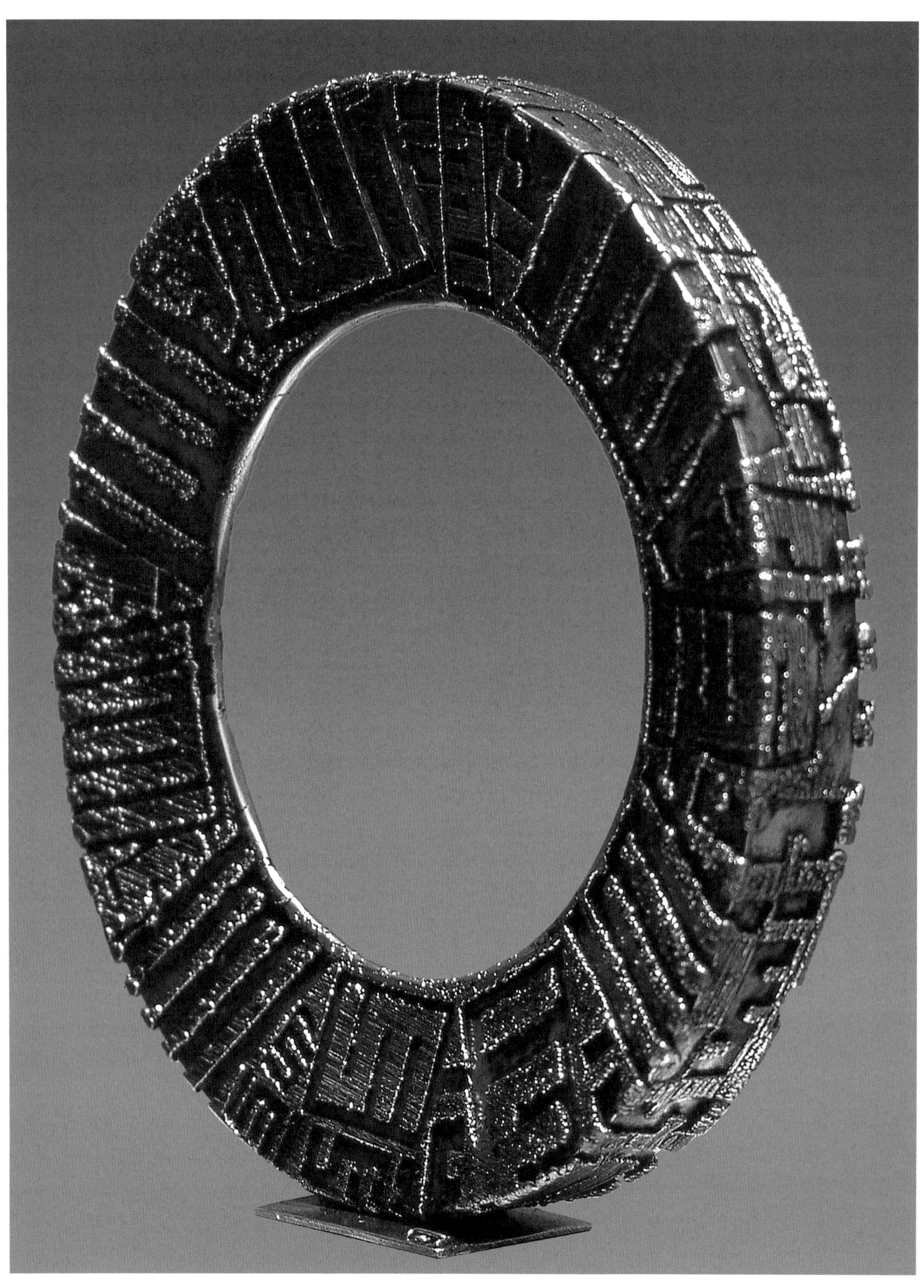

Circle II, 1995. Copper. 30.4 × 30.4 × 10 cm. Photo by Nafees

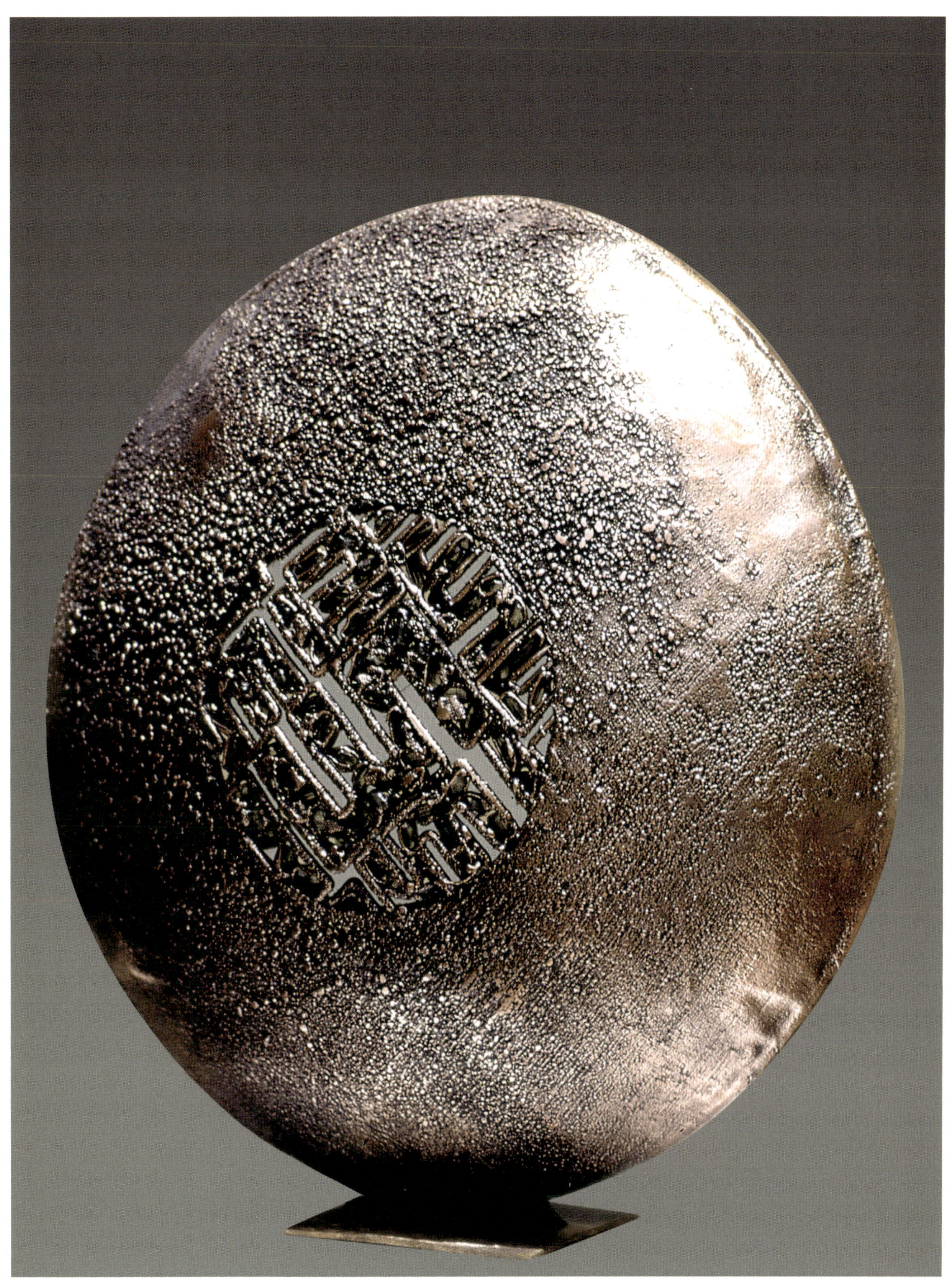

Shield, 1997. Copper and rock crystal. 45.7 × 45.7 × 10 cm. Photo by Nafees

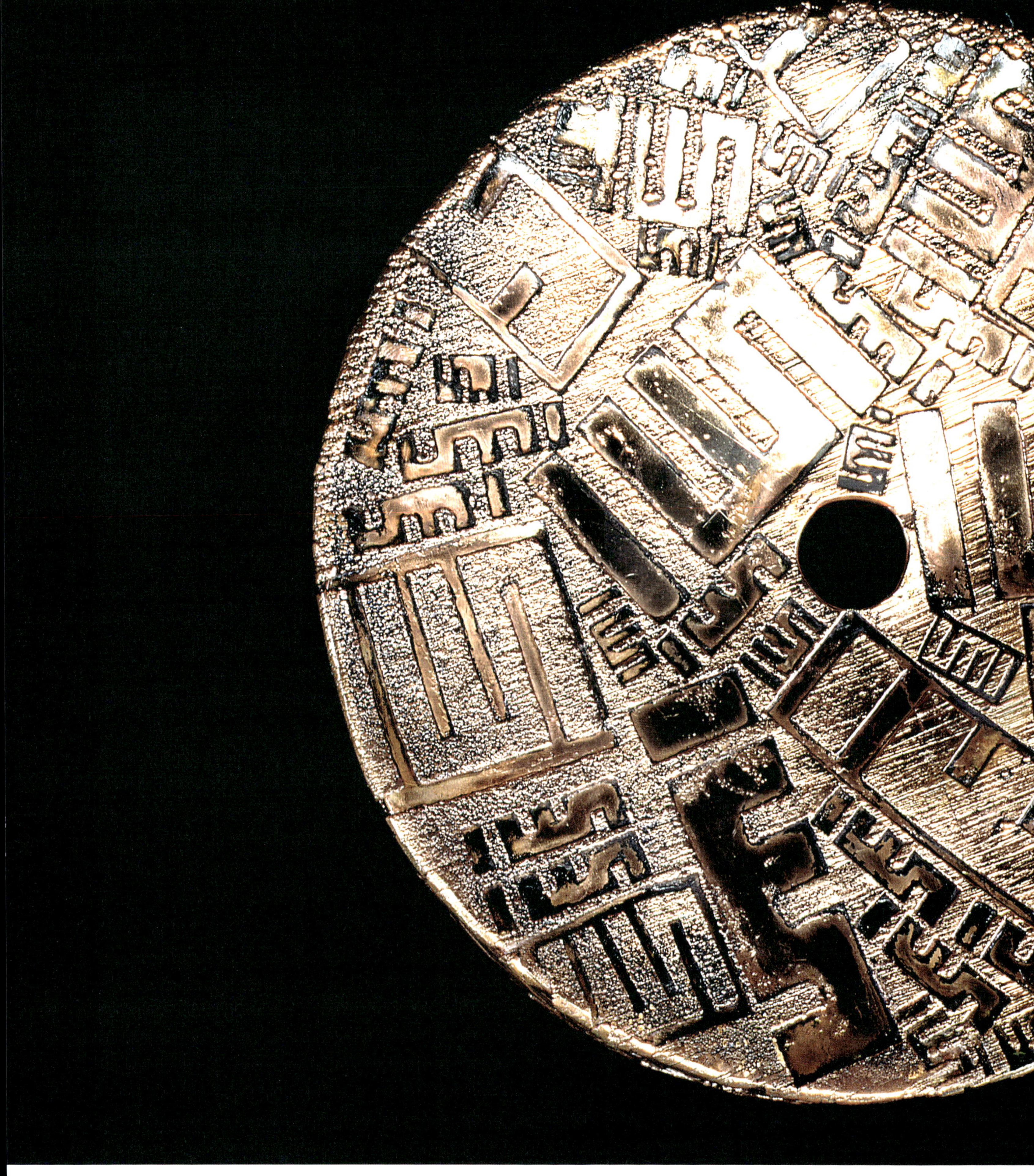

Wheel, 1999. Copper. 45.7 × 45.7 × 7.6 cm. Photo by Tapu Javeri

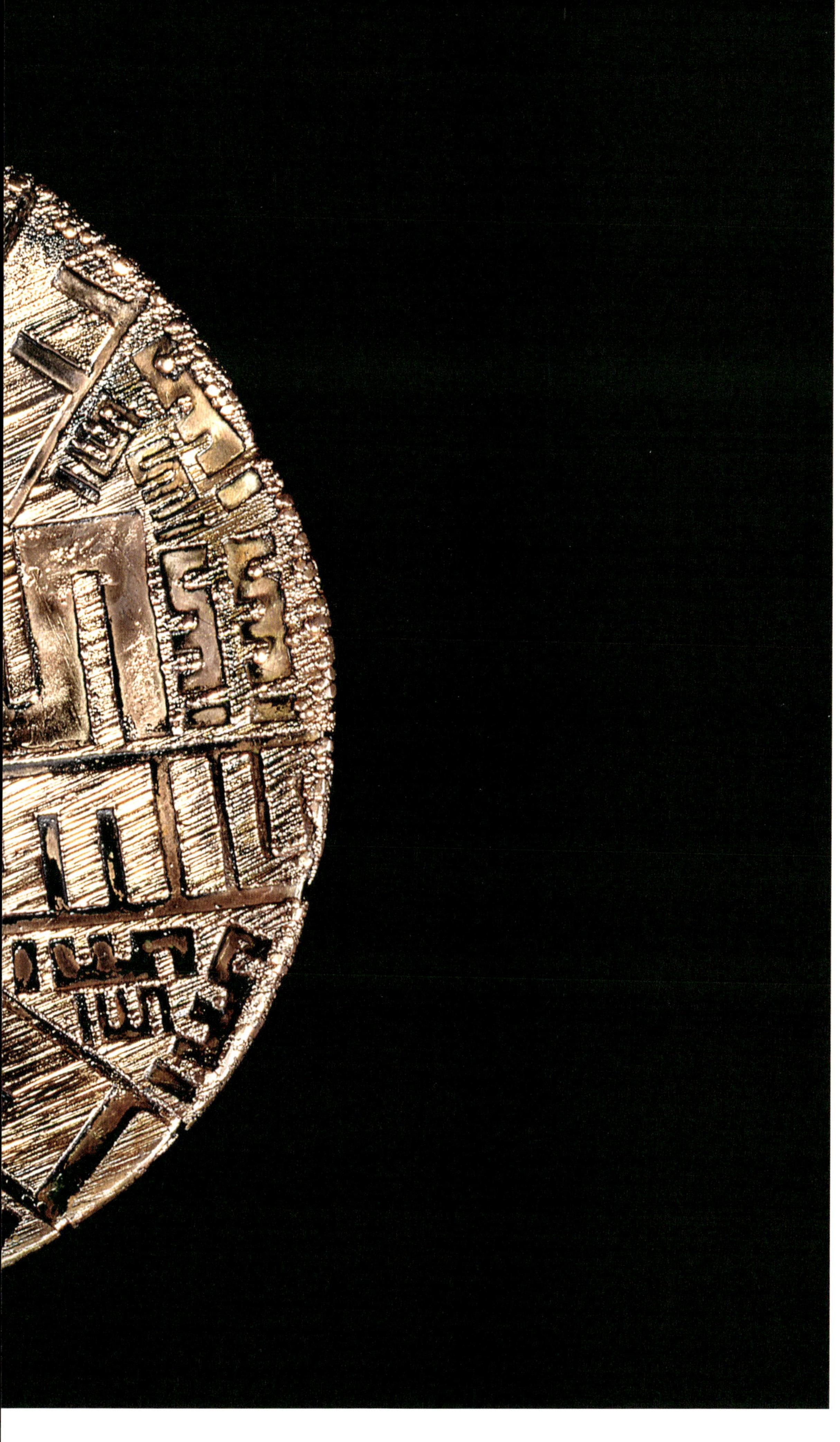

Energy, 1999. Copper. 35.5 × 35.5 × 35.5 cm. Photo by Tapu Javeri

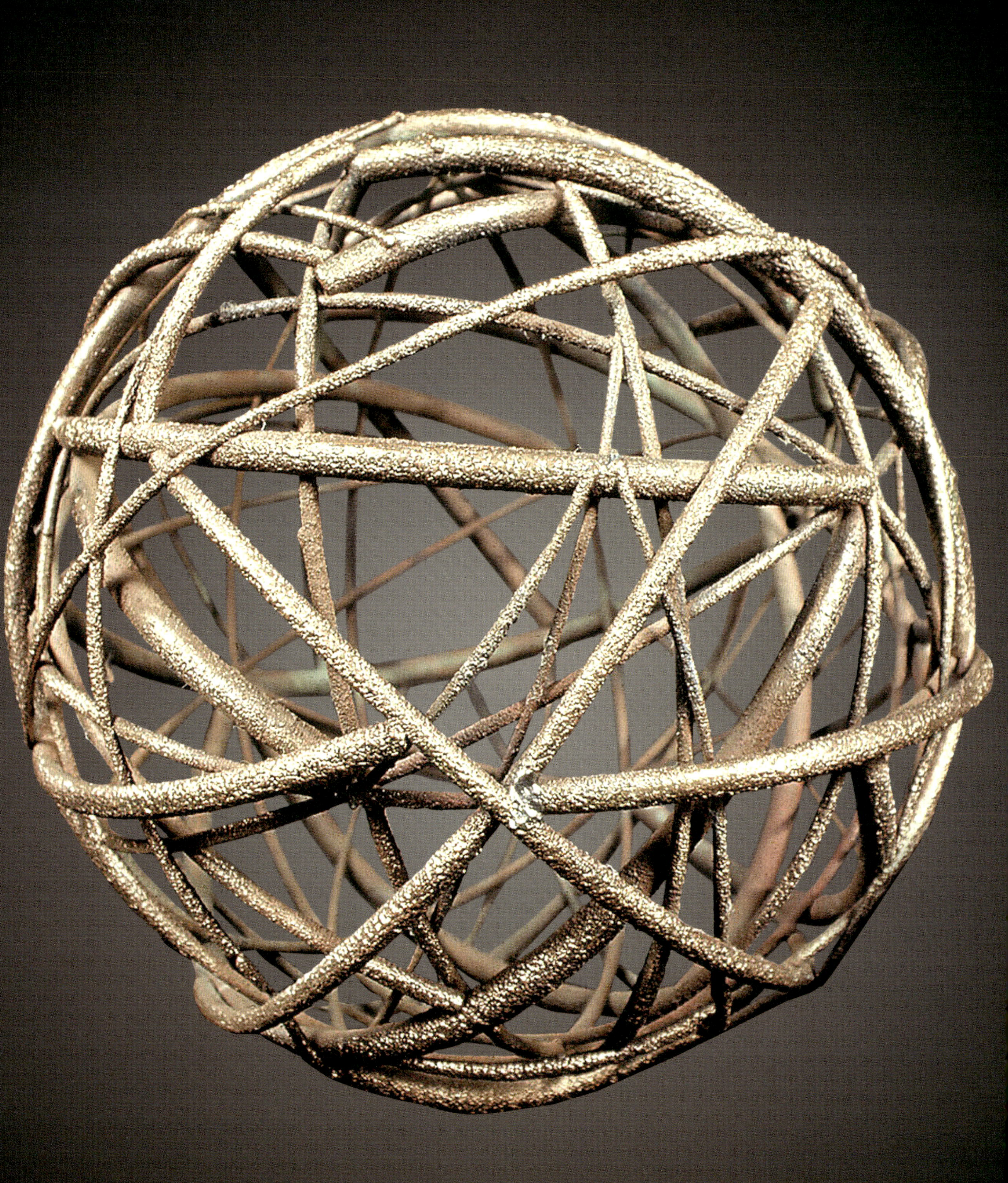

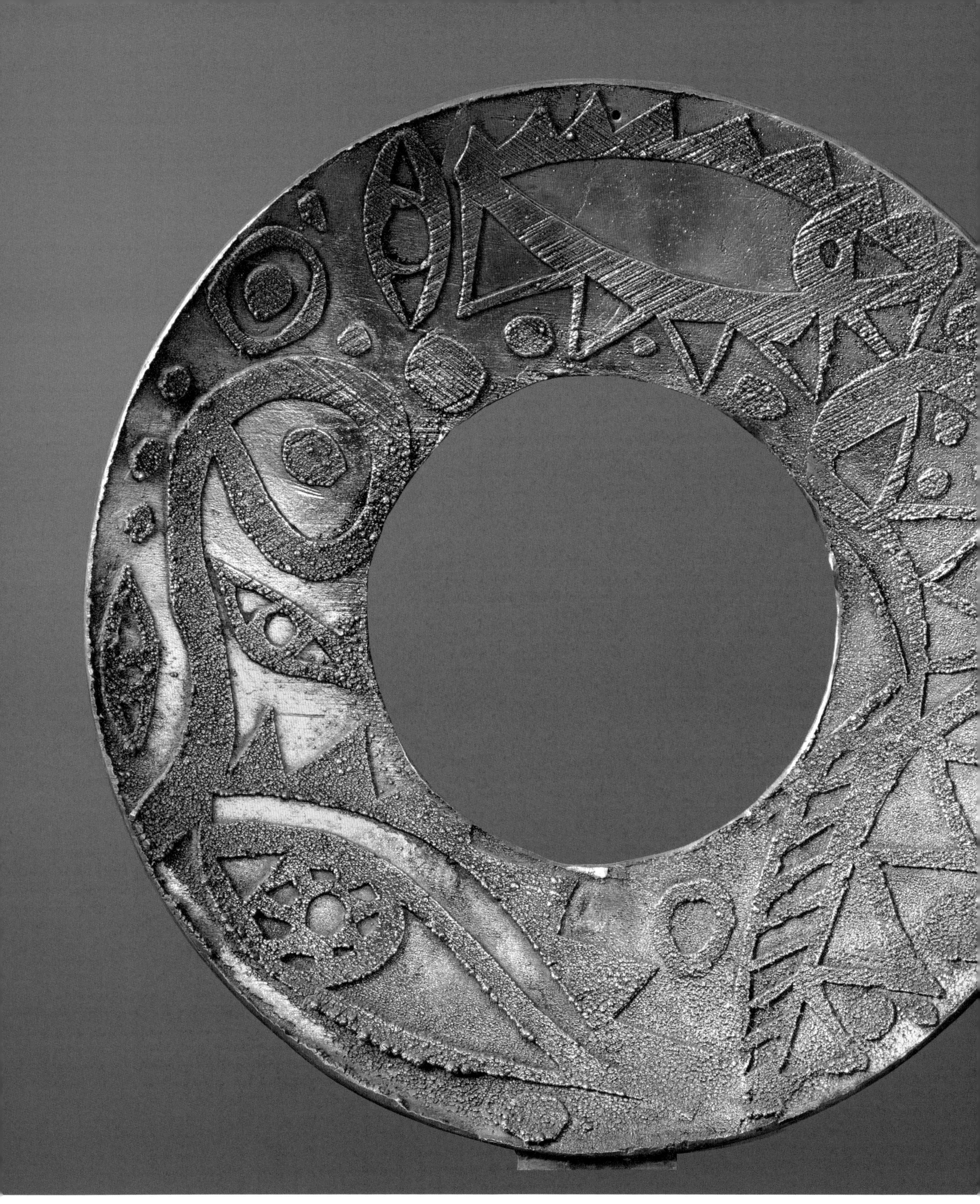

Worn Ring, 2007. Copper. 51 × 51 × 10 cm. Photo by Tapu Javeri

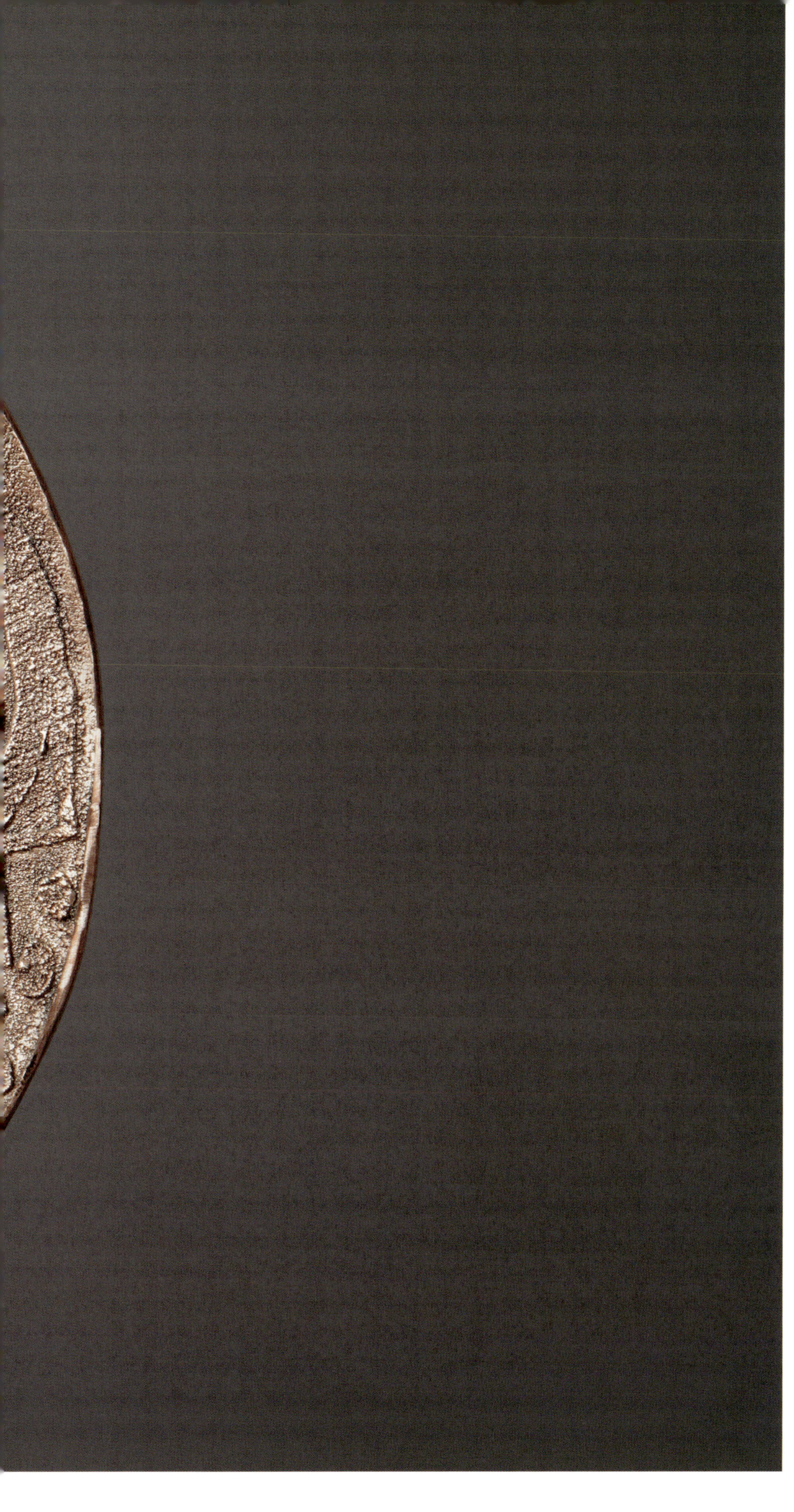

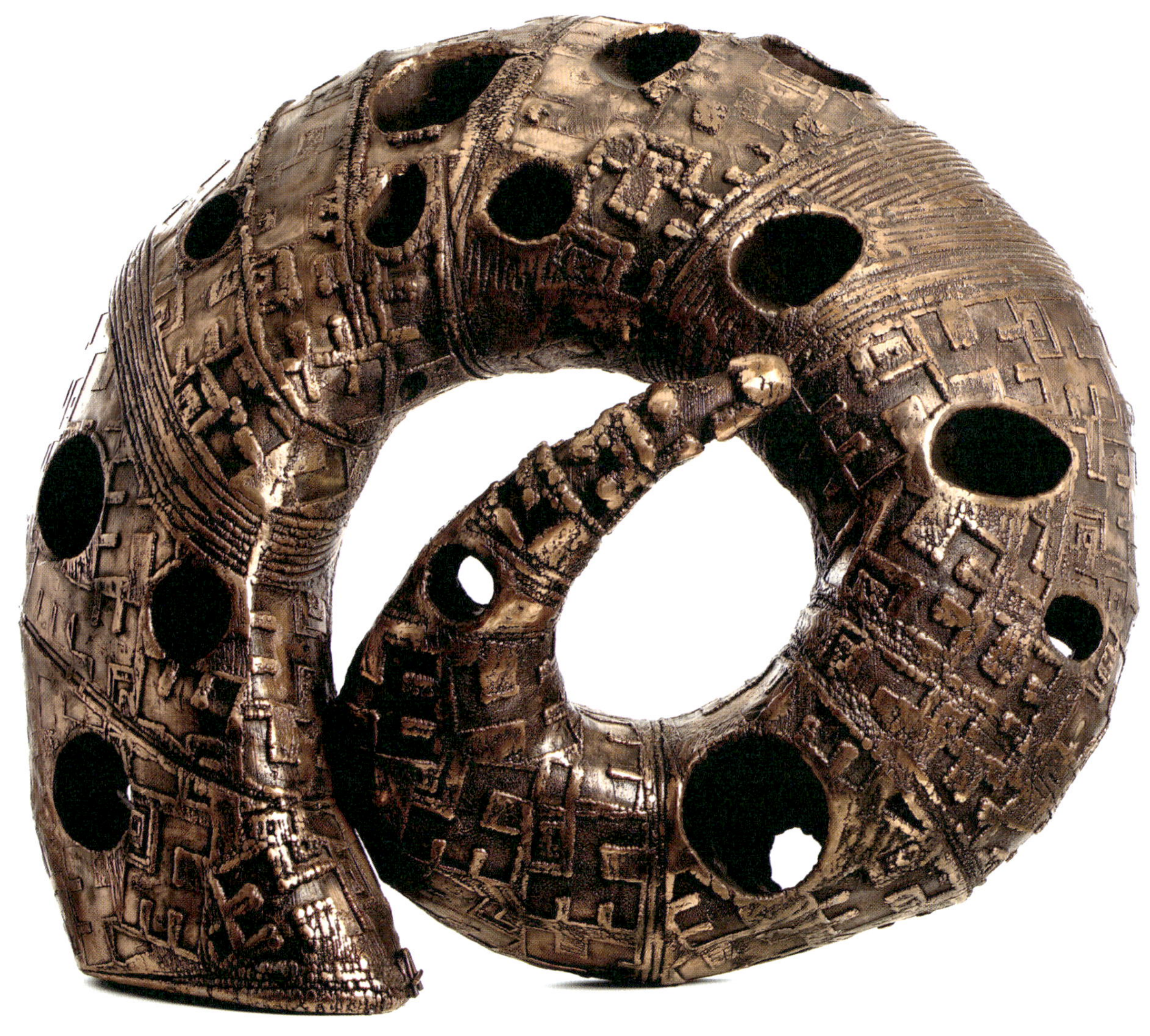

Horn I, 2014. Copper. 75 × 89 × 46 cm. Photo by Shamyl Khuhro

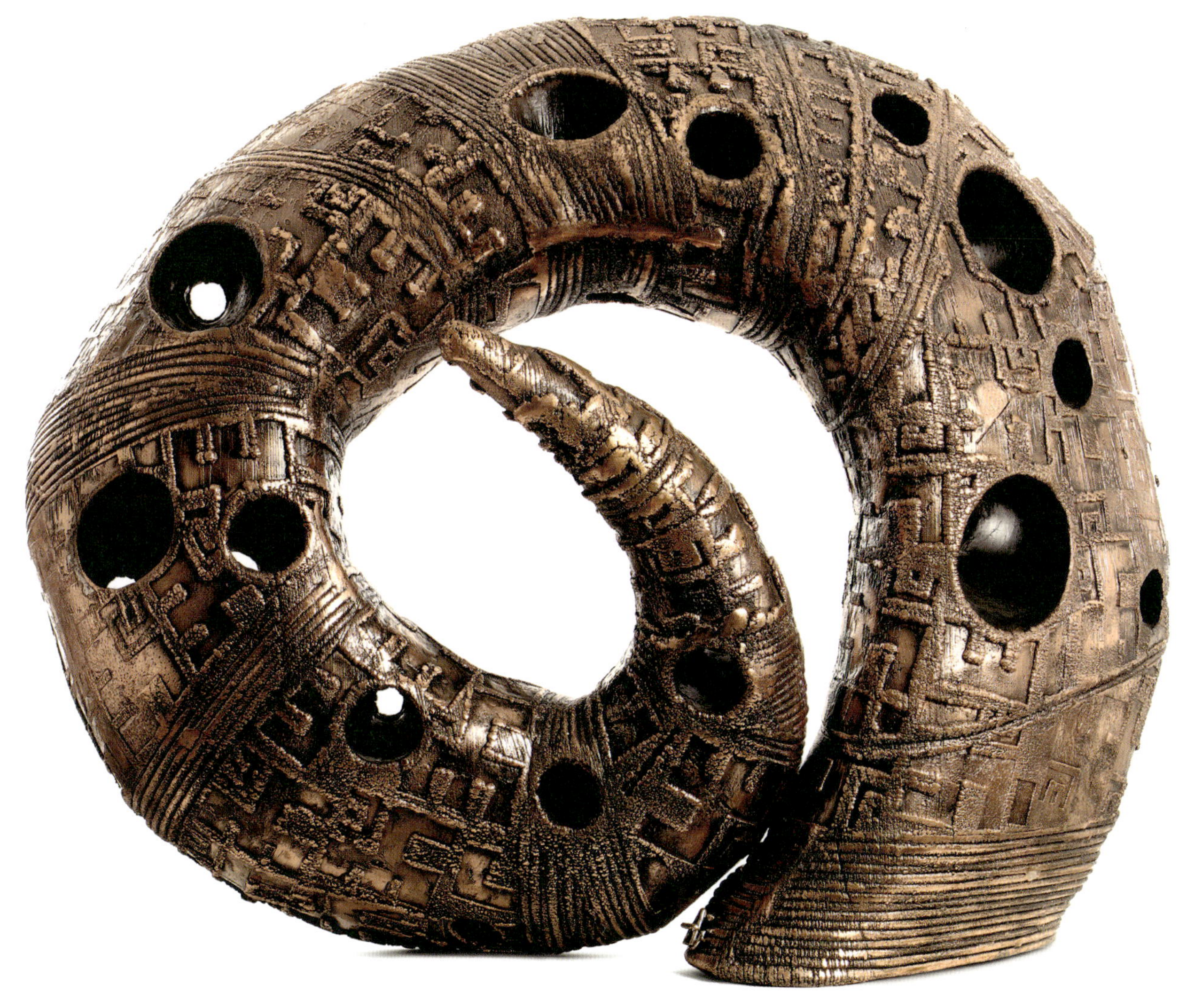

Horn II, 2014. Copper. 75 × 89 × 46 cm. Photo by Shamyl Khuhro

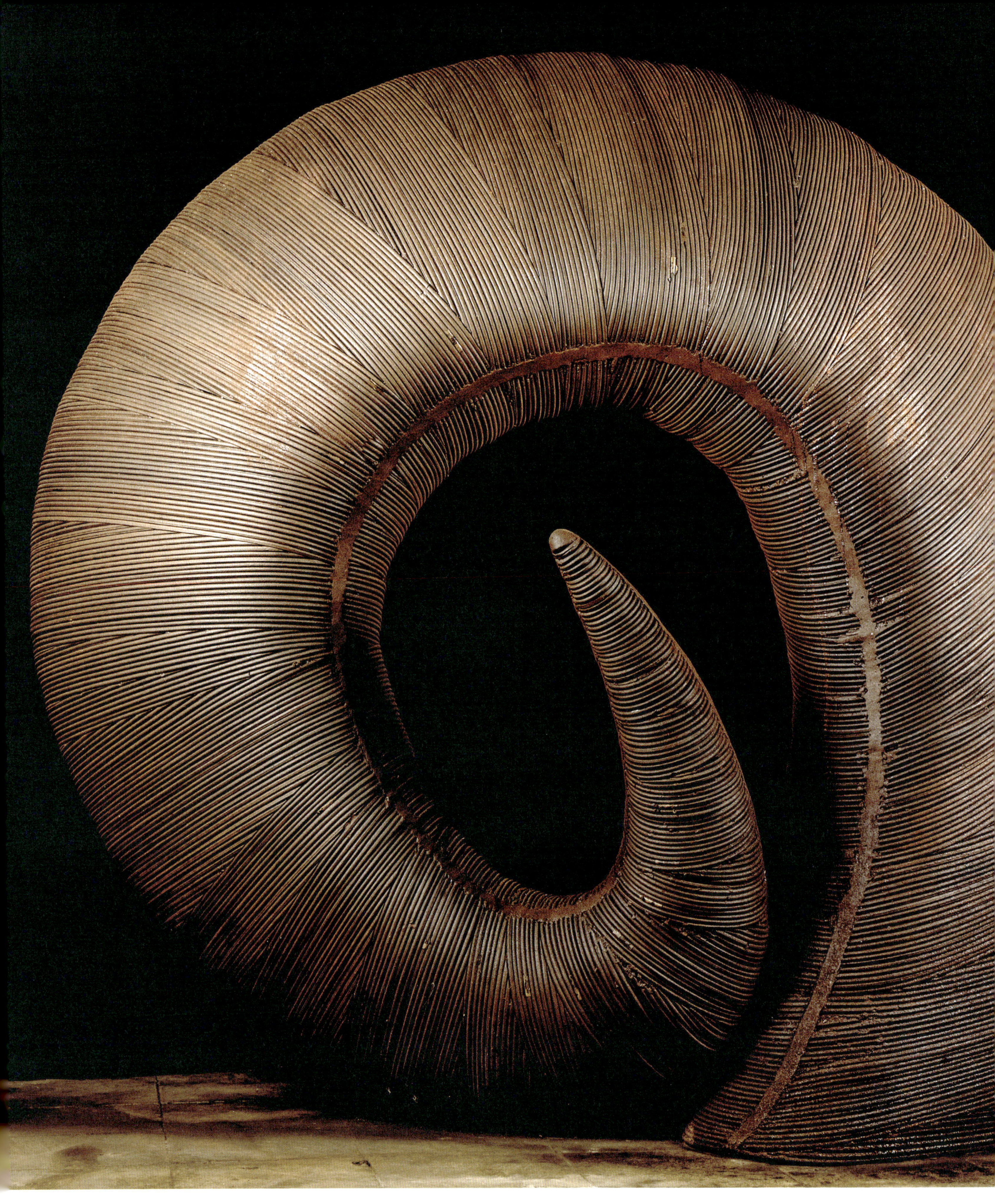

The Iron Horn, 2023. Iron. 108 × 195.5 × 61 cm. Photo by Humayun Memon

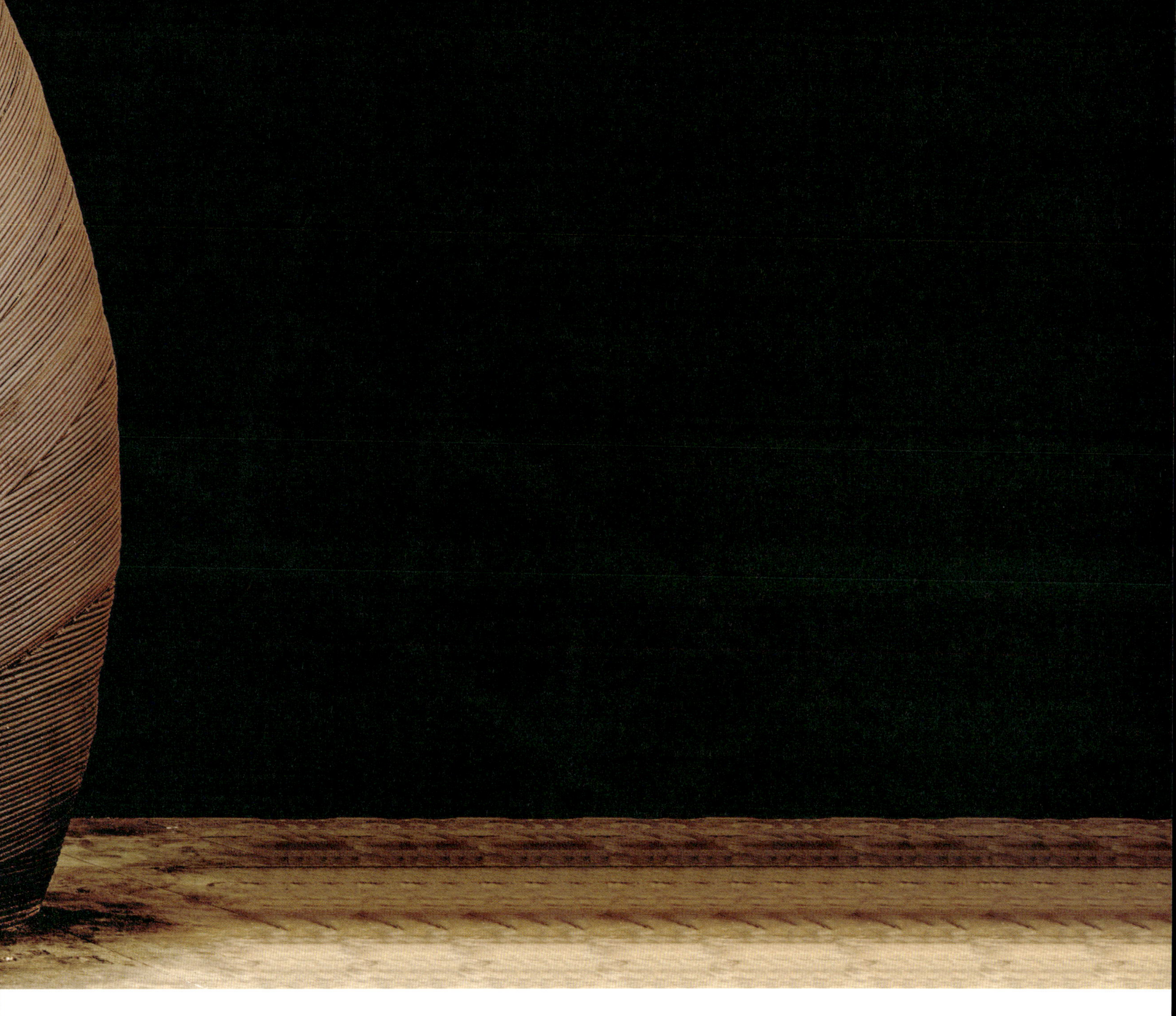

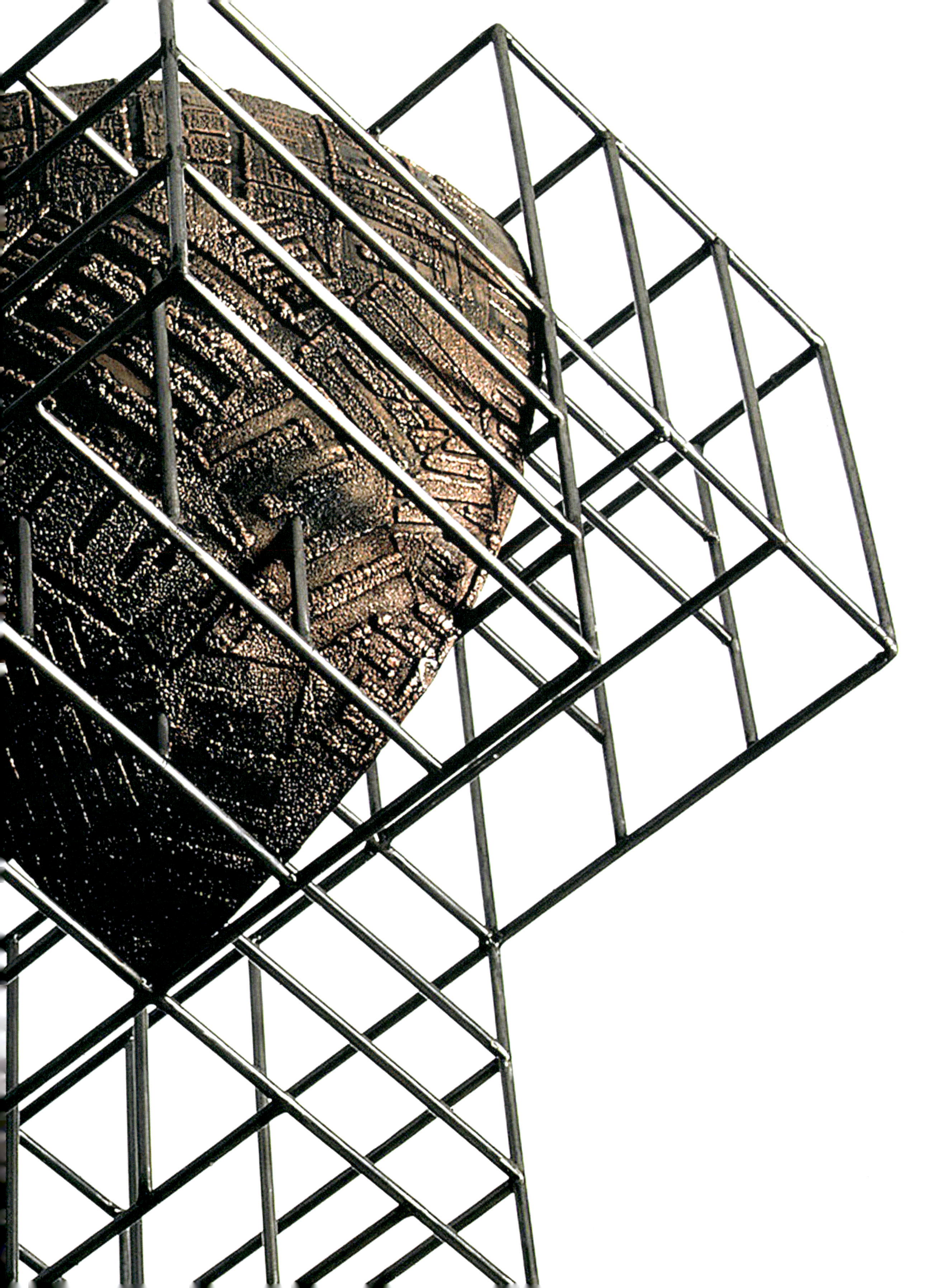

Char Bagh

2002 - 2003

Photo by Tapu Javeri

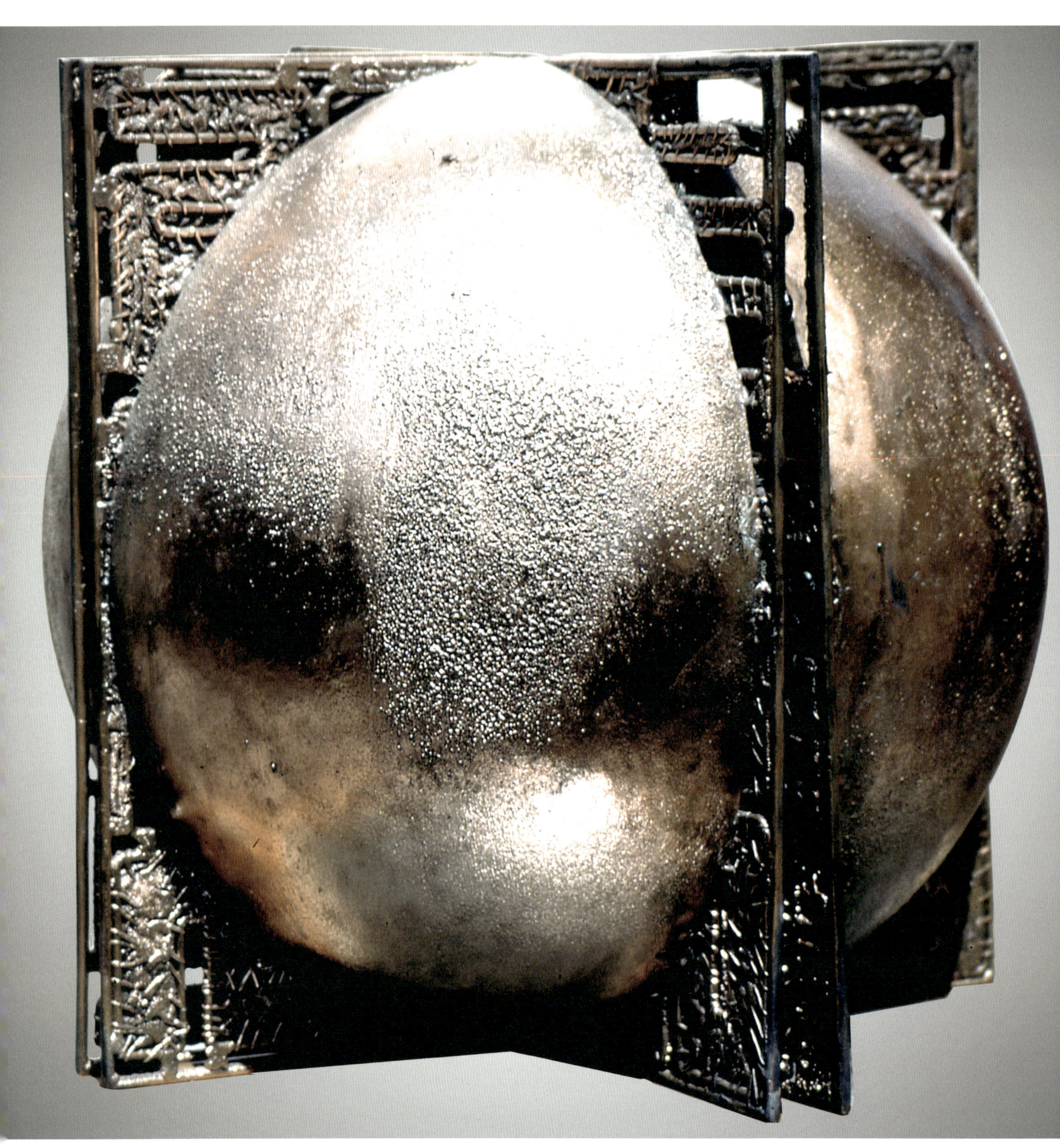

Char Bagh I, 2003. Copper. h. 51 cm. Photo by Tapu Javeri

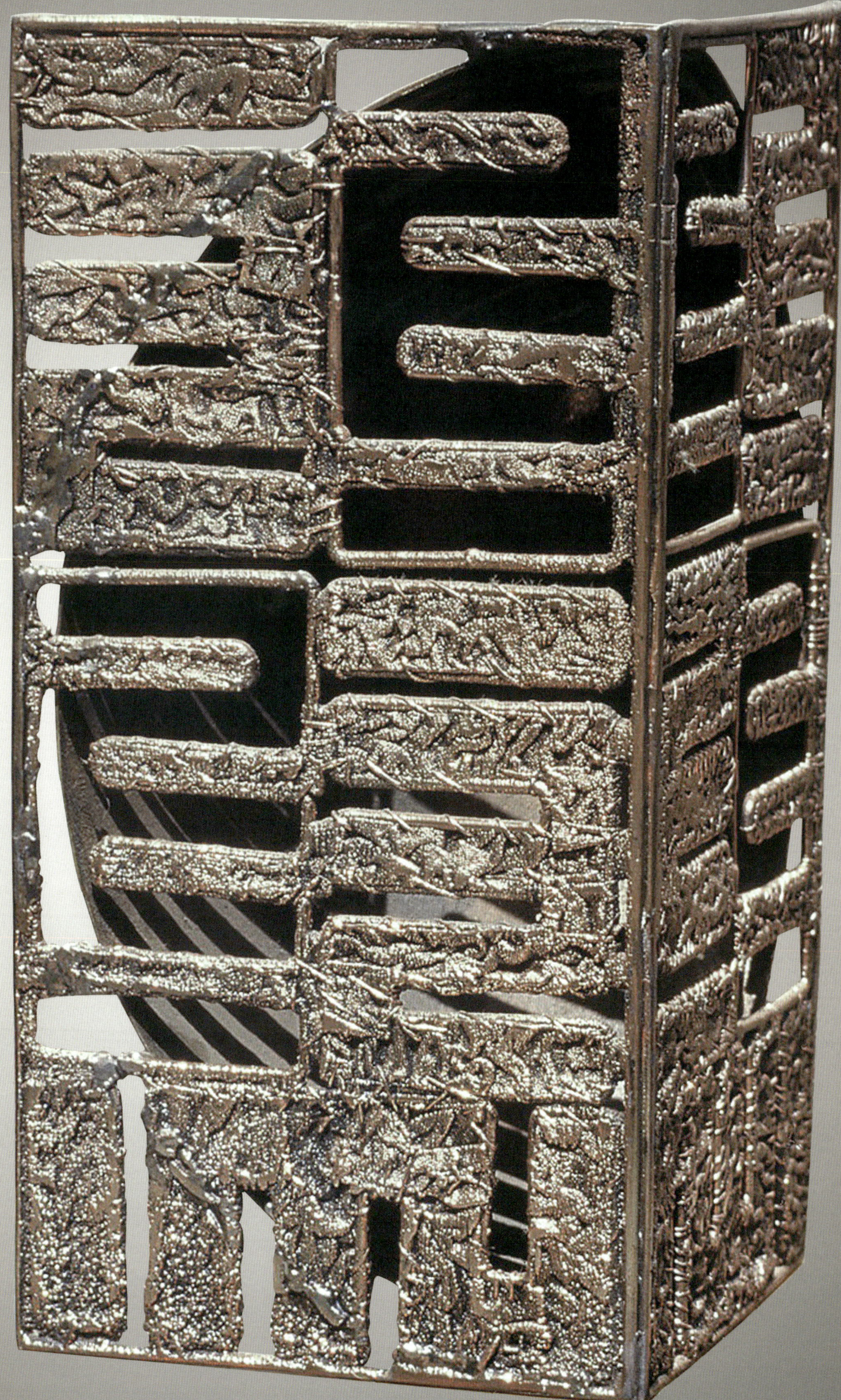

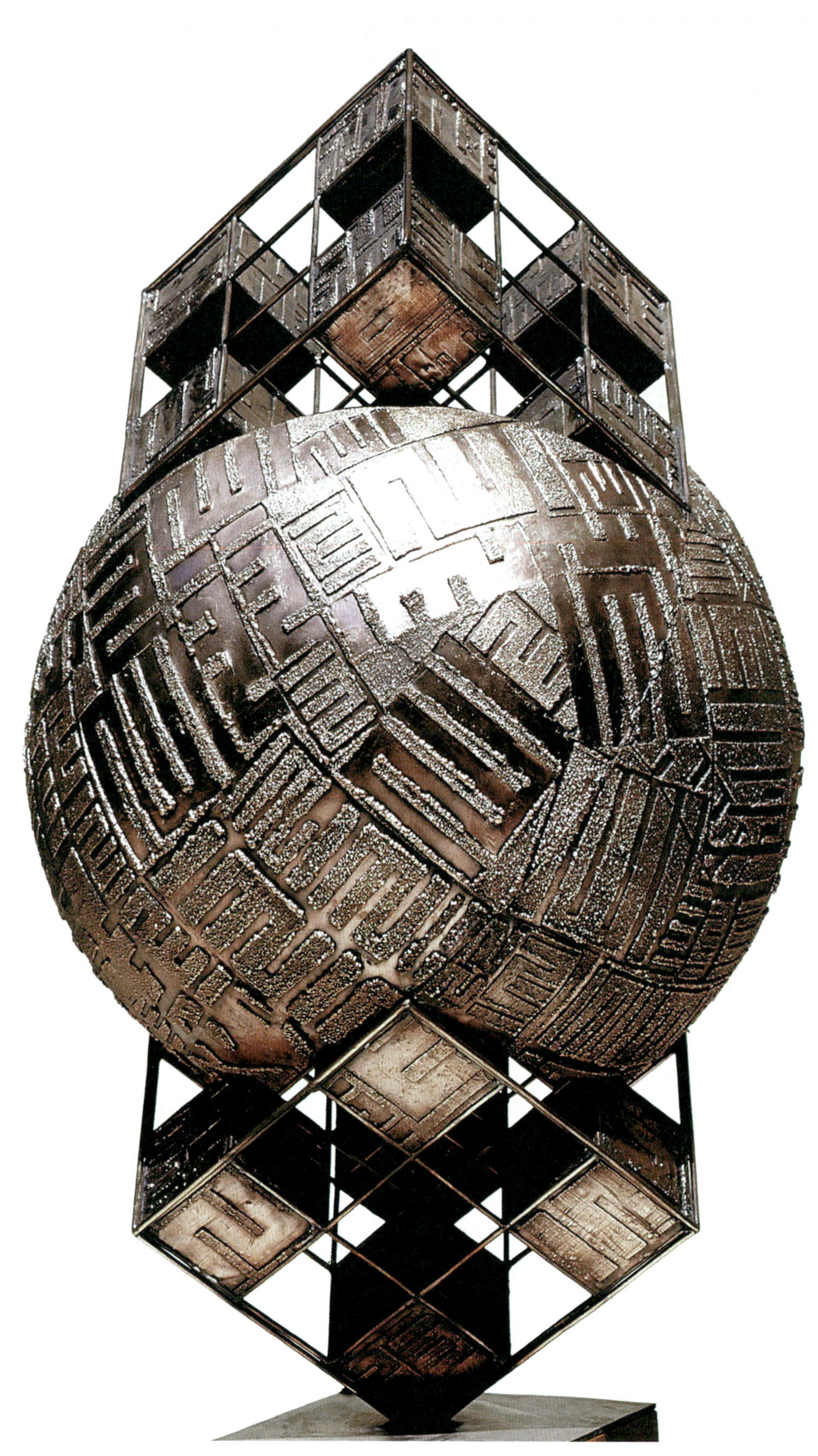

Balance, 2003. Copper and gold leaf. 118 × 68 × 68 cm. Photo by Tapu Javeri

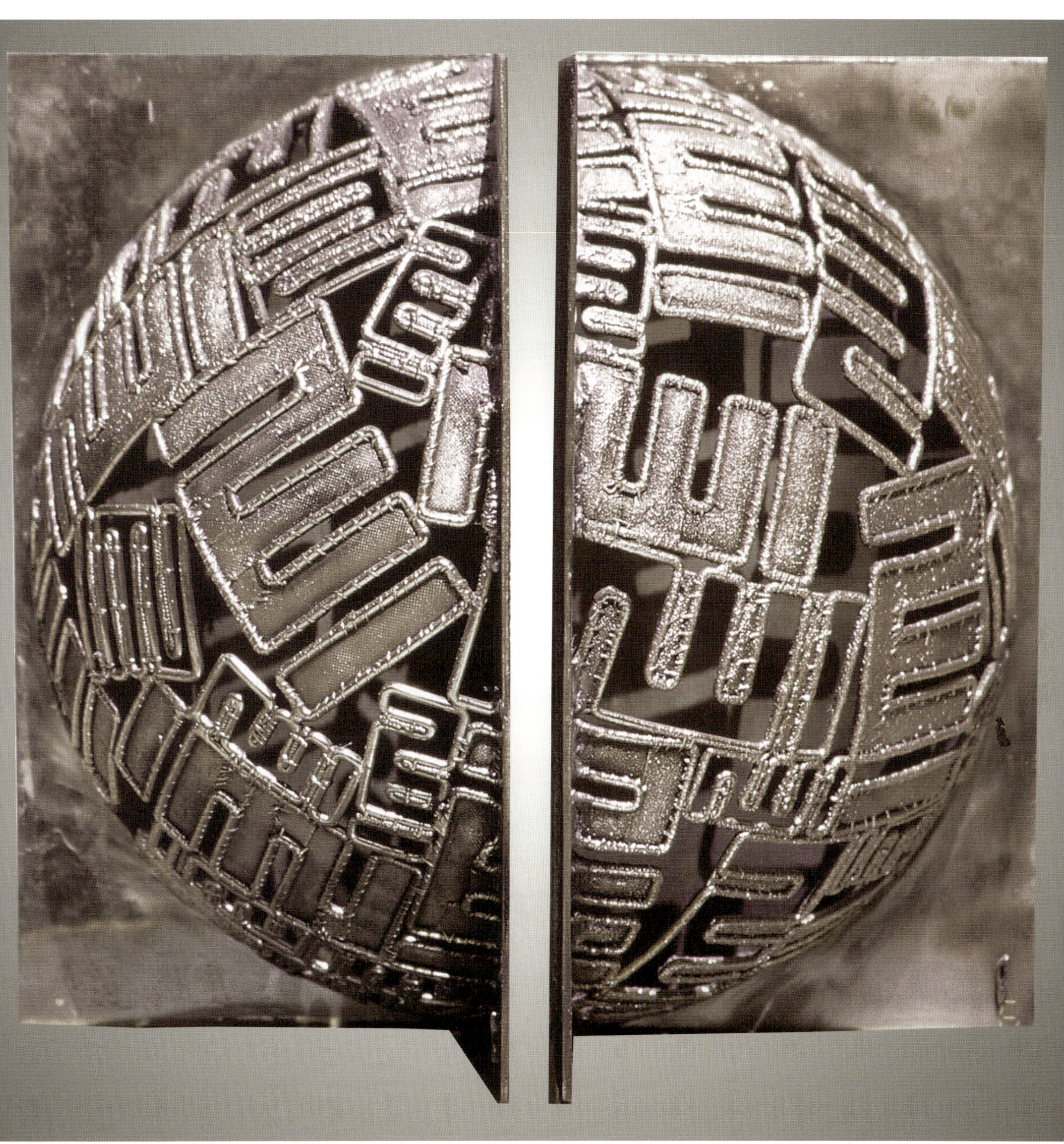

Char Bagh II, 2003. Copper. h. 51 cm. Photo by Tapu Javeri

Quarter, 2003. Copper and iron. 119 × 106.6 × 106.6 cm. Photo by Tapu Javeri

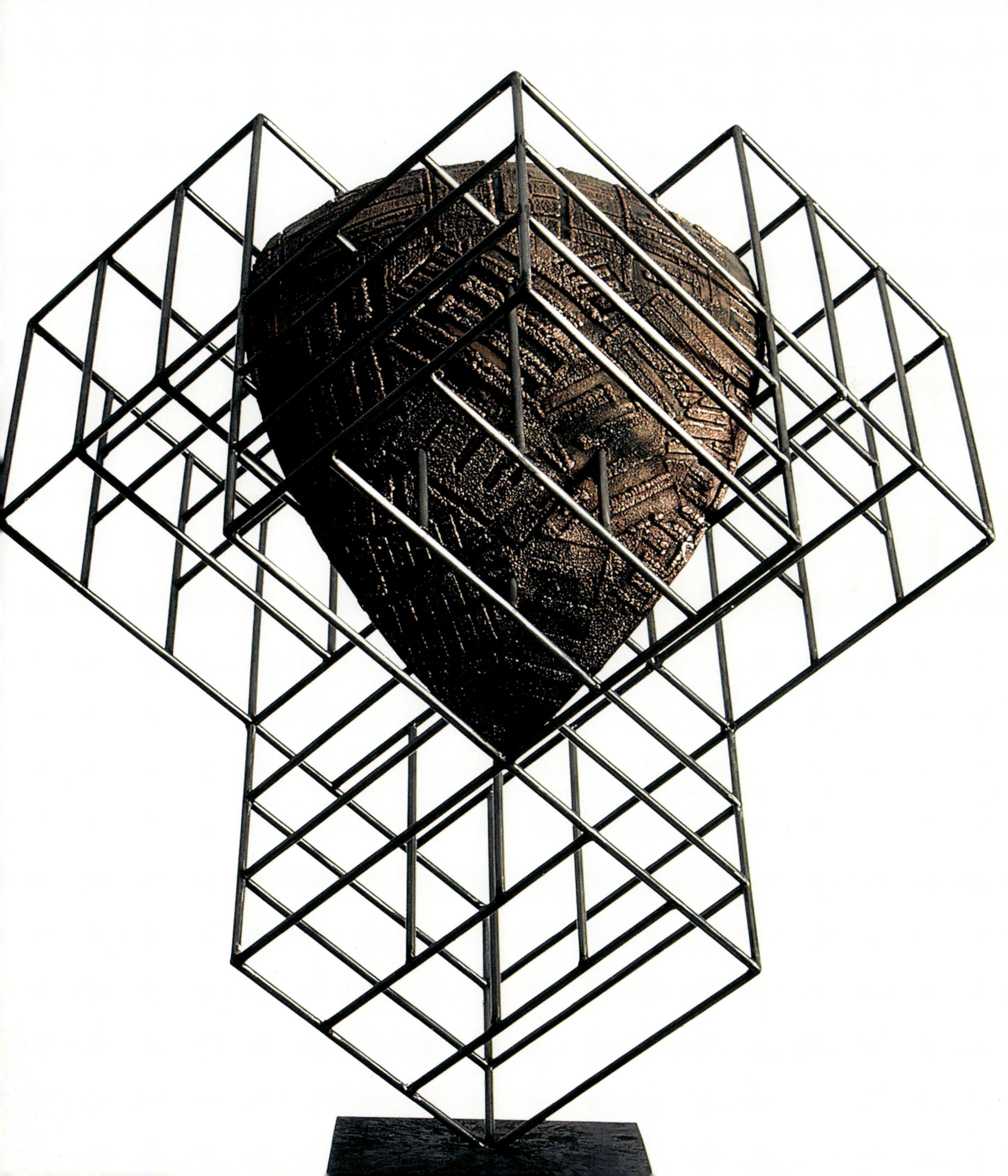

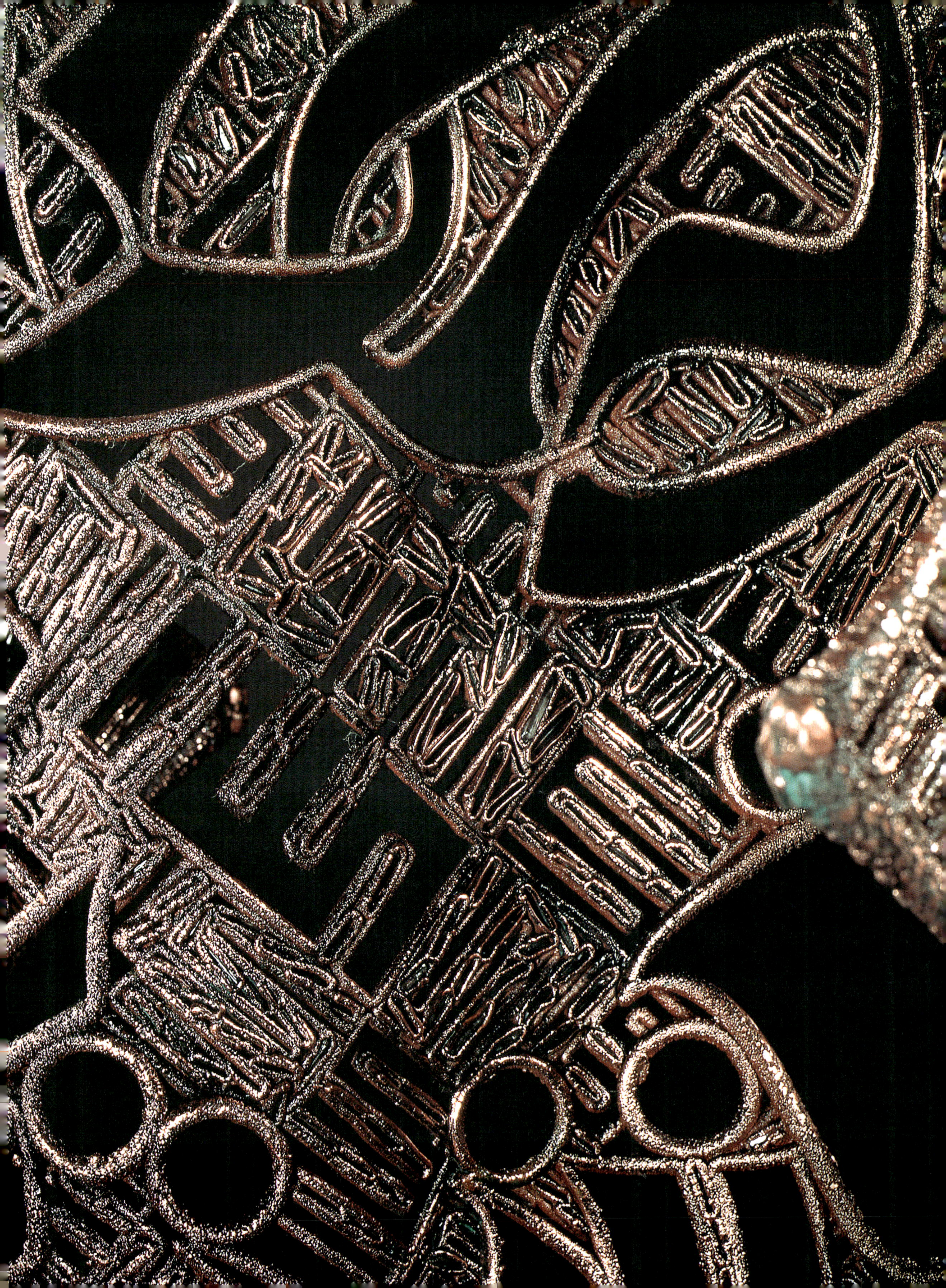

Surah-e-Rehman

1994 - 2008

Photo by Tapu Javeri

Rung I, 1994. Copper, rock crystals and glass. 61 × 38 × 22.8 cm. Photo by Humayun Memon

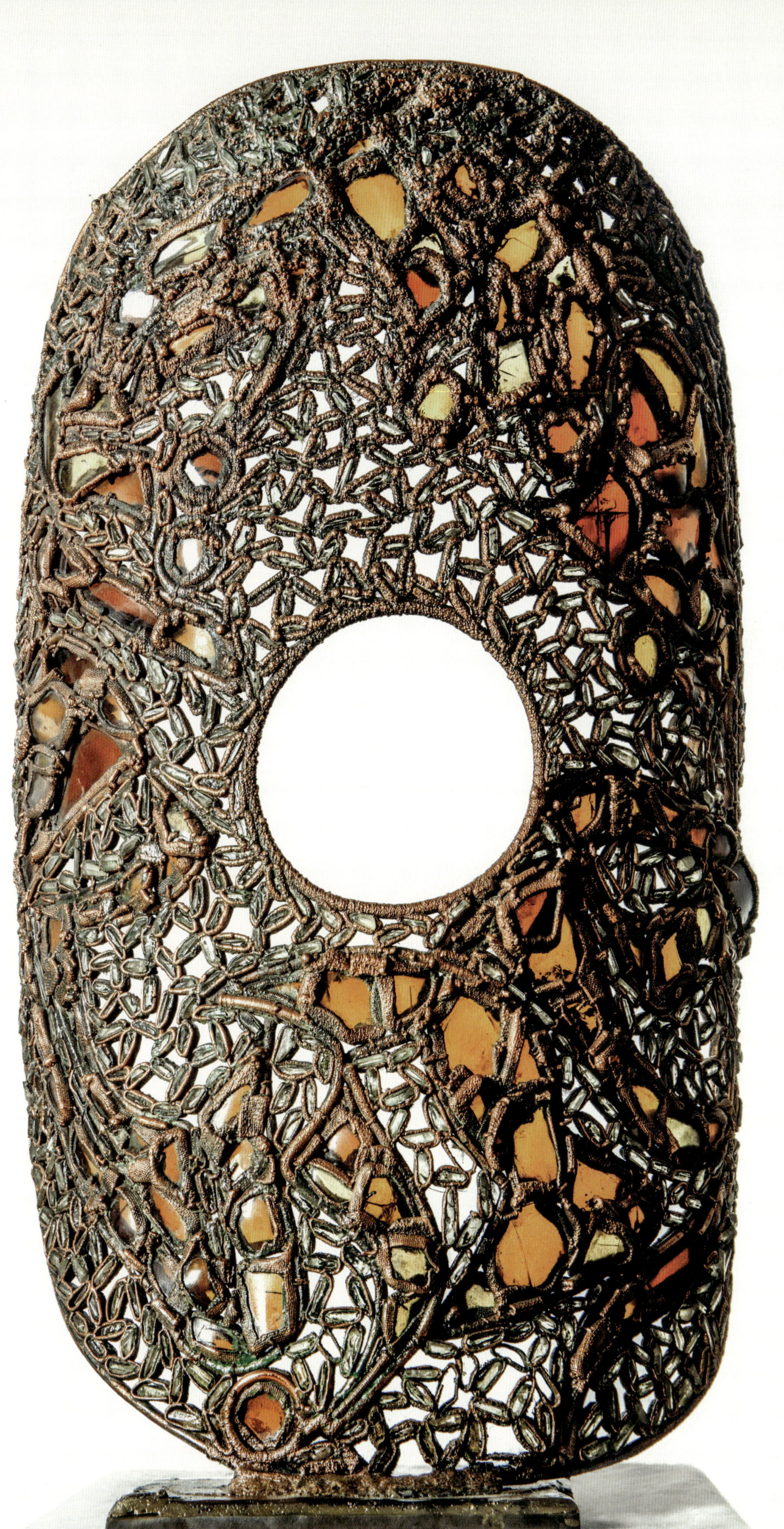

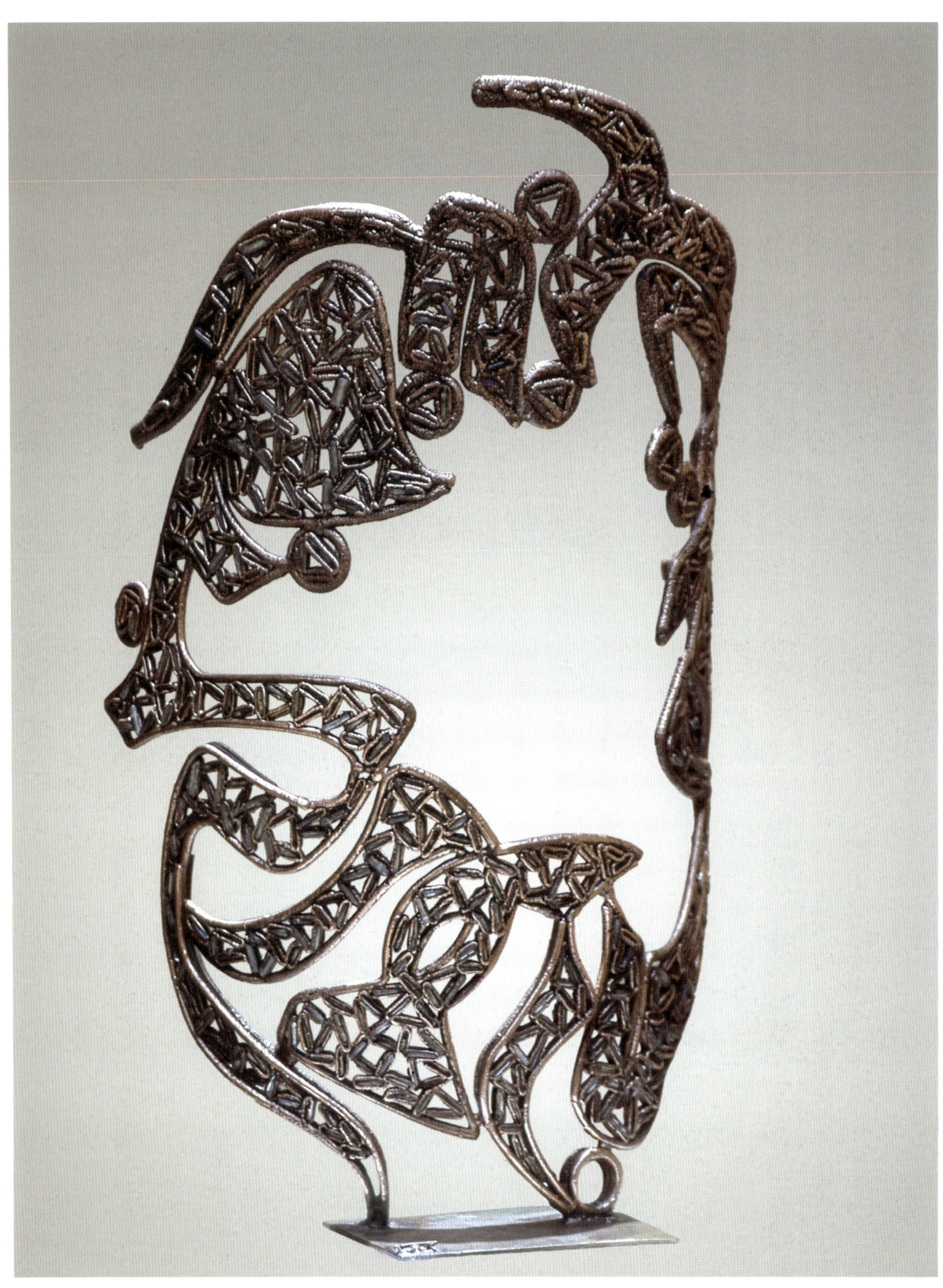

Connected I, 1996. Copper and rock crystals. 62.4 × 30.4 × 20.3 cm. Photo by Nafees

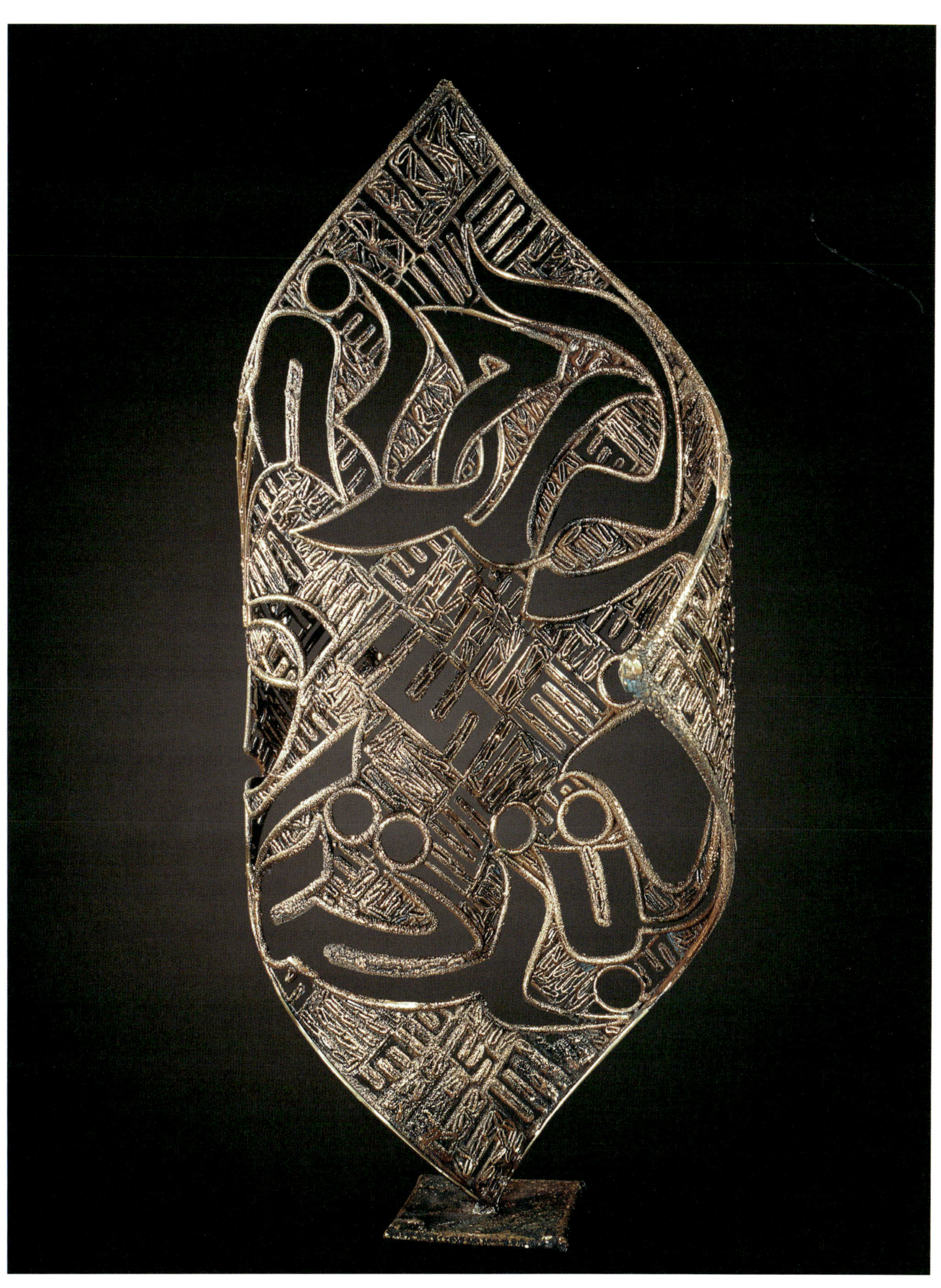

Air, 1999. Copper and rock crystals. 99 × 48.2 × 22.8 cm. Photo by Tapu Javeri

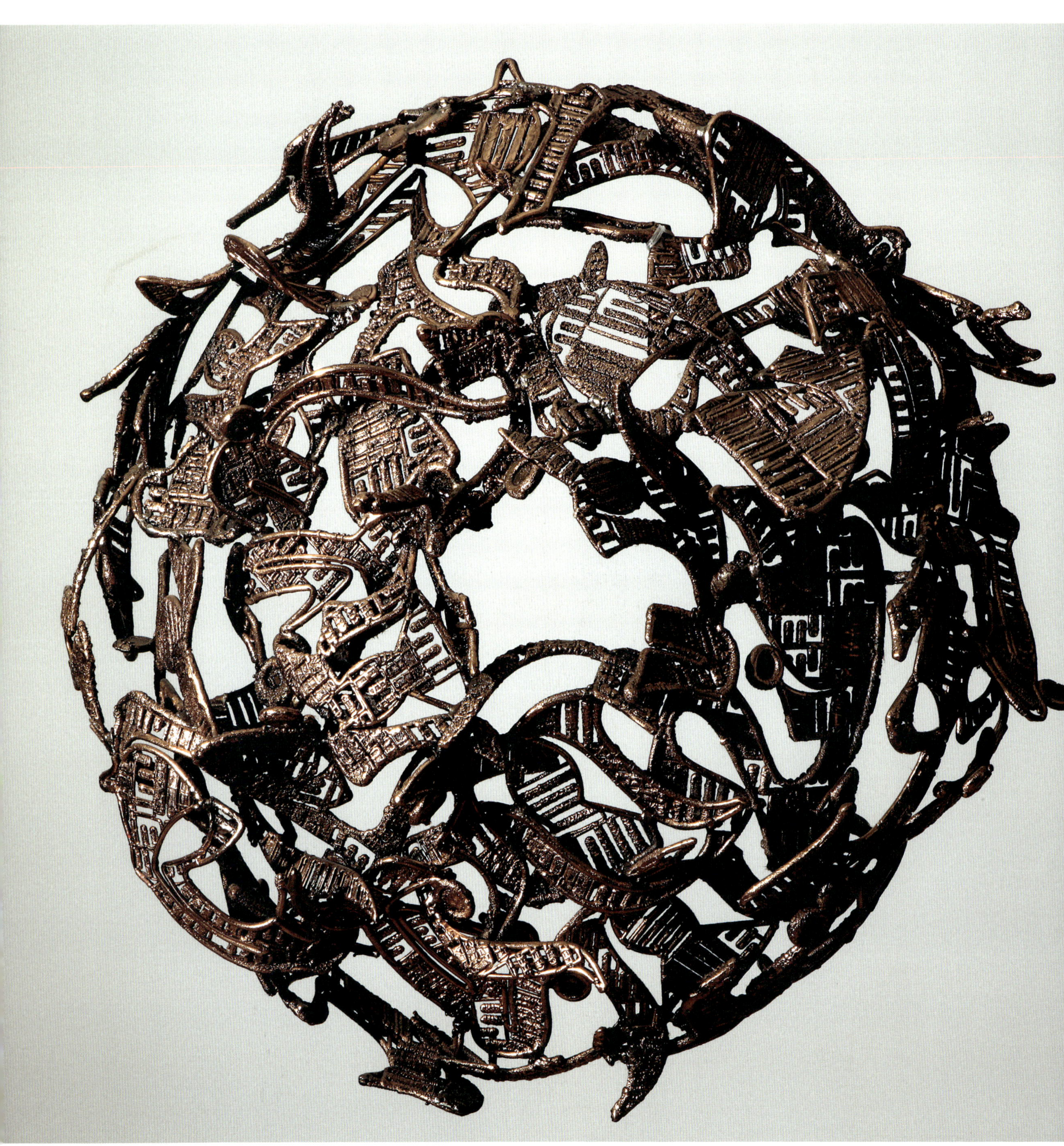

Ocean IV, 2008. Copper. 111.7 × 111.7 × 55.8 cm. Photo by Tapu Javeri

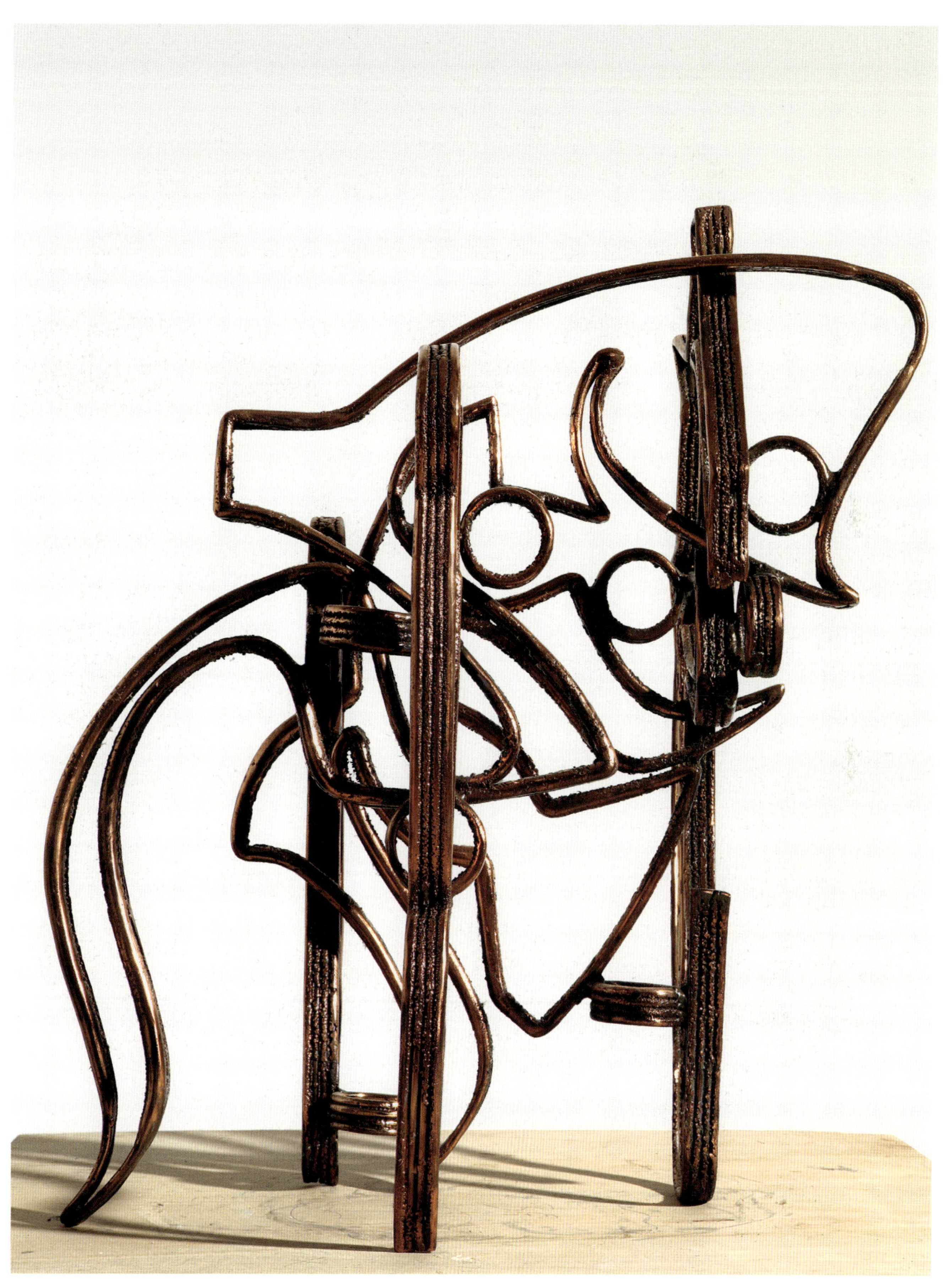

Embedded Line IV, 2008. Copper. 76 × 53 × 68.5 cm. Photo by Shamyl Khuhro

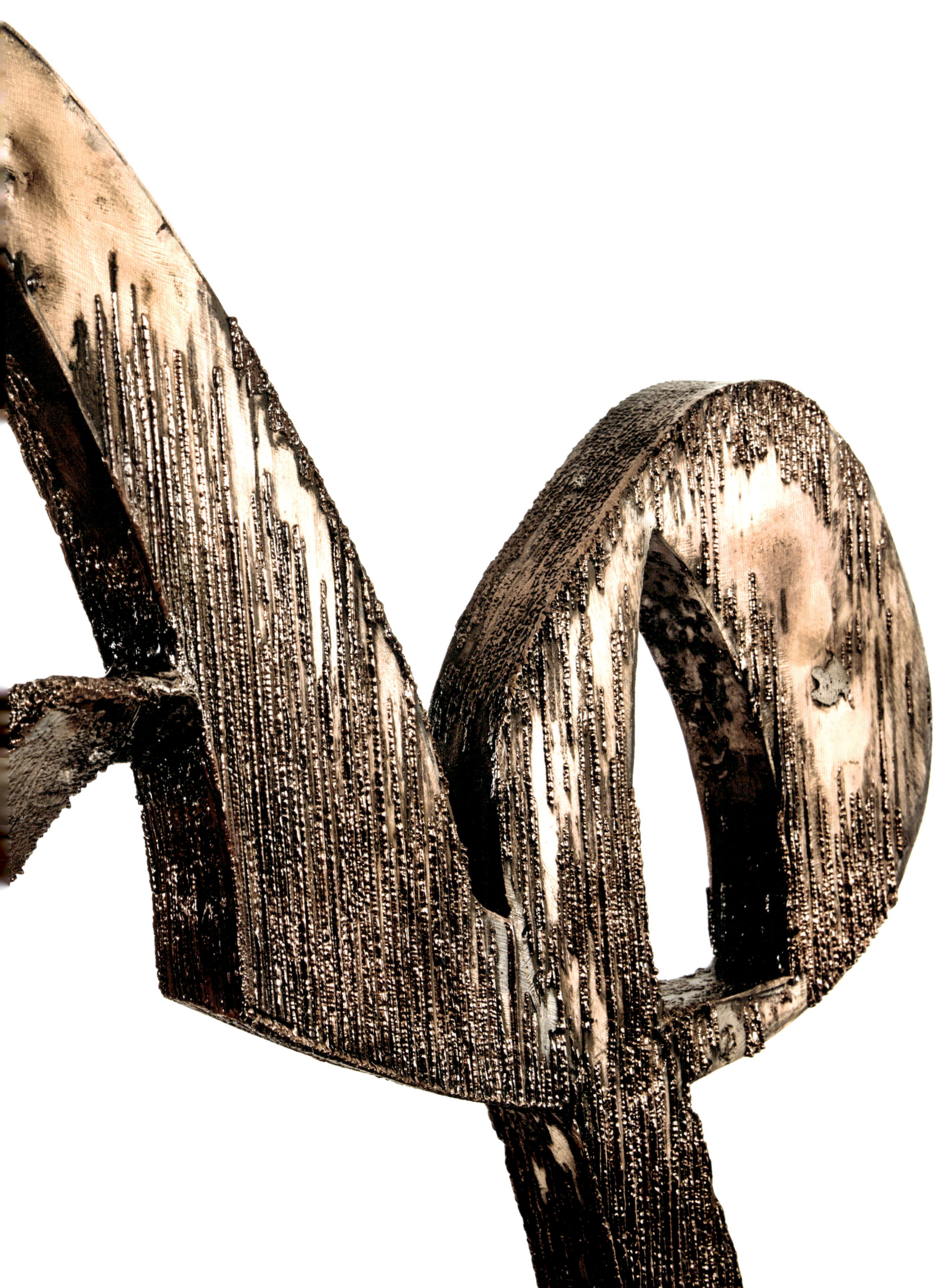

Iqra

1992 - 2018

Photo by Humayun Memon

The Binding, 1992. Copper and rock crystals. 61 × 17.7 × 10 cm. Photo by Nafees

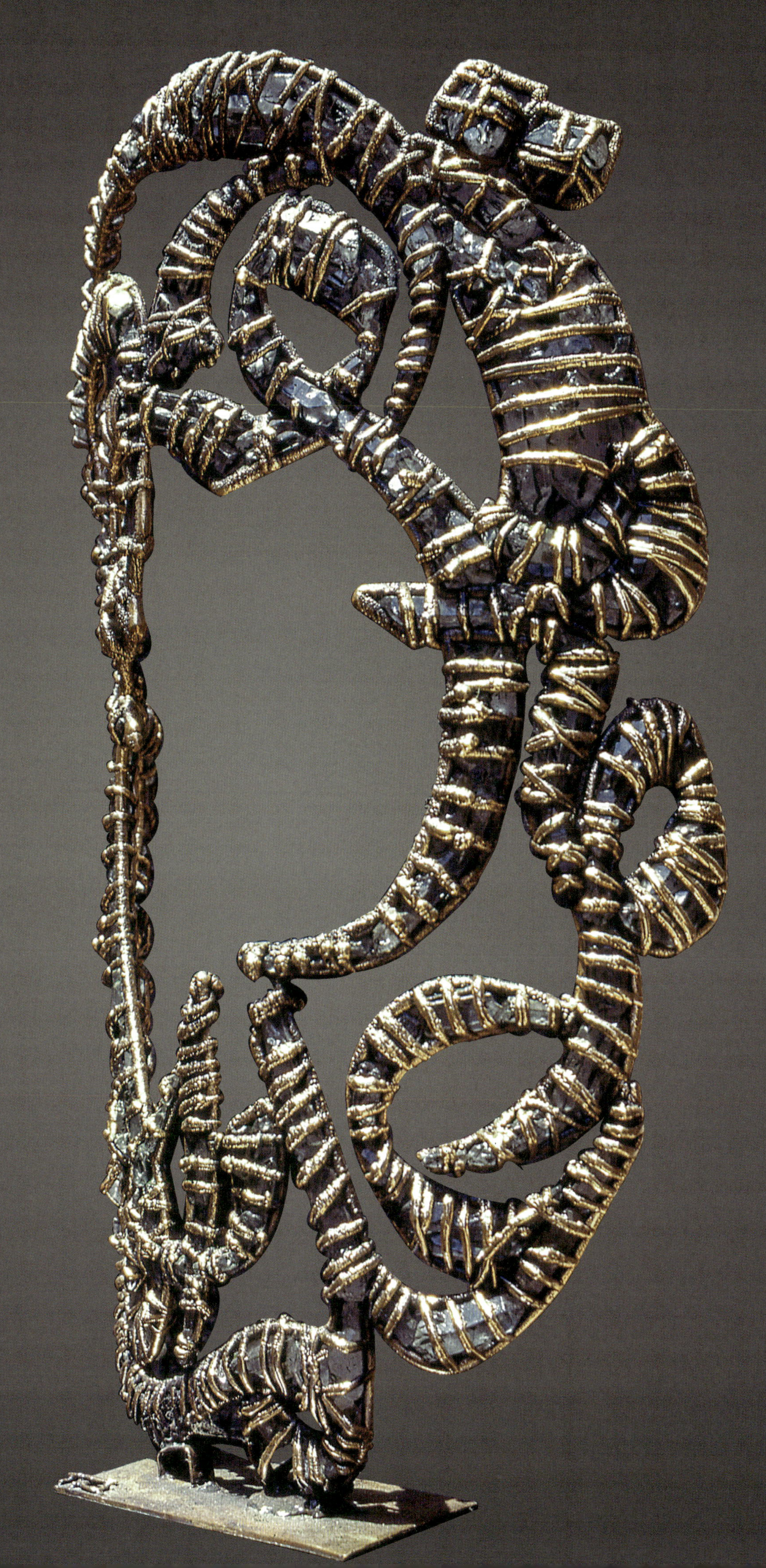

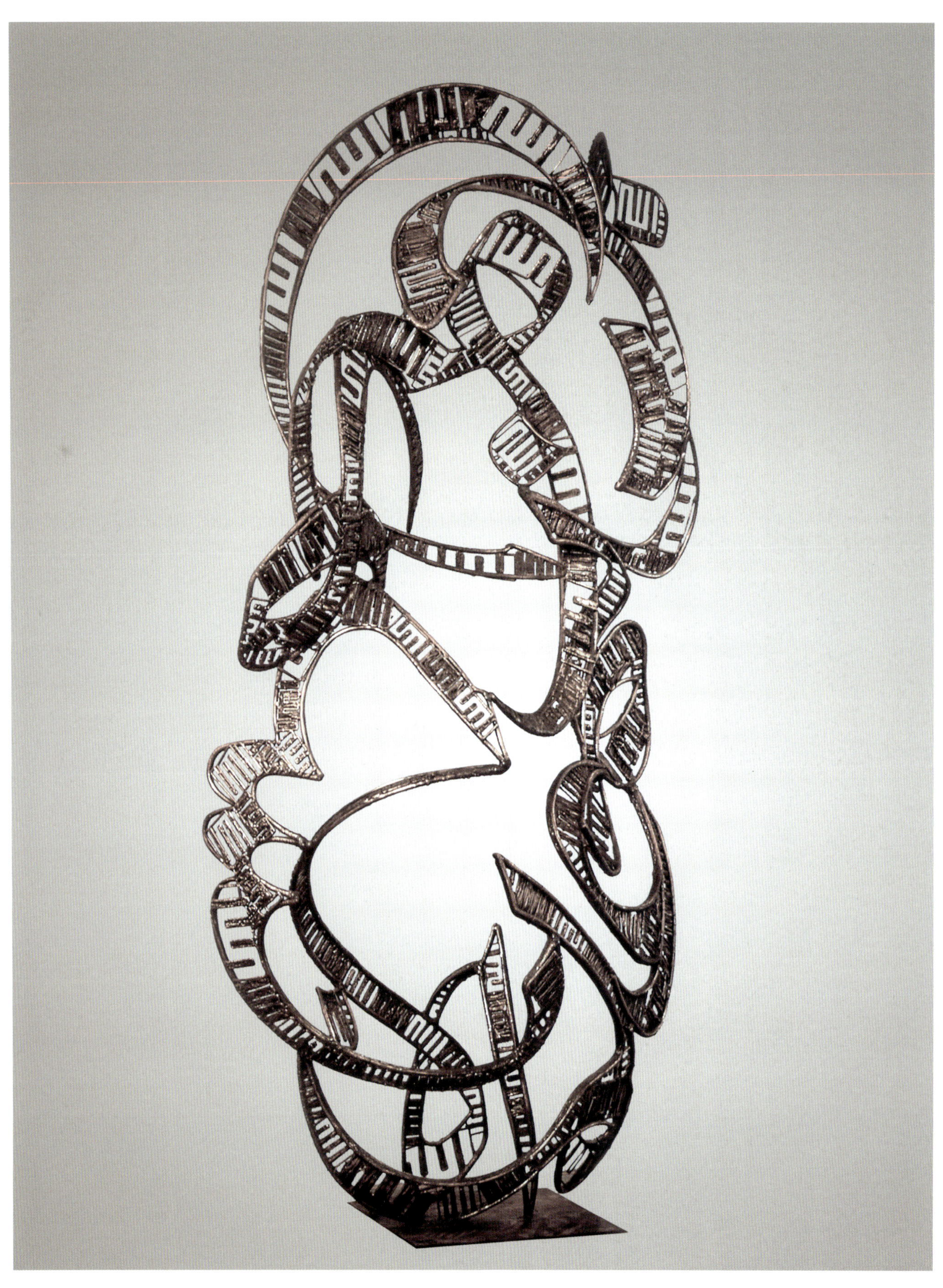

The Web, 2002. Copper. 213 × 127 × 22.8 cm. Photo by Nafees

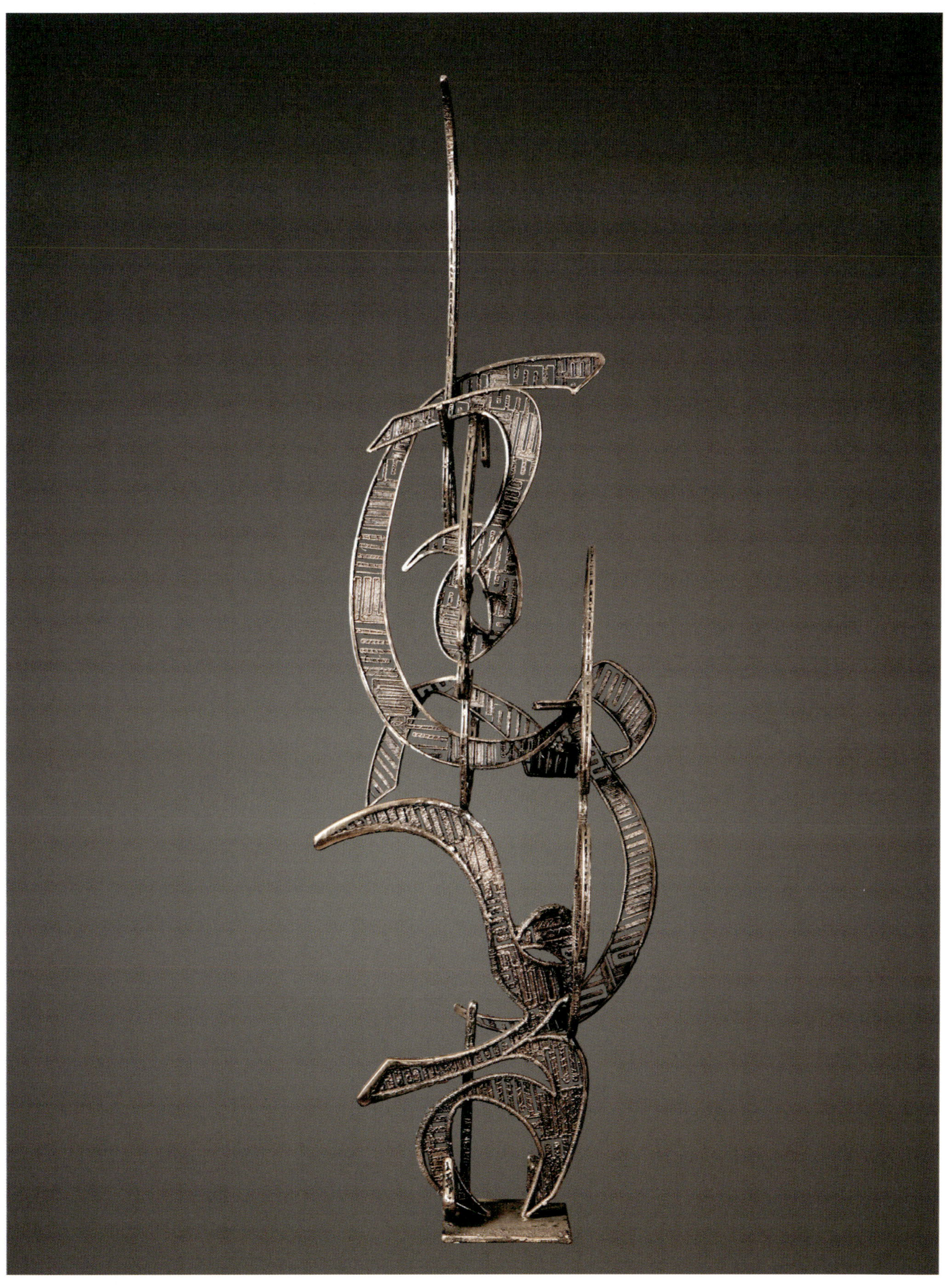

Flight I, 2007. Copper. 127 × 58.4 × 55.8 cm. Photo by Tapu Javeri

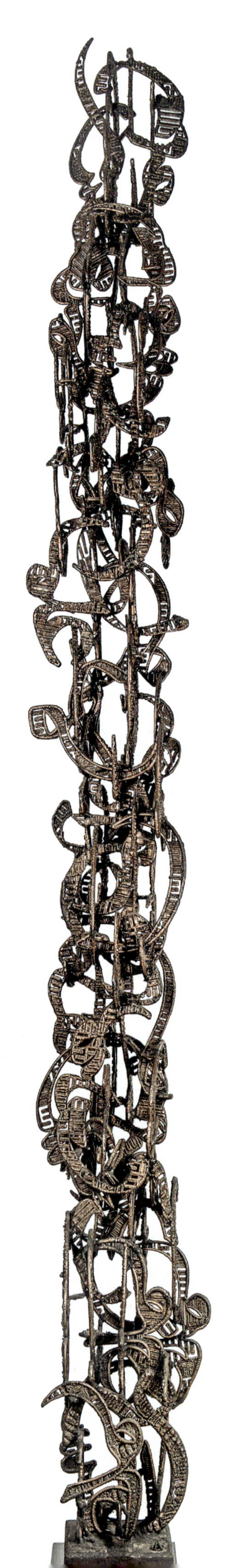

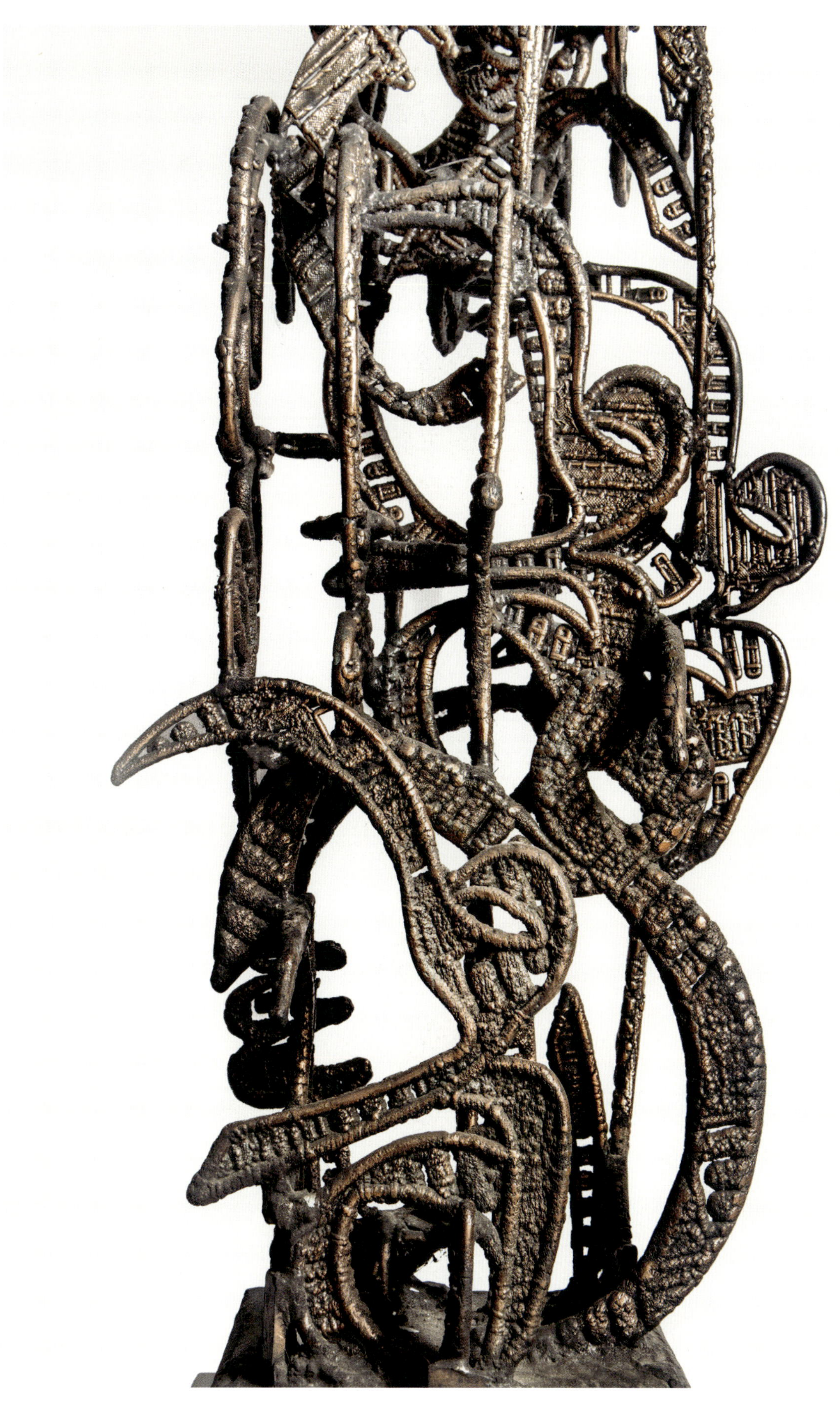

Link V: Stitches, 2008. Copper. 381 × 48 × 48 cm. Photo by Humayun Memon

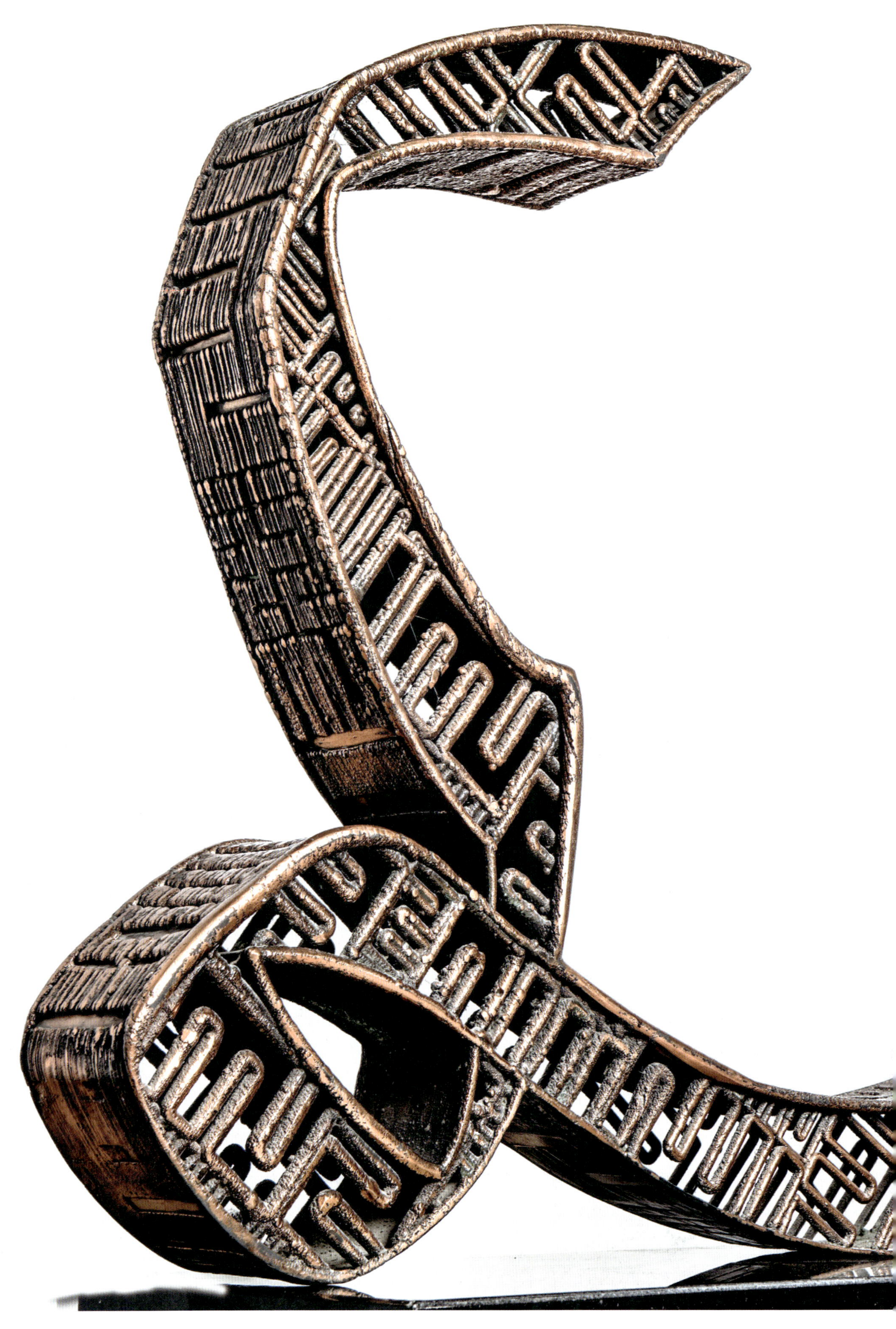

Fragment III, 2008. Copper. 67 × 91.4 × 11 cm. Photo by Humayun Memon

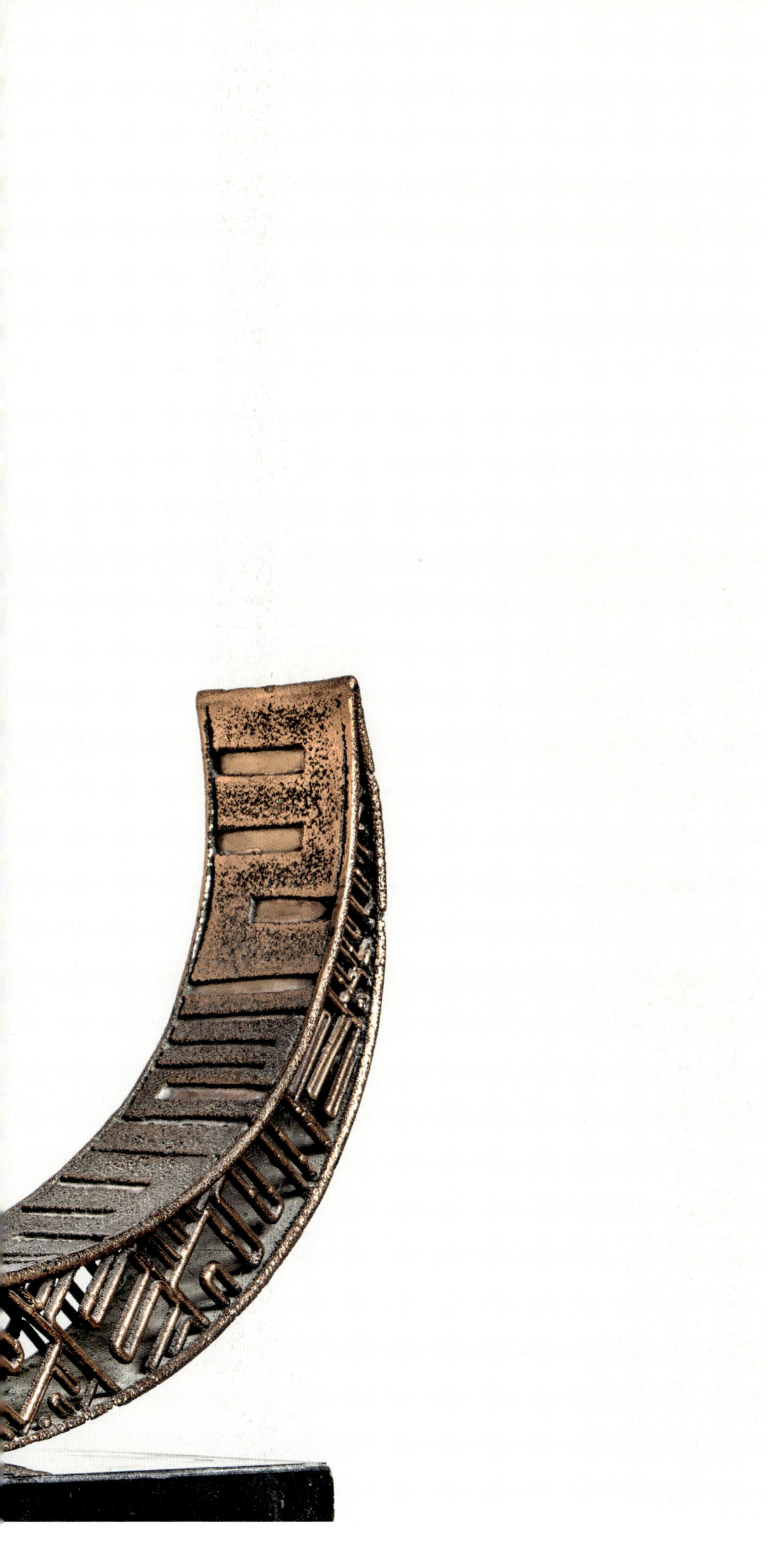

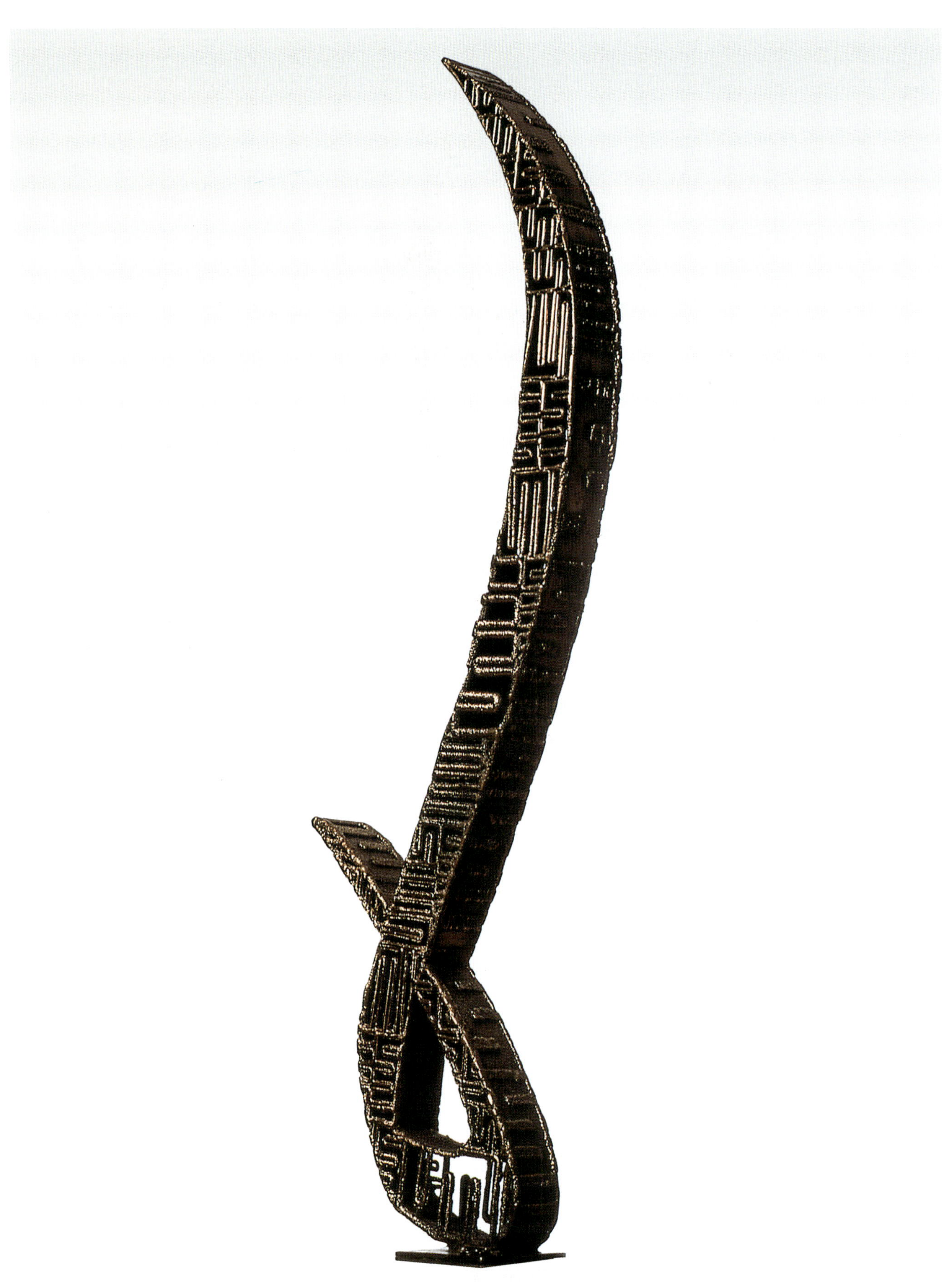

Fragment V, 2009. Copper. 73.6 × 25.4 × 7 cm. Photo by Shamyl Khuhro

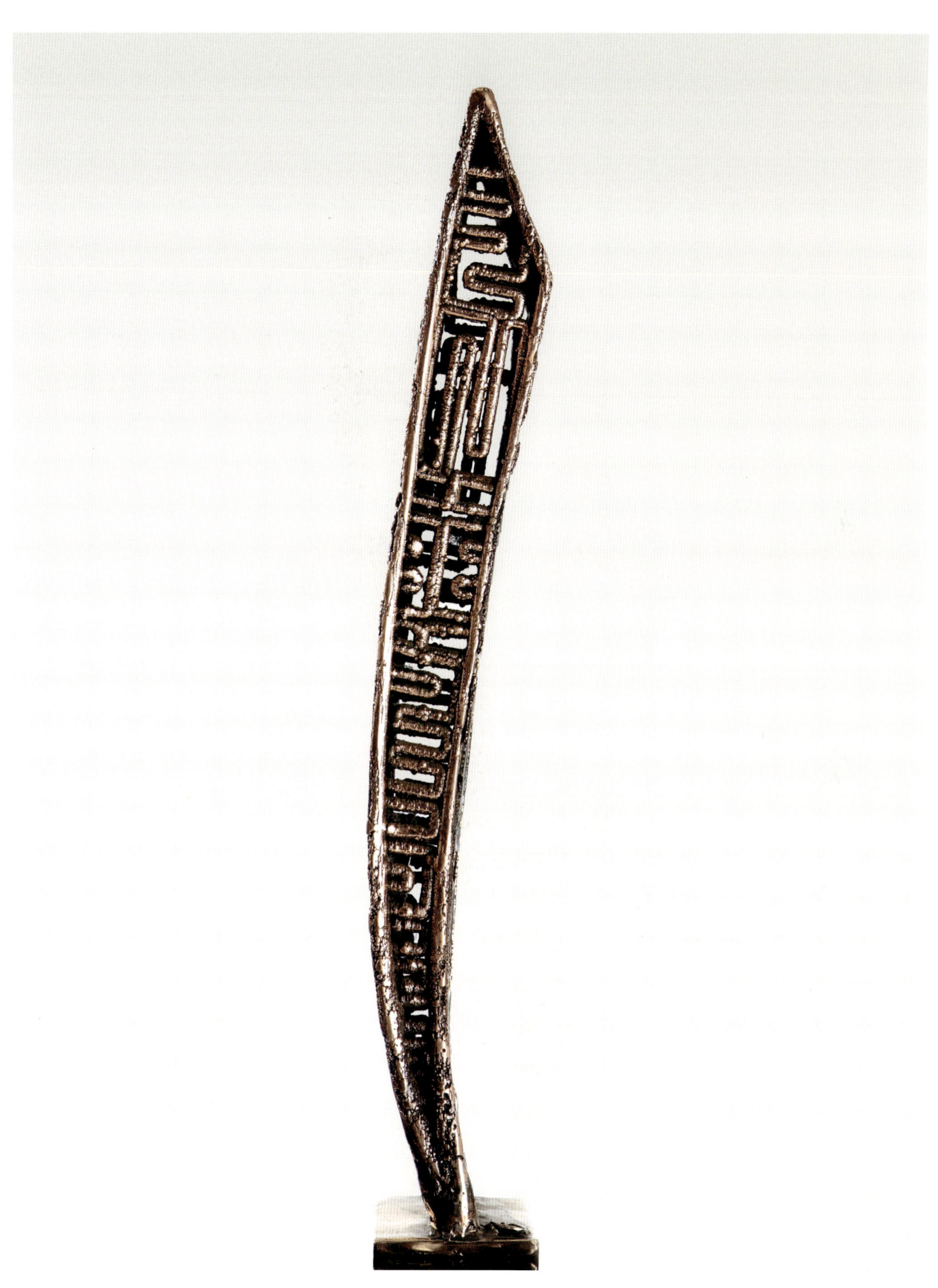

Aleph, 2014. Copper. 57 × 19 × 16.5 cm. Photo by Humayun Memon

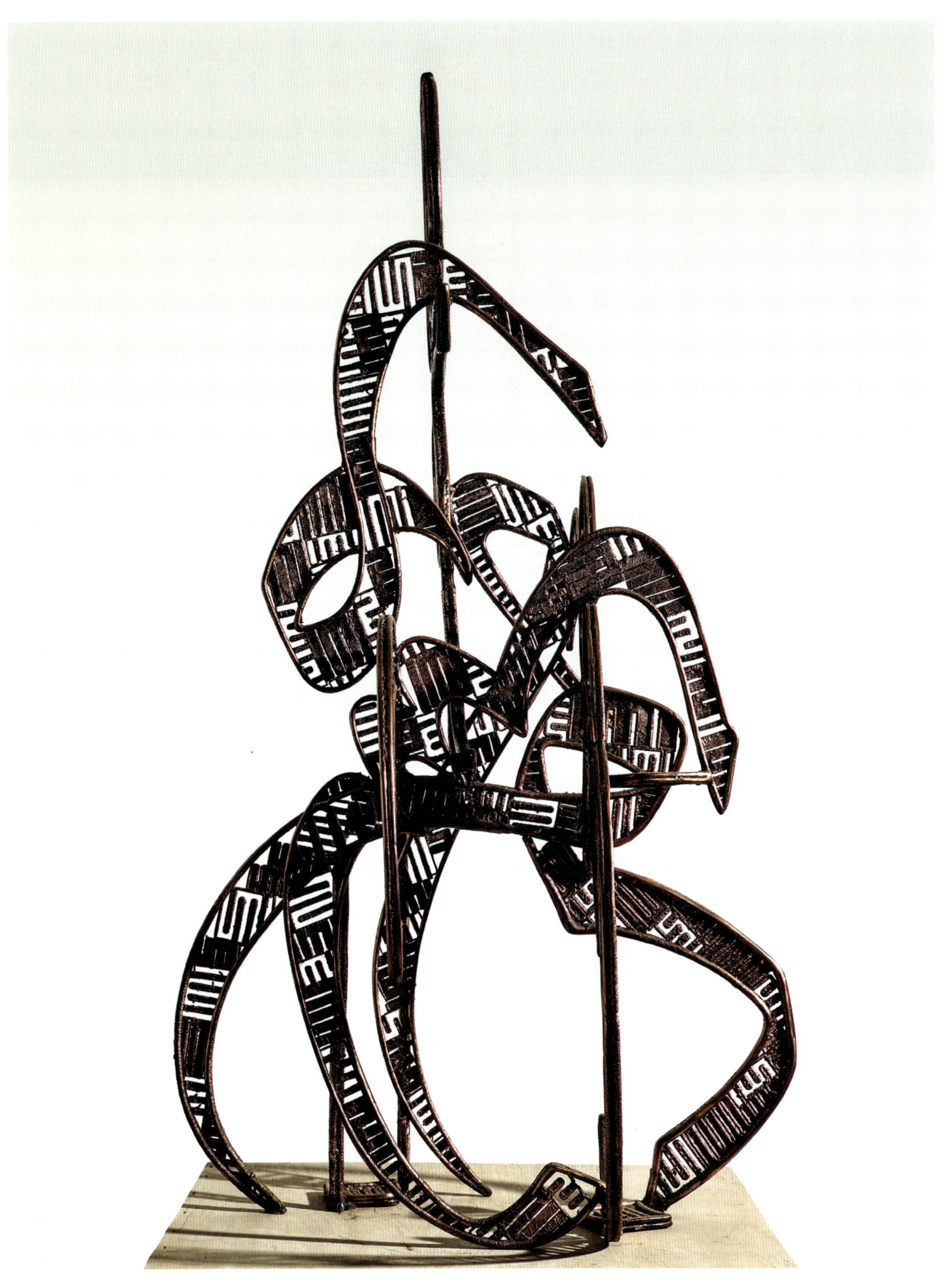

Spider II, 2009. Copper. 152 × 109 × 86 cm. Photo by Shamyl Khuhro

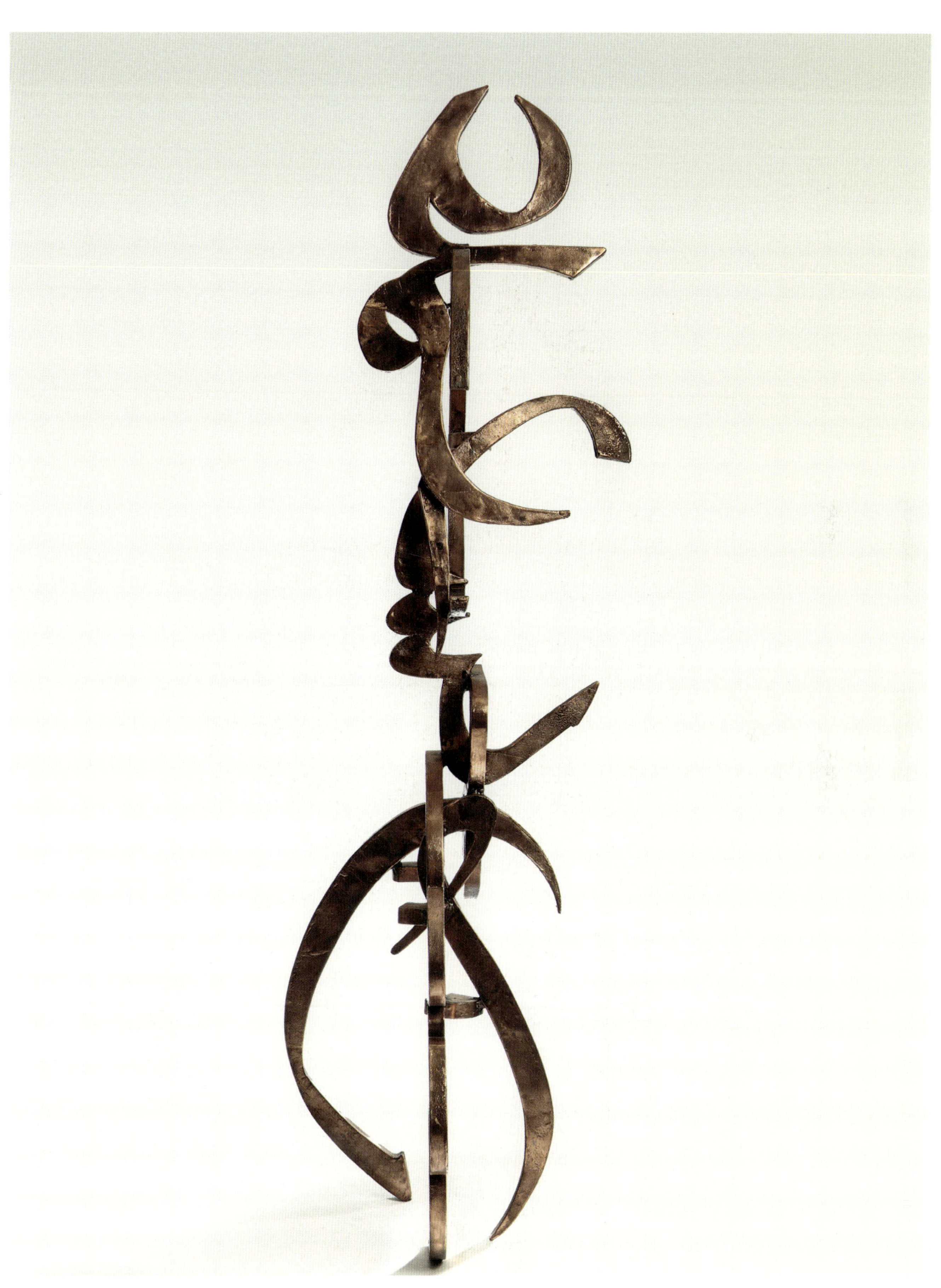

Spider Raga VIII, 2012. Copper. 188 × 61 × 54.6 cm. Photo by Shamyl Khuhro

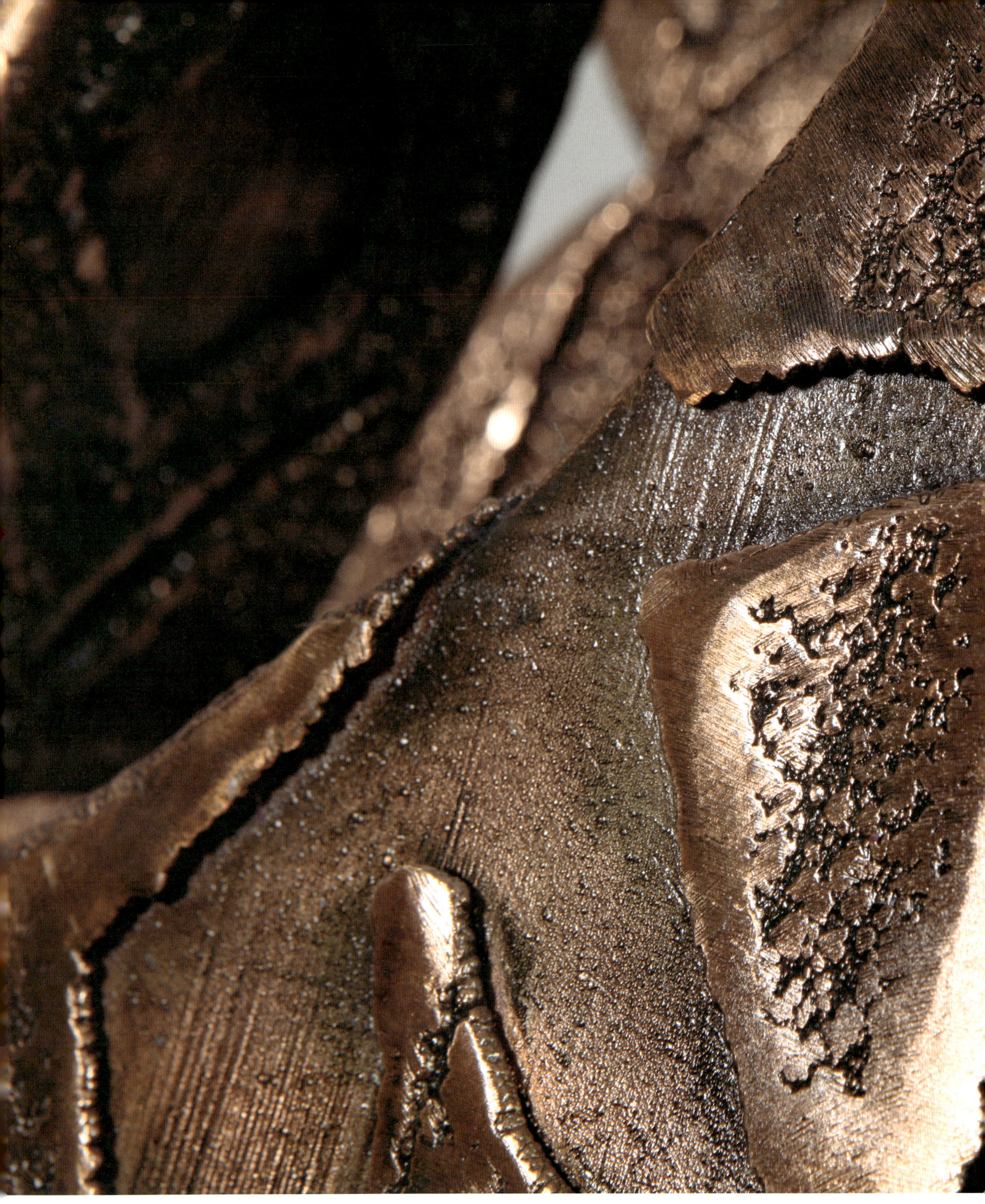

Dragon Spider, 2012. Detail. Copper. 251.4 × 78.7 × 81.2 cm. Photo by Shamyl Khuhro

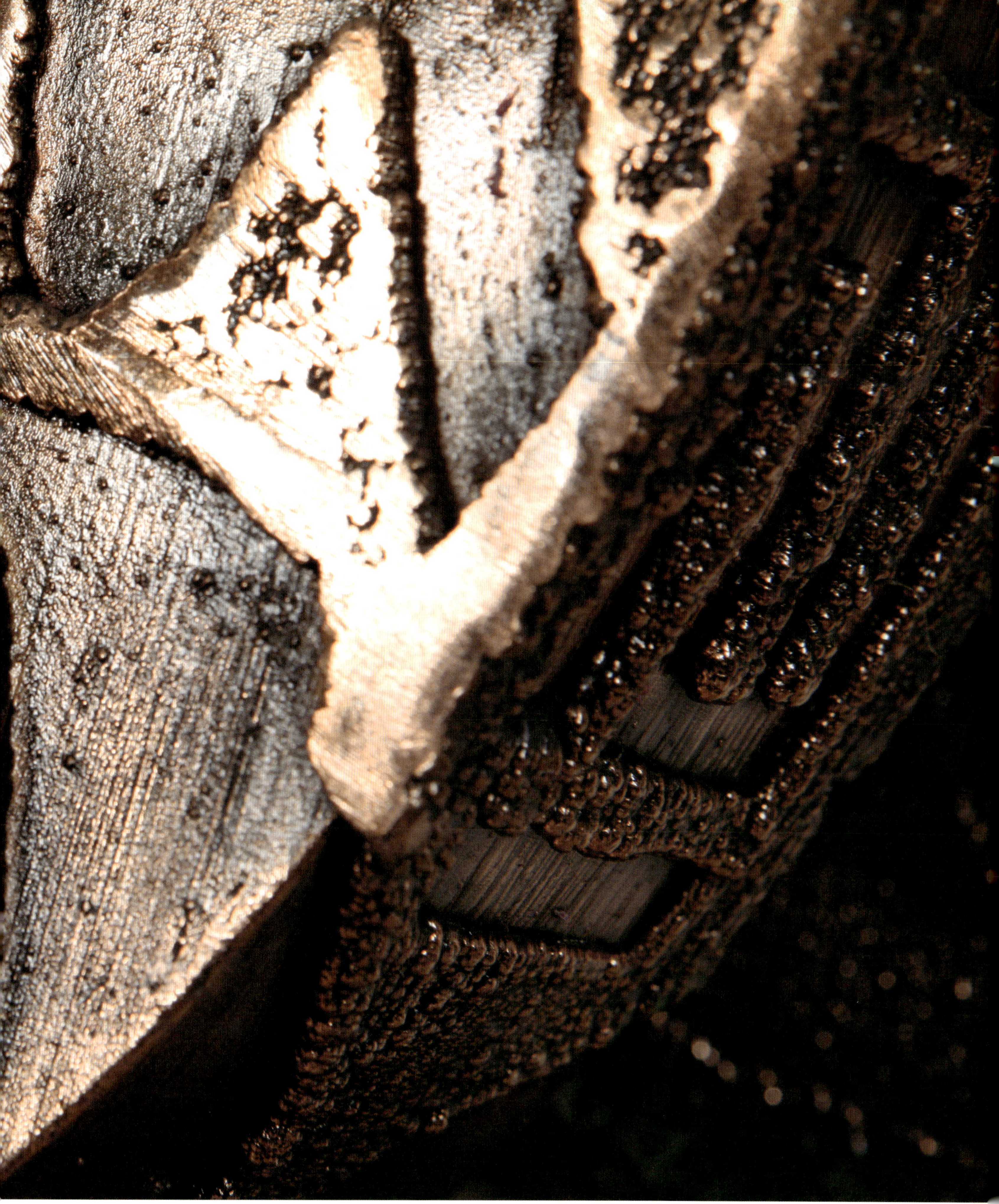

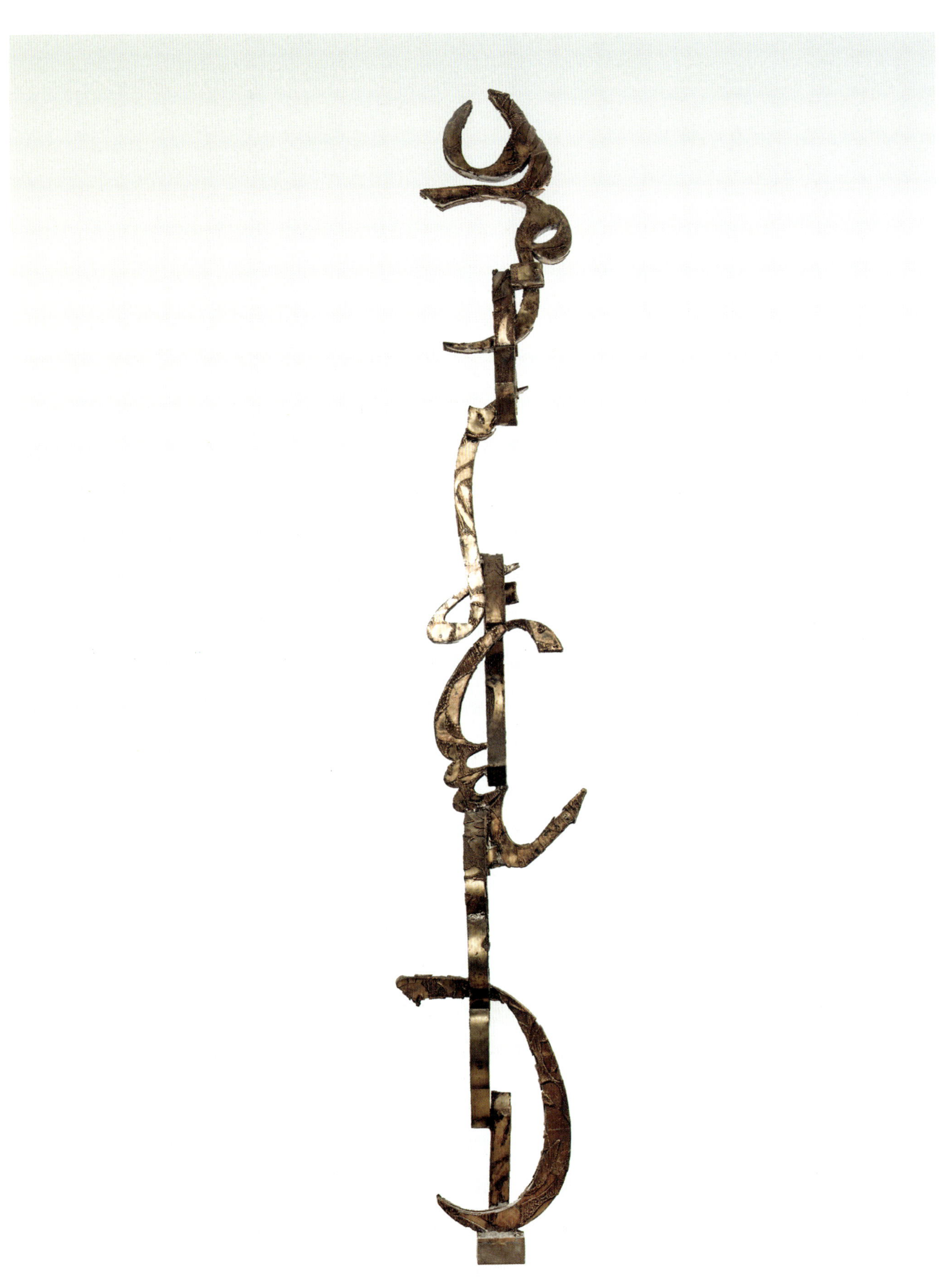

Zero Gravity II, 2016. Copper and steel. 305 × 53 × 51 cm. Photo by Humayun Memon

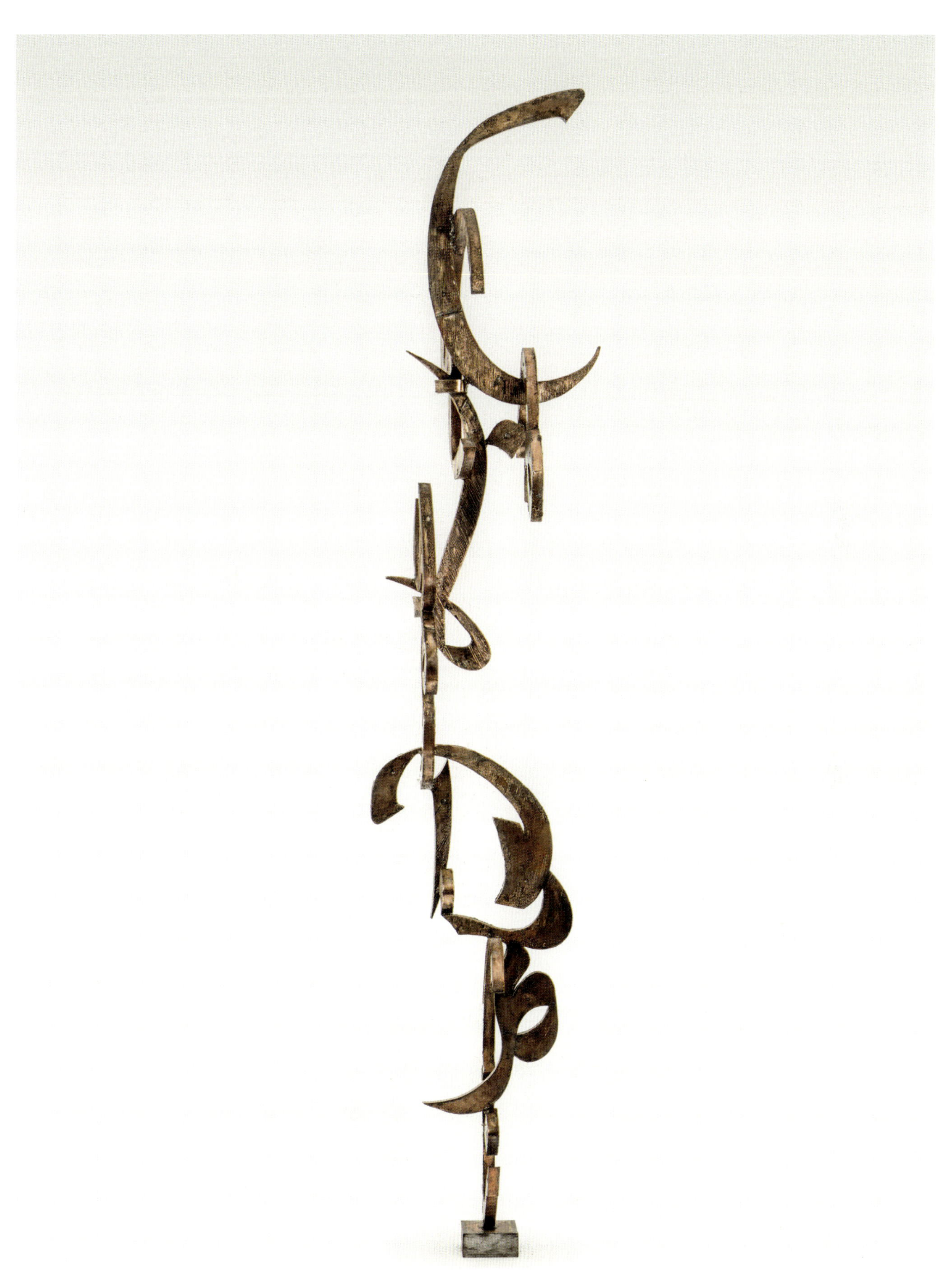

Ascension IV, 2018. Copper and steel. 267 × 71 × 68.5 cm. Photo by Humayun Memon

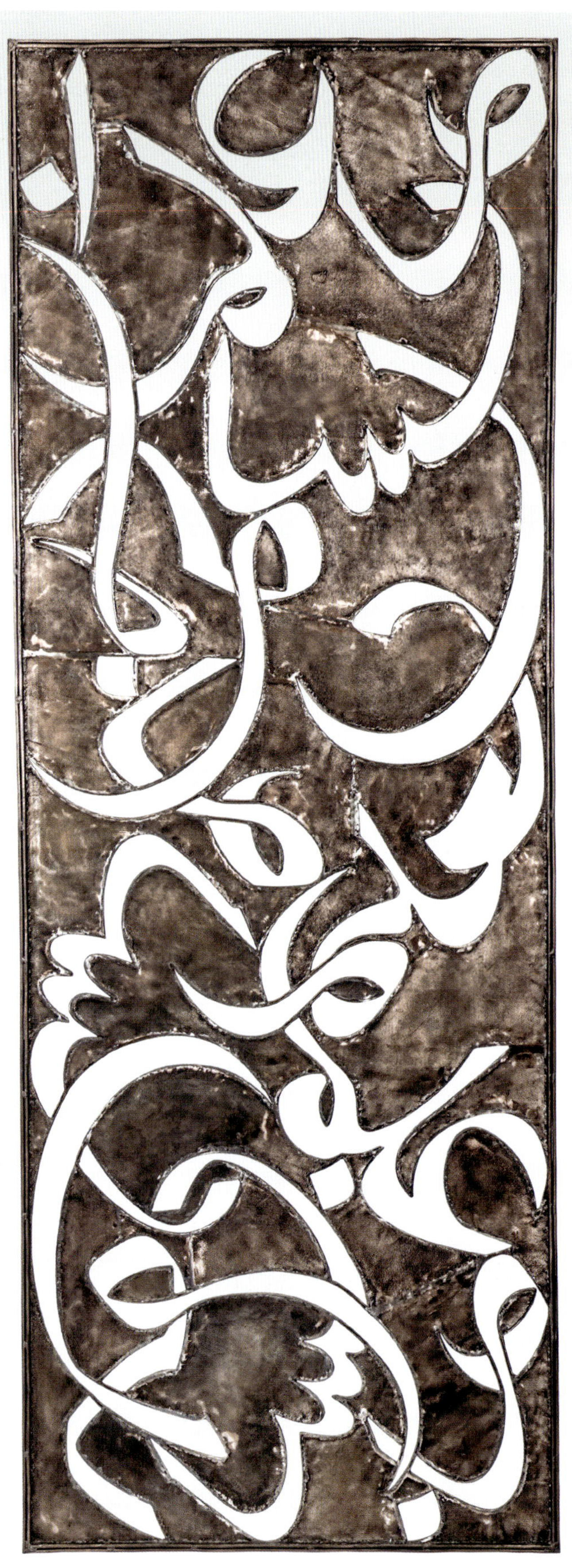

Perforated Scroll I, 2018. Copper and steel. 244 × 89 × 11 cm. Photo by Humayun Memon

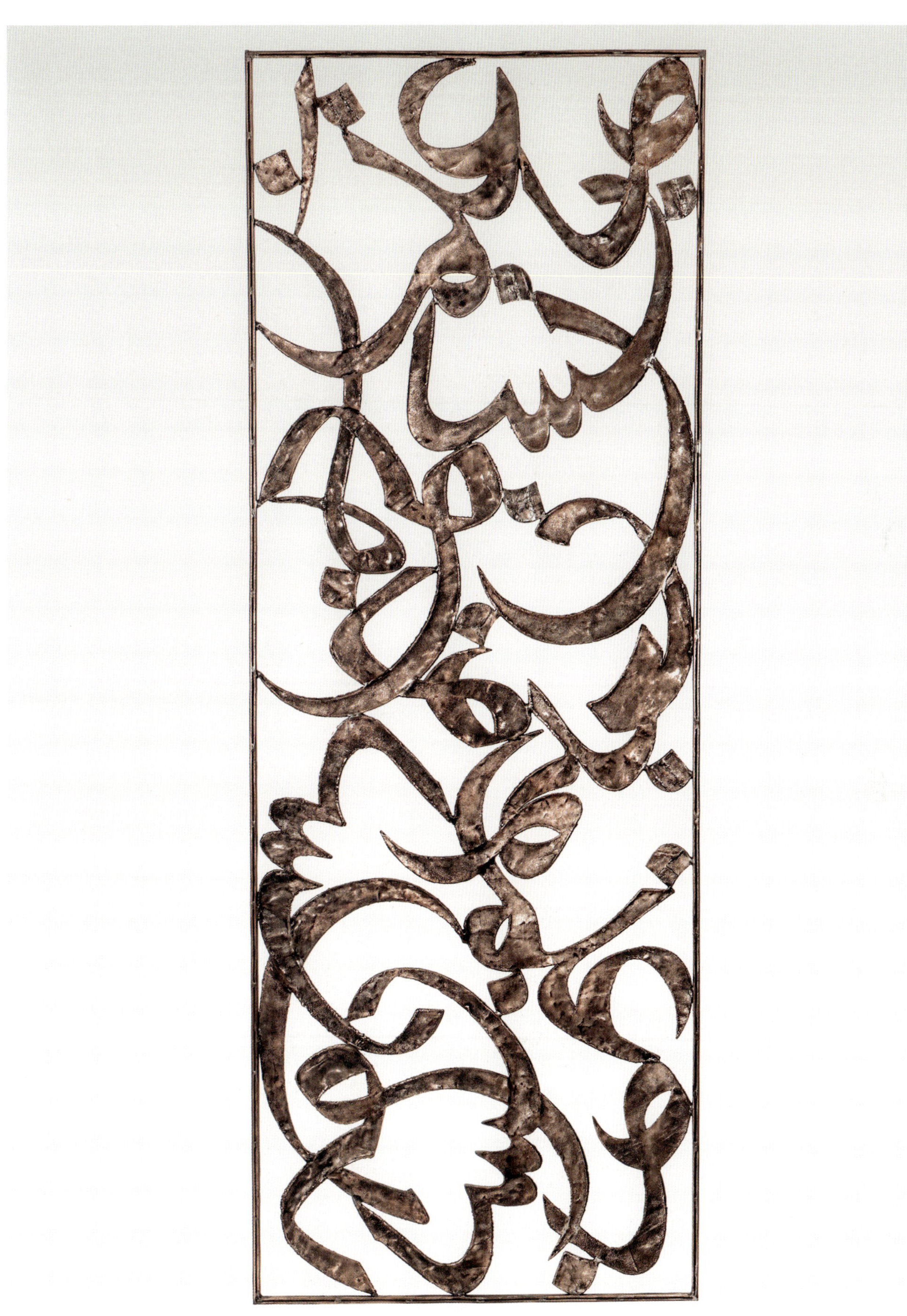

Perforated Scroll II, 2018. Copper and steel. 244 × 89 × 11 cm. Photo by Humayun Memon

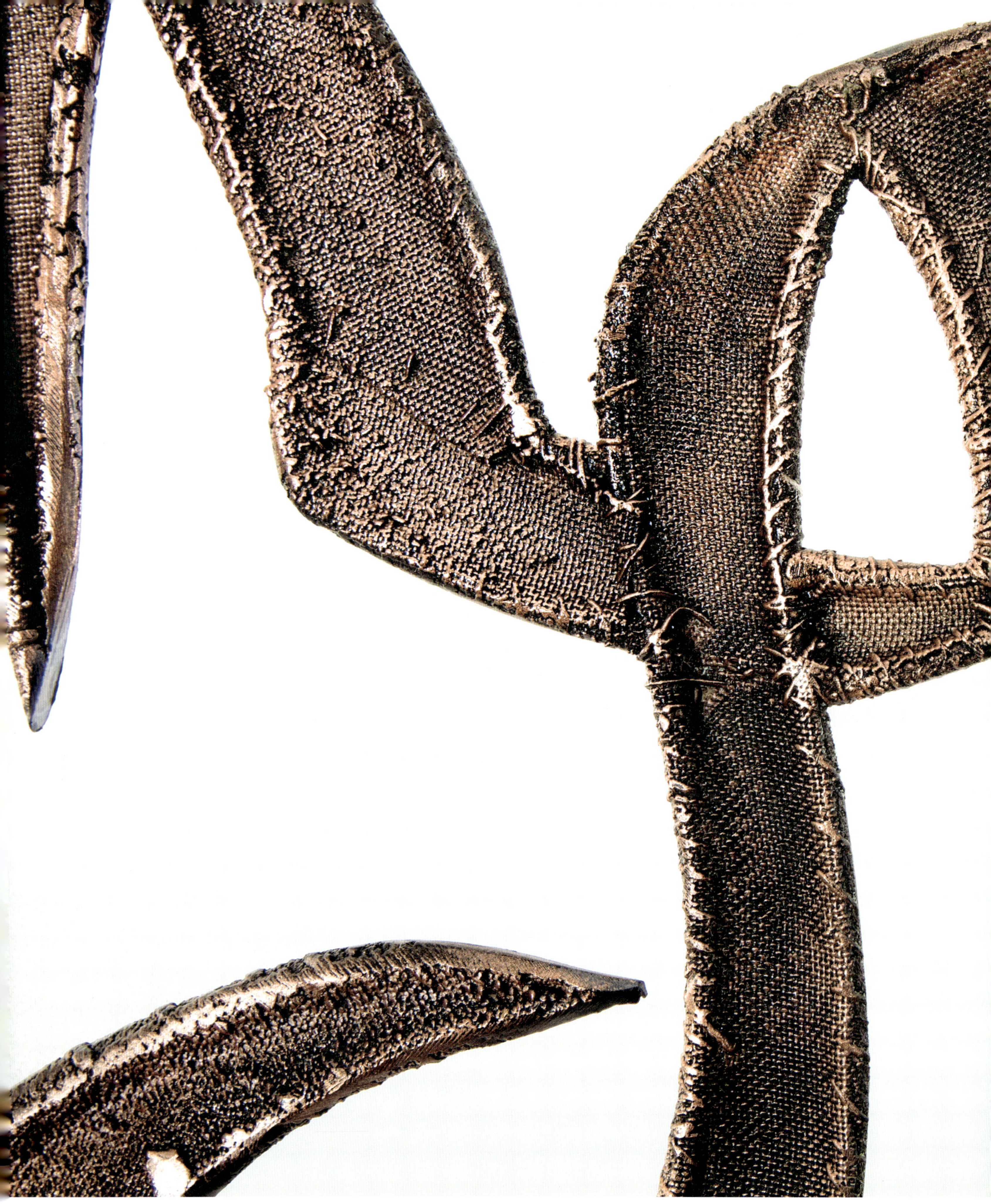

Perforated Scroll II. Detail. Photo by Humayun Memon

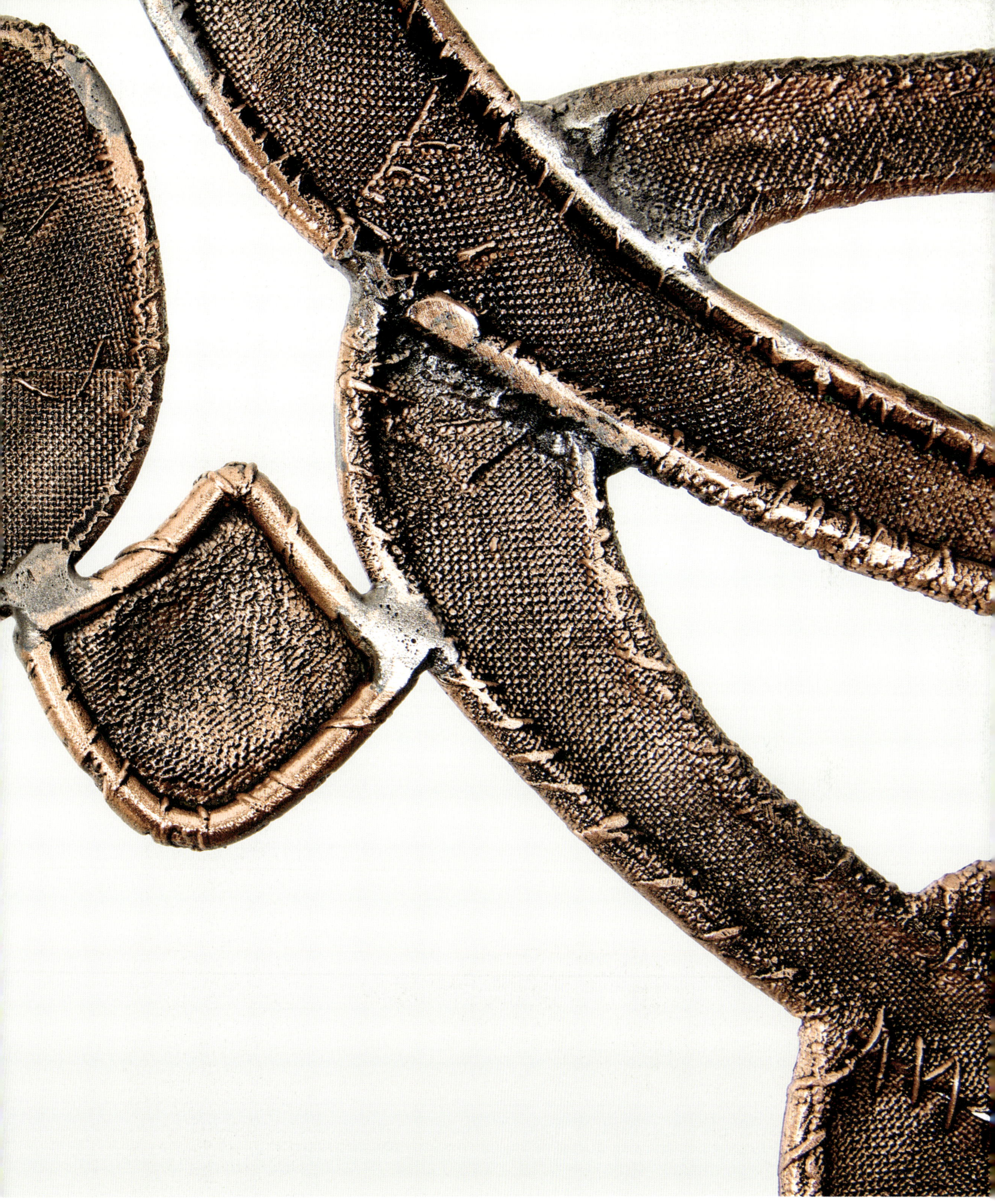

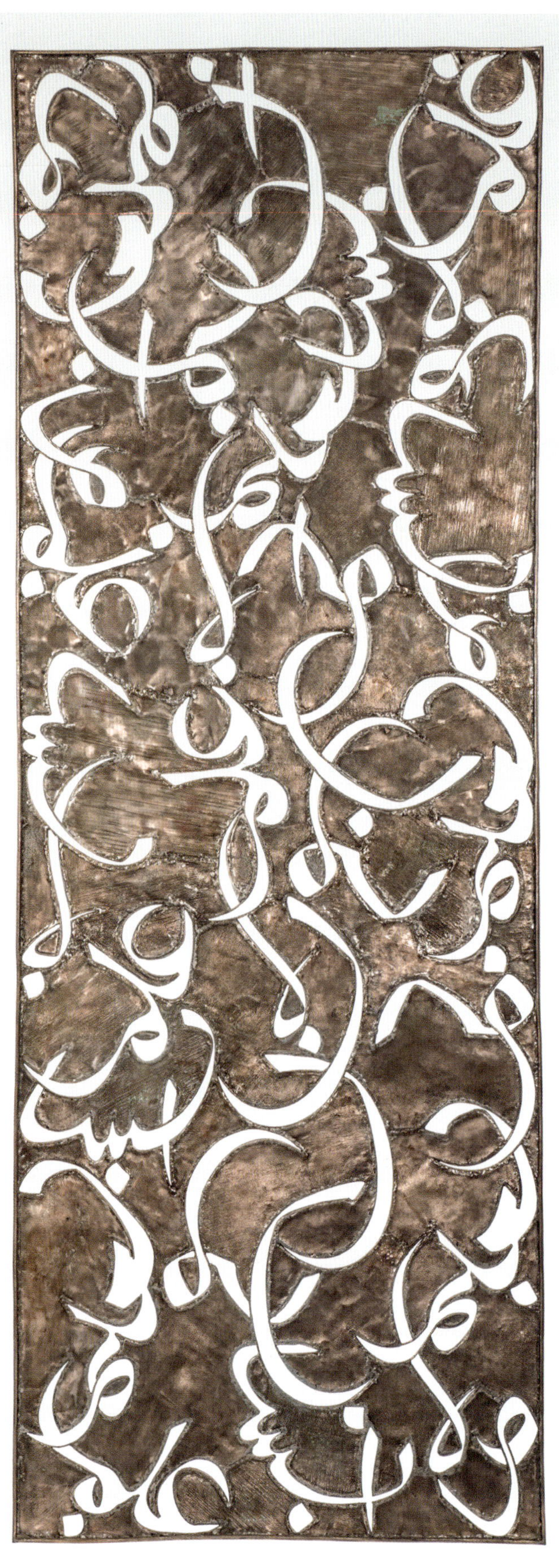

Perforated Scroll III, 2018. Copper and steel. 244 × 89 × 11 cm. Photo by Humayun Memon

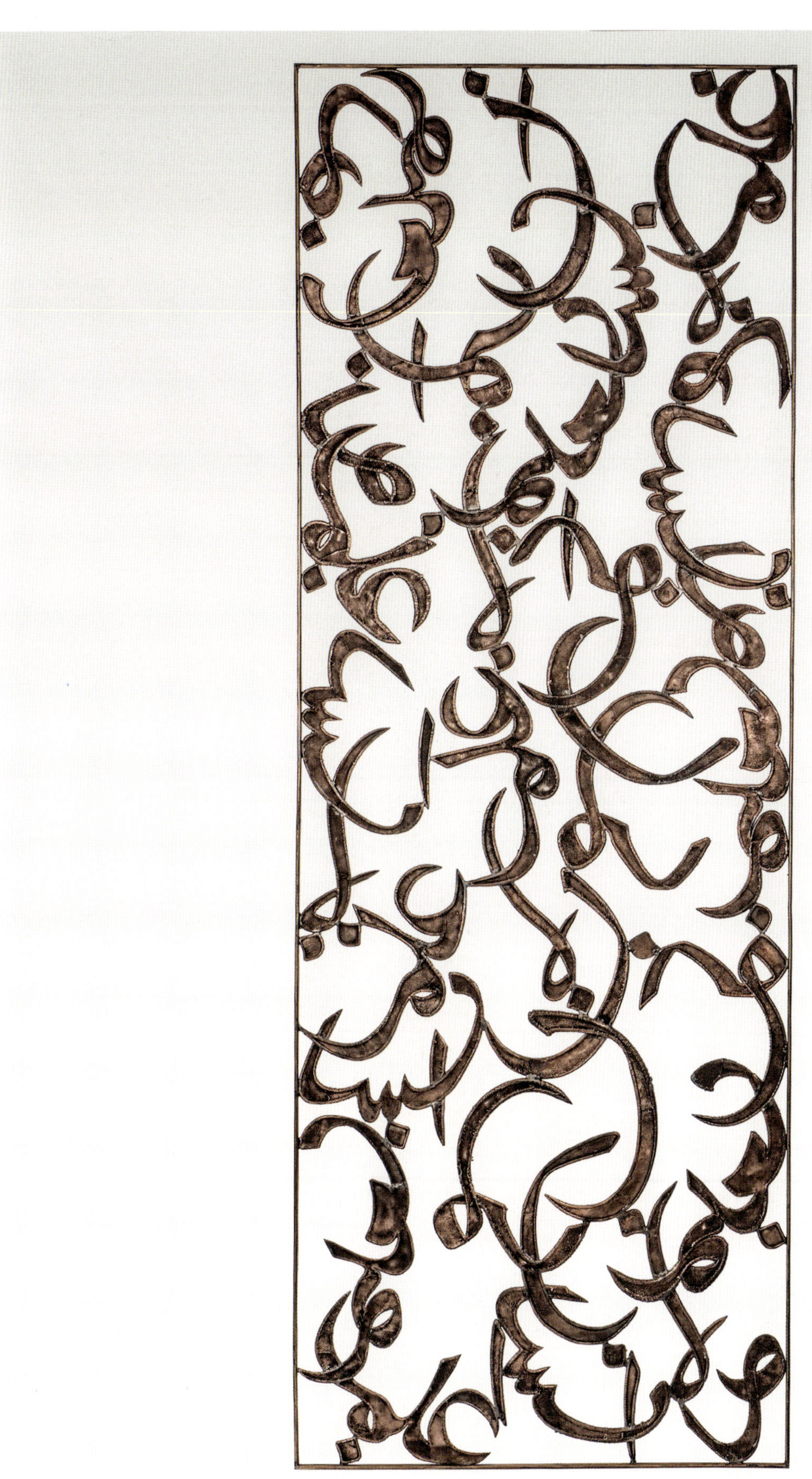

Perforated Scroll IV, 2018. Copper and steel. 244 × 89 × 11 cm. Photo by Humayun Memon

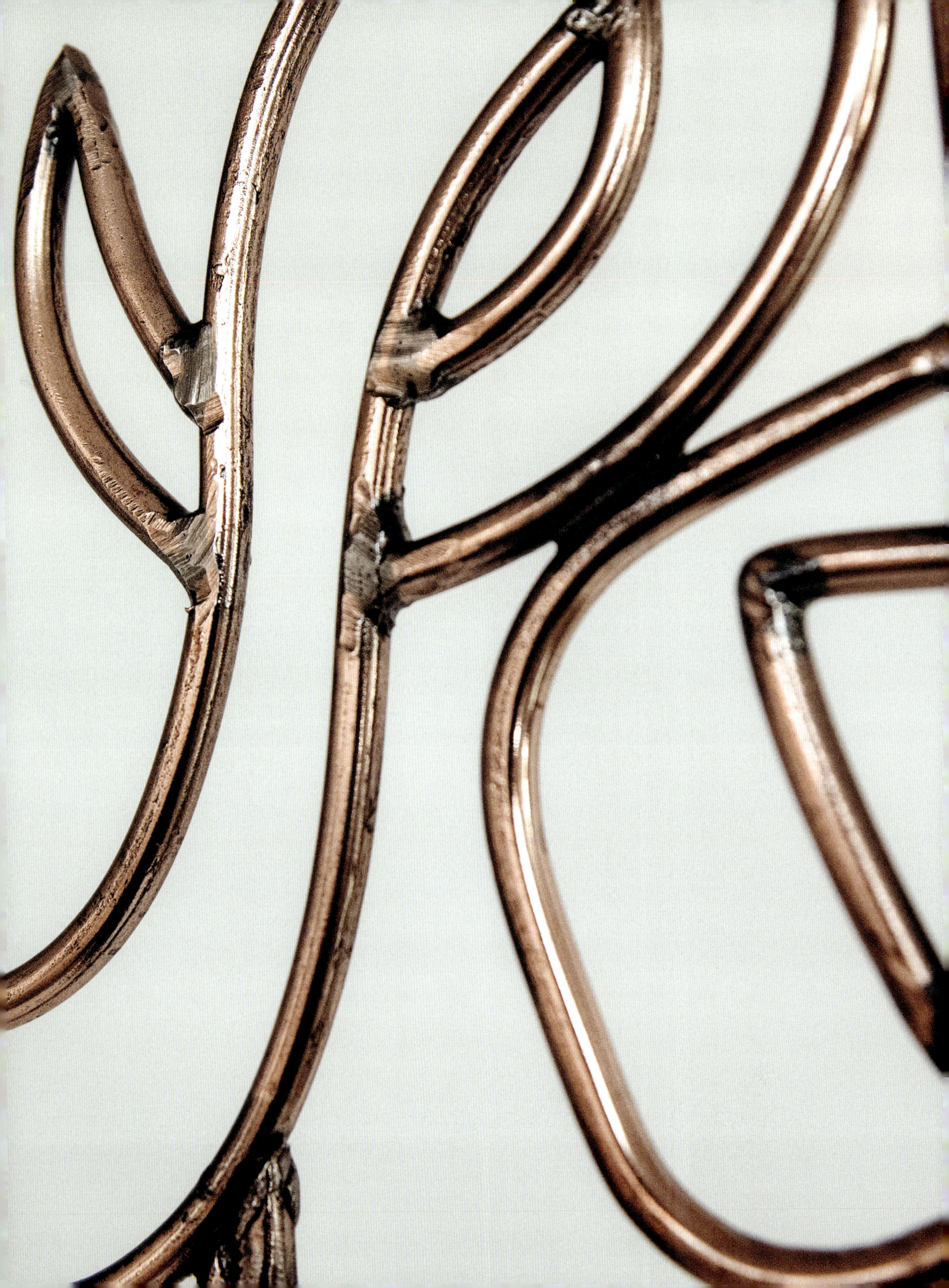

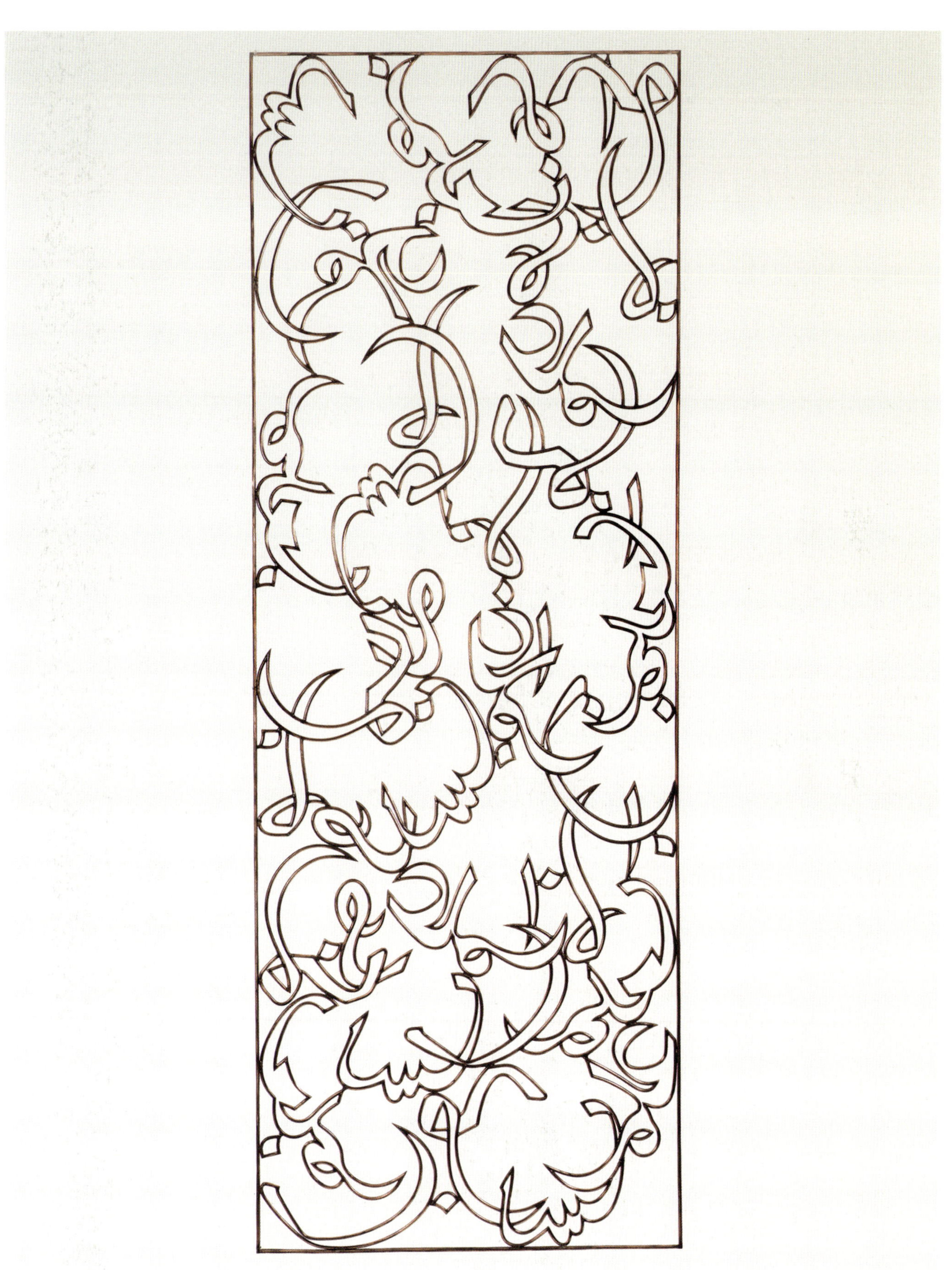

Salt Screen I, 2018. Copper and steel. 244 × 89 × 11 cm. Photo by Humayun Memon

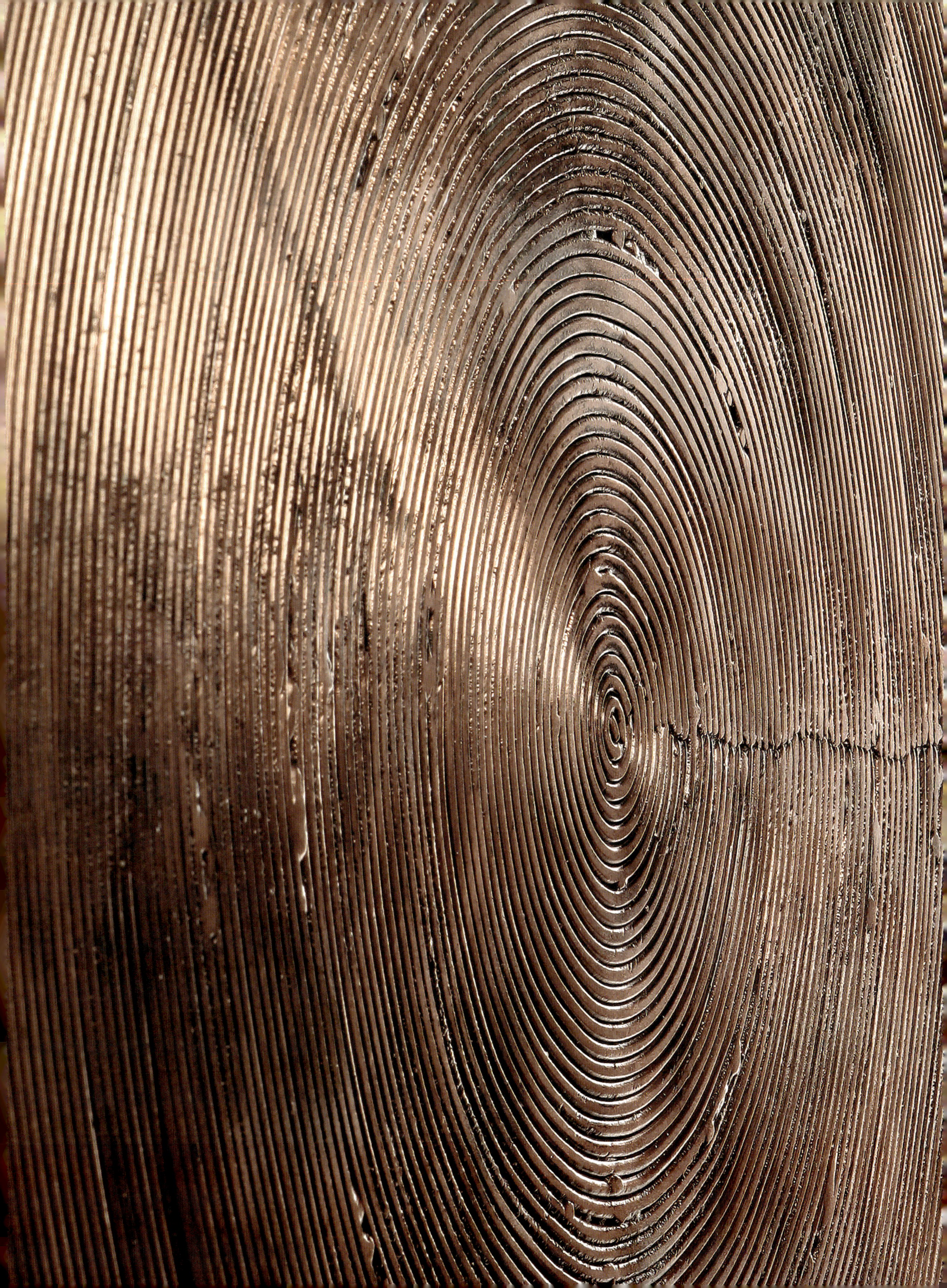

Cosmic Chapati

2011 - 2013

Photo by Shamyl Khuhro

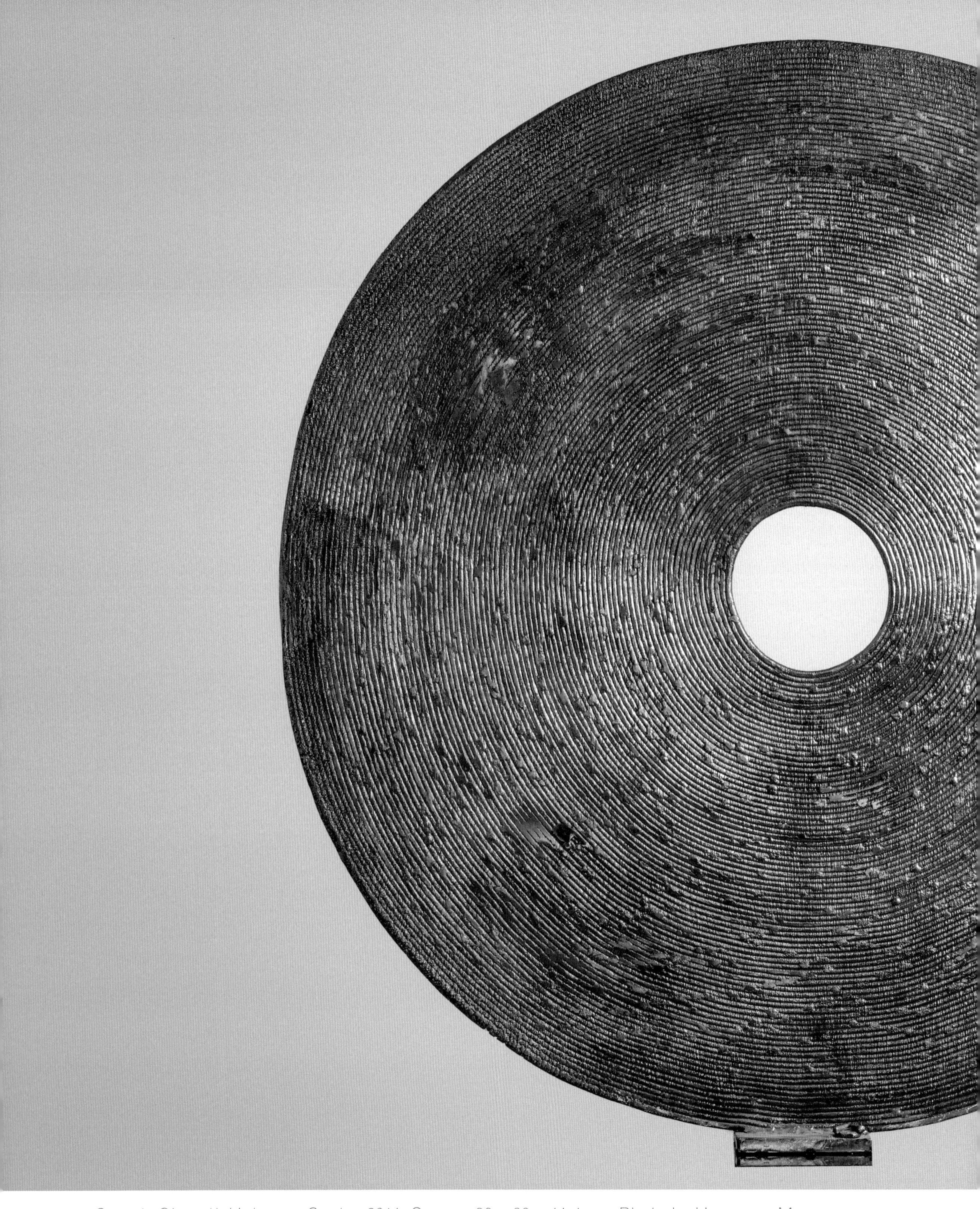

Cosmic Chapati: Unknown Centre, 2011. Copper. 90 × 90 × 11.4 cm. Photo by Humayun Memon

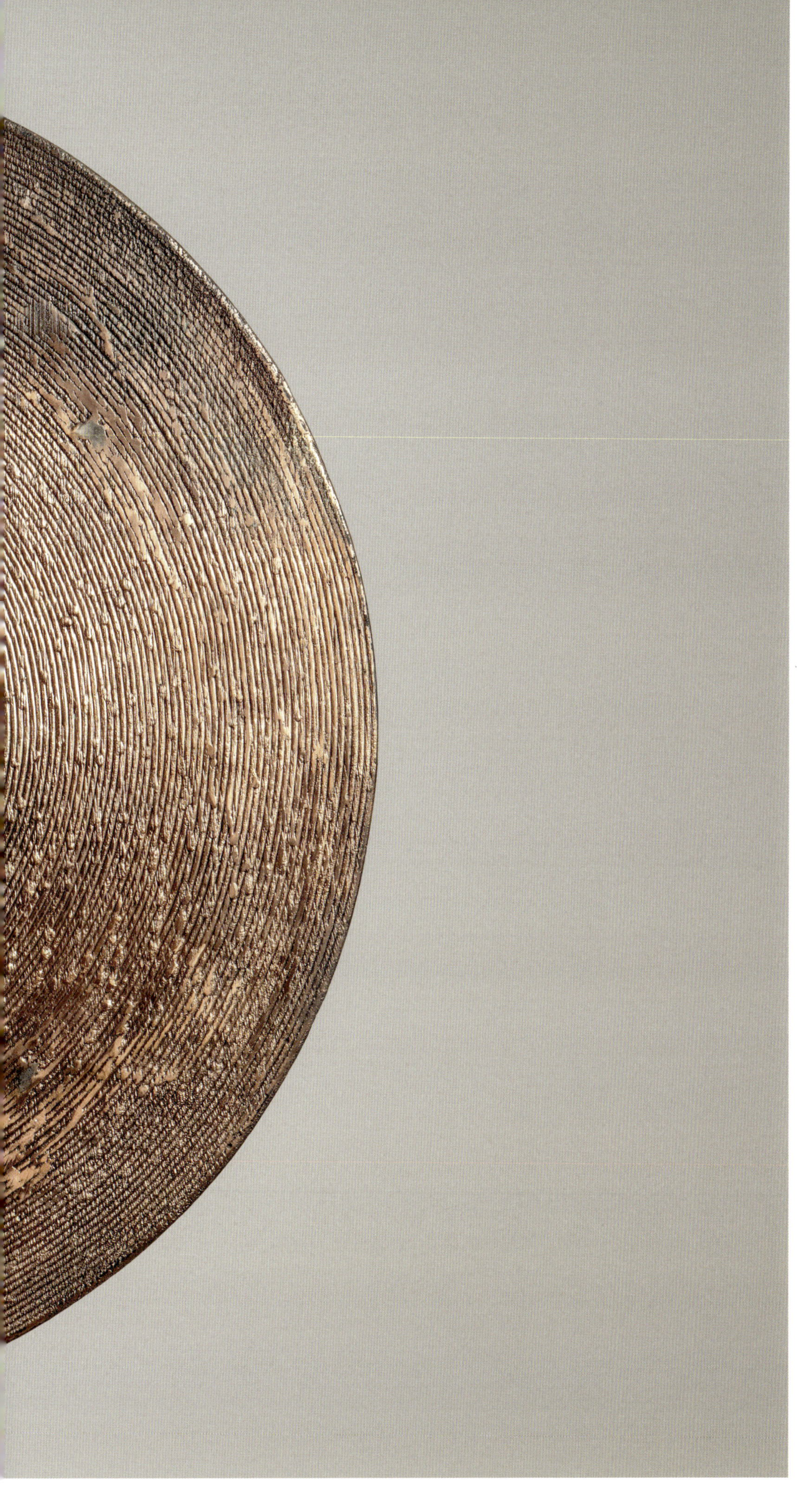

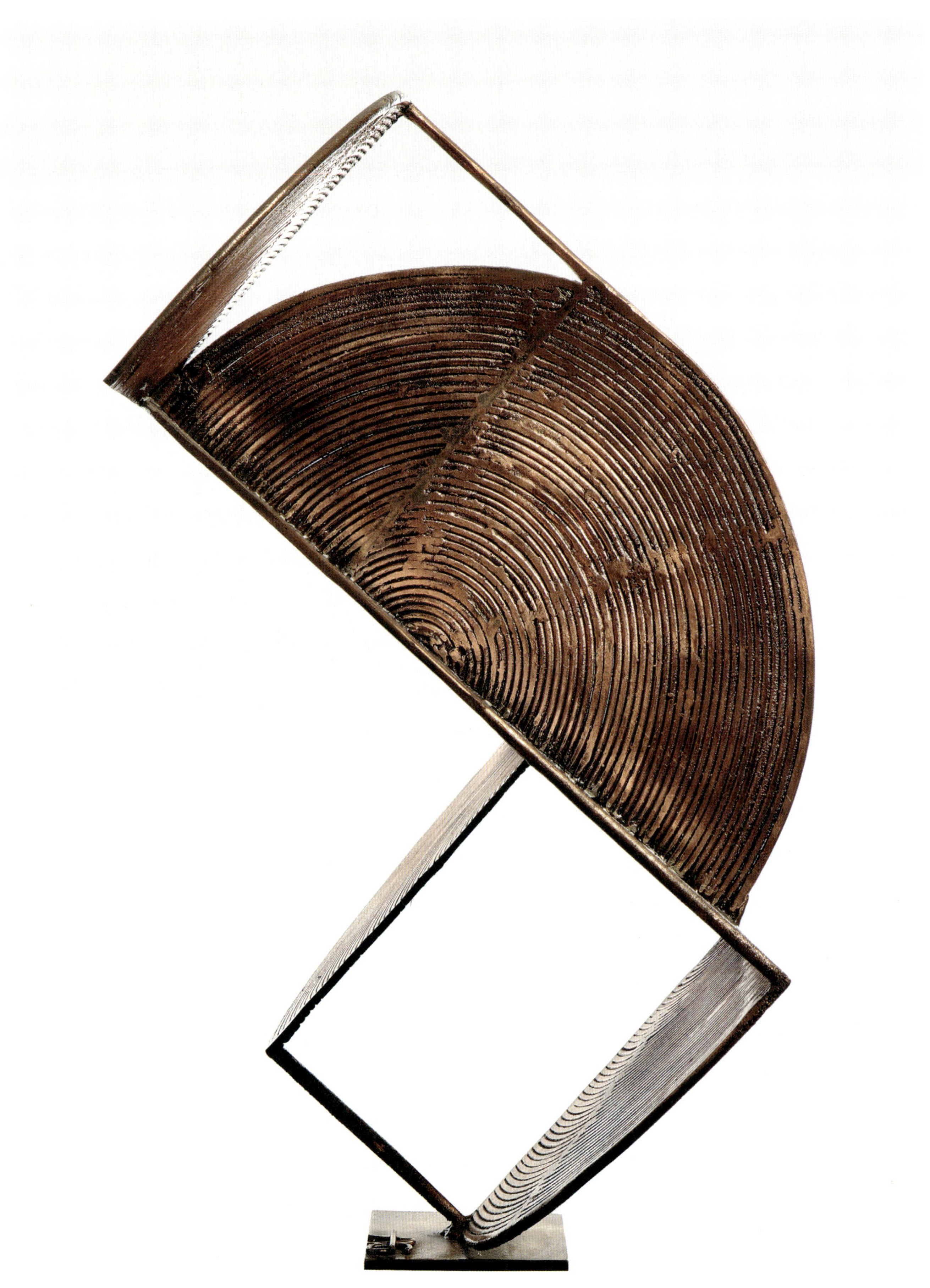

Four Quarter and Two Half Chapatis, 2011. Copper. 61 × 41 × 41 cm. Photo by Shamyl Khuhro

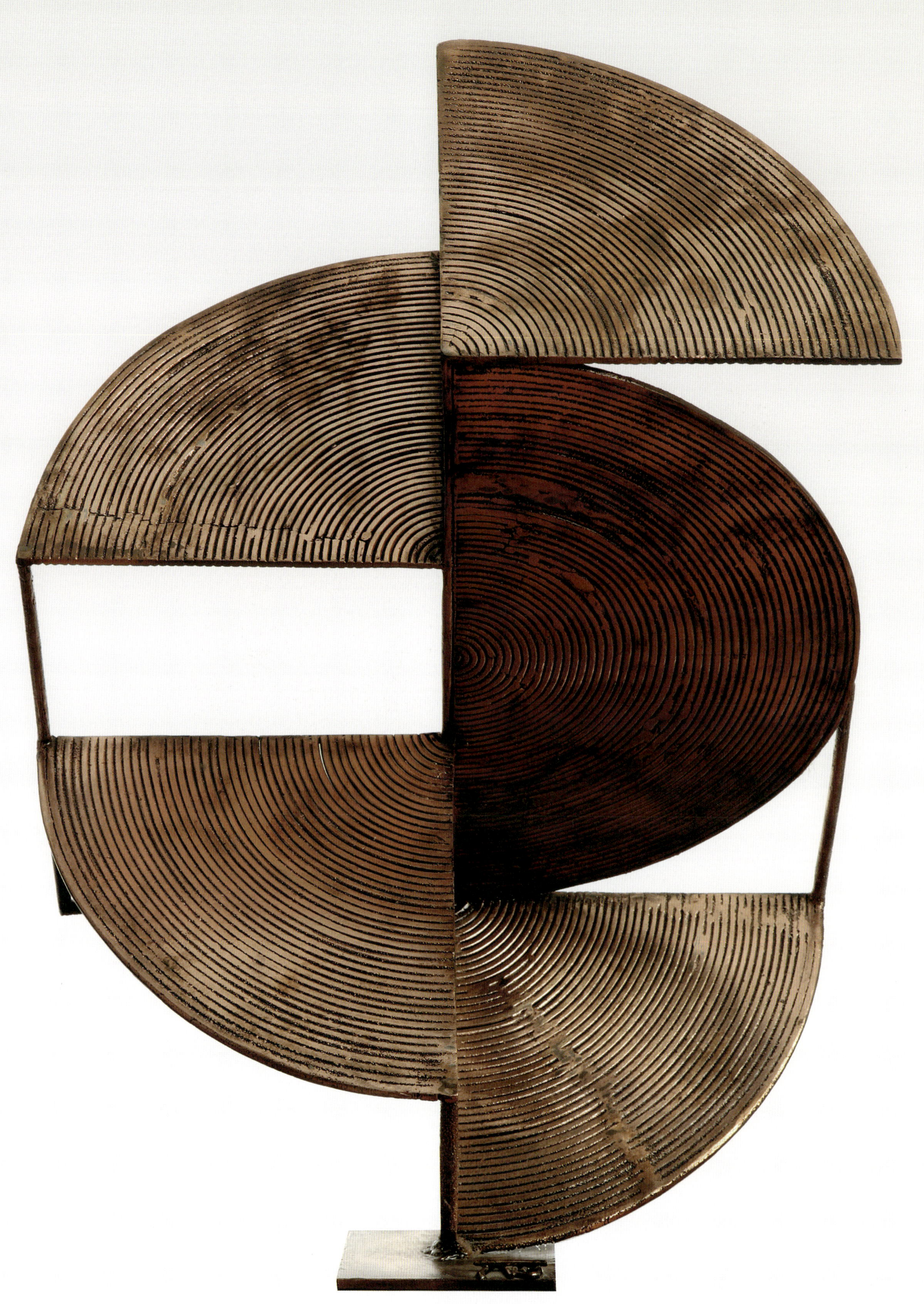

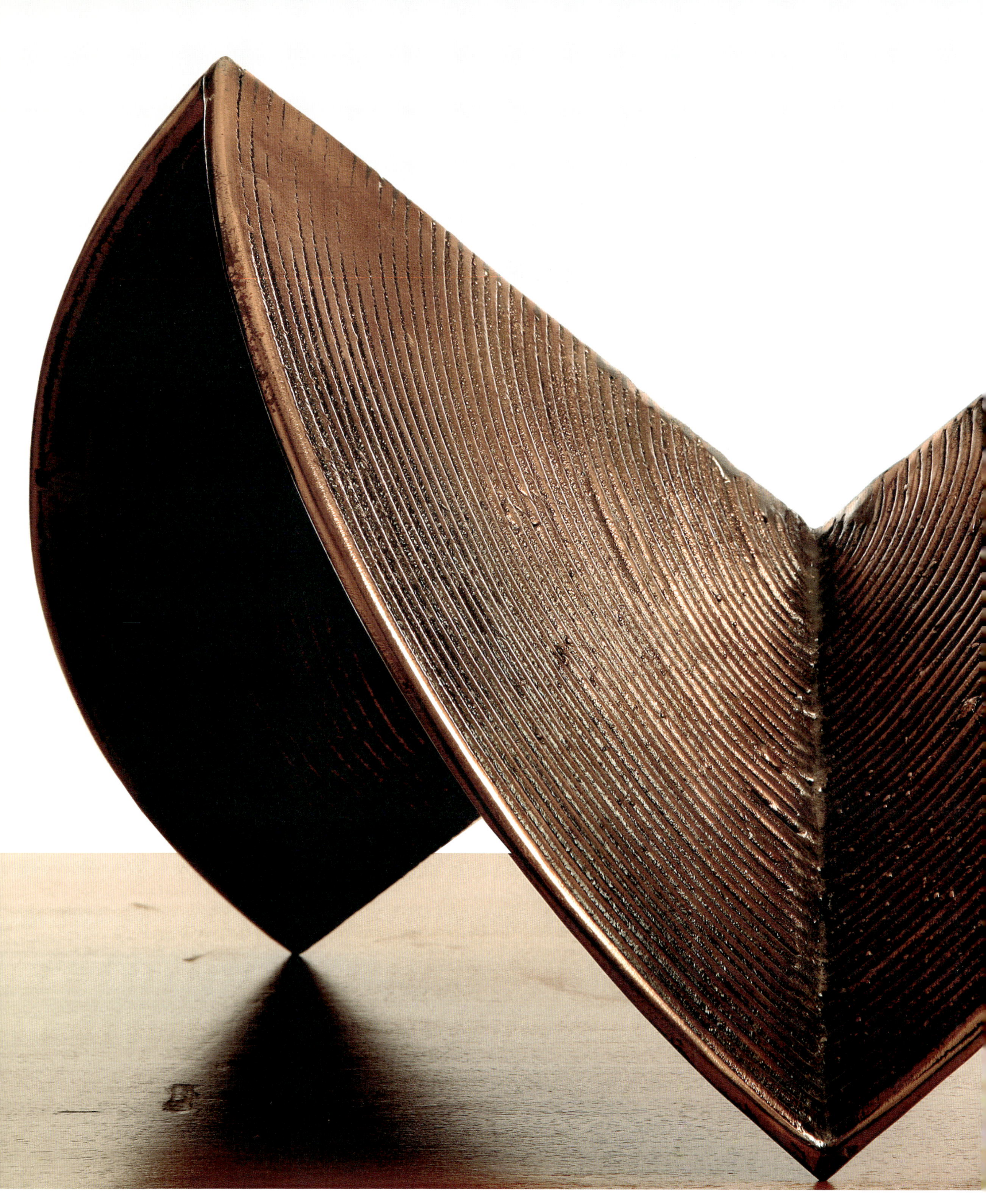

Folded Chapati II, 2011. Copper. 43 × 41 × 91 cm. Photo by Shamyl Khuhro

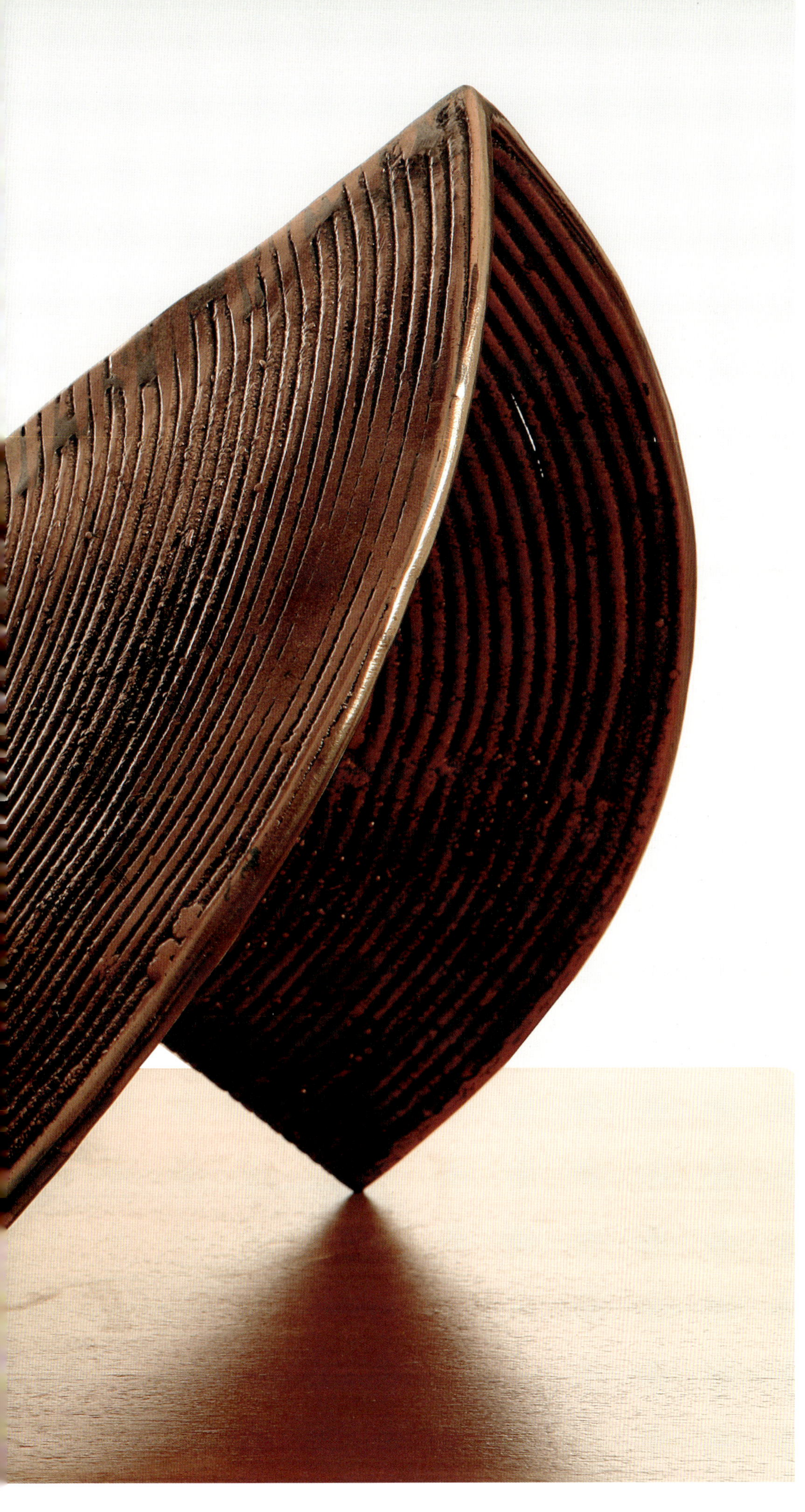

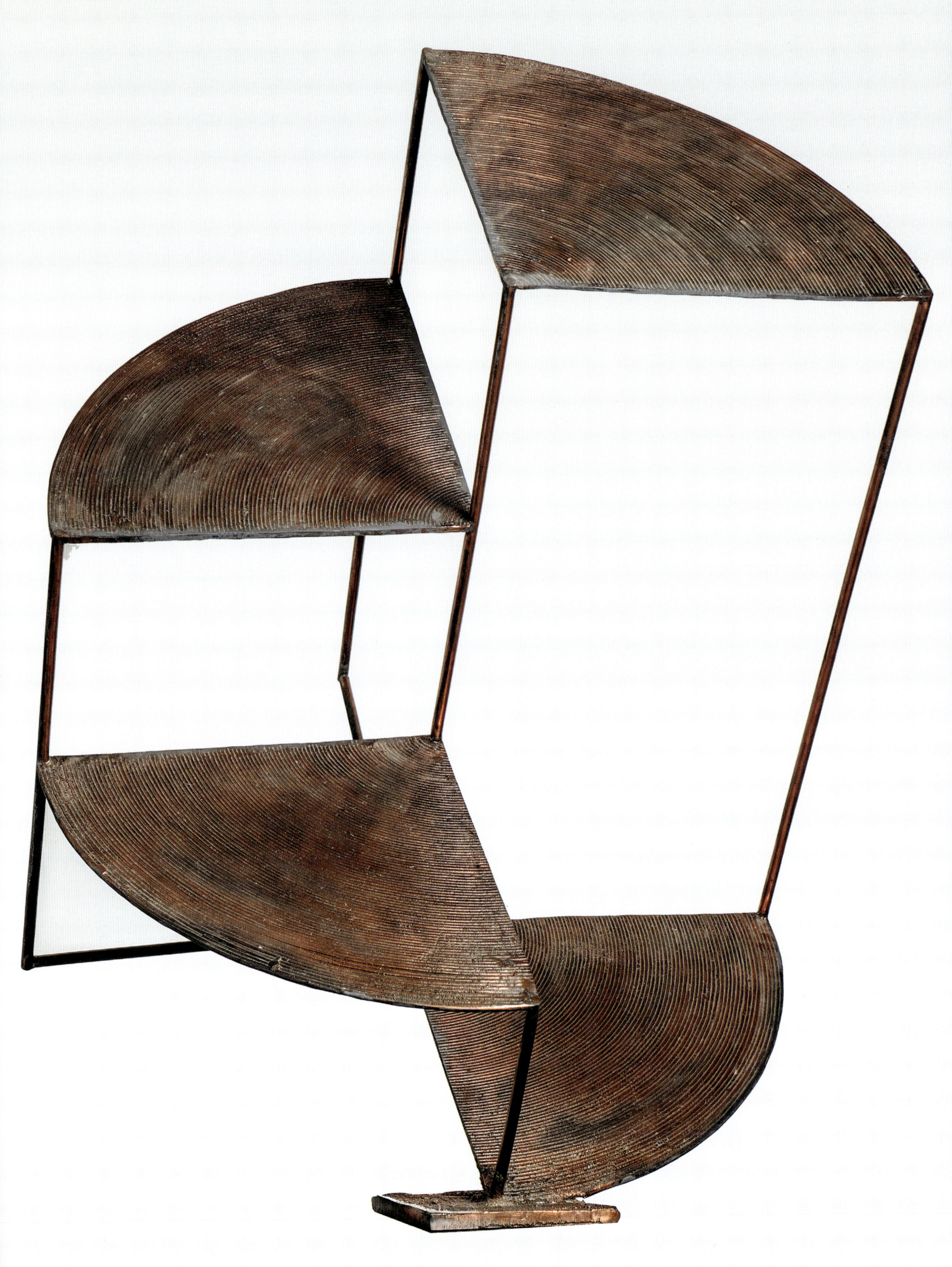

Four Quarter Chapatis II, 2012. Copper. 121.9 × 93.9 × 88.9 cm. Photo by Humayun Memon

Three Folded and Two Half Chapatis, 2013. Copper. 112 × 94 × 67 cm. Photo by Humayun Memon

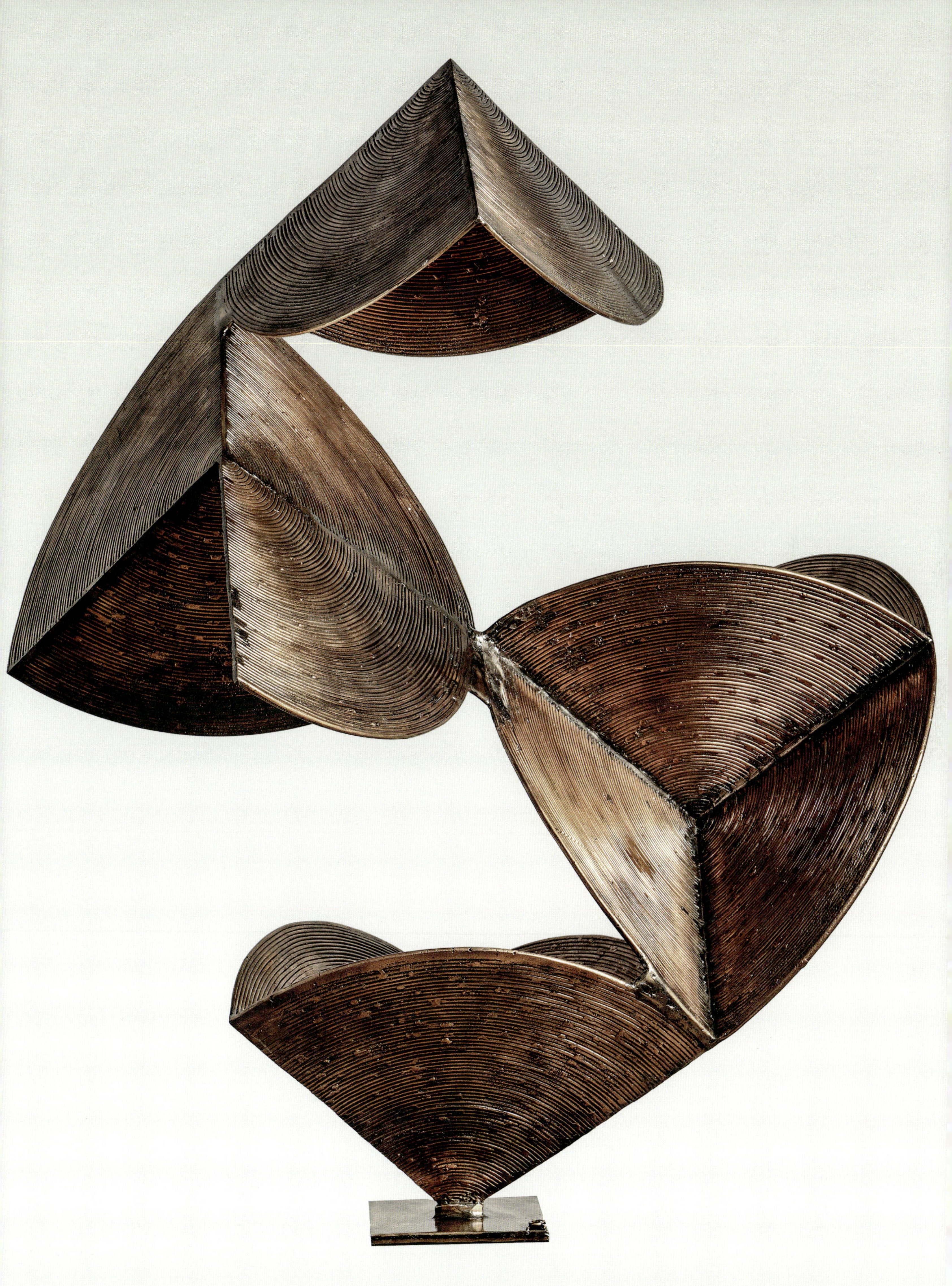

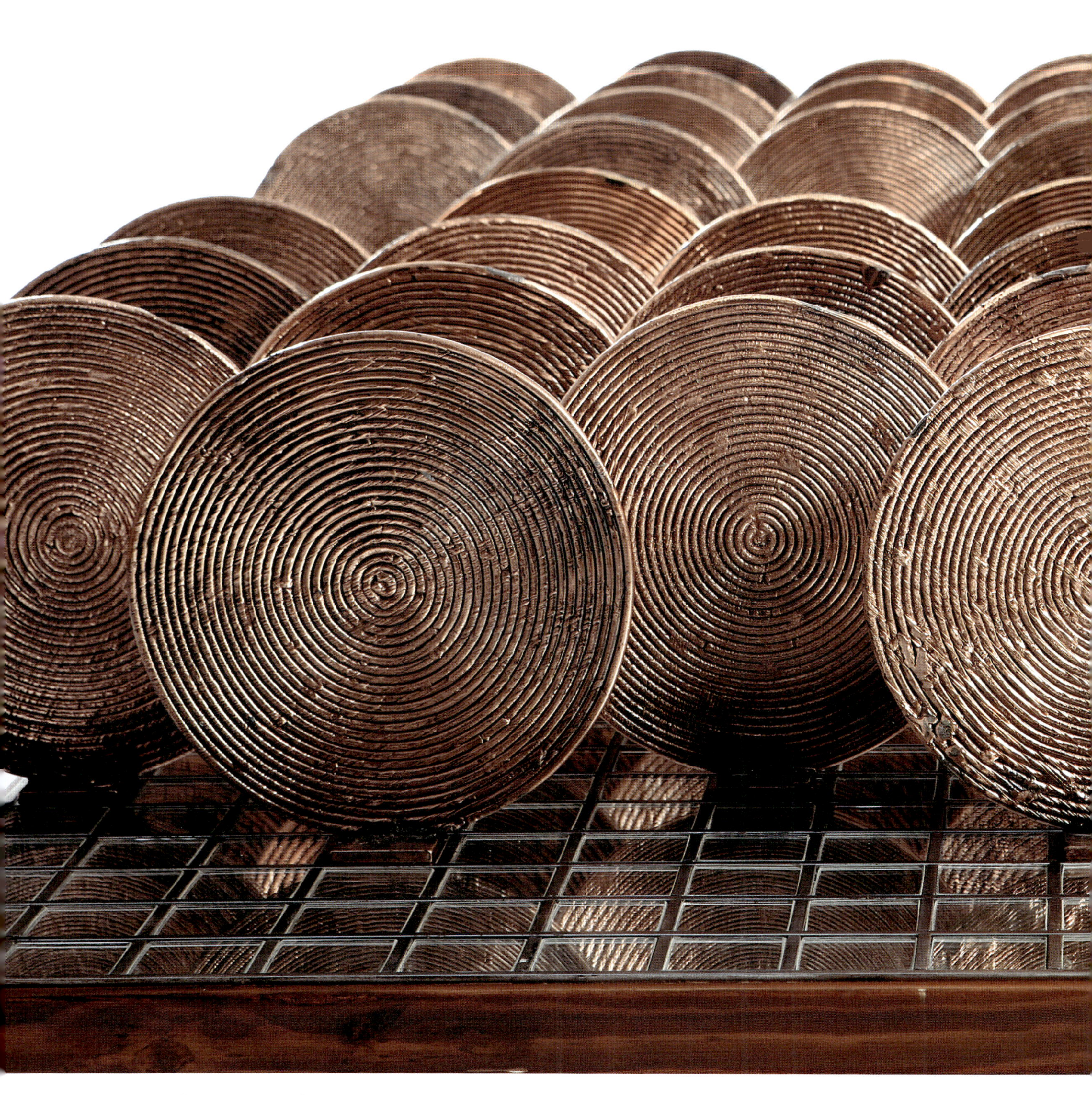

Hunger Games, 2013. Copper, steel, mirror and wood. 30.48 × 213.36 × 109.22 cm. Photo by Shamyl Khuhro

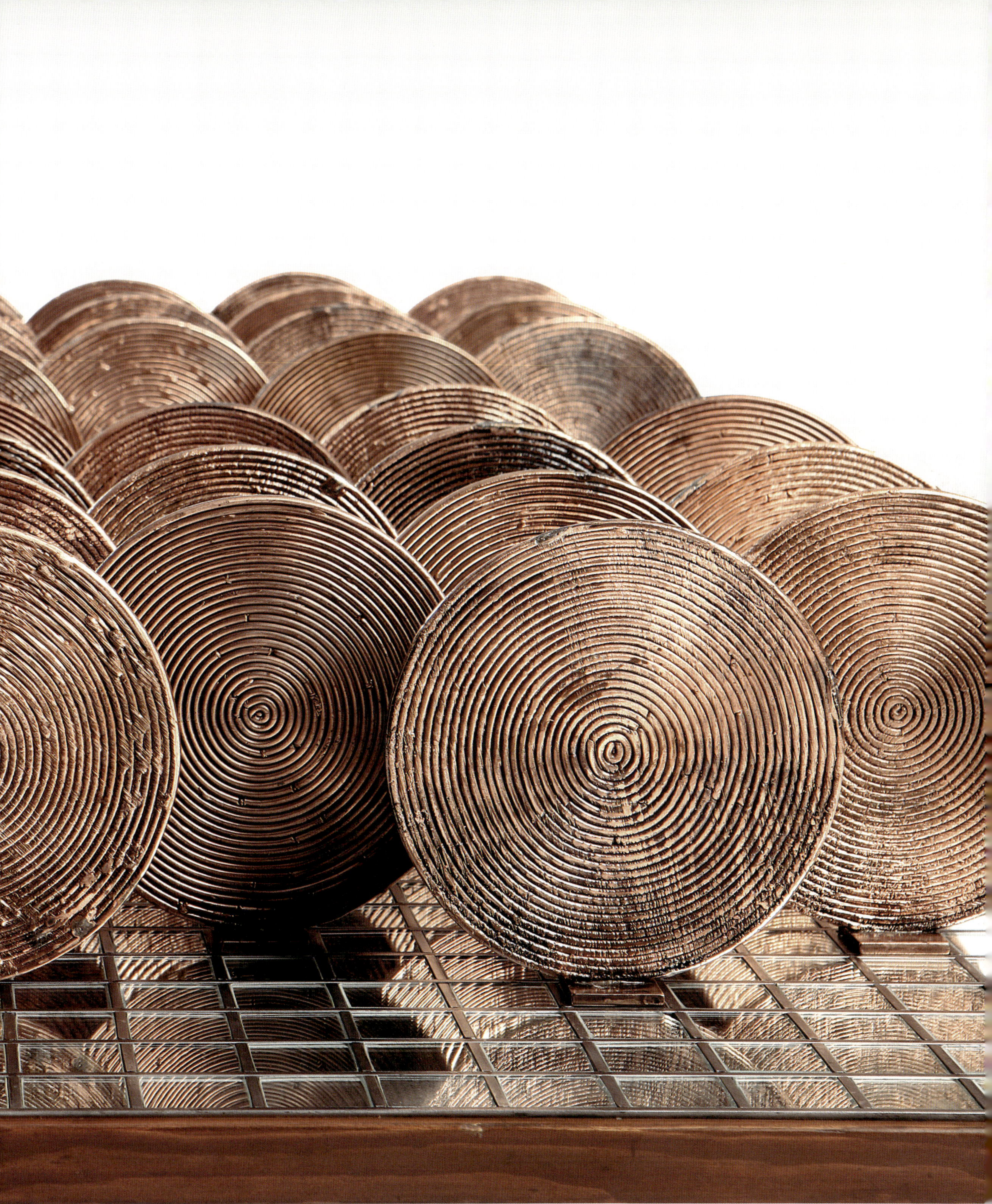

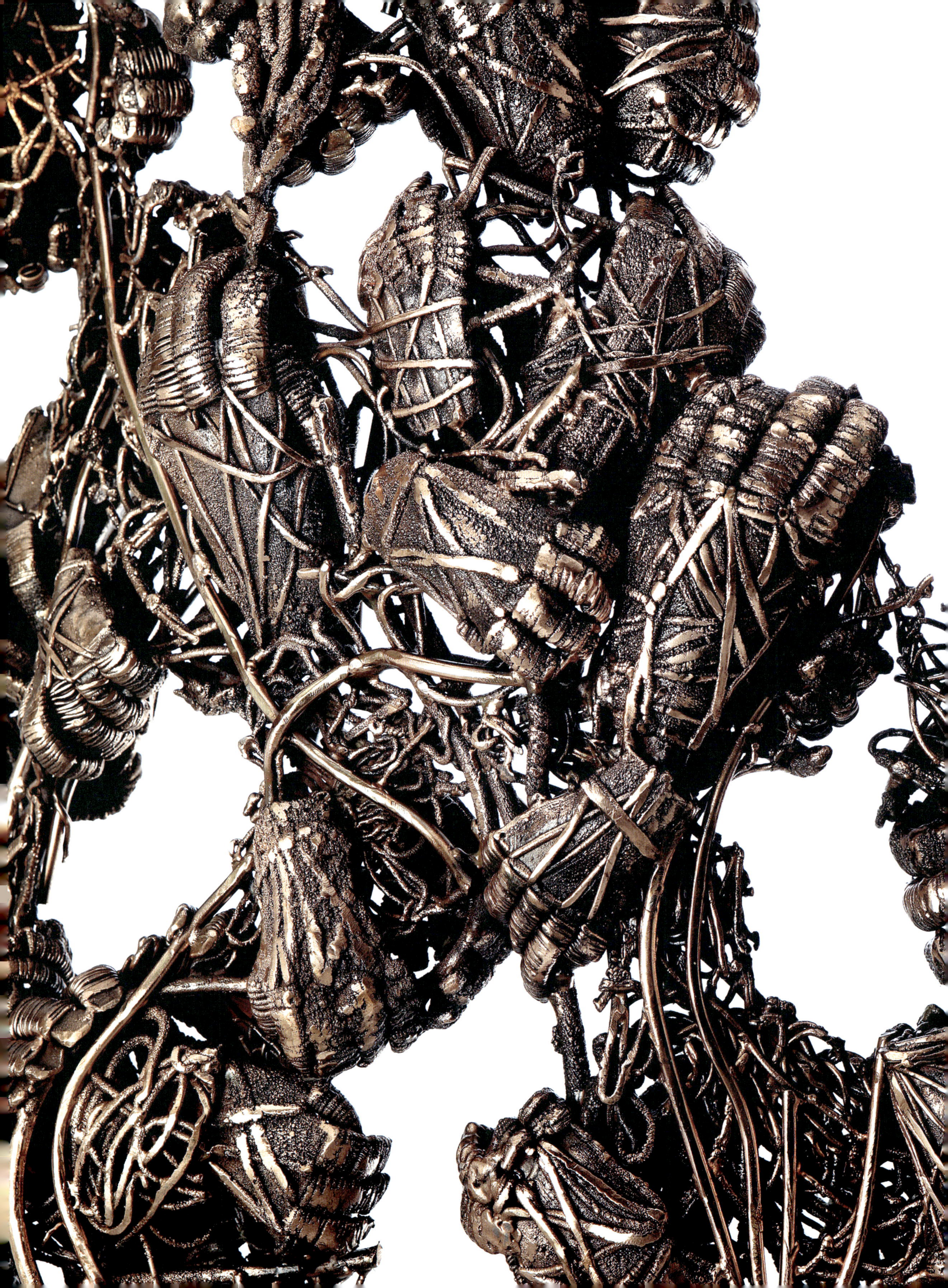

Hands

1993 - 2018

Photo by Shamyl Khuhro

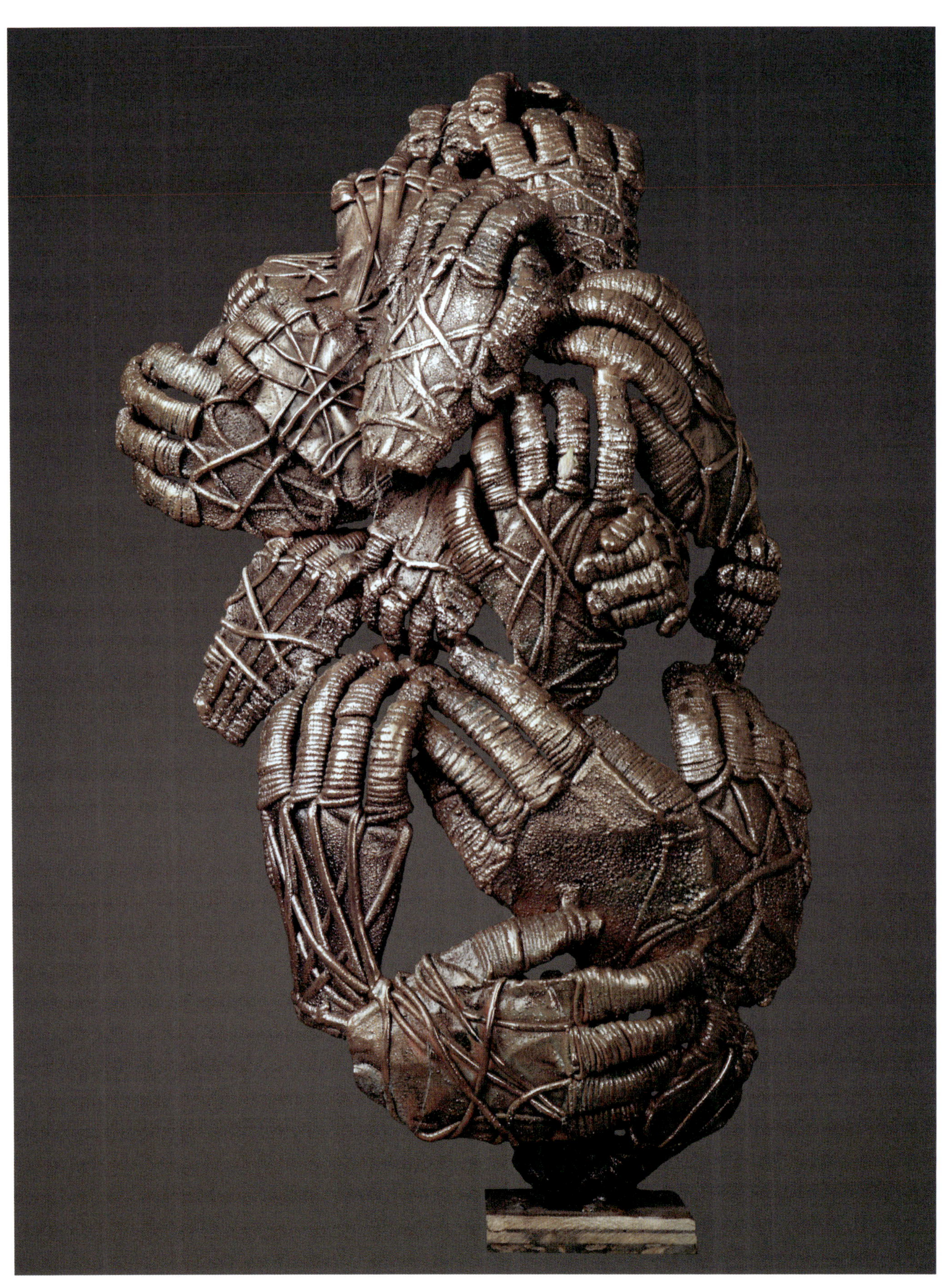

Touching Myself, 2007. Copper. 45.72 × 40.64 × 40.64 cm. Photo by Tapu Javeri

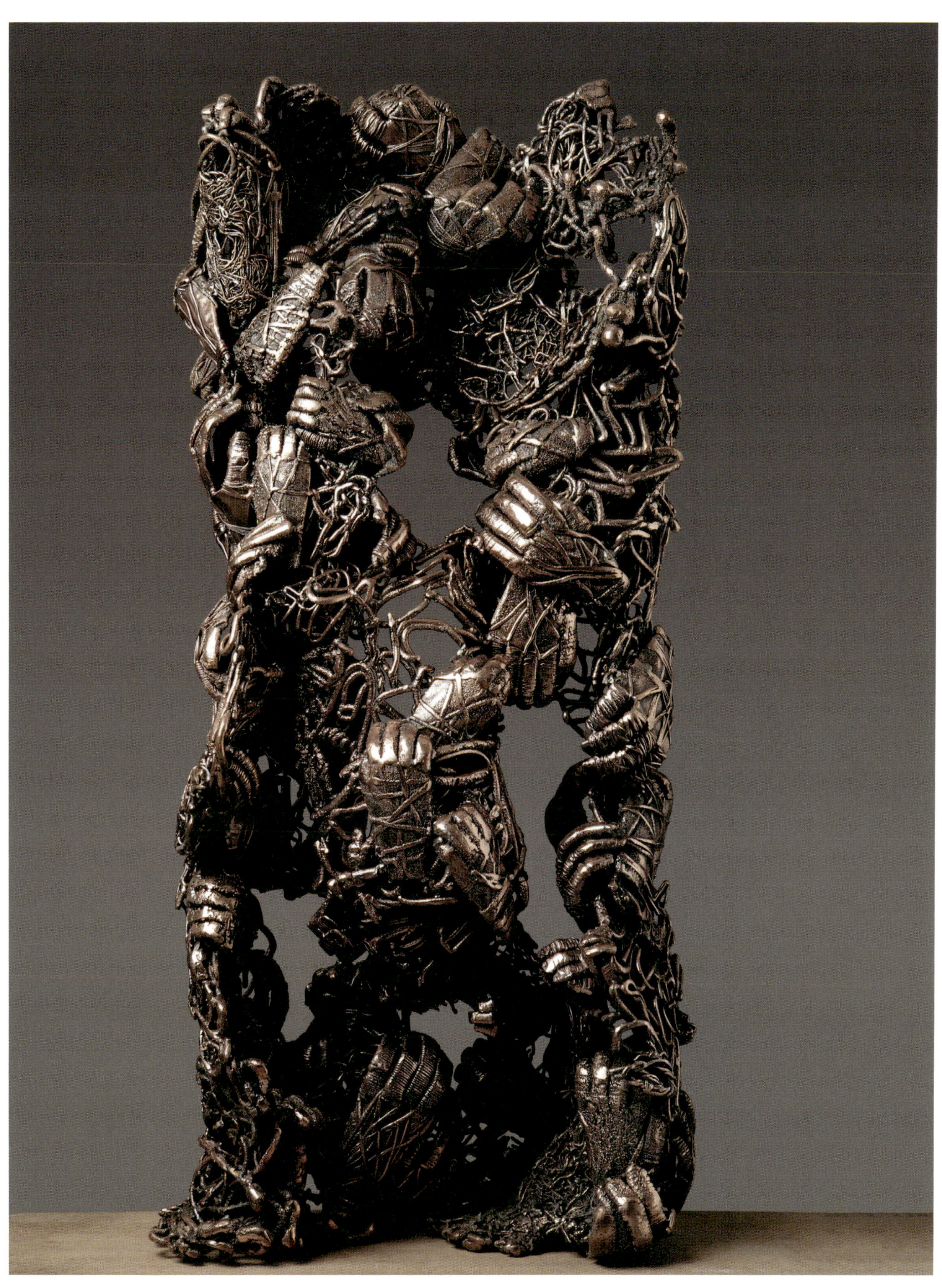

Ripping the Bird's Nest III, 2008. Copper and bronze. 116.84 × 53.34 × 33.02 cm. Photo by Tapu Javeri

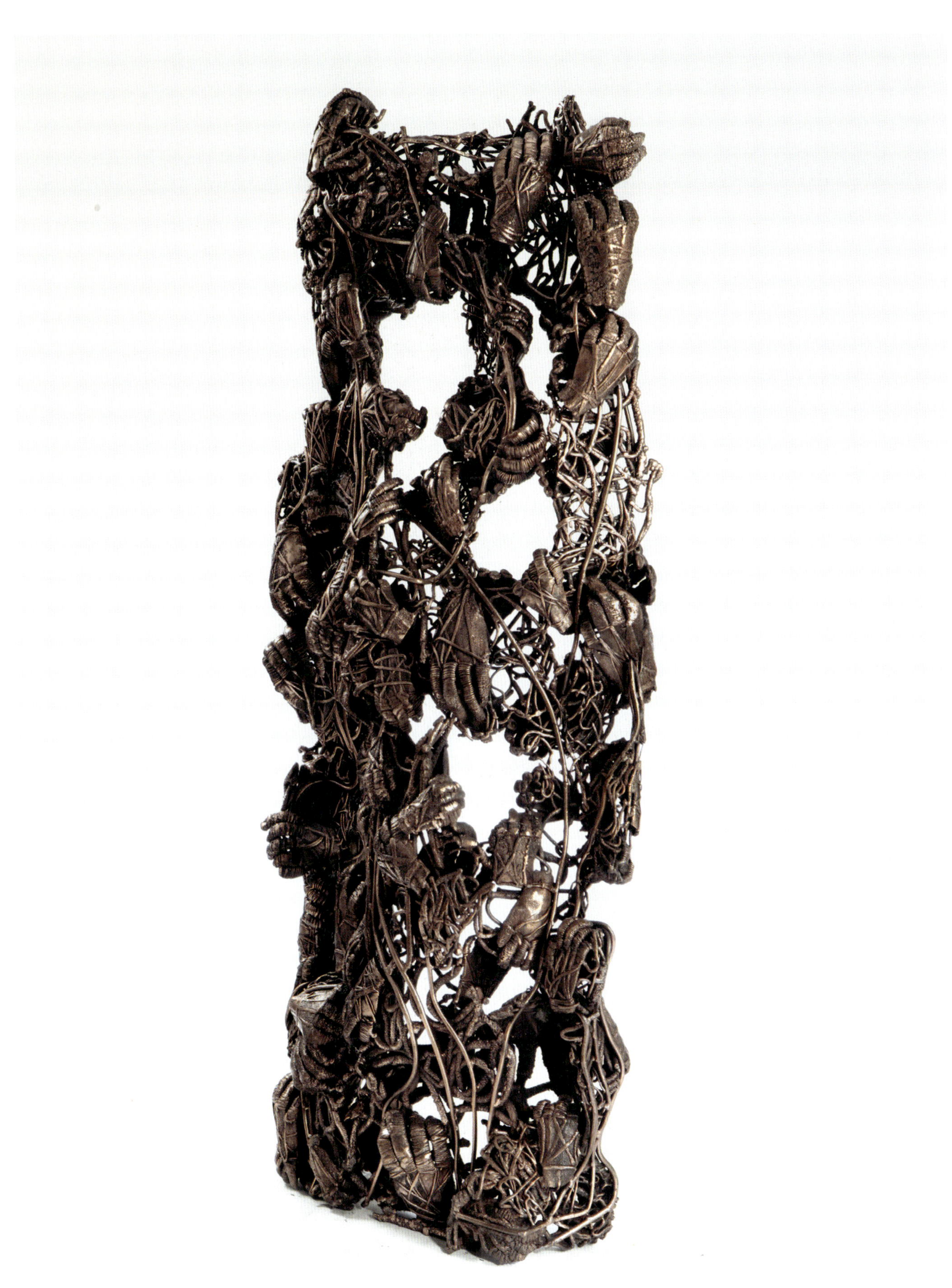

Ripping the Bird's Nest IV, 2013. Copper and bronze. 154.9 × 83.8 × 30.4 cm. Photo by Shamyl Khuhro

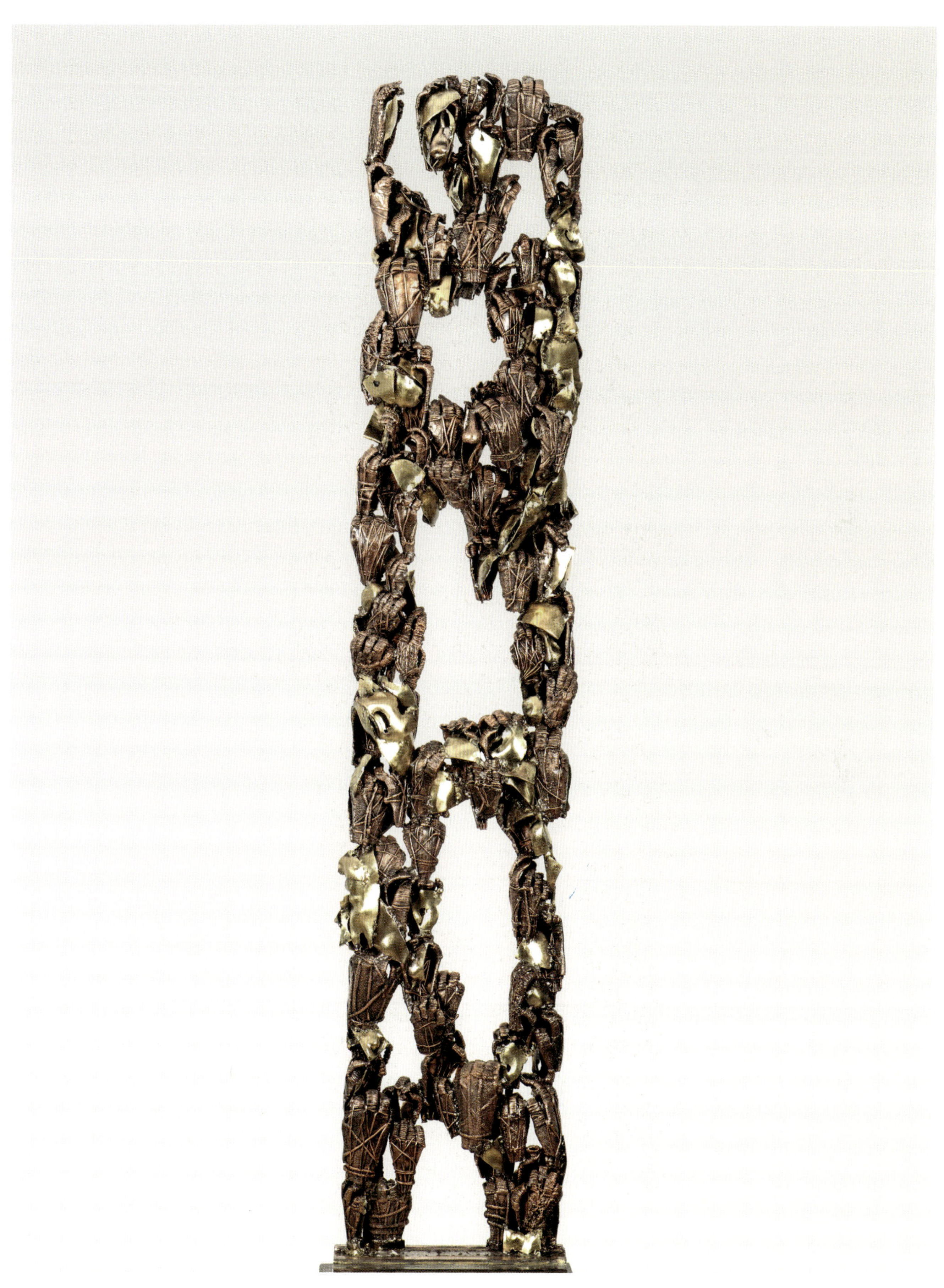

Entangled Tower, 2023. Copper and bronze. 231.14 × 45.72 × 17.78 cm. Photo by Humayun Memon

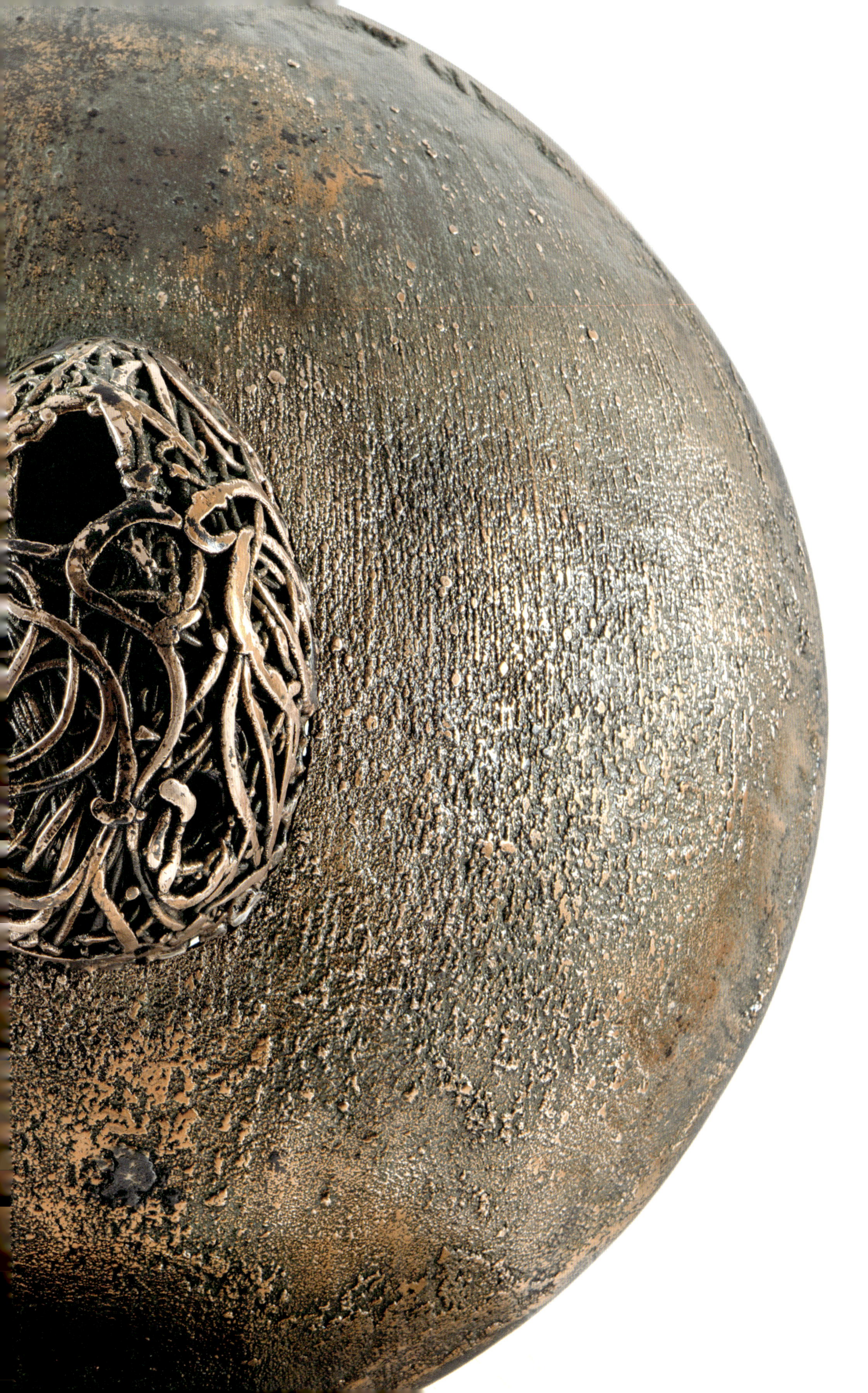

Egg

2003 - 2018

Photo by Humayun Memon

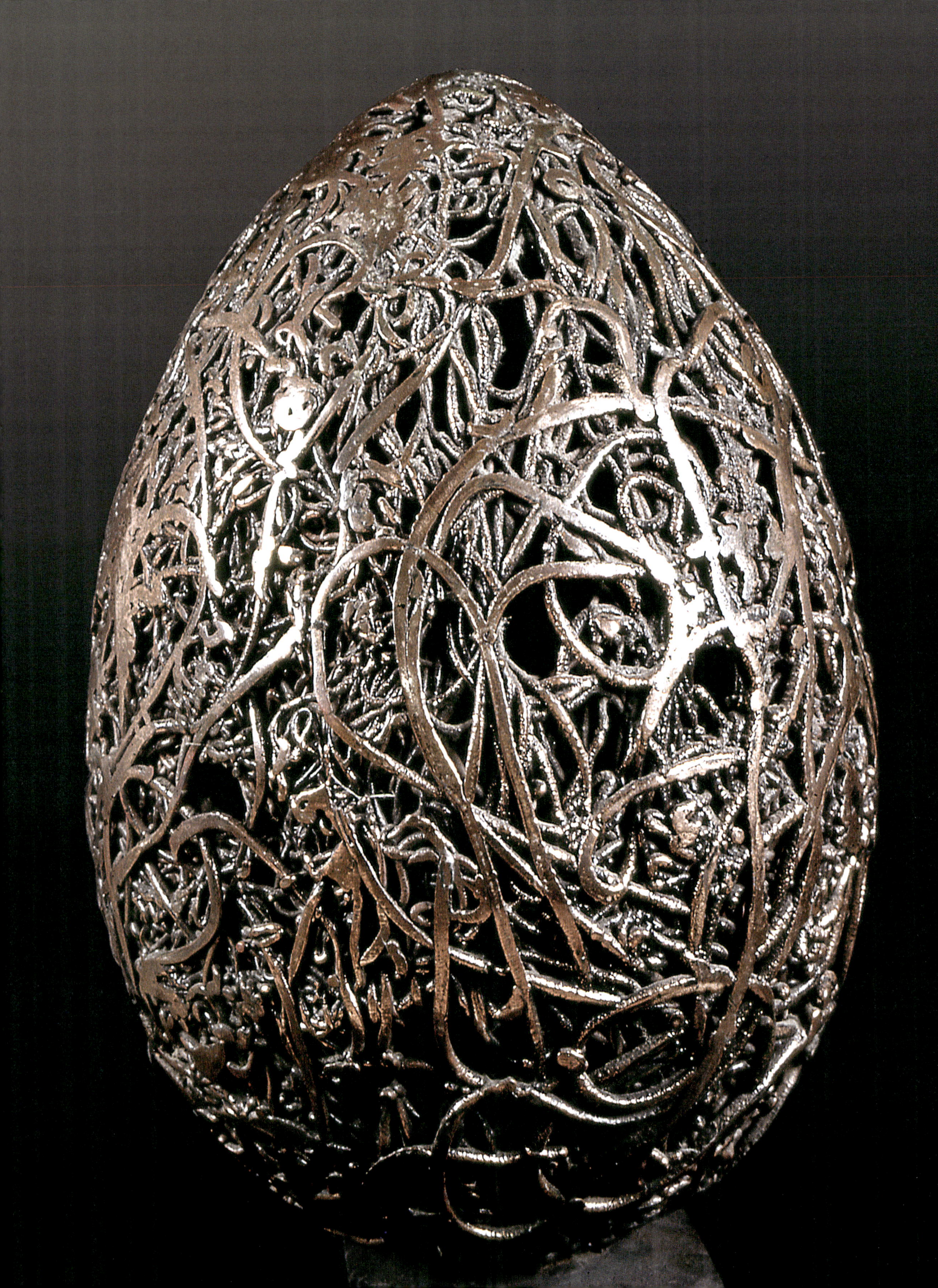

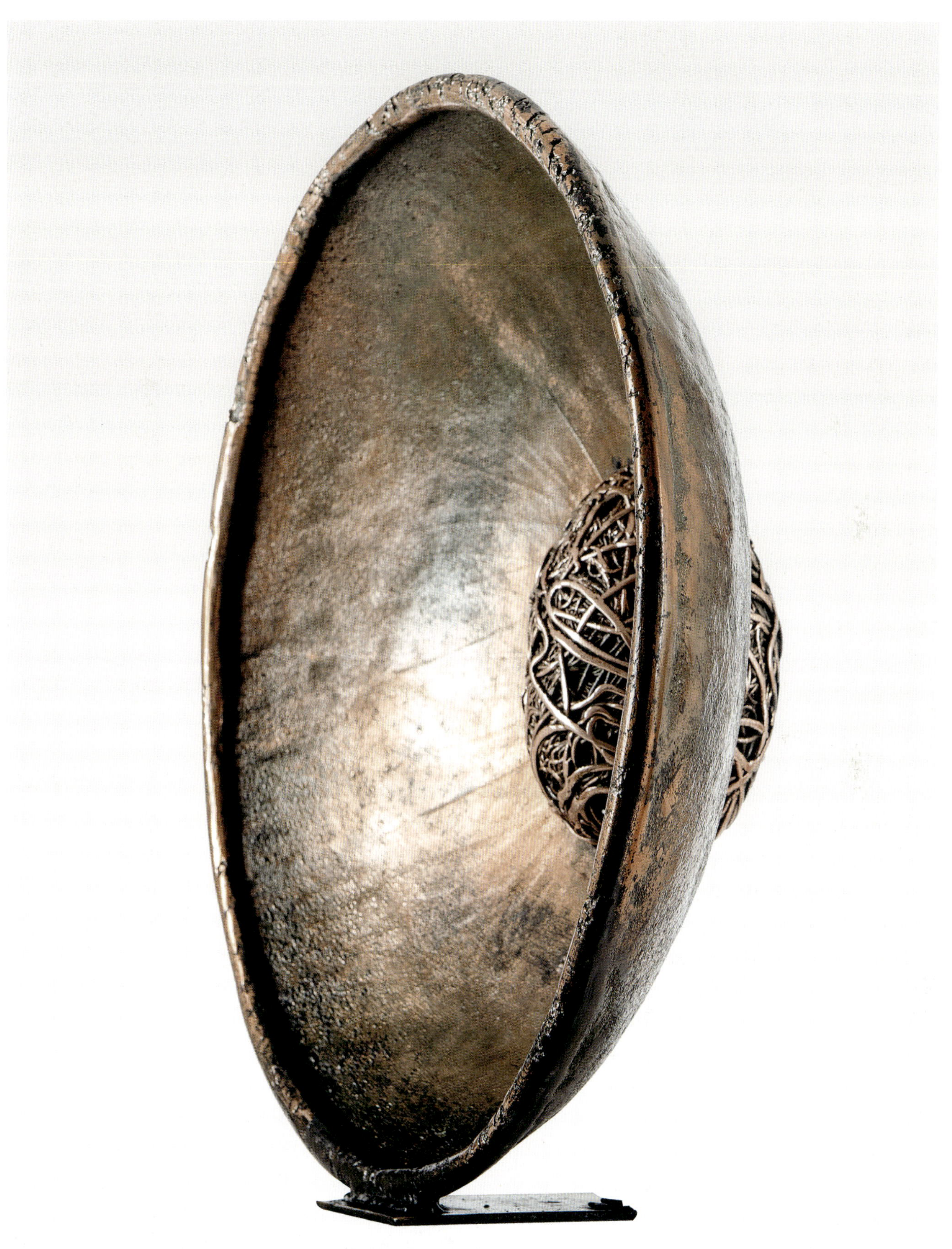

Egg V, 2003. Copper and silver leaf. 45.7 × 45.7 × 10 cm. Photo by Humayun Memon

Opposite page
Egg I, 2003. Copper. 20.32 × 33.02 × 33.02 cm. Photo by Tapu Javeri

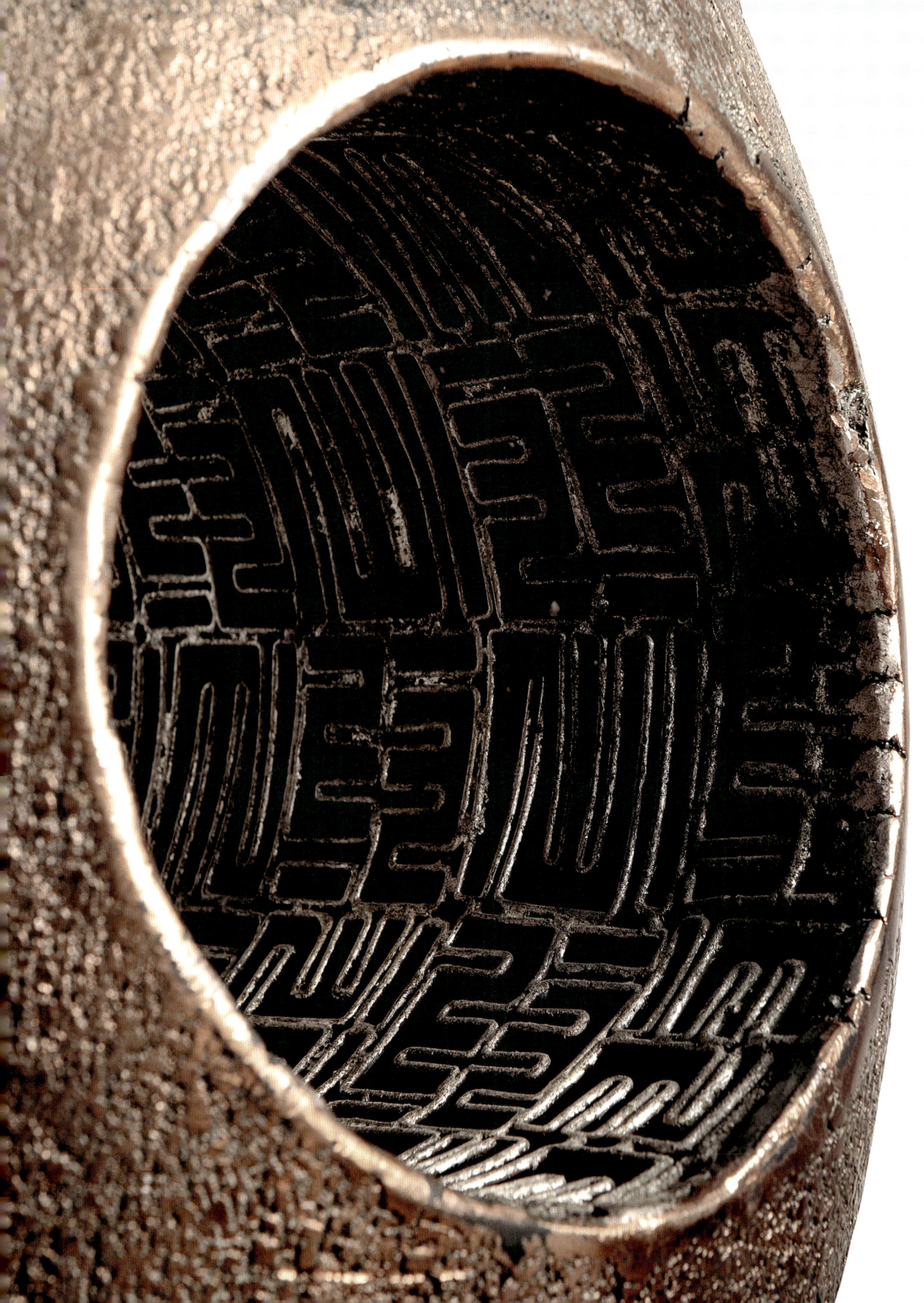

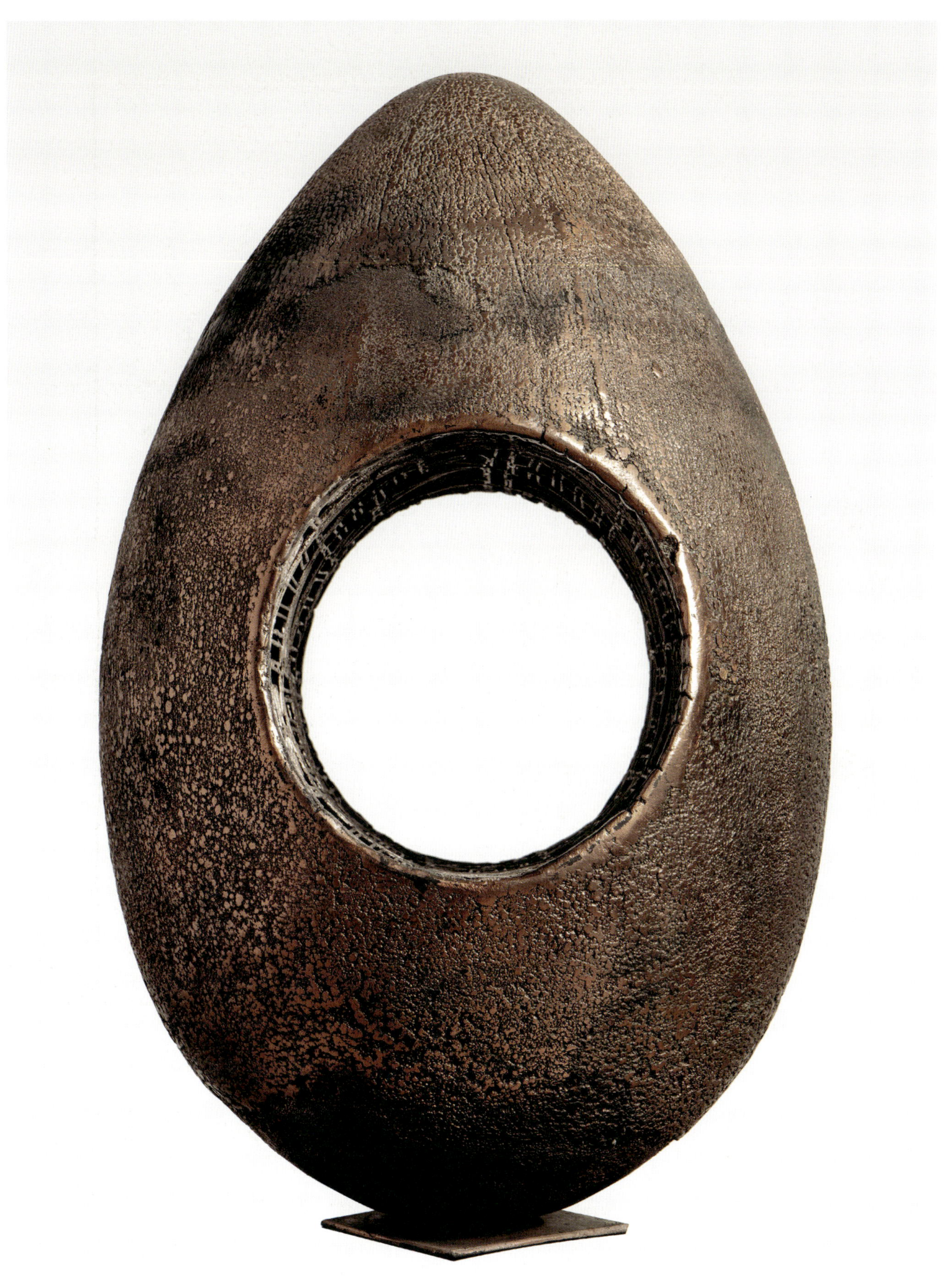

The Womb, 2003. Copper and silver leaf. 64 × 39.3 × 33 cm. Photo by Humayun Memon

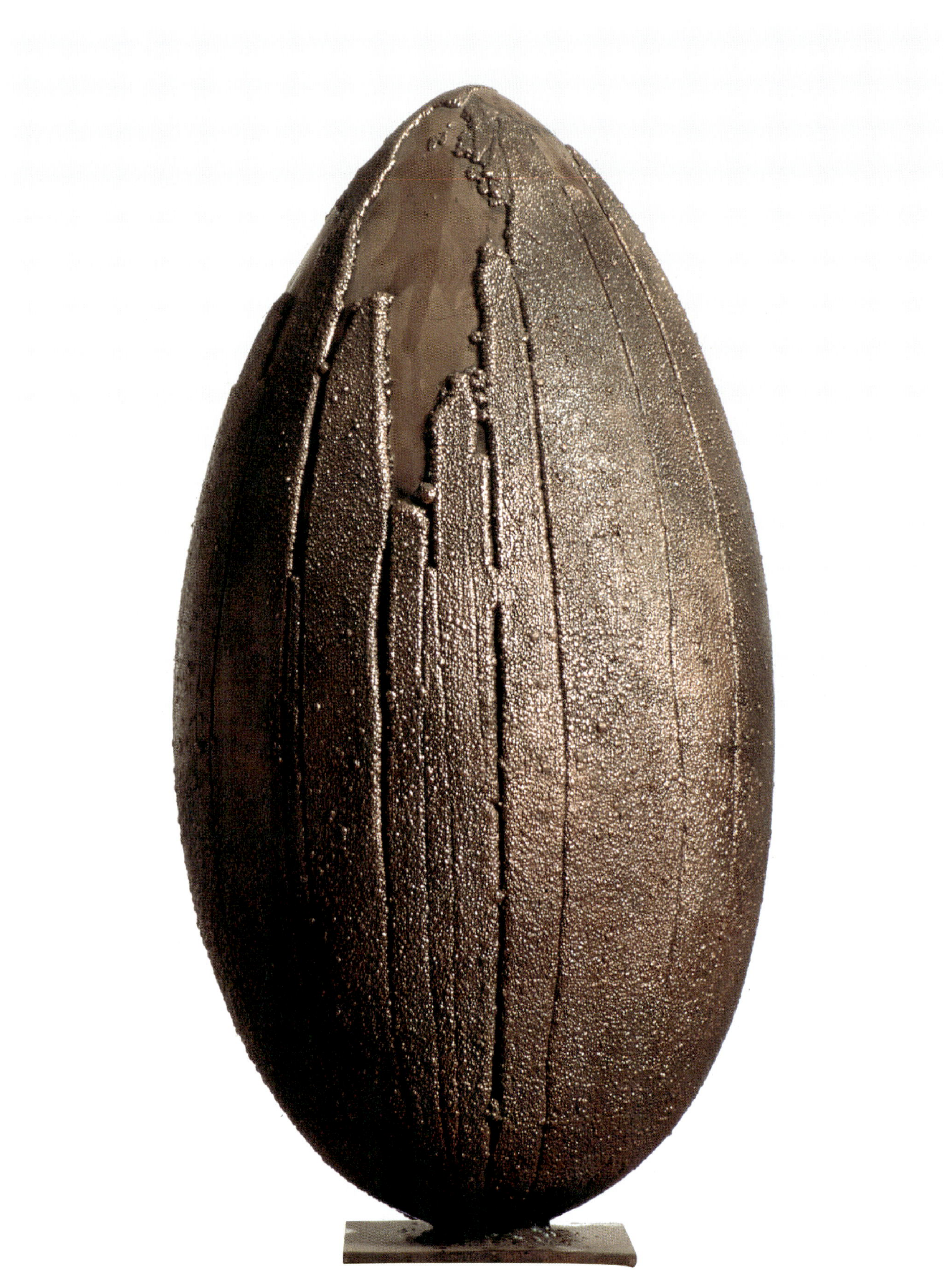

Melting Egg, 2007. Copper. 68.58 × 20.32 × 20.32 cm. Photo by Nafees

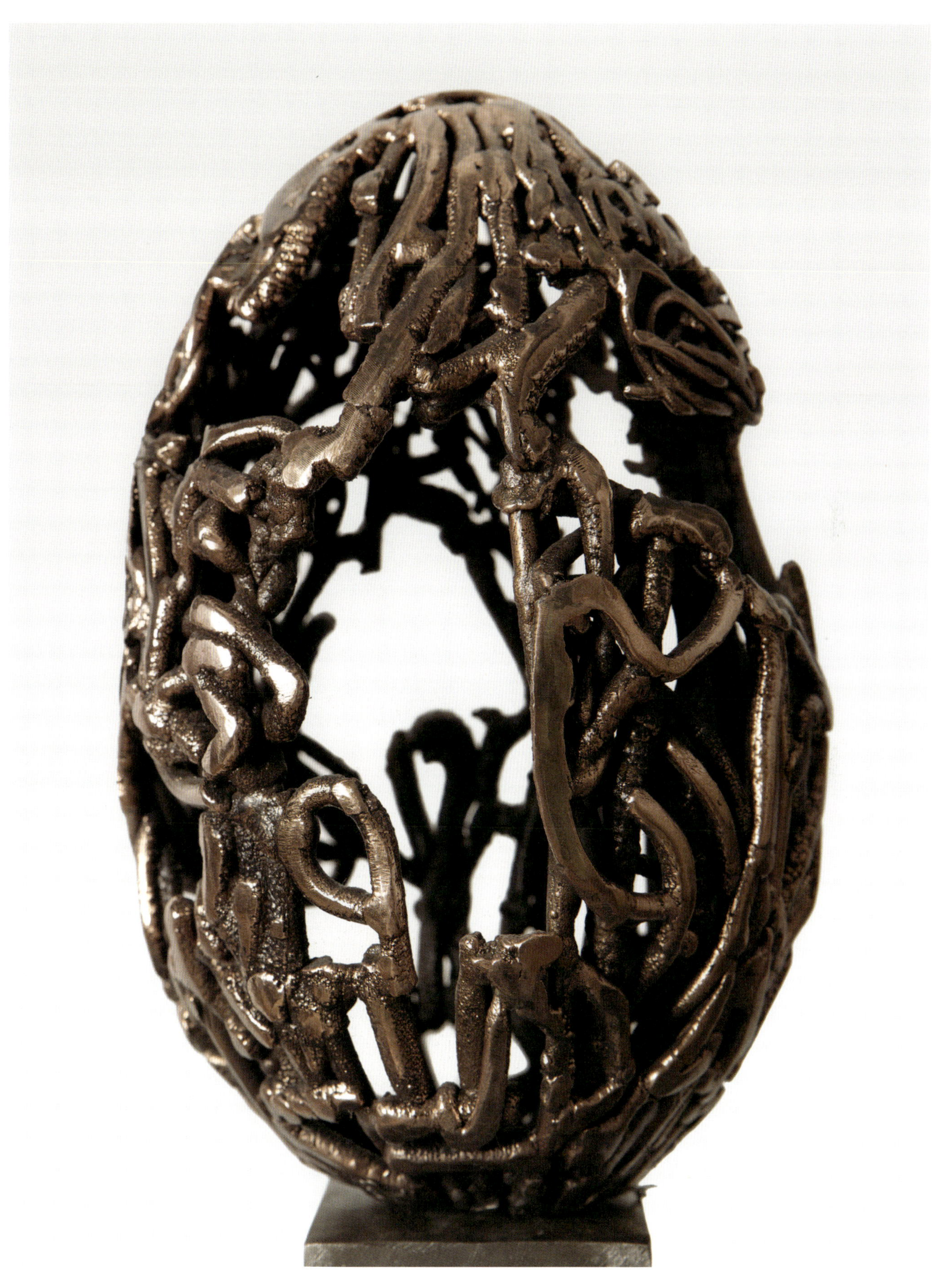

Empty Egg IV, 2015. Copper. 22.8 × 16 × 16 cm. Photo by Humayun Memon

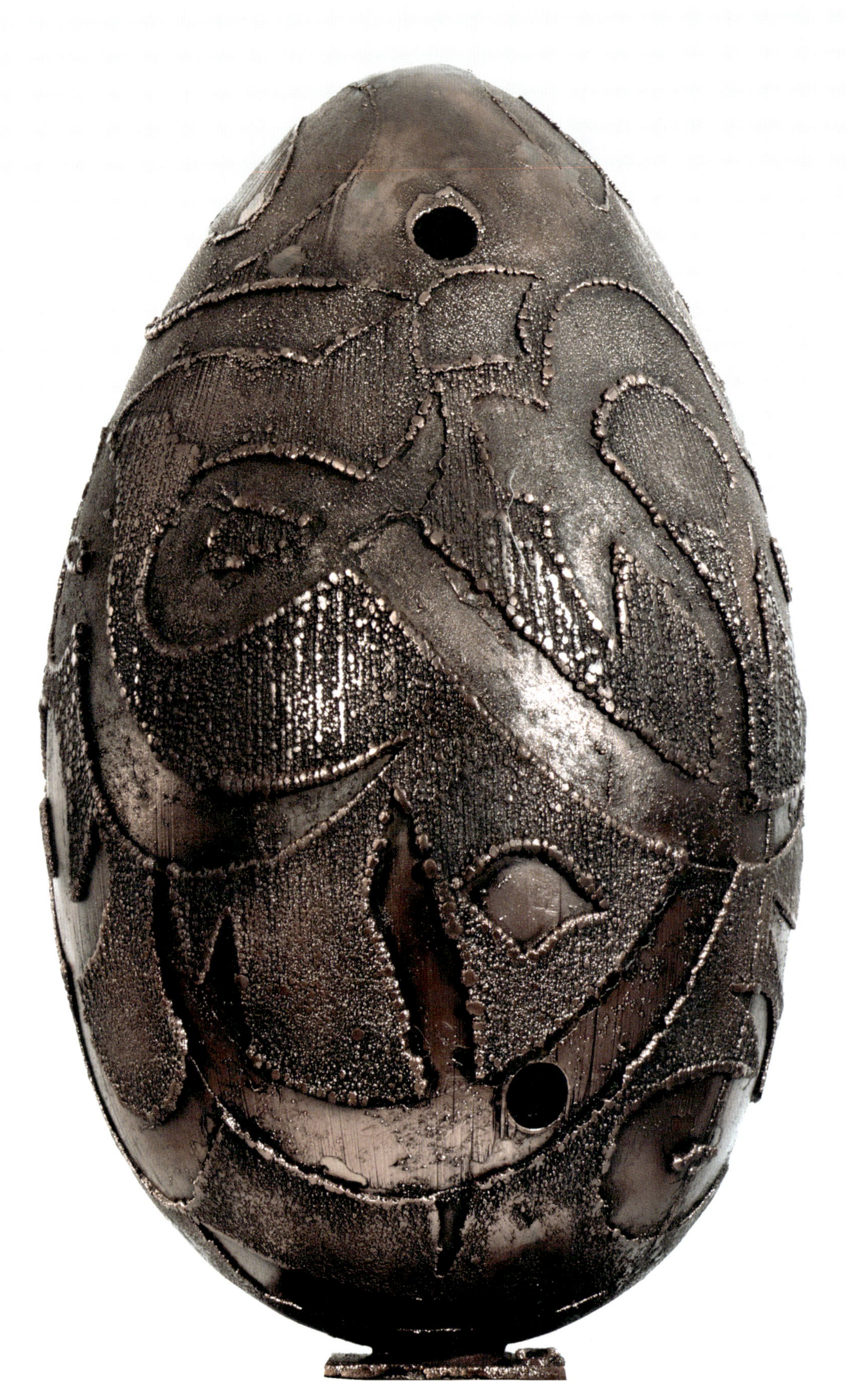

Infinity Egg I, 2018. Copper. 57 × 33 × 33 cm. Photo by Humayun Memon

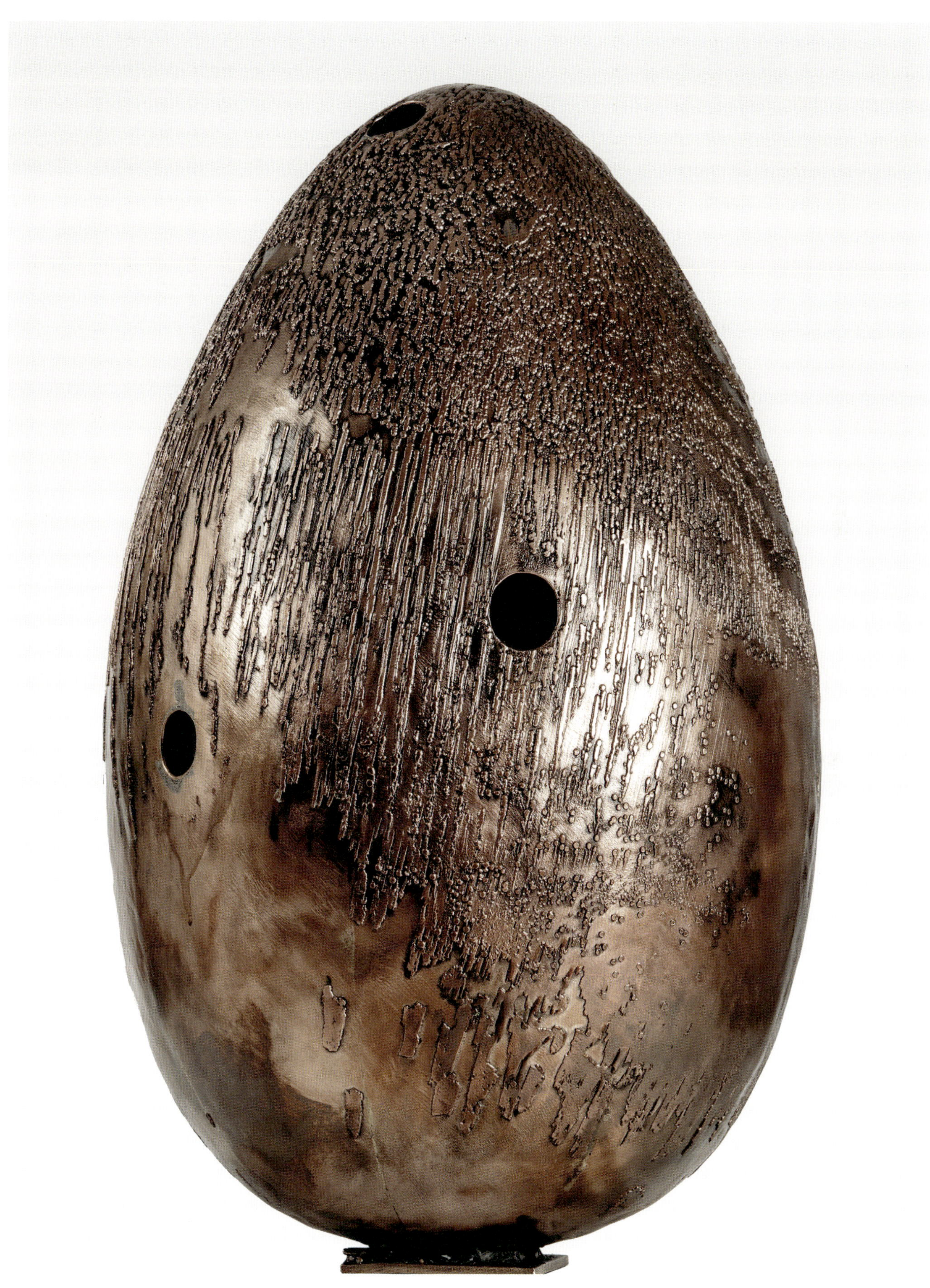

Infinity Egg III, 2018. Copper. 68.58 × 43.18 × 43.18 cm. Photo by Humayun Memon

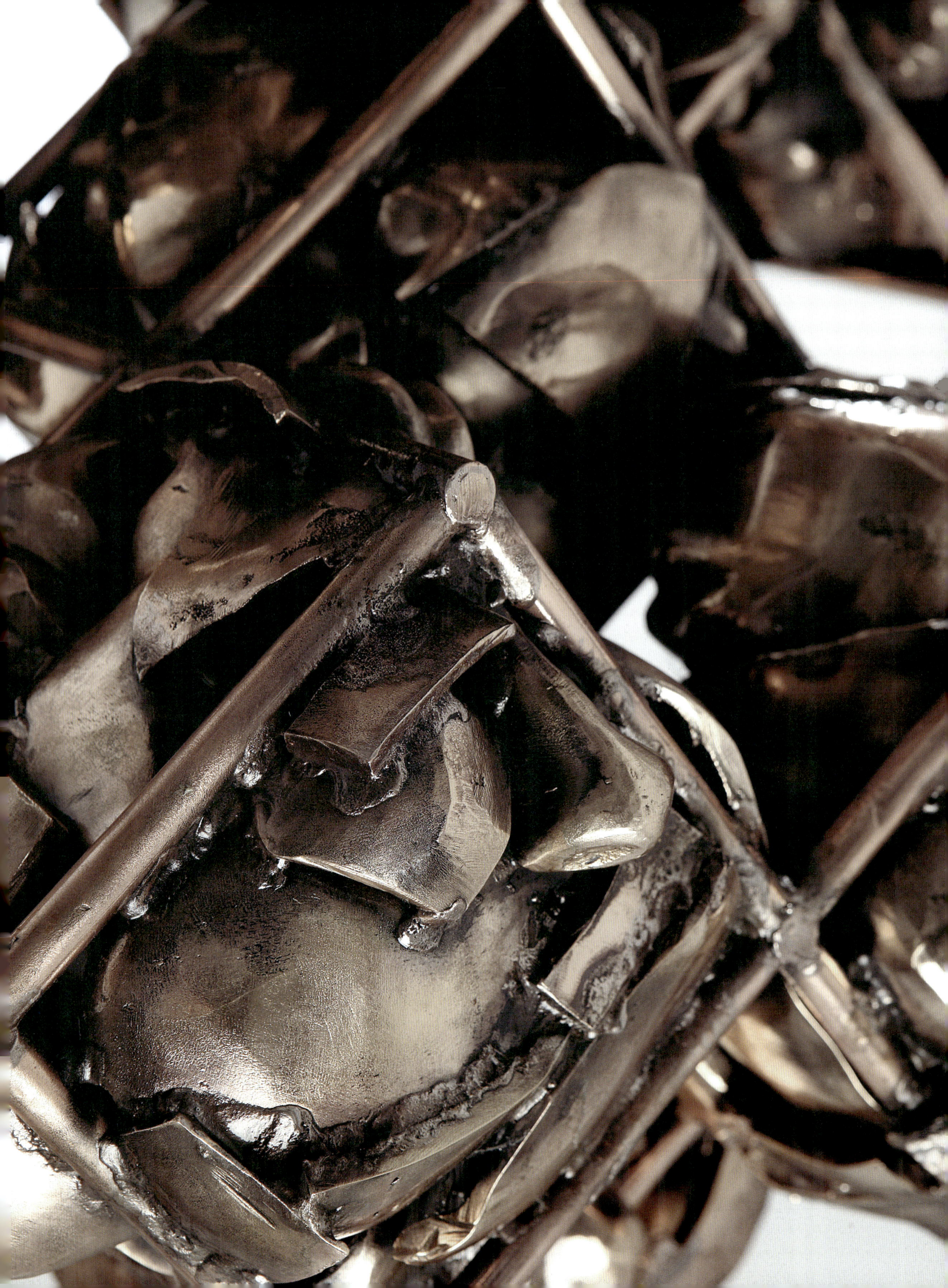

Self-Portraiture

1989 - 2017

Photo by Shamyl Khuhro

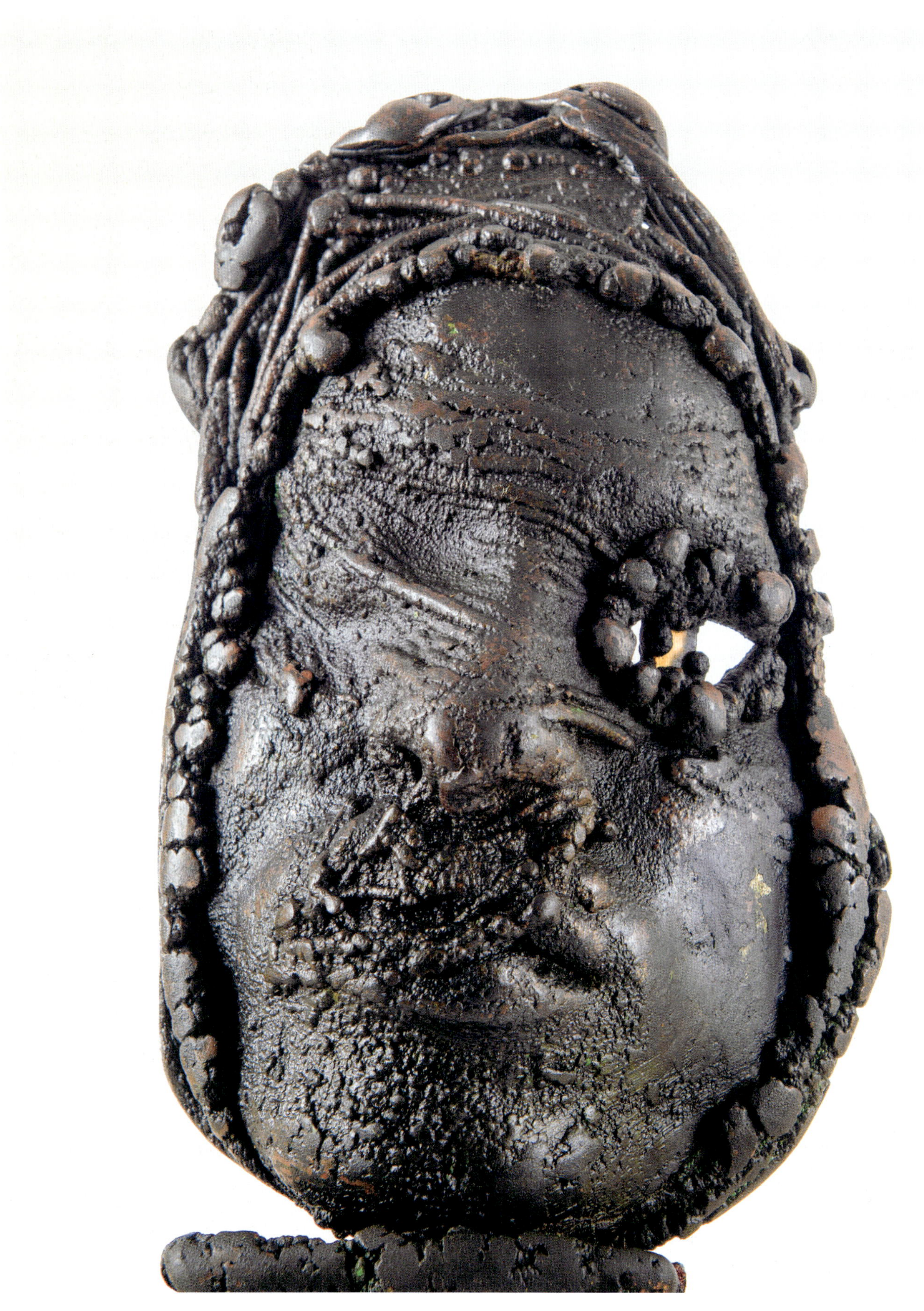

Me, 1989. Copper, bronze, rock crystal and gold leaf. 27.94 × 15.24 × 10.16 cm.
Photo by Humayun Memon

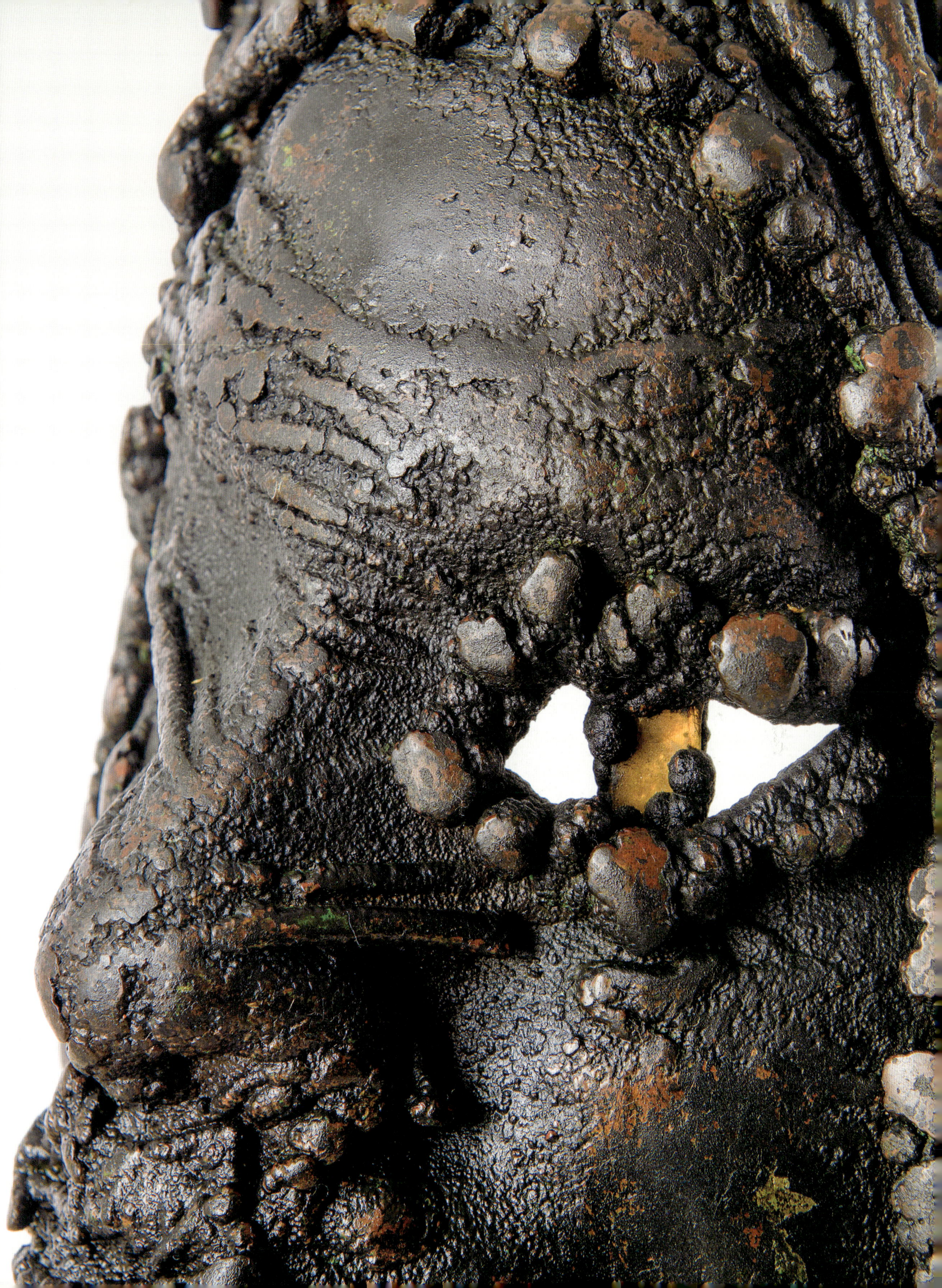

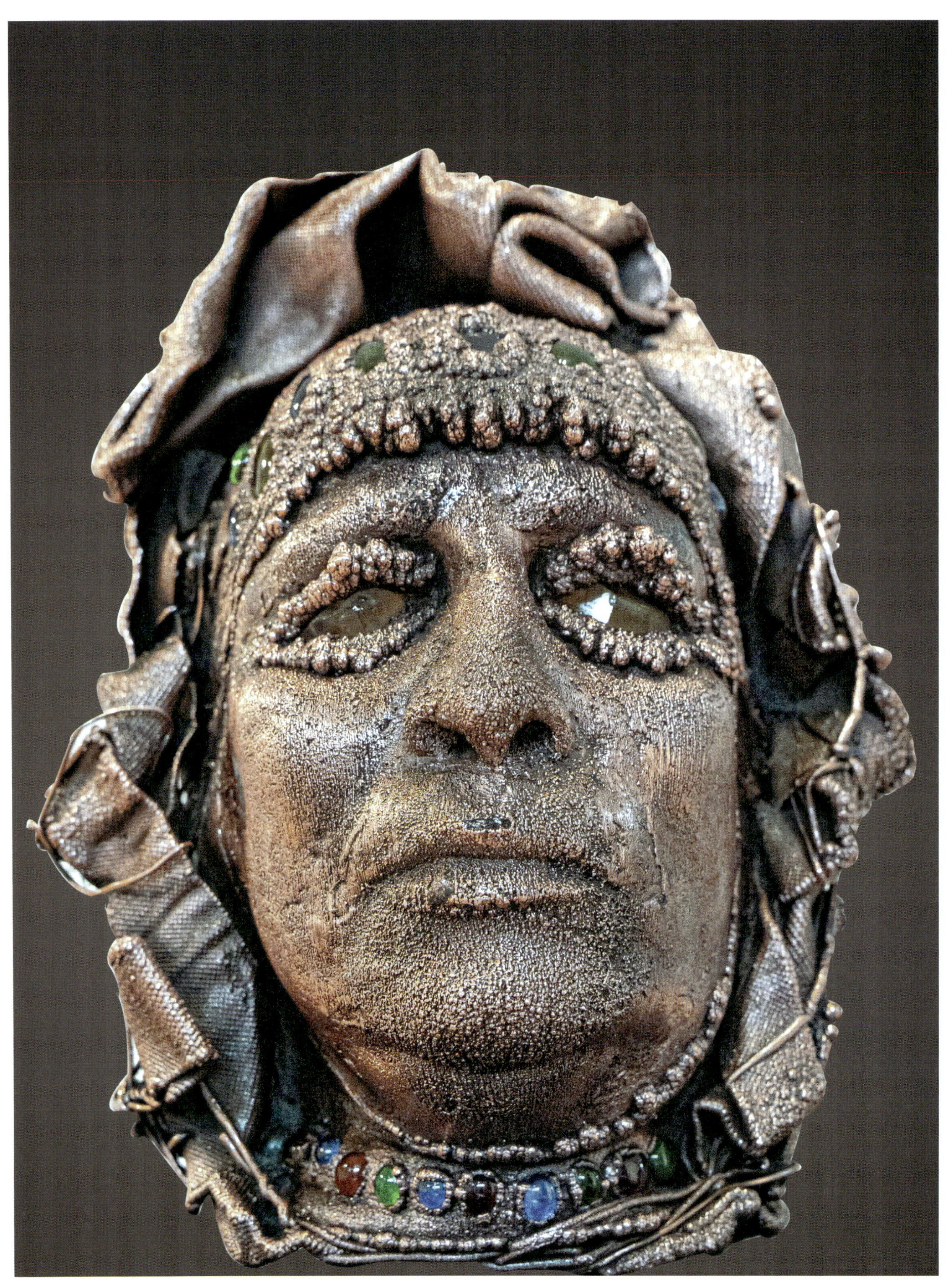

Mother, 1990. Copper, bronze and enamel. 33 × 20.3 × 25.4 cm. Photo by Farhan Baig

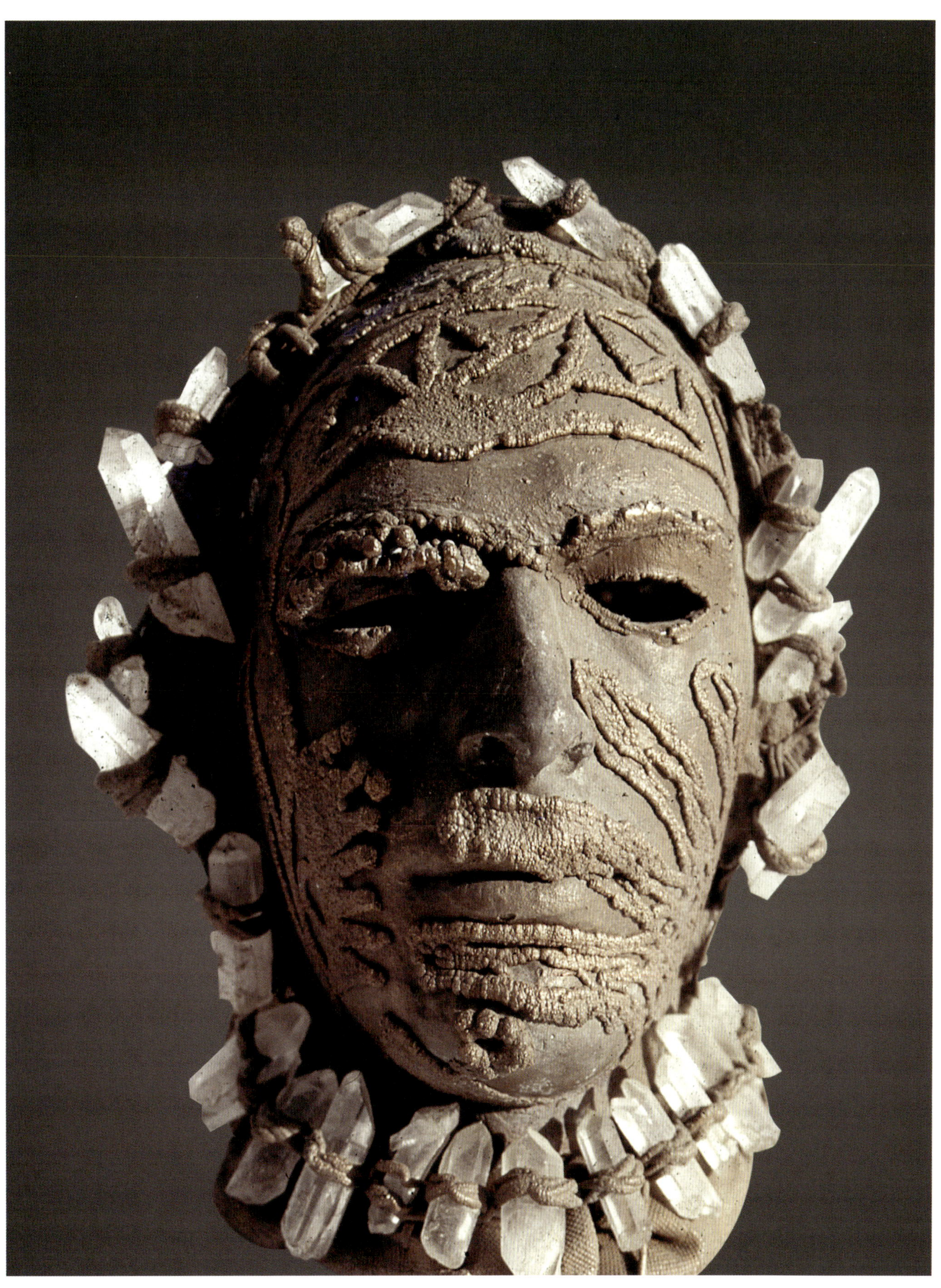

John, 1990. Copper, bronze and rock crystals. 31 × 19 × 25 cm. Photo by Nafees

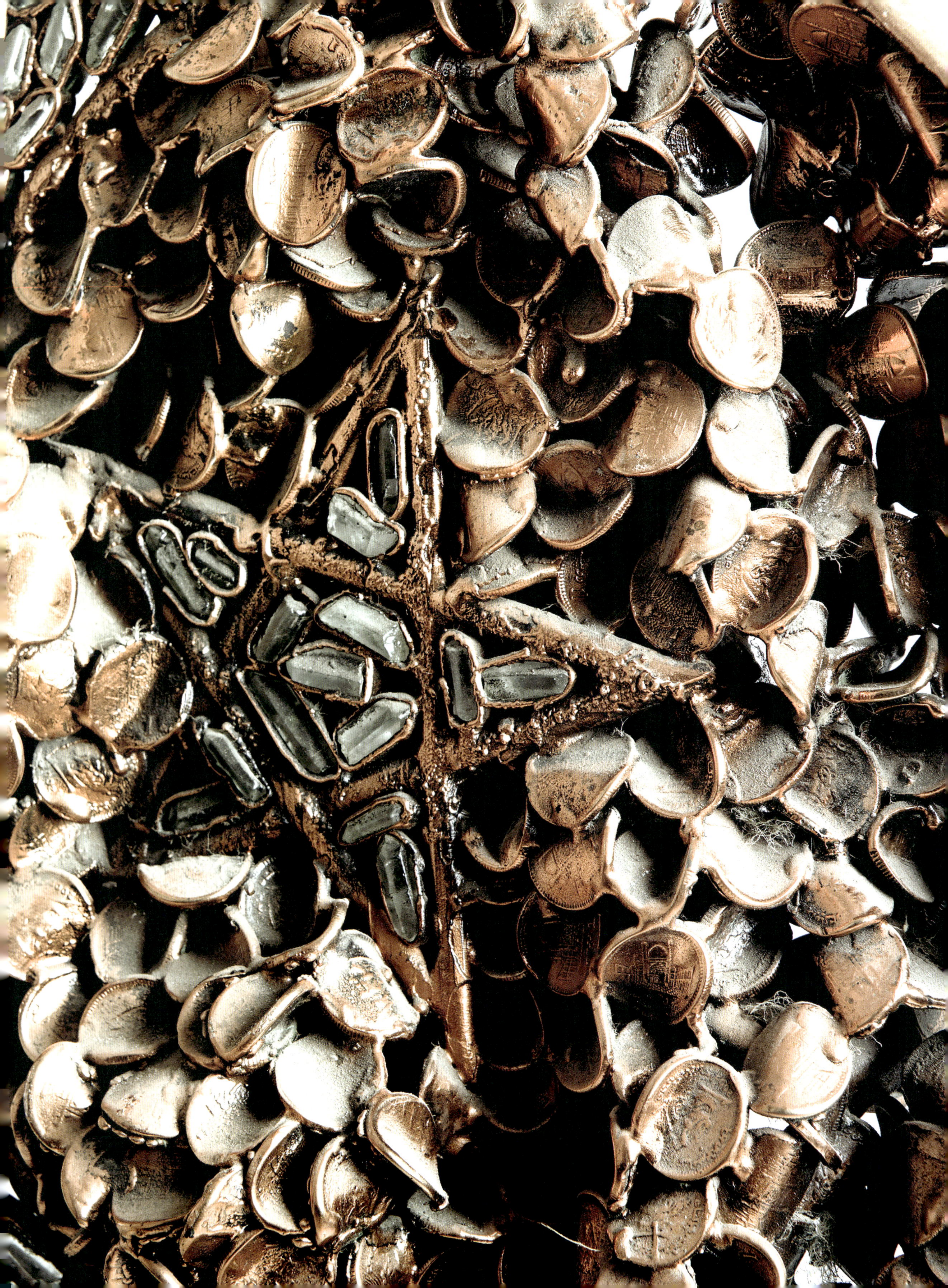

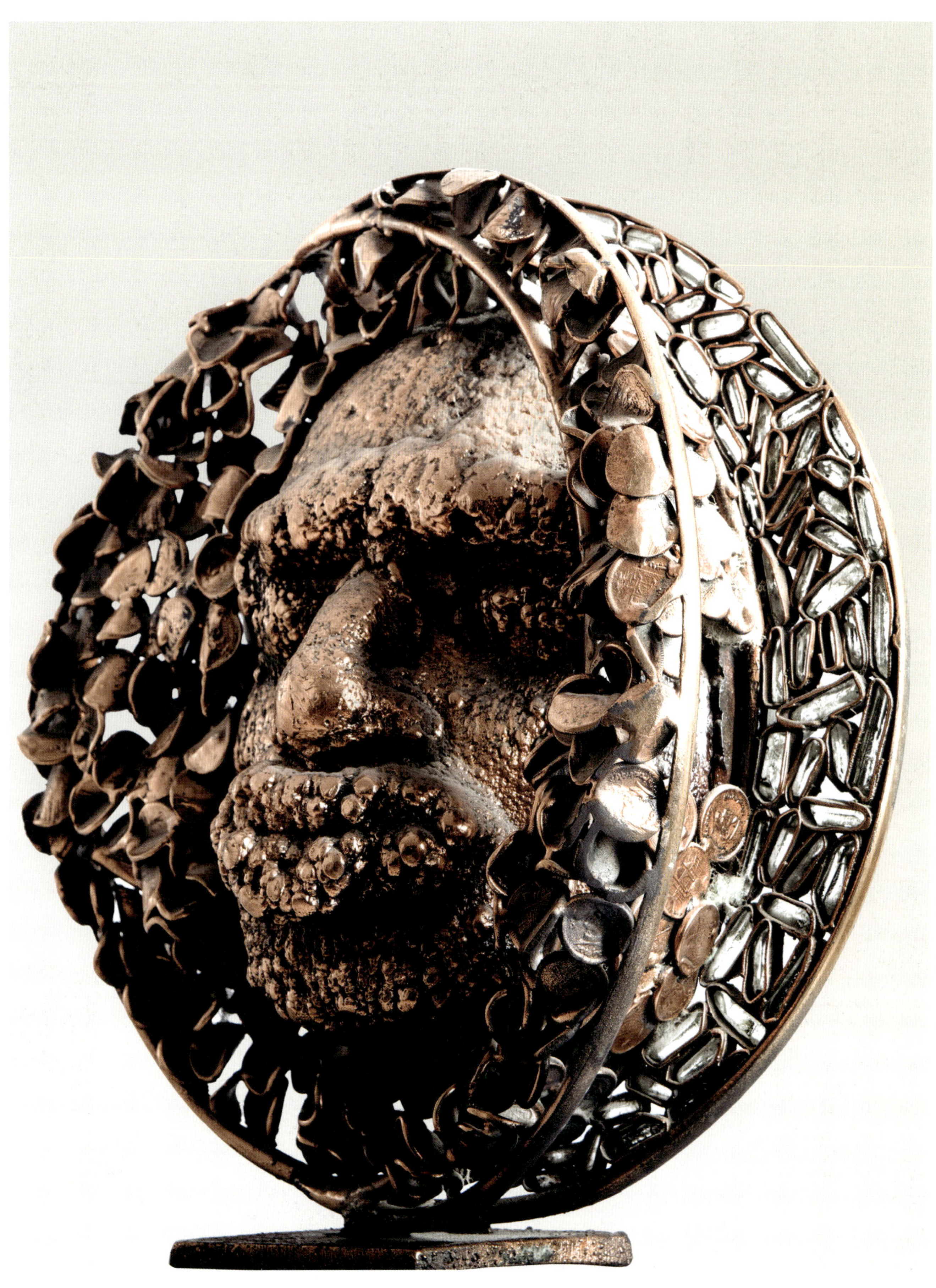

Father, 2001. Copper, bronze, coins and rock crystals. 30.4 × 30.4 × 15.2 cm.
Photo by Humayun Memon

Father and Son, 1999. Copper and bronze. 54 × 18 × 20 cm. Photo by Nafees

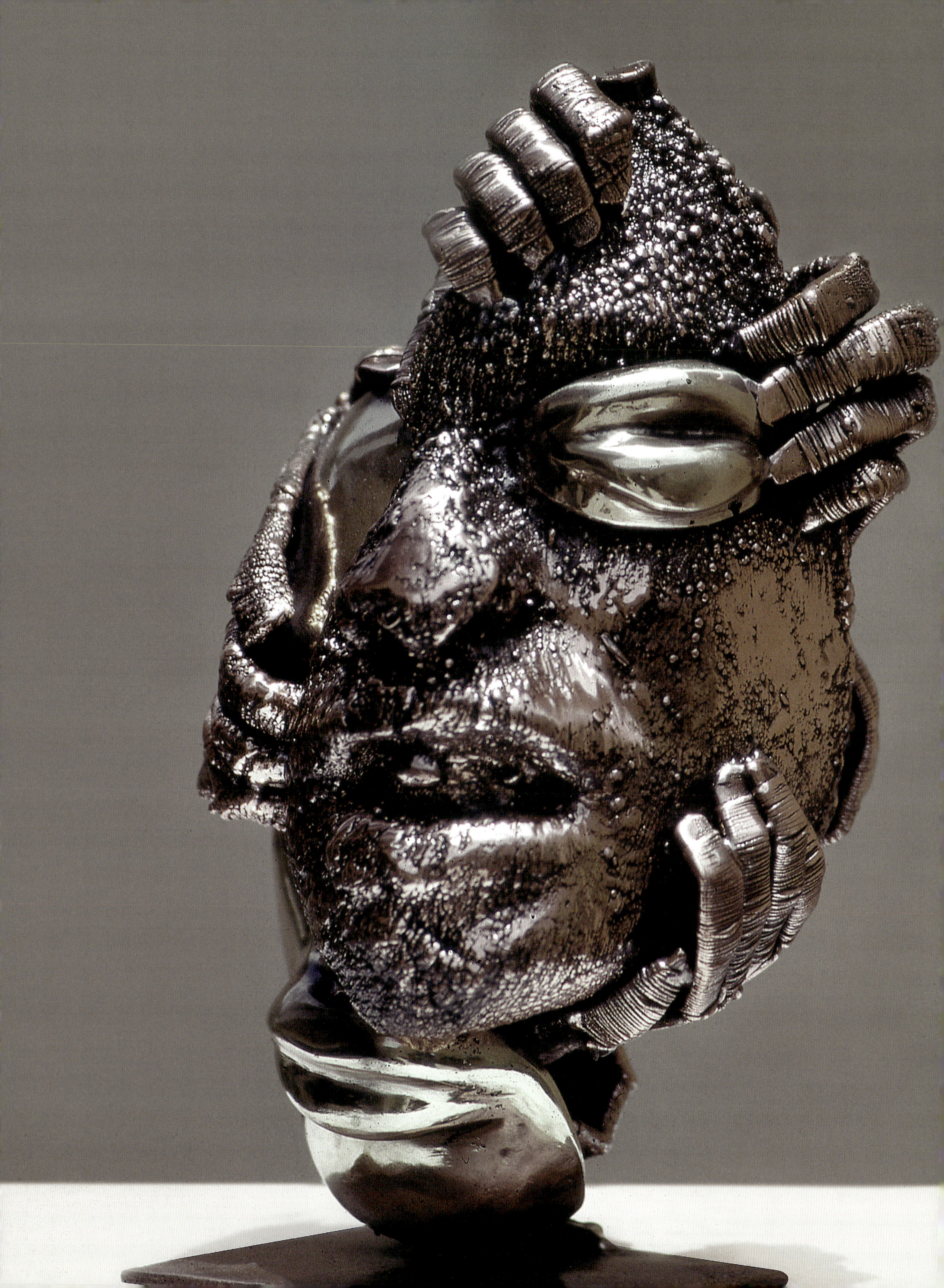

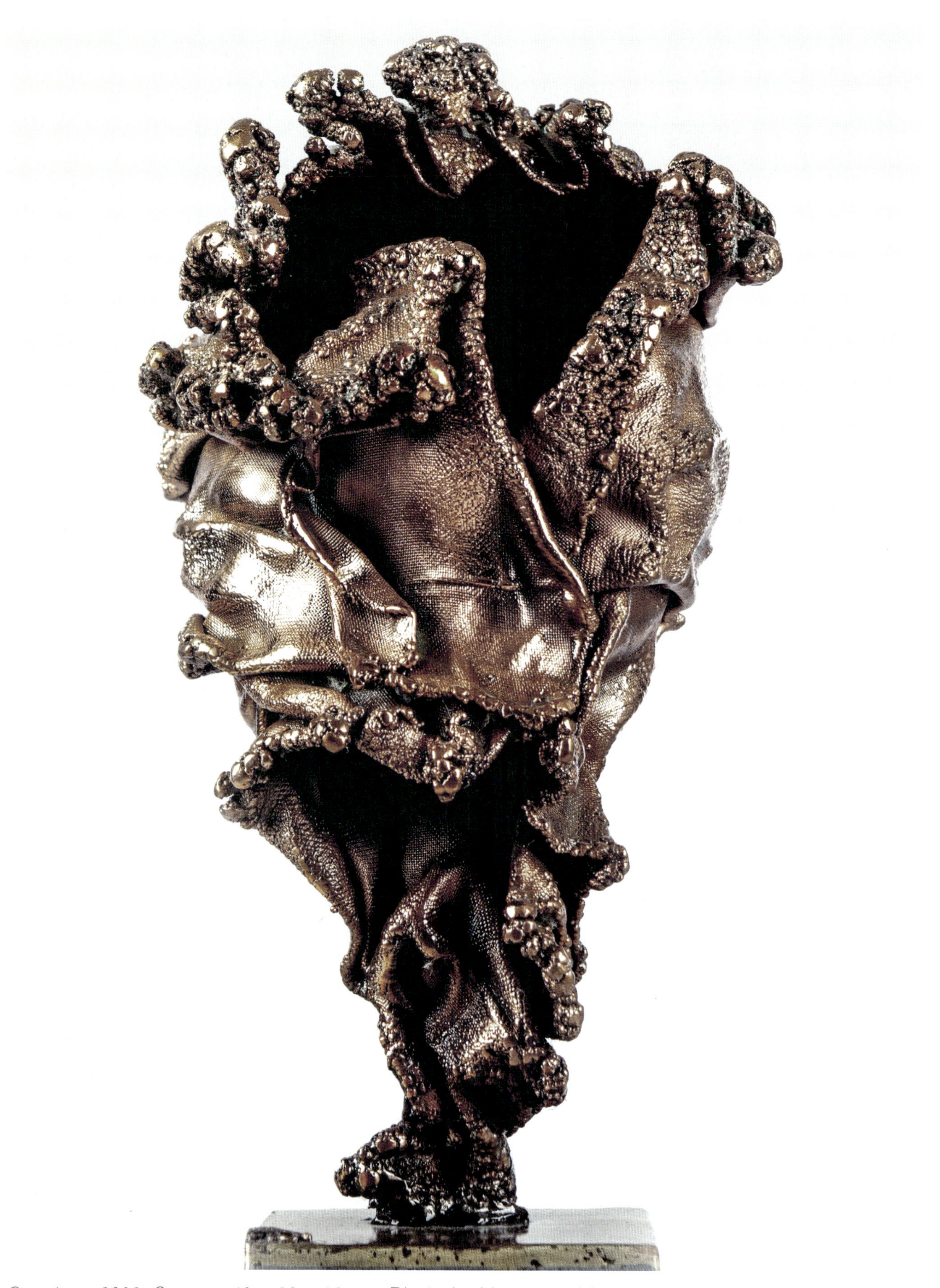

Cranium, 2002. Copper. 43 × 28 × 20 cm. Photo by Humayun Memon

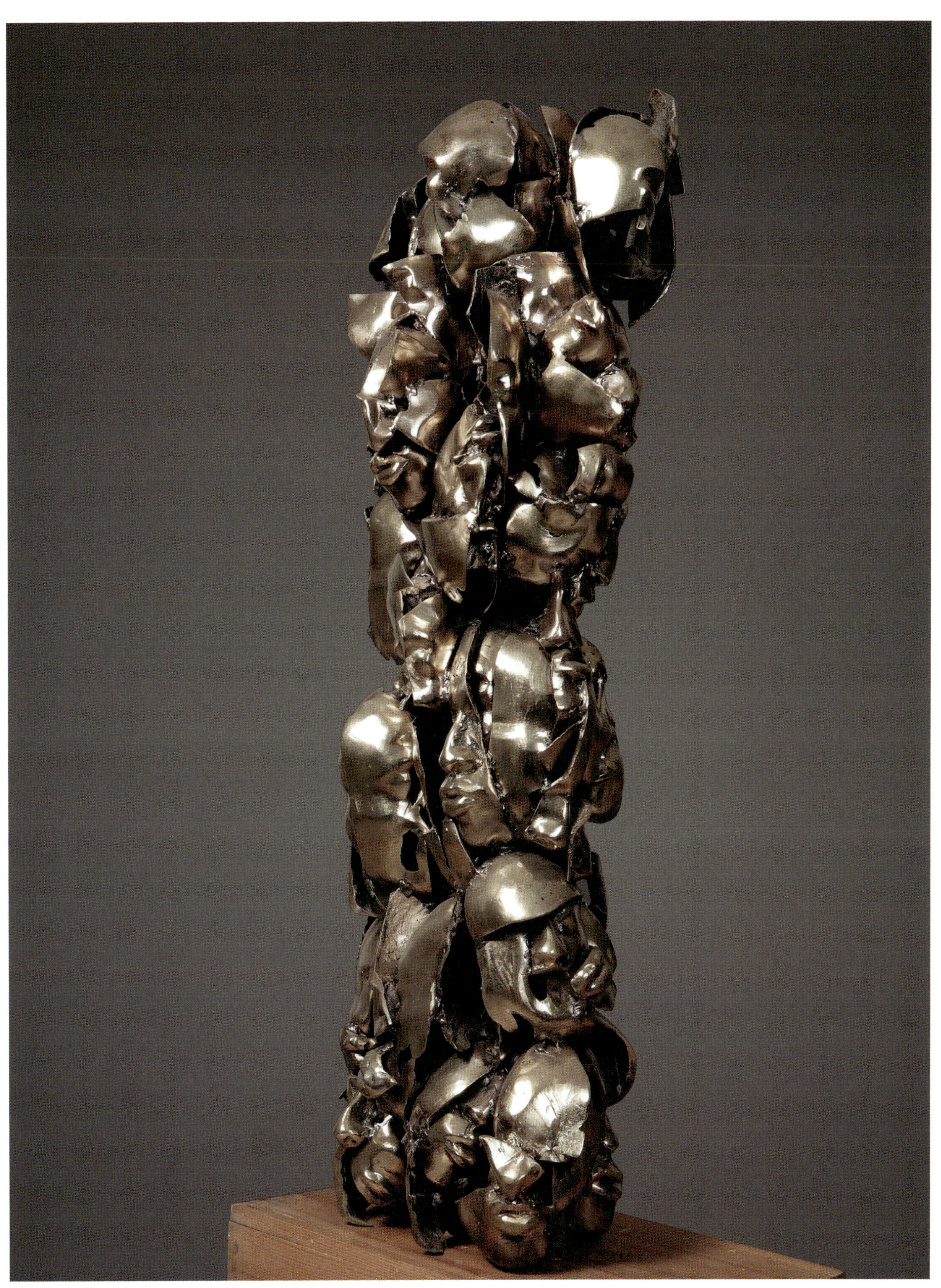

The Wall, 2007. Bronze. 114.3 × 43.18 × 30.48 cm. Photo by Tapu Javeri

47 Charbagh: The Resurrection, 2008. Copper and bronze. 132 × 125 × 30.4 cm. Photo by Shamyl Khuhro

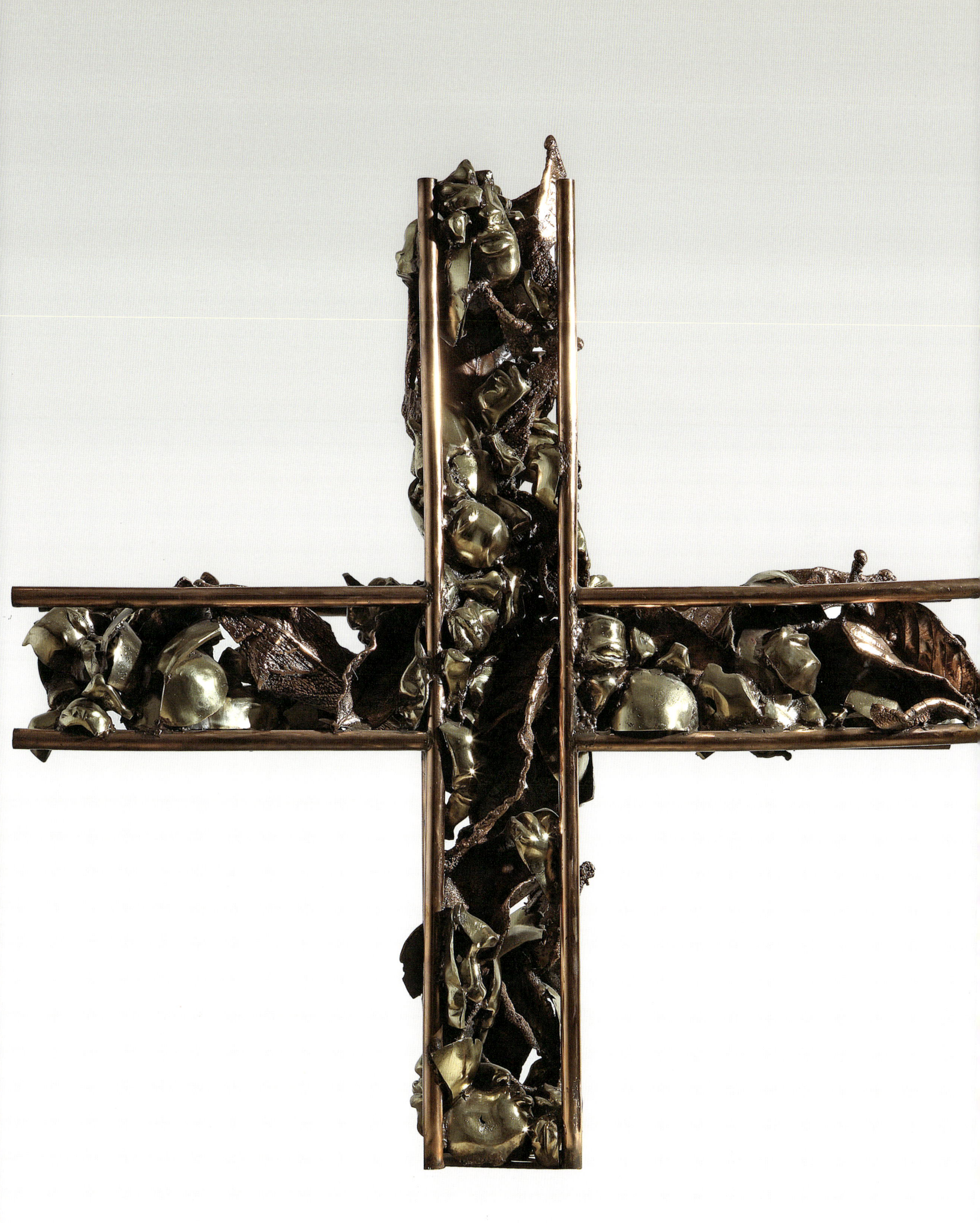

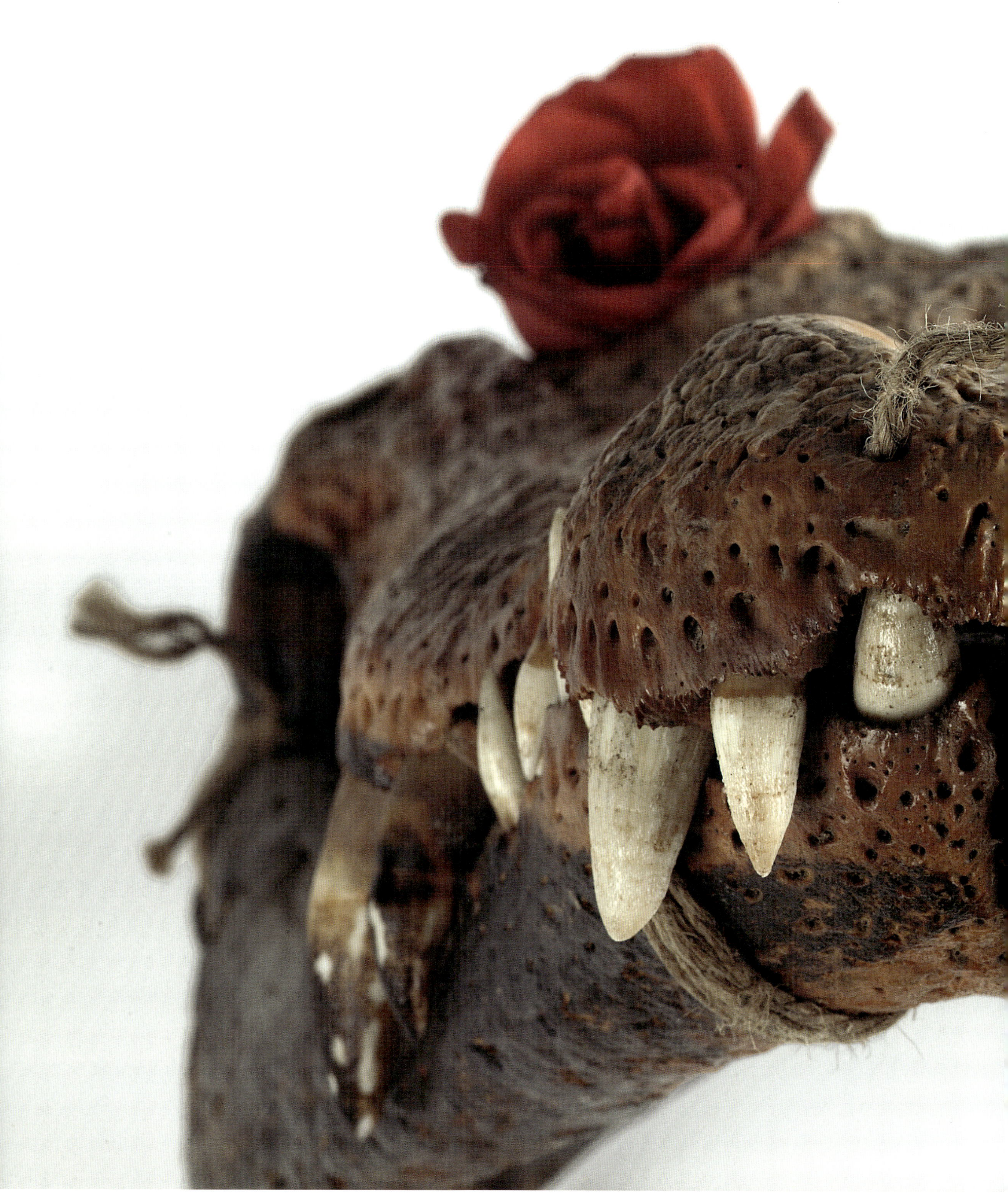

I Was Born This Way, 2012. Crocodile skull, roses and iron. 16 × 43 × 28 cm. Photo by Shamyl Khuhro

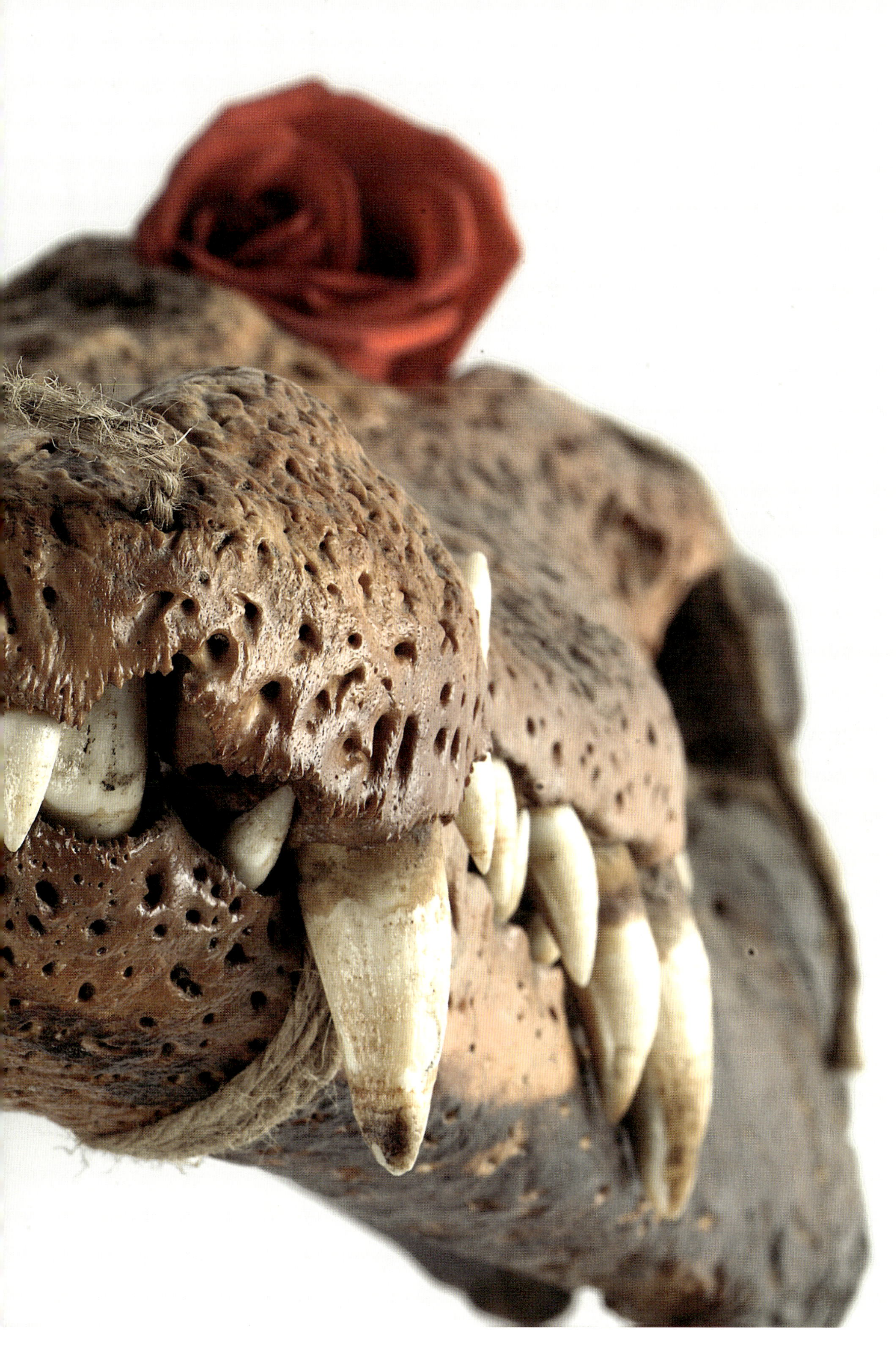

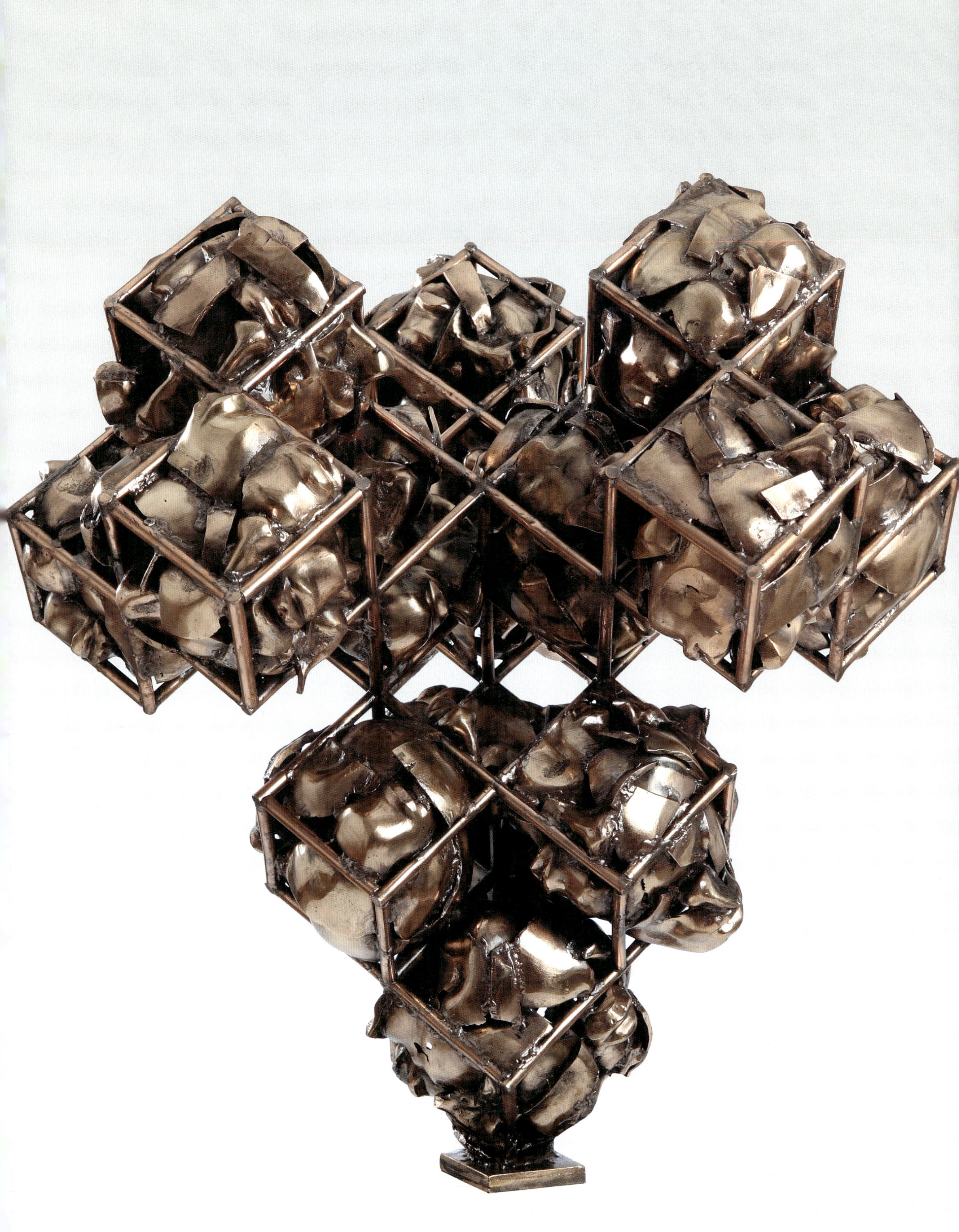

Me in the Matrix II, 2014. Copper and bronze. 91.4 × 91.4 × 91.4 cm. Photo by Shamyl Khuhro

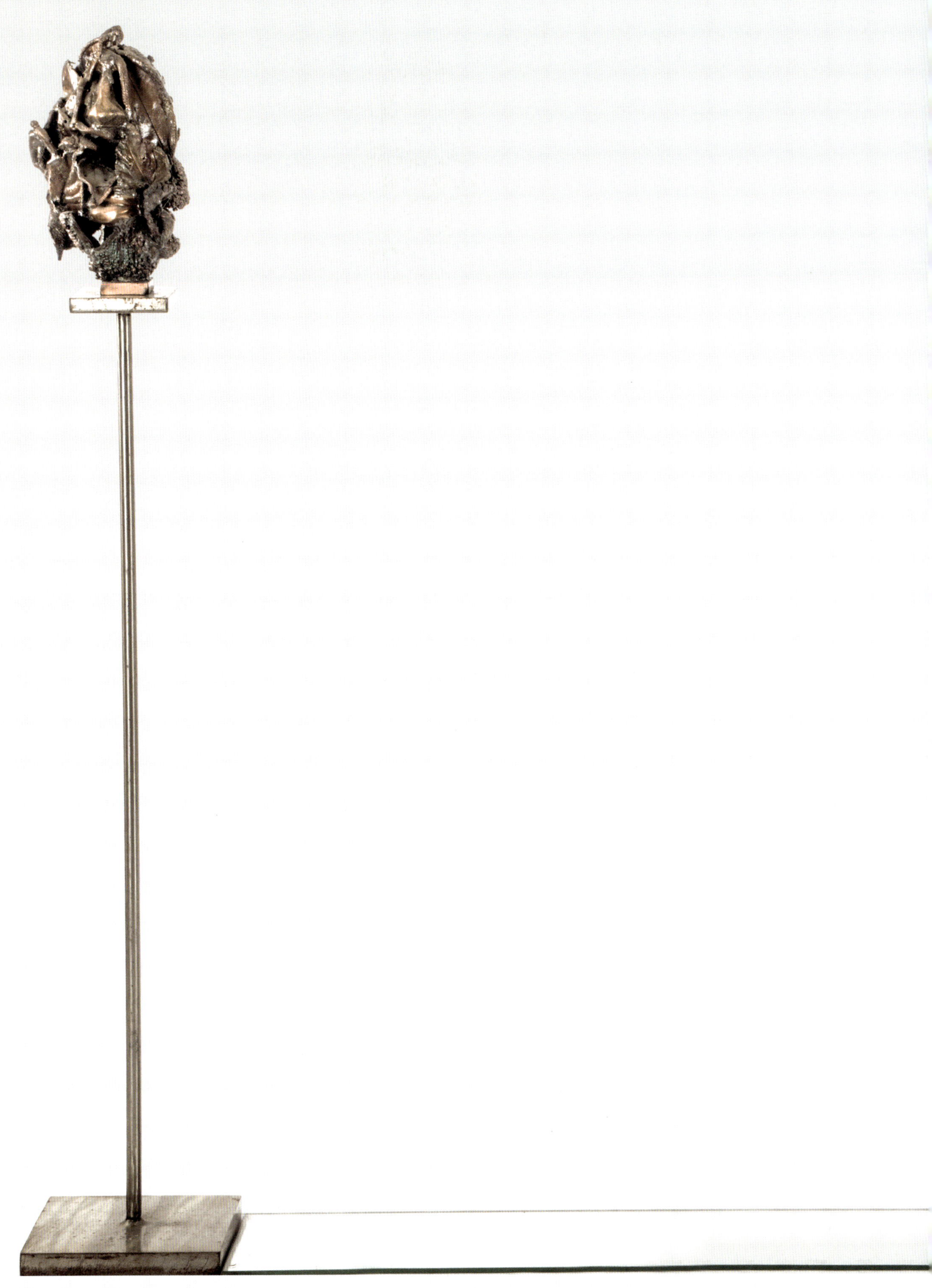

The Conversation, 2016. Copper, bronze, steel and mirror. 335 × 238.7 × 77.4 cm. Photo by Humayun Memon

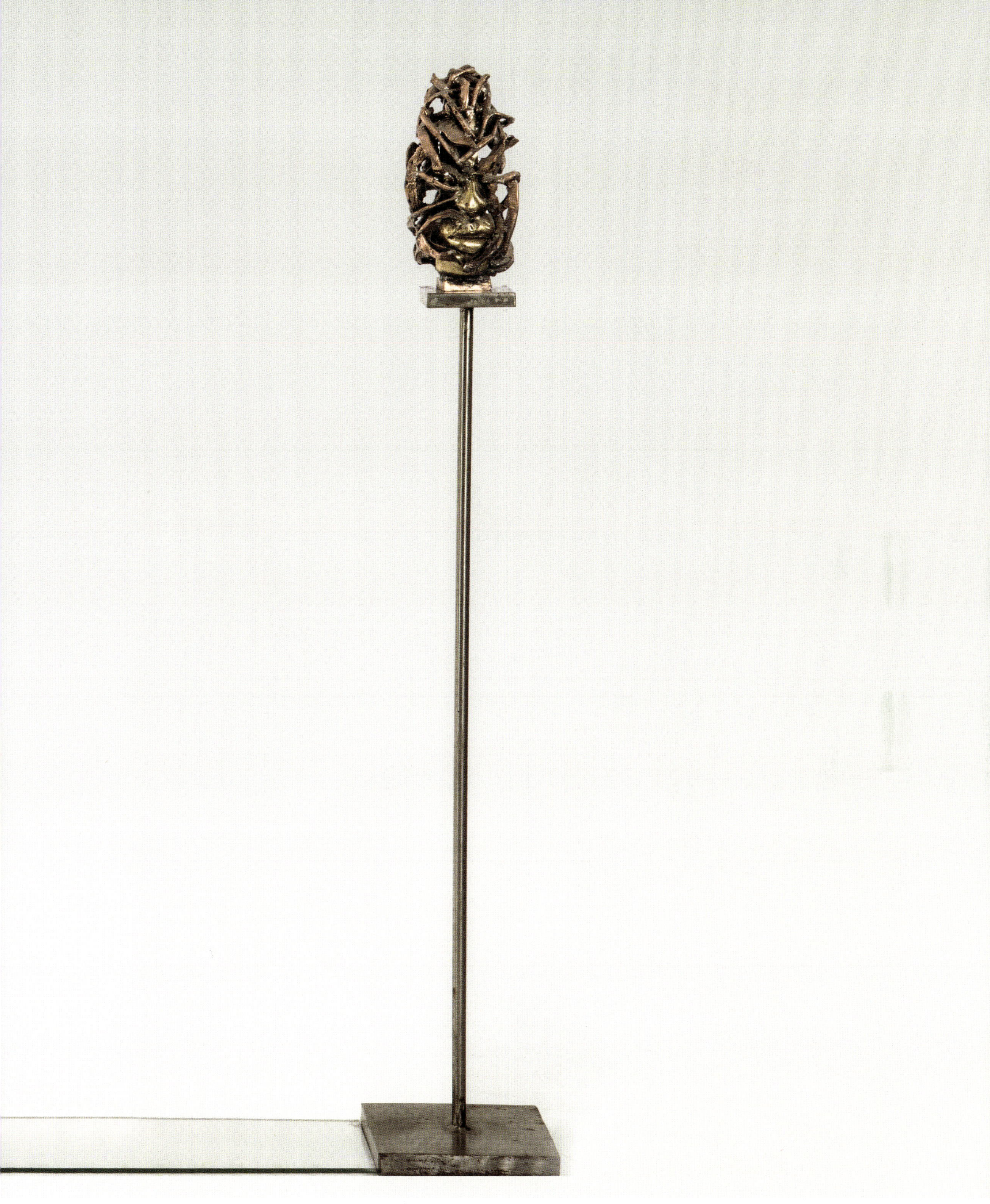

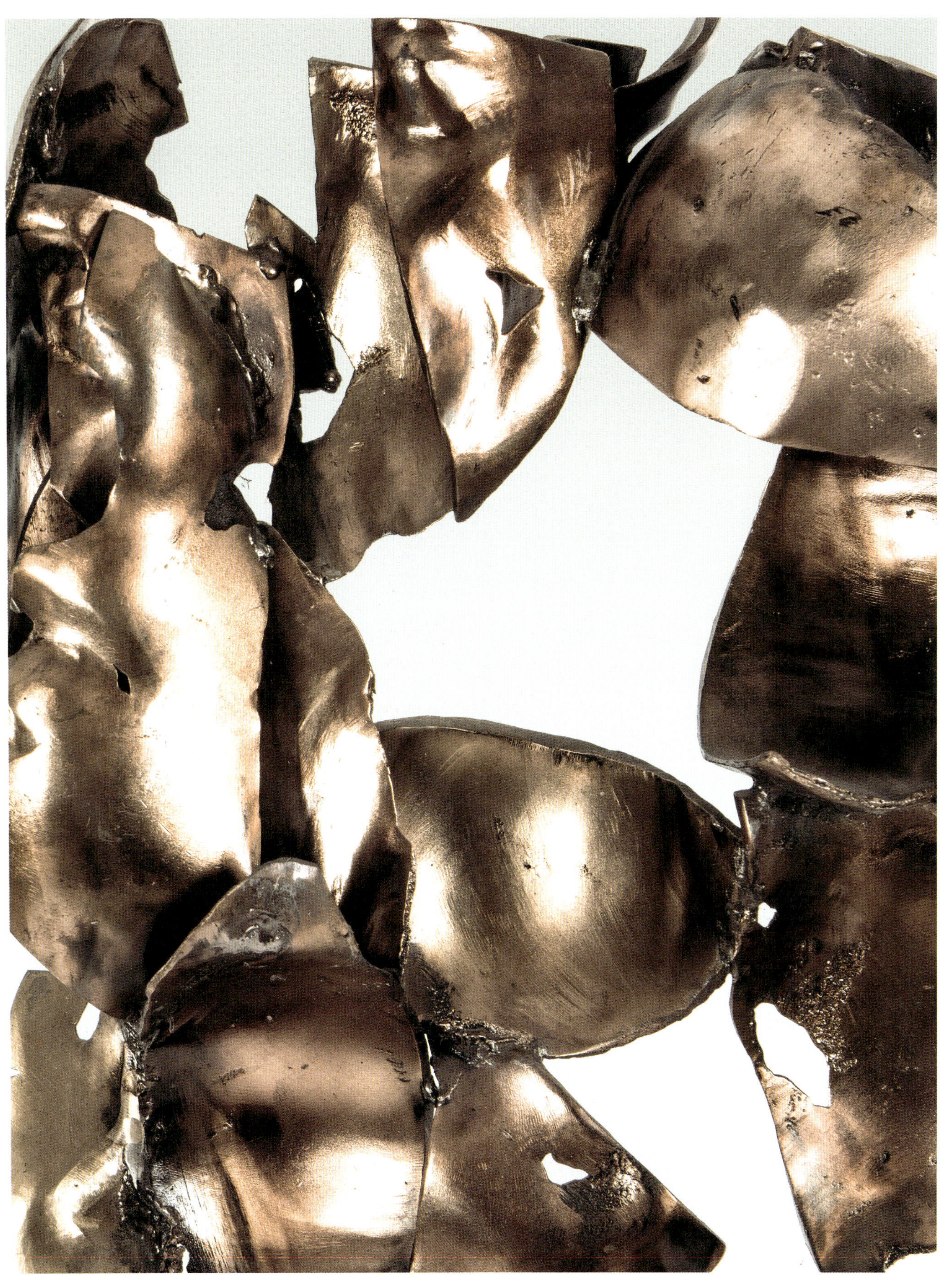

Loss of Face, 2017. Bronze. 91.4 × 43 × 17.7 cm. Photo by Humayun Memon

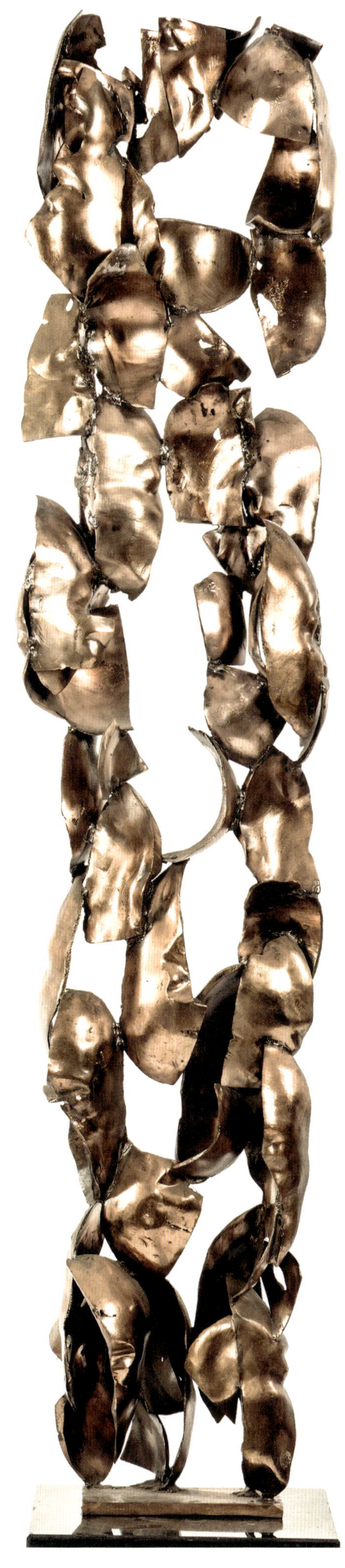

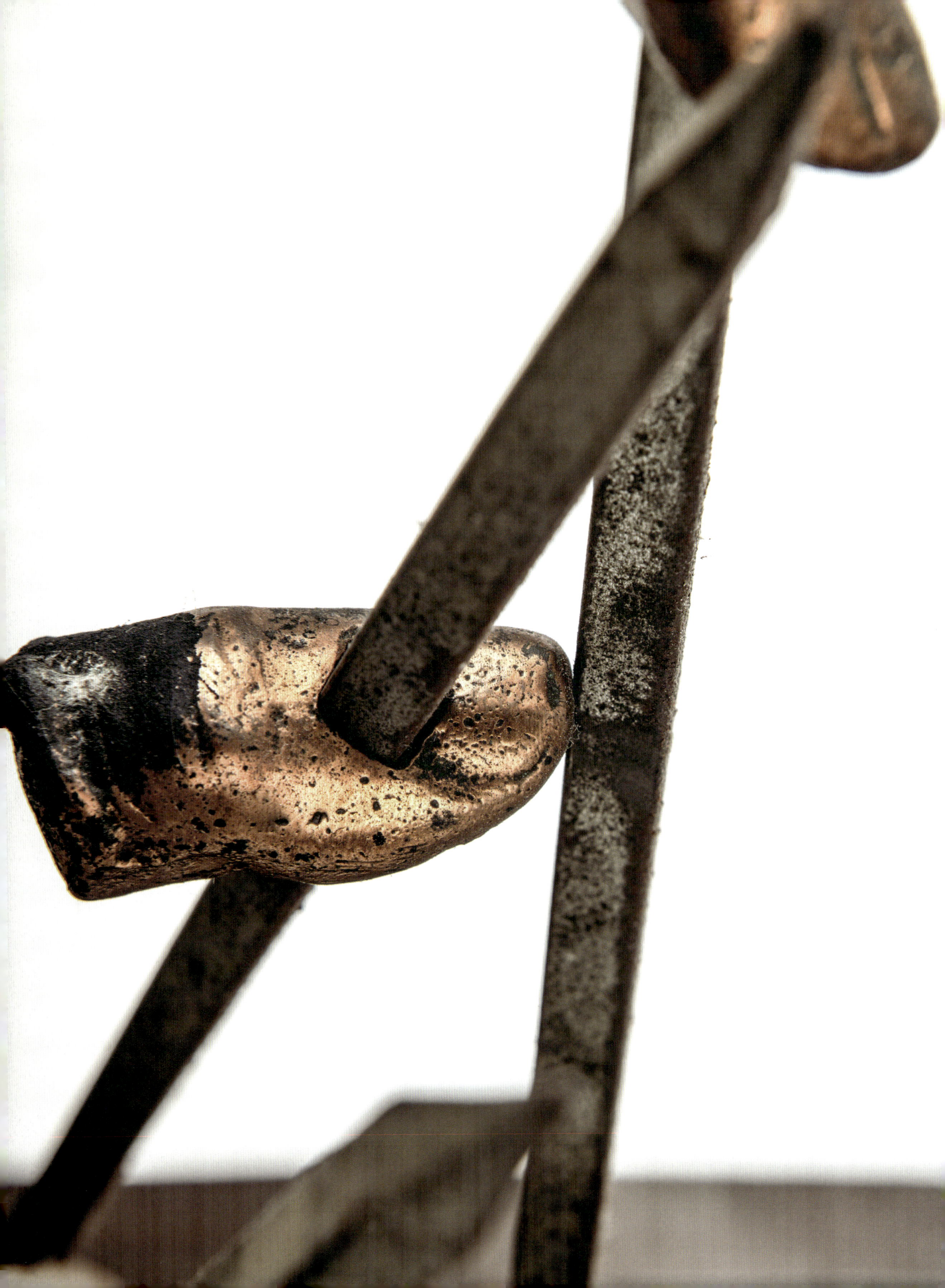

Other Works

1990 - 2019

Photo by Humayun Memon

Amin Gulgee Gallery Doors, 2000. Copper, bronze, glass and computer motherboards.
234 × 112 × 28 cm. Photo by Humayun Memon

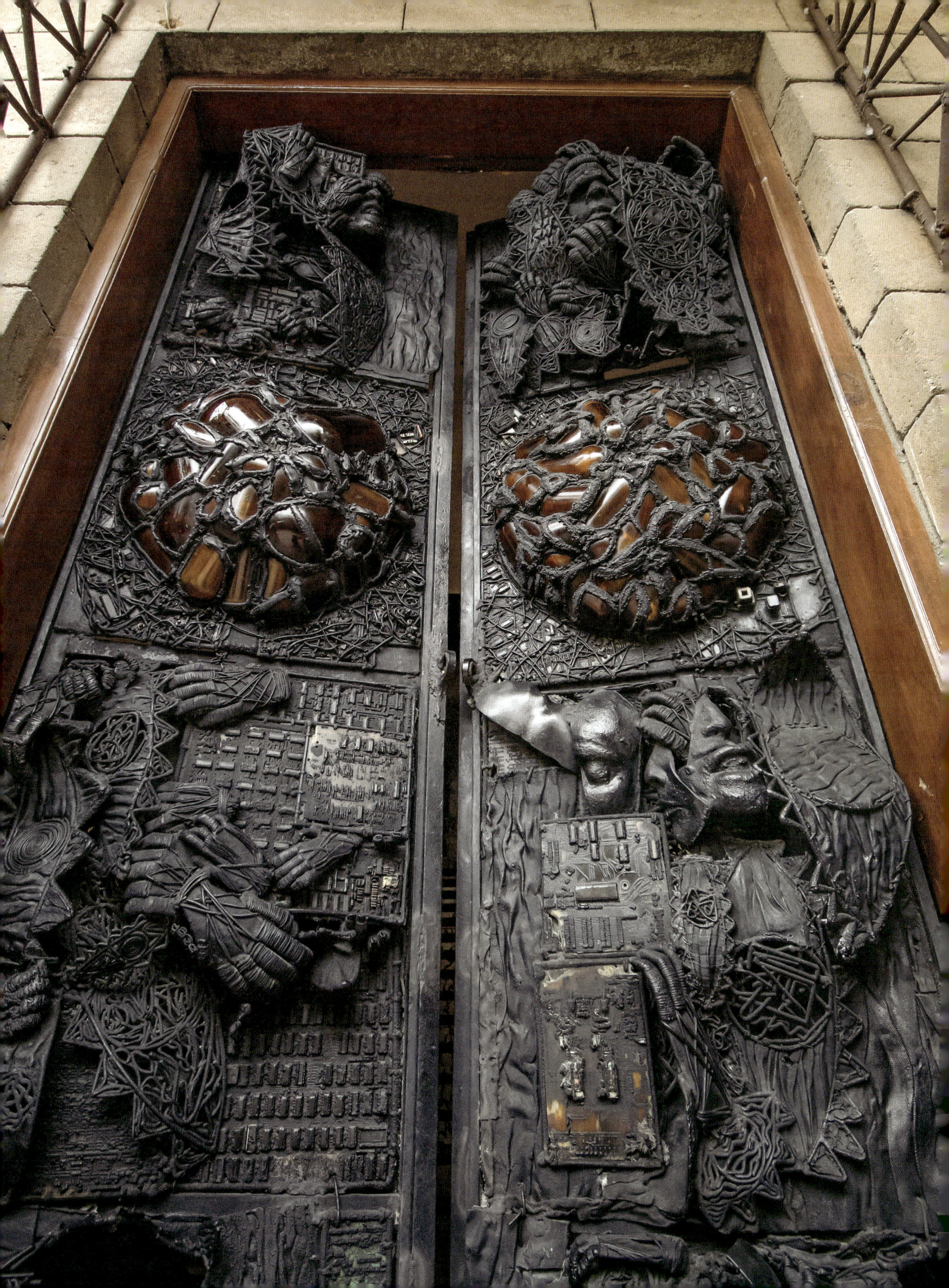

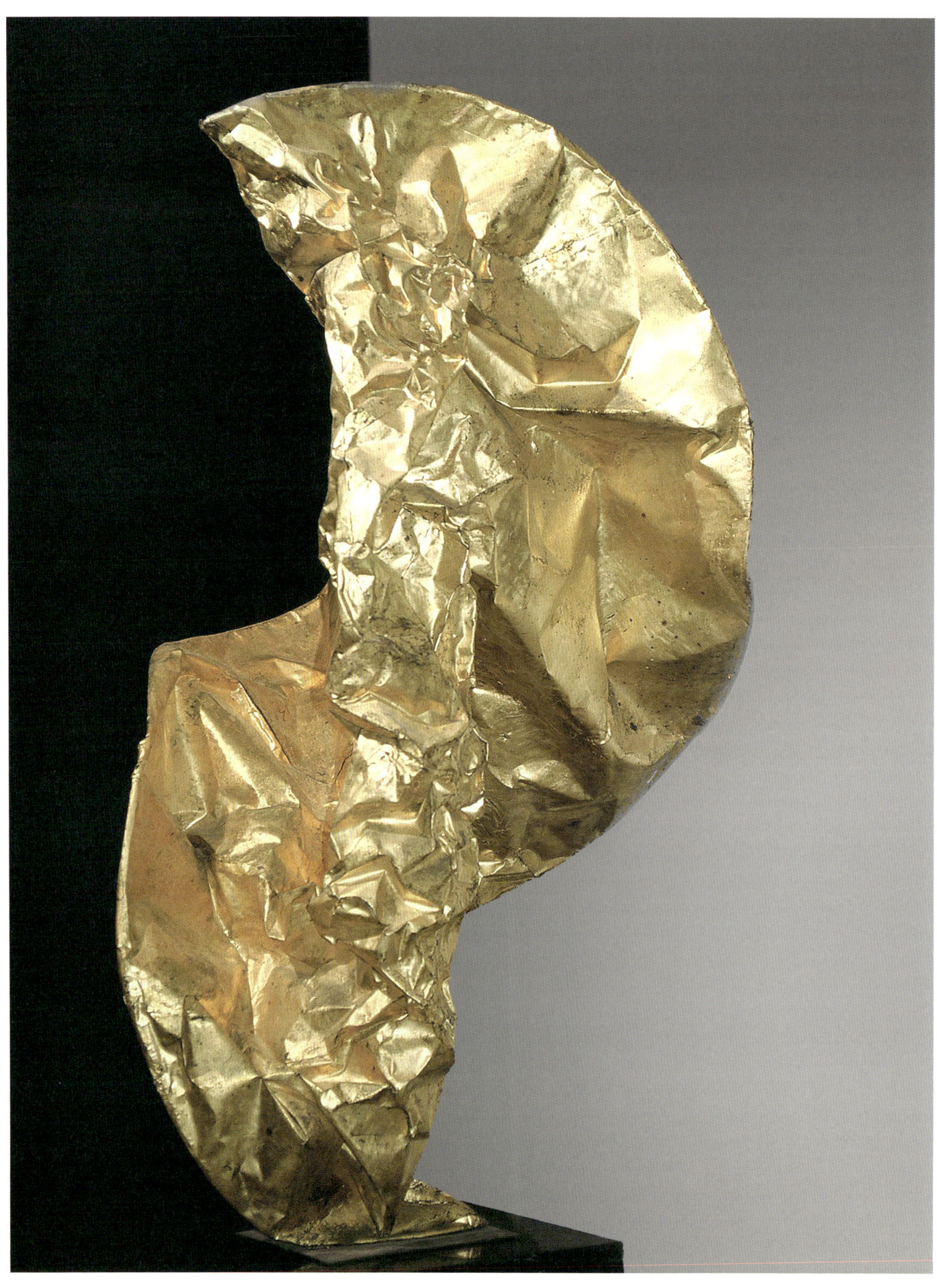

Crashed Sun, 2000. Copper and gold leaf. 203 × 10 × 124.5 cm. Photo by Nafees

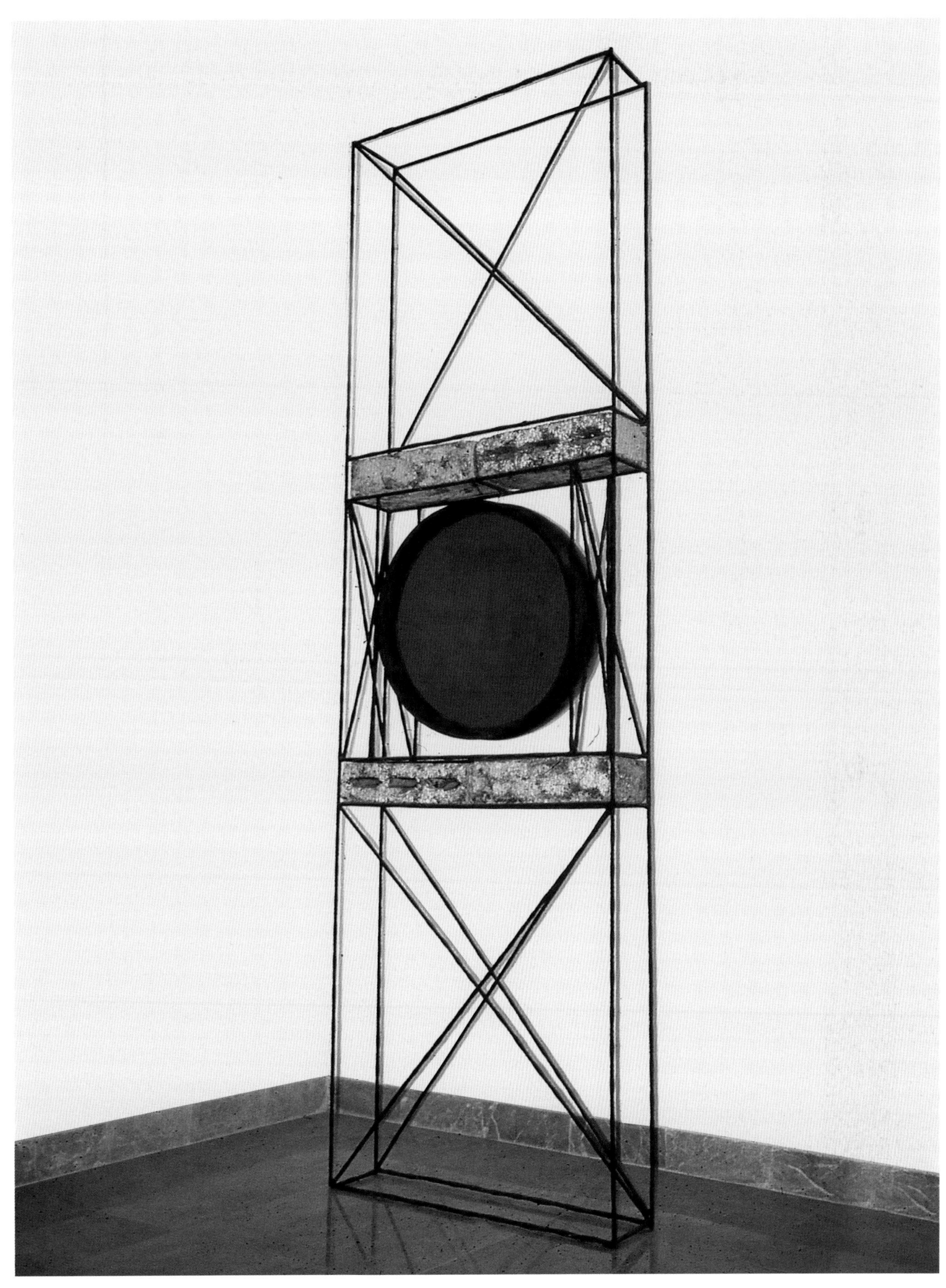

Construction, 2001. Iron, brick, silver leaf, cayenne pepper and found cauldron.
274.3 × 83.8 × 33 cm. Photo by Nafees

Afghan Tikka II, 2003. Copper, bronze and iron skewers. 114.3 × 45.7 × 27.9 cm.
Photo by Humayun Memon

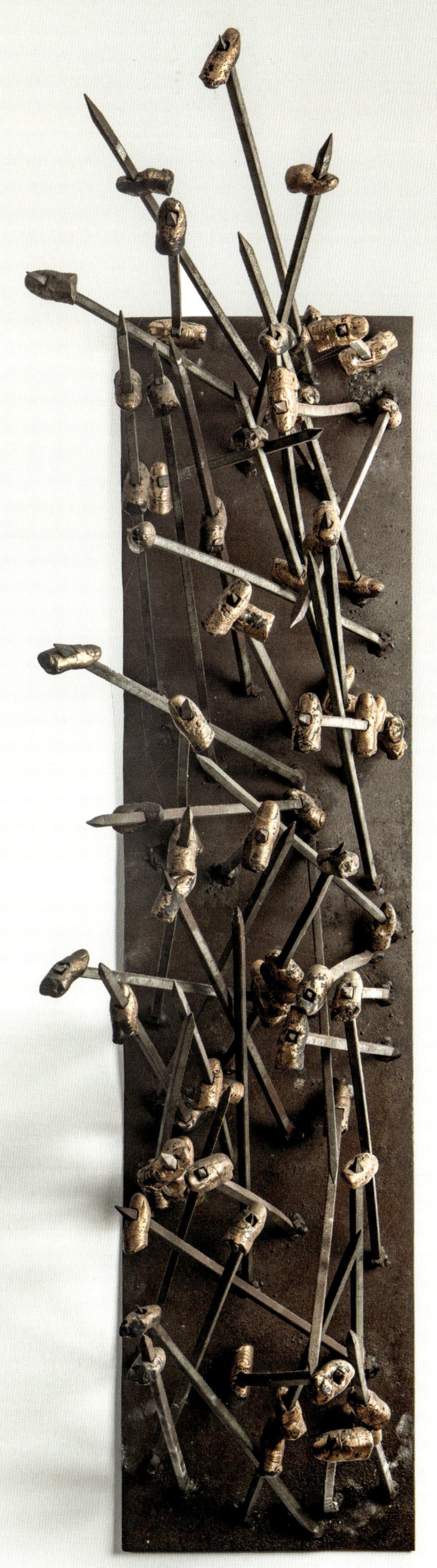

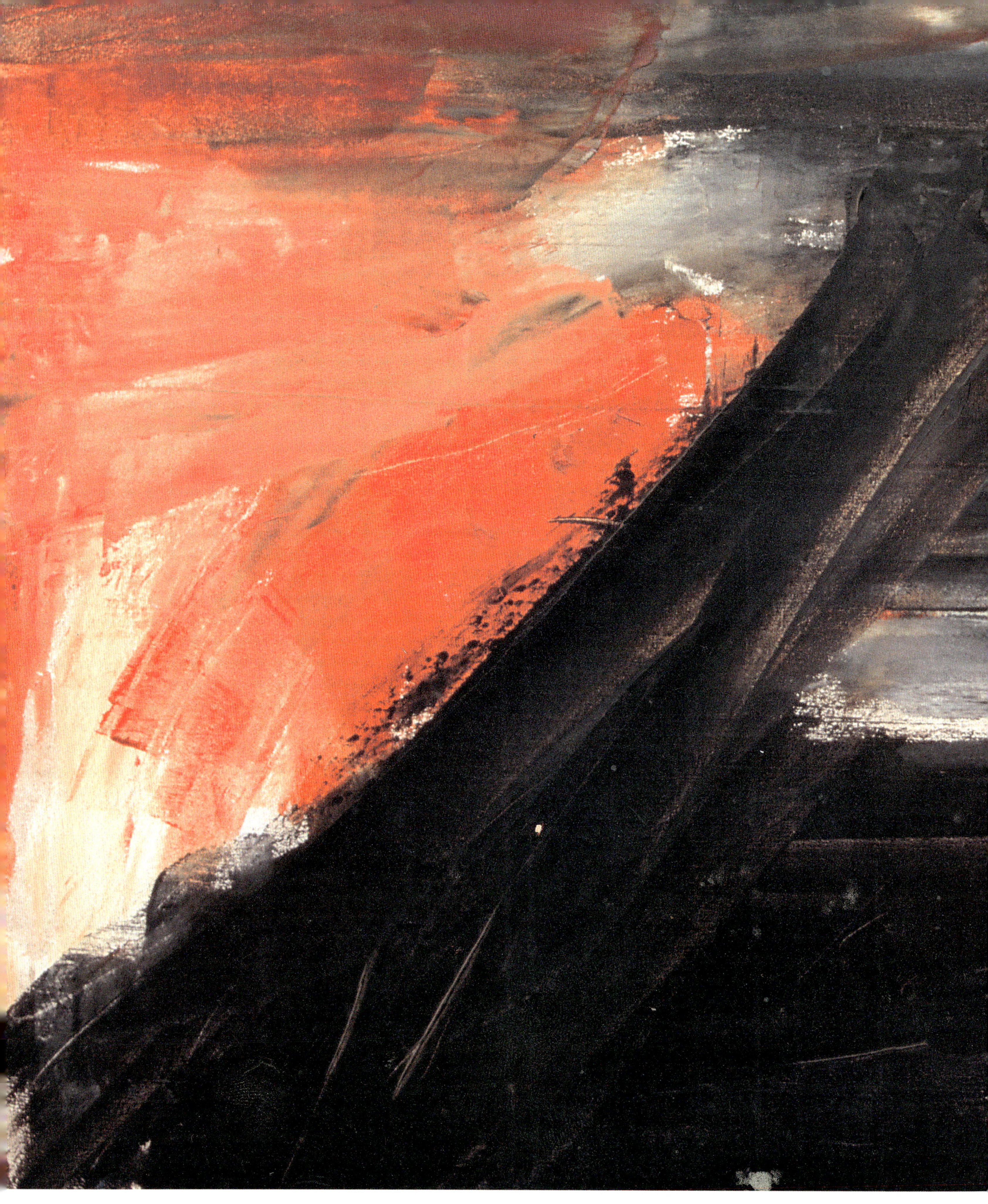

The Mountain, 2004. Oil on canvas. 91.4 × 122 cm. Photo by Shamyl Khuhro

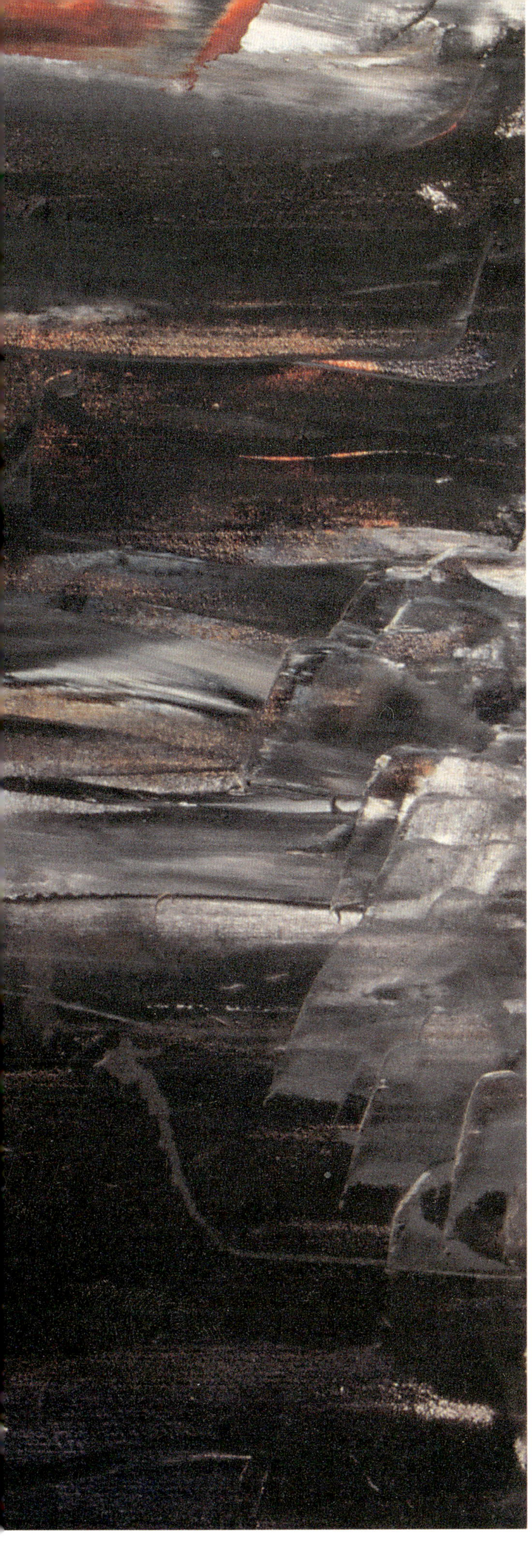

Forest Walk, 2004. Oil on canvas and silver leaf. 122 × 61 cm. Photo by Shamyl Khuhro

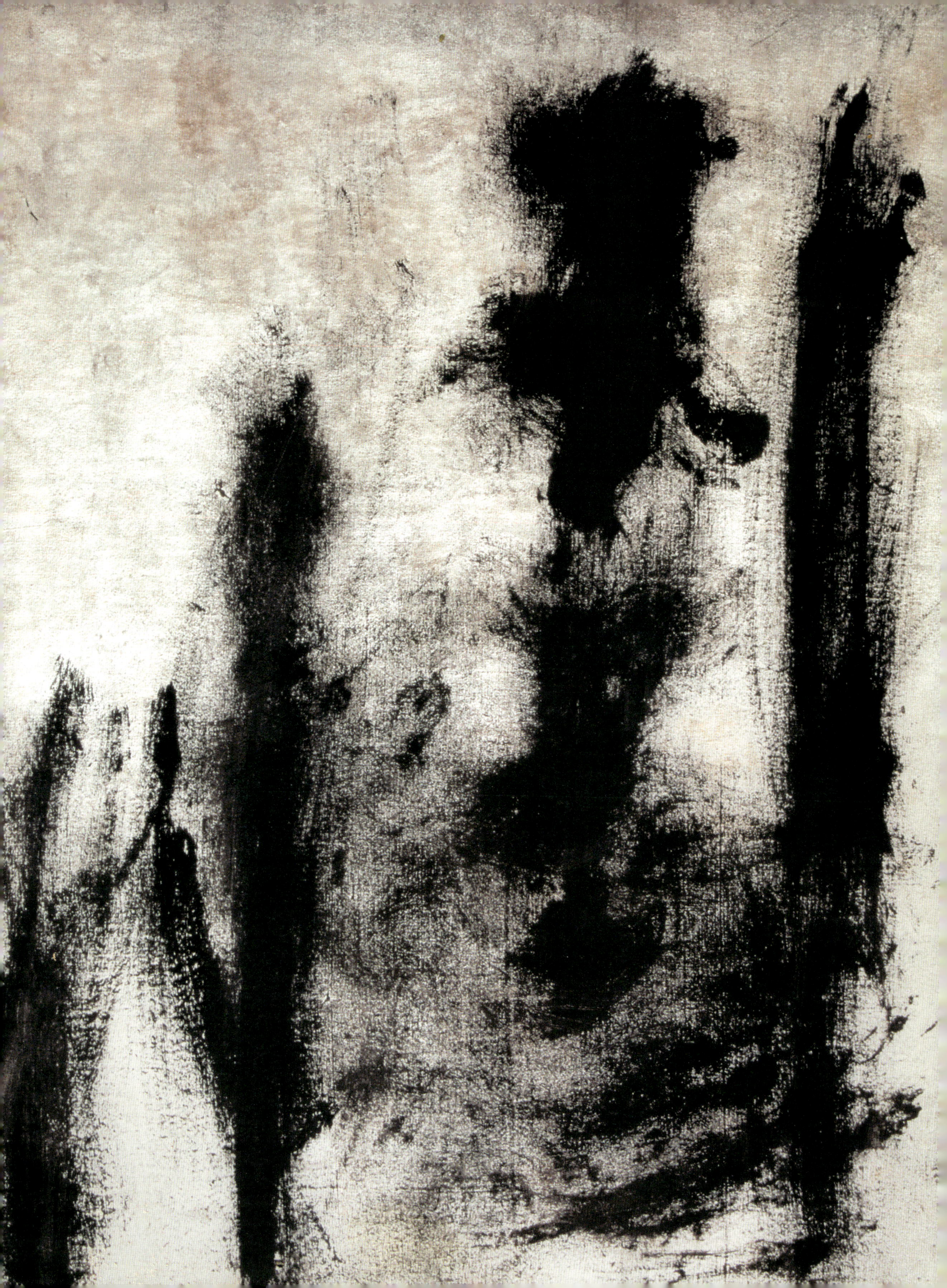

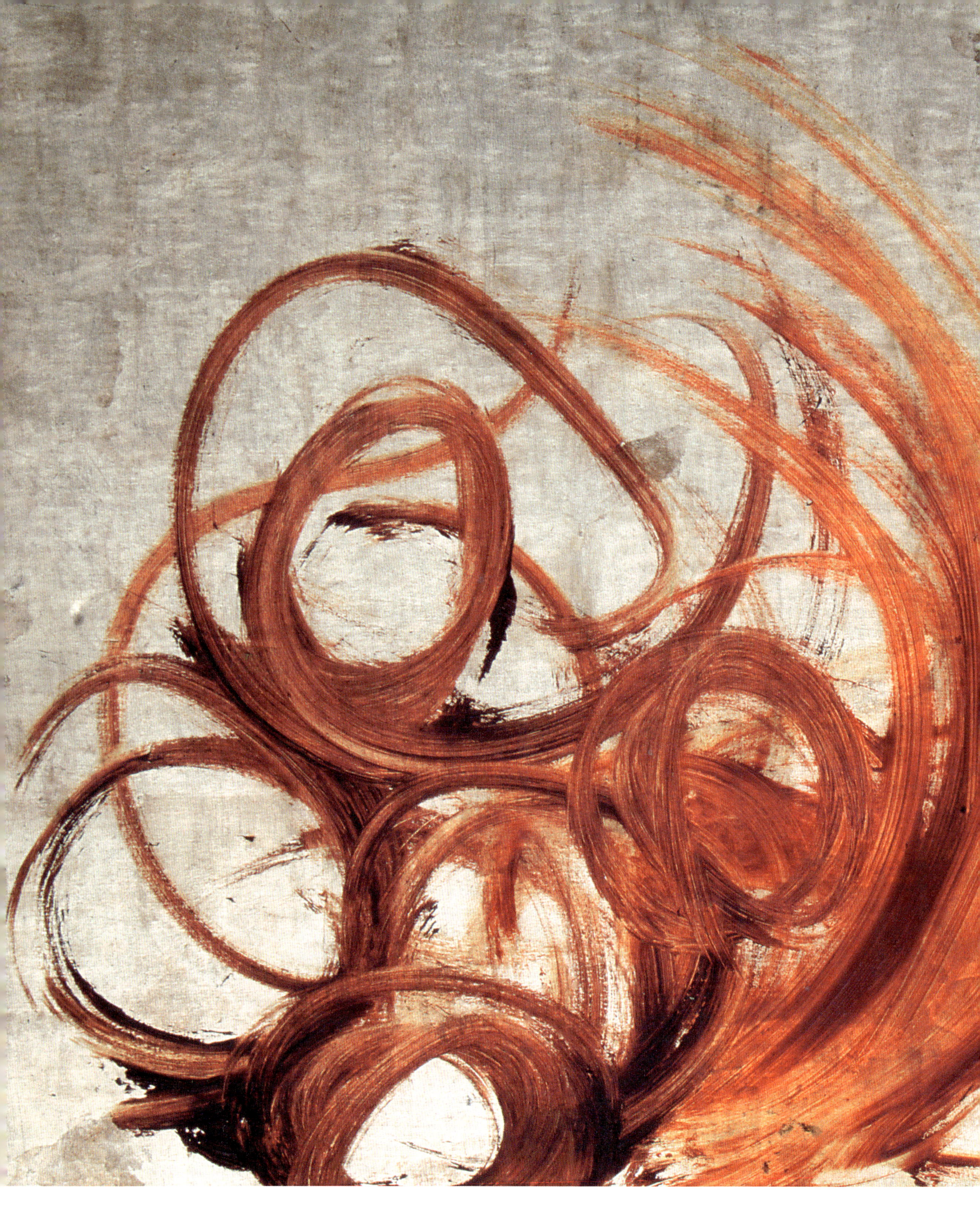

I Wish I Was a Fish, 2004. Oil on canvas and silver leaf. 91.4 × 152.4 cm. Photo by Shamyl Khuhro

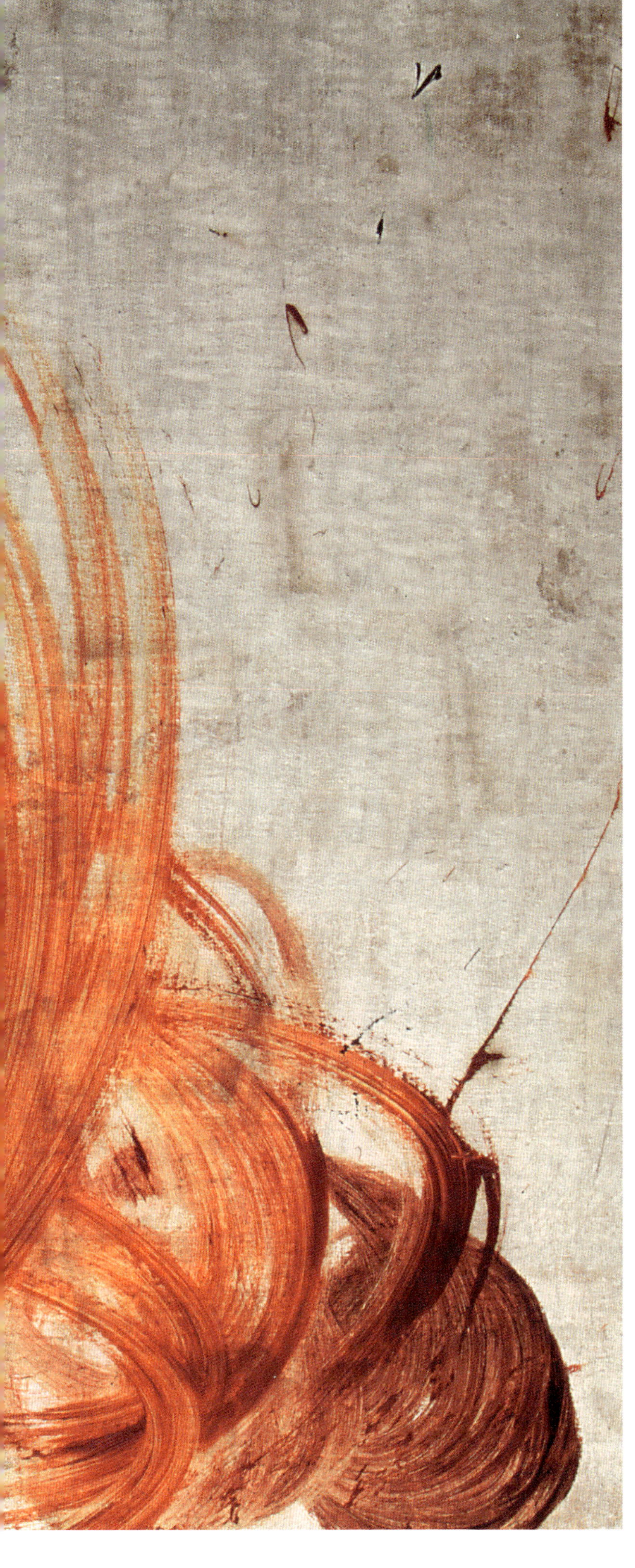

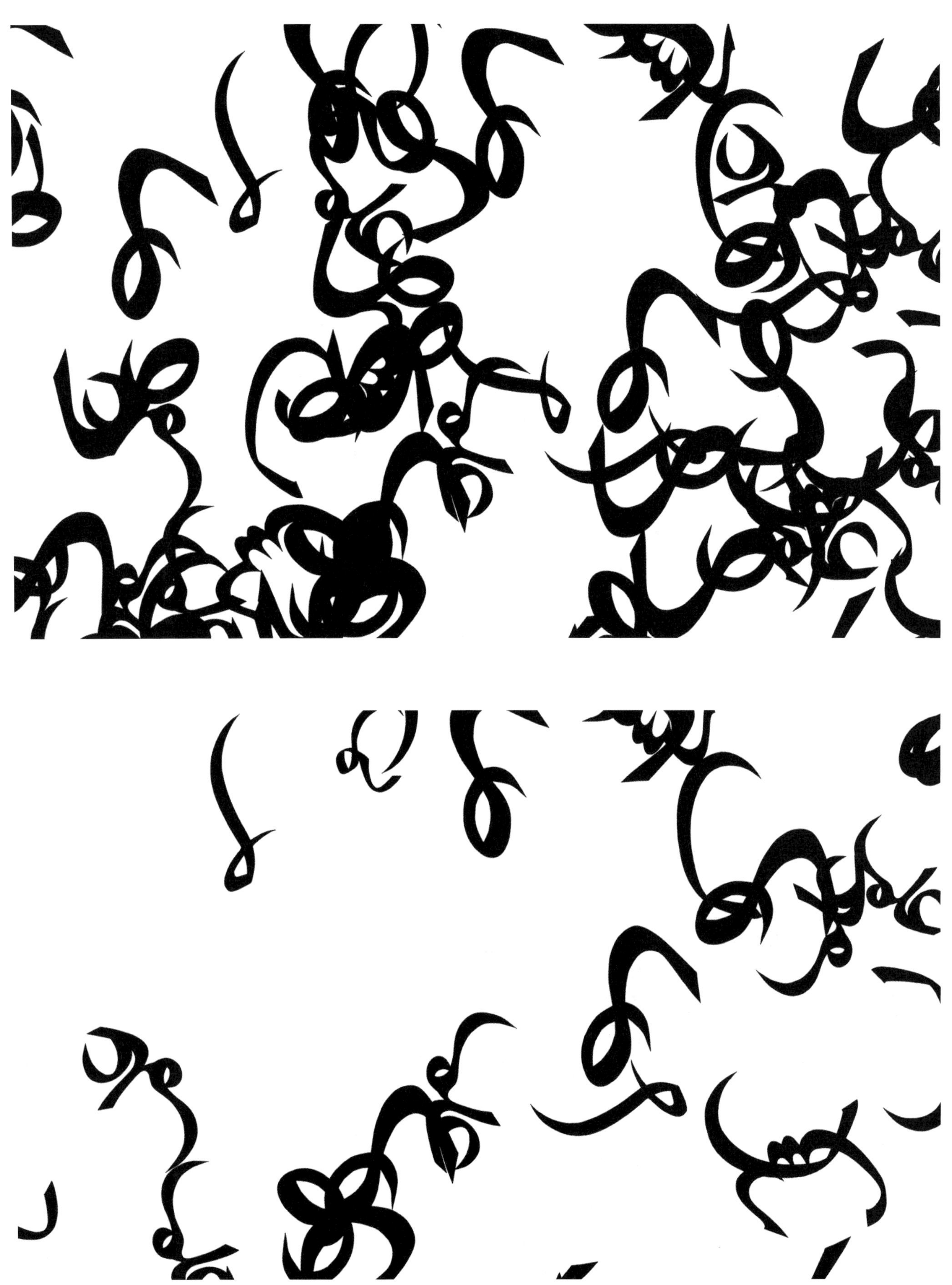

Algorythm VII, 2018. Computer-generated program/stimulation. Infinite. Stills courtesy Amin Gulgee

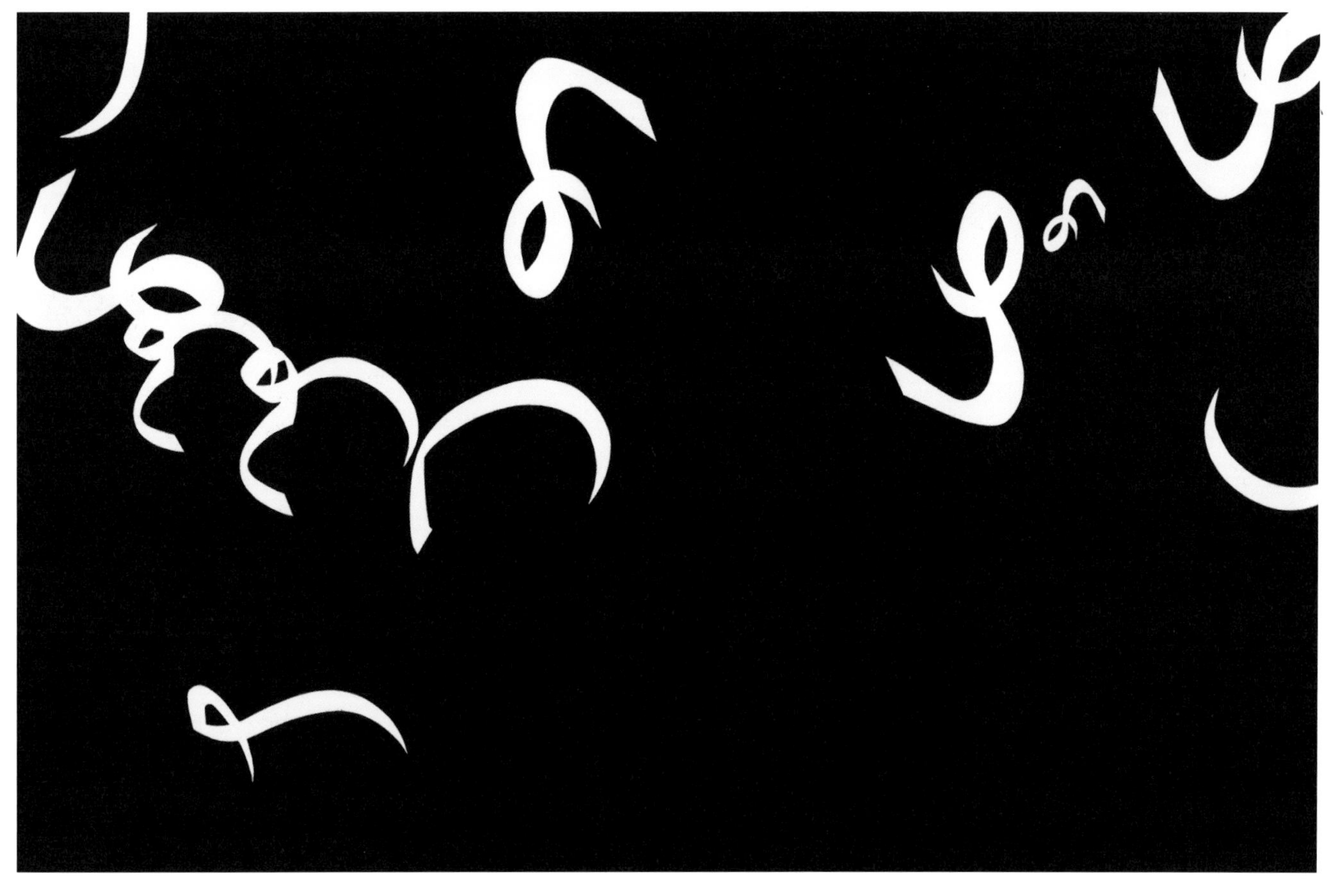

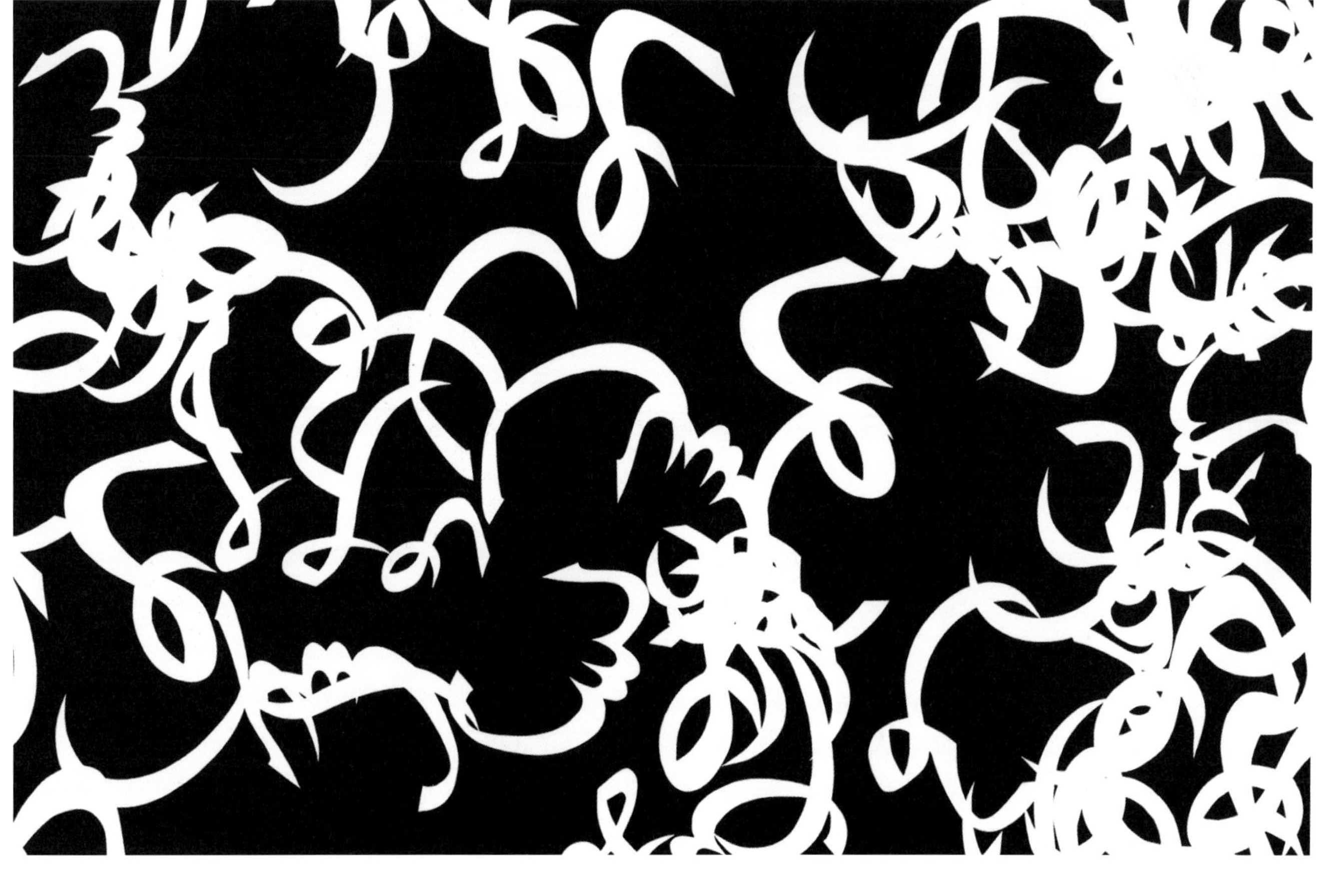

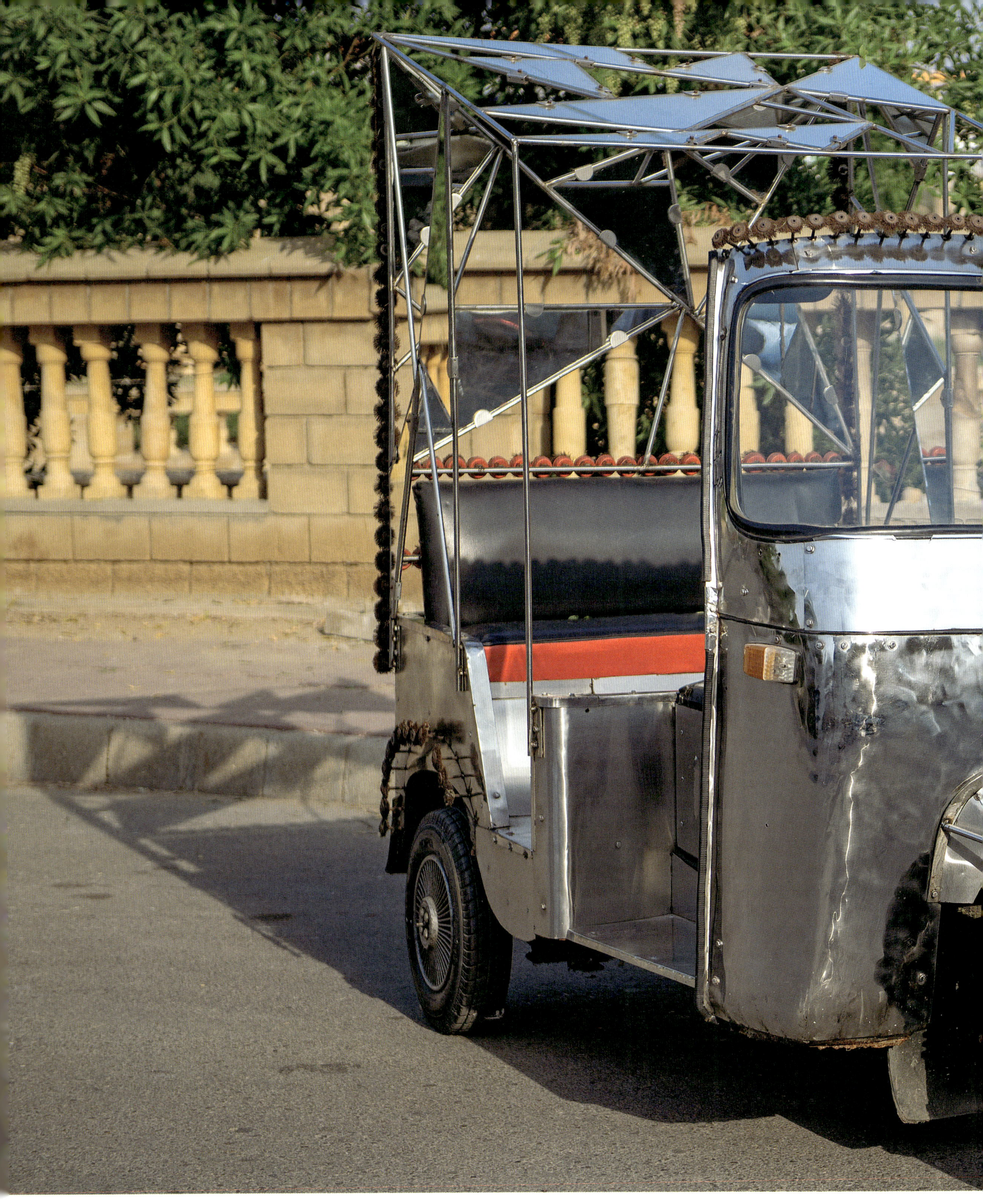

The Quantum Rickshaw, 2019. Copper, steel, mirror, rickshaw and wire buff. 218.4 × 266.7 × 132 cm. Photo by Humayun Memon

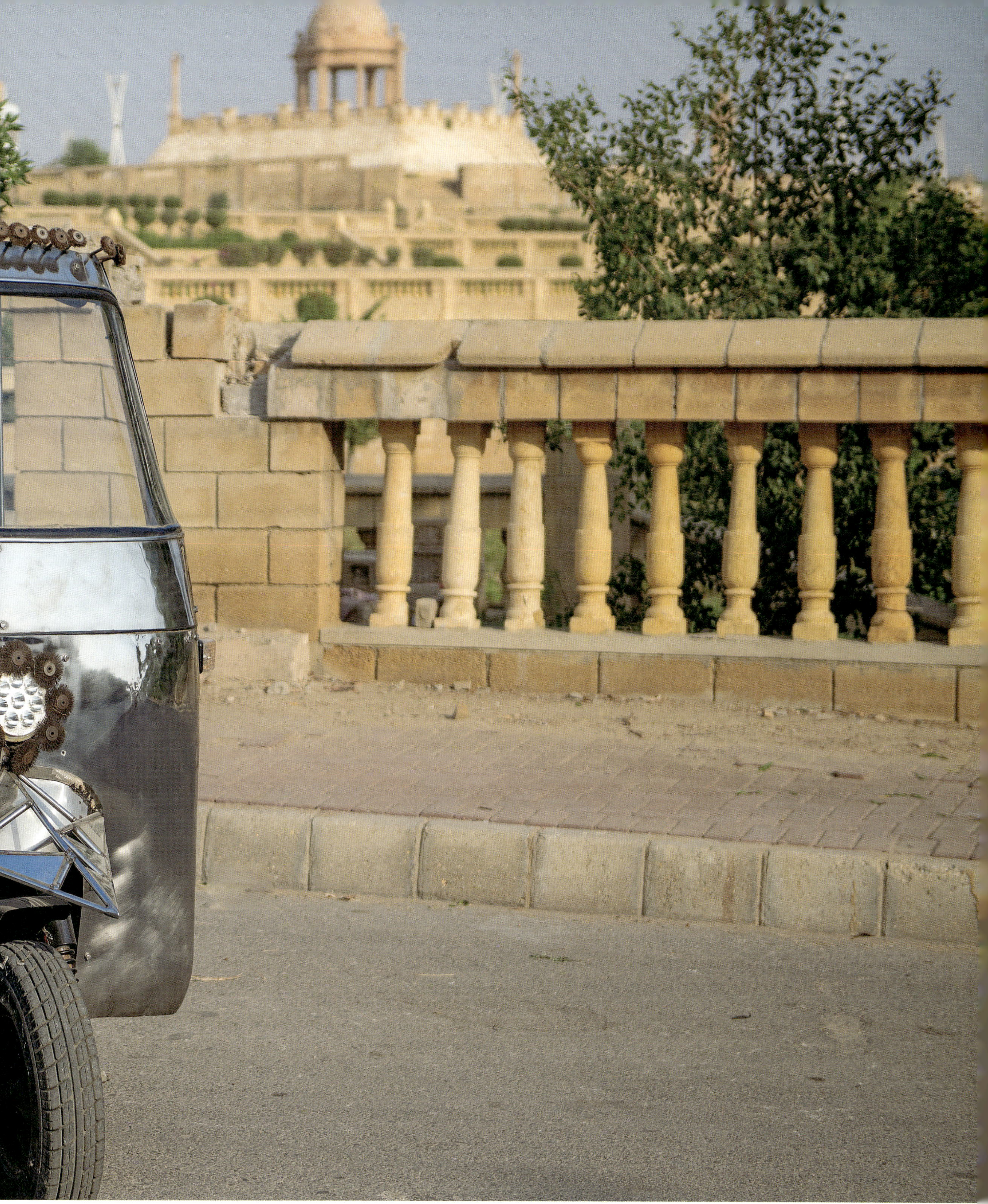

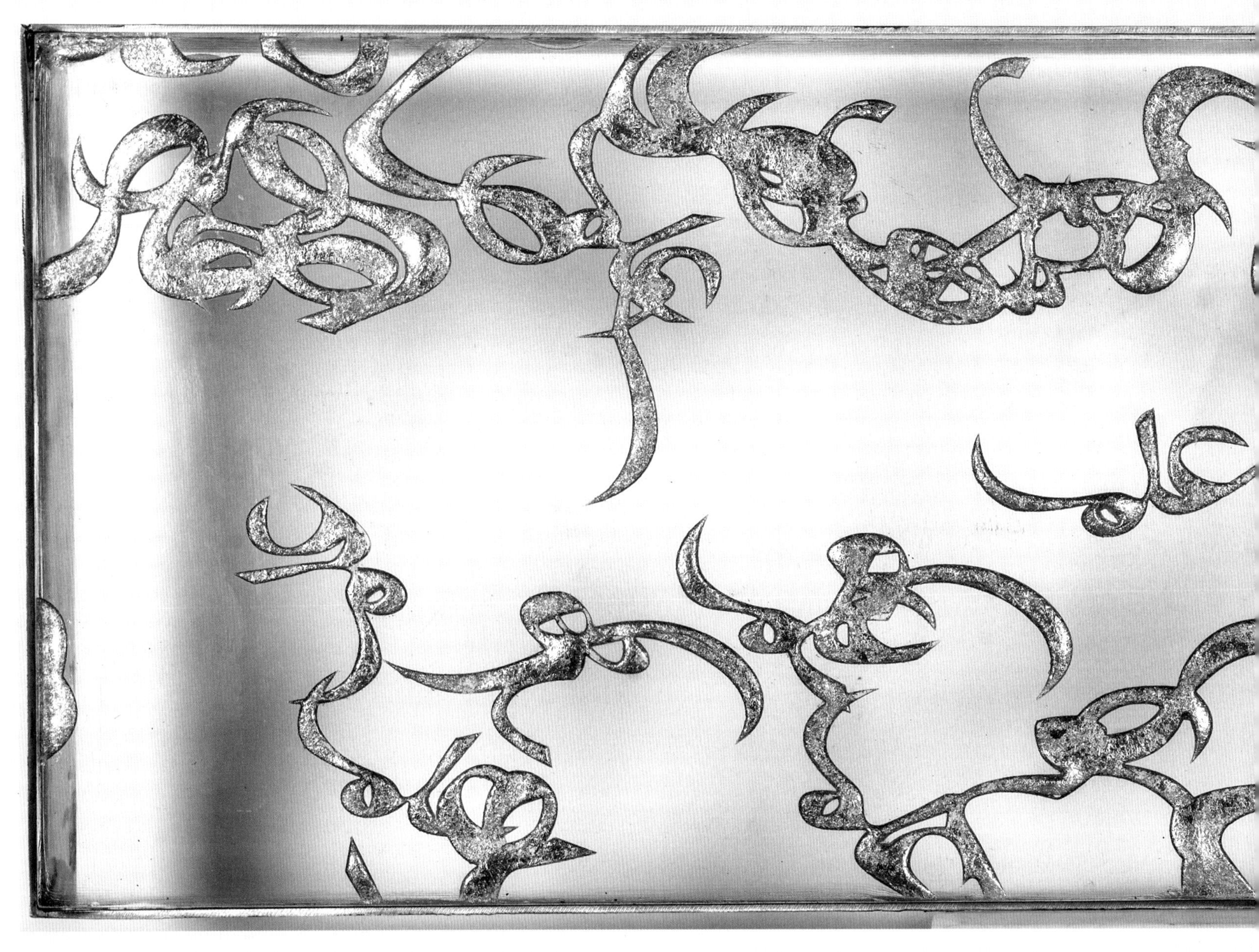

Shadow Letters II, 2023. Steel, glass and silver leaf. 91.4 × 30.5 × 7.6 cm.
Photo by Humayun Memon

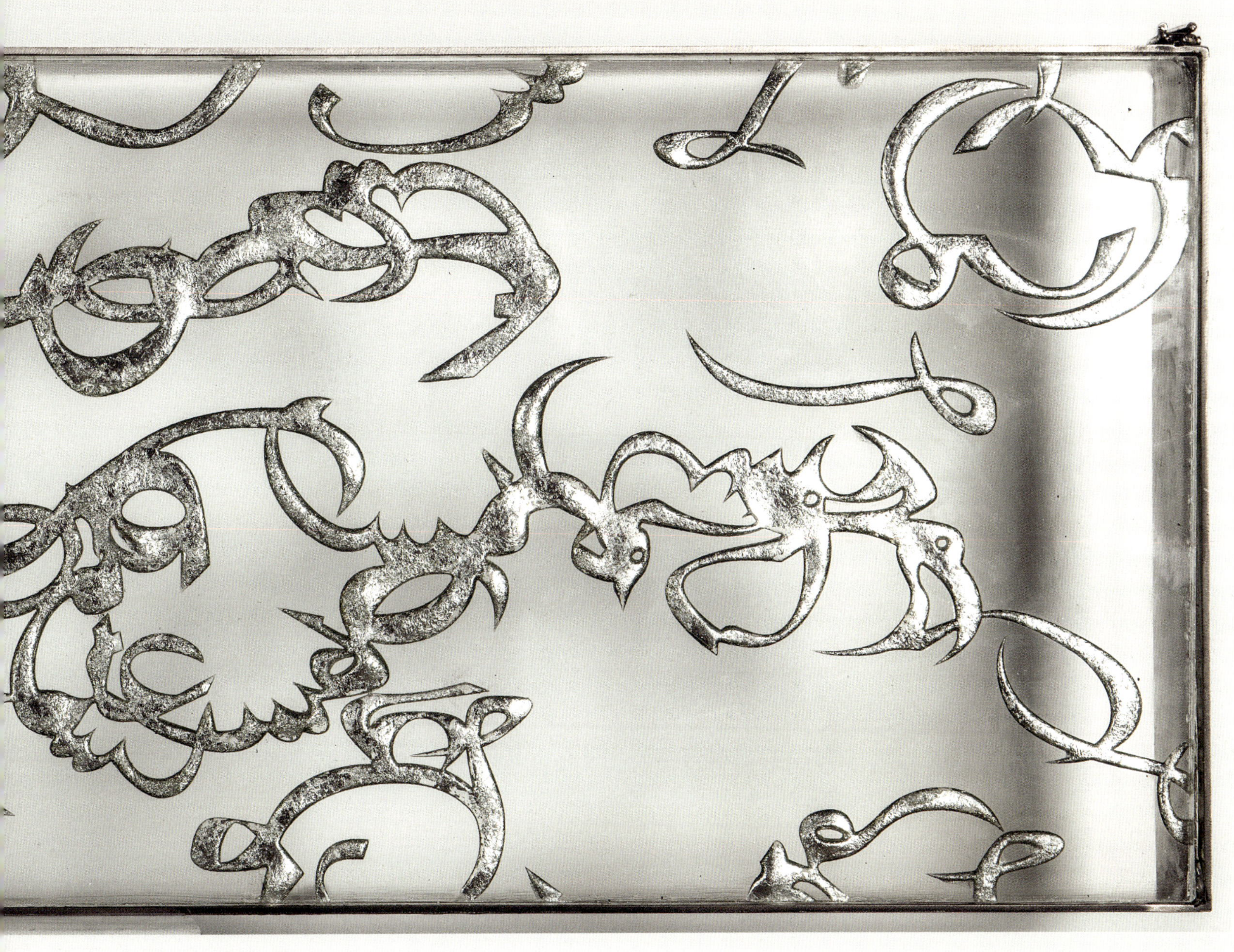

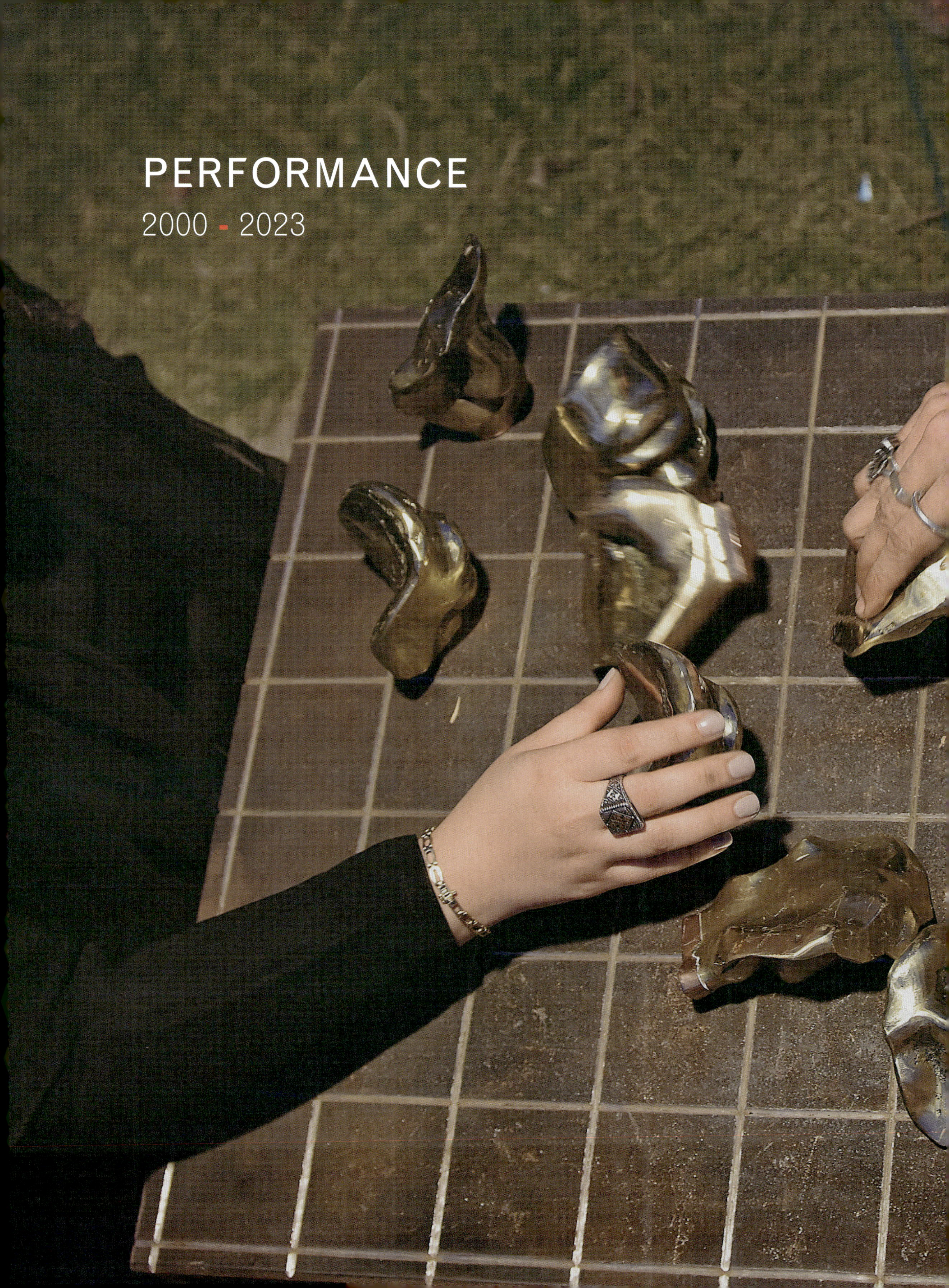

PERFORMANCE

2000 - 2023

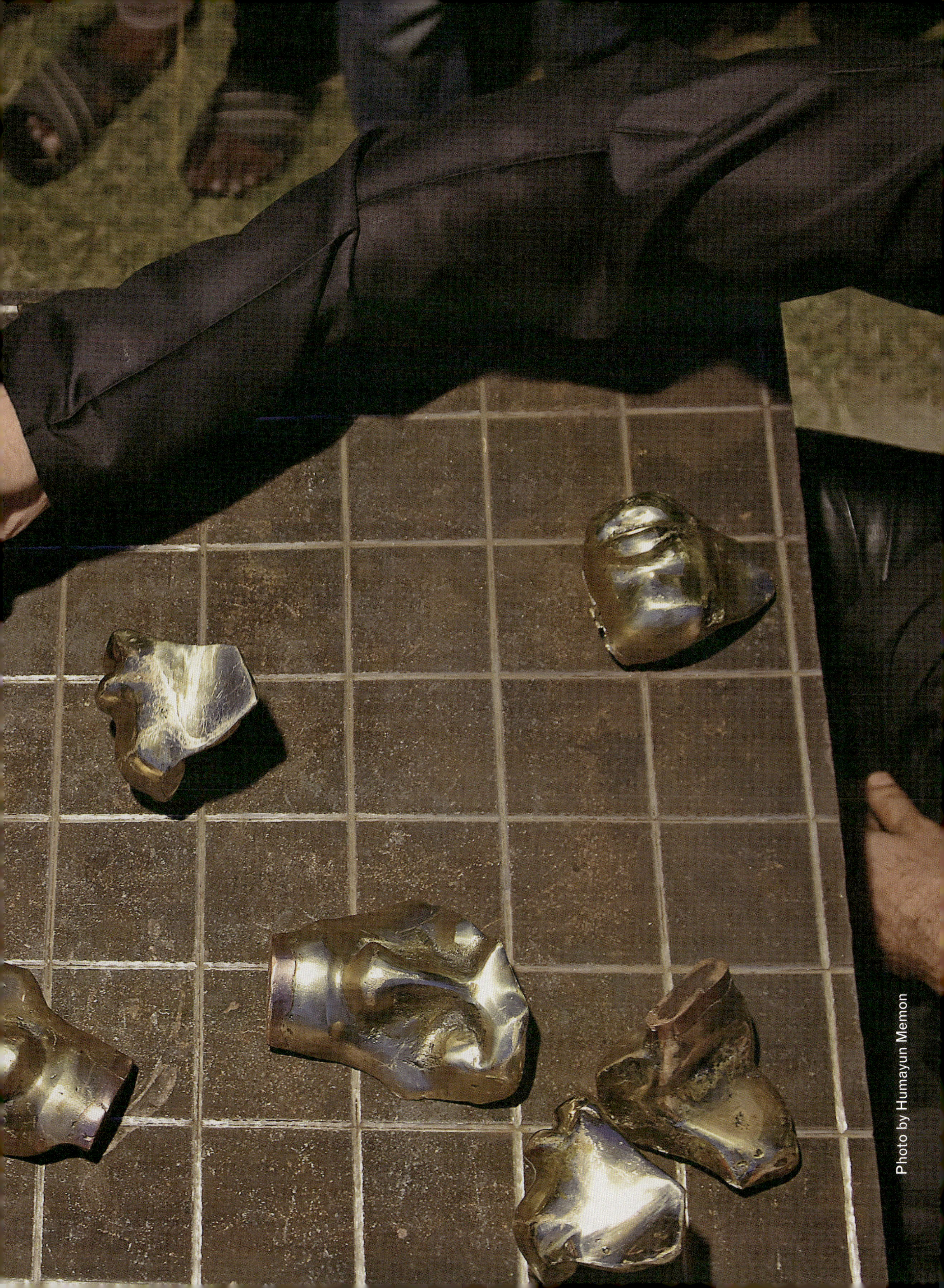
Photo by Humayun Memon

Alchemy | 2000

ArtFest, Sheraton Hotel, Karachi
47 minutes

Alchemy was a catwalk-based presentation of Amin Gulgee's jewelry and sculpture that took place at the former Karachi Sheraton Hotel and later at the Moghul-era Lahore Fort. Sonya Battla designed the clothes for the show; Pomme Amina Gohar was the producer; Ustaaz created the original music. *Alchemy* was divided into three sections: Bronze, Silver and Gold. Each was introduced by a performance work. In the first, Amin, covered in mud, appeared on the runway with a bronze, Janus-like mask hinged to his head as Shakila Khorasani sang a morning raga offstage. The artist briefly danced, released a powerful scream then ran backstage. In the second section, sculptor Syed Munawar Ali repeatedly fell on his face before somersaulting off the end of the catwalk. In the third, an architecture student strode down the runway with a large gold-plated copper disc strapped to his back, rattling it with outstretched arms. The three main parts of the show were no less performative. In Bronze, female fashion models carried or wore copper sculptural pieces that Amin had created. These objects appeared organic, almost soft. In Silver, the women were dressed in his copper bustiers and other geometric objects plated in nickel, all of which had a cold, linear feel. In Gold, they were adorned with Amin's gold-plated copper jewelry including his bold, unconventional earrings, pendants and necklaces. *Alchemy* was ostensibly a fashion show, but was much more than that. Amin's engagement with art jewelry, and the rebellious fashion scene of the time, took advantage of the heady atmosphere of the 1990s when democracy had been restored in Pakistan after a decade of religiously conservative military rule. Creatives in various fields pushed the envelope to test boundaries. *Alchemy* was not only a testament to Amin's generation's aspirations, but sowed the seeds for what would prove to be his deepening engagement with performance art.

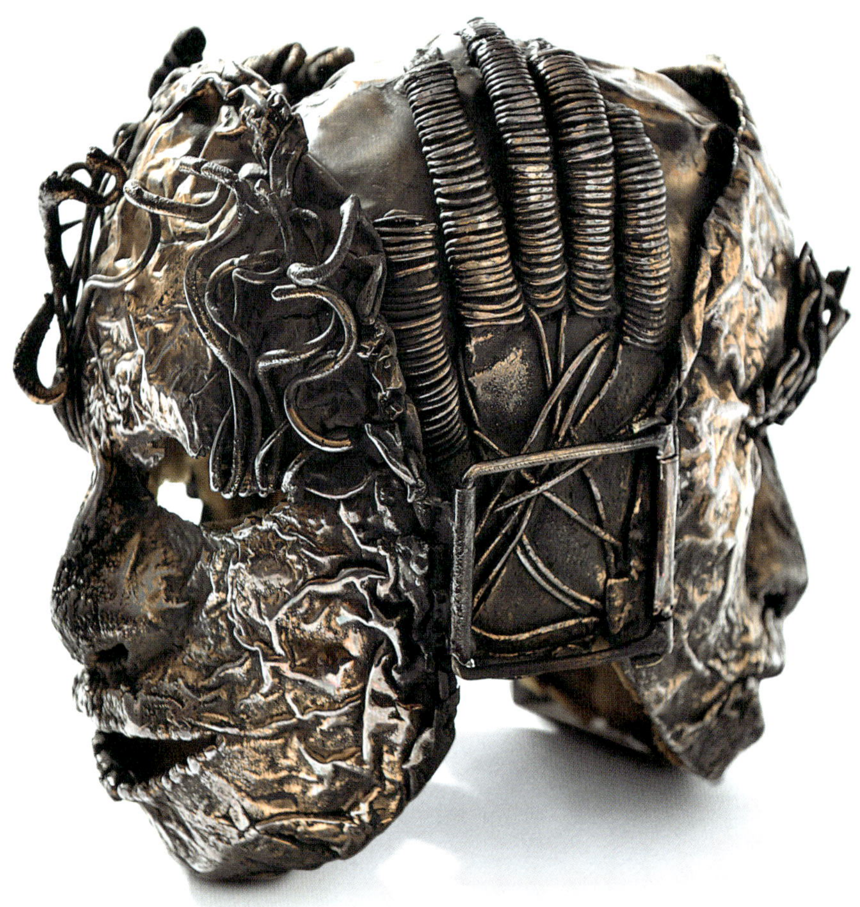

The Copper Mask, 2000. Copper. 25.4 × 20.3 × 28 cm. Photo by Humayun Memon

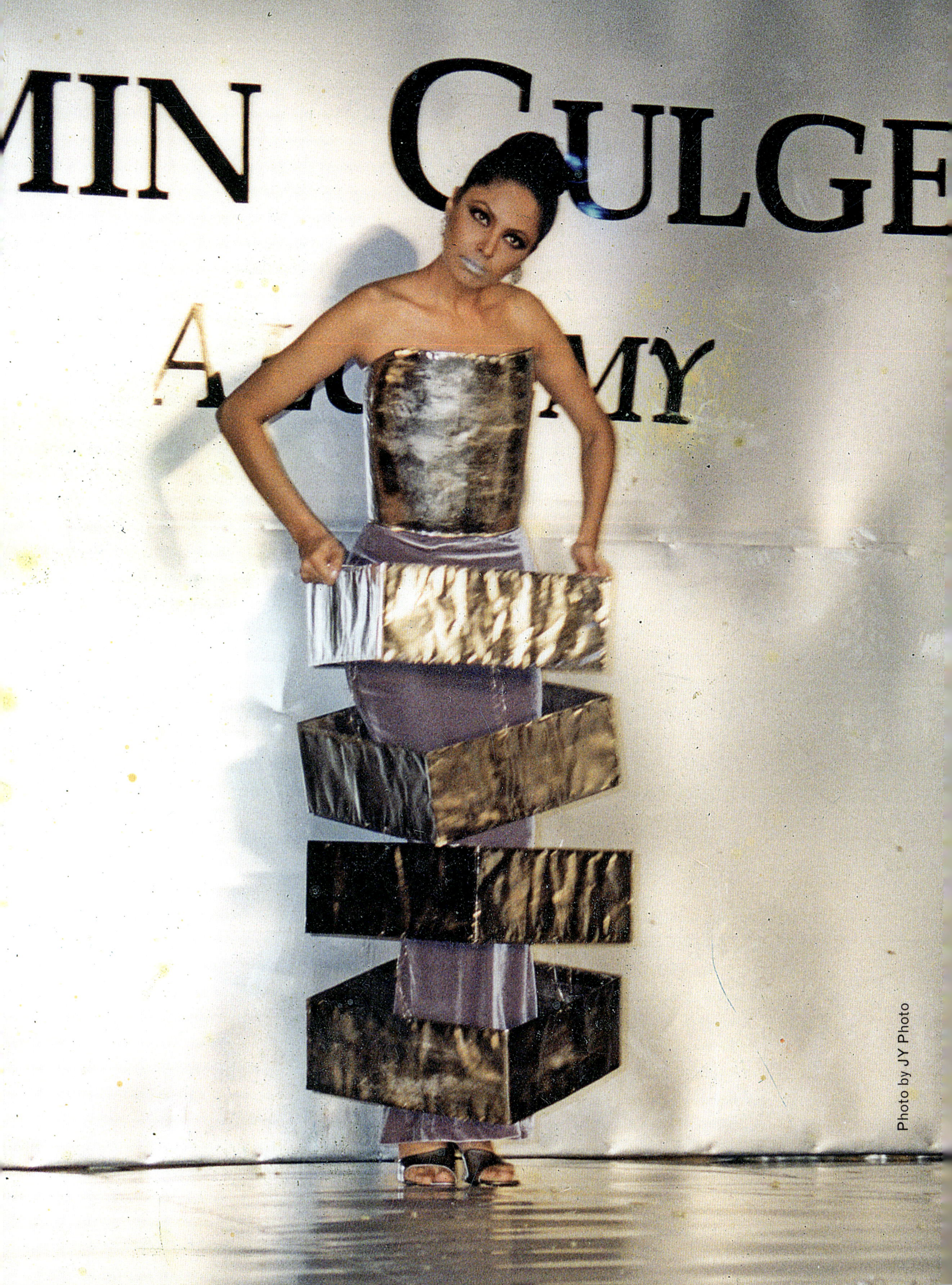

Photo by JY Photo

Calculate | 2004

Other Works, Canvas Gallery, Karachi
180 minutes

Amin Gulgee's performance *Calculate* was his first to take place in a gallery rather than on the catwalk. It was also the first—and only—time he showed his oil paintings. The performance, and paintings, were integrated into his solo exhibition of sculpture and installation, *Other Works*, at Canvas Gallery in Karachi, which featured dolls' heads cast in bronze, many of which appeared pocked, torn or burnt. The exhibit, which opened soon after the American invasion of Iraq, seemed to capture the foreboding climate of the times. The heads Amin cast were from toys he had discovered at Disposal House, a dusty, cluttered store of bric-a-brac in Saddar, a colonial-era Karachi bazaar. He wished the viewer to be disoriented, even alarmed, by the show, which had an apocalyptic feel. In the driveway, a coughing rickshaw whose body he had refashioned in copper drove back and forth, spitting fumes. Inside the gallery, a discordant sound piece the artist had asked Mehdi Rizvi to compose played at full volume as lights blindingly flashed. Amid this cacophonous chaos, the sculptor Seema Nusrat, who had just finished art school, systematically flung the found dolls' heads across a 213-cm, horizontal abacus with five rungs that Amin had fashioned out of steel. Stylist Tariq Amin had painted her face in exaggerated makeup so that she, too, resembled a macabre plaything. Positioned behind Seema was a large, curved board painted in dark gray. Stenciled upon it, in silverleaf letters from a font borrowed from *Dawn*, Pakistan's leading English daily, was the word "Calculate," suggesting a timely headline. As Seema tossed the dolls' heads back and forth with increasing abandon, some shattered as they hit their mark, an unexpected yet disturbingly inevitable consequence of her actions.

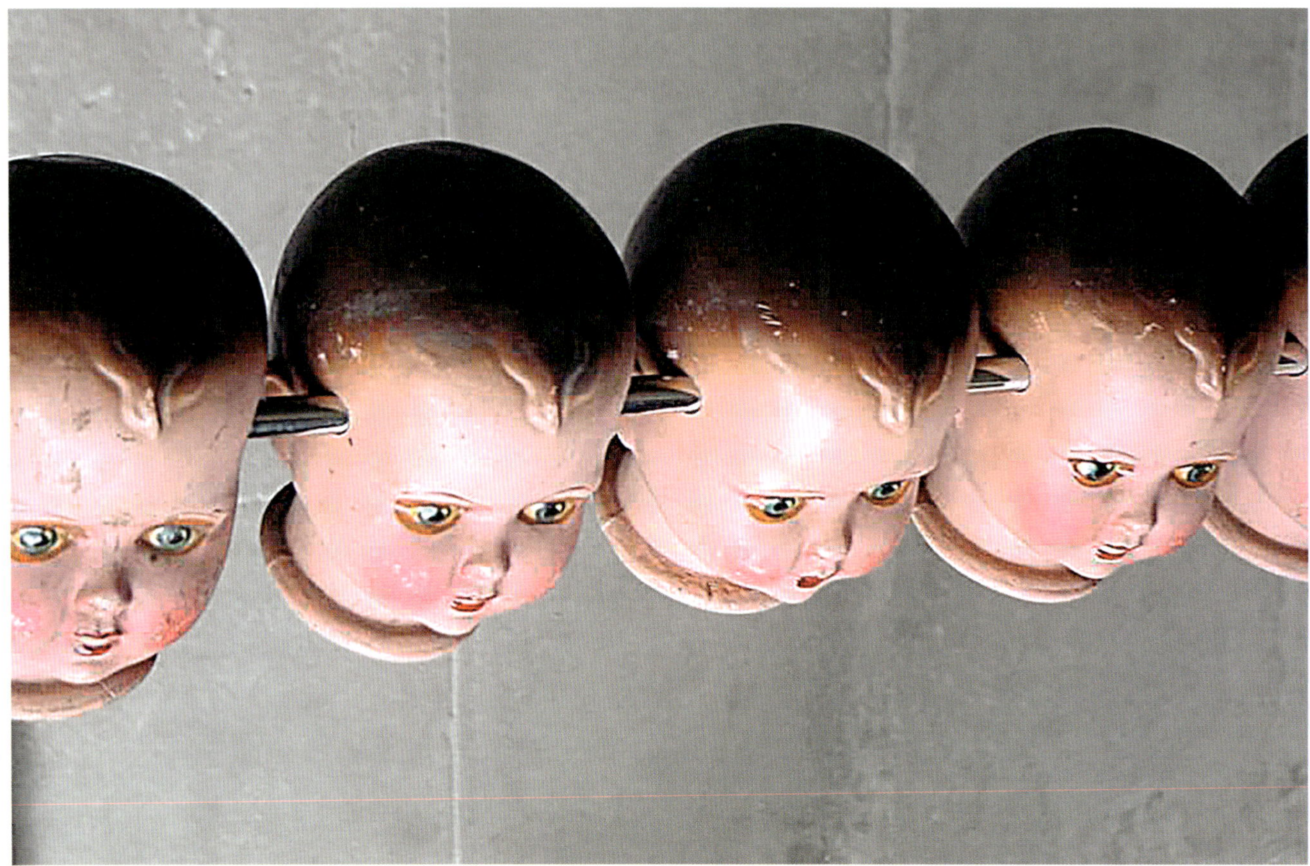

Photos by Auj Khan

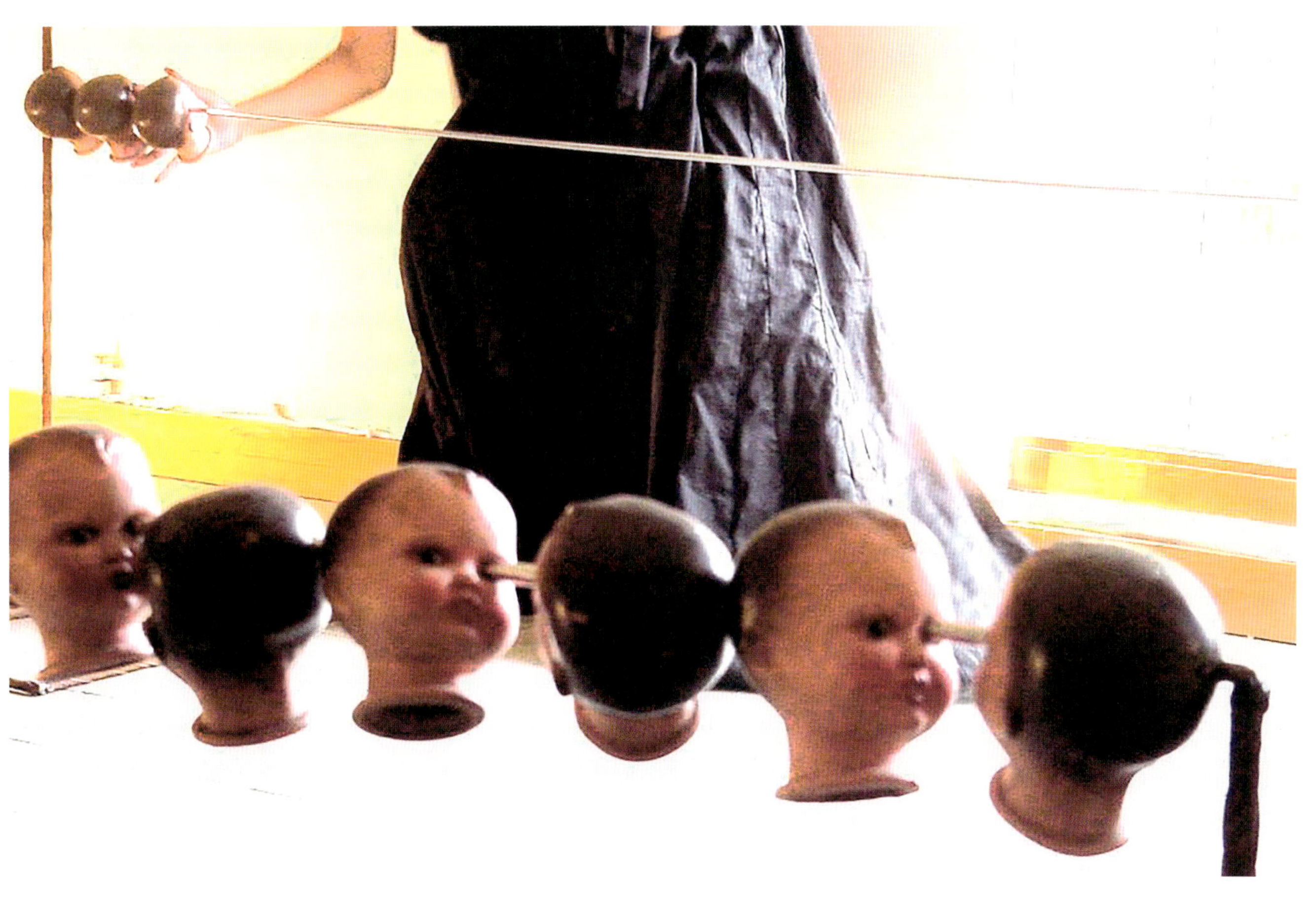

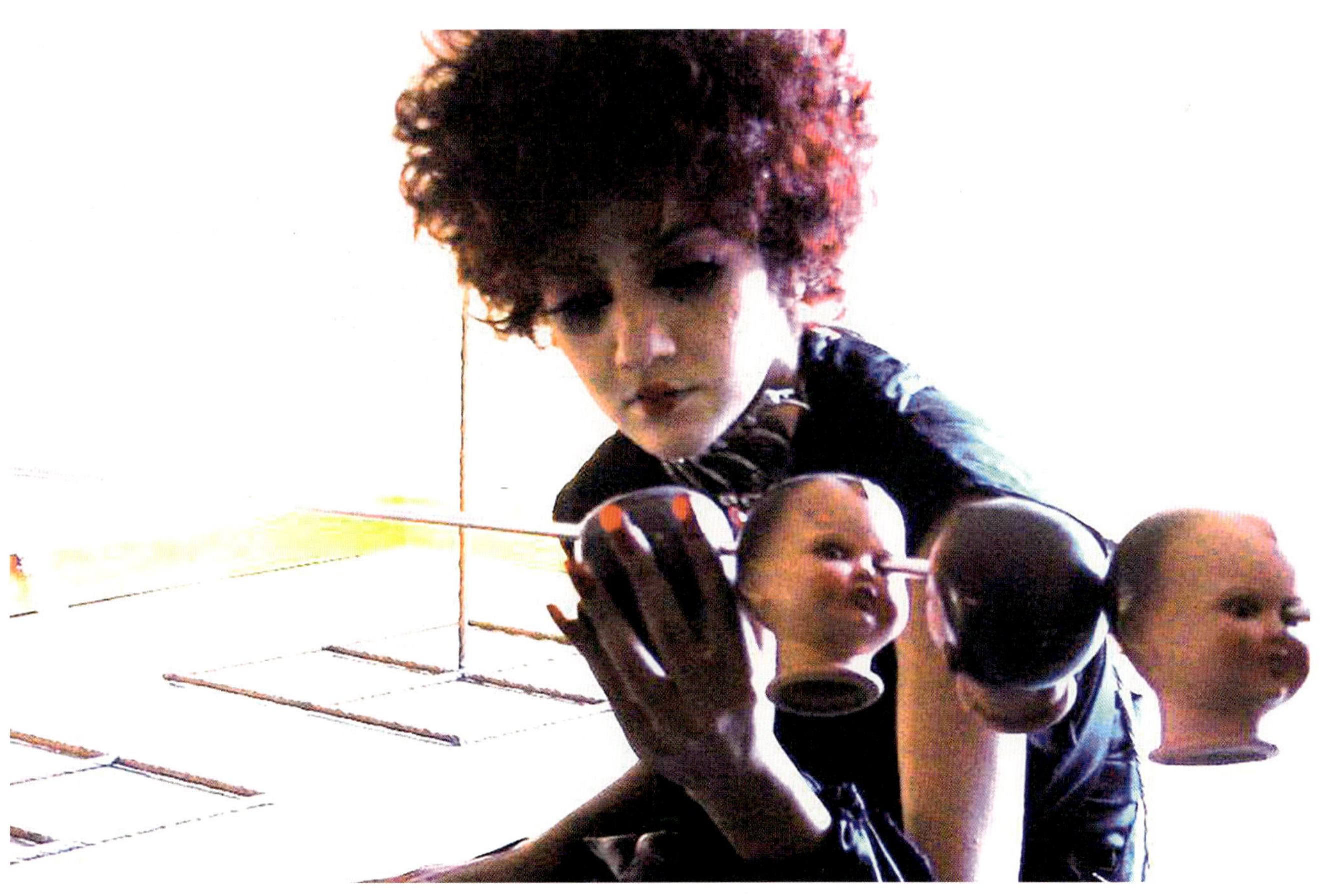

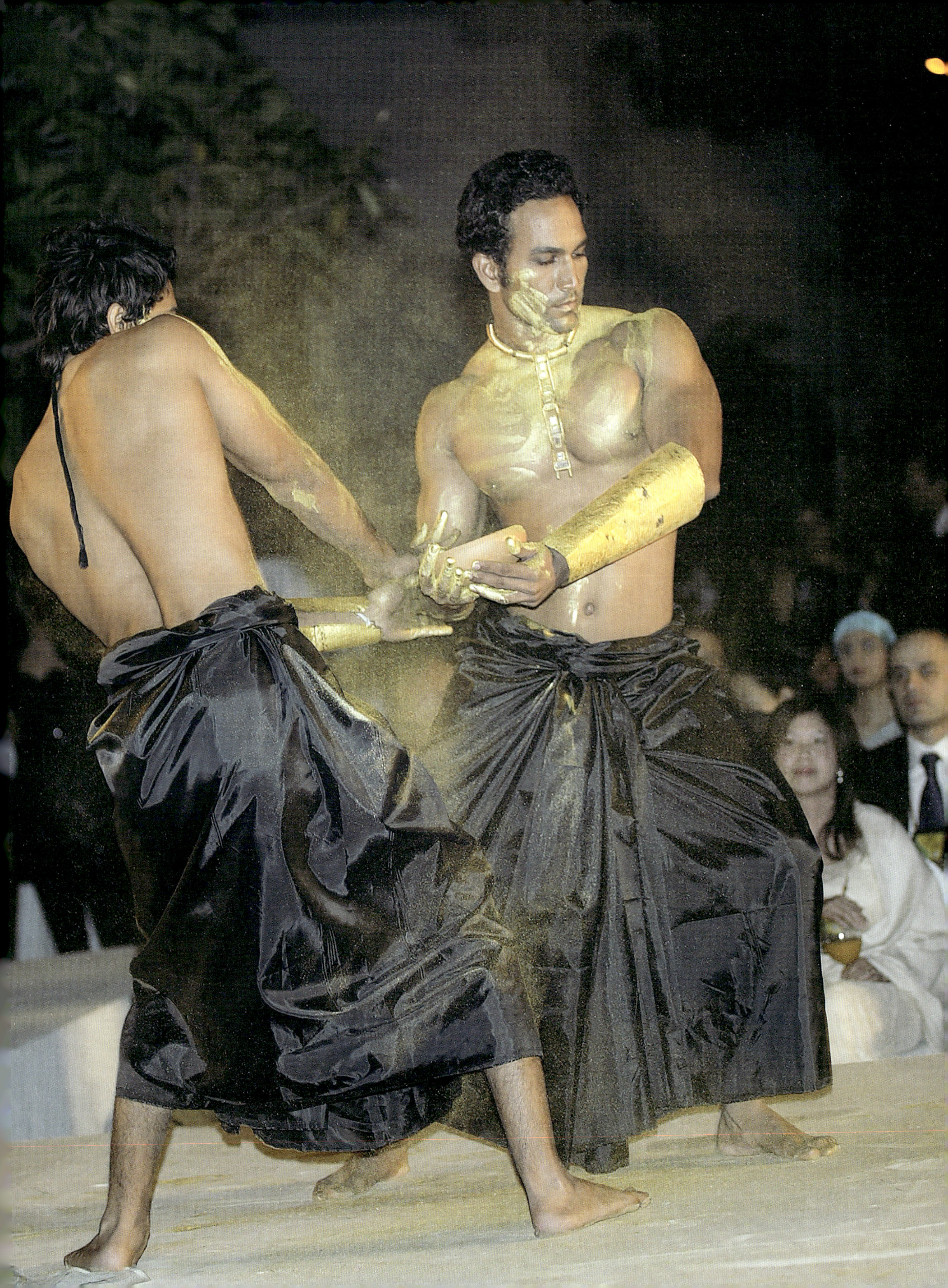

River Dreams of Alexander | 2006

Royal Palm Club, Lahore
57 minutes

River Dreams of Alexander was Amin's third and final catwalk-based performance. Like the other two, it was produced by Pomme Amina Gohar with original music by Ustaaz. It was presented in Lahore with clothes created by Yahsir Waheed, Deepak Perwani and Sheikh Amer Hassan. The show imagined the hallucinogenic dreams Alexander the Great might have experienced after he was gravely wounded in what is today the Pakistani city of Multan in 326 BCE. (Soon after, Alexander's armies mutinied, demanding to return home, frustrating his dream of conquering India, which he believed to be the land of Dionysius.) Amin's interpretation of this epic story was divided into three "acts": Death, Prophecy and Love. In Death, a woman, shrieking in disbelief, dragged a copper boat onstage that Amin had made. At its bow and stern were representations of bodhisattvas in the Greco-Roman style. Other women appeared and, reaching into the boat, retrieved a prone man lying within, whom they covered with gold dust. In Prophecy, the same man, wearing a loincloth and helmet embellished with leaves, rose and swayed. A woman appeared in a hooded white robe and copper mesh mask plated in nickel. Another woman in a martial bustier, also adorned with leaves, energetically kicked toward the audience. In Love, two men with black sarongs appeared on the catwalk and bathed one another's bare chests with gold powder from a clay pot. Their hands joined, they walked to the end of the stage then lay down facing one another as a *shehnai*, a wind instrument traditionally played at South Asian weddings, sounded, hinting at the union of Alexander with his lover Hephaestion. Women sensuously adorned one another with Amin's gold-plated jewelry. At the end of this section, and the show, the vocalist Areeb appeared on the catwalk and soulfully sang a Sufi *kalam*, a devotional poem, in his powerful voice.

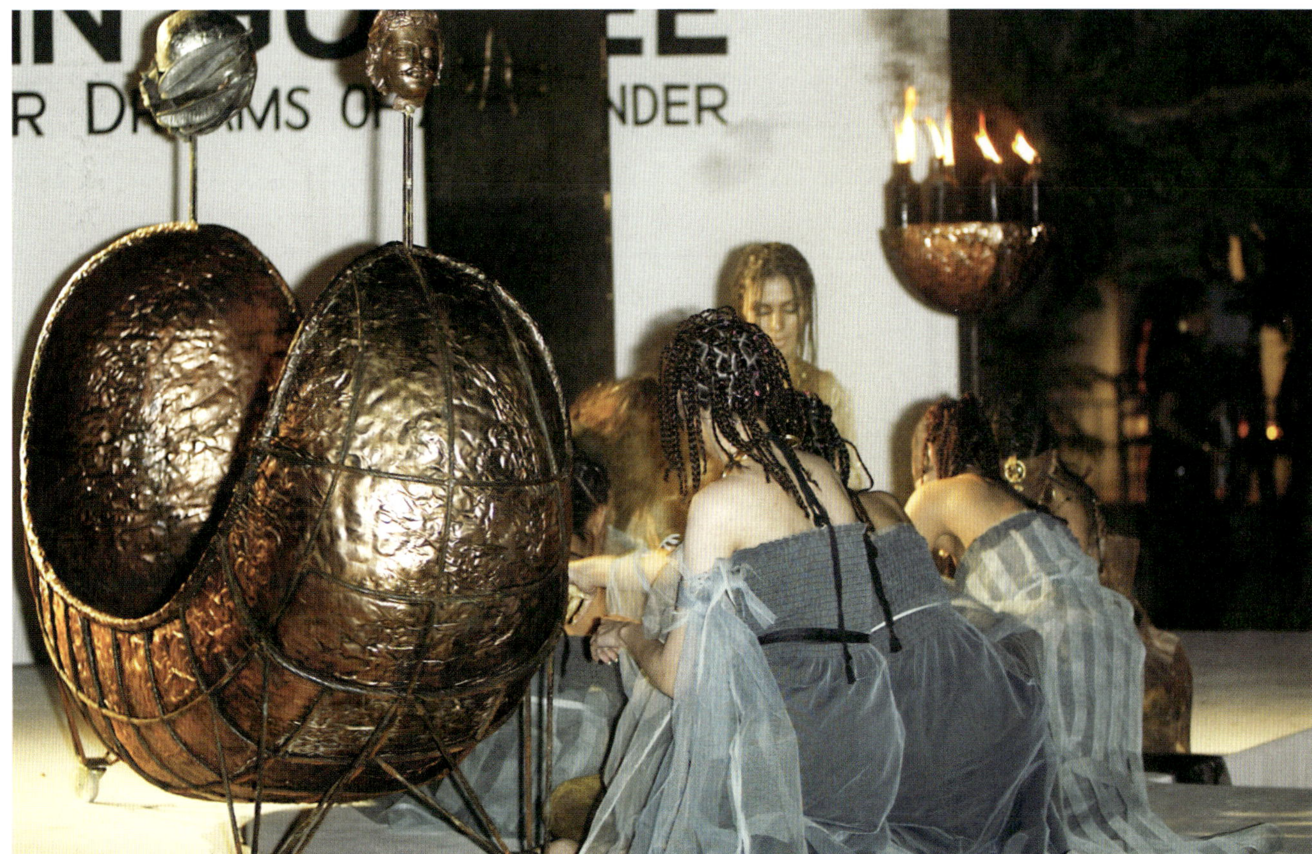

Photos by JY Photo

The Crucifixion | 2009

Looking for the Magic Center, ArtSpace Dubai
27 minutes

The Crucifixion occurred a little over a year after the murder of Amin's parents and their maid by a recently hired driver and his accomplice at their Karachi home. He revealed the performance at the opening of his solo exhibition of sculpture, *Looking for the Magic Center*, at ArtSpace Dubai. For this, Angeline Malik, an actor, director and producer for Pakistani television, appeared to crucify him upon his sculpture, *47 Charbagh: The Resurrection*, in which leaves and fragments of his own face cast in bronze compose a perpendicular grid. The title of the sculpture referenced the year of Pakistan's independence as well as the four-quadrant garden plan the Moghuls introduced to the subcontinent. As the performance began, Amin stood before his bronze and copper work in a black *sherwani*, a formal Pakistani coat. Angeline, wearing a long black skirt and blouse, slowly approached. Suddenly, she ripped open the buttons of Amin's jacket and snubbed out a burning cigarette onto his bare chest. Amin arched his back in pain, his arms spread, as he leaned against the sculpture in the form of a Greek cross, seeming to be nailed upon it. Angeline showered him with handfuls of gold dust, which billowed in clouds around them, obscuring their two forms. He slowly crumpled to the ground, where she knelt down to embrace him, holding him like a Pietà. After the performance, the startled audience trampled the thin layer of gold dust throughout the gallery, unconsciously leaving a ghostly presence of themselves in their wake.

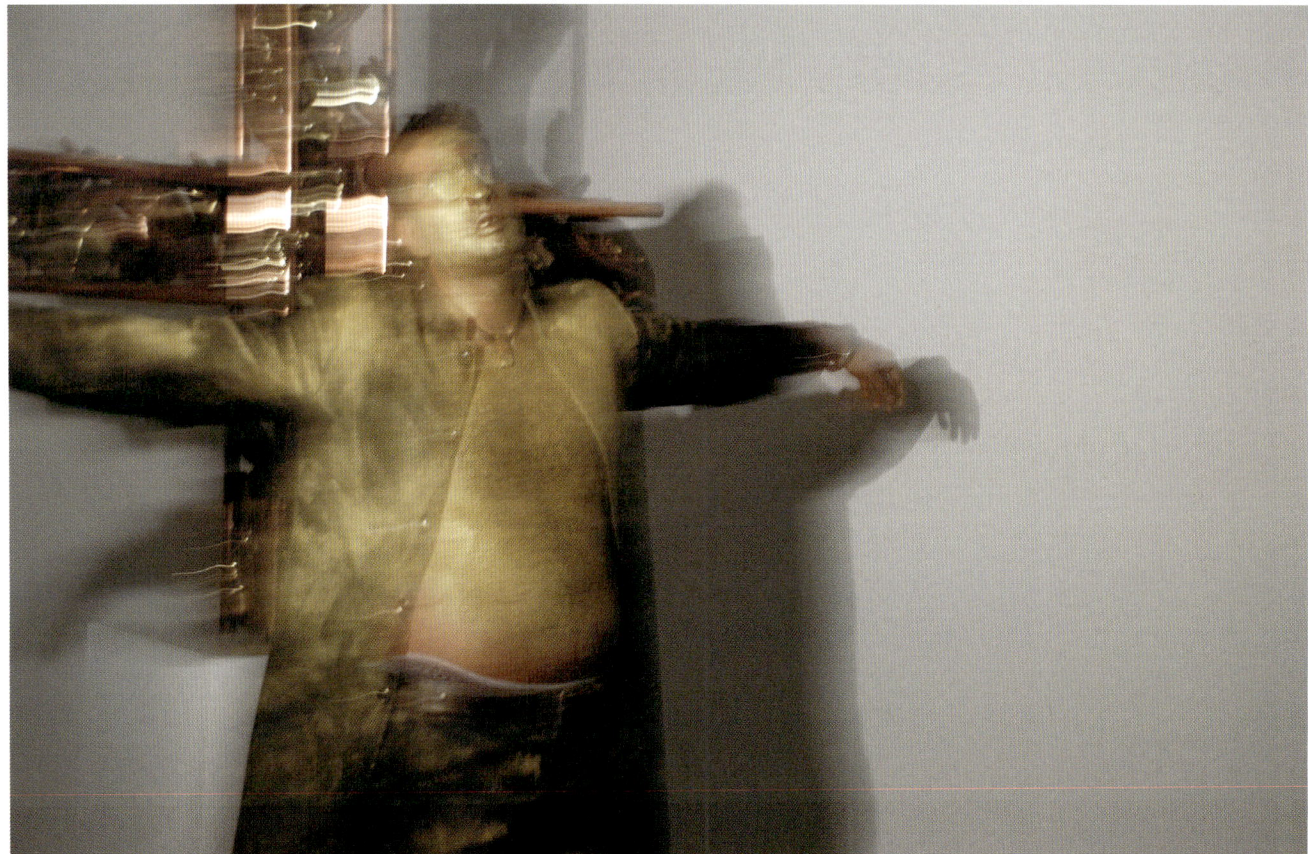

Photos courtesy ArtSpace Dubai

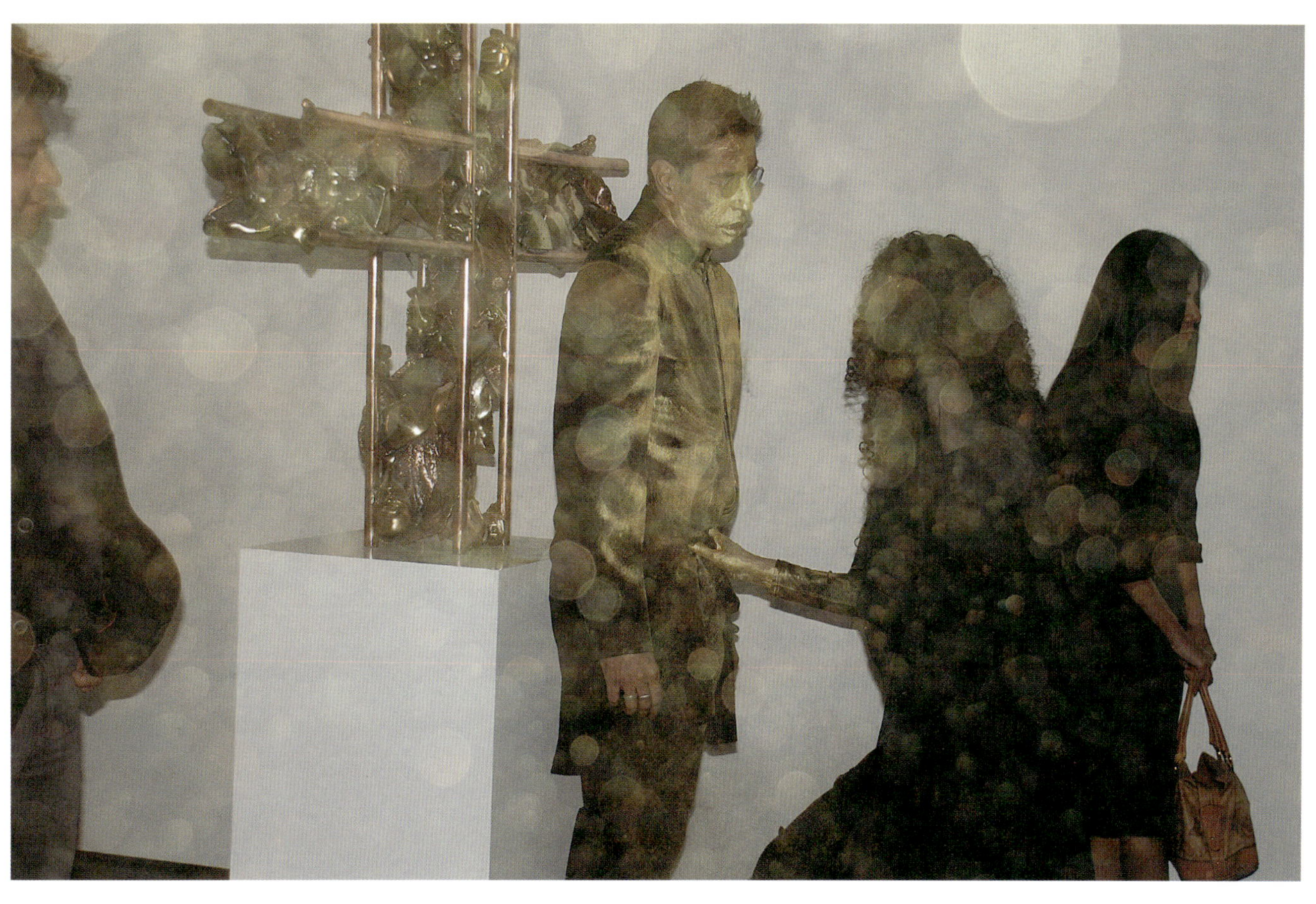

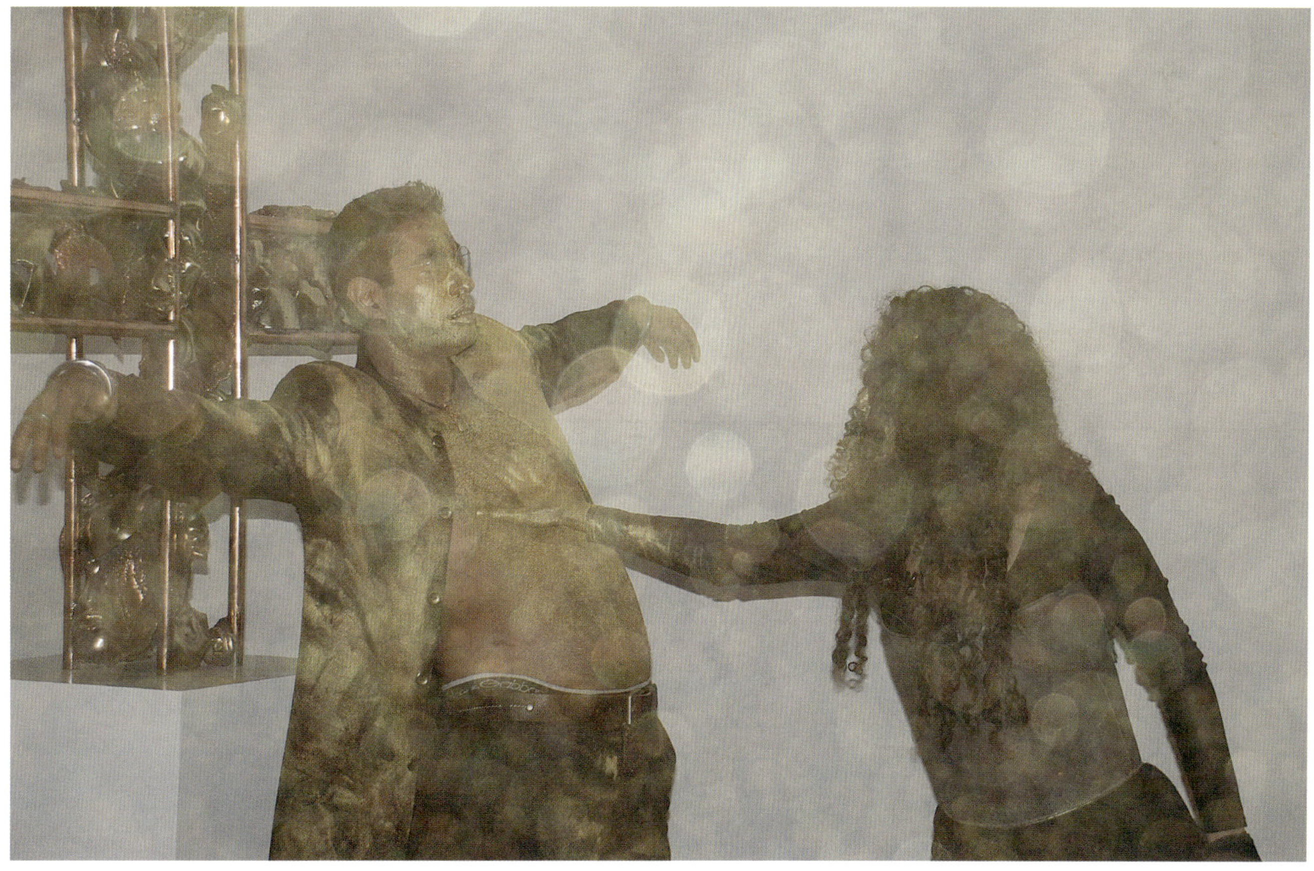

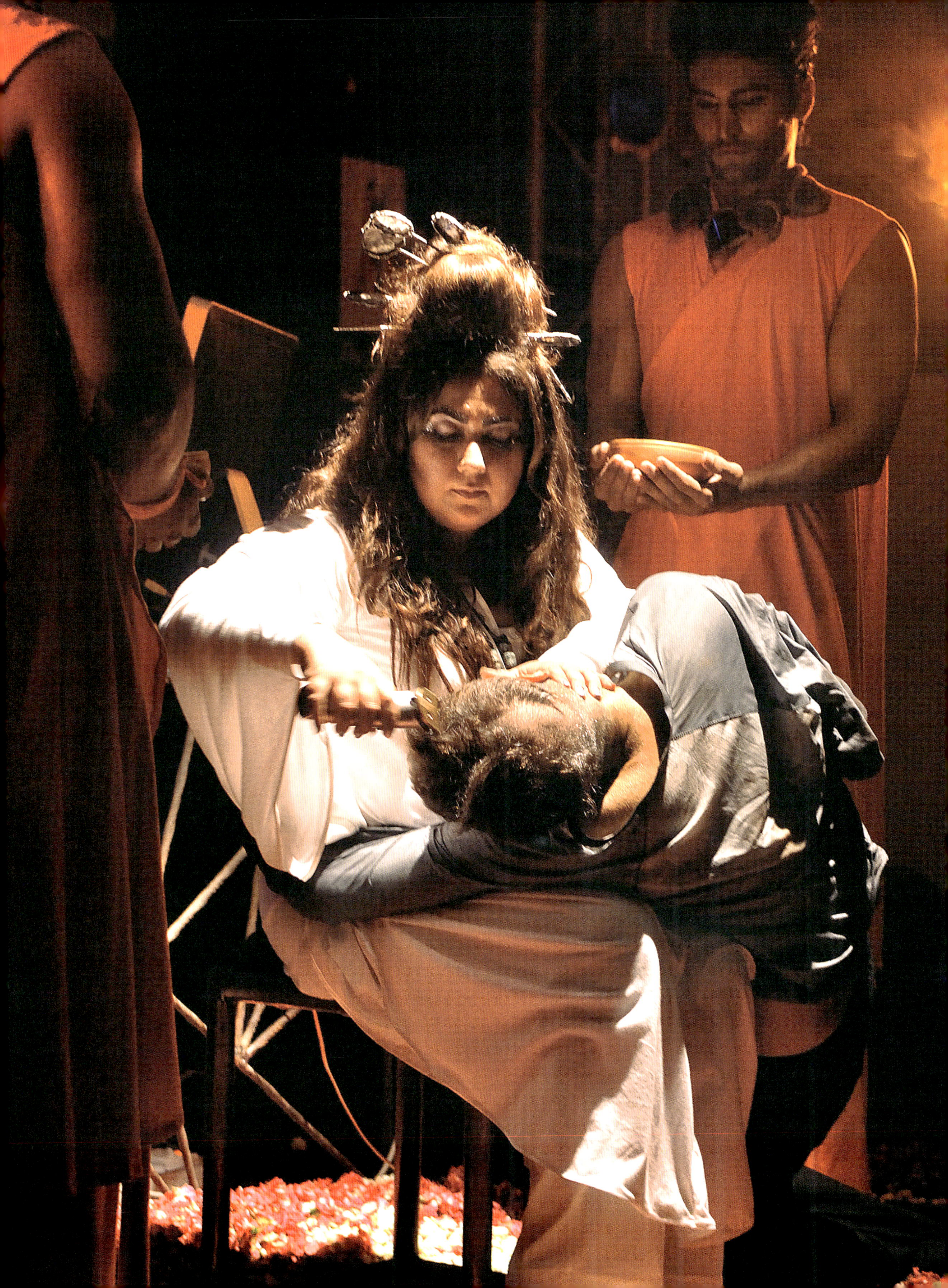

The Healing | 2010

Beach Luxury Hotel, Karachi
34 minutes

In Islam and in Hinduism, a baby's head is shaved seven days after its birth to protect it from evil. Referencing this ritual, Amin asked people close to him to help perform a vulnerable performance in which his head was shorn. Amin presented *The Healing* at the Beach Luxury Hotel in Karachi at an event honoring Ali Imam (1924-2002), a pioneering Karachi gallerist who was both a colleague and friend of Amin's mother and father. For this, a man carried Amin's inert body through the audience as another man bearing two lit copper torches followed. Amin wore severe black while the two men attending to him were attired in saffron robes and necklaces of copper set with shards of green glass. The man carrying Amin gingerly laid him in the lap of Rukaiya Adamjee, who, dressed in white, sat alone on a spot-lit chair within a circle of red rose petals. Nearby, a third man, also in saffron robes, and wearing a tall conical headpiece of copper, sat before a computer and performed an electronic composition. Rukaiya, a dear friend of Amin's whose mother was also a confidant of Amin's mother, tenderly shaved his head with a buzzing razor, handing his hair to the two men who had ceremoniously brought him forward. They gathered it in earthenware vessels found throughout Pakistan before burning it in the flames of the torches. His head denuded, a bereaved Amin slowly rose and danced before Rukaiya, who opened her arms, seeming to both protect and release him.

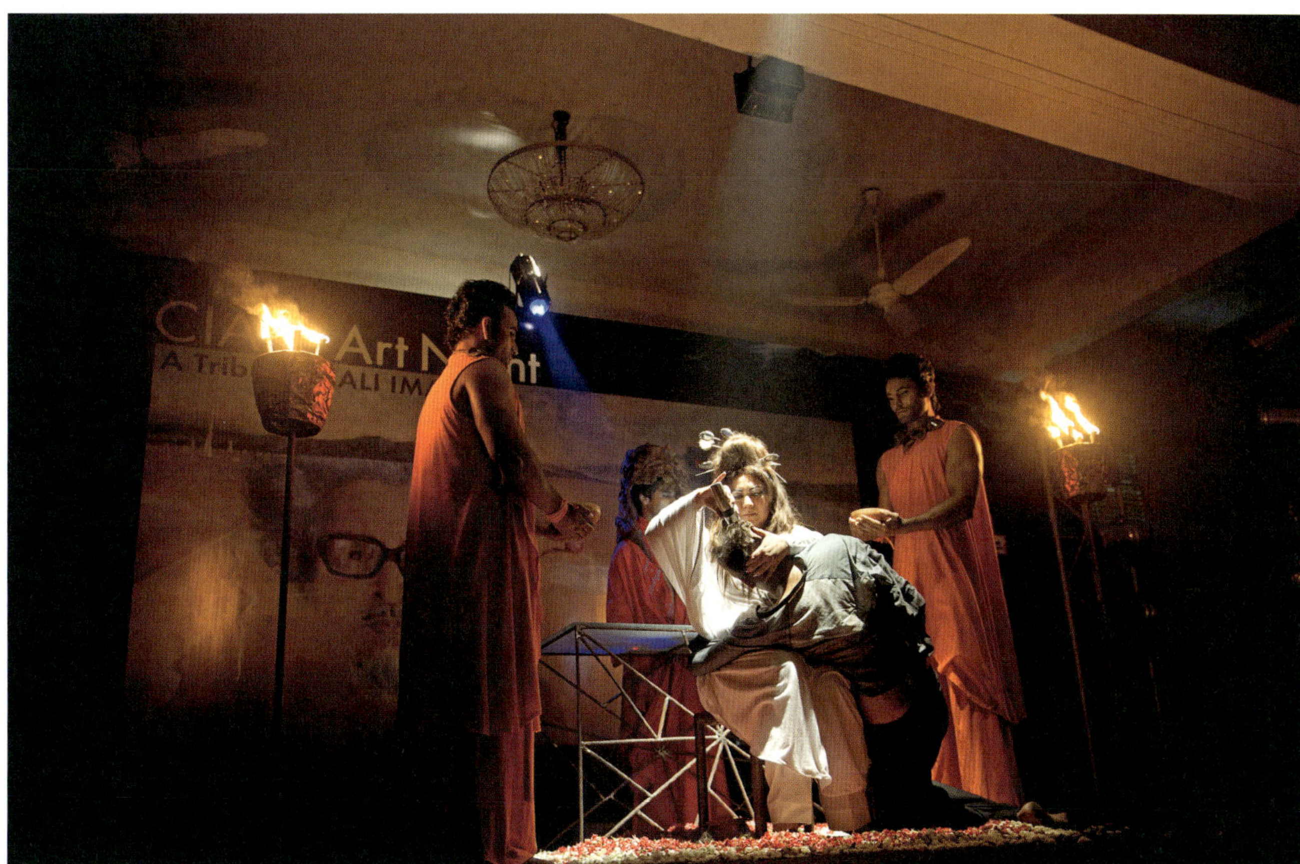

Photos by Nubain Ali

Love Marriage | 2012

Band, Baja, Baarat, Indus Valley School of Art and Architecture, Karachi
43 minutes

Amin created *Love Mariage* for *Band, Baja, Baarat*, a group exhibition curated by gallerist Sameera Raja at the Indus Valley School of Art and Architecture in Karachi. Sameera most likely borrowed the title of the exhibition, which translates as "band, music, procession," from the 2010 hit Bollywood rom-com about two rival wedding planners who inevitably marry. Amin's work subversively upended such tropes. The title was confrontational—a marriage in South Asia is assumed to be an arranged one while the term "love marriage" refers to couples who choose their own partners, sometimes against their families' wishes. Here the "couple" was played by Amin and fellow sculptor Saba Iqbal whose faces were painted an identical Kabuki white, effacing gender. Amin wore a gleaming copper helmet with a stiff plume atop that eventually fell off while Saba was strapped into an aggressive-looking nickel-plated copper bustier with nails protruding from it. Led by a group of musicians playing traditional drums that Amin had hired from a local Sufi shrine, the pair entered the courtyard of the school followed by male and female students dressed in gender-neutral white *shalwar kameez*, Pakistan's national attire, who played their joint baarat. Amin and Saba sat together within a metal frame strewn with fairy lights. Before them was a table with two large white bowls upon it, one filled with eggs, the other empty. Using elaborate, stylized gestures, they broke the eggs into each other's palms, pouring their contents into the barren bowl. Once the two had cracked open all the eggs, the procession gathered around them in a protective circle. Spontaneously, members of the audience came to sit on either side of the two to get their photos taken just as they would at a conventional wedding. Led by the drummers and the baarat, Amin and Saba performed their *rukhsati*, or formal departing, leaving the courtyard arm in arm.

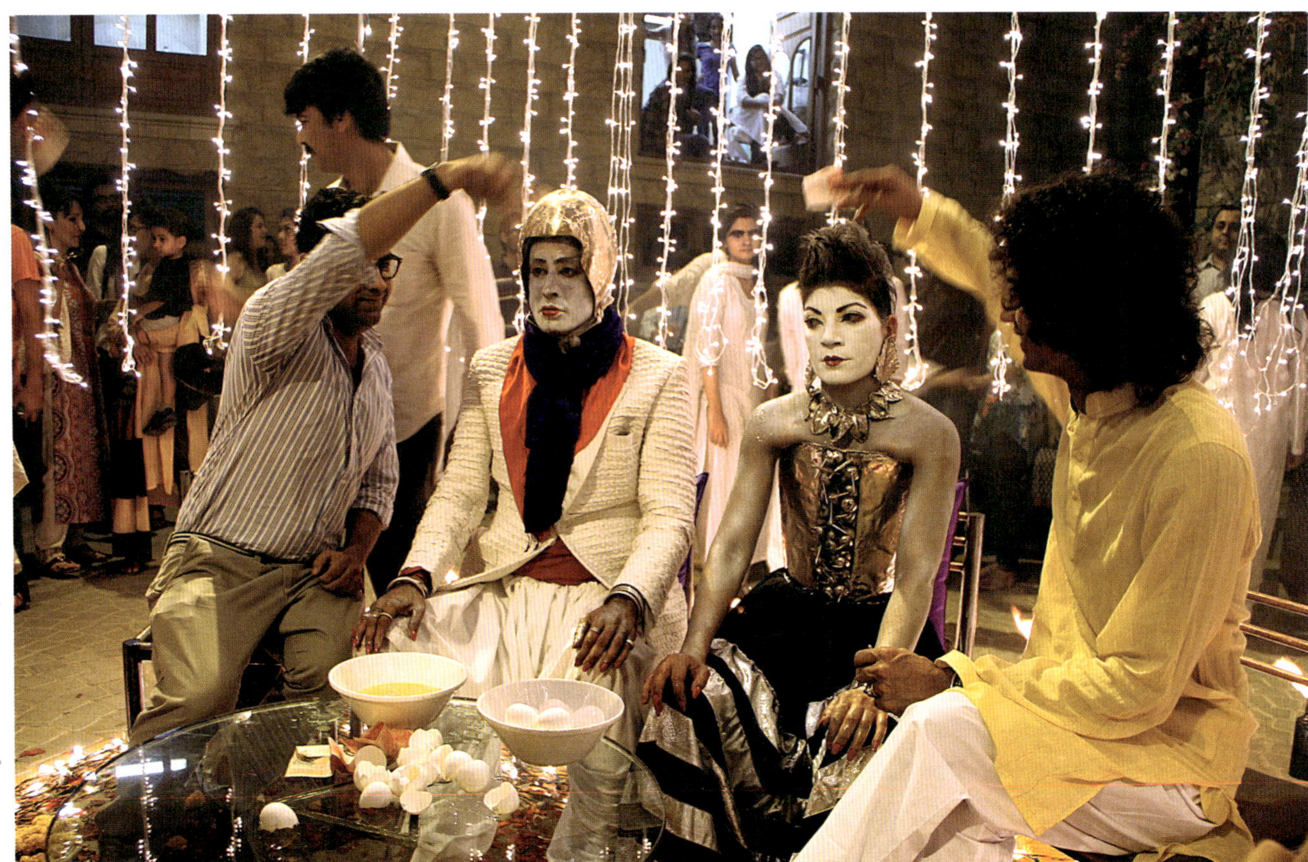

Photos by Jamal Ashiqain

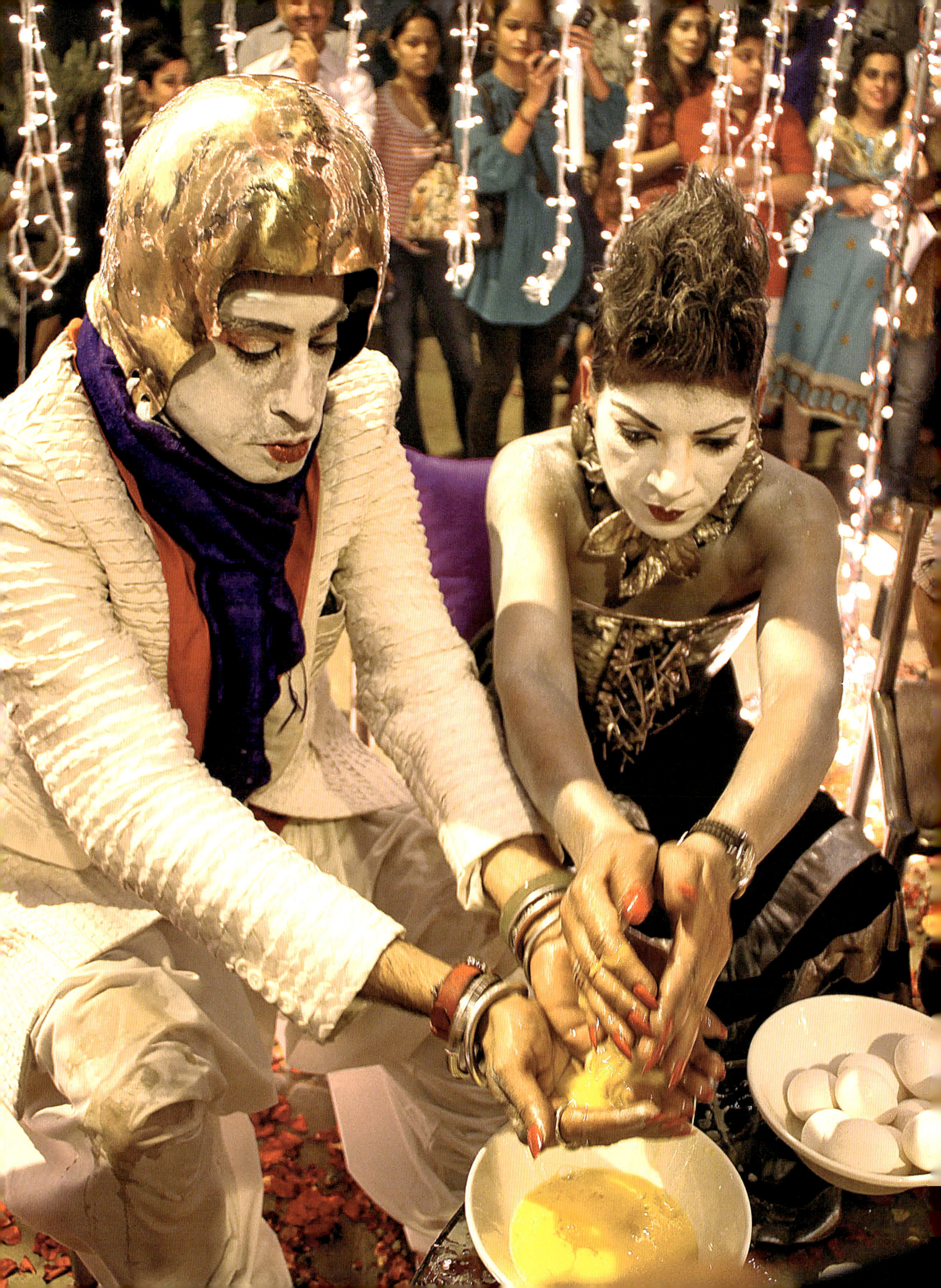

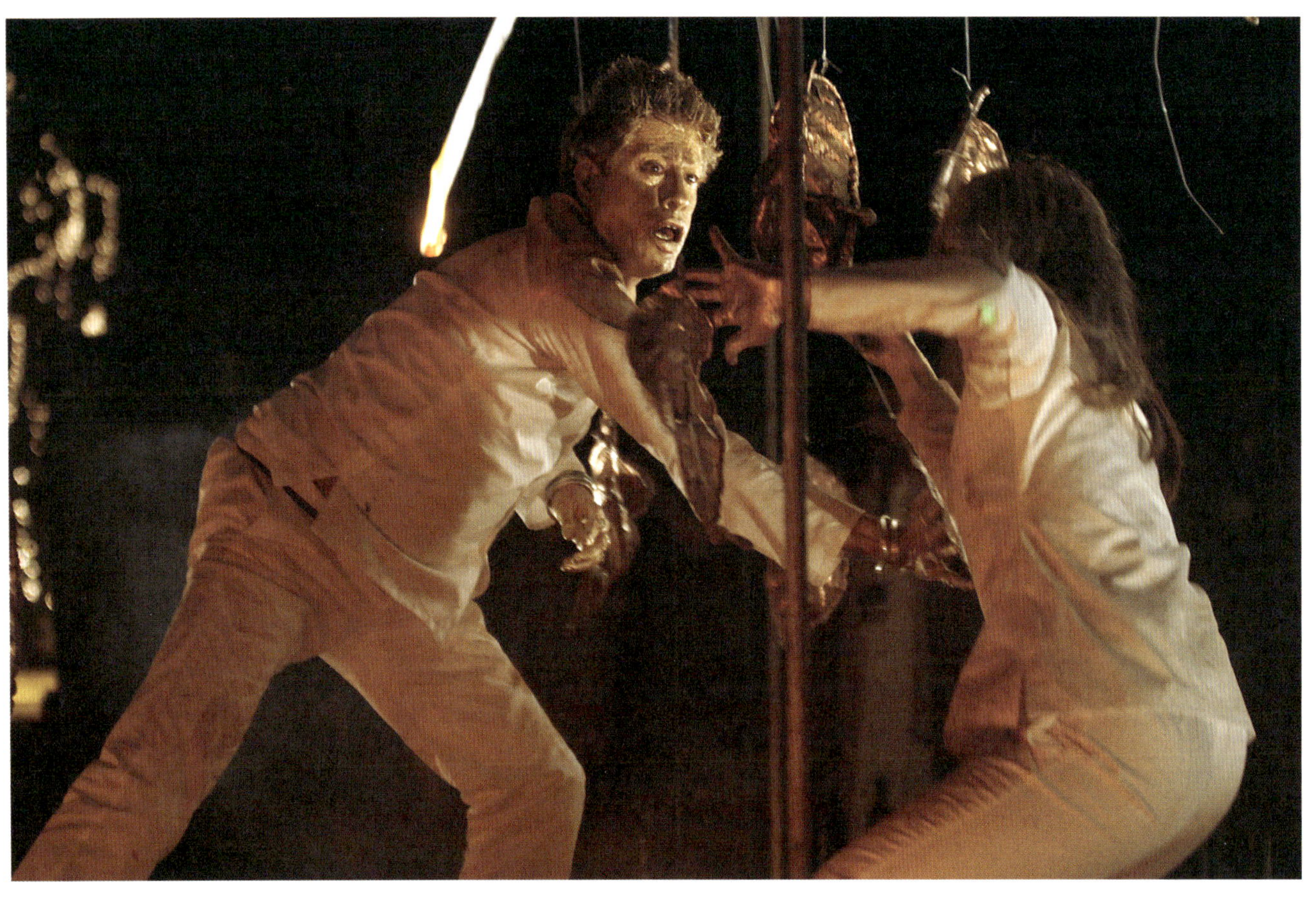

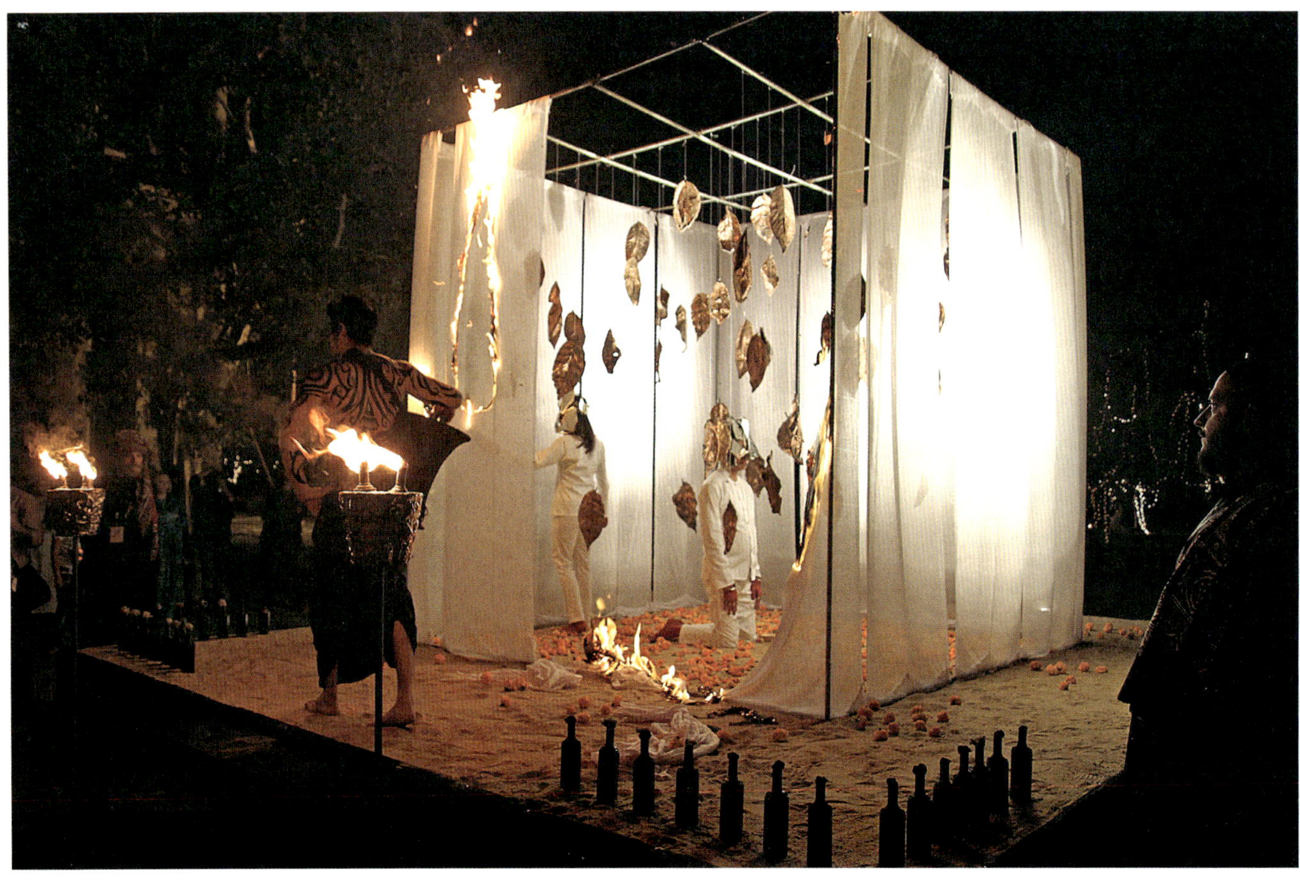

Paradise Lost | 2014

Sindh Art Festival, Frere Hall, Karachi
40 minutes

Paradise Lost was presented on the grounds of Frere Hall, a yellow limestone building in the Venetian-Gothic style that was the city's town hall during the British Raj. The 40-minute performance began at dusk inside a three-meter by three-meter steel frame from which copper leaves were suspended, many of which appeared in *Where's the Apple, Joshinder?* (The two performances occurred within weeks of each other.) The installation, which recalled a *Chahar Bagh*, the four-quadrant garden of the Moghuls, was sheathed on all sides by long strips of white muslin. Appropriate for its colonial setting, the work spoke of partition—not only of Pakistan from India, but of the sexes and of man and woman from the Garden of Eden. The work began with Haamid Rahim playing an original composition as Kashif Hussain, whose face and torso were painted in black arabesques, approached, bearing two lit copper torches created by Amin. He circumambulated the cube, lighting a ring of bottles stuffed with kerosene-soaked rags, then circled again, tossing marigolds from a rattan basket slung on his back. Hidden from view inside this wrapped structure were Amin and Joshinder Chaggar, dressed identically in unisex white coats and pants, both wearing silver masks comprised of irregular pieces of mirror. Amin sat motionless as Joshinder took one of the burning bottles and lit the muslin, which, wet with dew, slowly burned, producing clouds of black smoke. As the fabric smoldered, the nylon string suspending the leaves melt. One by one, the leaves crashed to the ground. Amid this shower of projectiles, the pair removed one another's masks, frantically calling out the other's name—Amin's Muslim, Joshinder's Sikh. They then faced off in a confrontational yet coordinated dance. Night fell, the muslin burnt to the ground and Amin and Joshinder left the ruined garden, heading off in different directions.

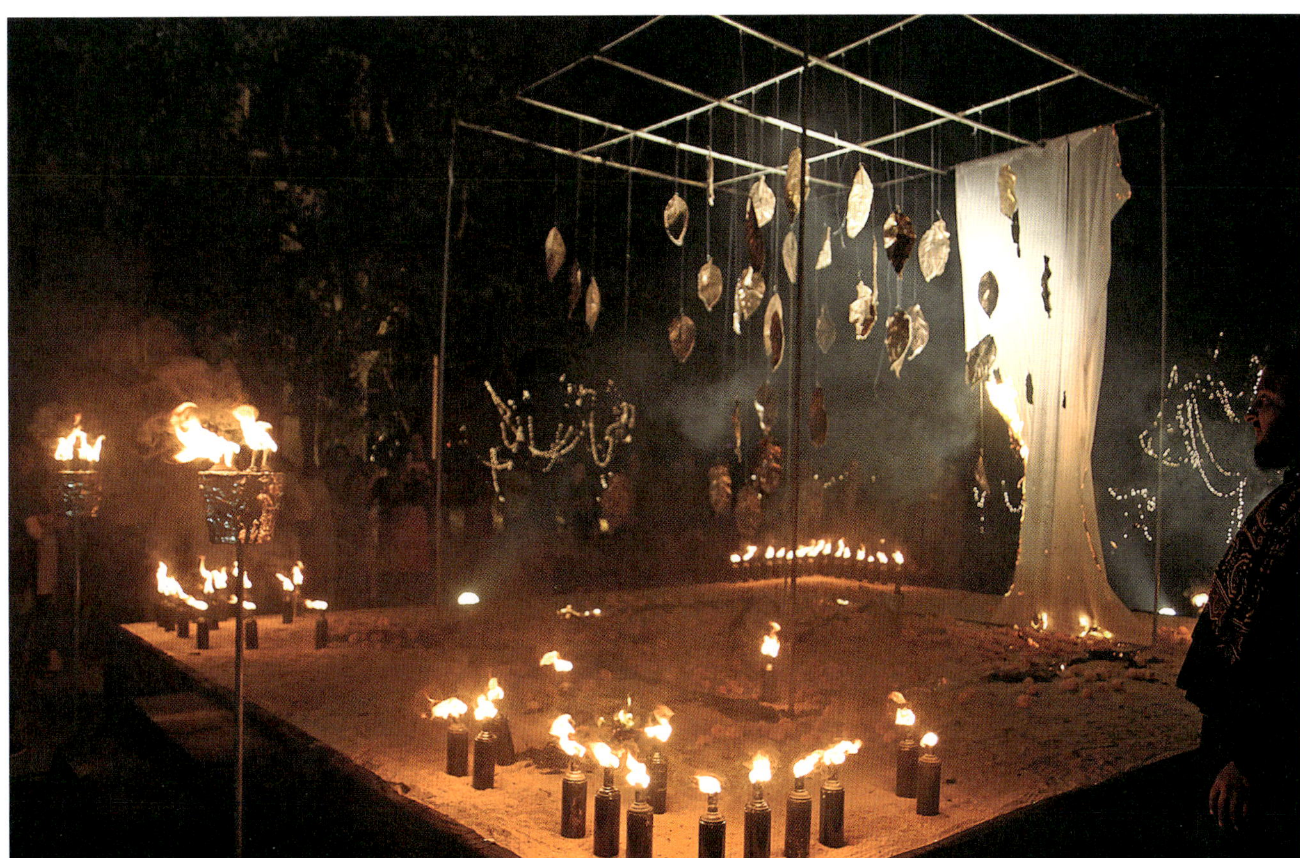

Photos by Jamal Ashiqain

Where's the Apple, Joshinder? | 2014

Karachi Arts Council
47 minutes

Where's the Apple, Joshinder? was a 47-minute movement-based performance conceived and choreographed by Amin that was presented for three consecutive nights at the auditorium of the Karachi Arts Council. It featured the dancer Joshinder Chaggar; the actors Sunil Shankar, Kashif Hussain, Erum Bashir and Vajdaan Shah; the musicians Haamid Rahim and Sikandar Mufti; and the painter and performance artist Syed Ammad Tahir. Amin worked with this multidisciplinary group for six months to create the work, which revolved around a large installation in the form of an Indo-Persian garden that he had recreated out of copper leaves hanging from steel beams above a 2.4 by 1.2 meter wedge of mirror. It began with Haamid wearing a black robe and copper helmet sitting within the audience with his back turned to it as he played his own electronic composition. Kashif, in an orange sarong and copper helmet with curving horns, emerged from the orchestra pit. His bare torso and legs painted in strokes of black paint, he moved back and forth across the stage, tossing his head like a bull. Wearing a mesh mask, Sunil then entered the stage on all fours, prowling catlike. He climbed onto the central, mirrored surface, constructed in a slant, seeming to recoil from his own image. Wearing an avian mask of looking glass and nickel-plated copper, Joshinder lifted her cocked head from behind the reflective slide. Sunil and Joshinder sparred and embraced. Erum and Vajdaan joined them on stage, pairing off with the two in various combinations of male with female, female with female, male with male. Ammad then appeared onstage dressed in formal South Asian bridalwear while Sikandar coaxed a tabla, a drum associated with courtesan dances of the 18th century. The action that occurred around and atop the installation explored gender and the non-binary. In the end, Sunil, Joshinder, Vajdaan and Erum burned the nylon from which the leaves hung, destroying the paradisical garden.

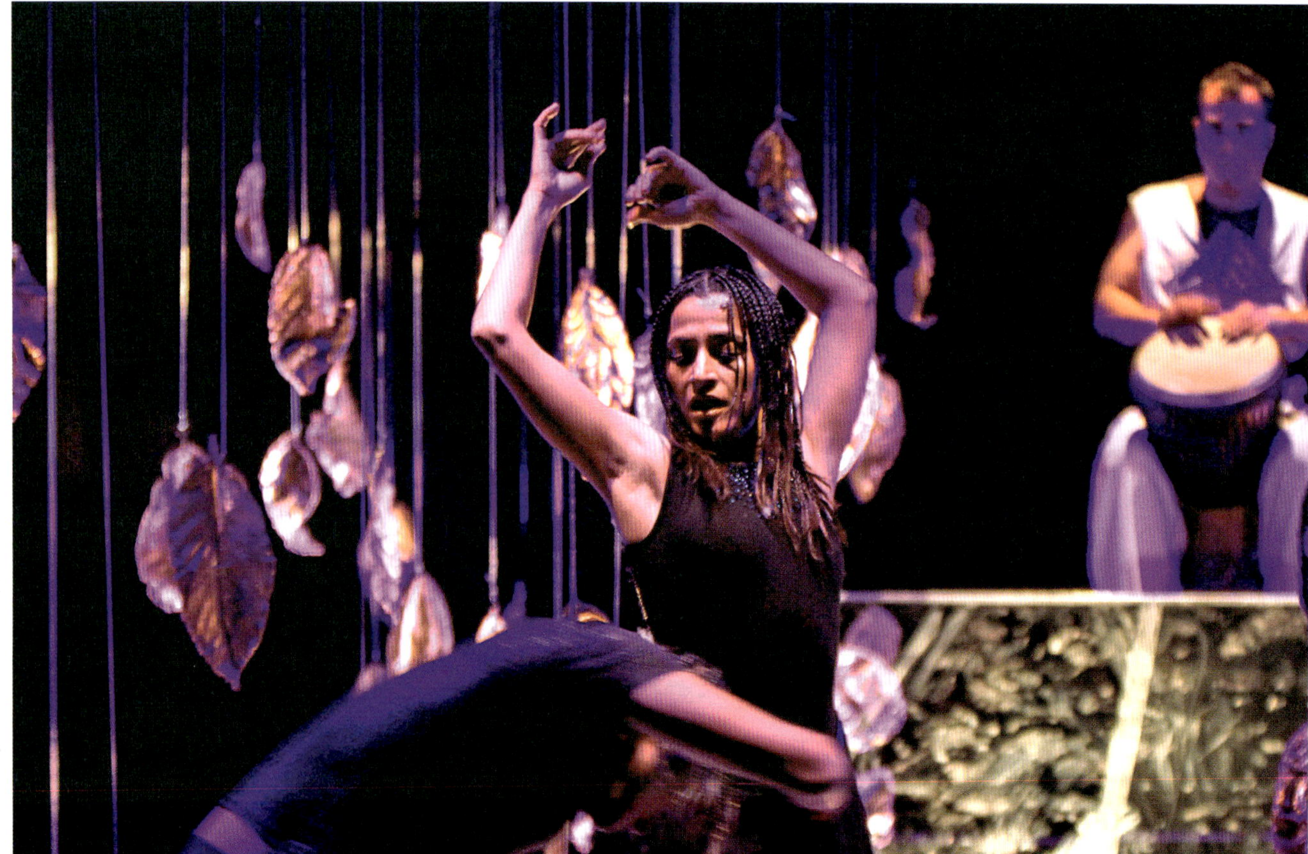

Photos by Jamal Ashiqain

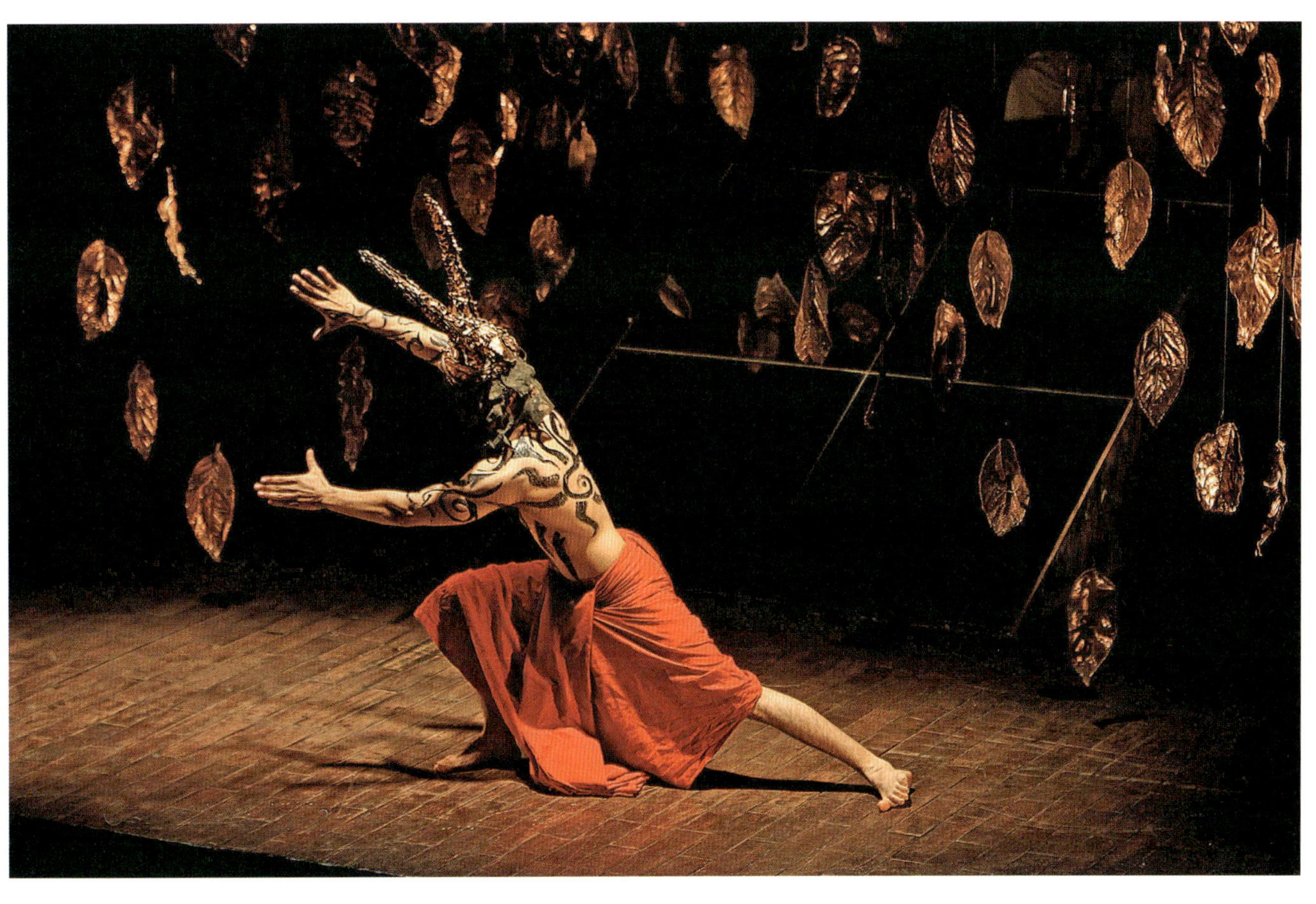

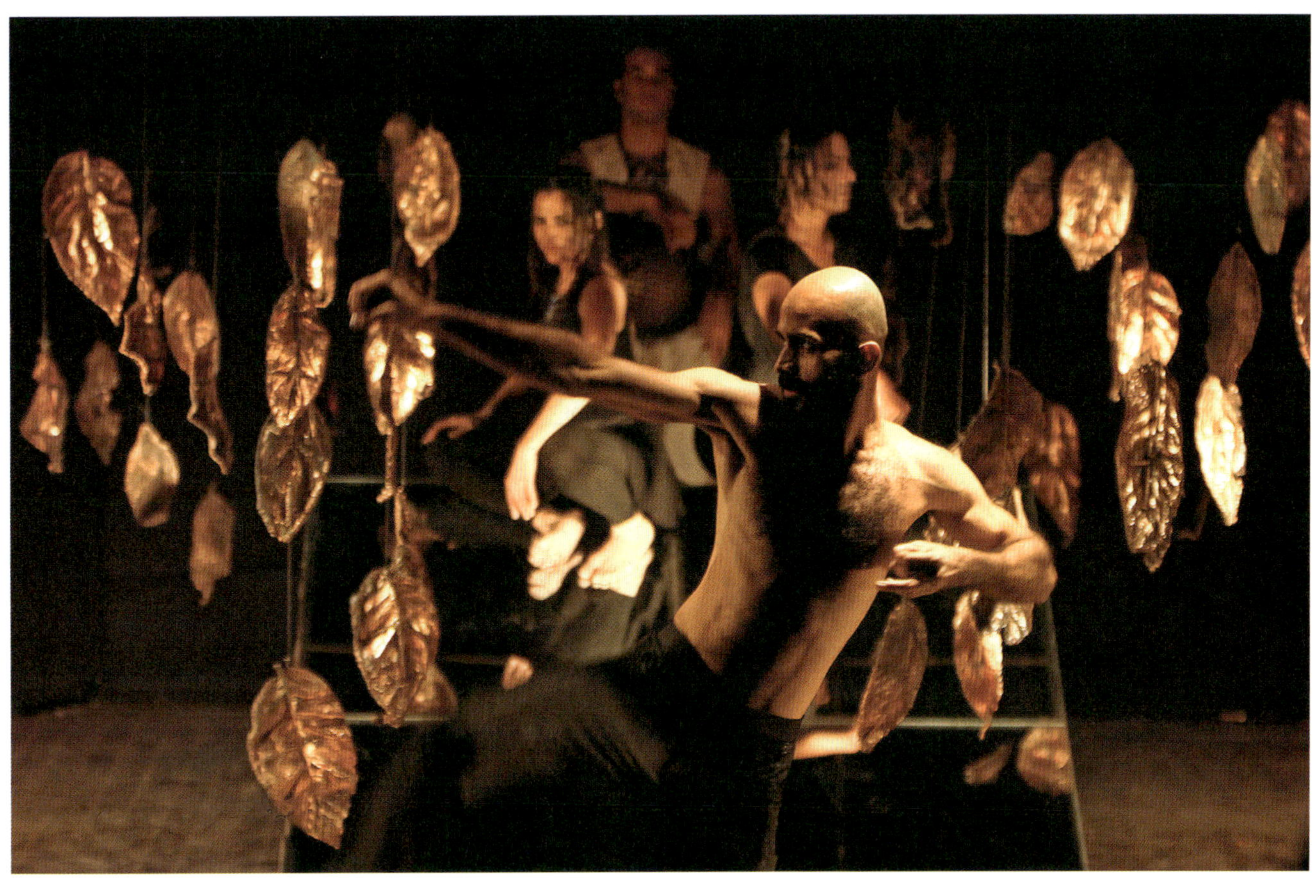

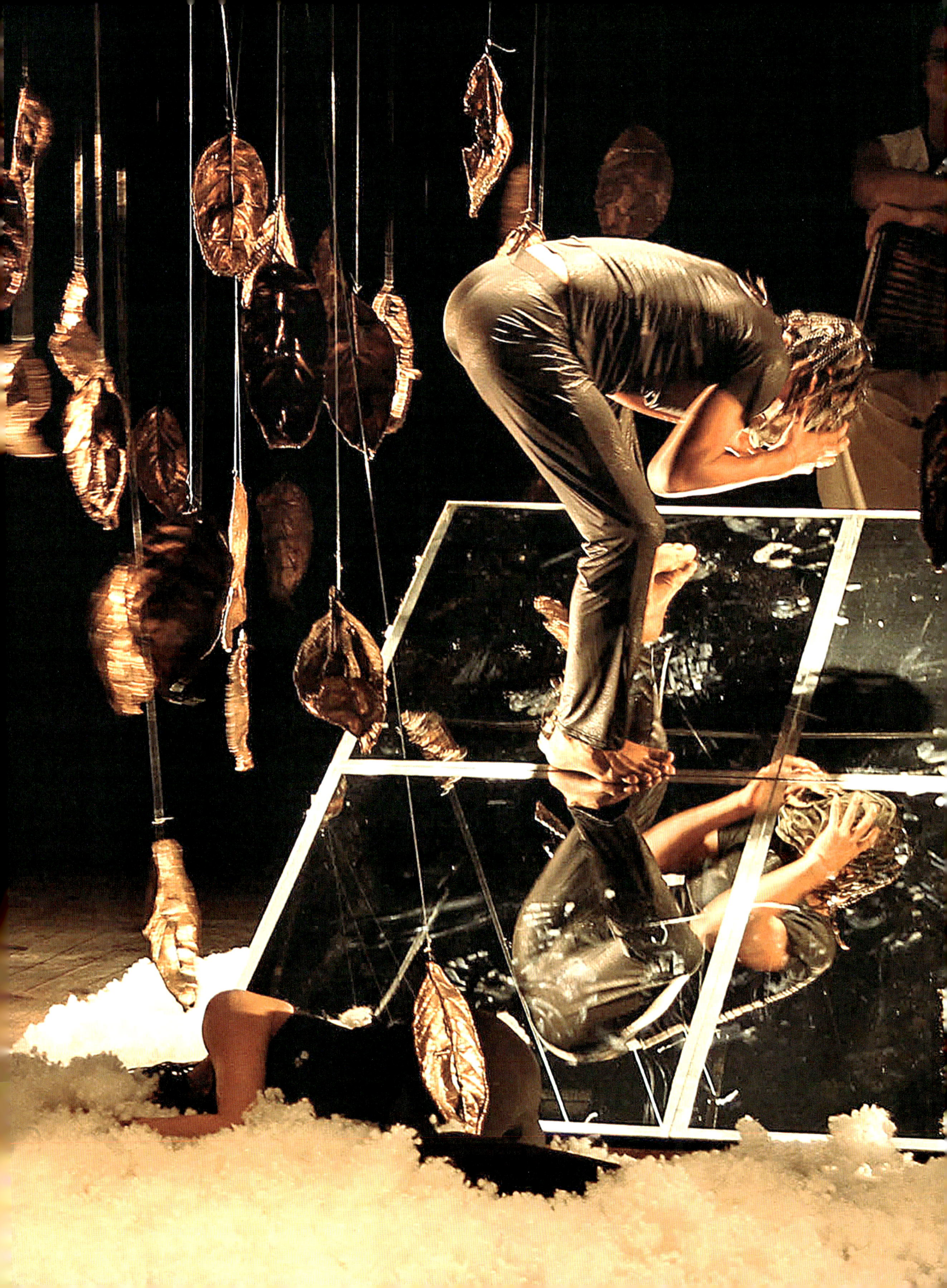

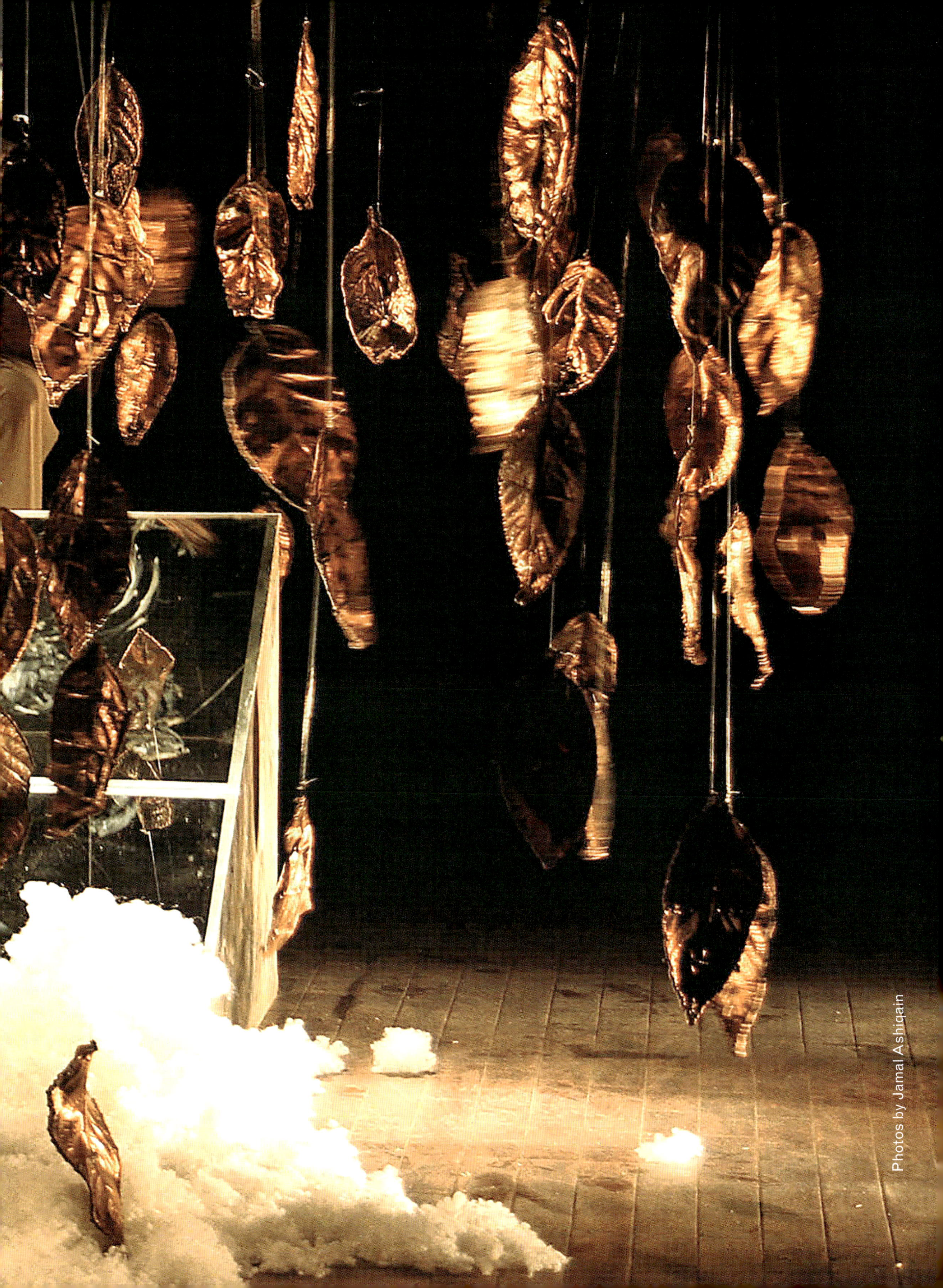

Photos by Jamal Ashiqain

Play Me | 2017

Karachi Art Summit, National Museum, Karachi
77 minutes

Amin cast parts of his own face in bronze for his performance *Play Me*, which took place at dusk on the grounds of the National Museum in Karachi. Sitting on steel and copper chairs on either end of a steel table with a brass grid on top, all created by Amin, he and Sara Vaqar Pagganwala faced off in a game whose rules they made up as they went along. Staring obstinately into one another's eyes, they slammed duplicates of Amin's cut-up features upon the board, shouting, "No!" as they aggressively advanced their own set. The antagonism between the two seemed only to build. Children who had gathered in the park to play soon huddled, fascinated by Amin and Sara's loud sparring. Some, gripping soccer balls, looked on in apparent disbelief as the weighty pieces flew from the table, thudding to the ground. After more than an hour, Sara and Amin rose, gravely shook hands then departed. The work brought to mind *Reunion*, a 1968 performance by Marcel Duchamp, his wife and John Cage. (Playing on an electronic chessboard, the three created an extemporaneous composition in which each move was reproduced as sound; they continued until the audience got so bored it left.) Amin returned to his performance for *Play Me* (*Duchamp is Dead*), in which he and Zarmeene Shah competed over the same chess-like game. The two, laughing maniacally at the absurdity of it all, was included in *Outsiders*, an exhibition they co-curated with Zeerak Ahmed at the Amin Gulgee Gallery in collaboration with the Goethe-Institut in 2018.

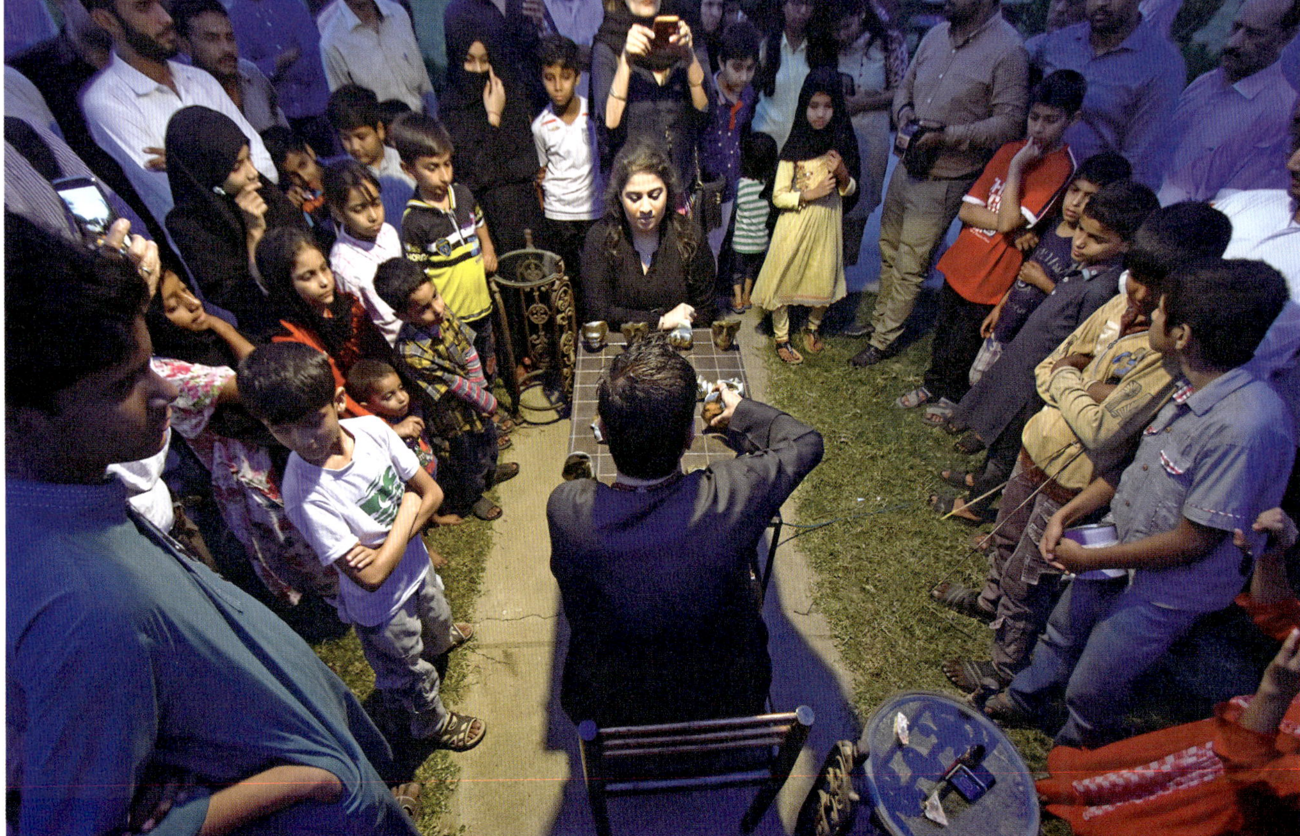

Photo by Humayun Memon

Love Letters | 2018

7 and *7.7*, Kuala Lumpur, Karachi, Rome
180 minutes

Love Letters was an instructional work repeated three times. It was part of Amin's installation, *7* and *7.7*, co-curated by Paolo De Grandis and Claudio Crescentini, which travelled from Wei-Ling Contemporary in Kuala Lumpur to the Amin Gulgee Gallery in Karachi and then on to Galleria d'Arte Moderna (GAM) and Mattatoio, both in Rome. For this interactive performance, the artist provided empty bottles and a postcard-size note that read: "Kindly write a declaration of love to a person, place or thing (past, present or future) on a piece of paper, roll it up and place it in one of the bottles. Take your bottle inside the gallery and place it against any one of its walls. These messages, which are to remain strictly private, will be destroyed at the end of the show." Amin had deconstructed a line from the Quran that has particular resonance for him for the itinerant show. He has used the words repeatedly in his sculpture. At first, they were readable, but over time they have been dissected to the point of illegibility. Here the verse was broken into seven fragments—hence the title *7*. Through this process of repetition and deconstruction, Amin has not only internalized the words' message, but reinforced the privacy of his attachment to it. These works became his private love letters. By asking viewers to write their own epistles and place them around his installation, he wished to confirm his belief in the privacy of love. Amin also wanted to draw attention to the specter of surveillance that prevails in our electronic age. At GAM, Claudio greeted the exhibition's arrival with a curatorial intervention: Roman poets took turns reciting declarations of love into a microphone. Amin cannot understand Italian. Their intent, however, was not lost on him, or anyone else in attendance.

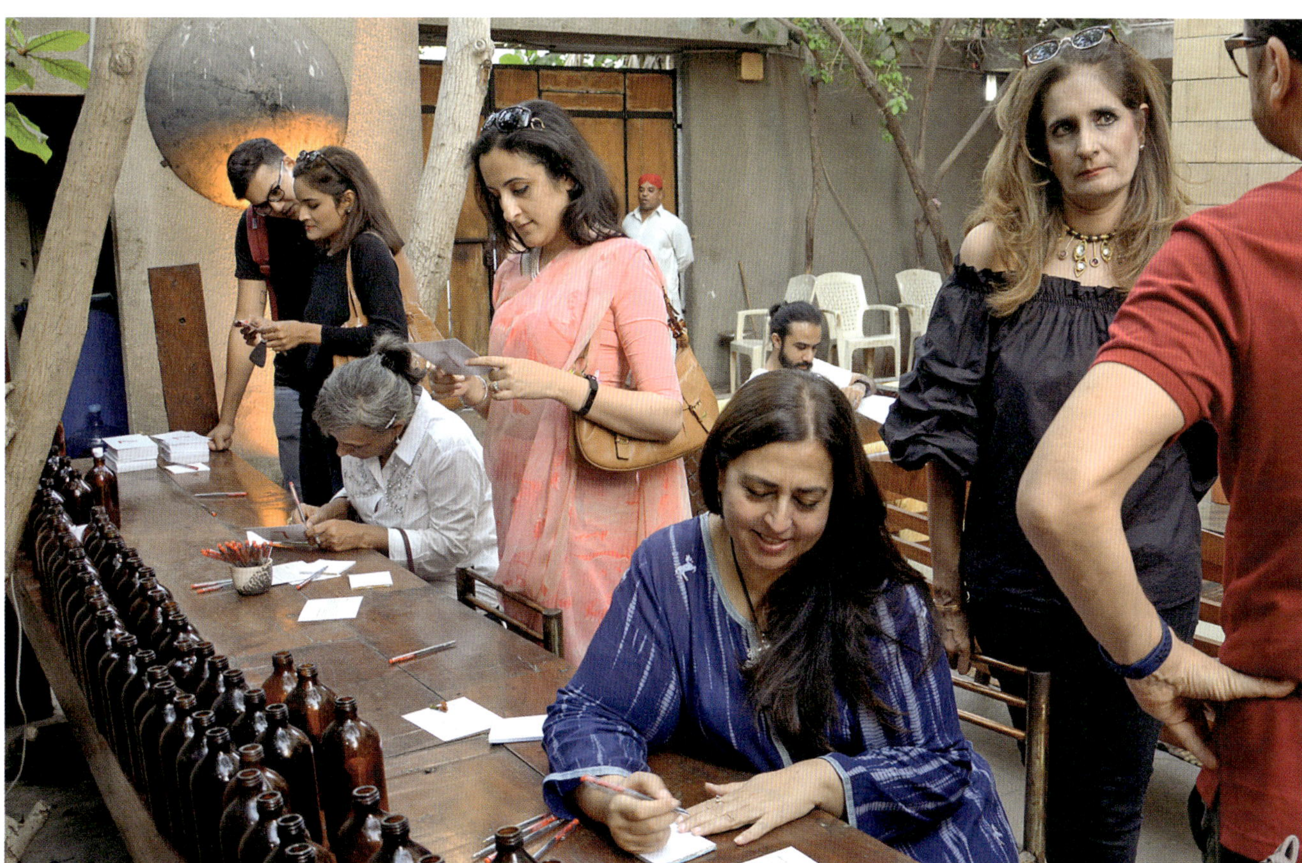

Amin Gulgee Gallery. Photo by Humayun Memon

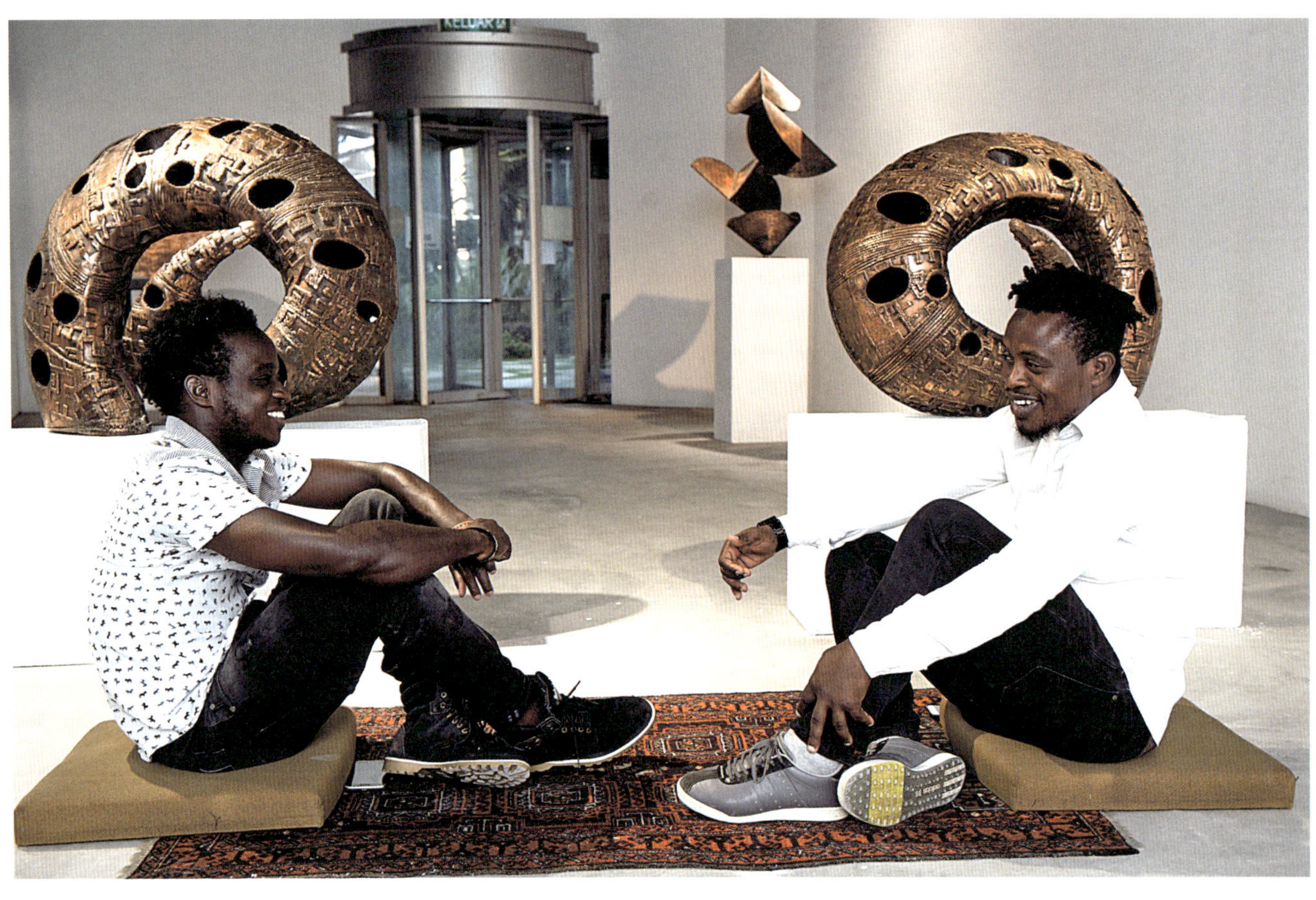

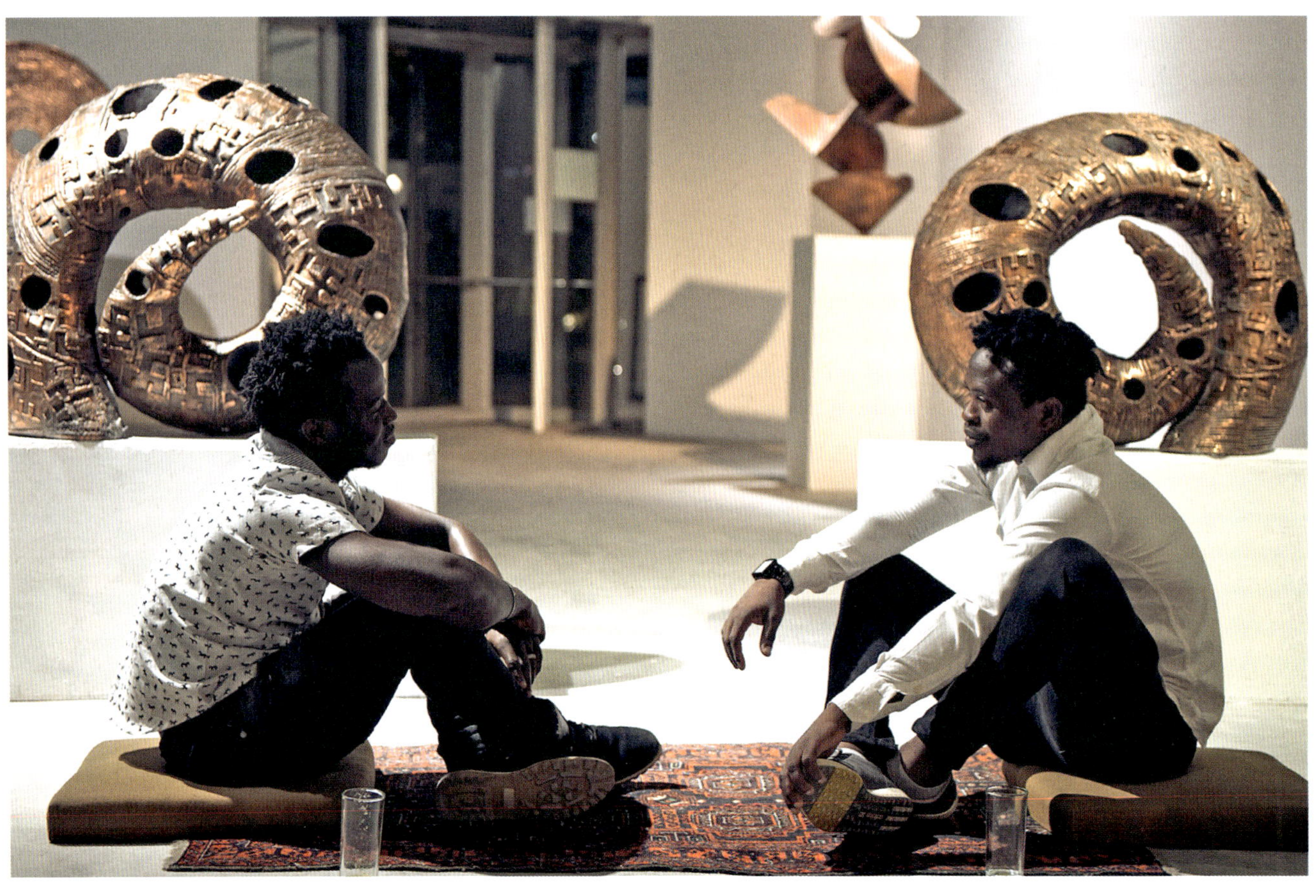

The Beloved Sun | 2018

Walking on the Moon, Wei-Ling Contemporary, Kuala Lumpur
180 minutes

The theme that united all the performances for *7* was the privacy of love. Within this greater narrative, individual accounts were also told. Some spoke of efforts to cross boundaries, many resistant to their breach. At Wei-Ling Contemporary in Kuala Lumpur, where the show was launched, Amin invited Suraj and Aziz, two Guinean refugees who are employed by the gallery, to perform a work that was inspired by them. Called *The Beloved Sun*, it was a play on their names: Suraj means "sun" in Arabic; Aziz means "beloved." The two, who have been friends since childhood, migrated to Malaysia together in search of a better life. Amin wished to celebrate their fraternal bond by having them face one another within an installation of a small Persian carpet placed before two of his imposing copper sculptures in the shape of water buffalo horns. Throughout the three-hour duration of the opening, they laughed and chatted with one another in a pidgin that no one at the gallery but they could grasp as attendants ceremoniously offered them food and drink. The performance made many attending the opening uncomfortable. Amin insisted that the privacy of Aziz and Suraj's conversation remain undisturbed.

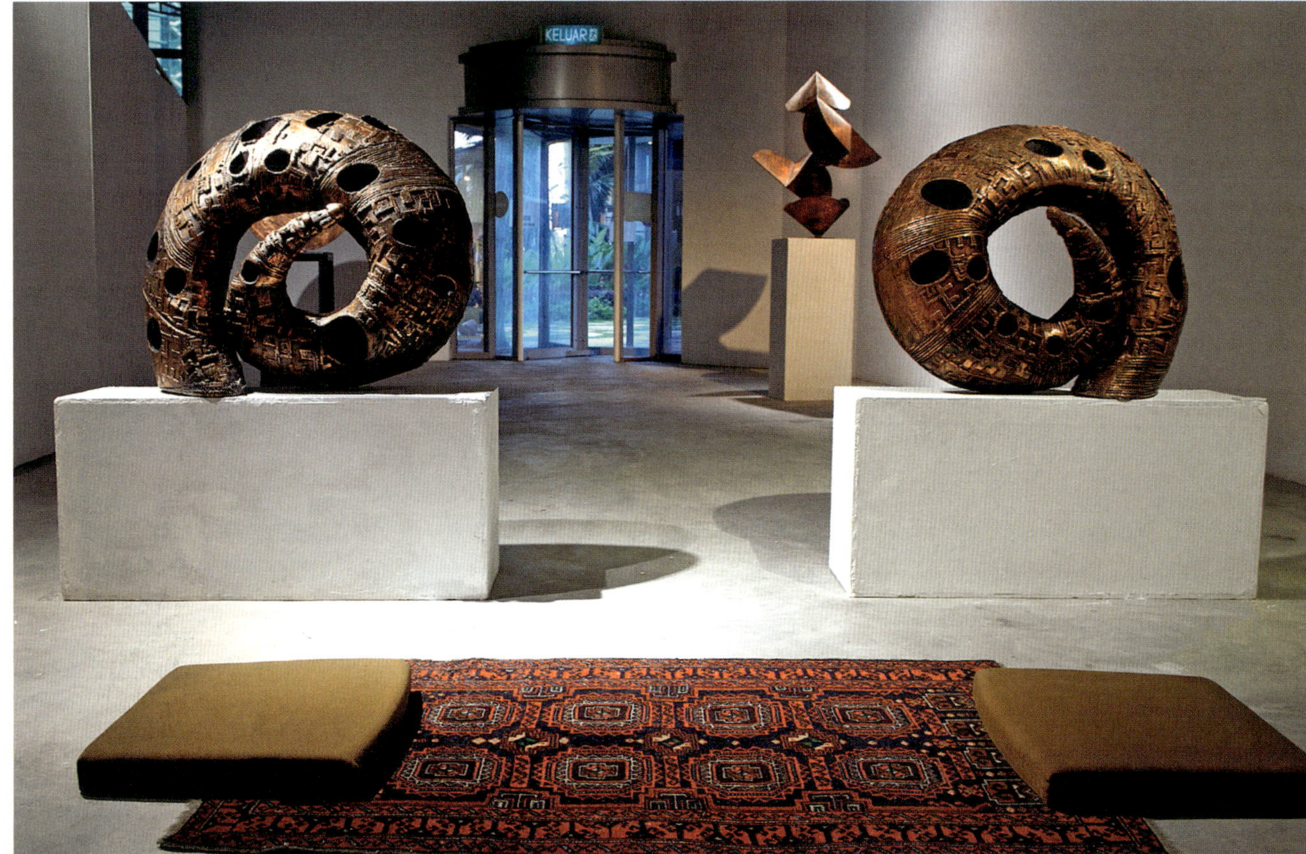

Photos courtesy Wei-Ling Contemporary

Paint Me | 2018

Mixed Tape [1], Canvas Gallery, Karachi
180 minutes

For *Mix Tape [1]*, an exhibition of group performance curated by Sara Vaqar Pagganwala at Canvas Gallery, Amin lay upon a red mattress in a pair of white shorts before an instruction stenciled upon the wall: "Paint me." A small abstract canvas in an ocean of color painted by his father hung high above his reclining form. On a tall table at his feet were acrylics in black and white as well as a palette knife. Early on in the show, someone hesitantly painted a stick figure upon his bare chest. Taking this as a clue as to how to proceed, others followed suit, some using the knife, others their fingers. By the end of the three-hour show, Amin was covered in paint. This instructional, interactive work was rooted in childhood memory. When Amin was little, his father would invite him into his studio, set up an easel next to his and permit him to use any of his oils. They would then show one another their finished canvases. Although his father never actively encouraged Amin to be an artist, this was their way of bonding. Through *Paint Me*, Amin's private and public worlds intersected. Lying prone and vulnerable, Amin, his eyes masked by purple-lensed aviator glasses and his head propped upon a violet pillow, quietly revisited his own tender moments of childhood as the public marked him in any way they chose.

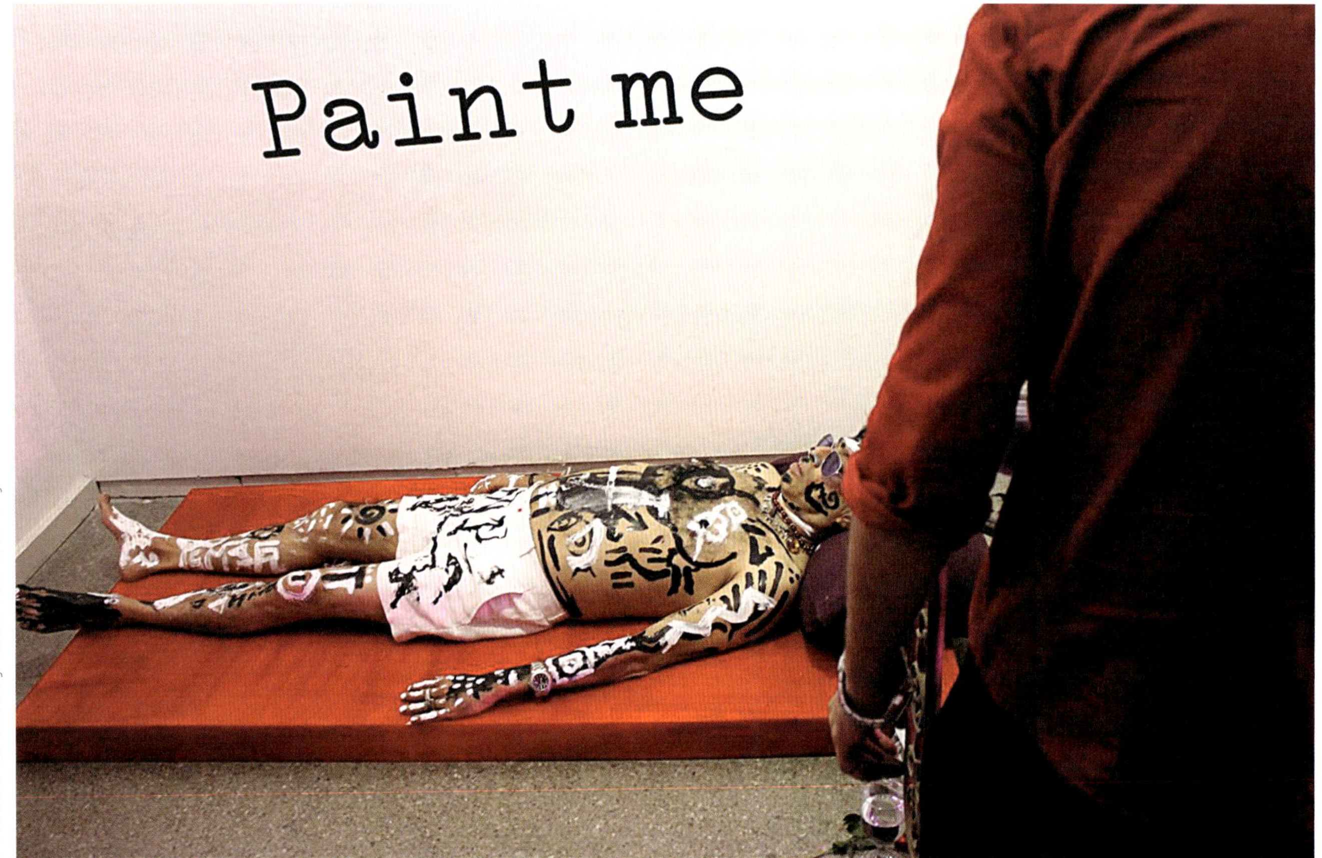

Photos courtesy Canvas Gallery

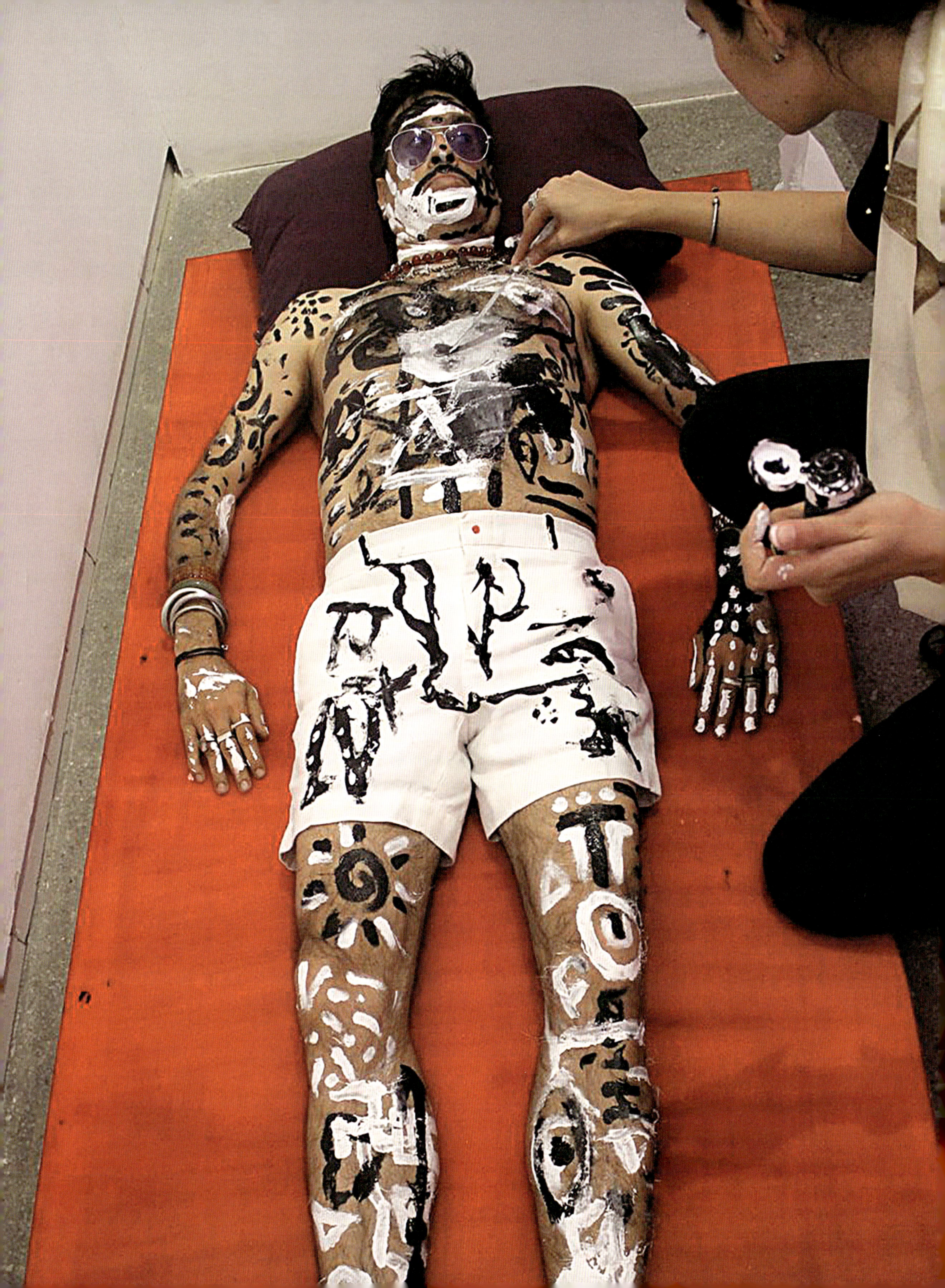

Call Me Fertile | 2019

Lahore Biennale 02 - Collateral Event, O Art Space, Lahore
180 minutes

Amin performed *Call Me Fertile* at O Art Space for a collateral event of the second Lahore Biennale, curated by Hoor Al Qasimi. For this work, he created a pregnant stomach out of copper to fit his body. He wanted it to feel like a natural extension of himself so that he inhabited it, and it him. On the opening of the group show, Amin, dressed in a somber business suit and polished dress shoes, tied the custom-made belly to his waist and moved throughout the milling crowd, making casual conversation. Some ignored his attire, others raised an eyebrow to it, while yet others fell into a familiar social pattern of congratulating him on his good fortune. The stomach was a recreation of one that Vinnie Ahmed had worn on the catwalk for *Sola Singhar* in 2001. (Amin had long ago remade the original work into a free-standing sculpture called *Empty Nest*.) Eggs, and the fertility they represent, have been a recurring motif for the artist. He has returned to the form again and again over the years in his sculpture, reimagining it in myriad ways. Through the transformative act of wearing the pregnant stomach, Amin appropriated the egg, furthering his investigation of gender through performance. To document the work, Amin asked Karachi-based photographer Omer Ehtisham to create formal portraits of him such as those routinely taken in studio settings to mark important life events.

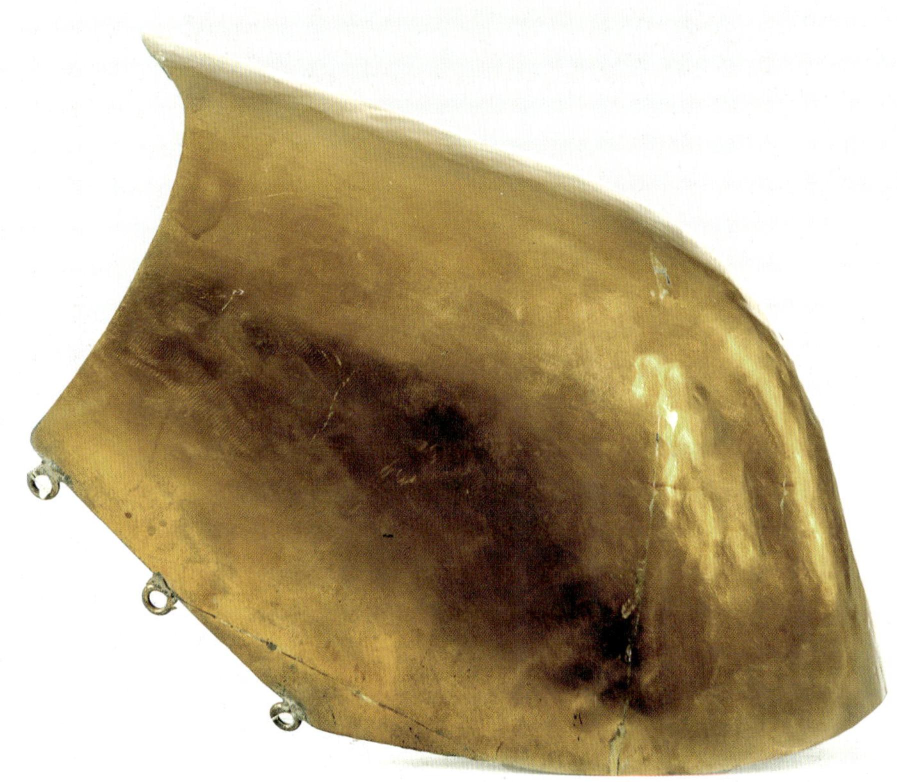

Stomach, 2019. Copper. 43 × 28 × 25.4 cm. Photo by Humayun Memon

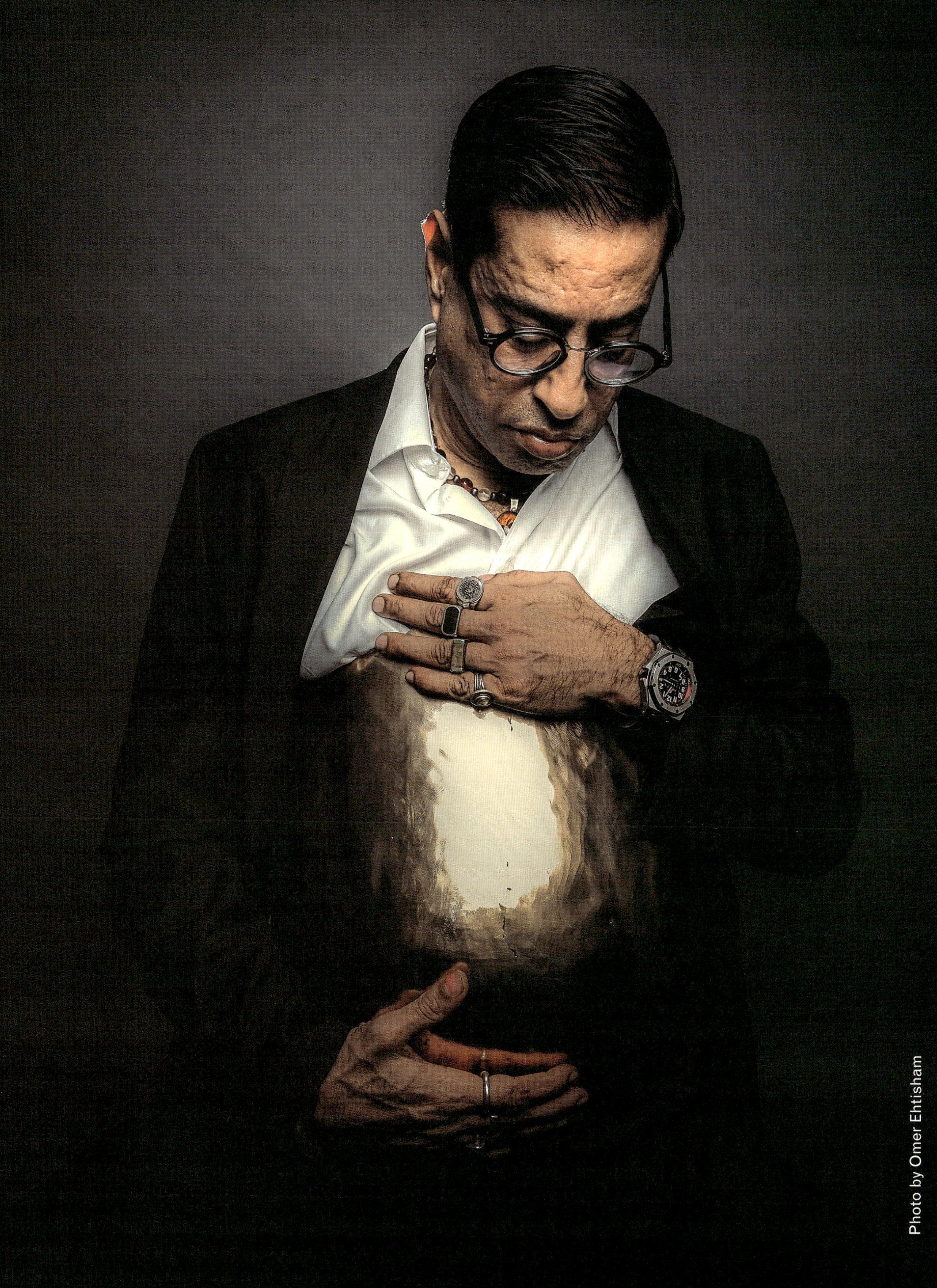

Photo by Omer Ehtisham

Healing II | 2020

Amin Gulgee Gallery, Karachi and V. DIGITAL ART SALON, Pinakothek der Moderne, Munich
34 minutes

At the height of the global lockdown due to the spread of COVID-19, Amin revisited his 2010 performance *The Healing*. This new work was part of what he came to call *The Corona Chronicles,* which also included his curatorial projects *LAL JADOO/RED MAGIC*, *The Trojan Donkey* and *If These Walls Could Talk*. *Healing II* occurred on the rooftop of Amin's home/gallery capped by his largescale mosaic *Salaam Gaudi*, installed in 2005. There was no audience present; rather, it was made specifically for video and photography and captured in a single take. As in the original performance, *Healing II* occurred during a time of terrible loss. And as in the first, Amin asked people close to him to help perform it. While Zarmeene Shah stood on a plinth reading a passage she chose from Albert Camus' *The Plague*, Adam Fahy-Majeed drew Amin, who was crouched upon a small cart into view. Adam and all other performers—except Amin—wore a perforated copper "plague mask." Amin brandished long copper fingernails, a spiked helmet of copper and steel and wings of copper, steel and gold leaf. Graffiti artist Sanki King had also marked his face and torso with Maori-like patterns. Australian-born Adam removed Amin's helmet and sheared his head with an electric shaver, handing the clumps of hair to Sara Vaqar Pagganwala, who gathered them in four terra-cotta bowls. Amin precariously navigated his pinions up and around a narrow spiral staircase to a terrace above, where, higher still, Muhammad Osama Saeed and Sanki King reclined on the base of a soaring iron and glass sculpture in the shape of an eye. Amin rocked back and forth, allowing his earth-bound wings to caress the wind, a dance as hopeful as it was sad. In a baptismal gesture, Sanki King poured milk over Amin's head from a clay vase that he had also brushed with black paint. He then tossed the terra-cotta vessel in a long arc to the terrace floor, where it shattered.

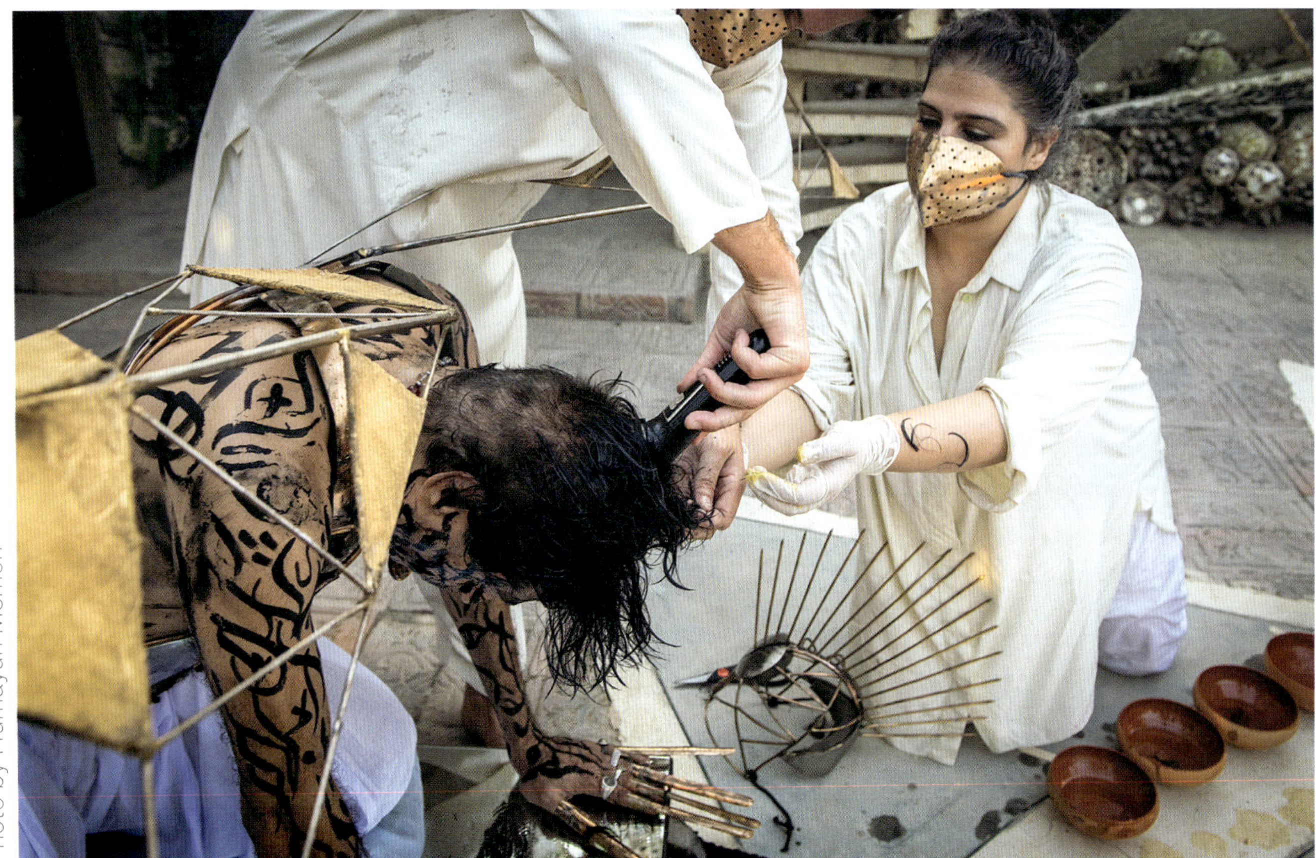

Photo by Humayun Memon

Q | 2020

Drawing Room Diamonds, Sanat Initiative, Karachi
95 minutes

Amin created *Q* for a group exhibition curated by Champa at Sanat Initiative in Karachi. Champa is a fictitious character invented by Emaan Mahmud for her ongoing blog, which chronicles the random thoughts of a high society Karachi woman who imagines herself an expert on contemporary Pakistani art. Amin created an alter ego of his own for her show. An hour before the opening, Amin asked Sara Vaqar Pagganwala to rub his face, chest, arms and legs with Holi colors of green and purple. Wearing only a loincloth of red felt, he lay inside a copper boat that he had created for *River Dreams of Alexander* in 2006. For this work, he had repurposed its interior with the same fabric as his lungi and stenciled a large black "Q" above his resting head. The night of the opening, "Champa" pulled the boat onto the floor of the gallery from behind a curtain. Fitted with a microphone, Amin called her name over and over again in an otherworldly voice as he fired two plastic toy guns that discharged soap bubbles. Following the curator's lead, others began to drag the boat this way and that. Soon he was being spun around in dizzying circles. Having relinquished control of his physical trajectory to the whims of the group, Amin focused on maintaining his own equilibrium. This is a survival mechanism commonly adopted by those who appear strange, unorthodox, or queer, to the majority. Amin's statement for the show was: "?".

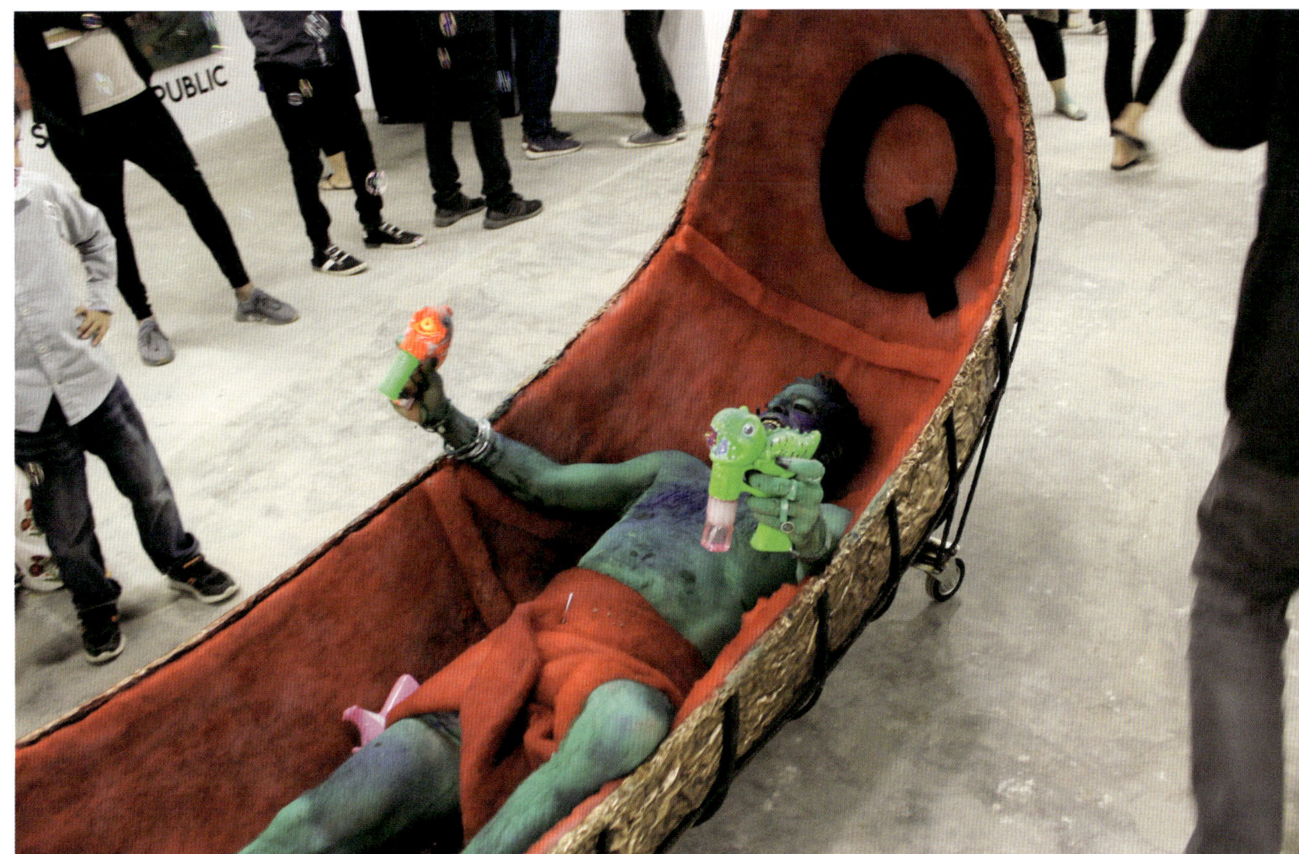

Photo courtesy Sanat Initiative

This Is Not Your El Dorado | 2021

Performative Utopias, Cité internationale des arts, Paris
77 minutes

Curators Dominique Malaquais and Julie Peghini gave Amin carte blanche for his collaborative performance *This Is Not Your El Dorado* which took place at the Cité internationale des arts in Paris on September 11, 2021 from 6:37 pm to 7:54 pm as part of their larger project, *Performative Utopias*, an academic conference on contemporary African performance. An obsessive reader of fiction, Amin saw this as an opportunity to write his own story through performance. He conceived each of the five levels of the Cité's gallery as a chapter within a novel running through the mind of the reader/observer. For this happening, 18 performances, both live and pre-recorded in sound or video, took place at the same time. Its prologue was a sound piece presented outside the gallery's doors in which Cameroonian writer Lionel Manga read aloud his short story in French about the American civil rights movement of the 1960s. Paris-based actor Olivier Llorden screeched as he interacted with a Minotaur-like helmet created by Amin. Once the doors to the show were officially opened, Congolese poet and rapper Vhan Olsen Dombo seemed to pull himself with a rope into the white cube, crawling through the churning legs of the crowd. Inside as out, Amin's sculptural pieces connected the varied performances as if by a thread. Multidisciplinary artists from across the globe adopted his helmets, masks, blindfolds, bustiers, fingernails, Arabic letters and ceremonial Hindu pigment to tell a story that was not only his, but part of their own. Dominique and Julie wrote in their curatorial note: "The dreams and myths of some are the source of marginalization and exile for others. *This Is Not Your El Dorado* confronts this terrible paradox."

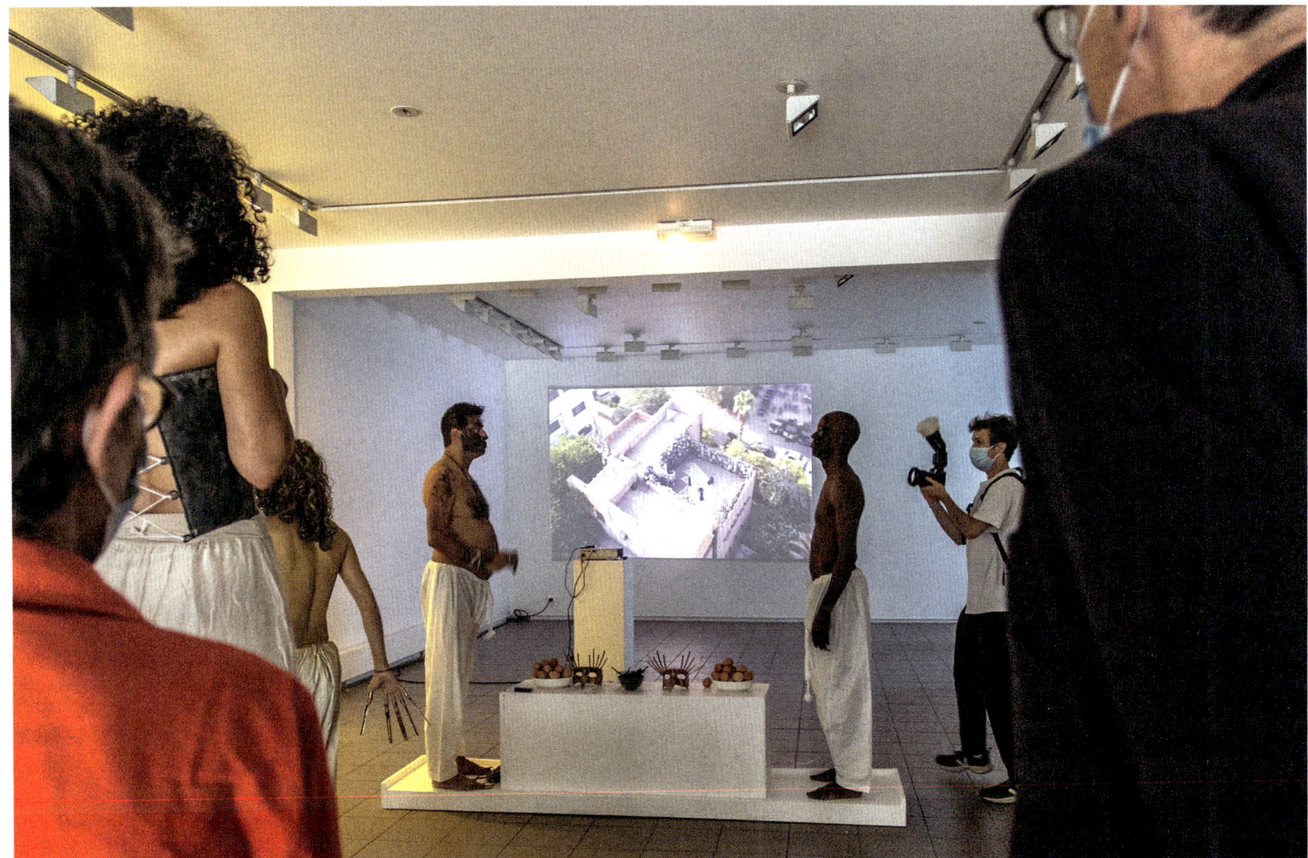

Photo by Nathalie Tiennot

Eating El Dorado | 2021

New Age Art, Indus Valley School of Art and Architecture, Karachi
27 minutes

Amin envisioned *Eating El Dorado* as an epilogue to *This Is Not Your El Dorado*. He worked on the two simultaneously. He performed the latter in the courtyard of the Indus Valley School of Art and Architecture four days after his return from Paris for a group show curated by Emaan Mahmud. The work included elements from his collaborative performance at the Cité internationale des arts, including his Minotaur helmet, bird masks and elongated nails. Eggs—70 in all—were central to *Eating El Doardo*. While in the earlier work Amin and the French-Cameroonian artist Lamyne M had inhabited the beaked and long-lashed masks to perform a solemn and sensuous ritual commemorating eggs, here Amin communed with the horned helmet to greedily devour them. In *Eating El Dorado*, Dostain Balach and Alina Sadaf Marri, their faces, arms and long curls dusted in gold, descended a flight of stairs. Wearing the aerial visors, the waif-like pair faced one another across two steel trays of eggs, making a series of harmonious gestures akin to a traditional Baloch dance. Amin, in the helmet and talons, pursued them down the steps, making guttural noises amplified by a mic. The two took turns feeding him raw eggs, which he hungrily took into his mouth, then spat out. Growling, he gathered more eggs in his nailed hands and broke them over his head. The yolks and whites ran slimily over his helmet and down the front of his black coat. Unsatisfied by their offering, he angrily smashed the remaining few before charging into the audience. The twin performances seemed to address our times. *This Is Not Your El Dorado* took place on the 20th anniversary of September 11, an event that brought loss, trauma and upheaval not only to America, but to the region where the artist lives. *Eating El Dorado* occurred in the midst of COVID-19, a pandemic that saw economic disparity yawn the world over.

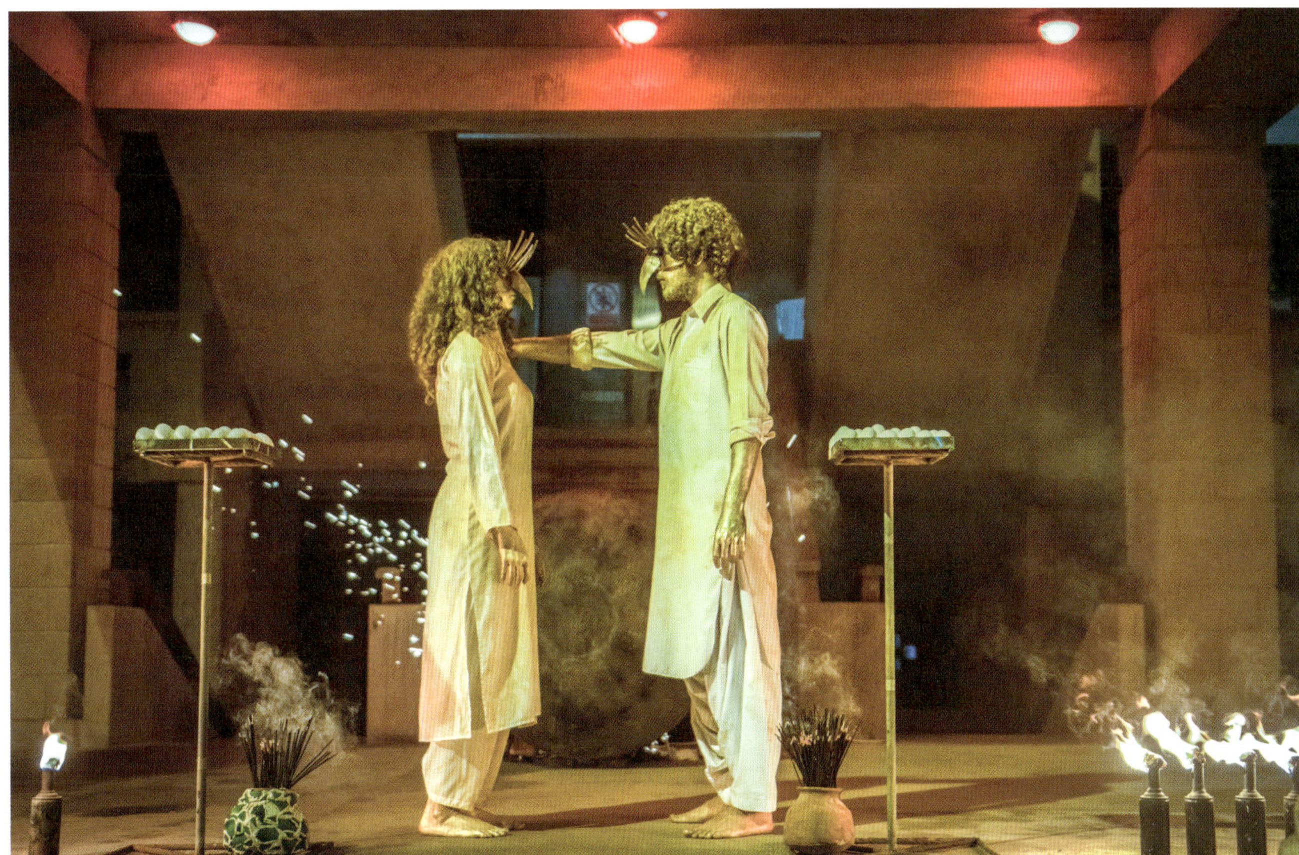

Photo by Humayun Memon

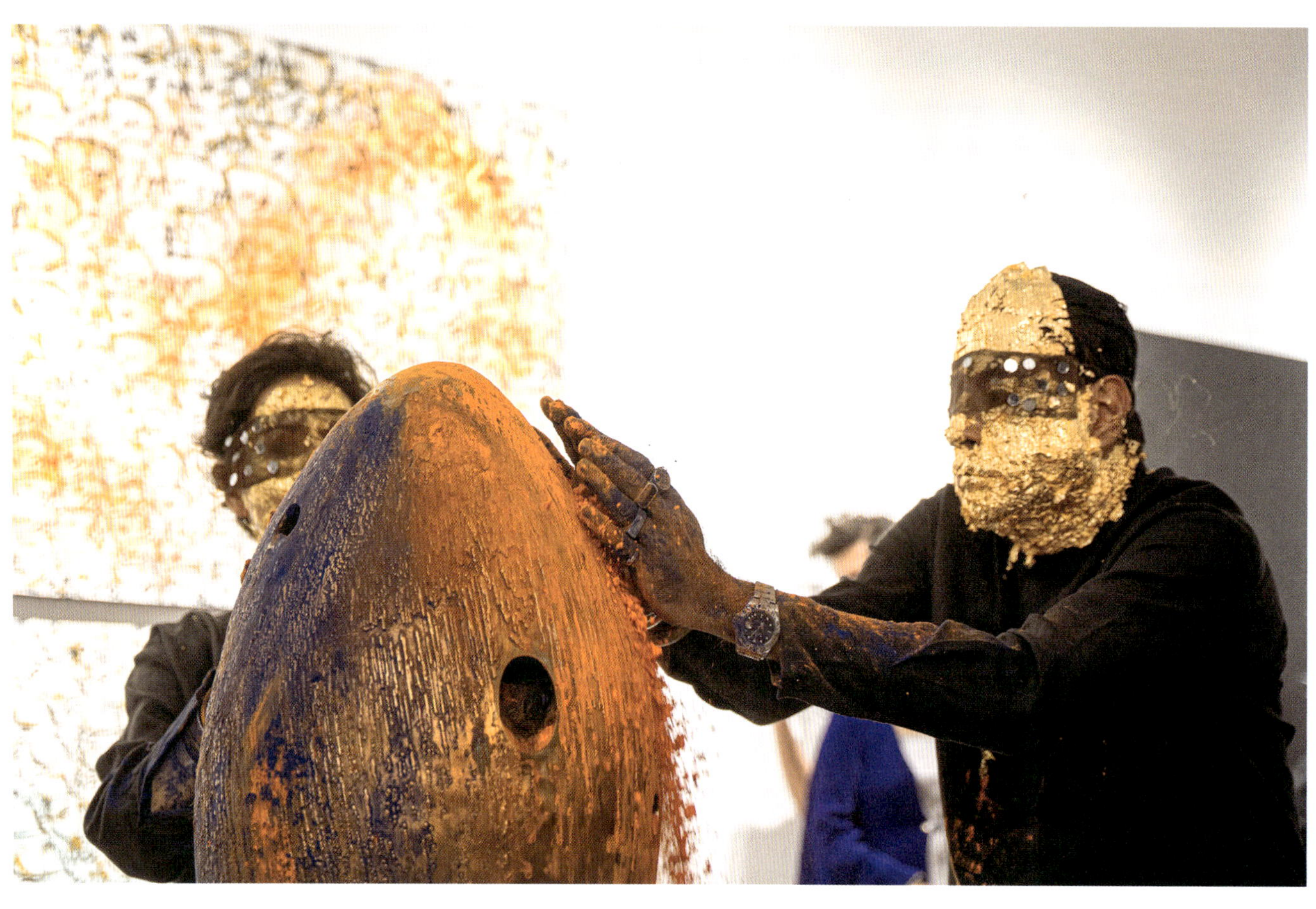

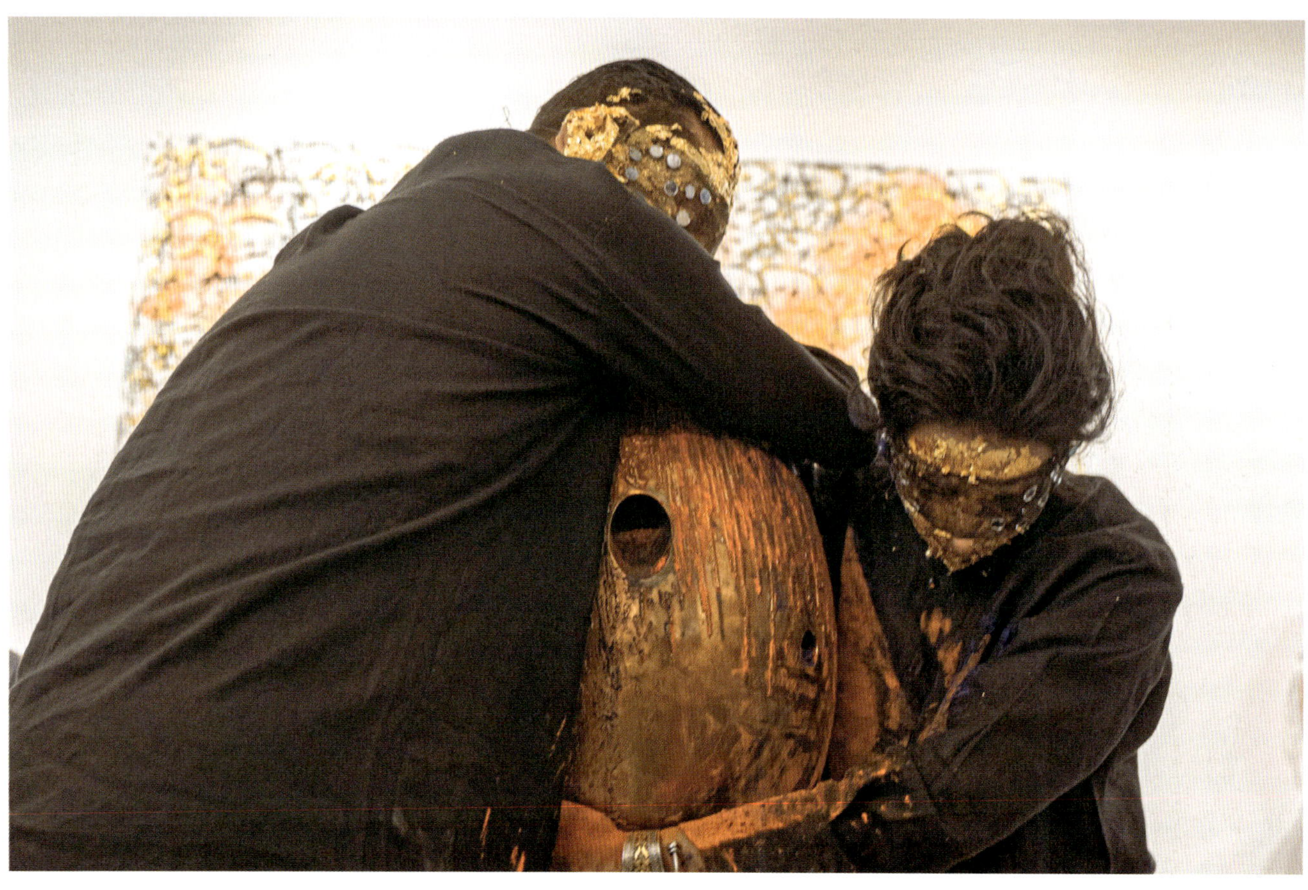

The Irritable Heart | 2022

Zenana-Mardana, Frere Hall, Karachi
25 minutes

Amin performed *The Irritable Heart* with the painter Nazia Ejaz, daughter of the legendary Pakistani singer Noor Jehan (1926-2000), for *Zenana-Mardana* (Feminine-Masculine), a group show organized by Pomme Amina Gohar at Karachi's Frere Hall in February 2022. The title of the work refers to a heart condition characterized by breathlessness, palpitation, weakness and exhaustion that is sometimes suffered by soldiers. Before the live performance, Amin and Nazia had recorded both their voices and layered them over the beating of a human heart, which first pounded rhythmically then sporadically. The night of the opening, as their sound piece played, Amin and Nazia, dressed in black *kurta pajama*, a genderless outfit, solemnly walked into Frere Hall's Galerie Sadequain and its assembled crowd. Their faces were covered in flaking gold leaf, their eyes unreadable through strips of copper mesh sewn with small round mirrors. They showed one another their open palms, then walked around Amin's sculpture, *Infinity Egg III*, which stood on a black granite pedestal. On either side were two terra-cotta bowls holding orange and purple powder. The two scooped up the pigment into their hands and took turns painting the egg, then wrapped their arms around it in a lingering embrace. After completing this ritual, they once again showed one another their palms, now streaked with color, as they stared into each other's eyes. They faced the audience, showing them their hands as well, before slowly walking out of the gallery and down the steps of Frere Hall. The work spoke of the blurring of male and female. Amin wished both Nazia and himself to find healing through their mutual appropriation of his egg.

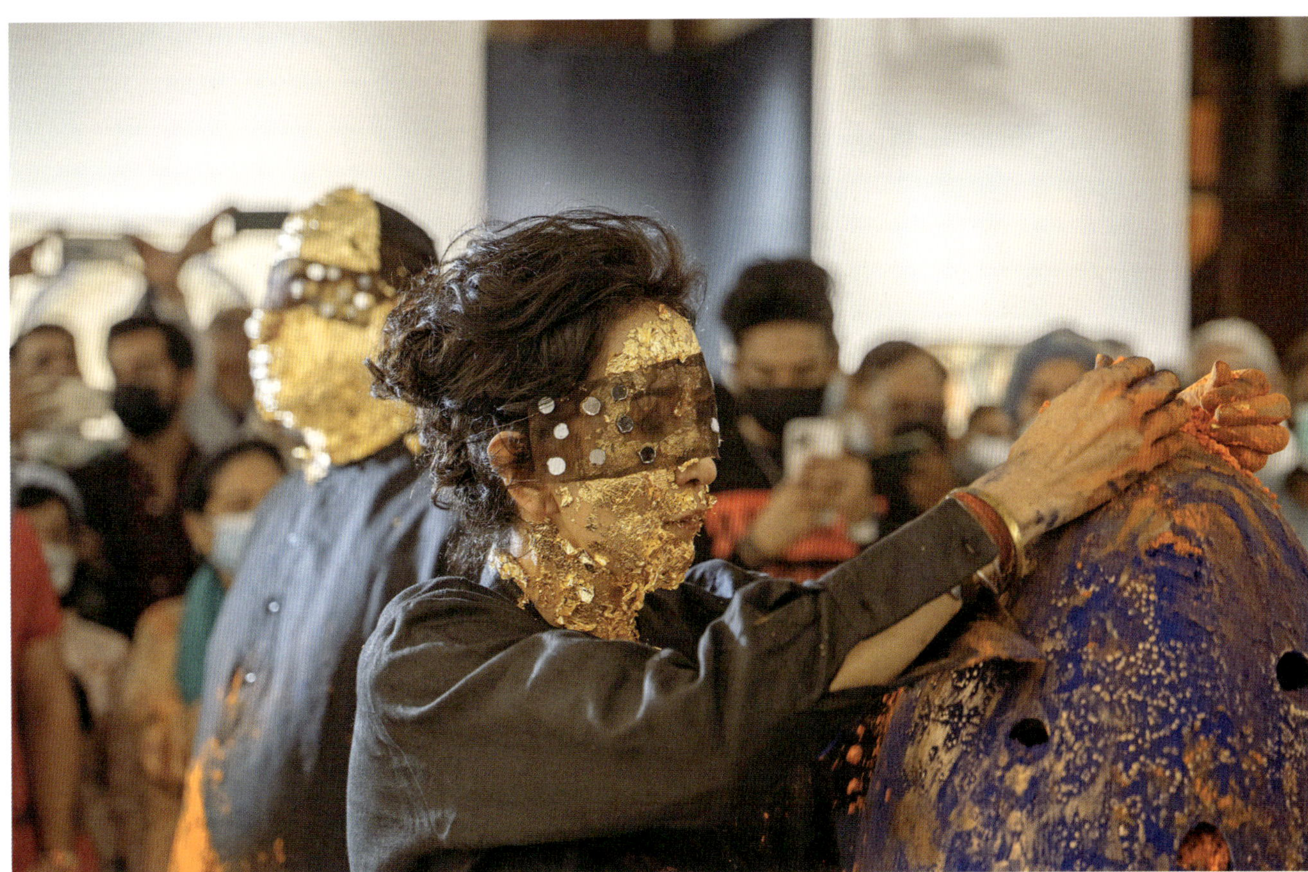

Photos by Farhan Baig

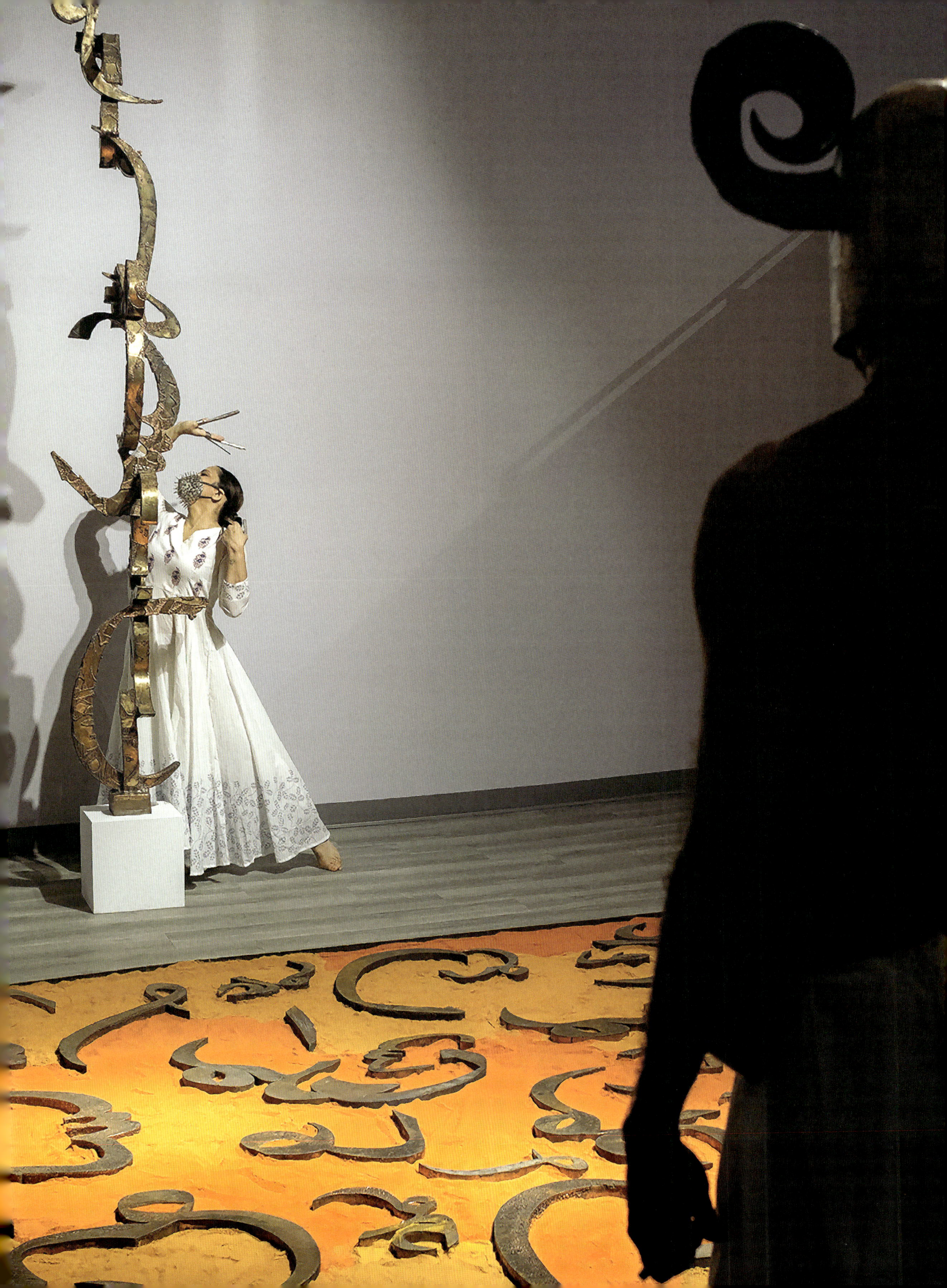

Kiss of the Spider Woman | 2022

The Spider Speaketh in Tongues, South Asia Institute, Chicago
77 minutes

Kiss of the Spider Woman was a collaborative performance that took place the night after the opening of Amin's solo exhibition, *The Spider Speaketh in Tongues*, curated by Adam Fahy-Majeed, at the South Asia Institute in Chicago. The performers included old friends of Amin's who had travelled from all over the United States to take part; young artists whom Adam had met as a graduate student at the School of the Art Institute of Chicago; and classical South Asian dancers based in the area. Amin held a series of conversations with each to determine how their individual narratives could merge with his. After jointly agreeing on how each performance would unfold, Amin selected one or more of his objects for them to wear. Nineteen performers enacted their works over 77 minutes. Some reacted to the work on display, which included sculpture, installation, sound and video. Shiwali Varshney Tenner, extended copper nails on her fingers, fluidly danced Kathak-like movements before *Zero Gravity*. An androgynous-looking Dominique Knowles, wrapped in a silver bustier and holding a single copper leaf, stood motionless before the installation *Liminal Letters*. Some interacted with the audience: Anene Ejikeme, dressed as a traditional Nigerian woman, cat-eye sunglasses and Amin's spiked mask obscuring her face, approached random people and asked, sotto voce, "What is your sexuality?" Irene Wa, flecked in gold leaf and wearing a silver helmet, placed her hands on people's backs and made sonar-like sounds. Amin, a crushed sheet of copper tied around his midriff, a horned helmet on his head, allowed Hassan Raazee, whose face was clouded by mesh, to flog him then place a hard-boiled egg into his mouth. The performers, whether floating or interacting with the work or each other, seemed to merge into one. As Amin said during a post-show discursive session over Zoom, "It was a shared belief." Keny De La Peña, who, like a medieval troubadour, walked back and forth before Amin's projection *Algorithm IV* singing an incomprehensible mix of Spanish, Portuguese and Catalan, wearing not only Amin's objects but a sarong that he himself had silkscreened, added, "It was a caring for each other."

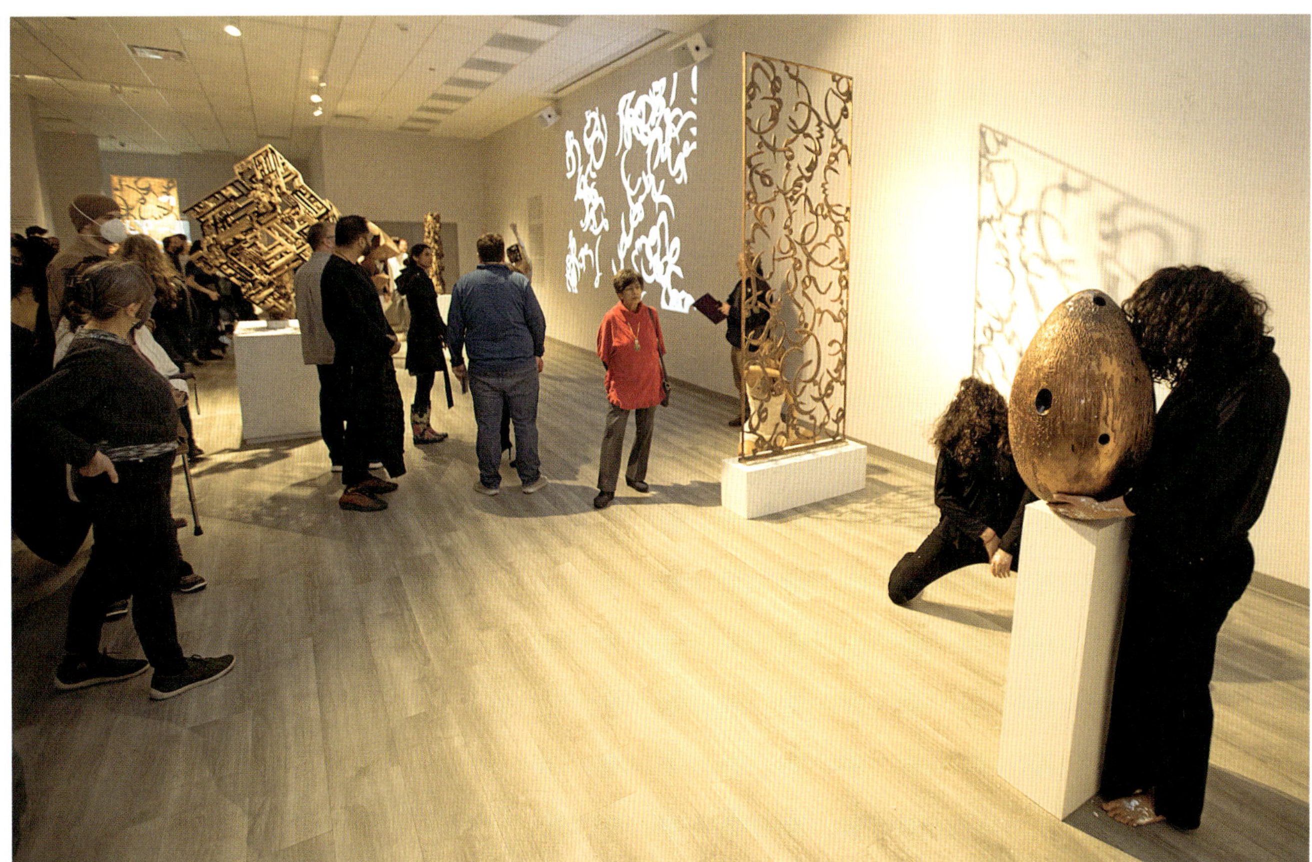

Photos by Ludvig Perés

The Requiem | 2022

ENTERLACS/INTERLACED, Cité internationale des arts, Paris
34 minutes

In June 2022, Amin presented *The Requiem* for the inauguration of *ENTRELACS/INTERLACED* at the Cité internationale des arts in Paris. This was an exhibition, symposium and series of performances in memory of Dominique Malaquais (1964-2021). An art historian and political scientist, Dominique dedicated her life and work to African worlds. Amin, who had known Dominique since they were freshmen at Yale, performed *The Requiem* with Bart Legum, Dominque's widower. Bare-chested, both wore white *shalwar*. Anointed in gold leaf, Bart's head and shoulders were enveloped in a shroud of copper mesh that Amin had made for him. On Amin's head was a copper helmet with curved, ram-like horns, rectangular eyes and a long, triangular nose. Like so many of Amin's worn sculptures, these evoked a mythical era of his own making. (For this performance, they corresponded to his installation *Elysian Fields* for the accompanying show at the Cité's gallery, where he reimagined the resting place of the heroic and virtuous in Greek mythology as a bed of coal strewn with fragments of Arabic text.) Hidden on an upper terrace of the Cité's courtyard, Bart began the performance by producing screeching cords from an electric guitar. Amin frantically pushed himself through the assembled crowd below to a plastic sheet spread on the ground where nine plates holding powder of various colors had been placed in a circle. Crouching at their center, Amin slammed his palms to the ground and mournfully cried "Allah!" three times. He then grabbed handfuls of the pigment and tossed them over himself. Bart slowly descended a brief flight of steps, still playing his guitar, and perched on a high stool. Amin crawled towards him, marking the hem of his *shalwar*. Bart performed a song in both English and French that he had written, a kind of mantra that he sings to himself whenever Dominque's absence becomes particularly painful. Solemnly, he sang: "Rest with the angels, my wonderful Do / You are an angel, my wonderful Do / You are my love and my light and my life."

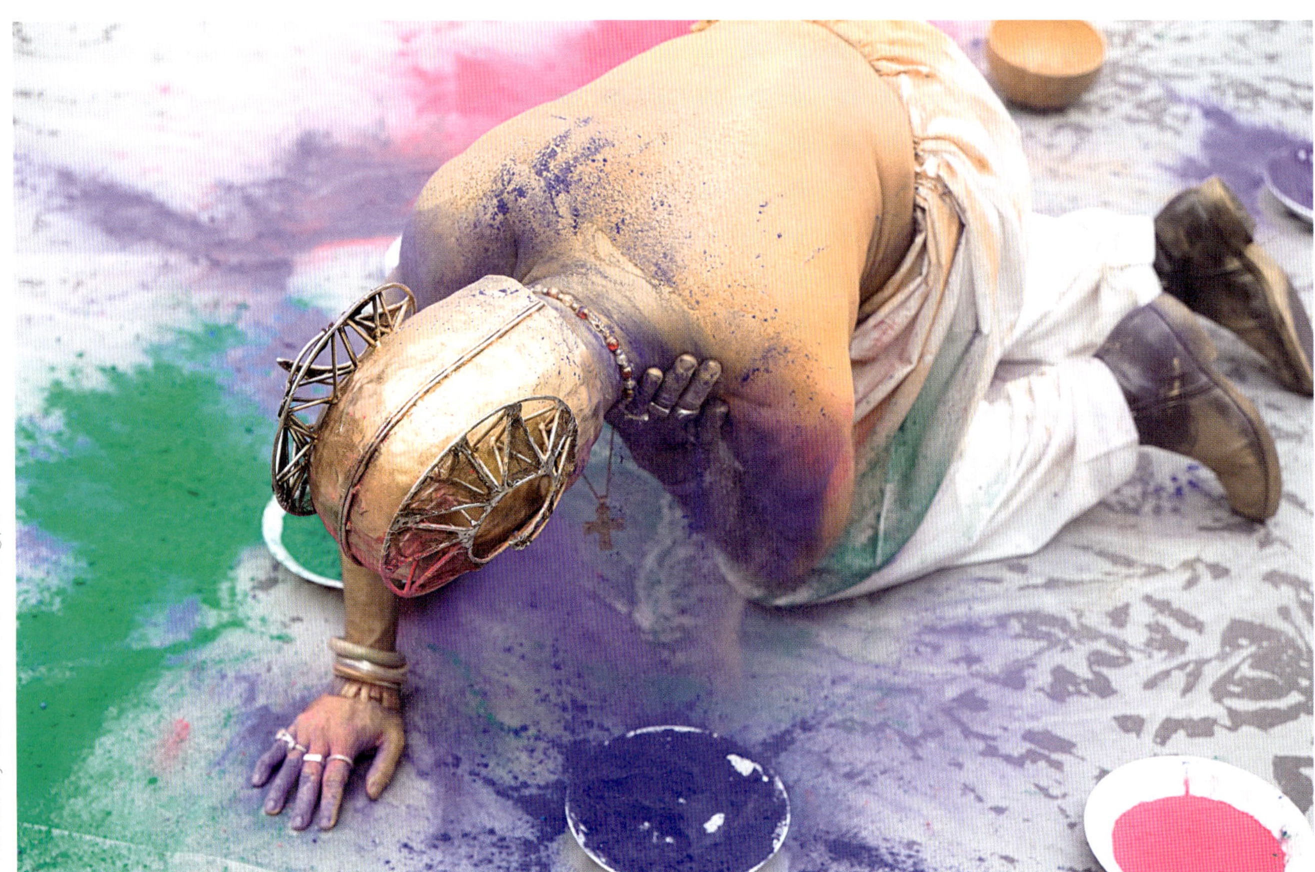

Photos by Maurine Tric-Adagp, Paris

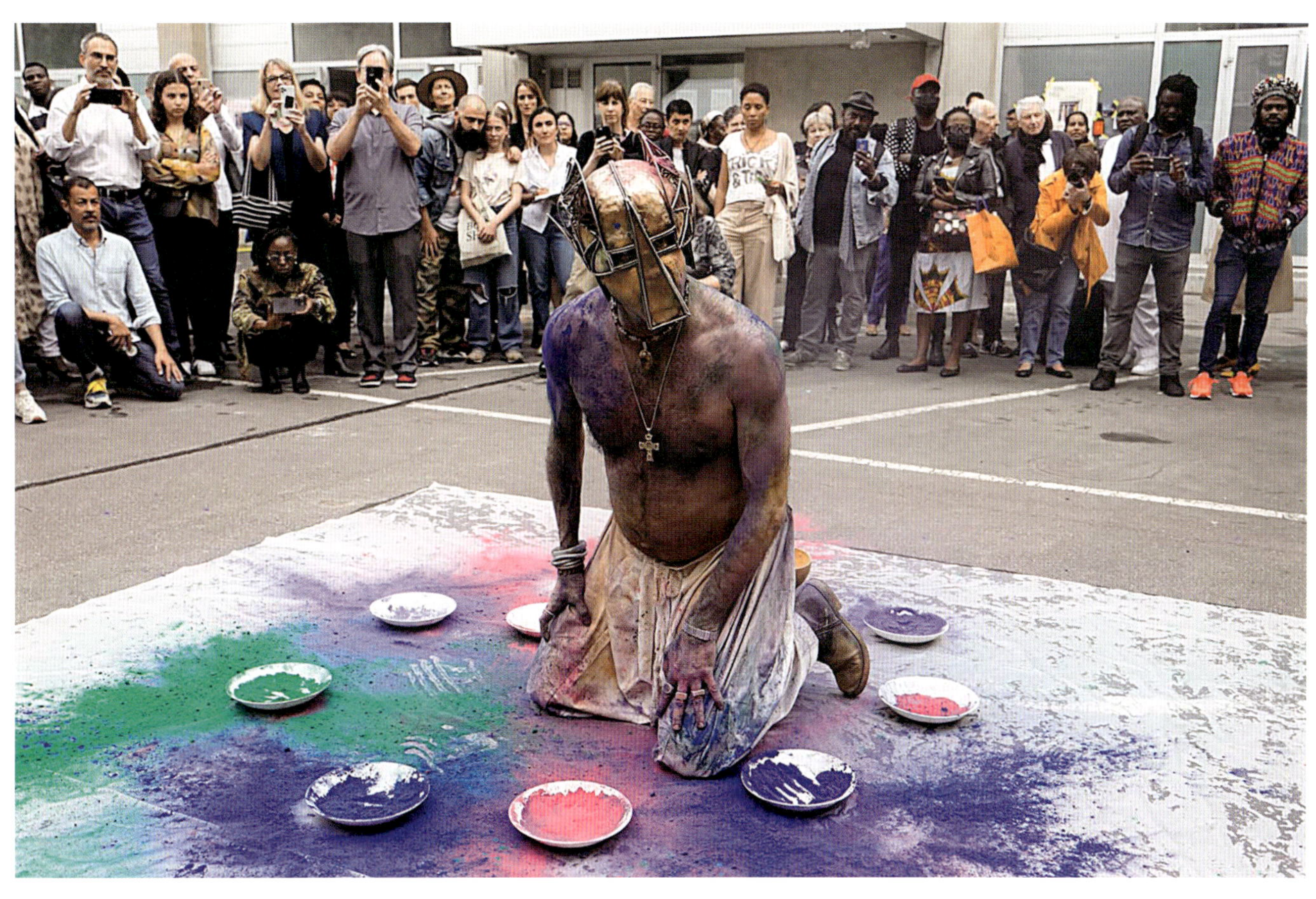

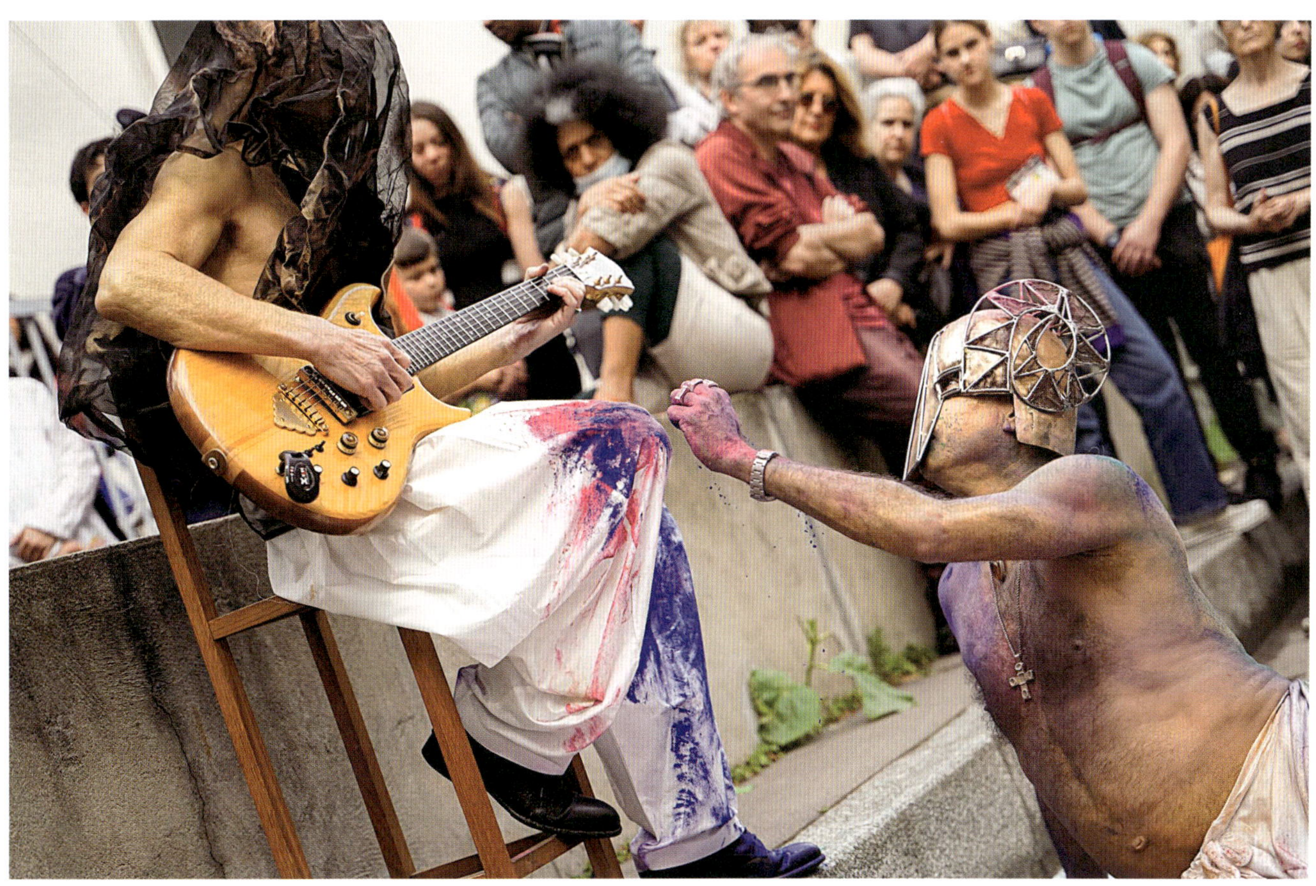

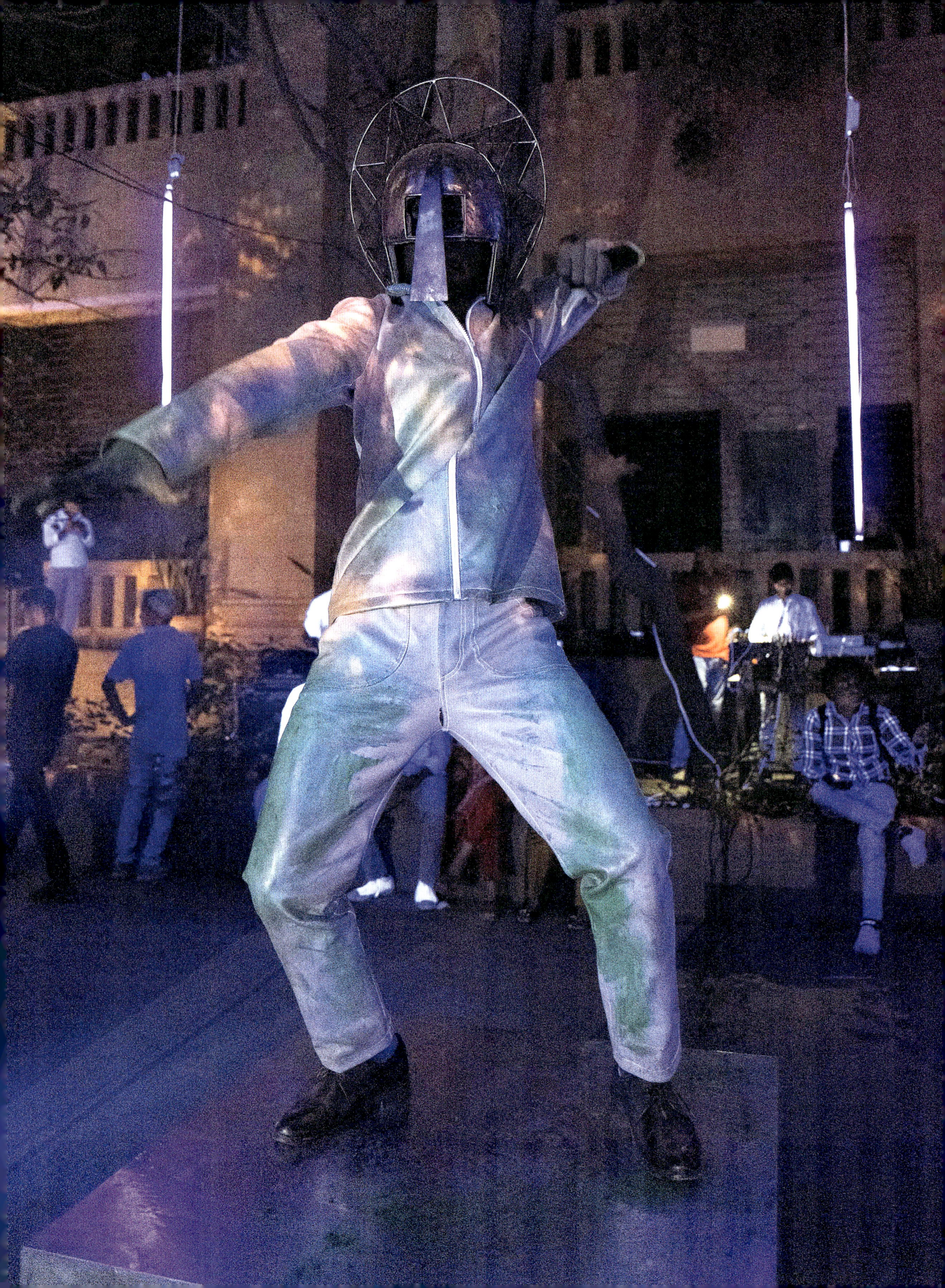

Forgotten March | 2022

Karachi Biennale 2022
34 minutes

In the fall of 2022, Amin conducted a workshop over a period of two months with students from Karachi's Narayan Jagannath Vaidya High School (NJV). Fifty pupils showed up for the open call. Amin eventually narrowed this down to a dozen boys and girls, age 14 to 17, all of whom were boarders from interior Sindh, which had just been devastated by unprecedented floods. Amin divided them into two groups: movement and sound. He positioned both batches, wearing Hellenistic helmets and other objects that he had created, on and around a line of plywood plinths covered in gleaming tin. The idea was to elevate them to the status of heroes. Amin, who performed alongside the children and four of their teachers, wanted them all to bond through this imagining of fantastical childhood games. One boy repeatedly jumped over another. Another boy climbed a tall ladder, stretching his arms wide once he reached the top. A girl and a boy revolved around one another, dancing, punching the air, throwing pigment. Dimly lit by black lights hanging from trees, the overwhelming impression of *Forgotten March* was one of sound. This was created by what Amin came to call The Memory Orchestra. The organist and *tabla* player were music teachers at the school. The other members of the ensemble were students at the NJV: three girls sang a wordless melody; two boys jammed on acoustic guitars; two other boys screamed periodically. Amin referred to this as "un-music." He wanted the teachers to unlearn their music, the students to improvise at will. Throughout his performance trajectory, Amin has engaged with sound, sometimes prerecording his own, sometimes asking professional musicians to perform classical South Asian pieces or create their own electronic compositions. This, however, was the first time he had conducted a live orchestra. *Forgotten March* took place at the NJV for the opening of the third Karachi Biennale. The audience moved around the performers, aloft on their plinths in a vertical format, enveloped in sound.

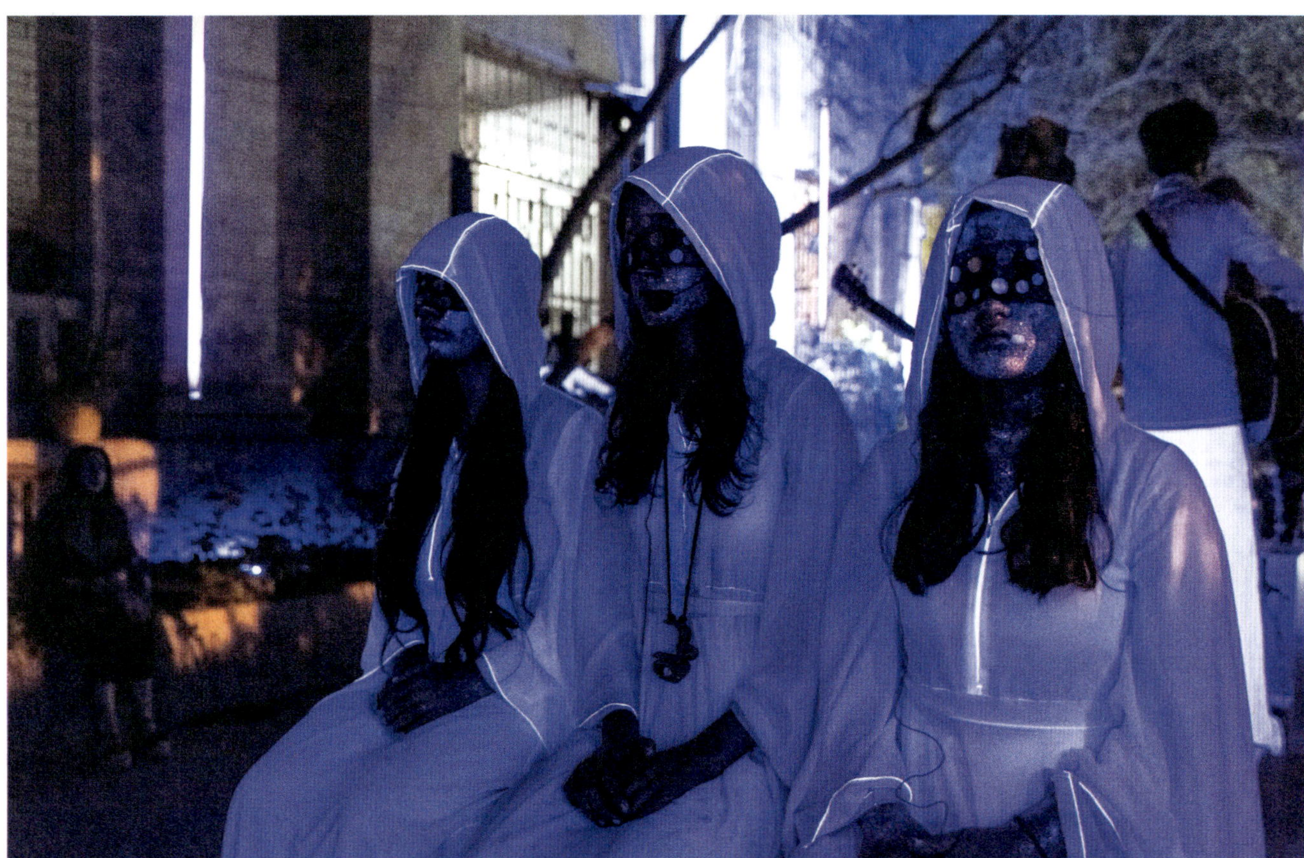

Photos by Farhan Baig

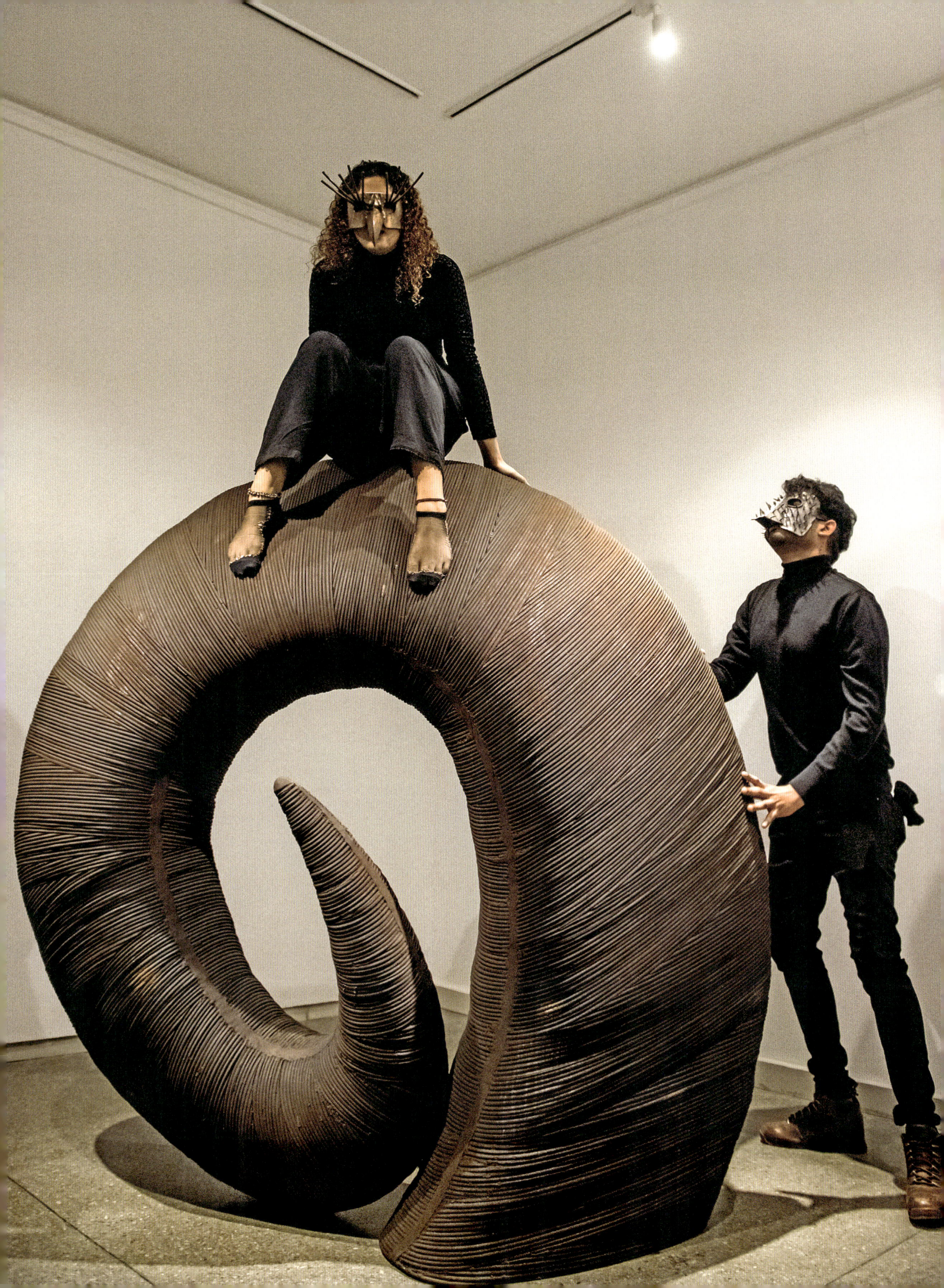

Fairytale 72 | 2023

Spooky Action at a Distance, Canvas Gallery, Karachi
27 minutes

Rather than a curated exhibition of simultaneous performance such as *The Q Rickshaw Project* or *Jagah Hai*, *Fairytale 72* was what Amin calls "a collaborative performance." Other examples include *This Is Not Your El Dorado* in Paris in 2021 and *Kiss of the Spider Woman* in Chicago in 2022. For these, Amin asks a multidisciplinary group to perform a work that he has conceived, usually, but not always, involving objects that he has made. Sometimes he takes part in these performances; sometimes he doesn't. Sometimes they occur within a display of his sculptures and installations; other times they don't. Amin presented *Fairytale 72* on the opening of his solo exhibition *Spooky Action at a Distance*, curated by Adam Fahy-Majeed on February 7, 2023 at Canvas Gallery in Karachi. For this collaborative work, he asked 17 others to enter another dimension with him for about an hour. (*Fairytale 72* began at the characteristically imprecise hour of 6:43 pm.) Safeer Jaffrey and Umaina Khan, both wearing masks that they had borrowed from shelves on the gallery's walls, performed with Amin's monumental sculpture, *The Iron Horn*. Sitting on top of it, Umaina, a painter, sang a line from a song in Saraiki that she had written: "Oh, I am looking for you." Safeer, a musician, moved around the horn, leaning against it, responding with another line from the song: "I am walking in the city alone." Actor Shaikh Faizan Chawla sat shirtless on a stool in a narrow alcove of the gallery. Wearing a helmet called *The Ram*, he wrapped his arms around his legs, seeming to retreat into himself. Her face covered in a copper shroud, Maha Minhaj confronted male spectators, shouting at them in Urdu: "Who are you?"; "Where do you come from?"; "What are you doing here?" The alarmed men often tried to explain themselves. In Pakistan, where most public spaces are male-dominated, this was her way of challenging their presence. Through their collaboration, Amin and his fellow performers created a story that had personal resonances for all those involved. Amin likens the process to his object making. His sculptures organically assemble themselves, he states, as do all his collaborative performances.

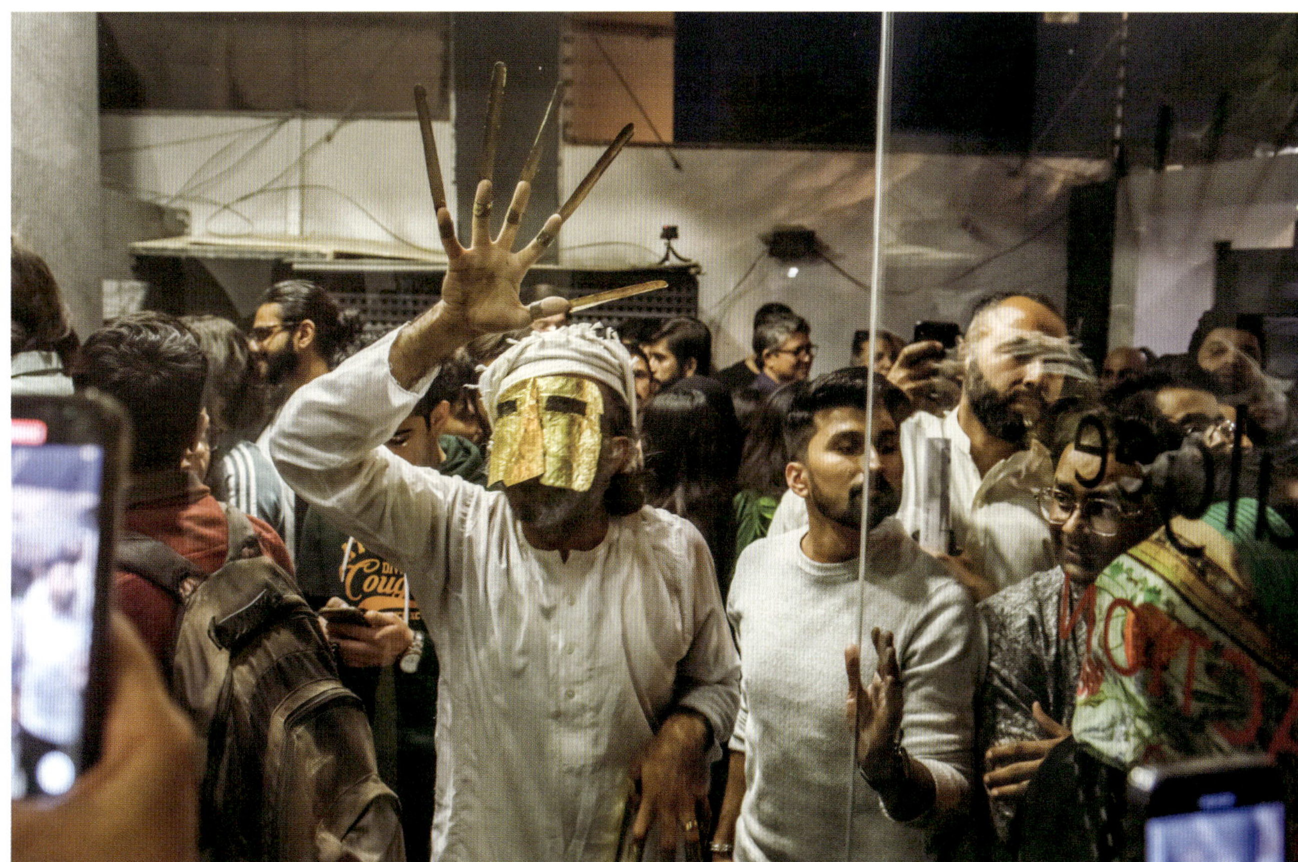

Photos by Humayun Memon

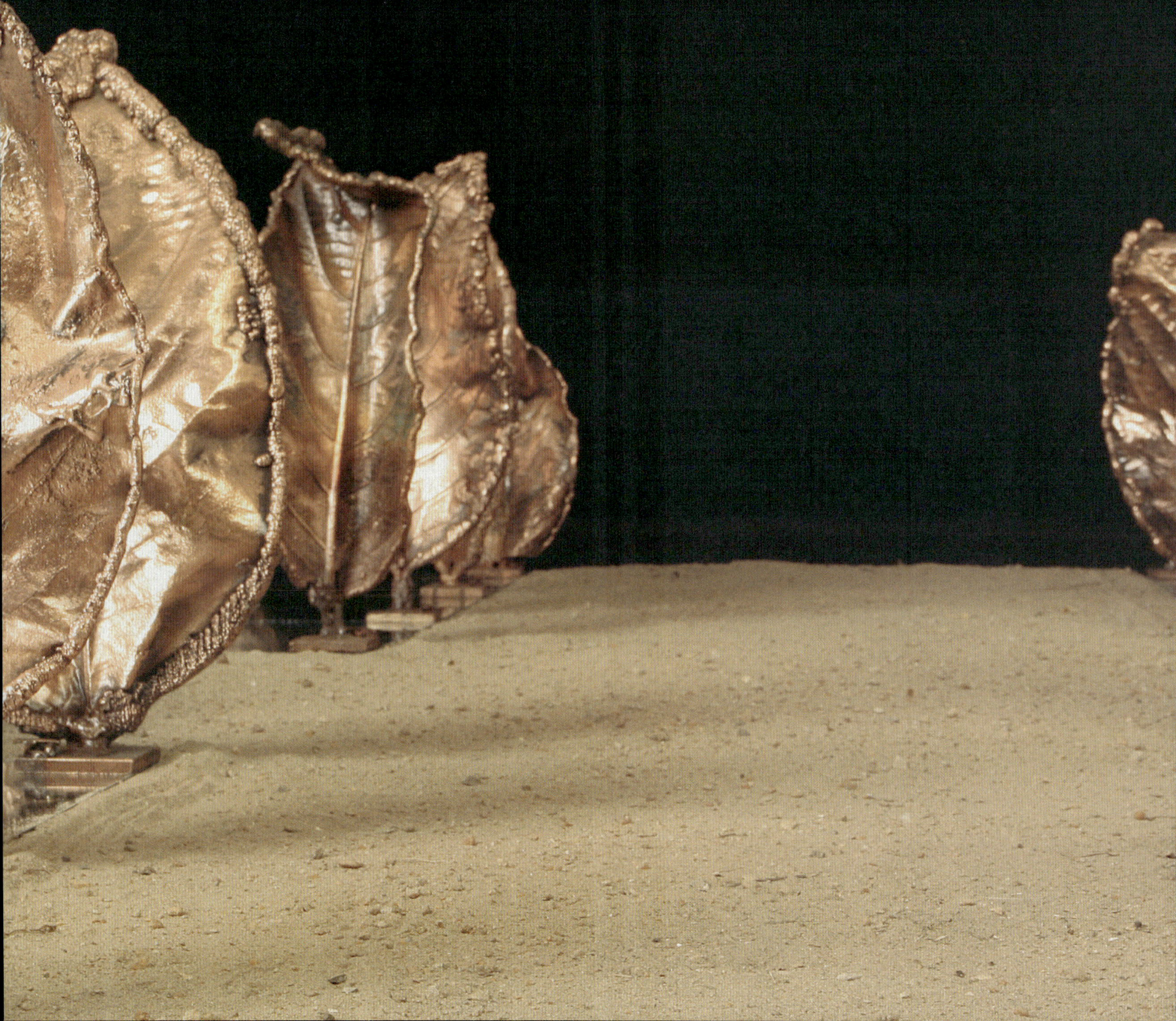

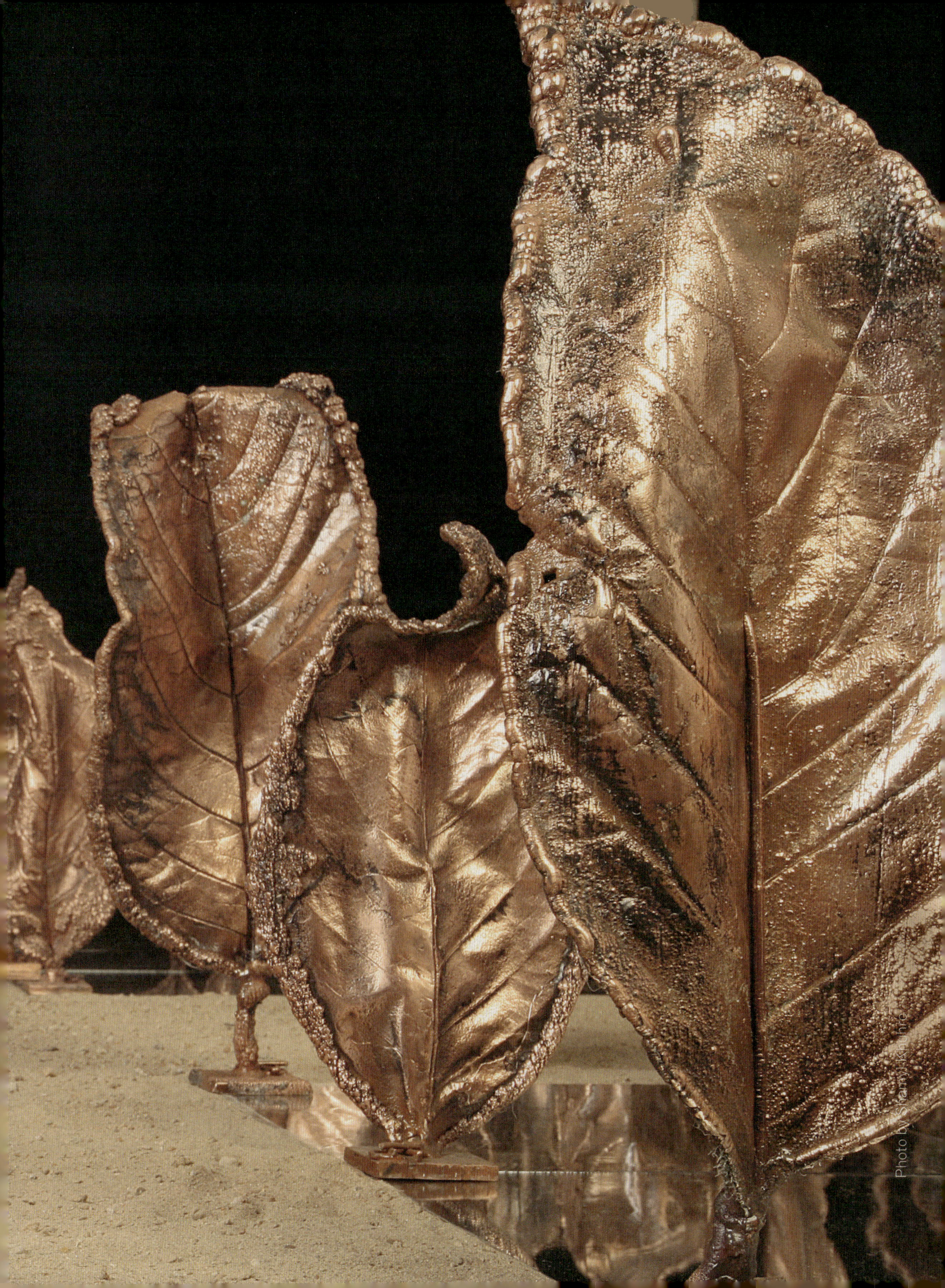

Photo by Shamyl Khuhro

Reflection

OPEN1

Esposizione Internazionale di Sculture e Installazioni

Venice, 1998

Copper and rock crystal. 152.4 × 122 × 63.5 cm (each work). Photo by Shamyl Khuhro

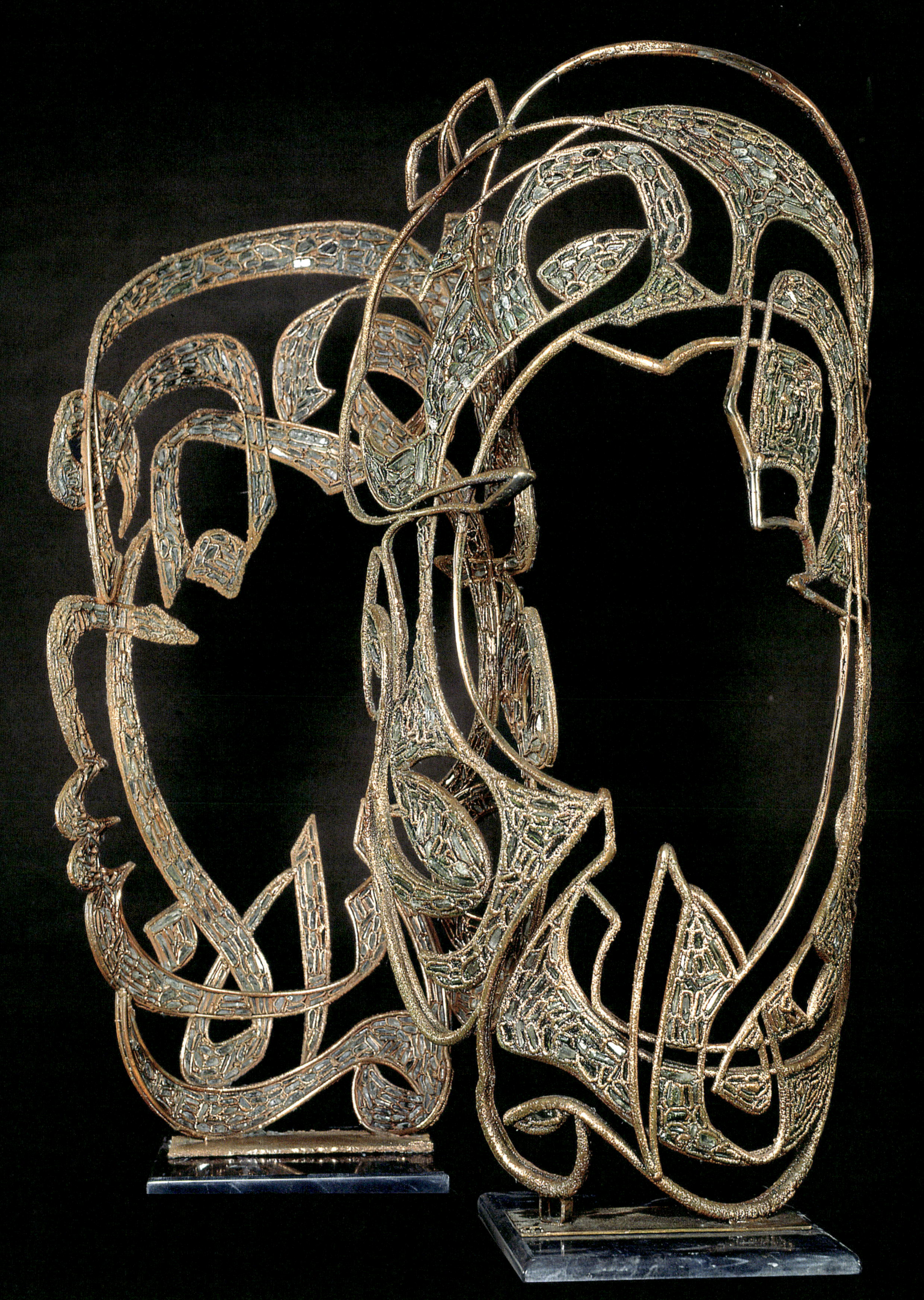

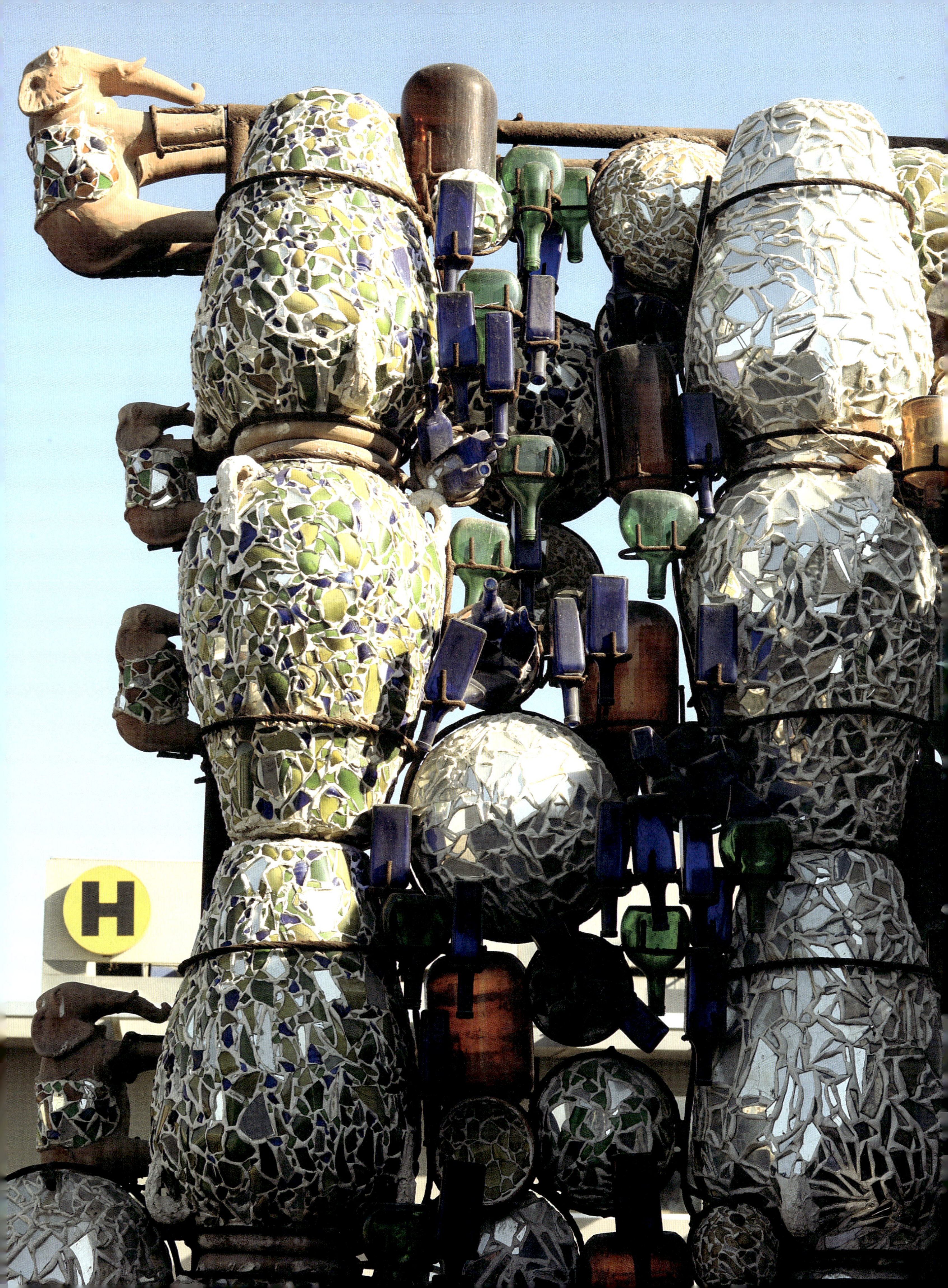
H

Salaam Gaudi

Amin Gulgee Gallery
Karachi, 2005

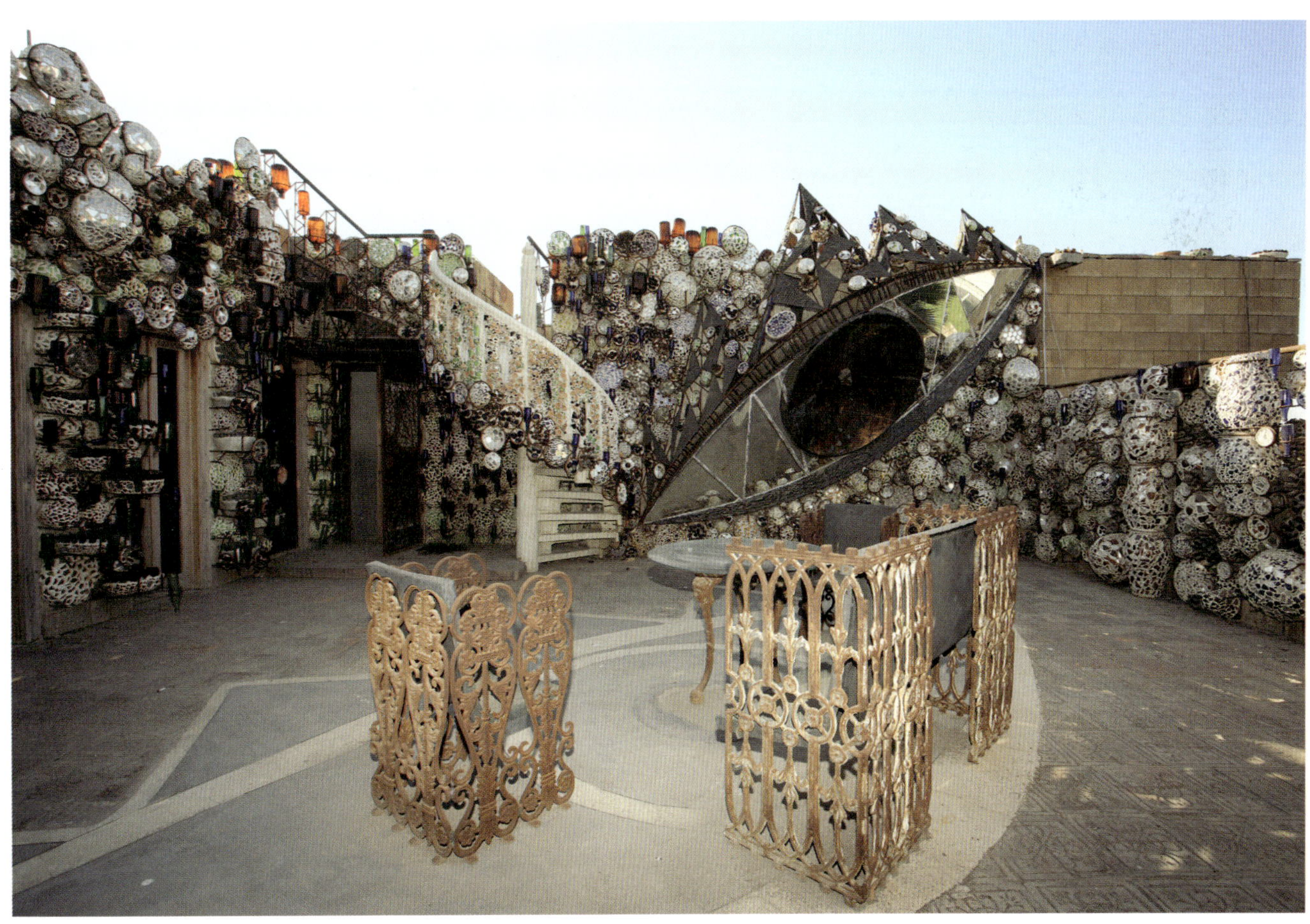

Earthernware, glass, mirror, bottles, cement, iron and copper. 792 × 792 × 373 cm.
Photo by Shamyl Khuhro

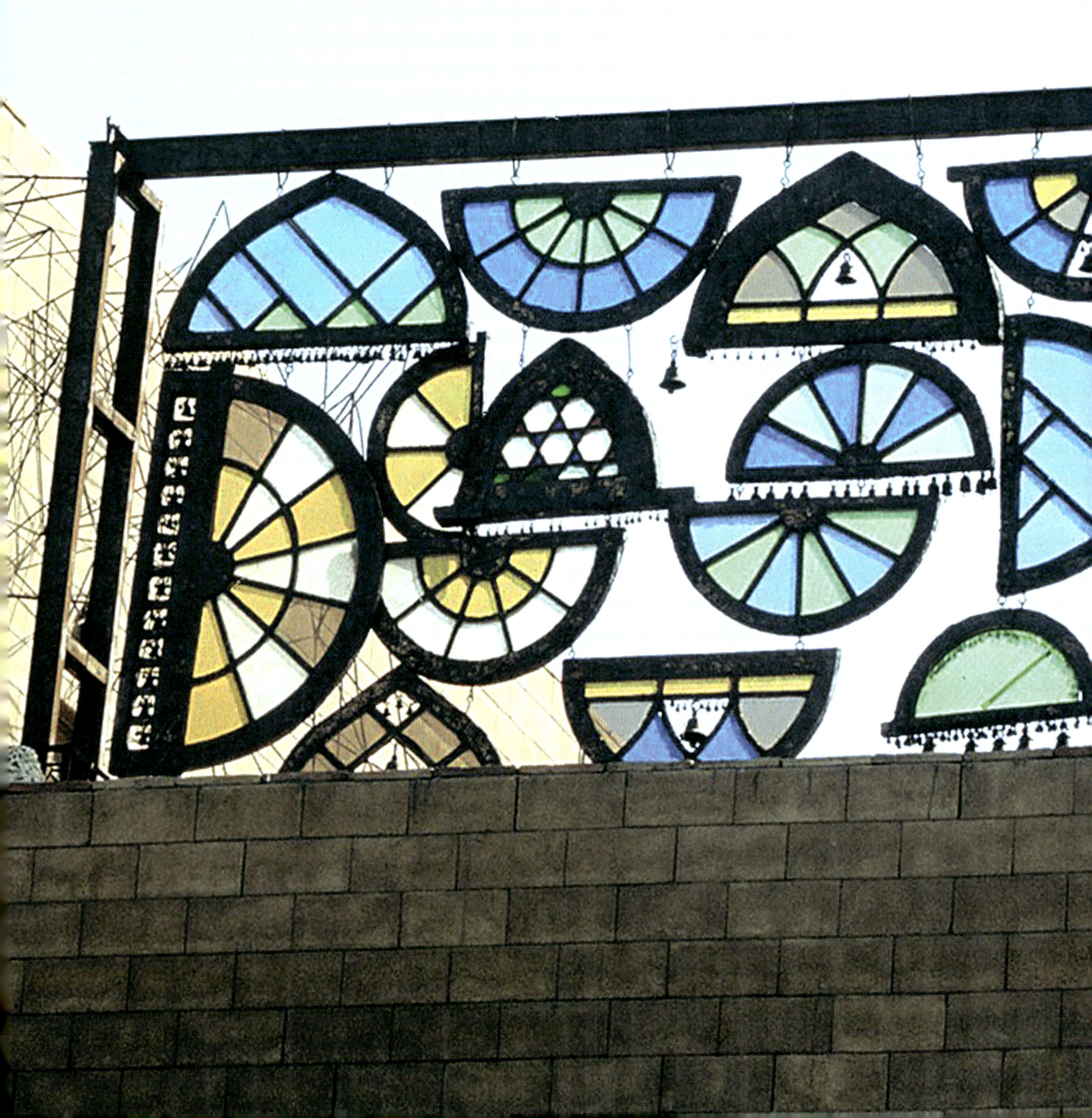

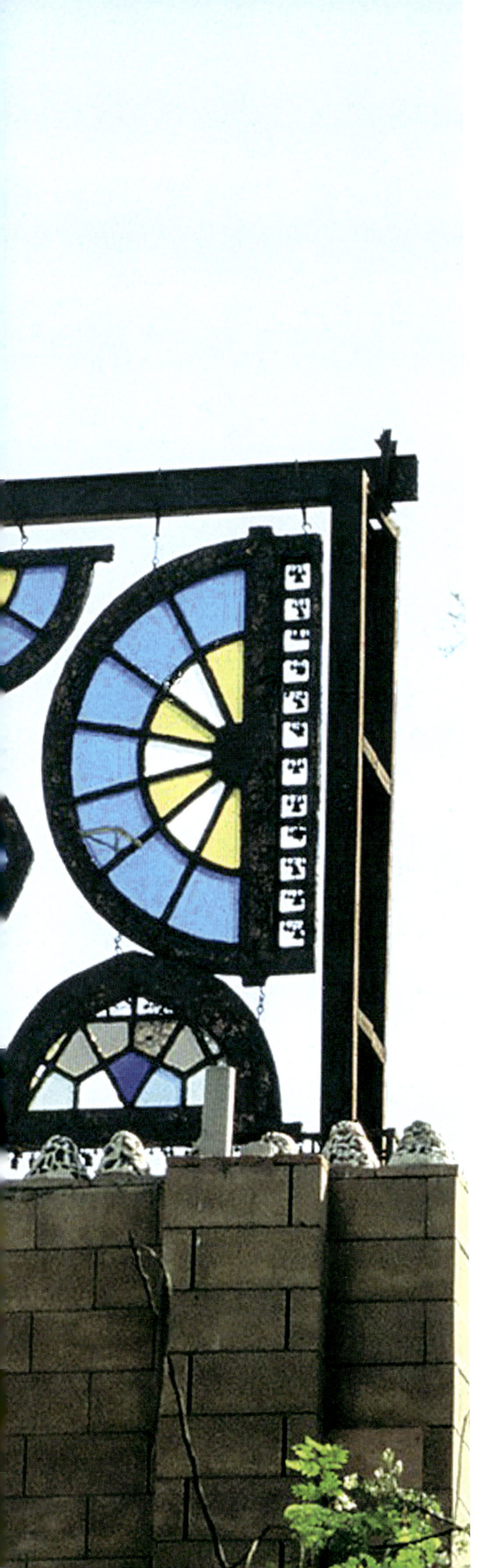

Purdah

Amin Gulgee Gallery
Karachi, 2006
Moving Ahead: Inaugural Exhibition
National Art Gallery
Islamabad, 2007

Lunettes, copper, glass and cow bells. 335 × 609.6 × 91.4 cm.
Photo by Nafees

Bustier, Helmet and Skirt

Black on Black
Koel Galley
Karachi, 2010

Copper with nickel plate, and garbage bags. 213.3 × 61 × 61 cm. Photo by Jamal Ashiqain

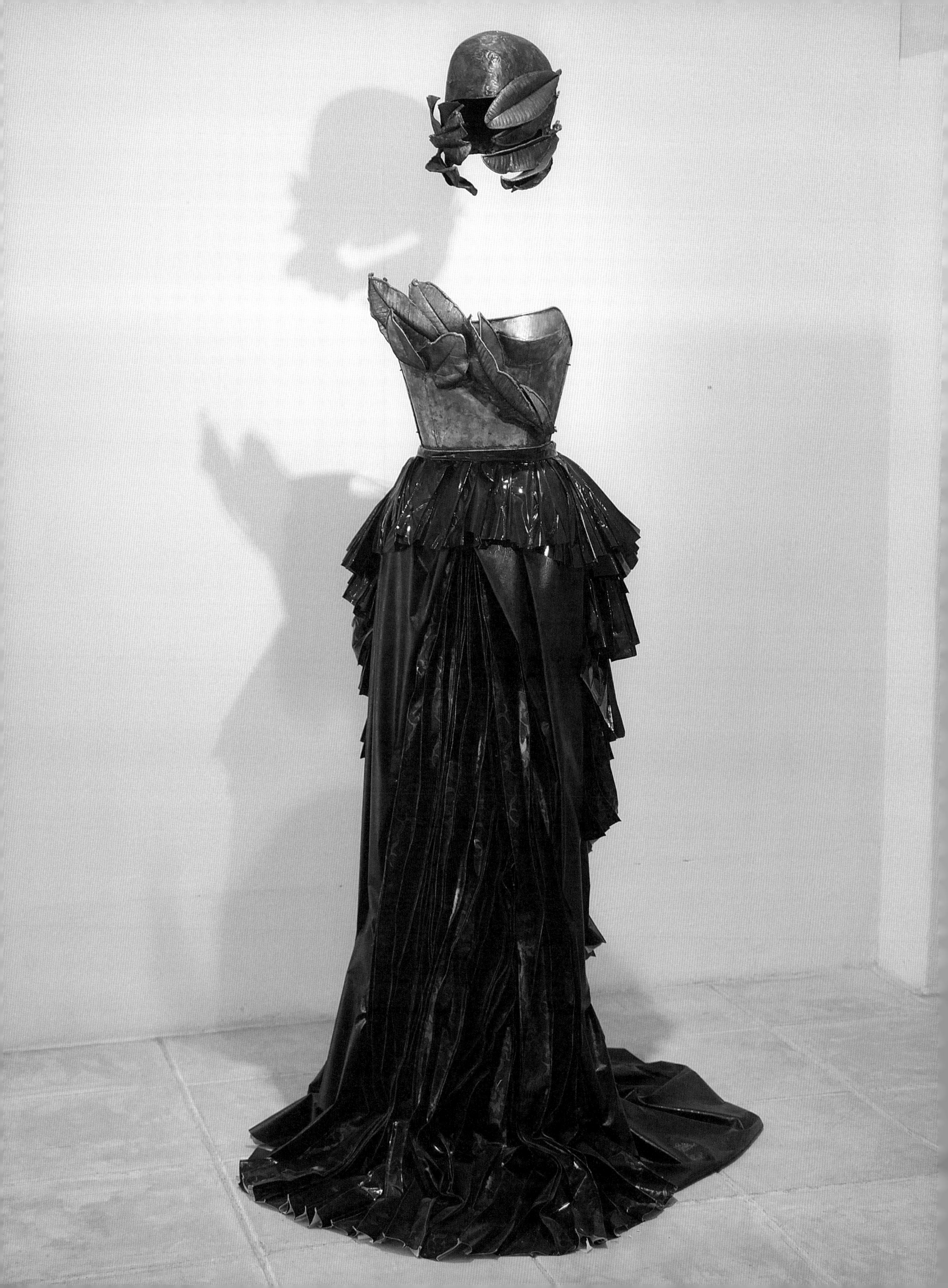

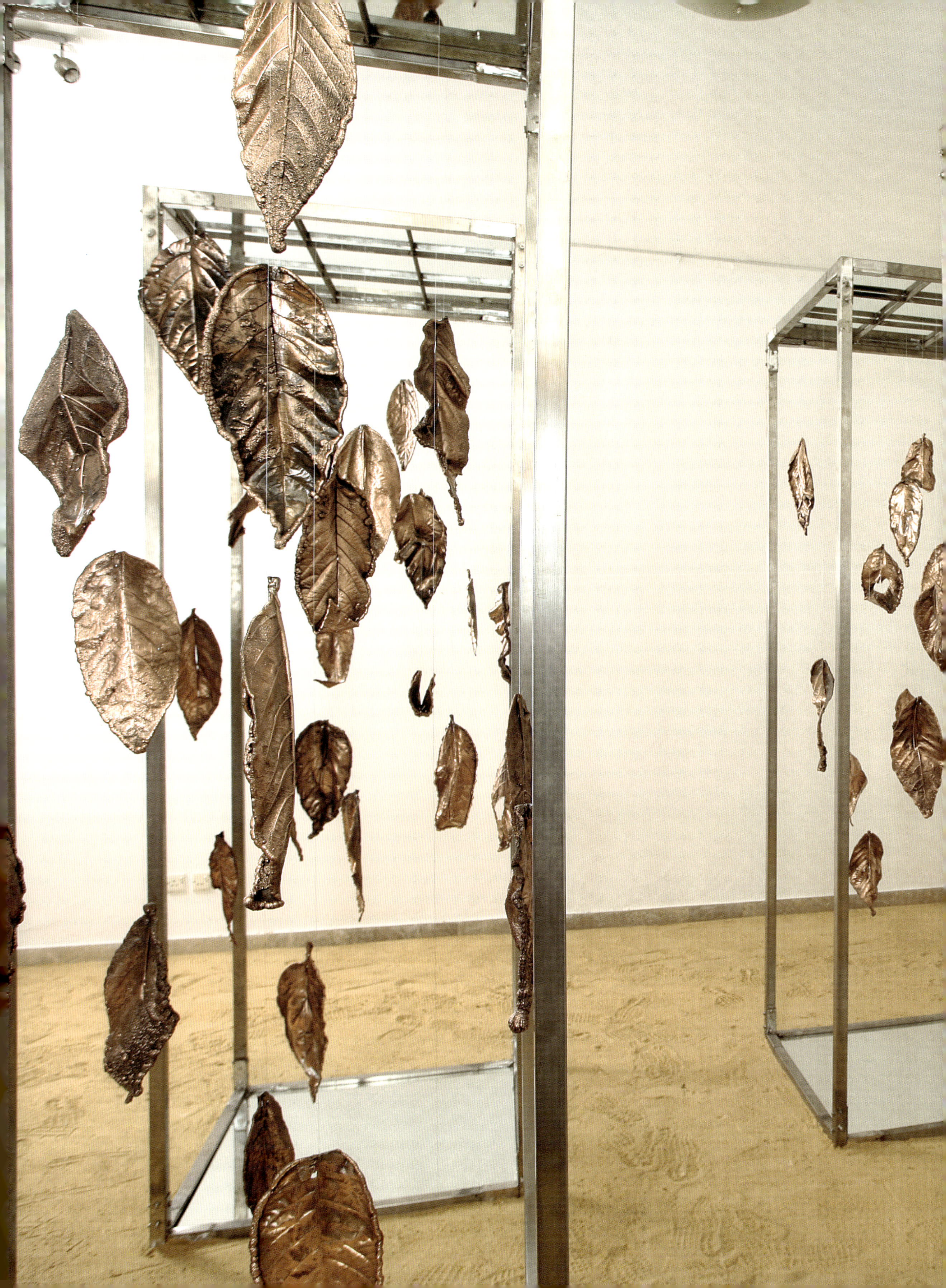

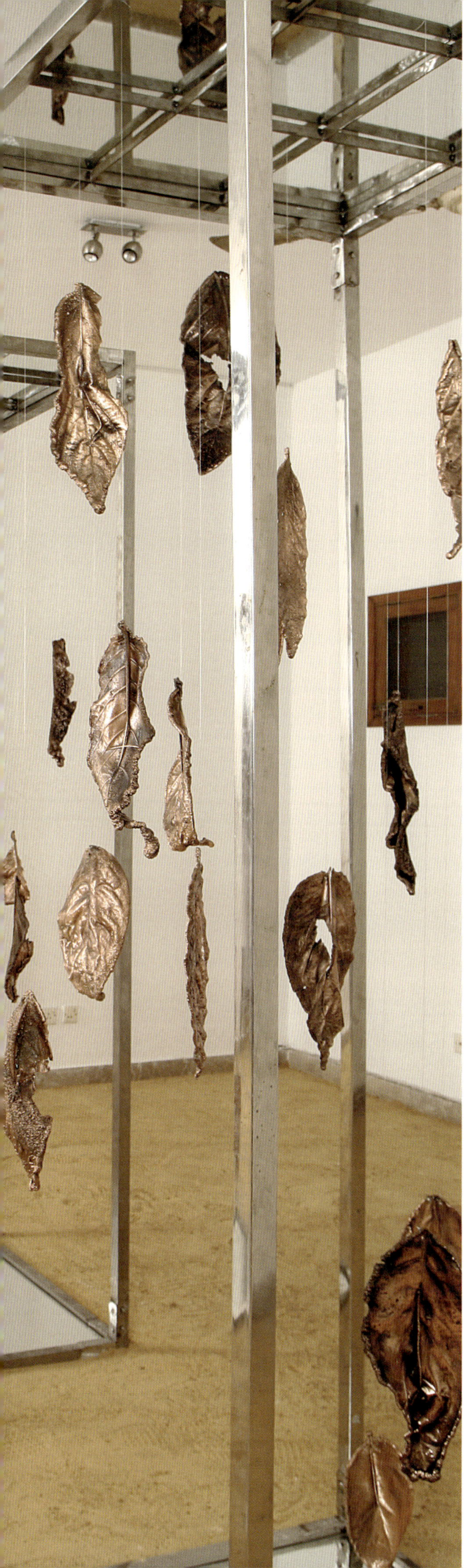

Charbagh II

Through the Looking Glass
Amin Gulgee Gallery
Karachi, 2013
Galerie Romain Rolland
Alliance Française de Delhi
2013

Copper, steel and mirror. 274 × 274 × 274 cm.
Photo by Shamyl Khuhro

Two Moons

Washed Upon the Shore
Canvas Gallery
Karachi, 2016

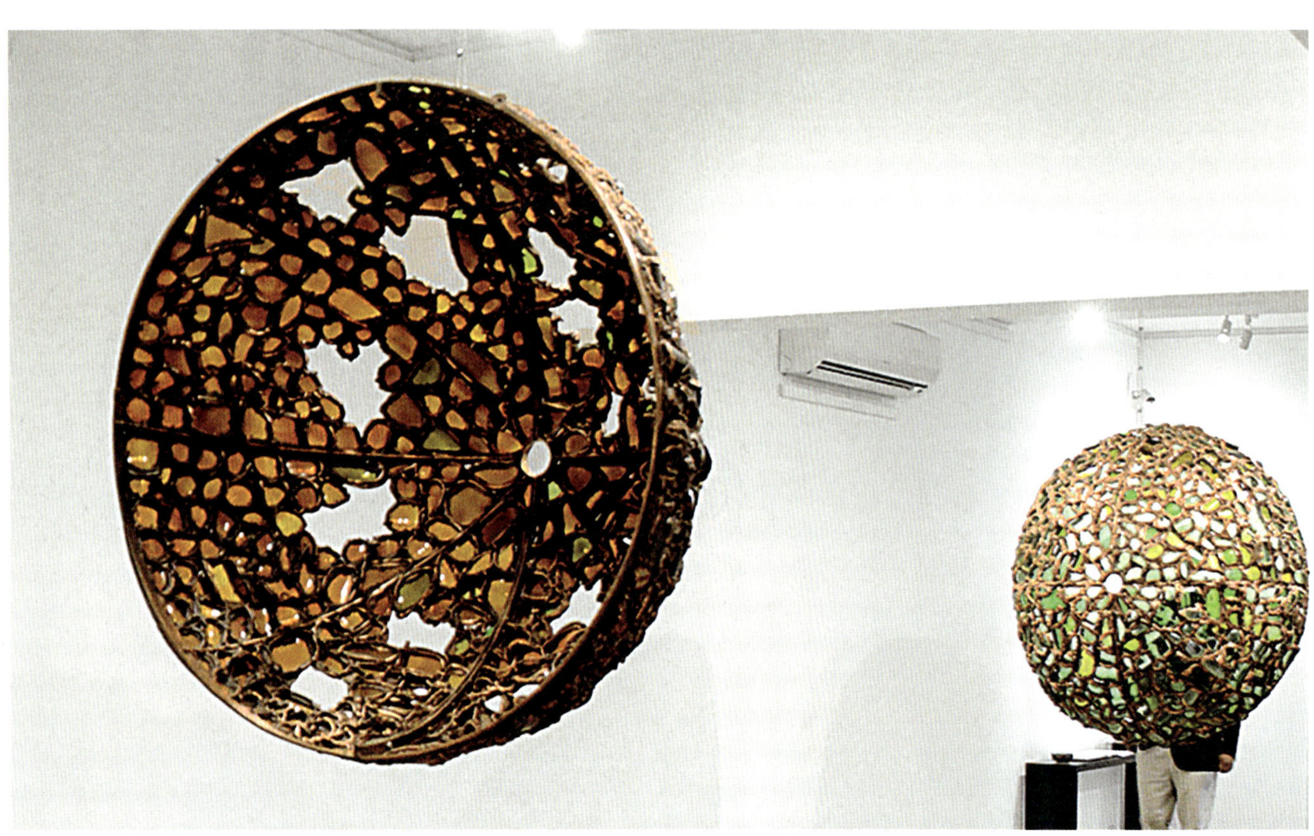

Copper, steel and glass. 122 × 122 × 63.5 cm (each work). Photos by Humayun Memon

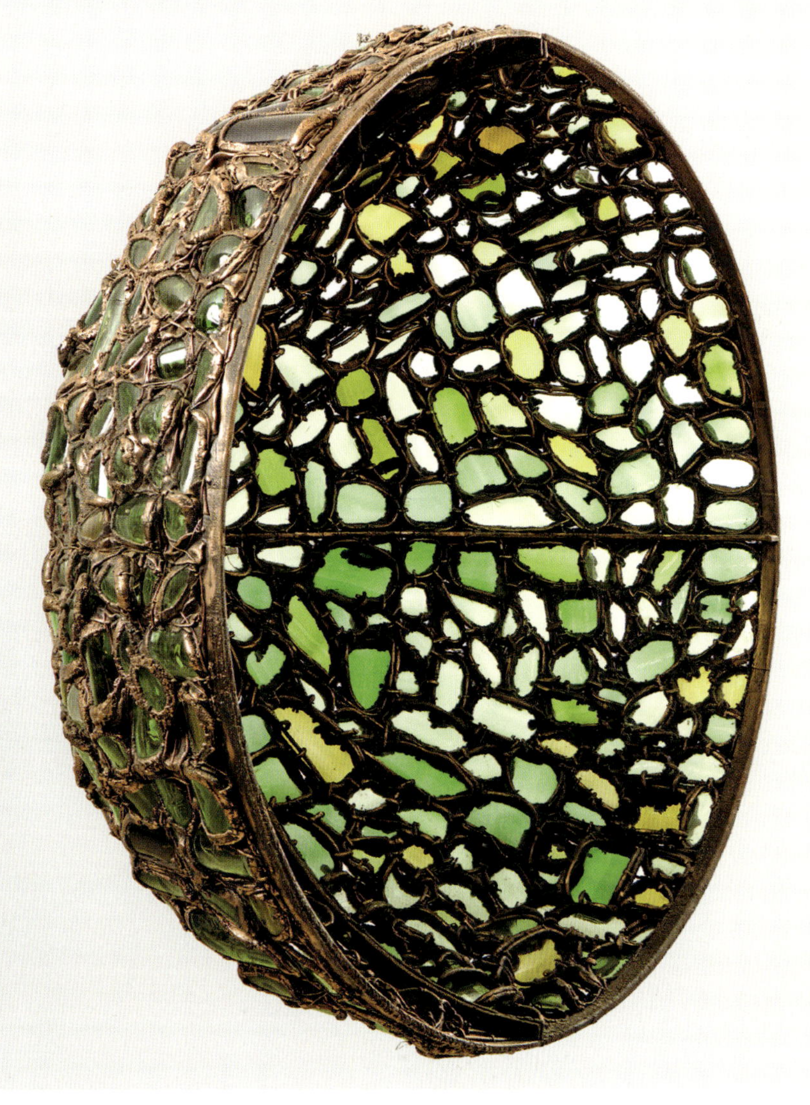

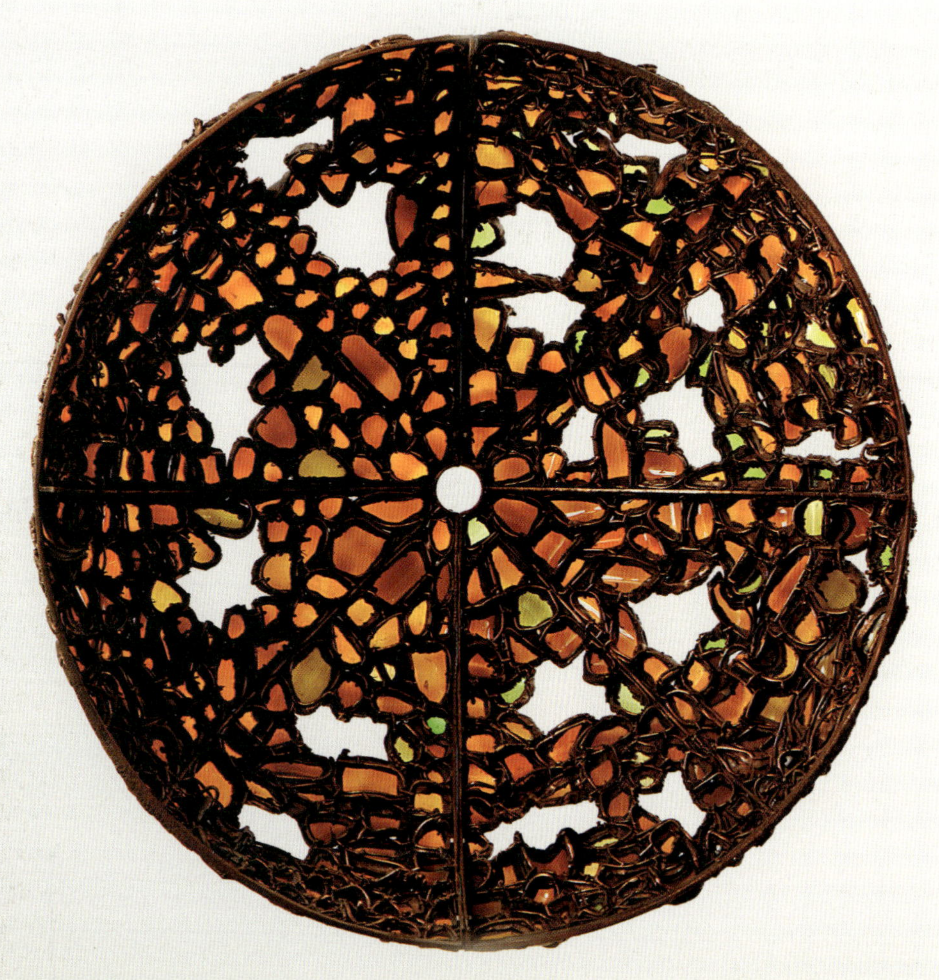

Third Moon
Washed Upon the Shore
Canvas Gallery
Karachi, 2016

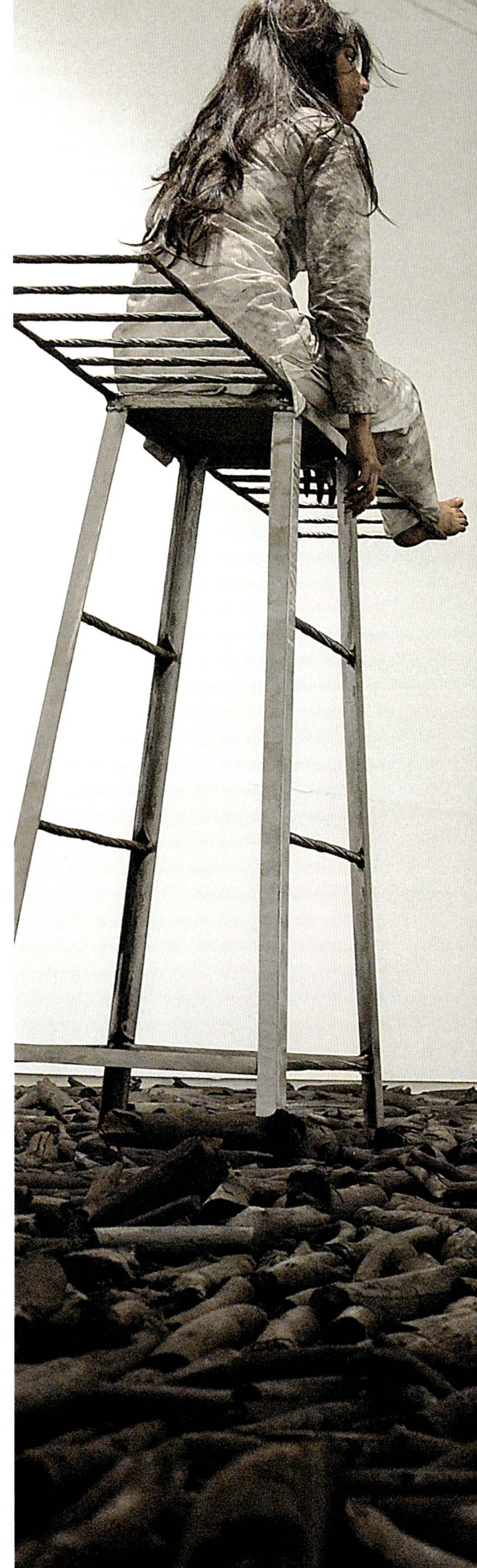

Copper, silver leaf, steel and coal. 327.6 × 528 × 439 cm.
Photo by Humayun Memon

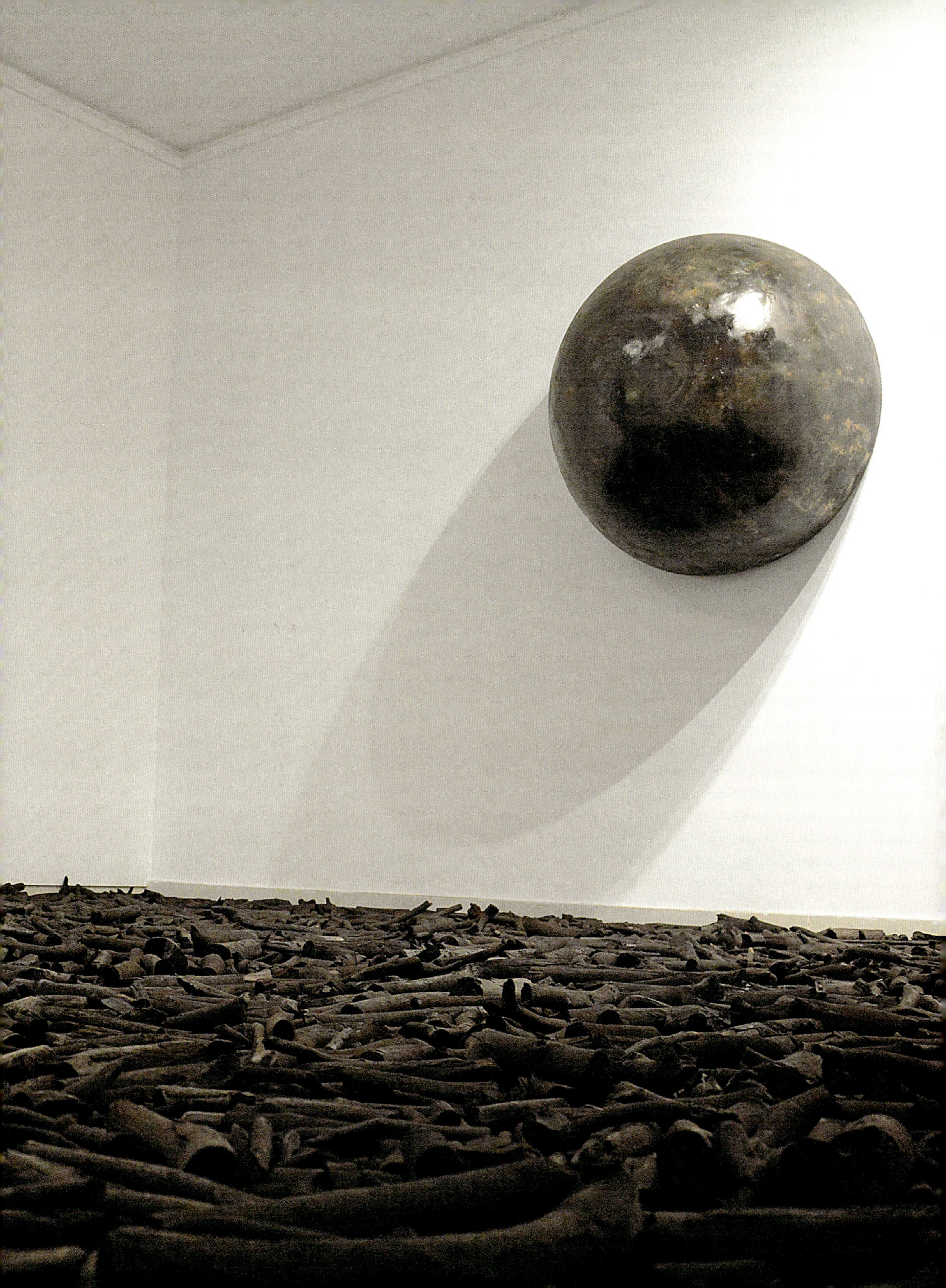

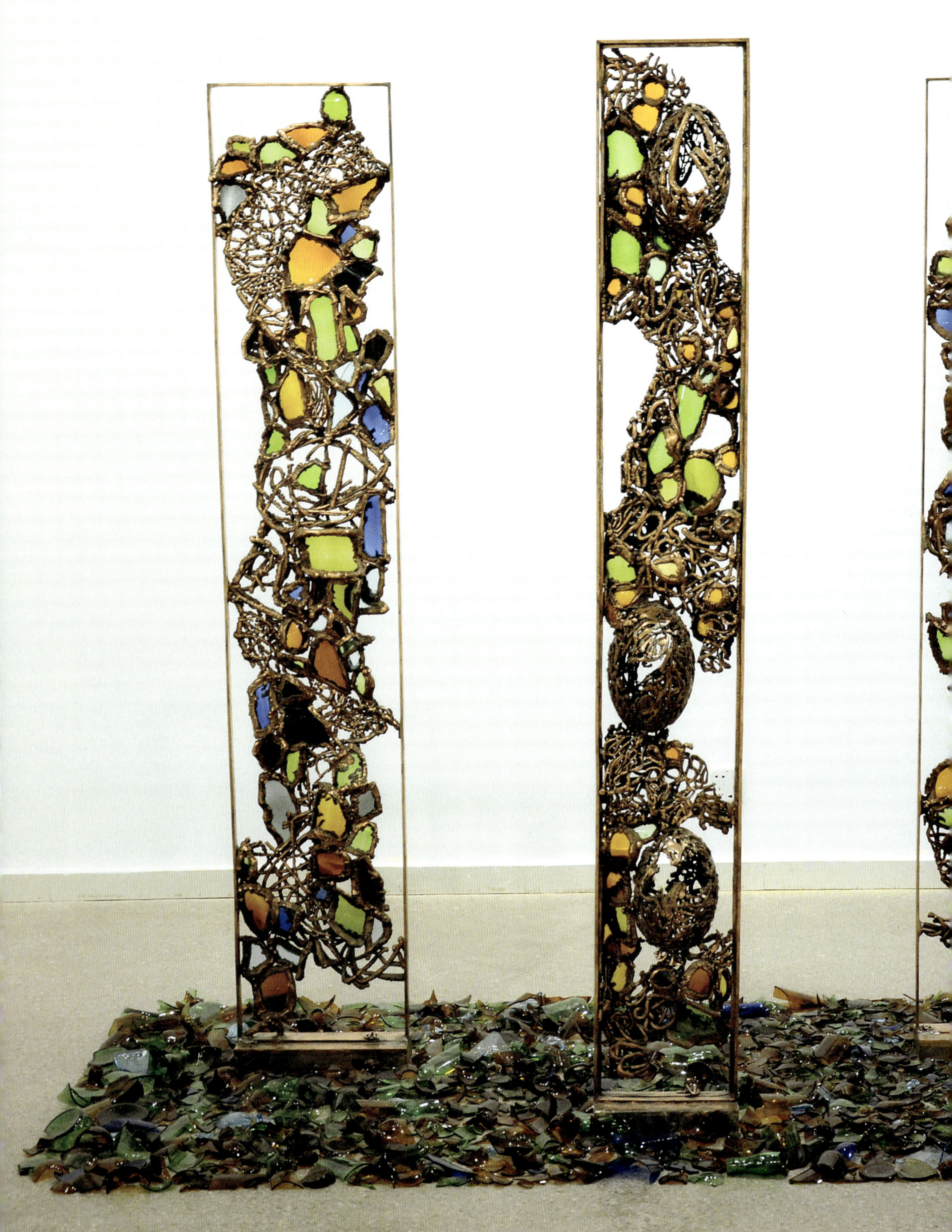

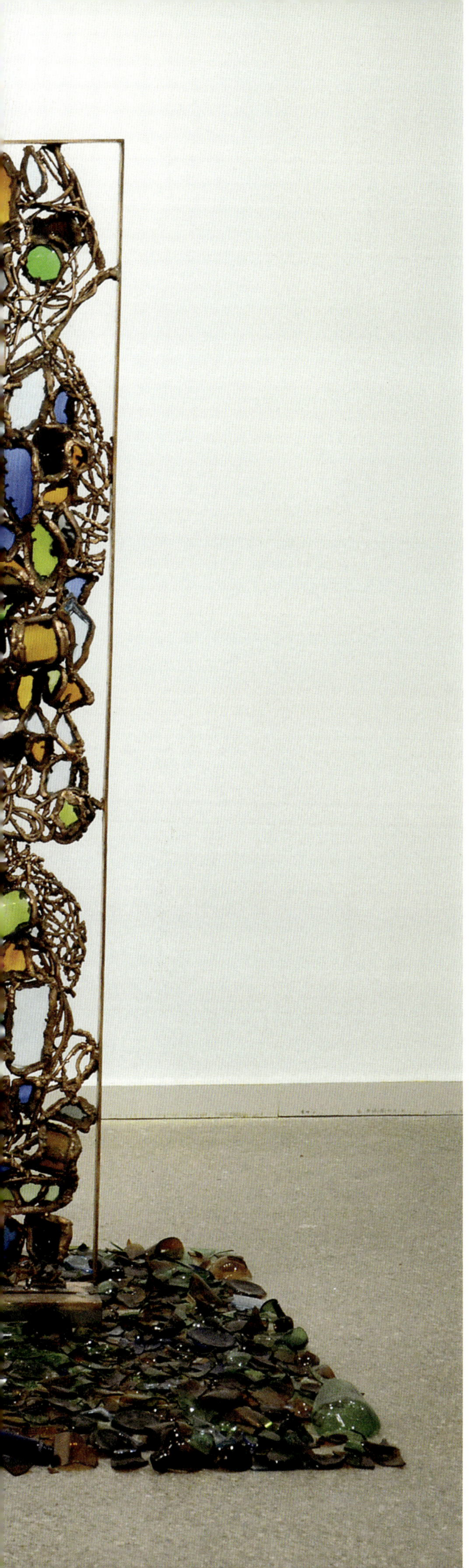

Garden Triptych: Fecund Landscape
Washed Upon the Shore
Canvas Gallery
Karachi, 2016

Copper and glass. 188 × 165 × 25.4 cm.
Photo by Humayun Memon

Char Bagh II: Falling Leaves

OPEN20

Esposizione Internazionale di Sculture e Installazioni

Venice, 2017

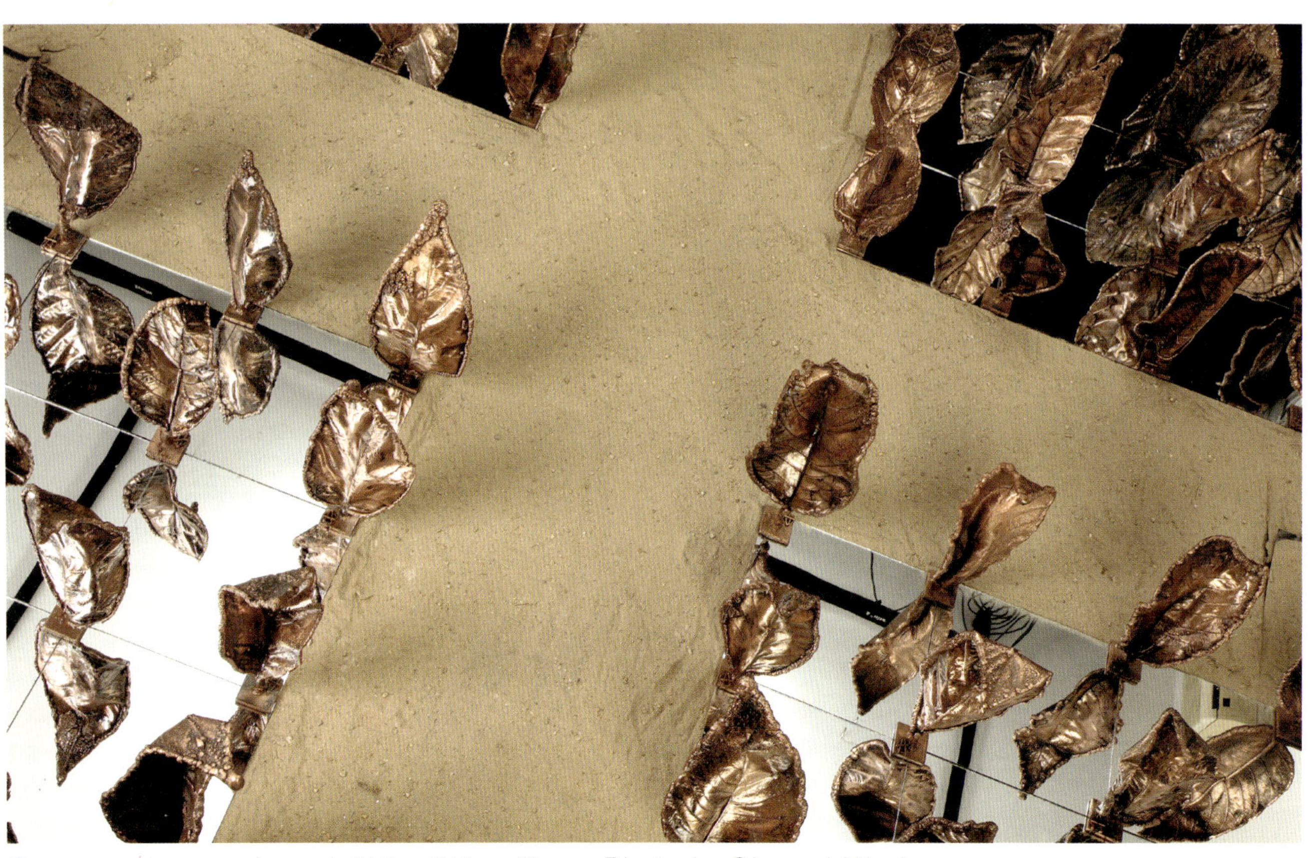

Copper, mirror and sand. 518 × 518 × 43 cm. Photo by Shamyl Khuhro

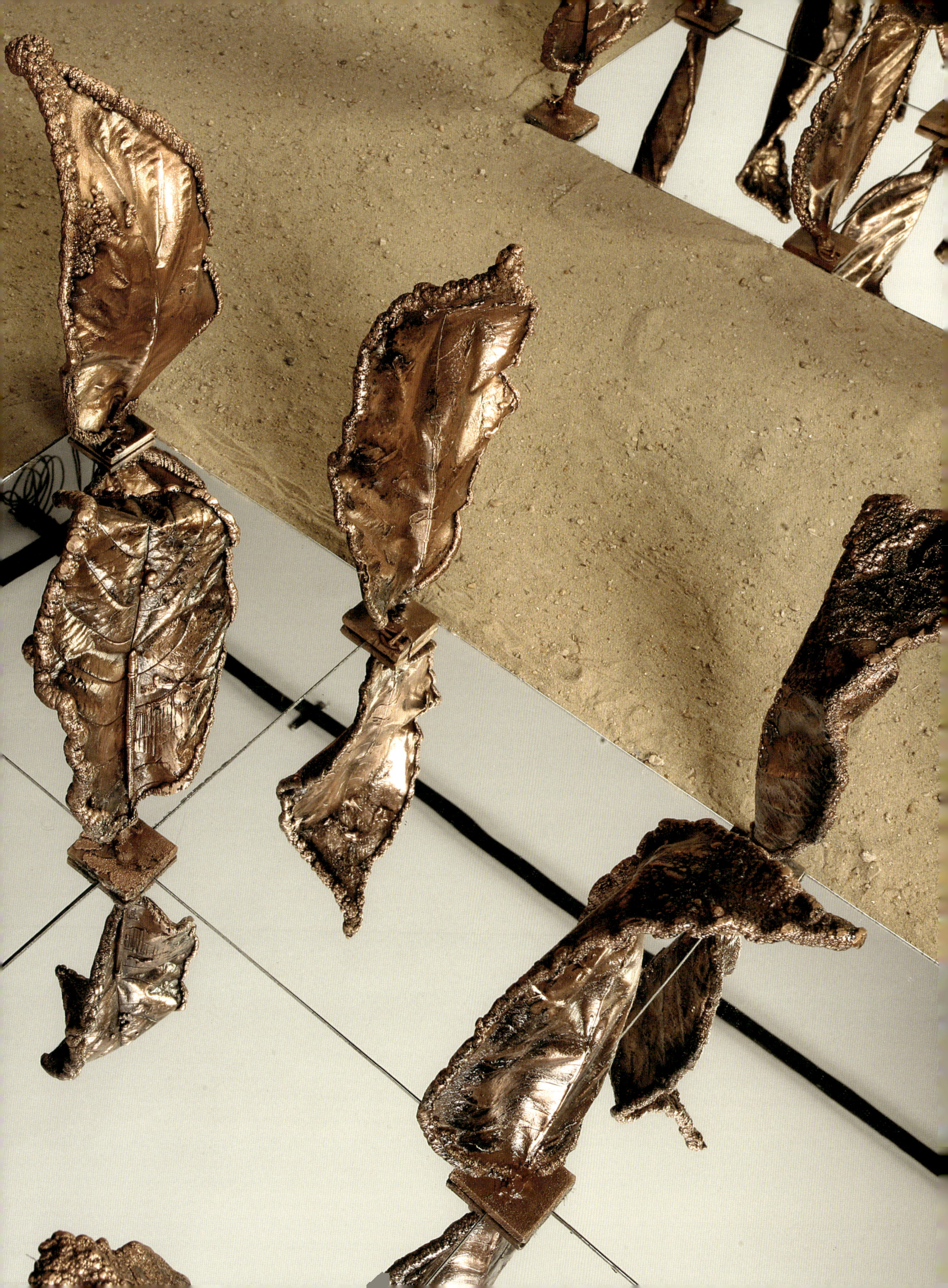

7
Amin Gulgee
Gallery
Karachi, 2018

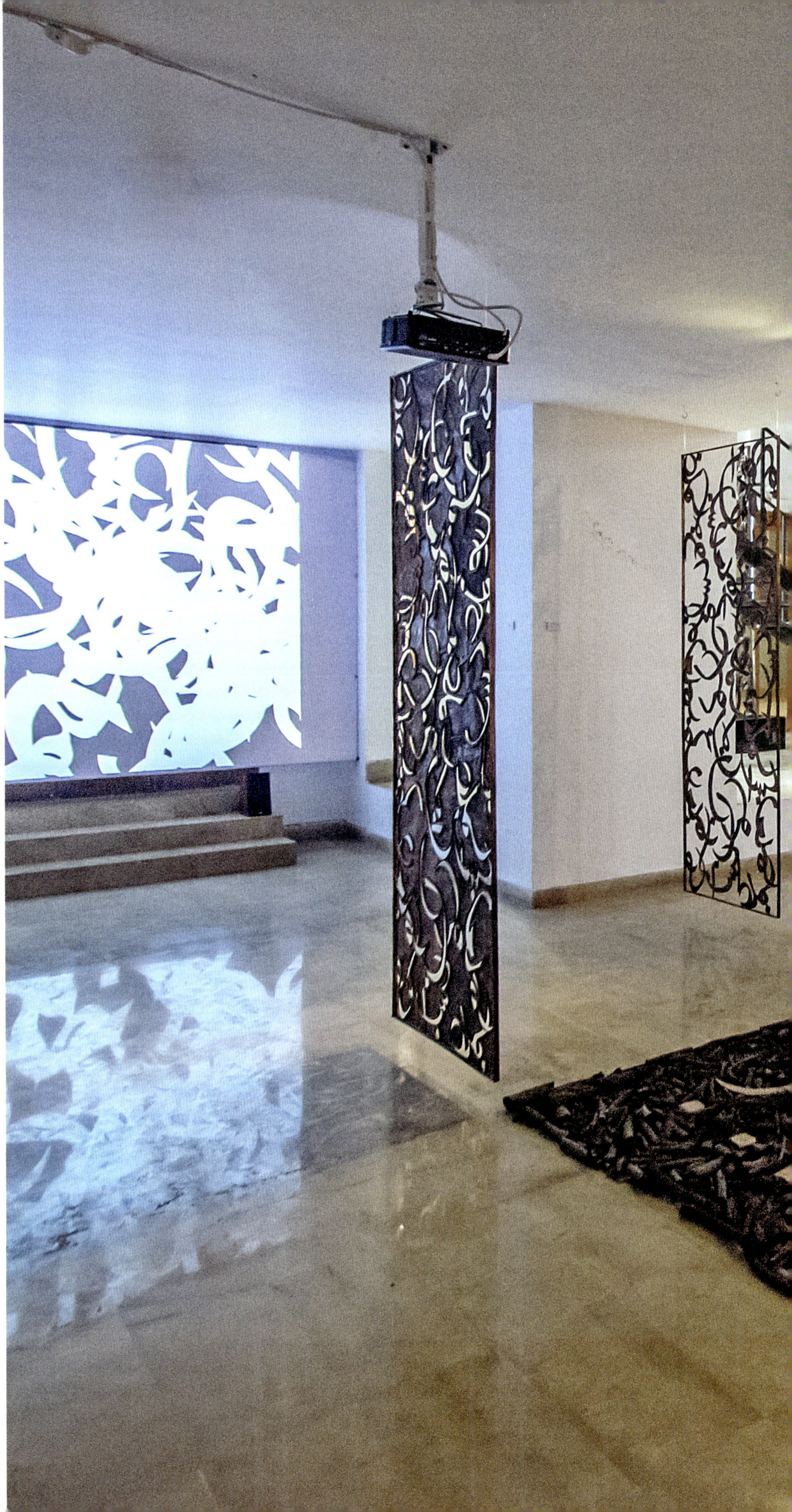

Copper, bronze,
coal and bottles.
1067 × 823 × 335 cm.
Photo by Humayun
Memon

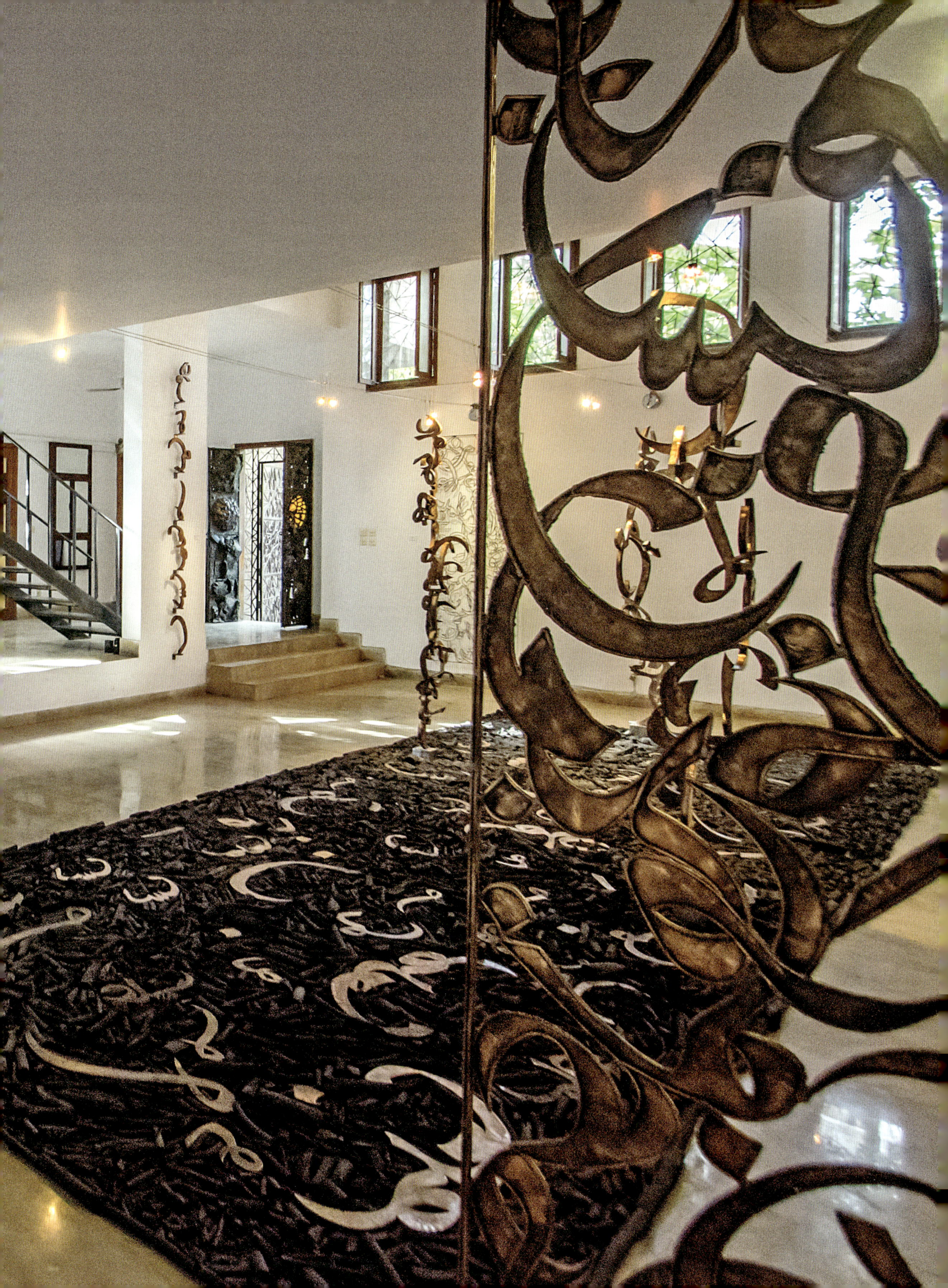

7
Galleria d'Arte Moderna
Rome, 2018

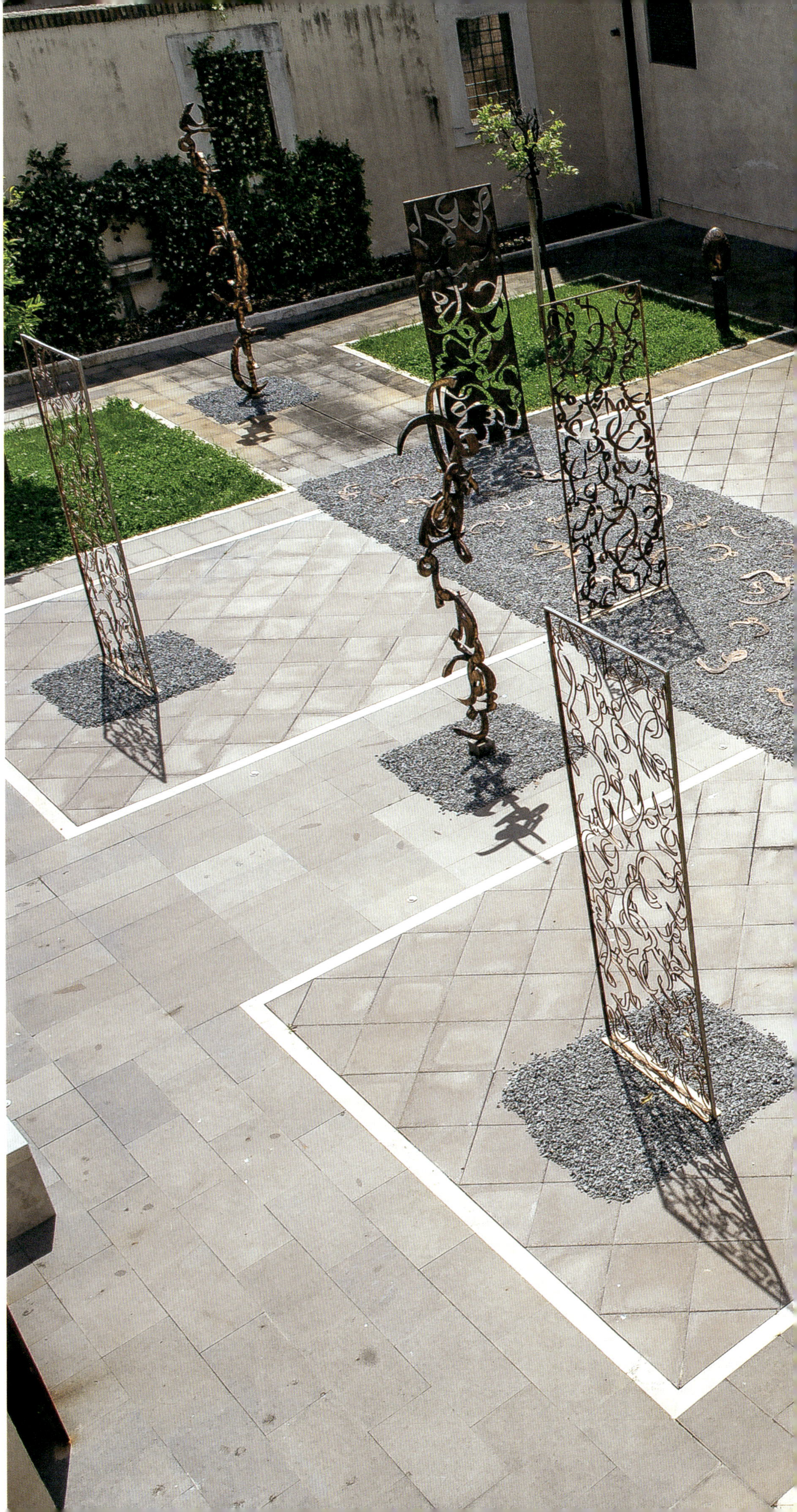

Copper, bronze and gravel. Photo by Fabrizio Piergiovanni

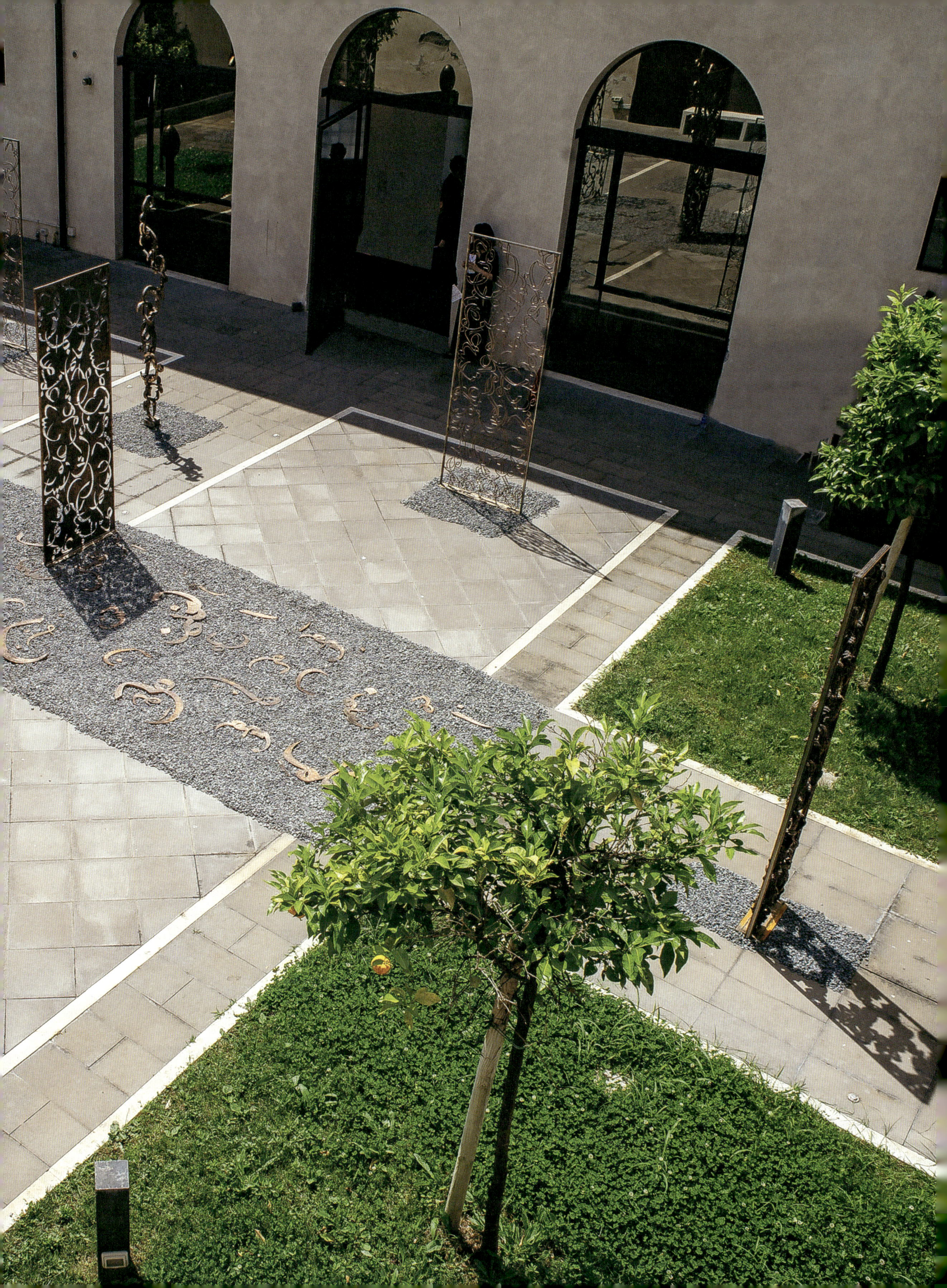

7.7
Mattatoio
Rome, 2018

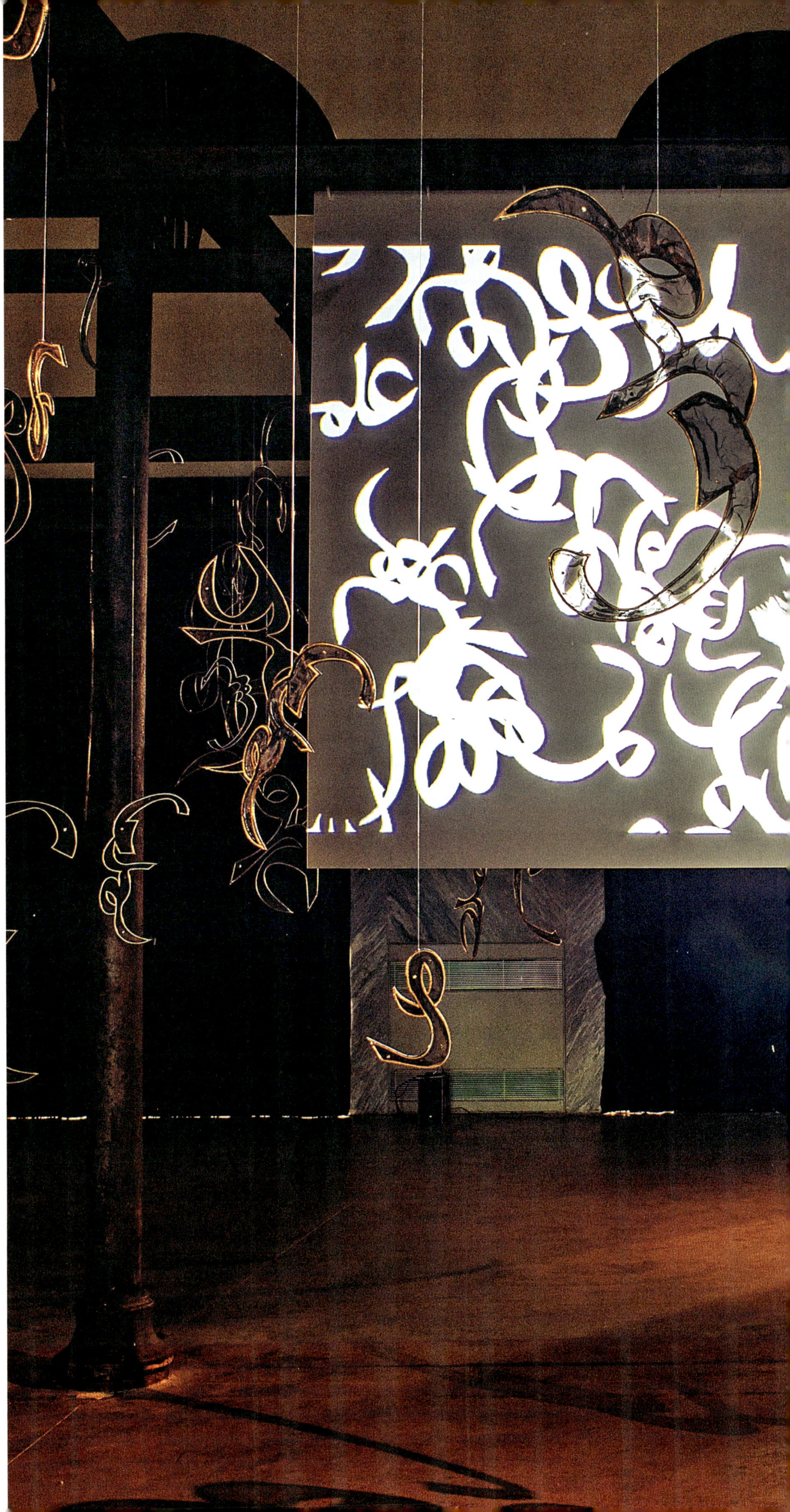

Copper, bronze, acrylic sheet, steel wire, coal and bottles. Photo by Fabrizio Piergiovanni

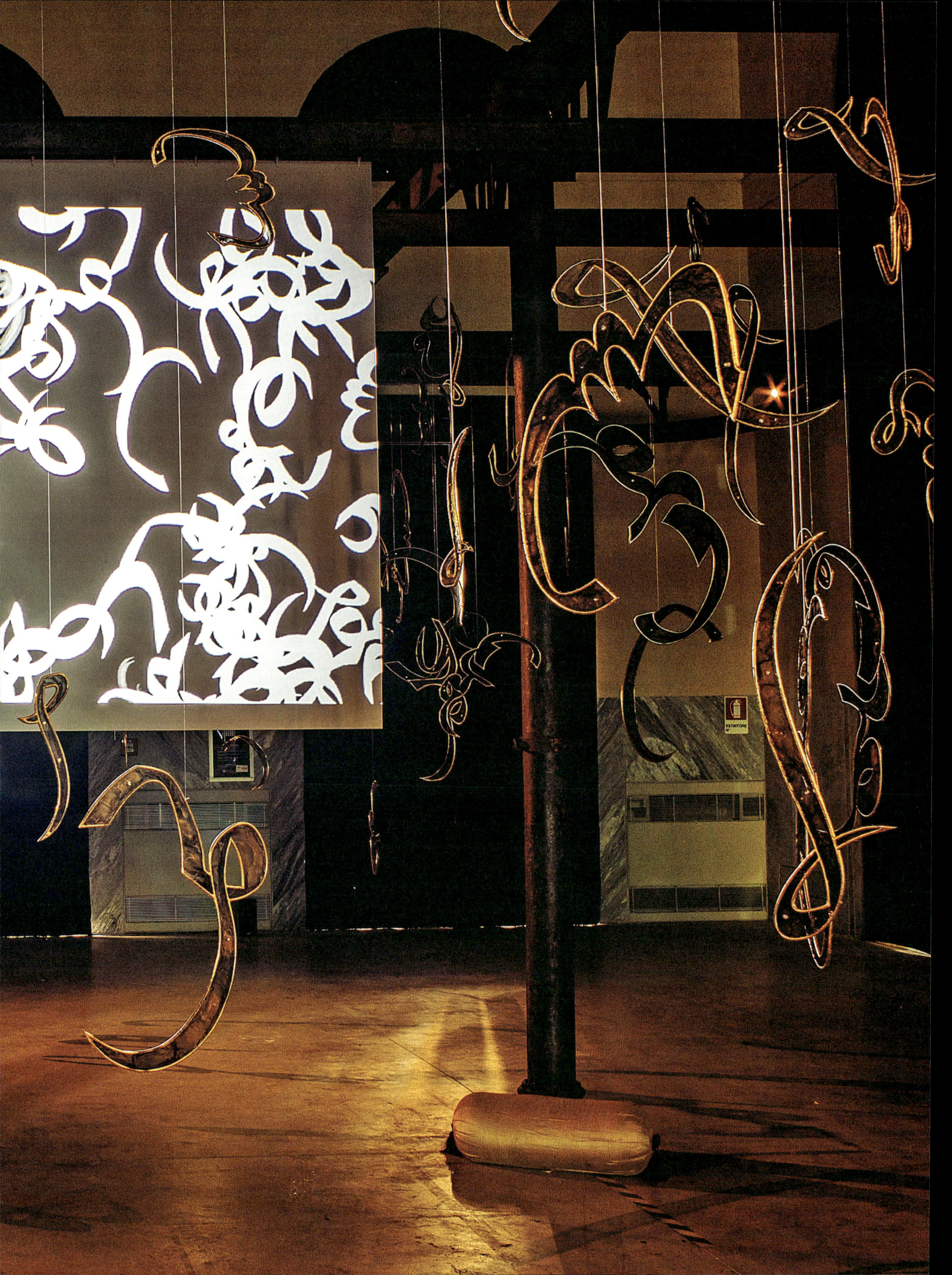
ESTINTORE
N°

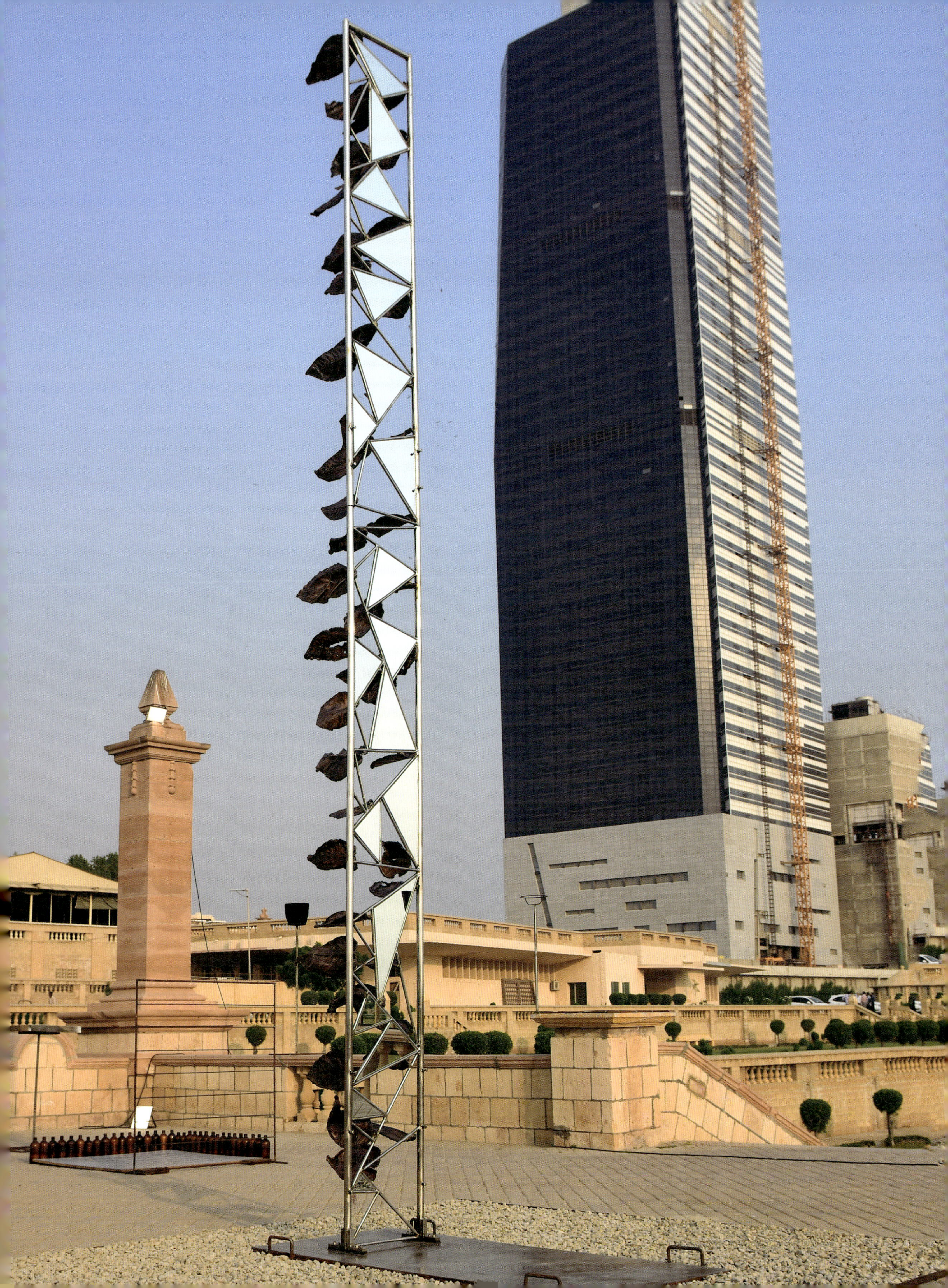

Impossible Growth

Karachi Biennale 2019

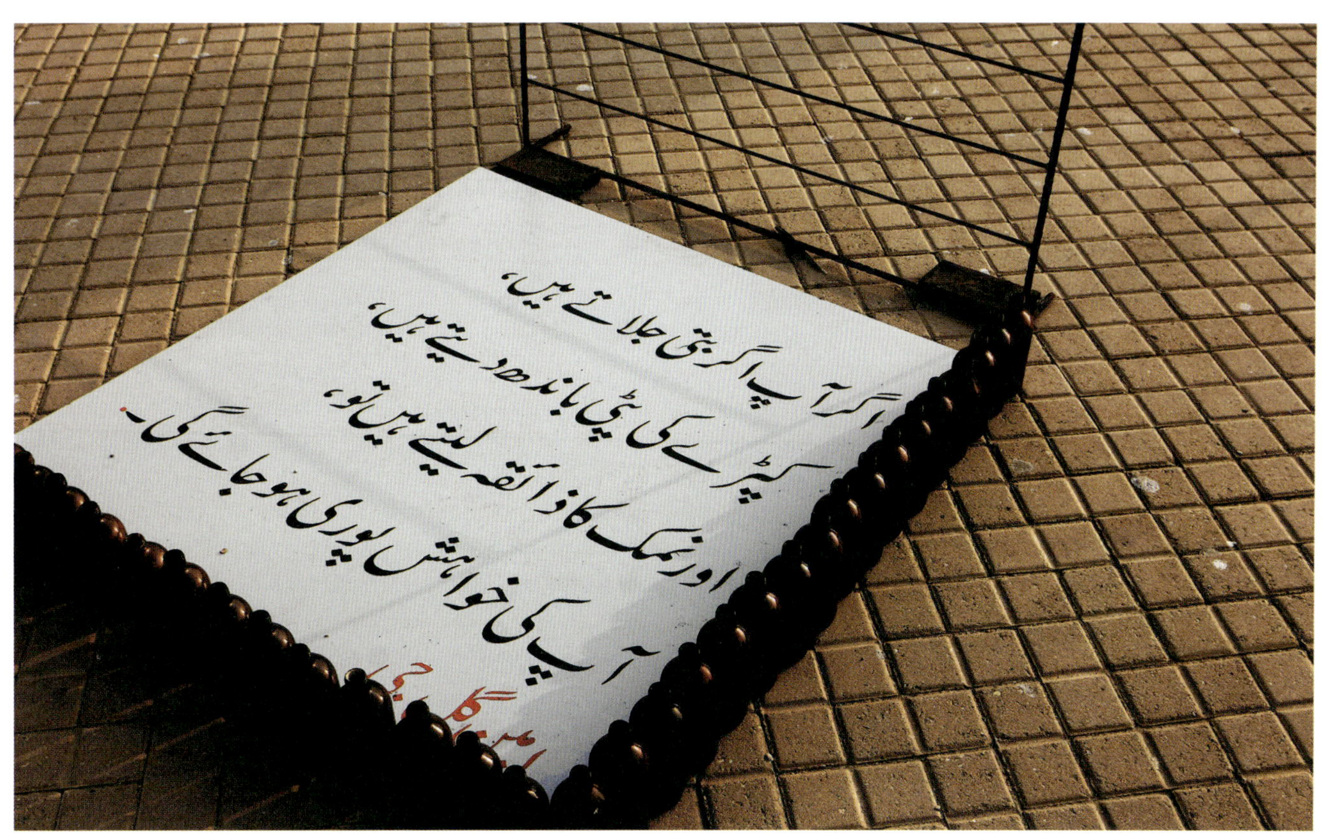

Copper, steel, iron, mirror, cloth, incense and bottles. 86 × 127 × 500 cm. Photos by Humayun Memon

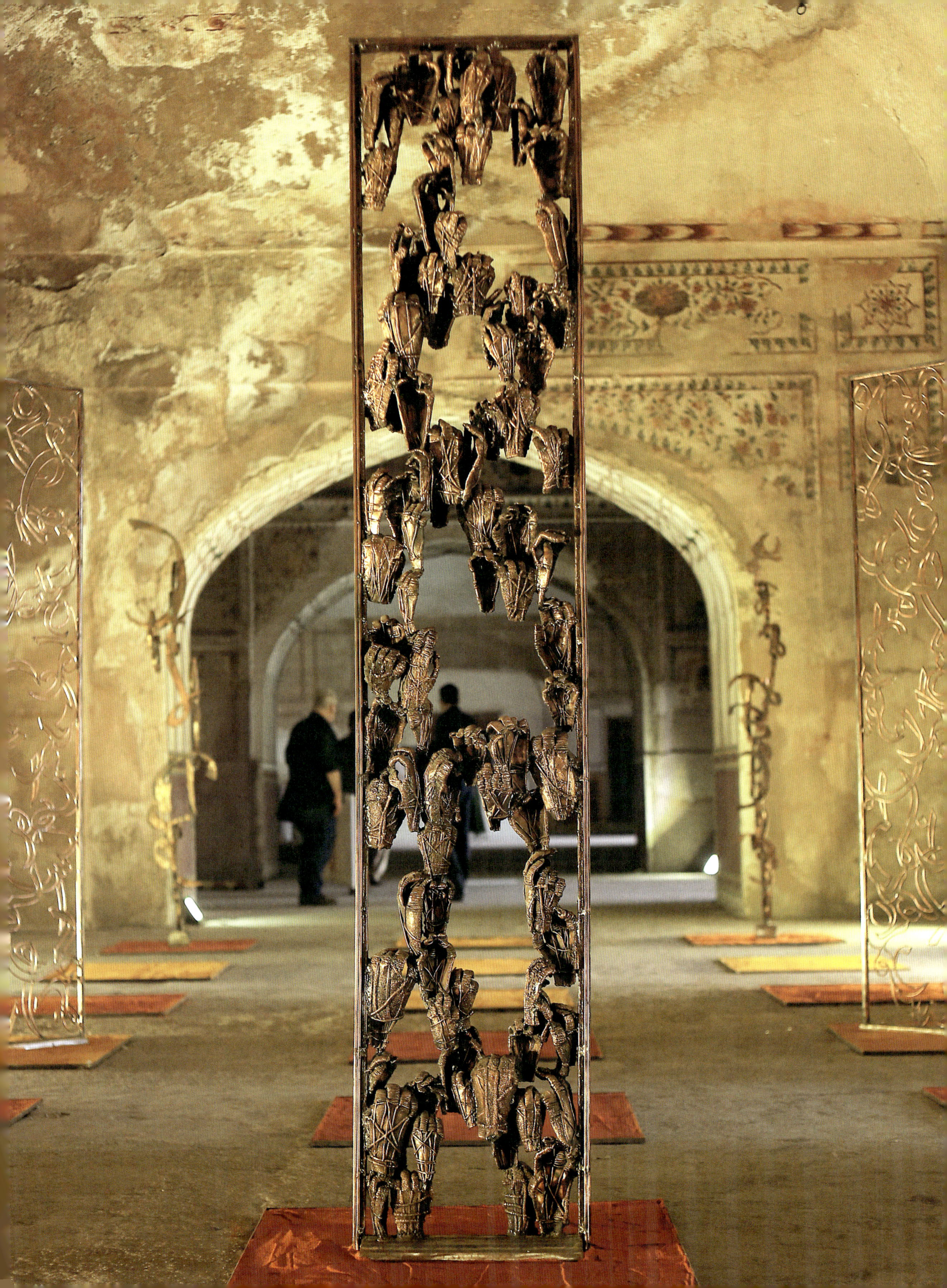

Spice

If There is Paradise on Earth
Art Lahore 22
Lahore Fort, 2022

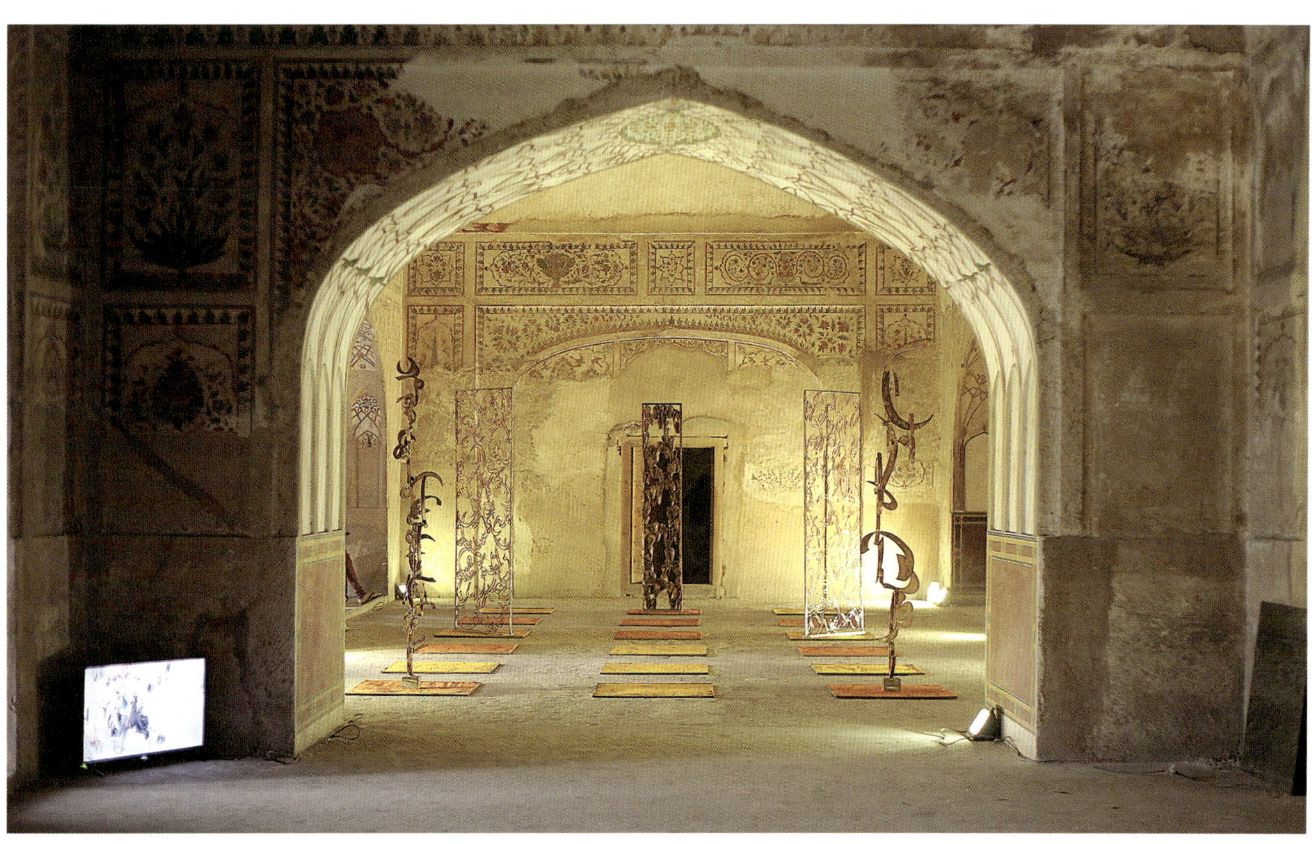

Copper, bronze, iron, turmeric and cayenne pepper. 457 × 998 × 335 cm. Photos by Ameer Hamxa

Spice Tray

The Spider Speaketh in Tongues
South Asia Institute
Chicago, 2022

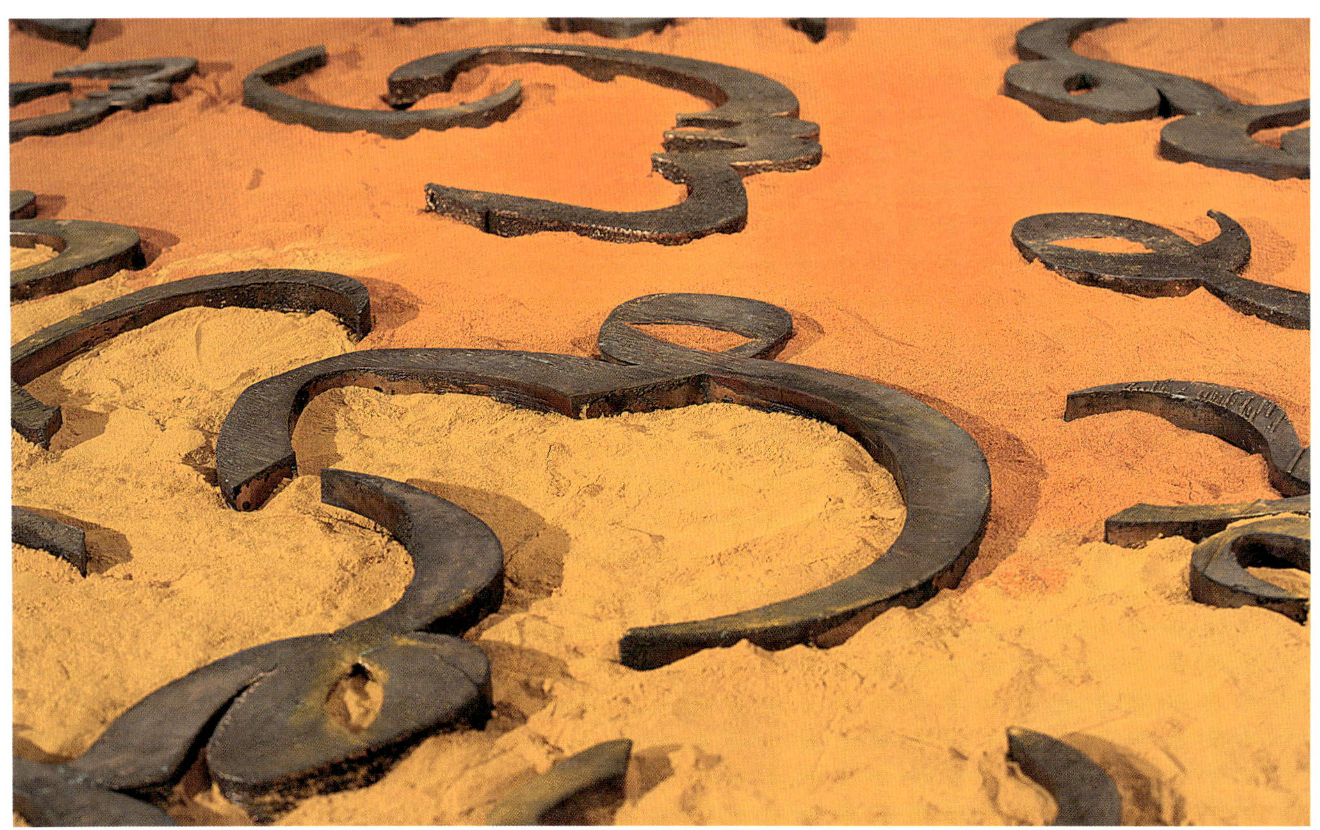

Copper, bronze, iron, turmeric and cayenne pepper. 335 × 335 × 7.6 cm. Photos by Ryan Bach

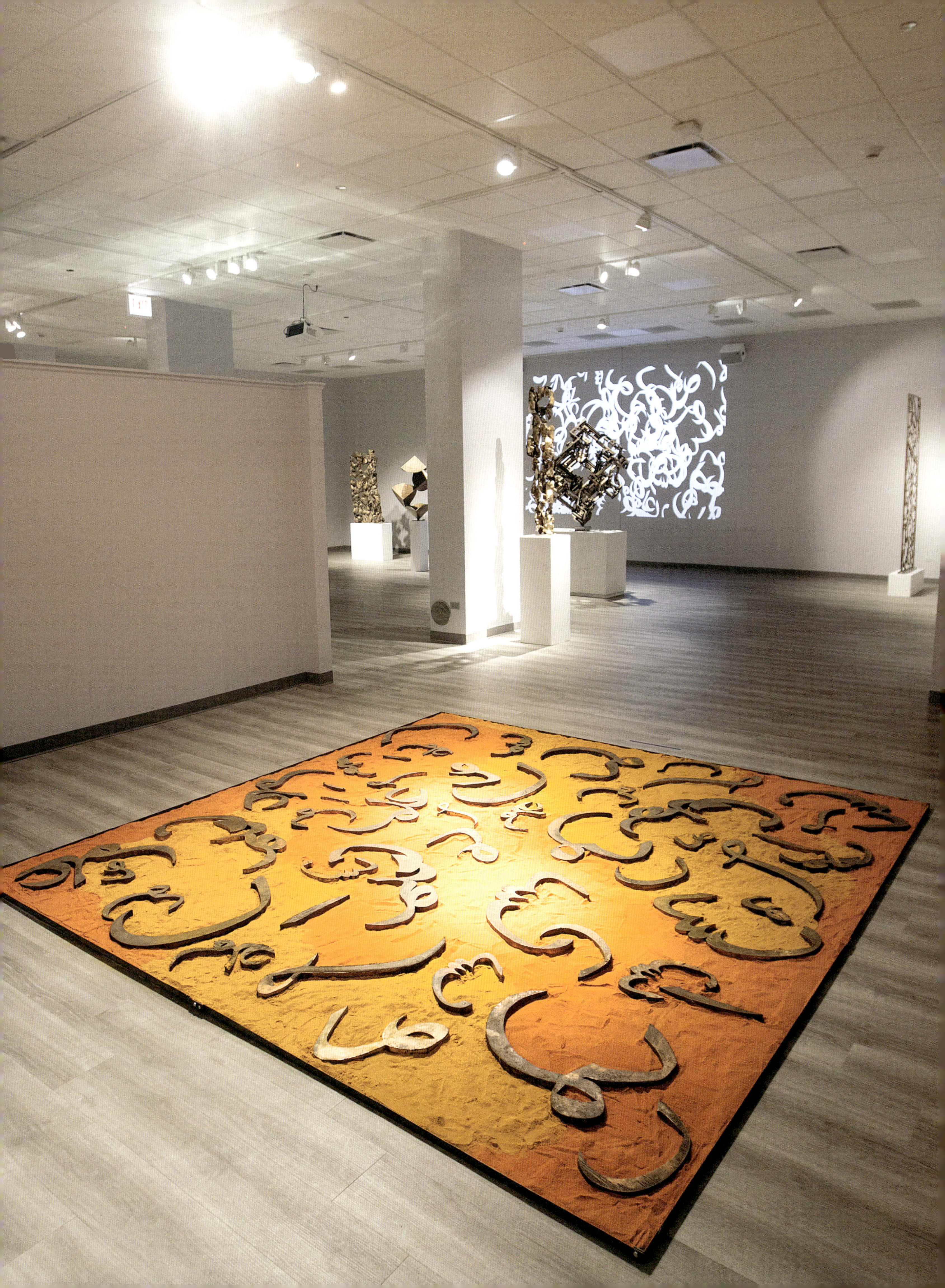

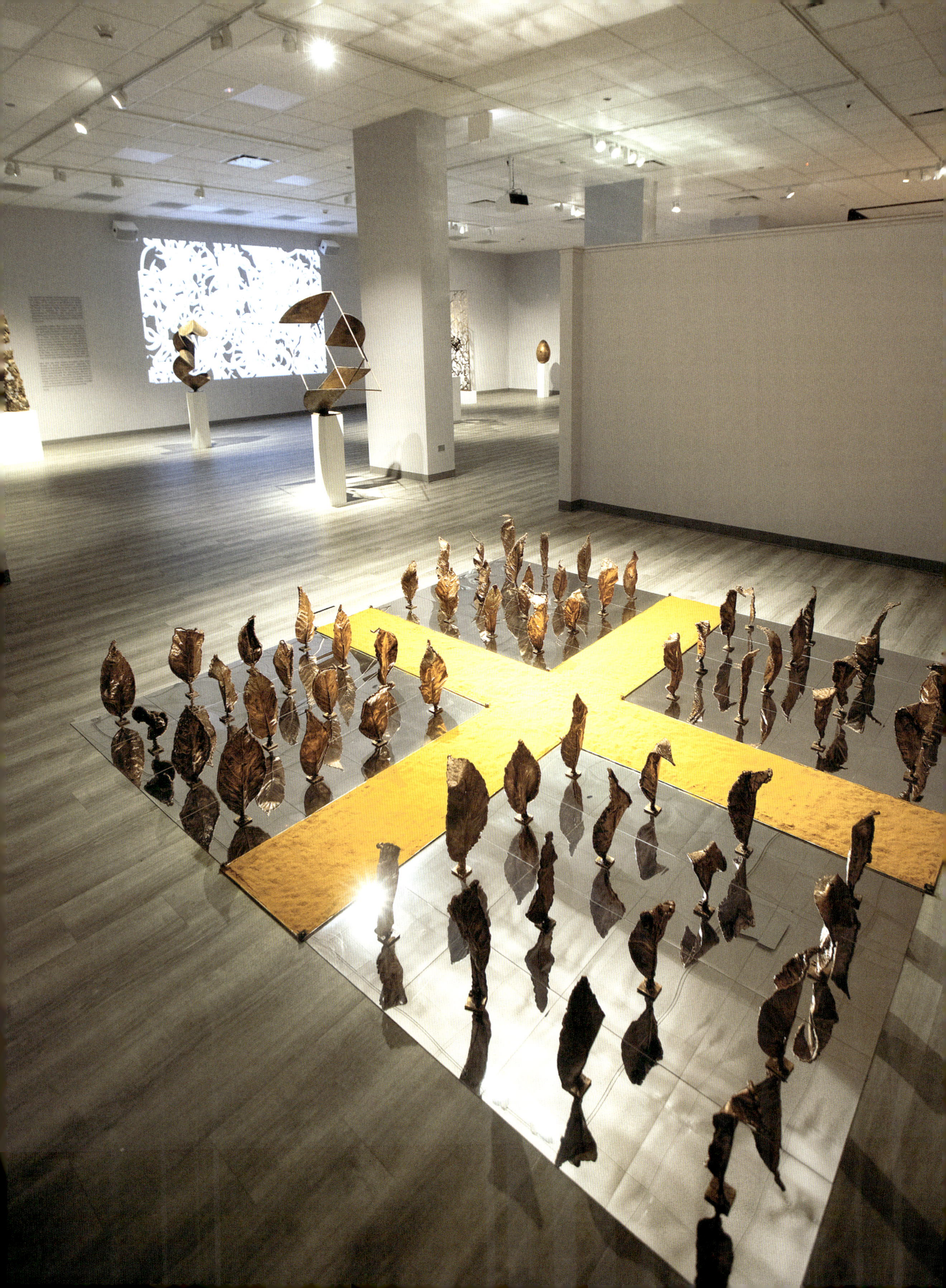

Char Bagh: The Spice Garden

The Spider Speaketh in Tongues

South Asia Institute

Chicago, 2022

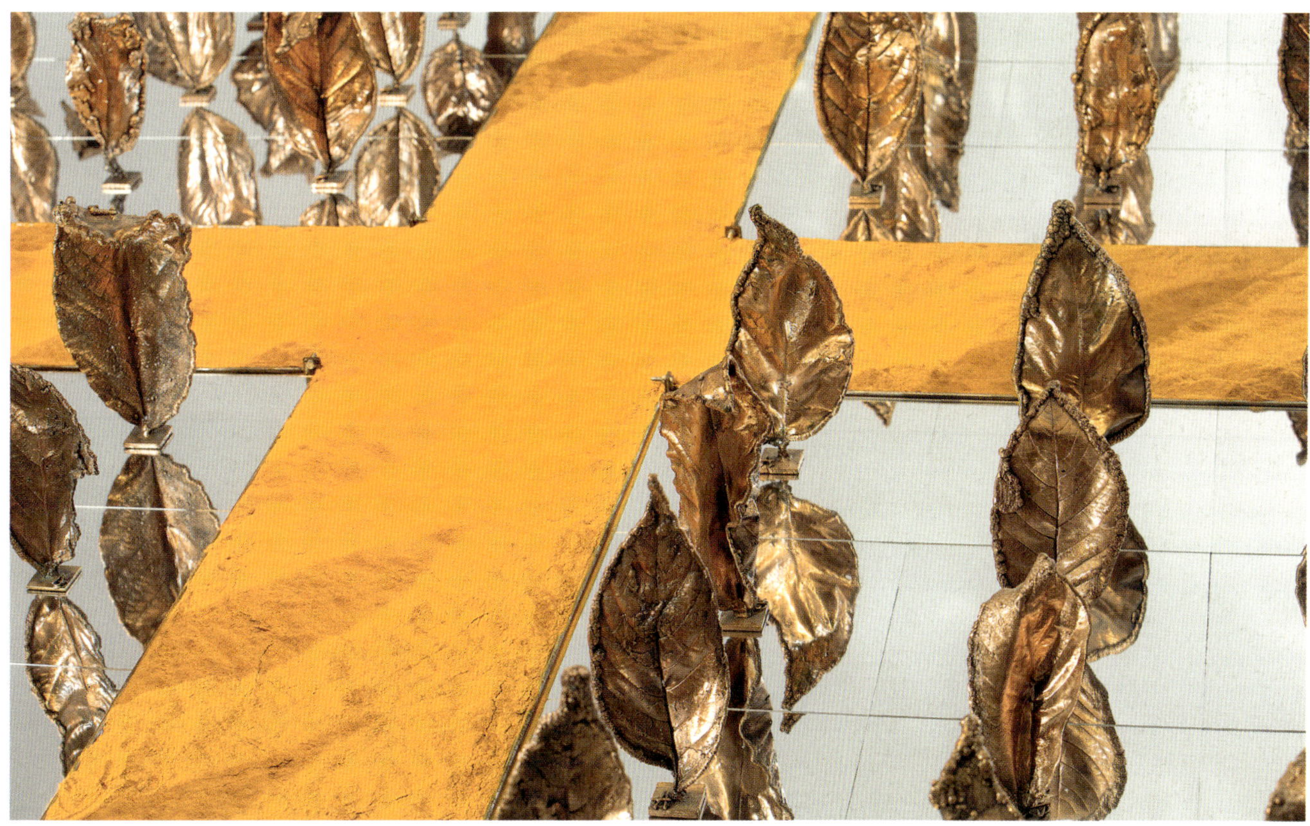

Copper, iron, turmeric and mirror. 335 × 335 × 68.5 cm. Photos by Ryan Bach

Liminal Letters

The Spider Speaketh in Tongues
South Asia Institute
Chicago, 2022

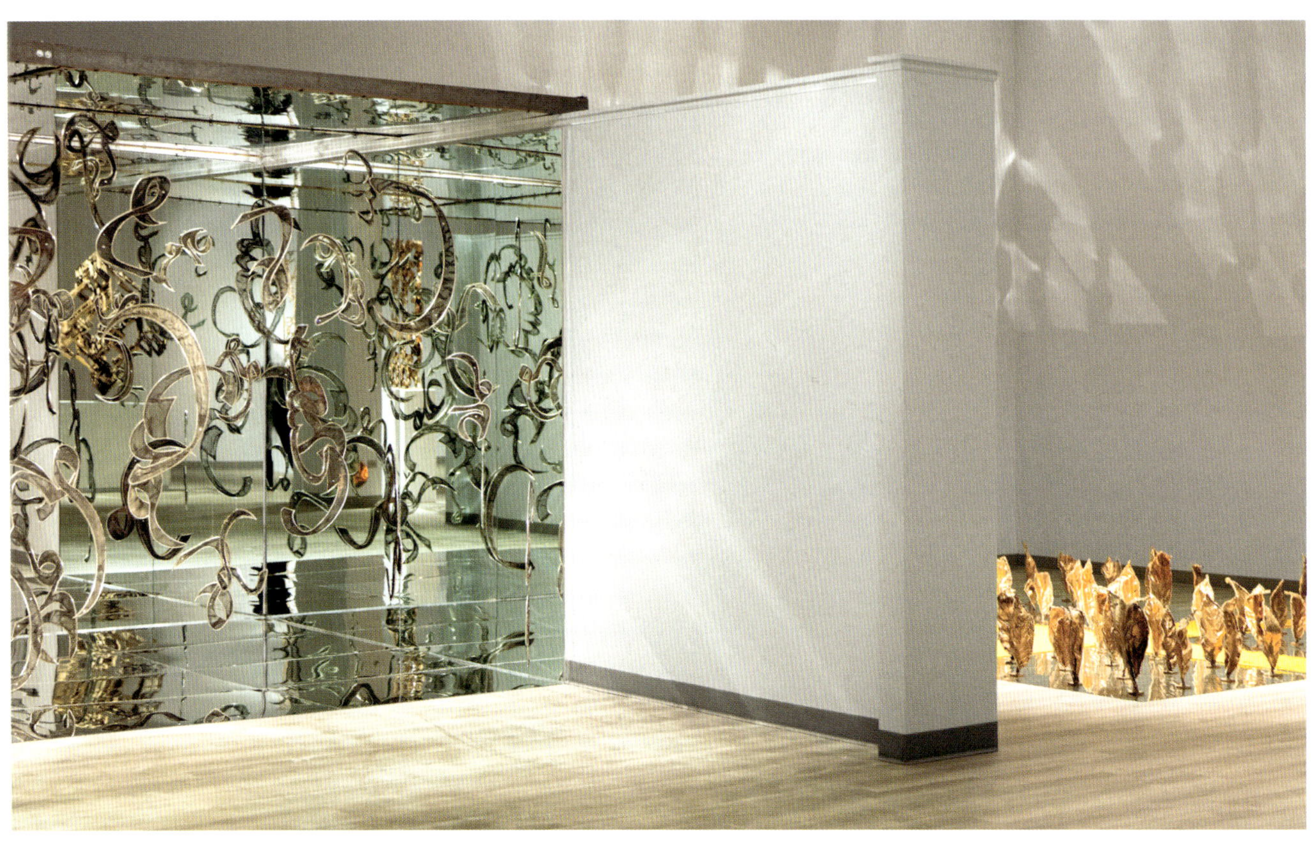

Copper with nickel plate, iron, zircon, fish wire and mirror. 457 × 457 × 304.8 cm. Photos by Ryan Bach

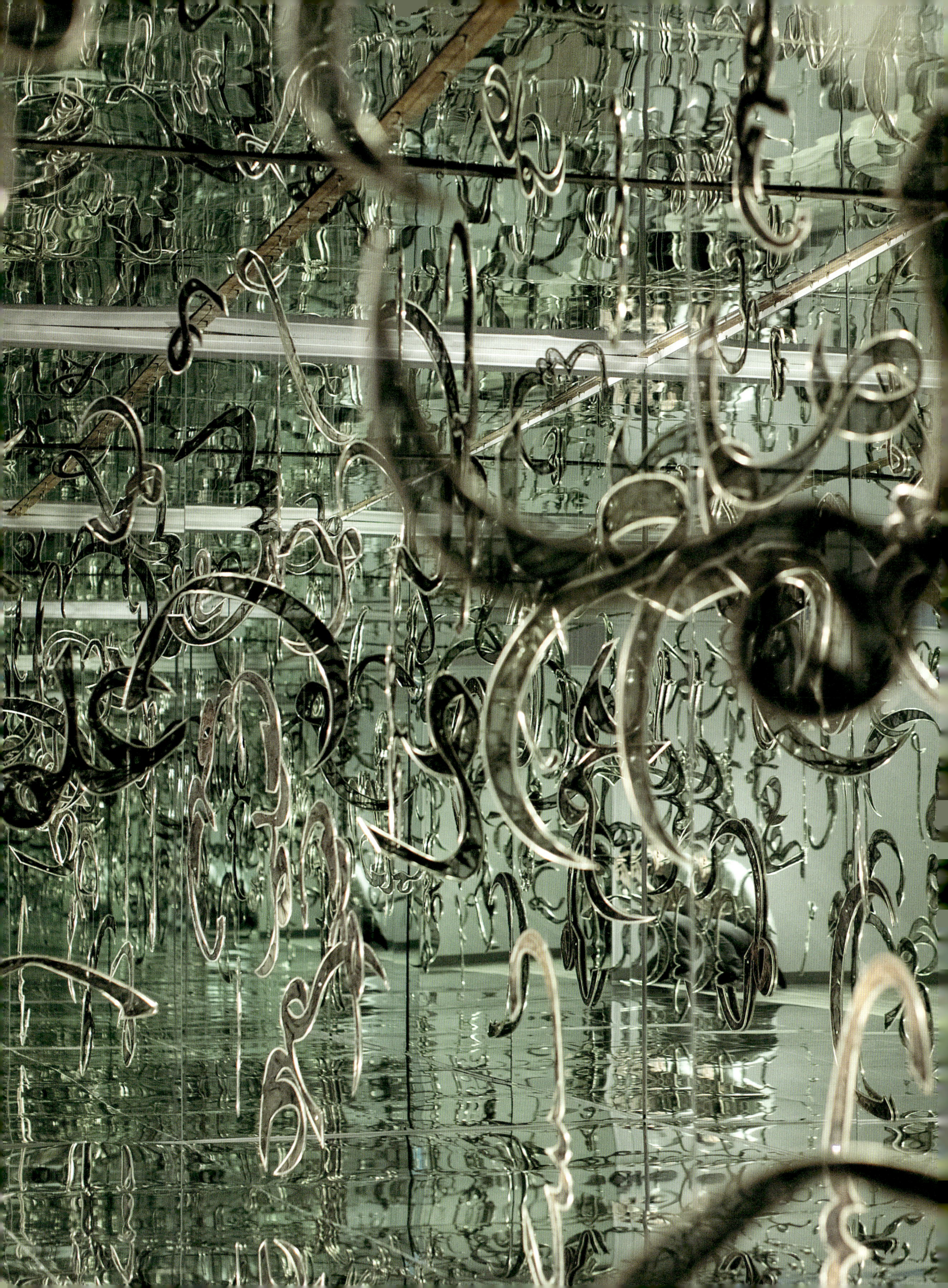

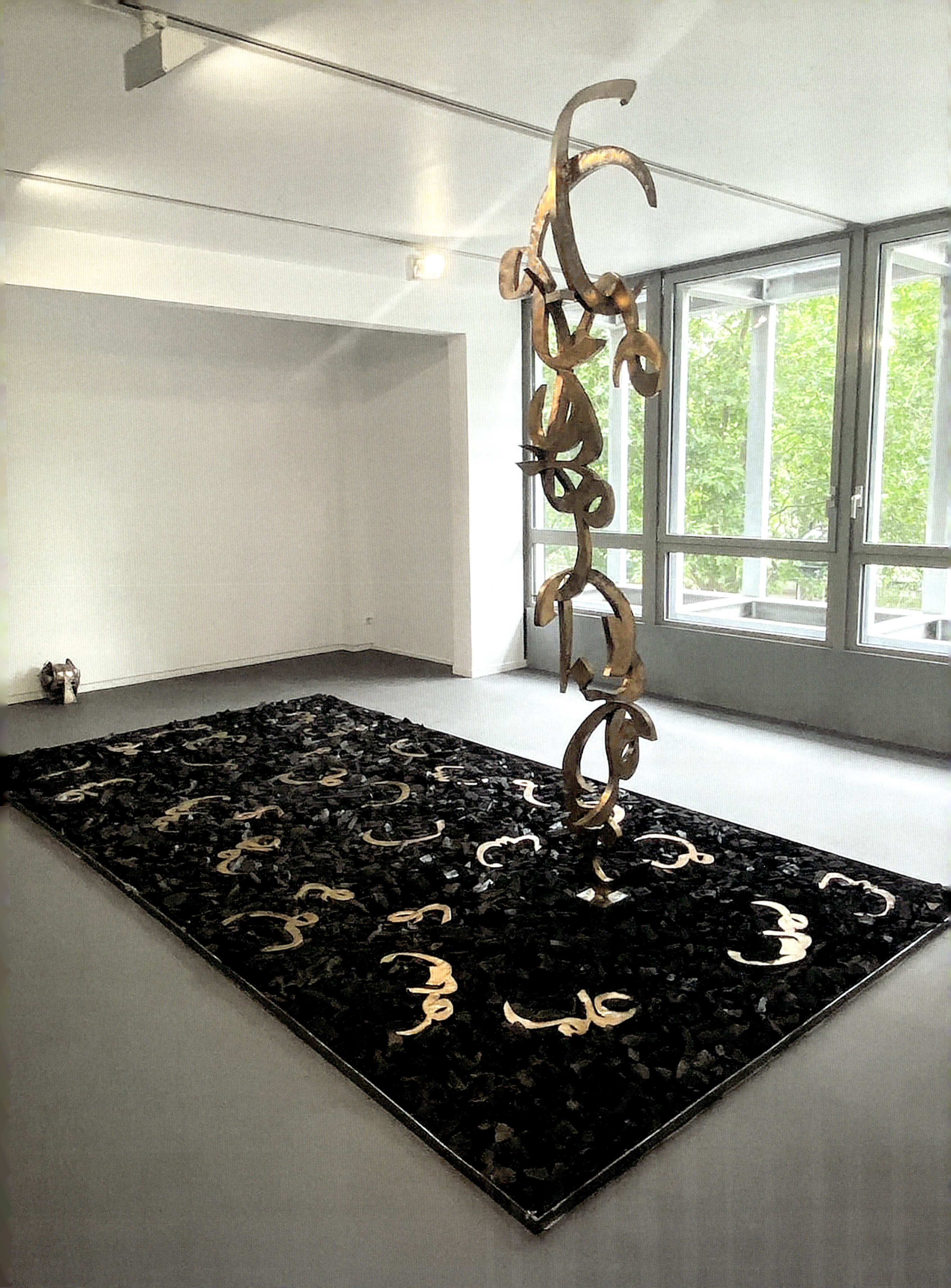

Elysian Fields

ENTRELACS|INTERLACED

Cité internationale des arts

Paris, 2022

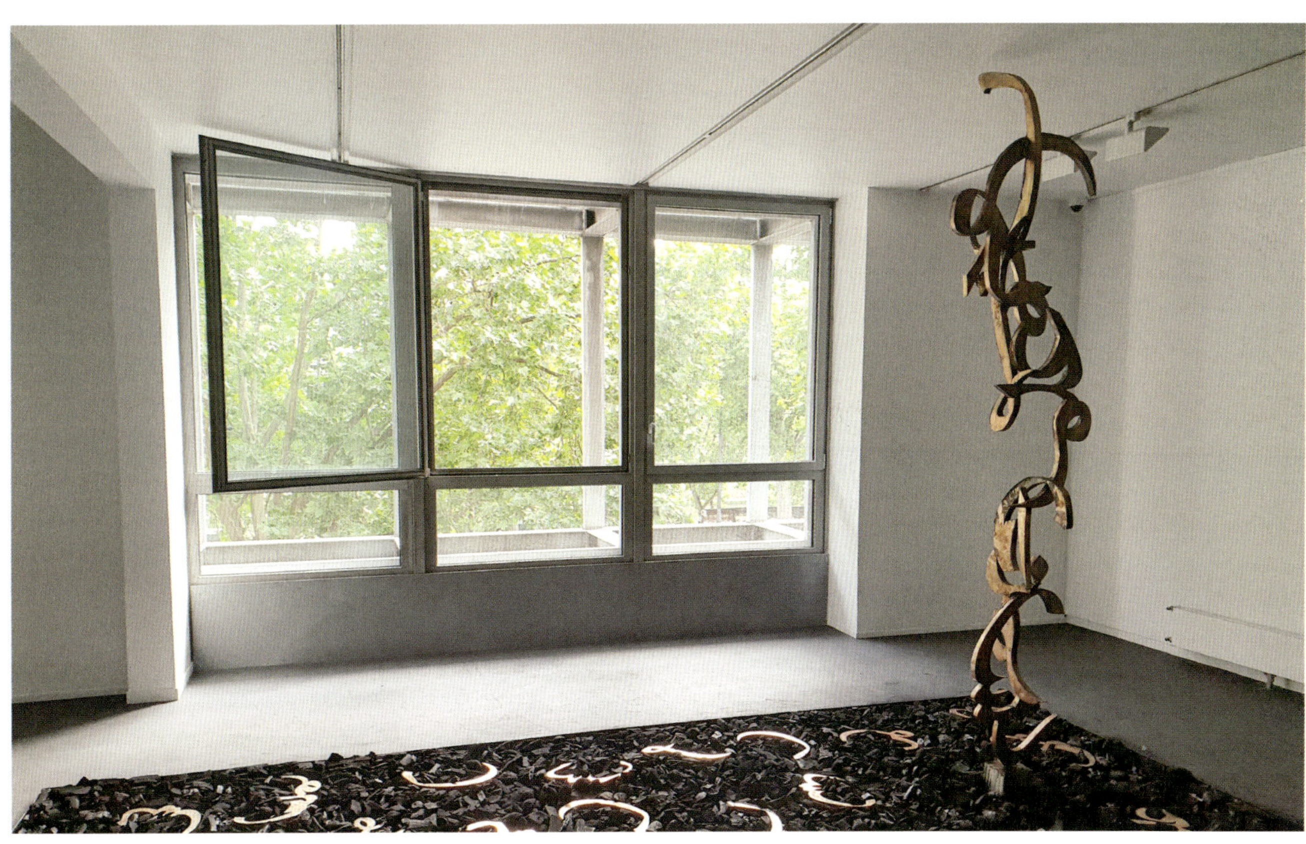

Copper, iron and coal. 205.7 × 426.7 × 274.3 cm. Photos by Laurent Malaquais

Memory Room 305

Karachi Biennale 2022

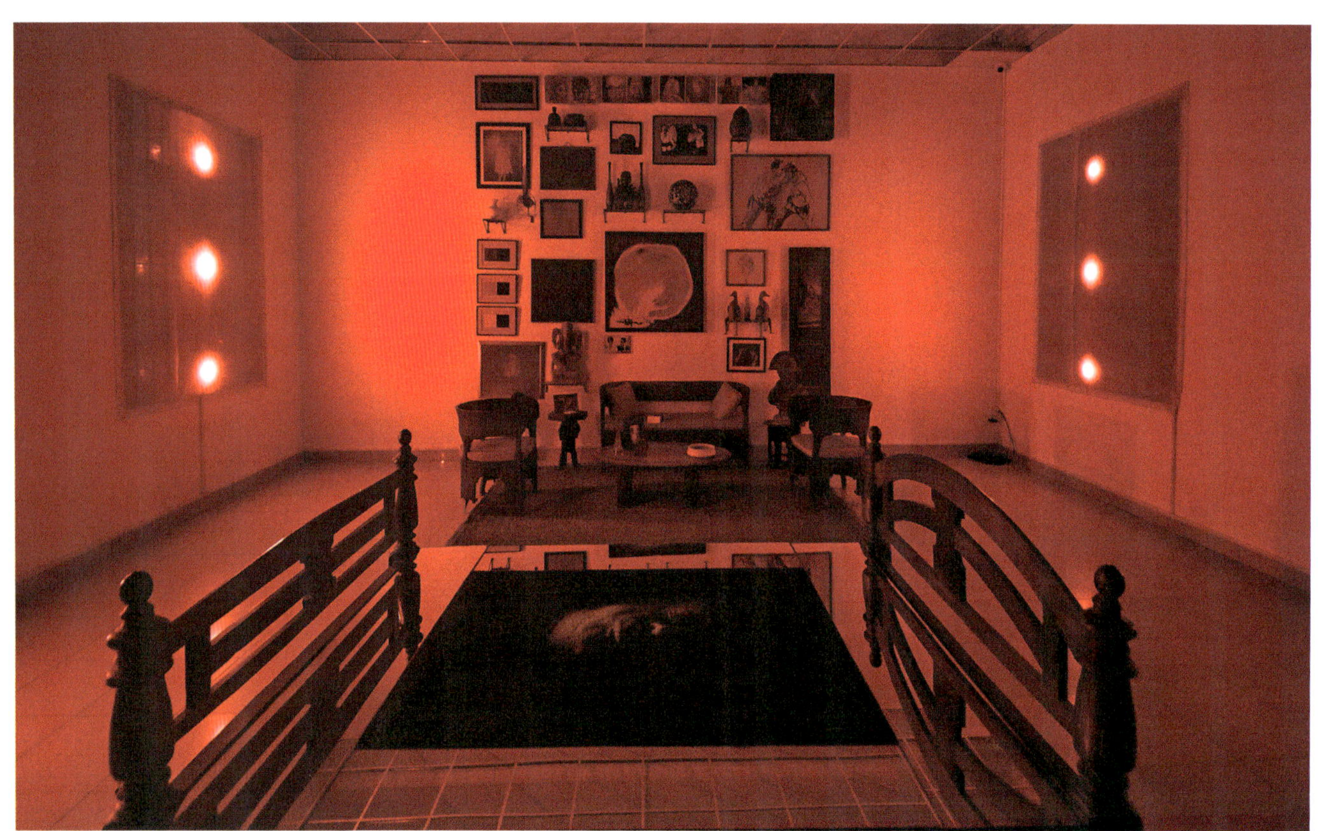

Mixed media. 914.4 × 762 × 304.8 cm. Photos by Humayun Memon

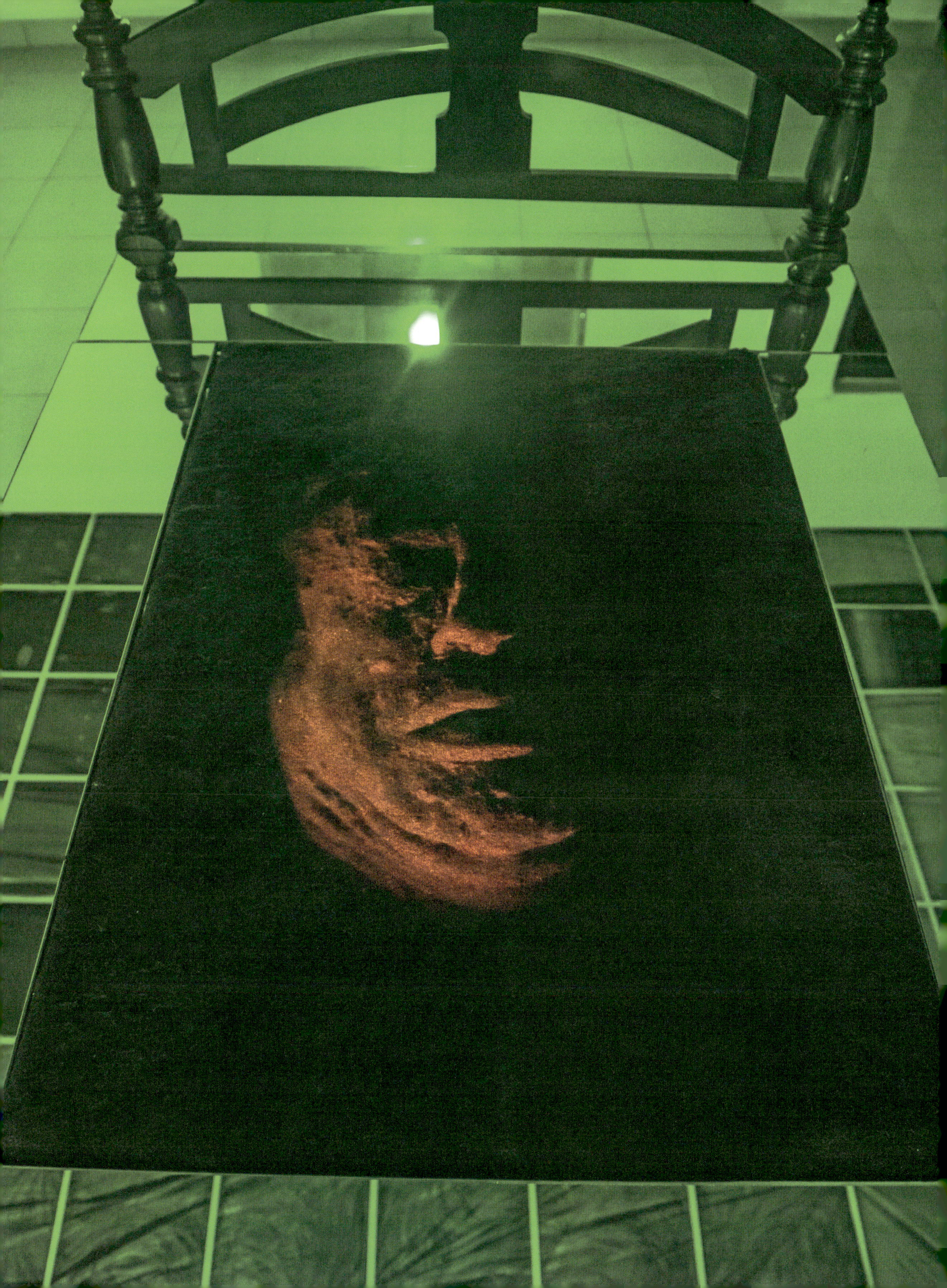

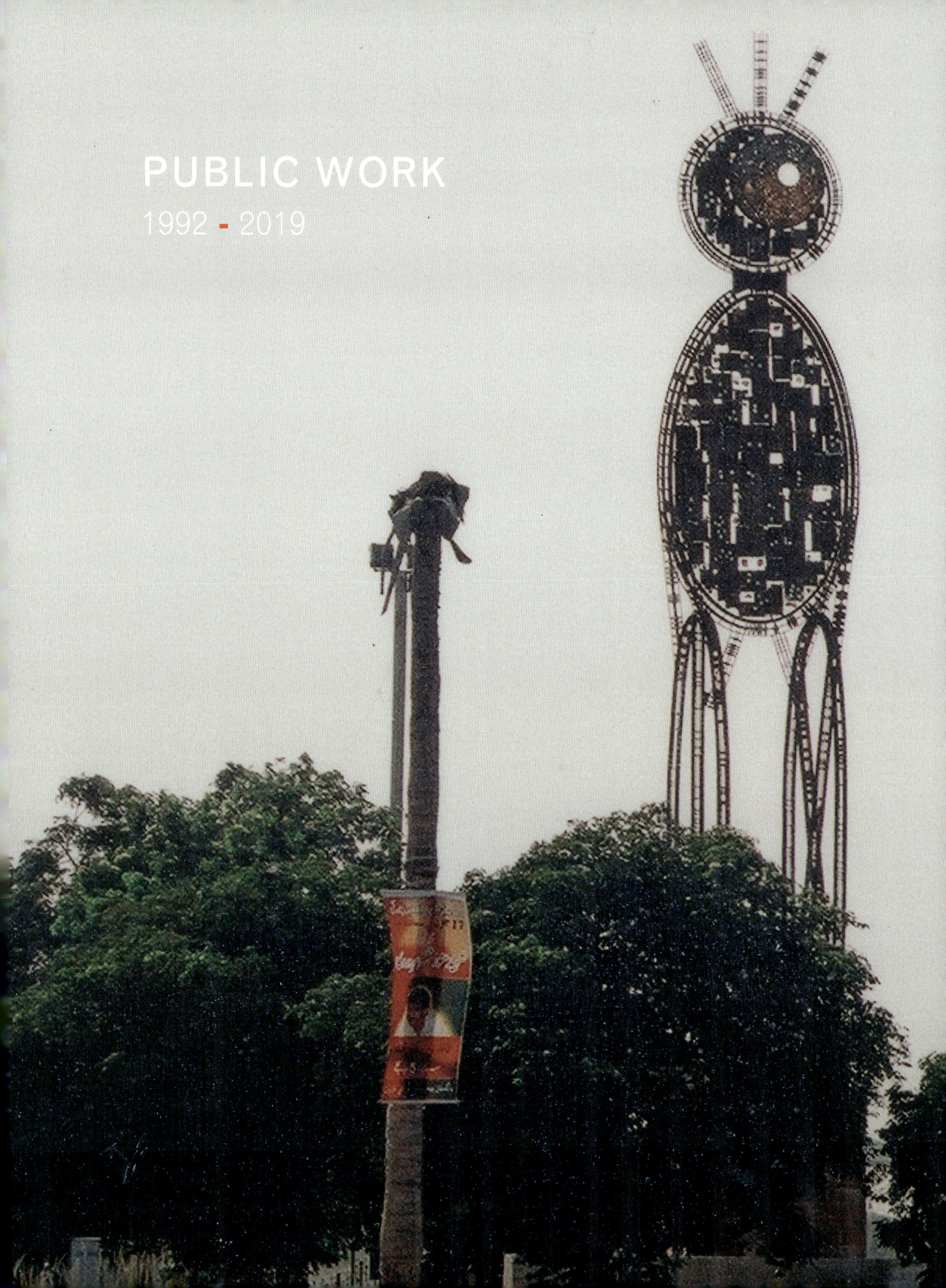

PUBLIC WORK

1992 - 2019

Photo by Nafees

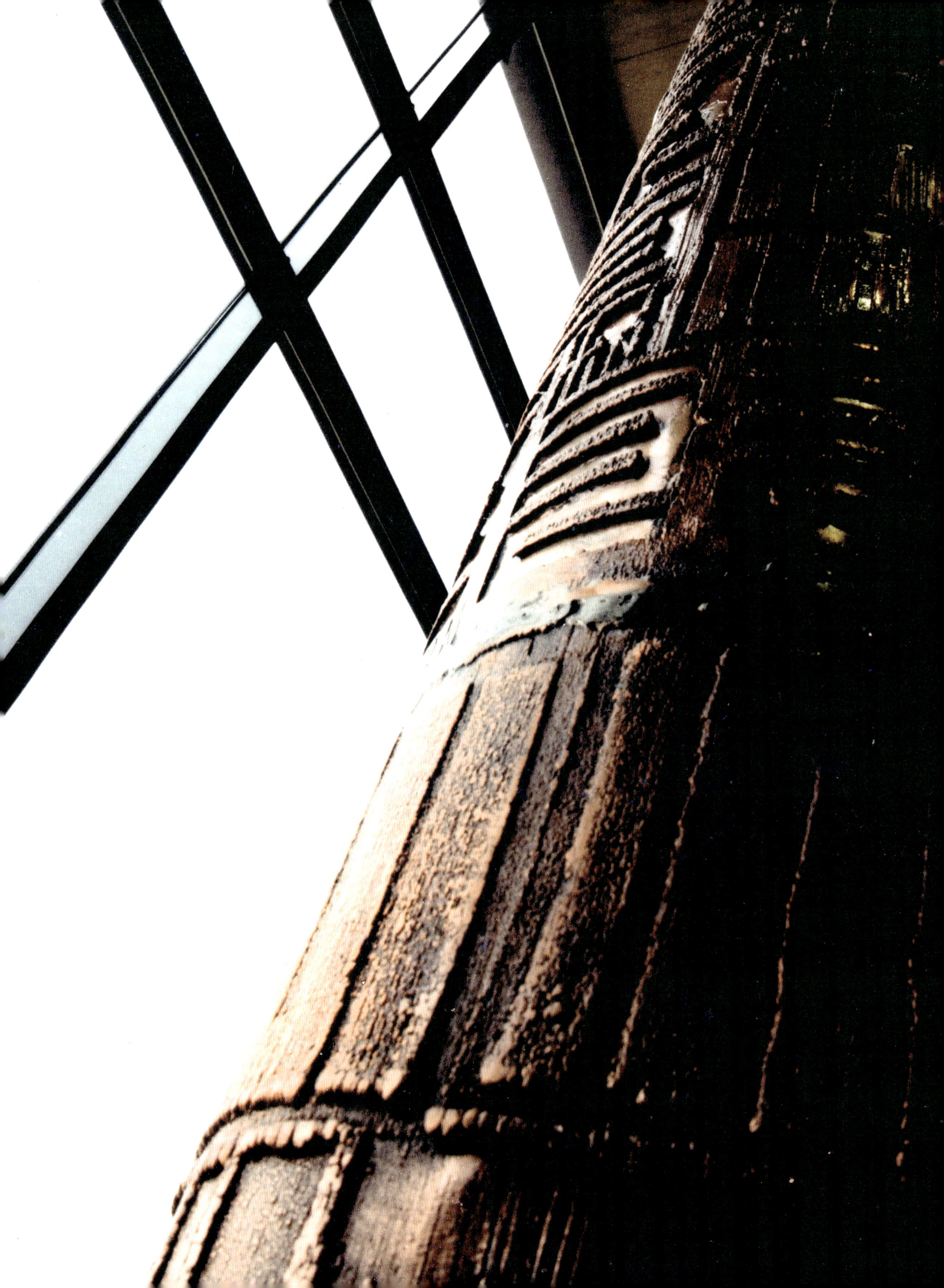

Minar II | 1998

Jinnah International Airport
Karachi

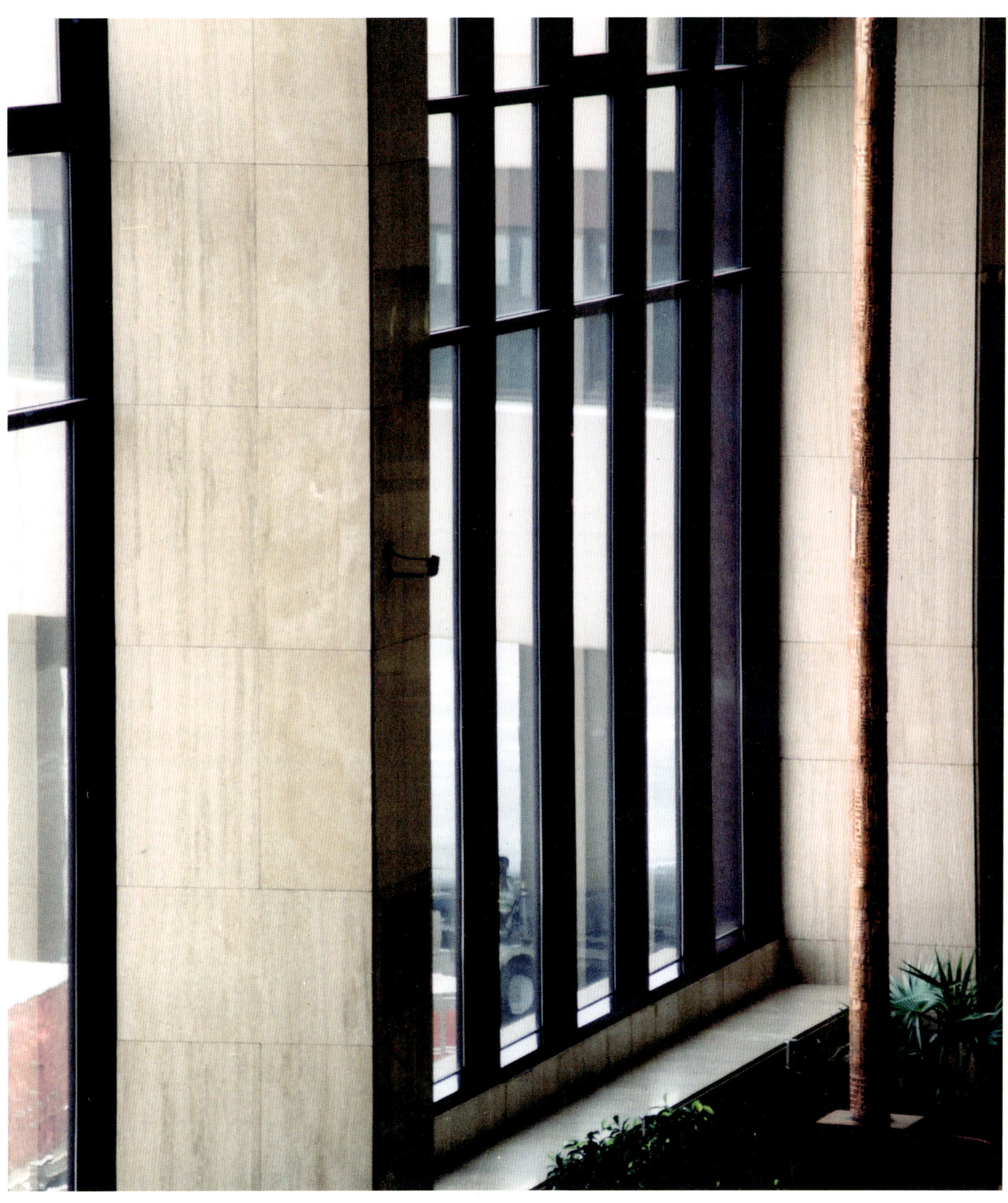

Copper. 609.6 × 22.8 × 22.8 cm. Photos by Shamyl Khuhro

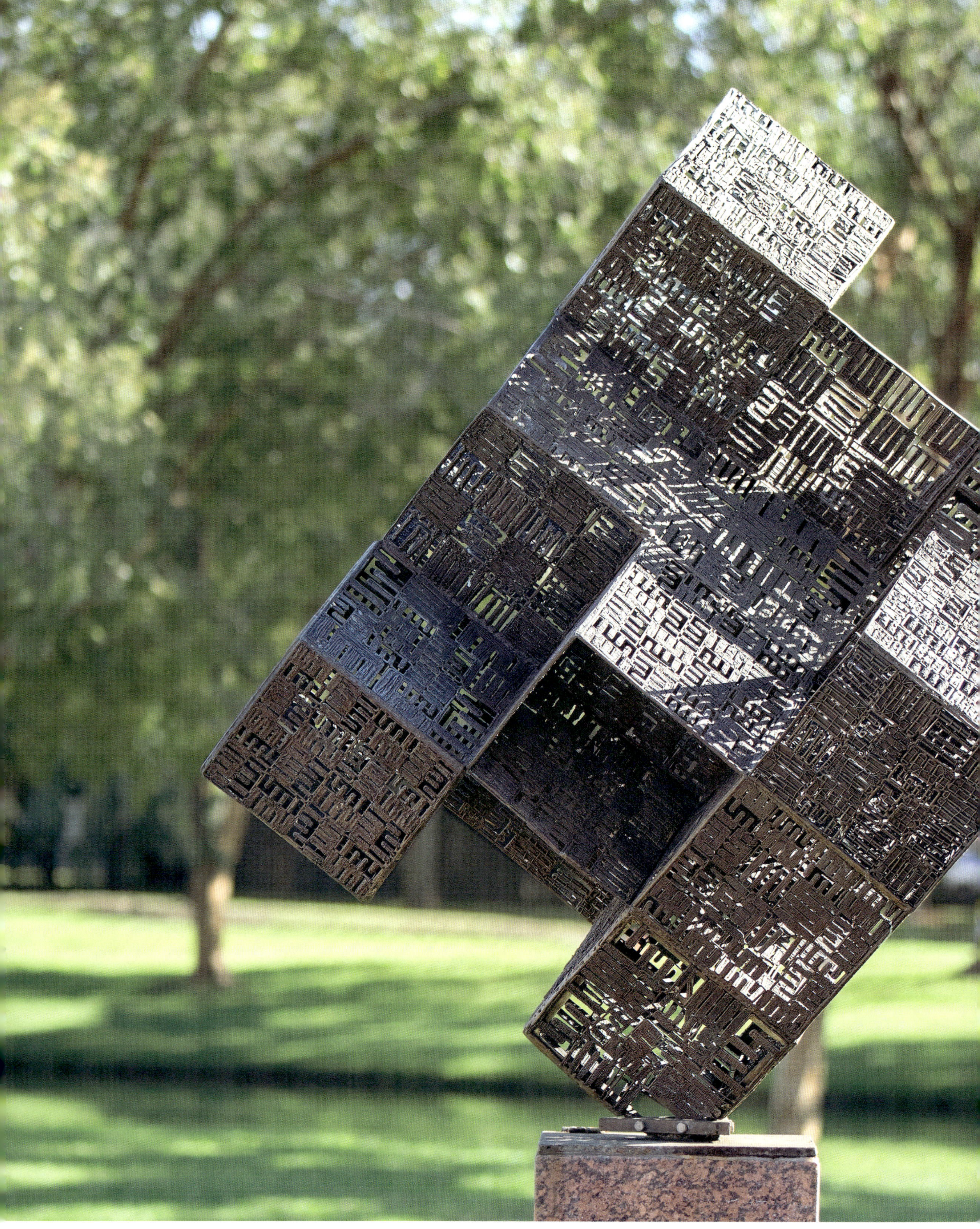

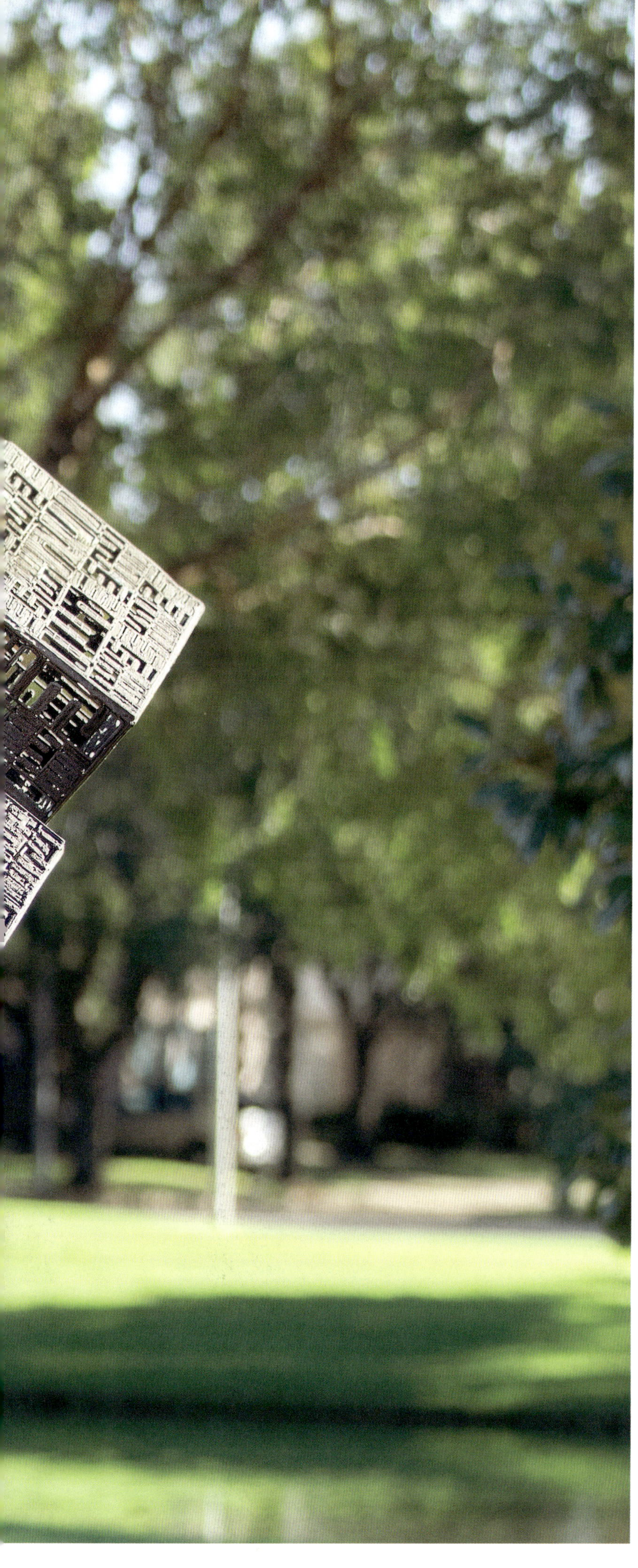

Habitat VII | 2002

Aga Khan Center
Houston

Copper. 241 × 228.6 × 228.6 cm.
Photo courtesy Aga Khan Center, Houston

Char Bagh III | 2003

Sindh Governor House

Karachi

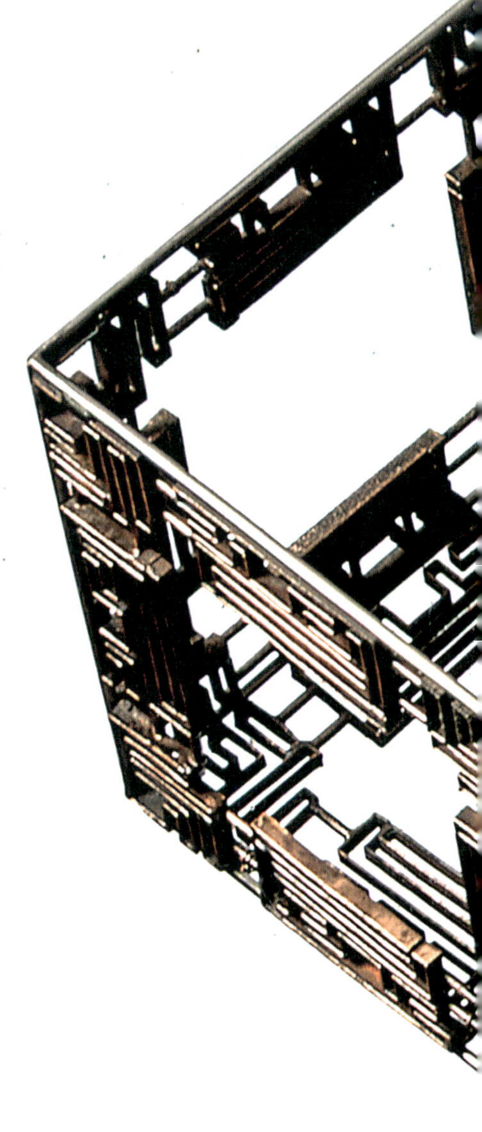

Copper. 119.3 × 101.6 × 101.6 cm. Photo by Shamyl Khuhro

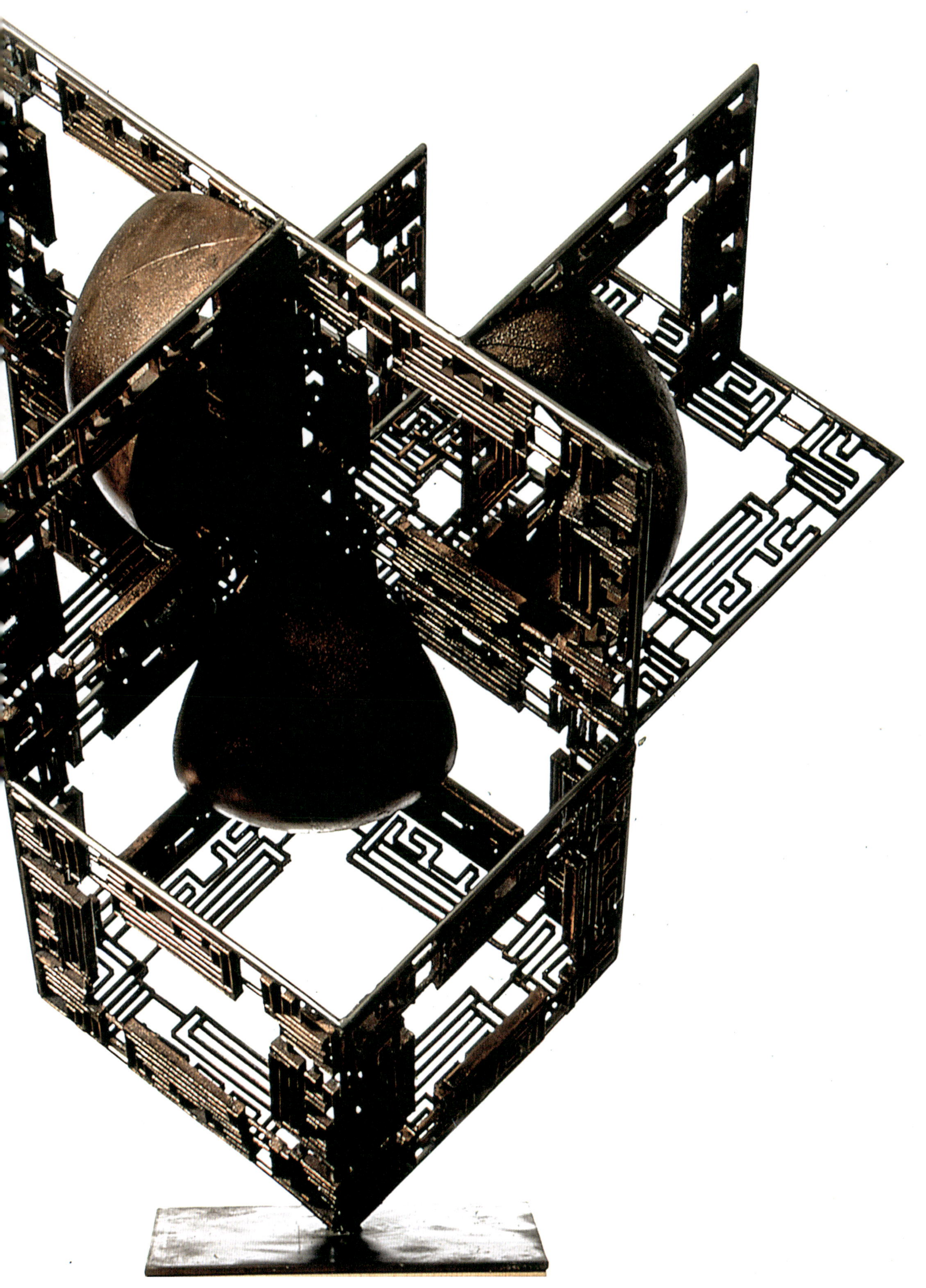

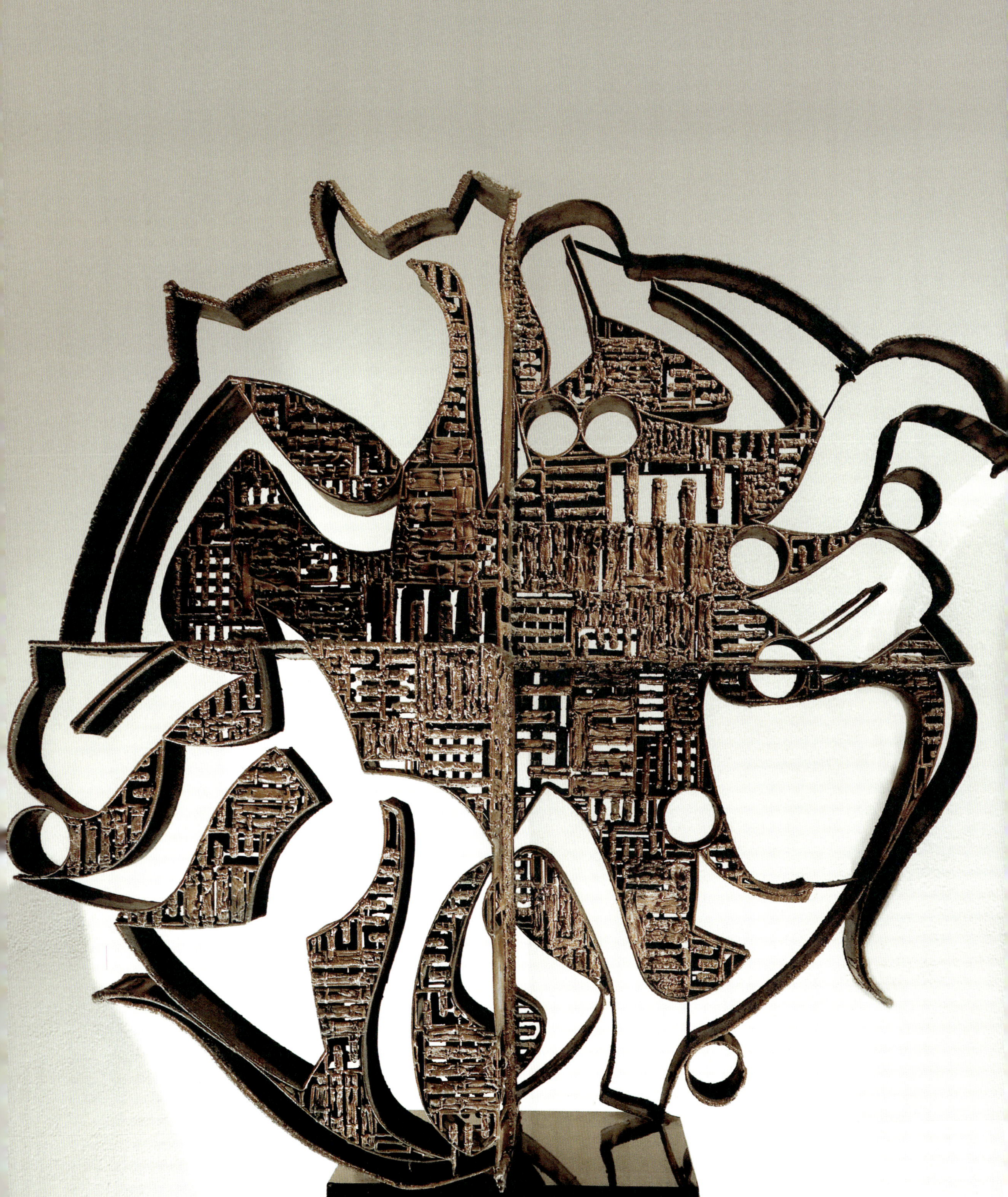

Char Bagh IV | 2003
Serena Hotel
Islamabad

Copper. 94 × 94 × 89 cm. Photo by Talha Zulfiqar

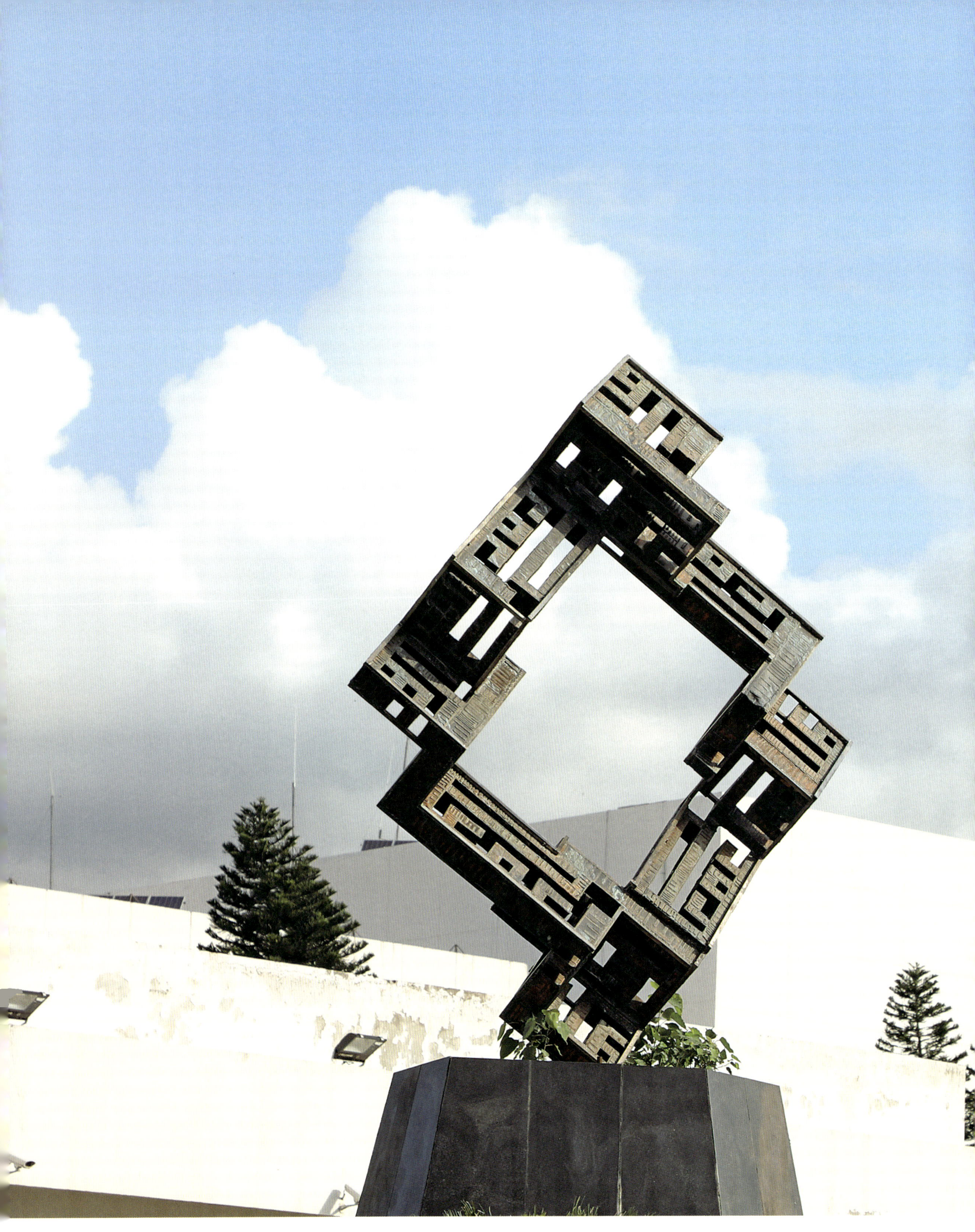

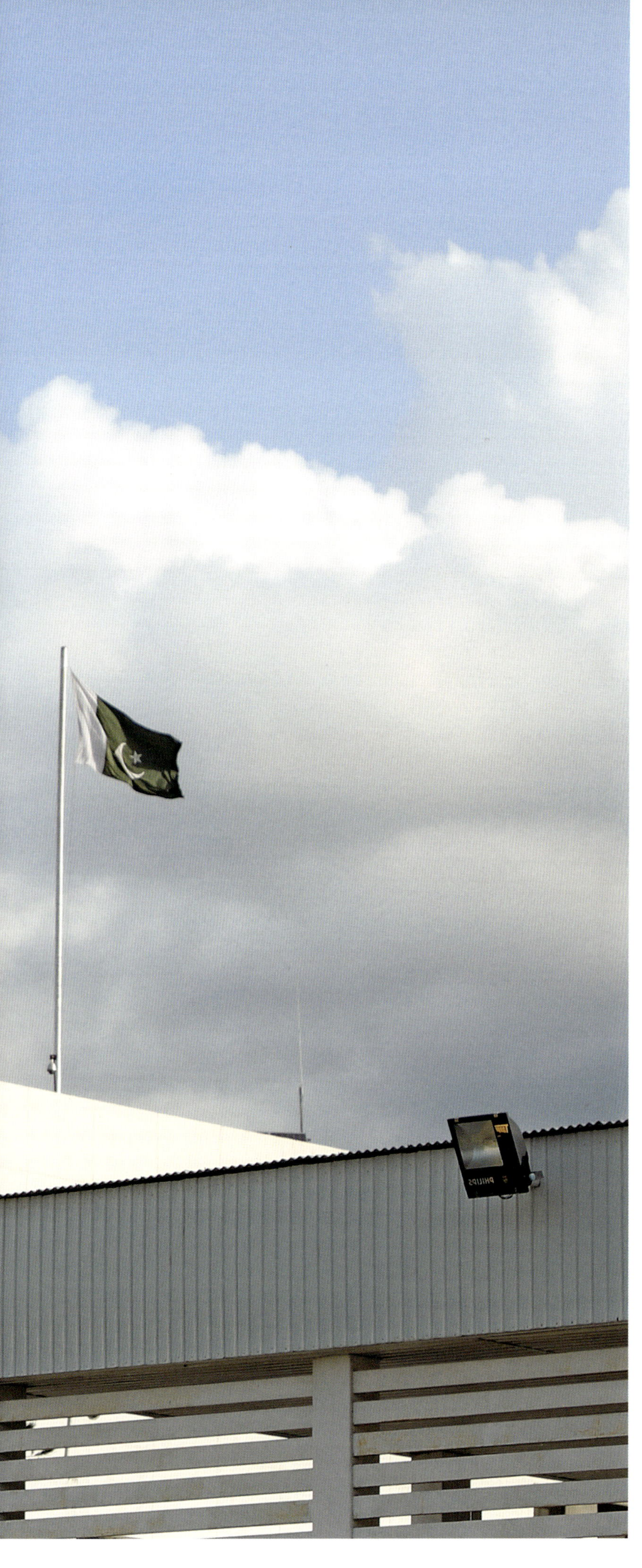

Steps VIII | 2003

Parliament House
Islamabad

Copper. 396 × 335 × 335 cm. Photo by Talha Zulfiqar

The Message | 2003

The Presidency
Islamabad

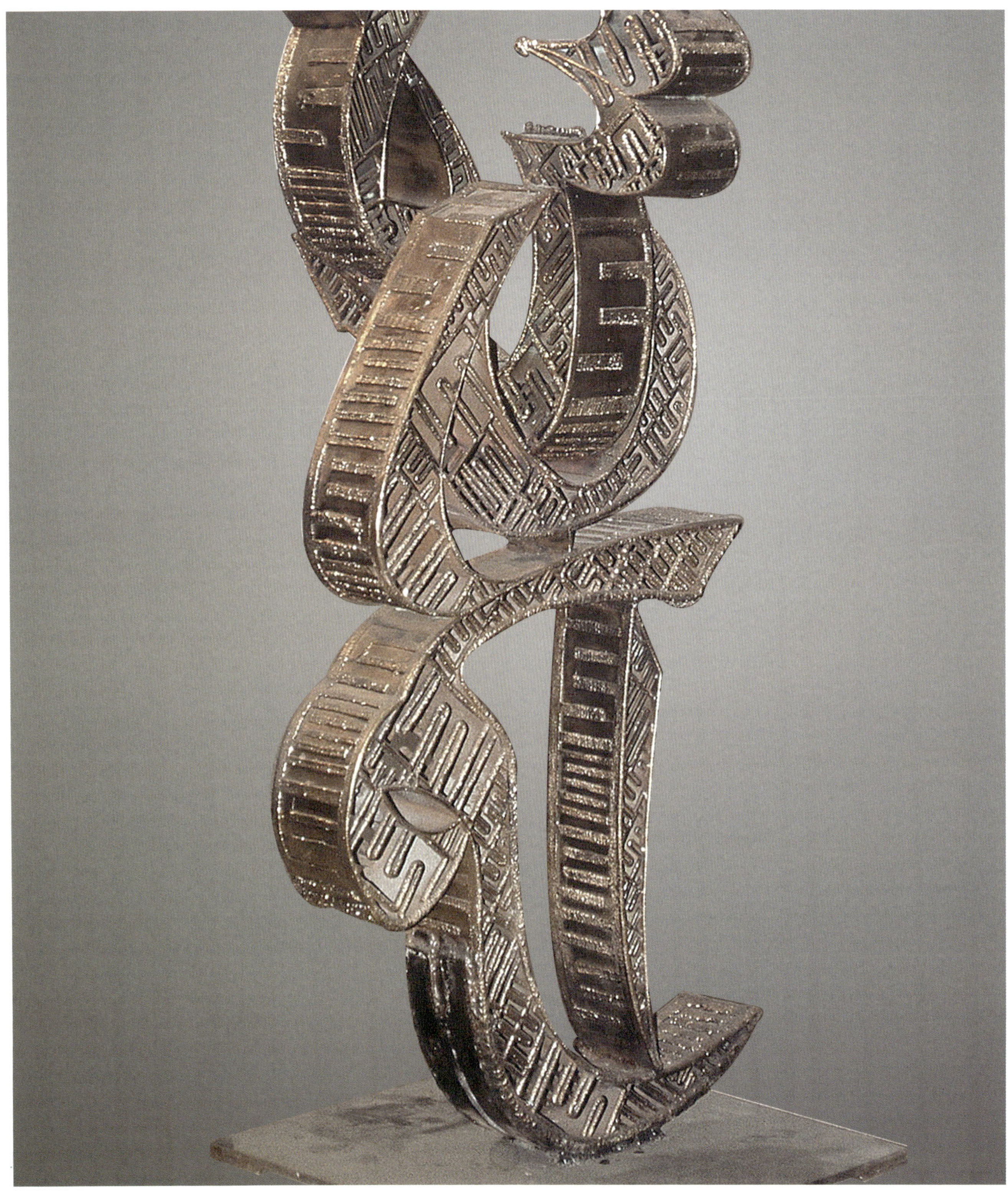

Copper. 335 × 68.5 × 78.7 cm. Photos by Ismail Gulgee

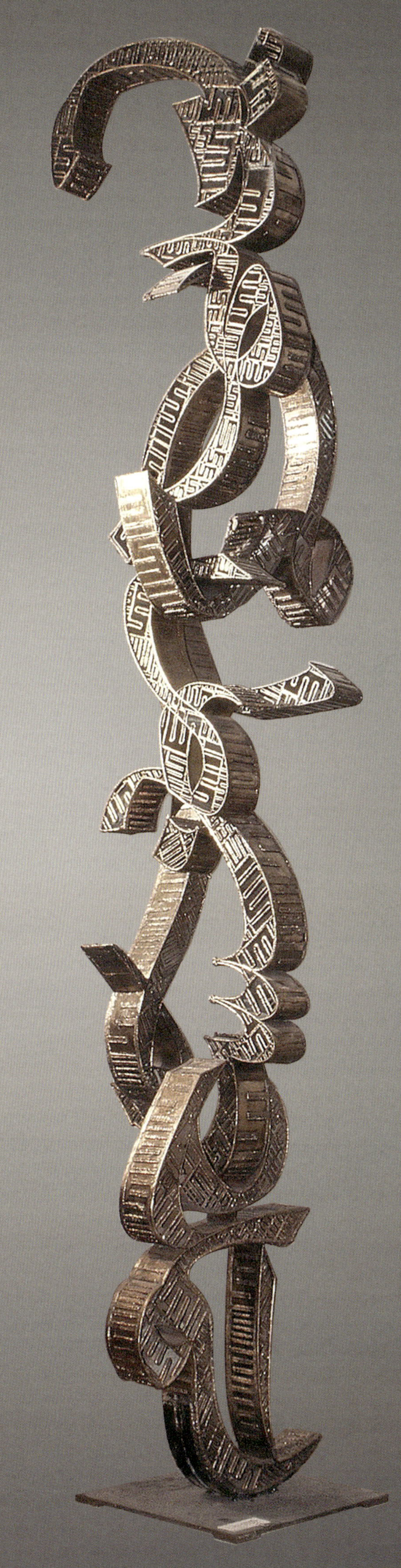

Photo by Nafees

Forgotten Text | 2004

Billawal Roundabout
Karachi

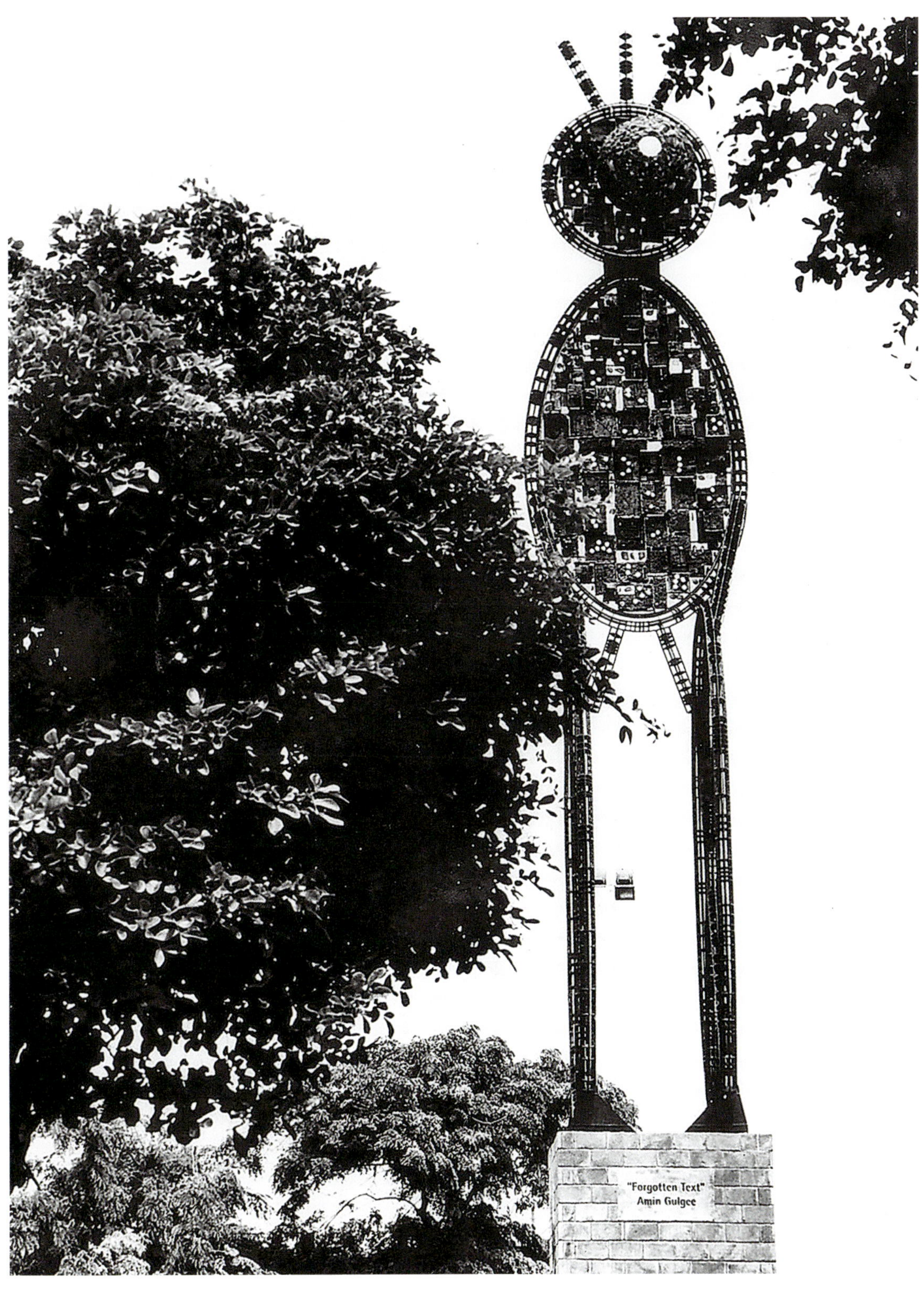

Glass, iron, steel, computer motherboards, mirror and copper.
1219 × 243.8 × 356.5 cm. Photo by Izdeyar Setna

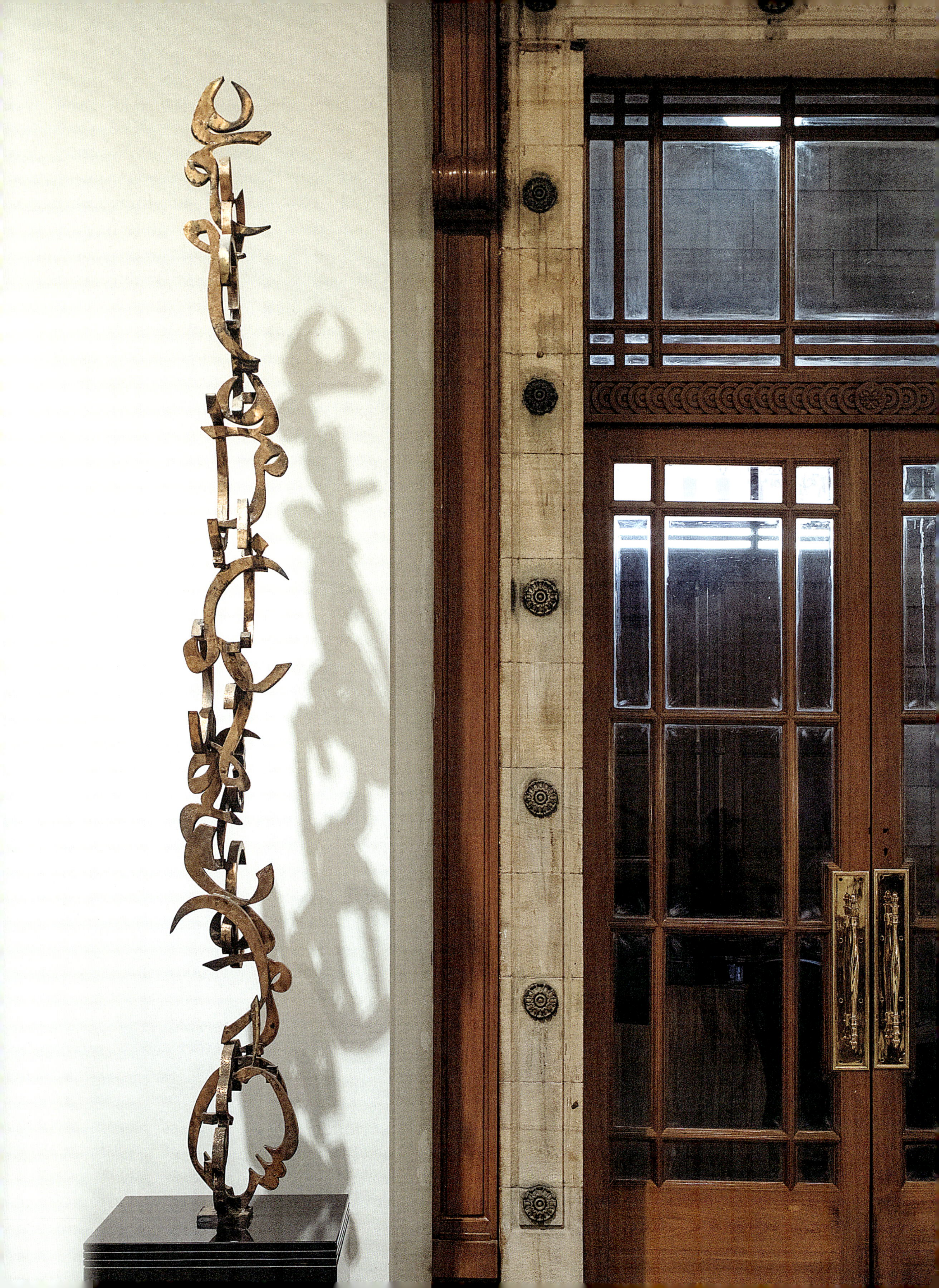

Ascension V | 2018

State Bank Museum and Art Gallery
Karachi

Copper. 267 × 71 × 68.5 cm. Photo by Humayun Memon

Grasping for Air: Reaching for the Skies | 2019

United Nations
New York

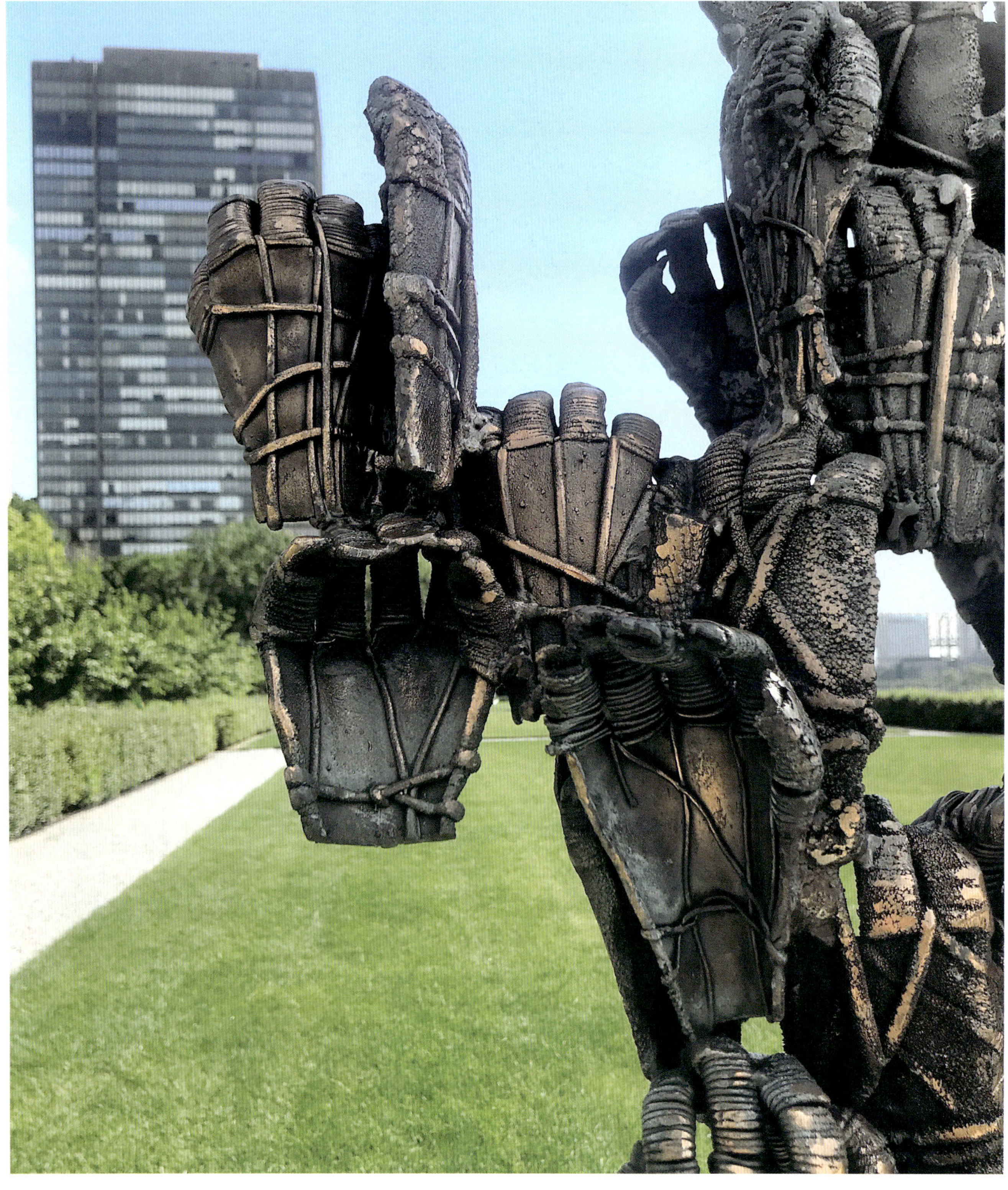

Copper and bronze. 216 × 66 × 20 cm. Photo by Amin Gulgee

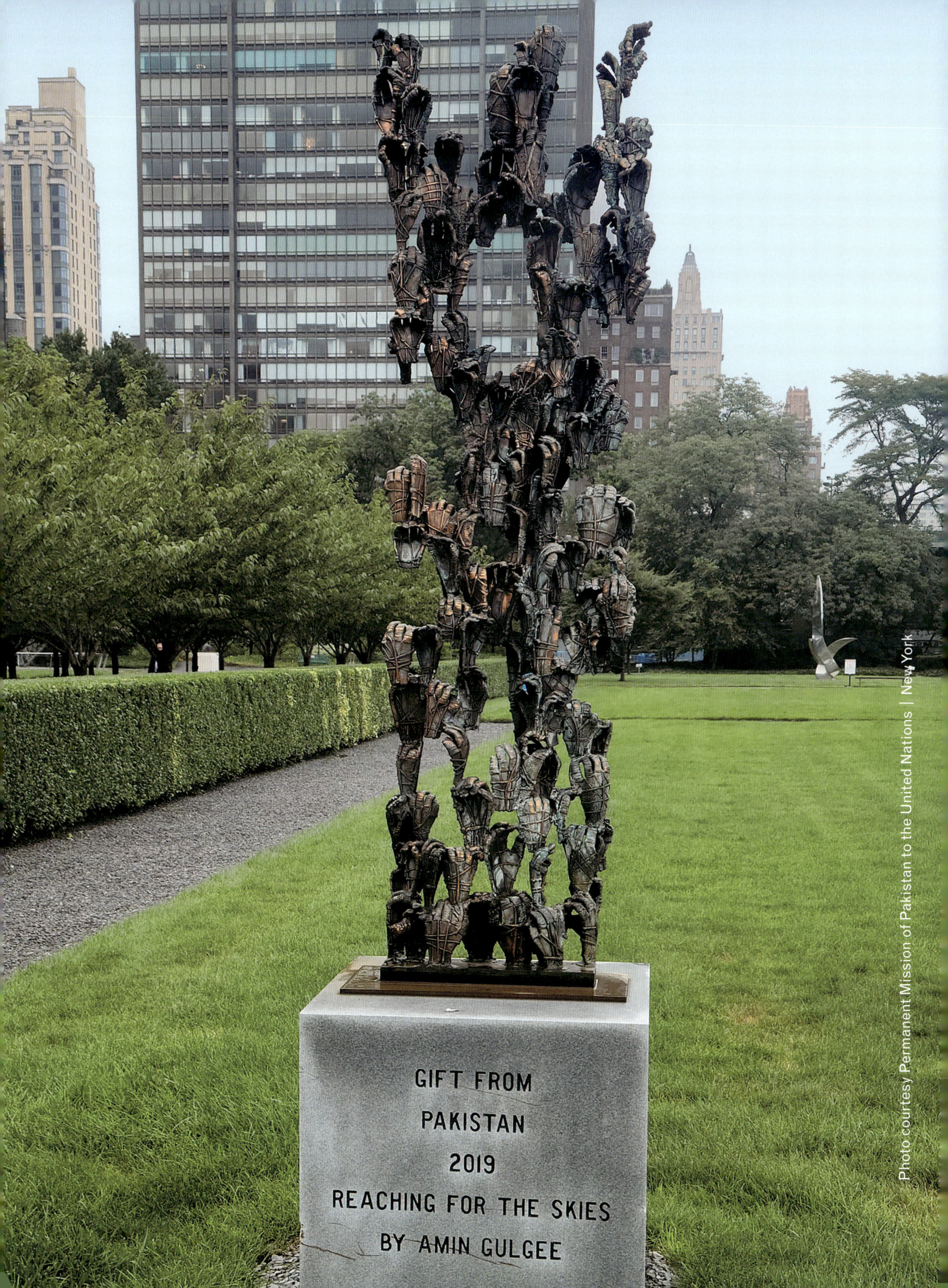

Photo courtesy Permanent Mission of Pakistan to the United Nations | New York

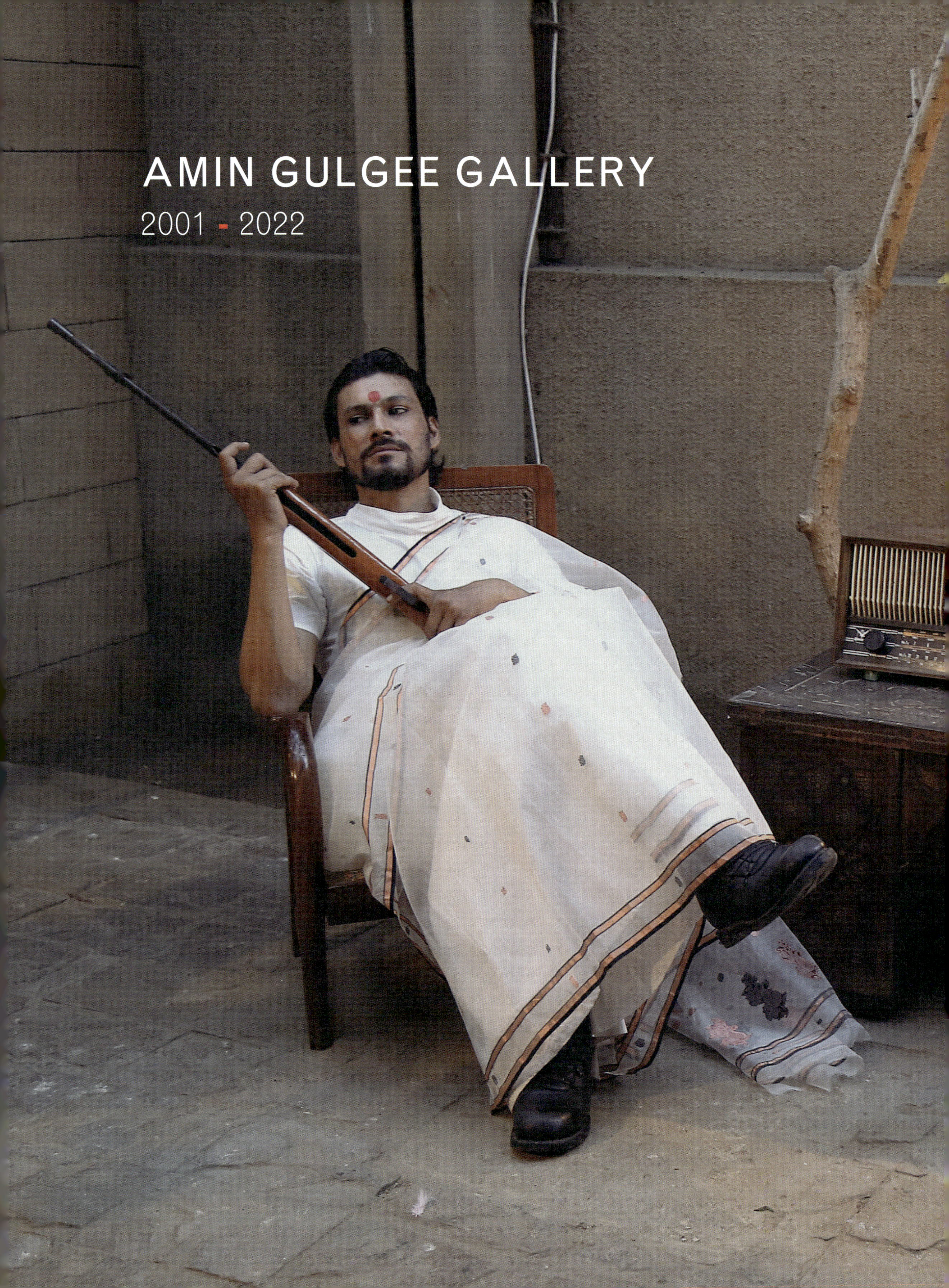
AMIN GULGEE GALLERY
2001 - 2022

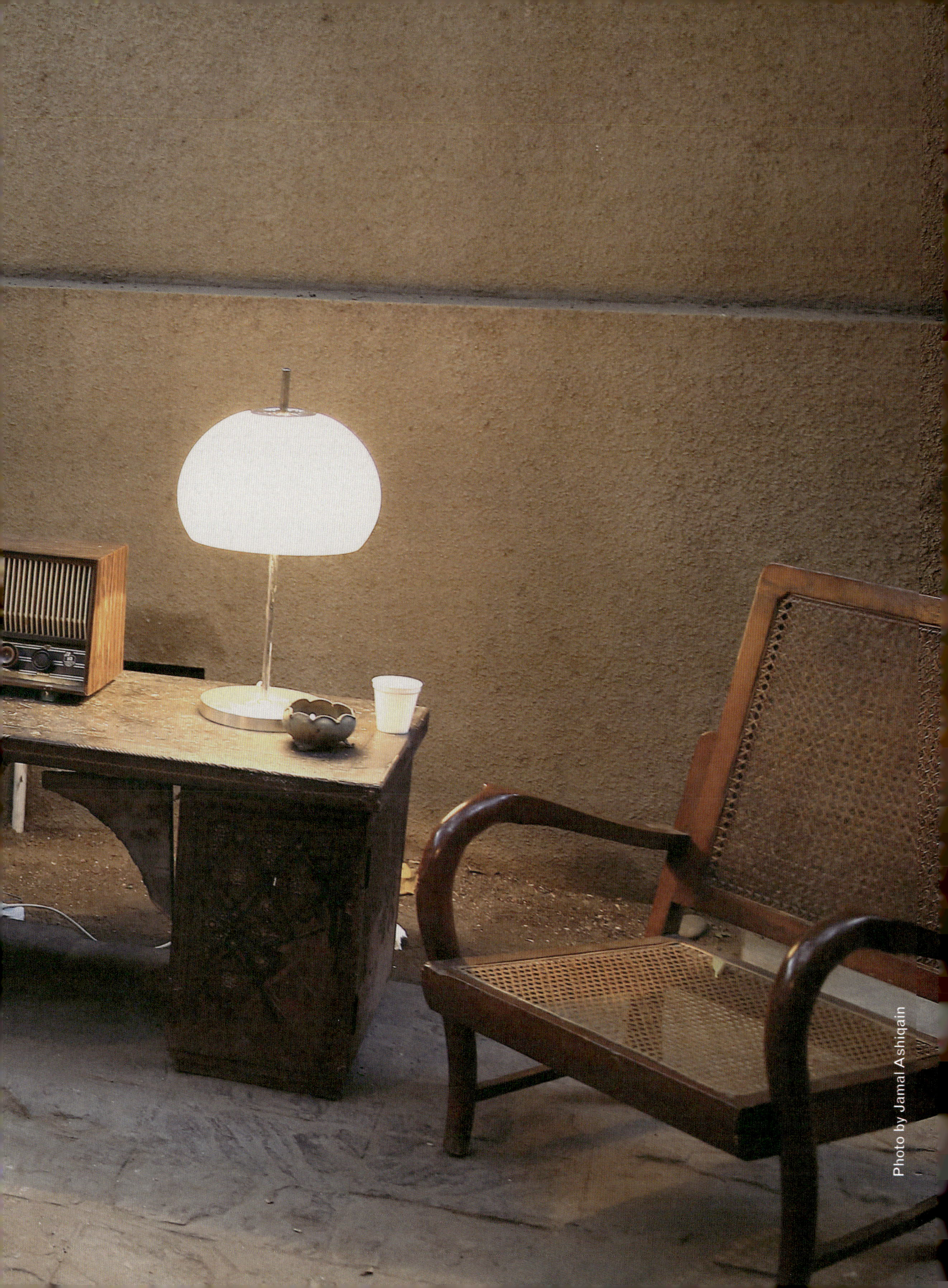
Photo by Jamal Ashiqain

Vasl | 2001

Work from the first Gadani Residency

The Amin Gulgee Gallery is a non-commercial, artist-led space in Karachi that was launched in 2000 with an exhibition of Amin's sculpture. The artist, who lives upstairs, continues to show his work there, but also sees the need to collaborate with outside curators to organize large-scale thematic exhibitions of his contemporaries. *Vasl* was an exhibition of the work produced during the first Vasl International Artists' Workshop at Gadani, a coastal town in Balochistan that is home to the world's third largest shipbreaking yard. Amin took part in the two-week workshop and was also one of the original trustees who established Vasl Artists' Association, which is affiliated with the Triangle Network (UK), host to the longest running international residency program in Pakistan. A seminar was held in tandem with the exhibition at the adjoining Gulgee Museum. Participating artist Nayan Kulkarni introduced it with a performance in which he washed blue sequins from his face. The exhibition featured the work of 12 Pakistani artists as well as 10 artists from the Netherlands, Nigeria, Sri Lanka, the US, the UK, Bangladesh, Egypt, China and India.

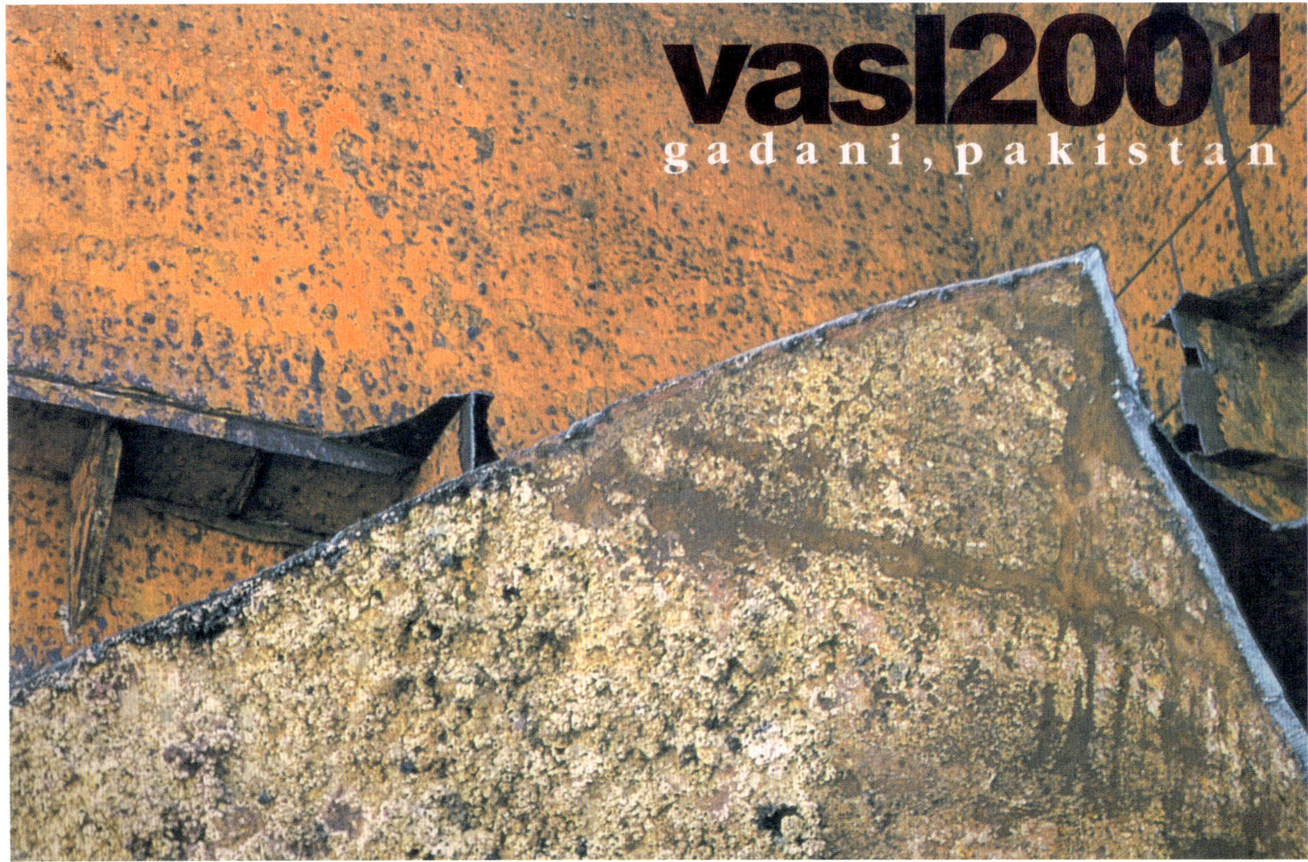

Photo courtesy Vasl

Uraan | 2002

Curated by Sairah Irshad Khan and Niilofur Farrukh

The Amin Gulgee Gallery hosted *Uraan,* which means "flight" in Urdu, in the spring of 2002. Curated by gallerist Sairah Irshad Khan and art historian Niilofur Farrukh, this was an exhibition of painting, ceramics and sculpture by 33 artists from across Pakistan, including Gulgee, Jamil Naqsh, Imran Qureshi, Rashid Rana and Unver Shafi Khan, among others. A survey of trends in Pakistani art, the exhibit was originally intended to be displayed at a prominent gallery in New Delhi. However, the political climate between the two countries was such at the time that the show was unable to travel to India. The curators decided that the ambitious exhibition should be seen by a Pakistani audience instead. They initially thought of installing it at Frere Hall, a public space in Karachi that is widely accessible. However, due to the nature of some of the figurative work, the concerned authorities balked. Amin opened his gallery to the show.

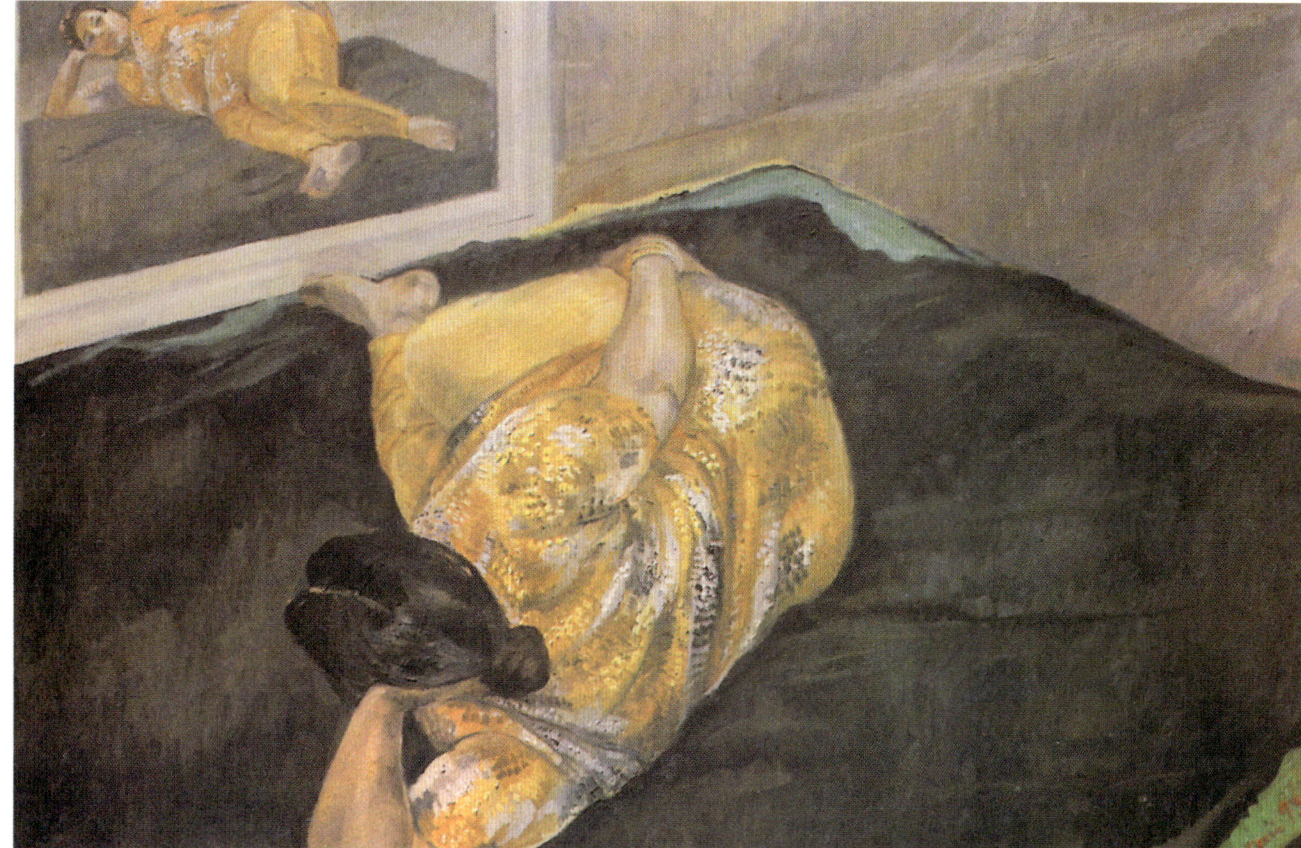

Photo courtesy Iqbal Hussain

Dish Dhamaka | 2002

Curated by Amin Gulgee

Amin took on the mantle of curator at his gallery for the first time with *Dish Dhamaka.* This was not his first curatorial effort, however. He had curated three iterations of *Urban Voices* at the Karachi Sheraton Hotel in the late 1990s, transforming its main lobby into a pop-up art space. These shows juxtaposed work by established Pakistani artists with that of recent graduates from local art schools. For *Dish Dhamaka,* or "dish explosion," he asked 20 sculptors, painters and architects to appropriate a satellite dish and create a work from it. (Syed Munawar Ali saw the dish as a plate proffering a tempting red apple; Abdul Jabbar Gull reimagined it as a beggar's bowl holding three foreign coins randomly tossed within.) Amin's curatorial proposition was unusual at a time when Karachi's art scene was largely comprised of commercial galleries showing painting and drawing. The sculptor was drawn to the satellite dish for two reasons. First, it was three-dimensional, allowing him to curate one of the city's first shows of large-scale objects. Second, these parabolic antennas proliferated at the turn of the last century, bringing a wide range of mostly Western content into Pakistani homes for the first time. With the advent of cable TV a few years later, dishes became as quickly obsolete as they had been desirable. The bowl-shaped receivers continued to stubbornly sit upon Karachi's rooftops, however, pointing to the sky, transforming the silhouette of the city. Amin asked each of the artists to write statements, pondering what these aerials symbolized to them. Some saw them as messengers of information, others as conveyors of dreams, and yet others as a harbinger of obtrusive foreign influence.

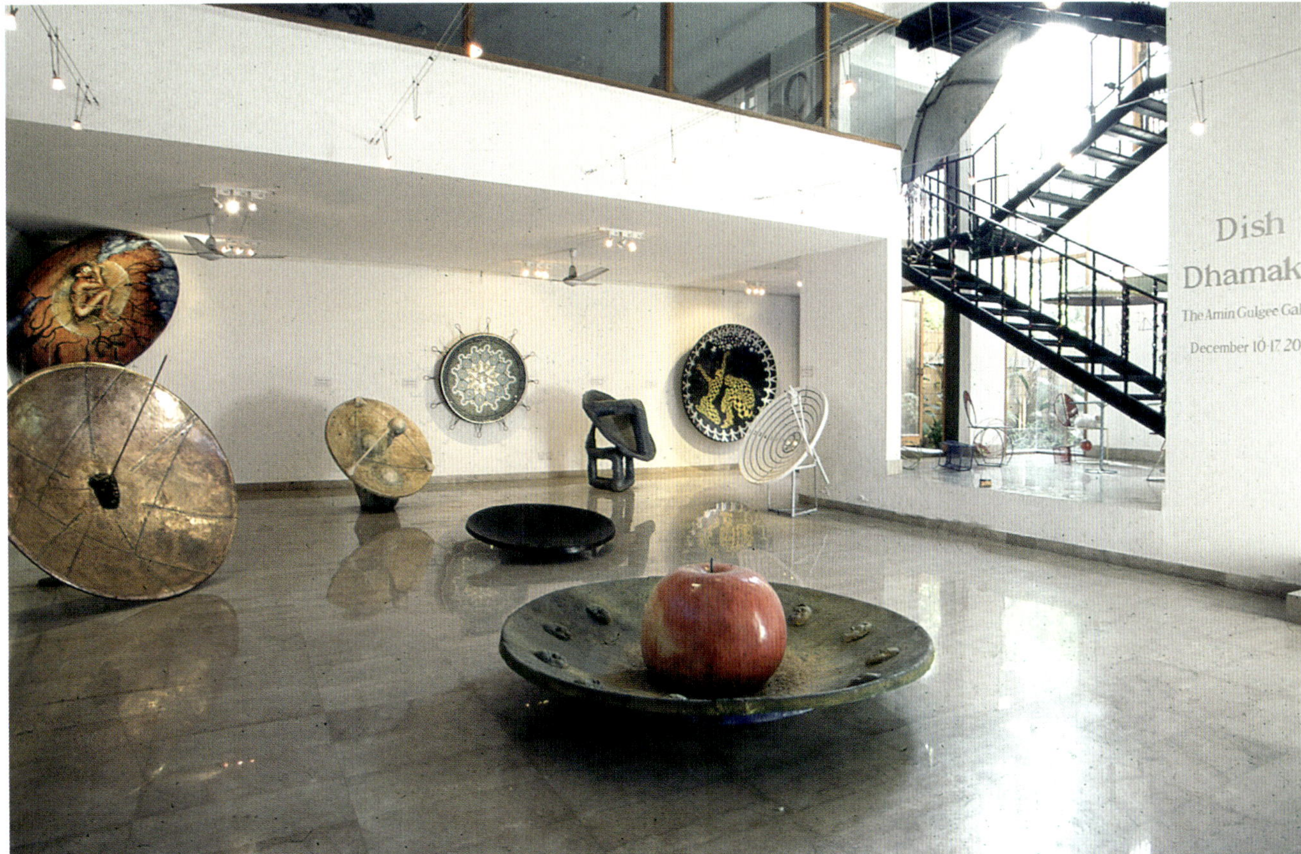

Photo by Shamyl Khuhro

Gino Marotta: The Color of Light | 2003

Travelling exhibition under the patronage of the Italian Ministry of Foreign Affairs

The Amin Gulgee Gallery, together with the Italian Ministry of Foreign Affairs, presented *Gino Marotta: The Color of Light,* an exhibition of 12 new paintings by the Rome-based multimedia artist Gino Marotta (1935-2012). The show travelled from Seoul to New Delhi to Karachi and then on to Taipei. During his long and storied career, Marotta experimented with many techniques and materials as he explored the avant-garde movements that emerged in Italy in the 1960s, including Pop, New Dada and Arte Povera. Marotta wrote in the handout that accompanied the show: "The works displayed in this exhibition are made with an industrial product that has neither history nor memory and it is just for this reason that I have chosen it as a mute means to show a way of creating art that has its roots in distant times... I am very grateful... to show my paintings in the gallery of the great artist Amin Gulgee, whose intense and suggestive artistic production I highly appreciate."

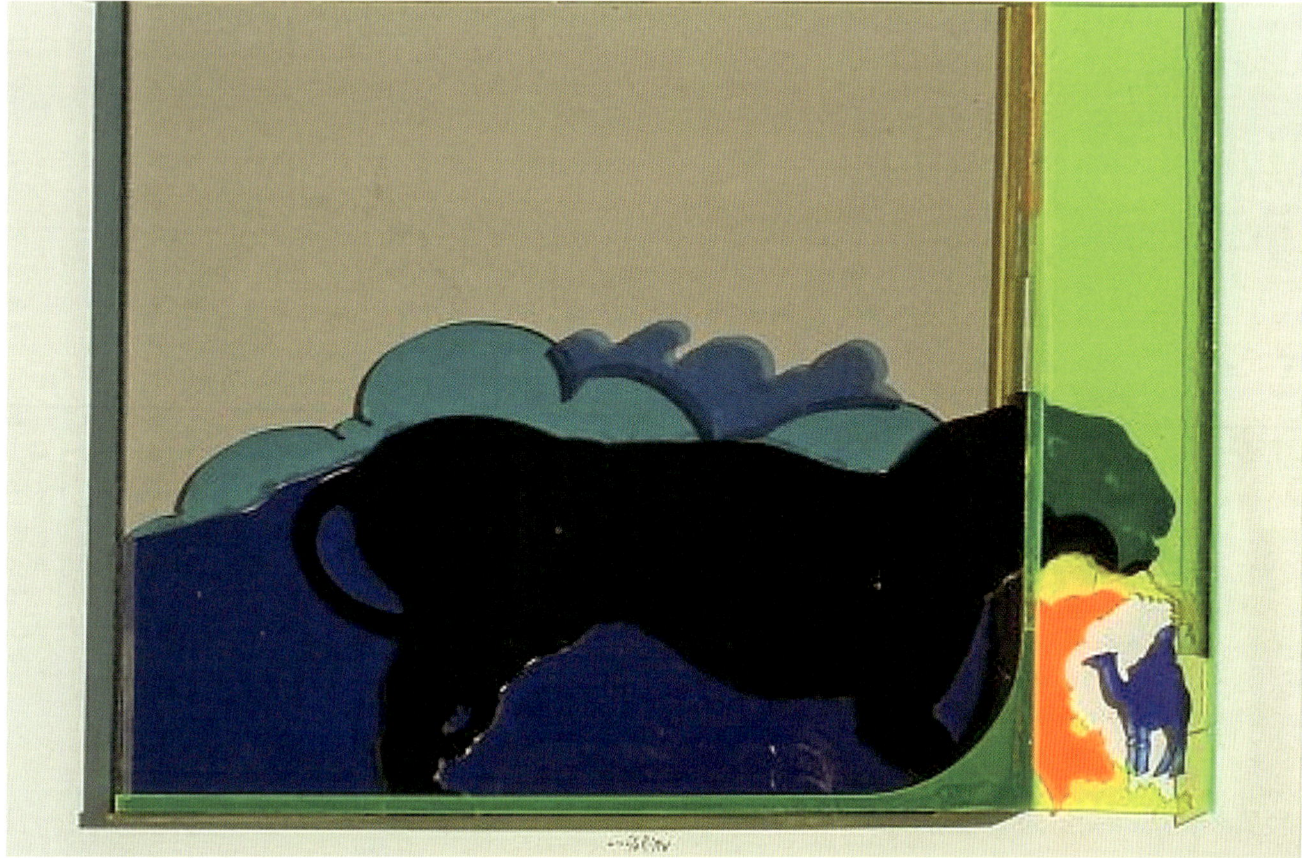

Photo courtesy Gino Marotta

Photo courtesy Saeed Rahman

Artists' Voices | 2006

Curated by Amin Gulgee and Sheherbano Hussain

Artists' Voices were a pair of exhibitions co-curated by Amin Gulgee and artist/art critic Sheherbano Husain. The two curators asked over 30 artists from across Pakistan to create one work inspired by Islamic calligraphy, either religious or secular, and another by the human body. The back-to-back exhibitions were accompanied by the publication of two books bearing the exhibitions' titles, *Artists' Voices: Calligraphy* and *Artists' Voices: Body* (Oxford University Press, 2006), which included texts by the artists as well as scholarly essays creating a dialogue about these two topics. The premise of each show was charged, their juxtaposition combustible. The human body can be a problematic subject in a conservative Muslim society like Pakistan's. Equally controversial for Pakistan's contemporary artists is calligraphy, which is often associated with the Islamization of Pakistan promoted by General Muhammad Zia-ul-Haq during his strict military rule from 1978 to 1988. Although most of the artists included in the two shows had engaged with the body in their practices, almost none had attempted calligraphy. The curators' proposal was not to ask them to become calligraphers overnight—this is a discipline that takes a lifetime to develop—but simply to engage with a great art historical tradition. As Lala Rukh (1948-2017), the pioneering feminist artist, academic and women's rights activist, wrote in her statement for the book on calligraphy: "Beyond all the hype for and against Islamic calligraphy, the much maligned, much adored art, lies the reality of a highly sophisticated art form."

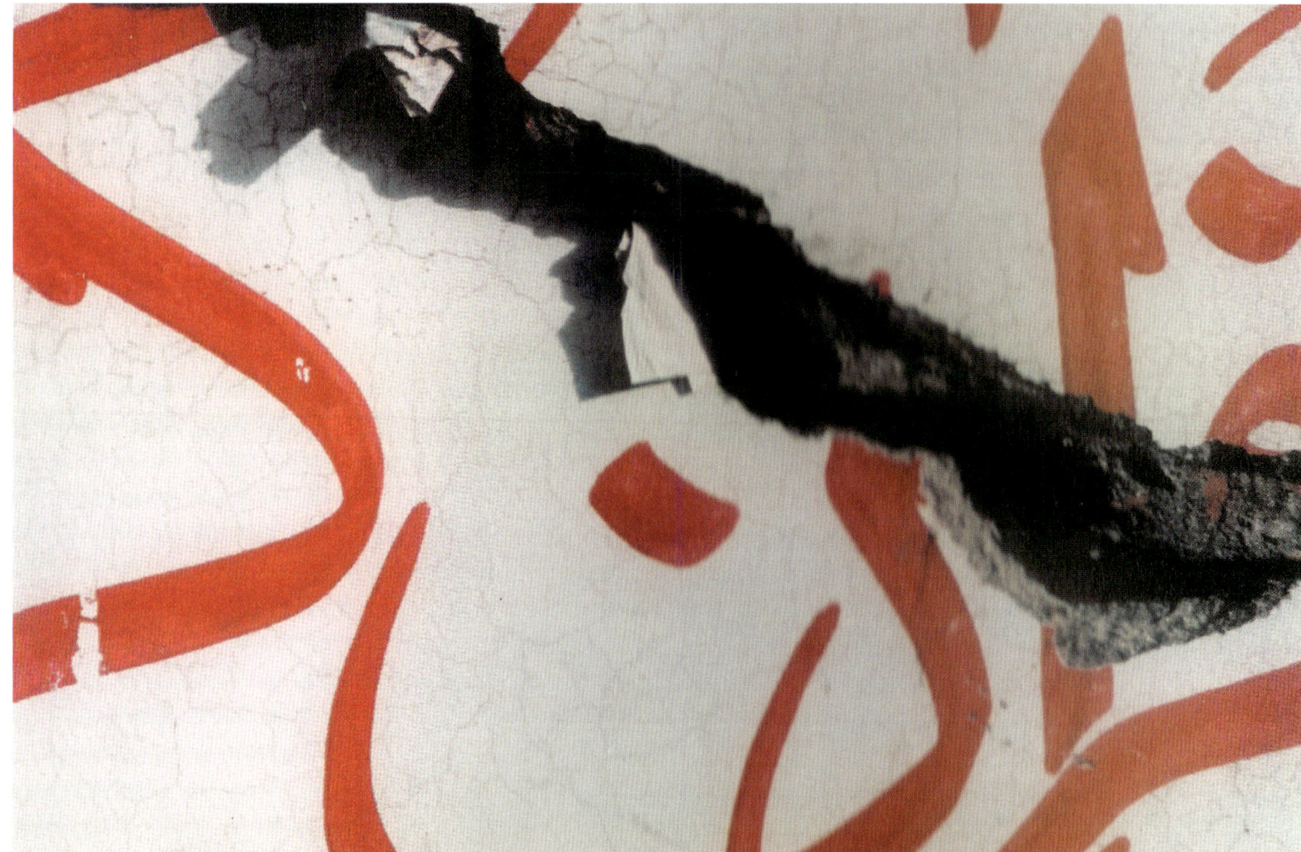

Photo courtesy Aasim Akhtar

18@8: KUL-KHI | 2006

Curated by Lim Wei-Ling

18@8: KUL-KHI was the first significant show of contemporary Malaysian art to travel outside that country's borders, according to its curator, Lim Wei-Ling. (Wei-Ling would go on to curate Malaysia's inaugural national pavilion at the 58th Venice Biennale.) She first met Amin during a trip to Karachi in 2003. A year later, Amin had his first solo show at Wei-Ling Gallery in Kuala Lumpur. In 2005, she opened a new space in a heritage shophouse at 8 Jalan Scott in the city's Brickfields neighborhood, also known as Little India, with an exhibition of 18 artists from Malaysia and beyond, including Amin. She called the show *18@8*. Amin invited her to present the second iteration of *18@8* at the Amin Gulgee Gallery the following year. For this show, Wei-Ling selected works by 18 Malaysian artists born between 1950 and 1980 whom she felt best represented the direction in which contemporary Malaysian art was heading. *18@8: KUL-KHI* included painting, drawing, sculpture, woodcut and video. The work addressed, among other concerns, questions of identity in a multiethnic country like Malaysia; racial profiling in a post-9/11 world; and the looming environmental crisis.

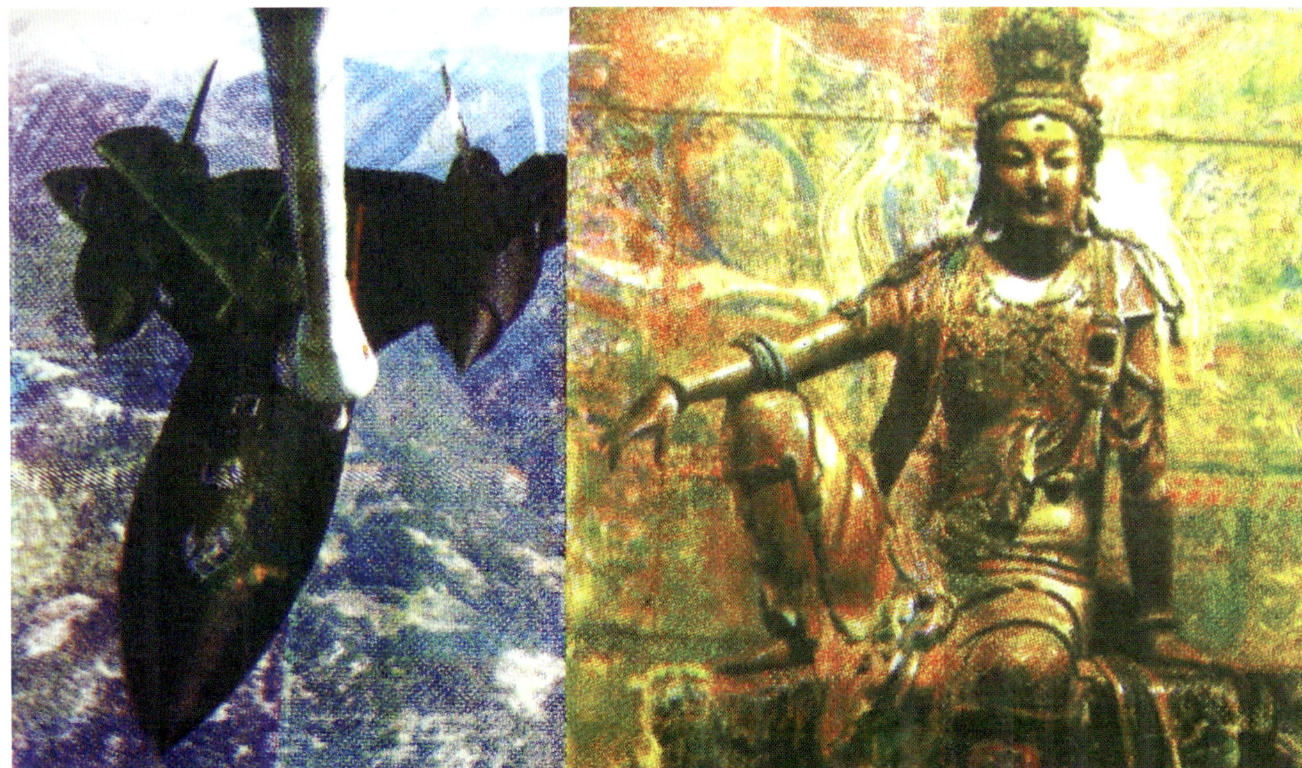

Photo courtesy Ivan Lam

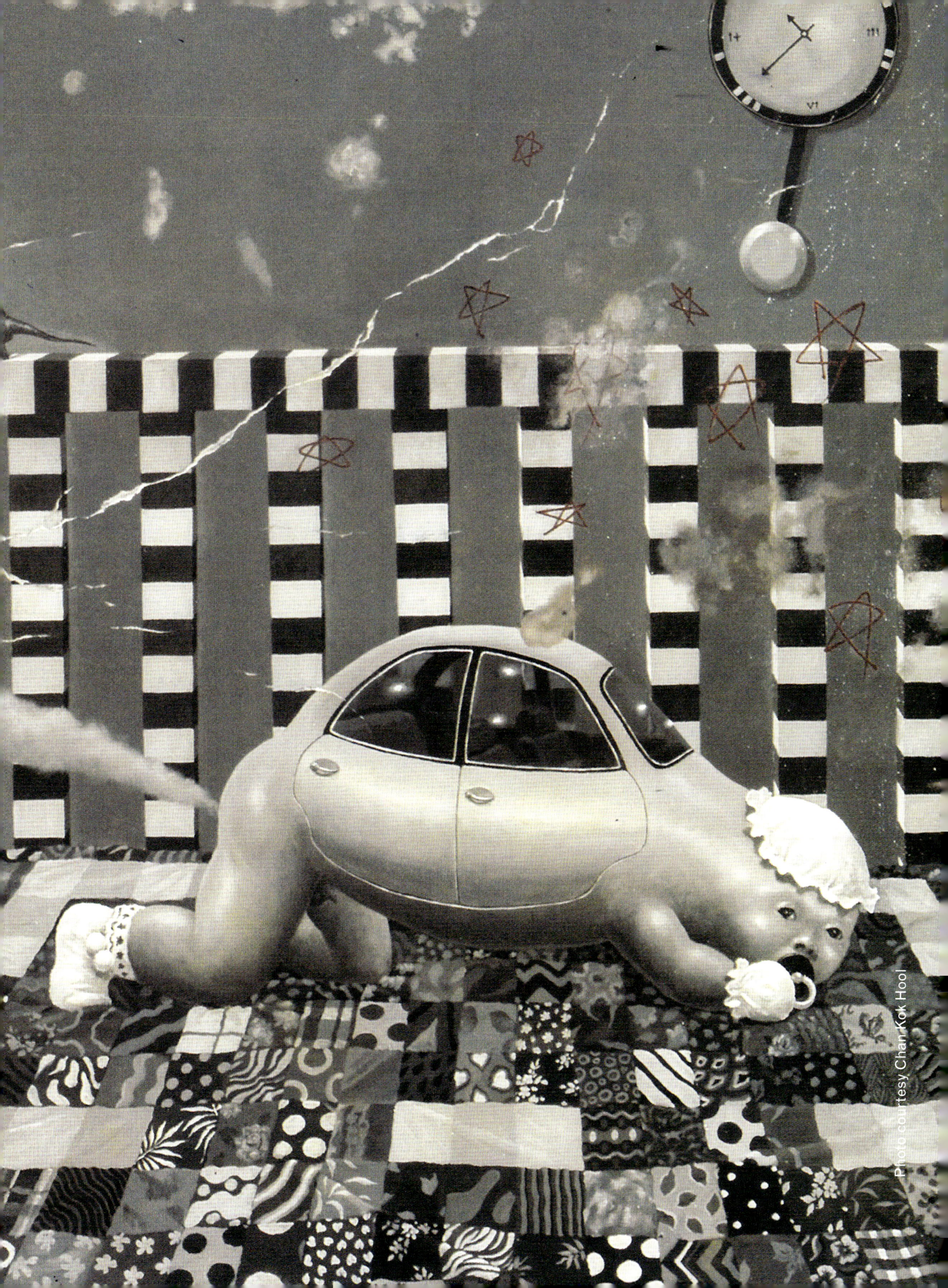

Photo courtesy Chan Kok Hool

Imag[IN]ing Cities | 2011

Curated by Kadiatou Diallo, Dominique Malaquais and Amin Gulgee

After a hiatus of five years following the murder of his parents and their maid by two fly-by-night domestics in 2007, Amin reopened his gallery with *Imag[IN]ing Cities*. He co-curated the exhibition with Kadiatou Diallo and Dominique Malaquais, co-founders of SPARCK, a Pan-African initiative of experimental multi-disciplinary residencies, workshops, symposia, exhibitions, publications and performances. An encounter between new media artists from Africa and South Asia, this was an exhibition of video, photography and sound in which over 50 African and South Asian artists from some 20 countries entered into a South-South dialogue about our increasingly urbanized world. Videos were looped on TVs and projected onto walls. Sound boomed from speakers or whispered through headphones. Photographs hung on the walls or rotated through slideshows. Throughout the gallery, South Asian artworks were interspersed with African pieces. In the main gallery, an early video by Pakistani artist Bani Abidi, in which a young woman randomly recounts the plots of various Bollywood movies, played from a flat-screen; in an adjacent, darkened room, Cameroonian artist Goddy Leye's naked, writhing image was projected onto a bed of sesame seeds on the floor as a disembodied, Hitlerian voice from Fritz Lang's *Metropolis* (1927) intermittently thundered. Dominique wrote in her curatorial essay for the digital catalogue that accompanied the show: "*Imag[IN]ing Cities* does not seek to explicate. It is not a show about individual cities or citiness, an exploration of given urban themes, histories or problematics. It is, rather, a reflection – a pearl-string of questions, queries, interrogations and musings about the contemporary urban condition."

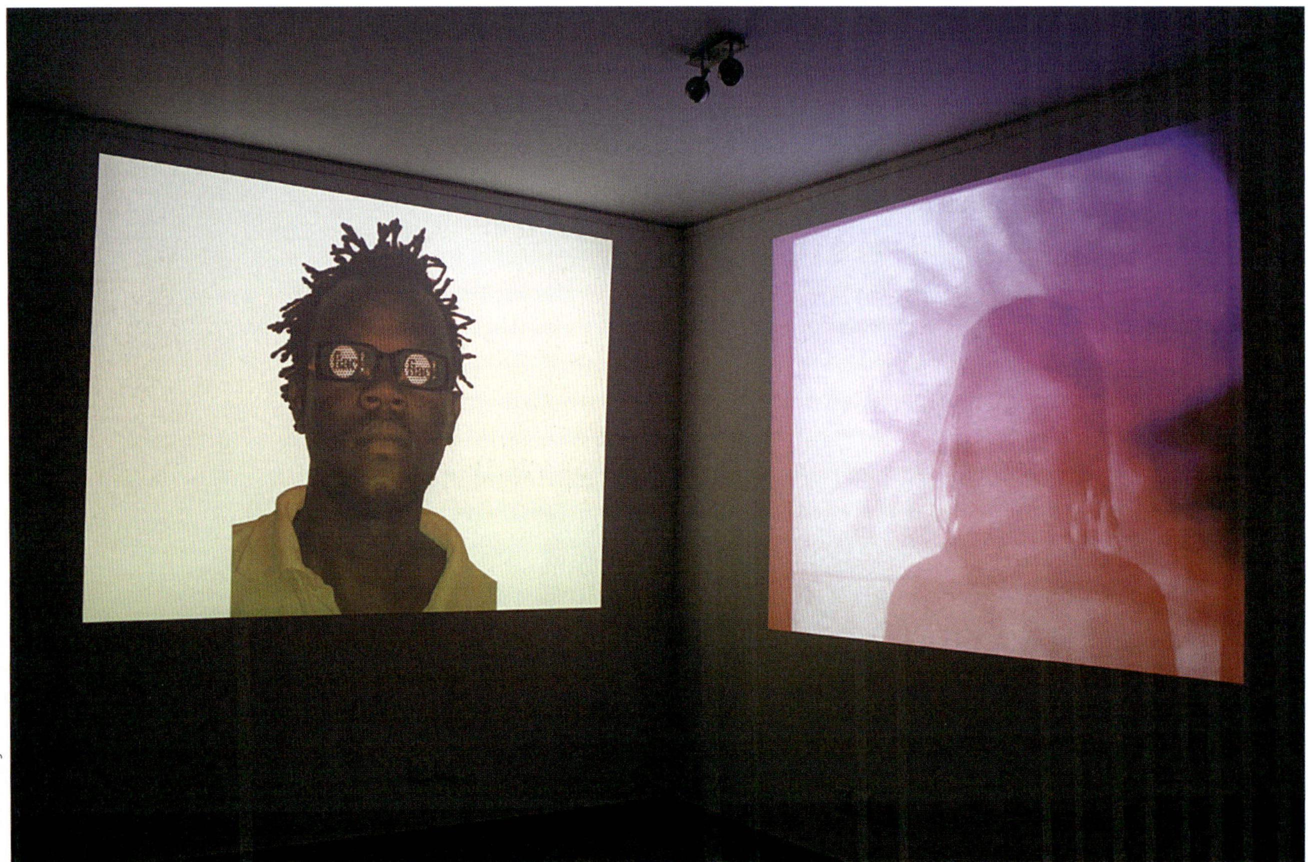

Photos by JY Photo

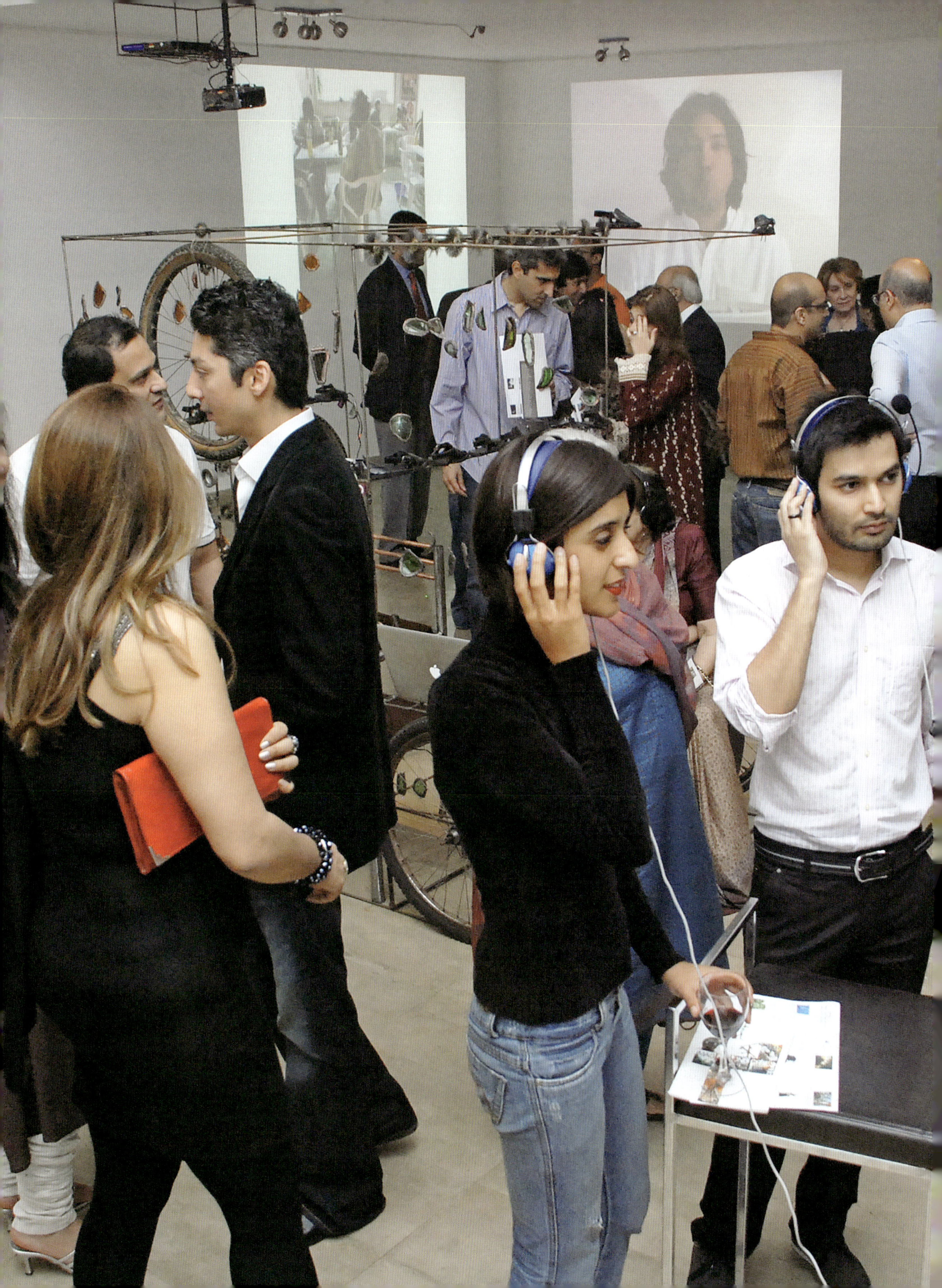

Riwhyti: One Night Stand | 2014

Curated by Amin Gulgee

Riwhyti: One Night Stand was the first exhibition of group performance in Pakistan. (The Urdu word in the title means tradition; its juxtaposition with the English phrase was suggestive.) Curator Amin invited 26 visual artists, musicians, filmmakers, actors, and architects to simultaneously perform 19 works over a period of two hours. The public was invited to walk throughout the gallery and its courtyards and watch the live performances in no particular order. In Syed Ammad Tahir's *Mirror, Mirror on the Wall*, the artist enacted a piece that allowed the public to peer into the privacy of his bedroom. Audience members took turns sitting on benches to watch him dance before a mirror as he adorned himself with makeup, a wig, jewelry and stilettos. Danish Raza's *Sacrifice and Surrogates* was a sly take on Pakistani democracy, or periodical lack of. Carrying a cardboard box, he led a goat, a Pakistani flag tied around its neck, through the bustling gallery handing onlookers a slip of paper that asked: "Should we sacrifice the goat or not?" The audience was asked to tick a box and then cast their "vote." Filmmaker Madiha Aijaz (1981-2019) and actor Nimra Bucha performed the interactive, narrative piece *Swimming Pool*. Madiha, wearing a floppy hat and sunglasses, sat behind Nimra, who, sporting a swimming cap and goggles, lounged on a beach chair, gesturing to audience members to sit down in the empty chaise longue next to hers and put on a pair of headphones. Madiha then switched on a story she wrote and narrated about a swimming instructor who marries into a religious family who insist she abandon her passion for swimming. As the story was told, Nimra slowly covered herself in an *abaya*. The crowd, which numbered in the hundreds by the end of the evening, was at once perturbed, amused, baffled and intrigued.

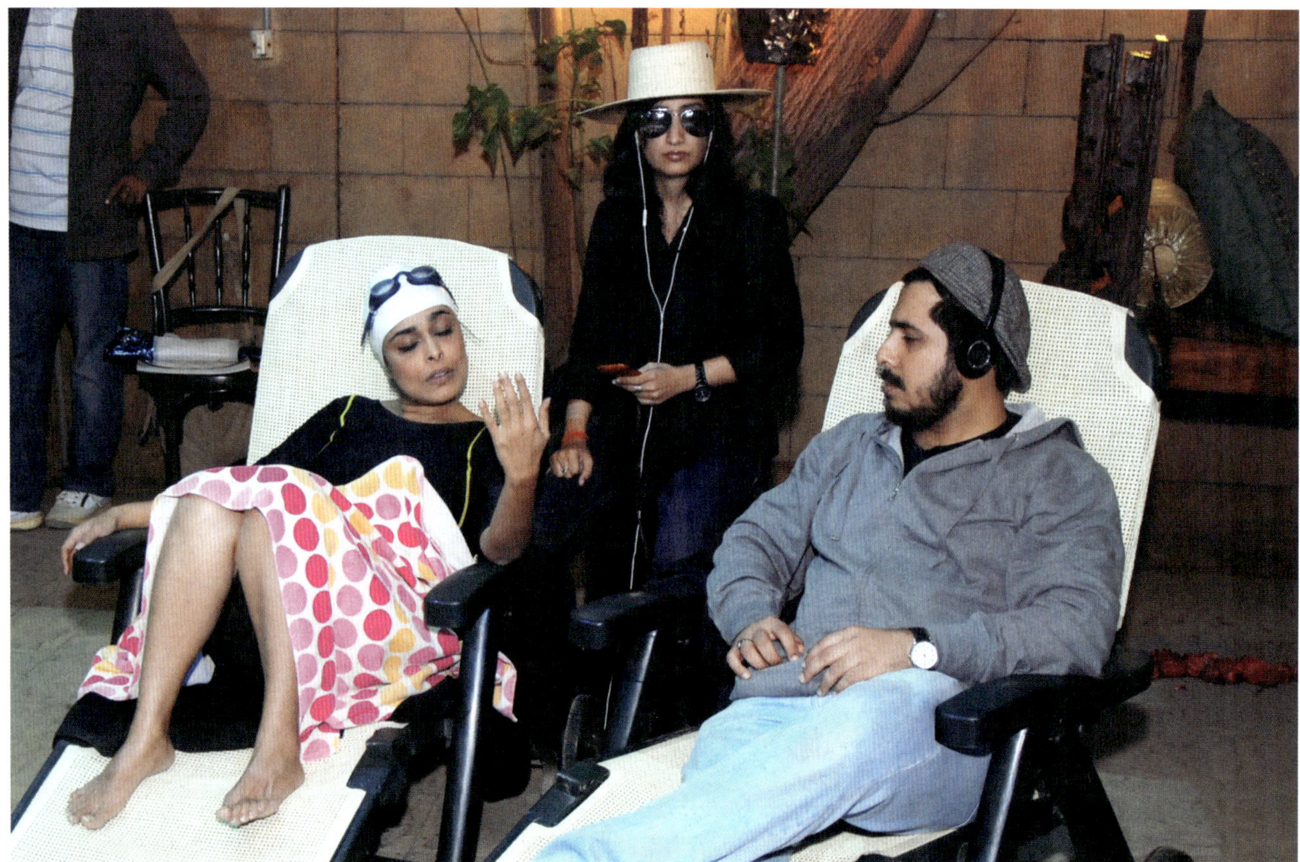

Photo by JY Photo

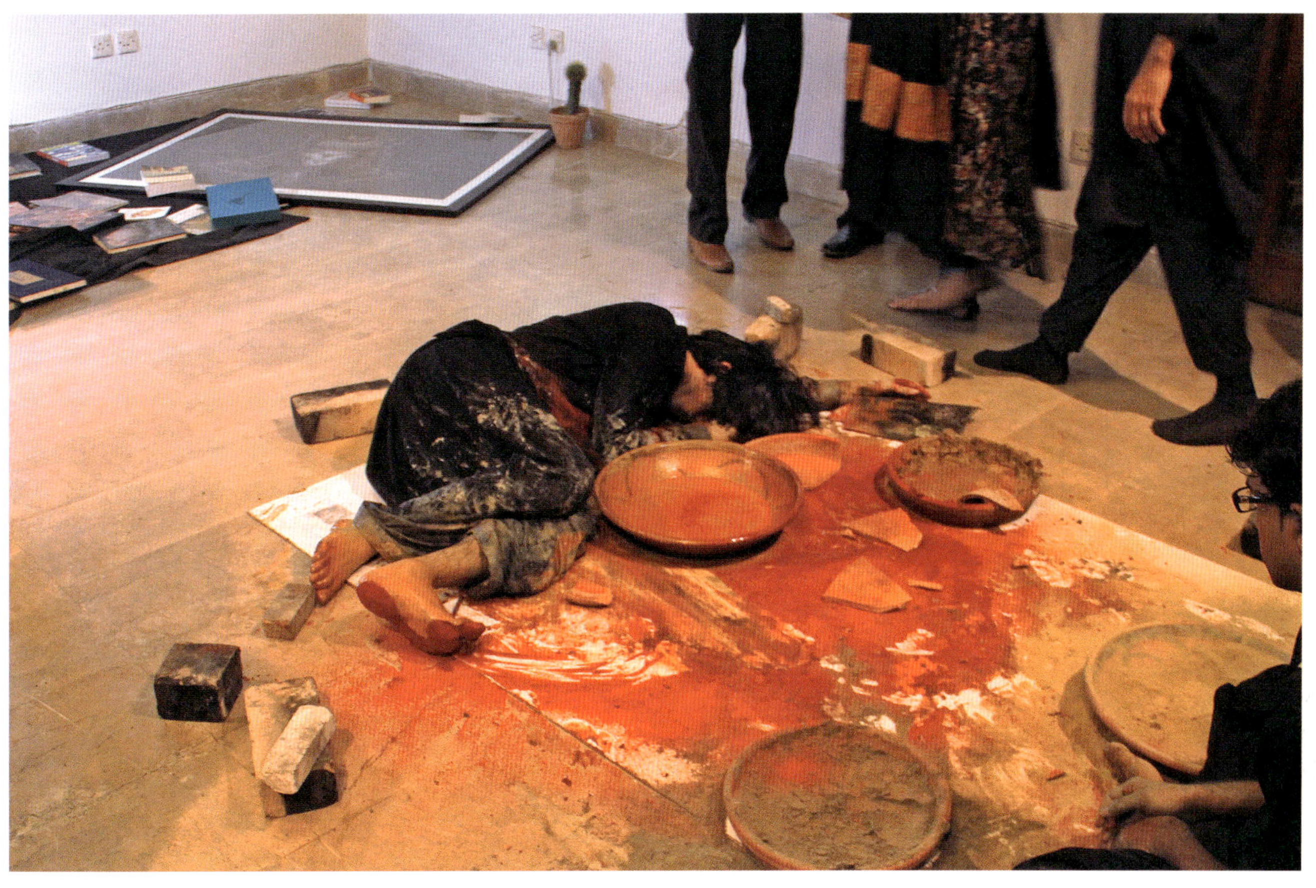

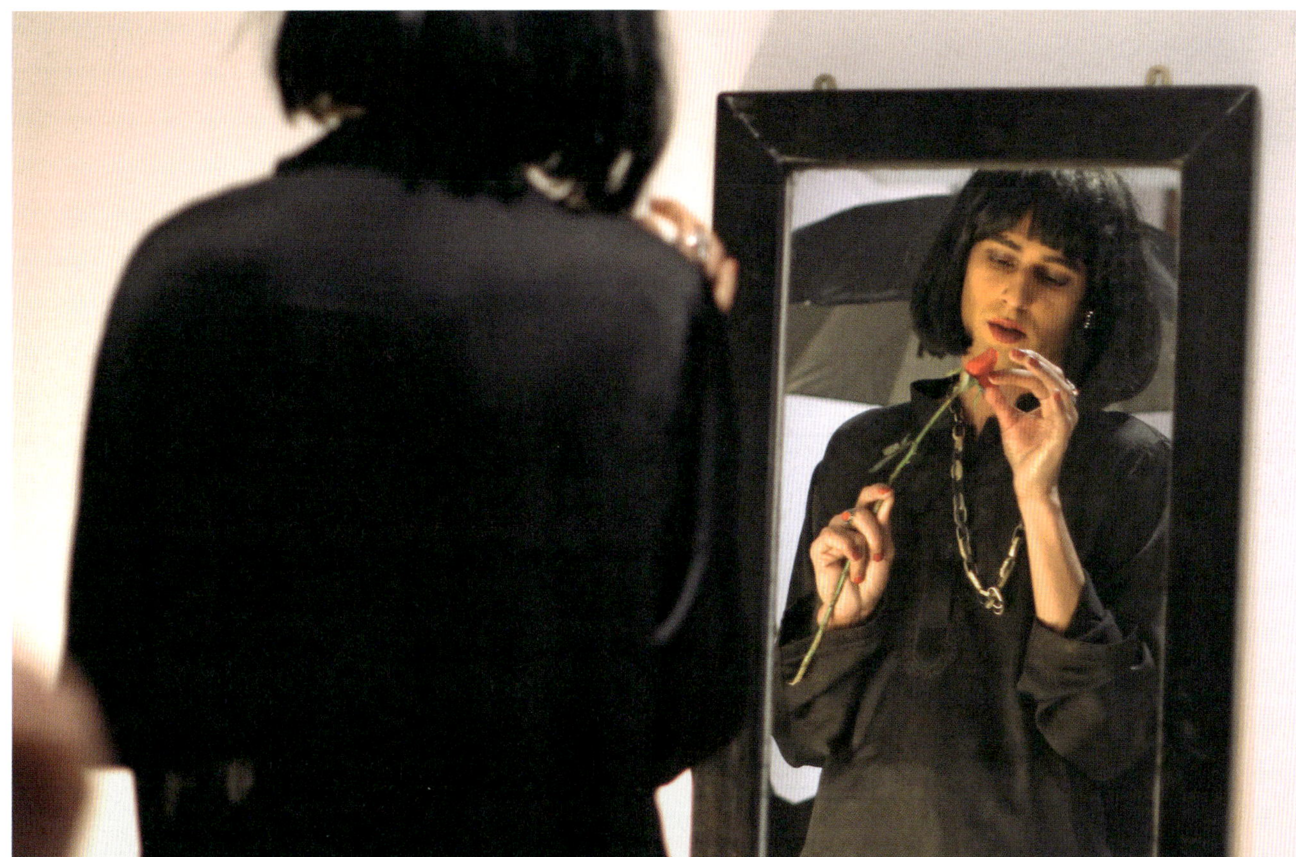

Photos by Jamal Ashiqain

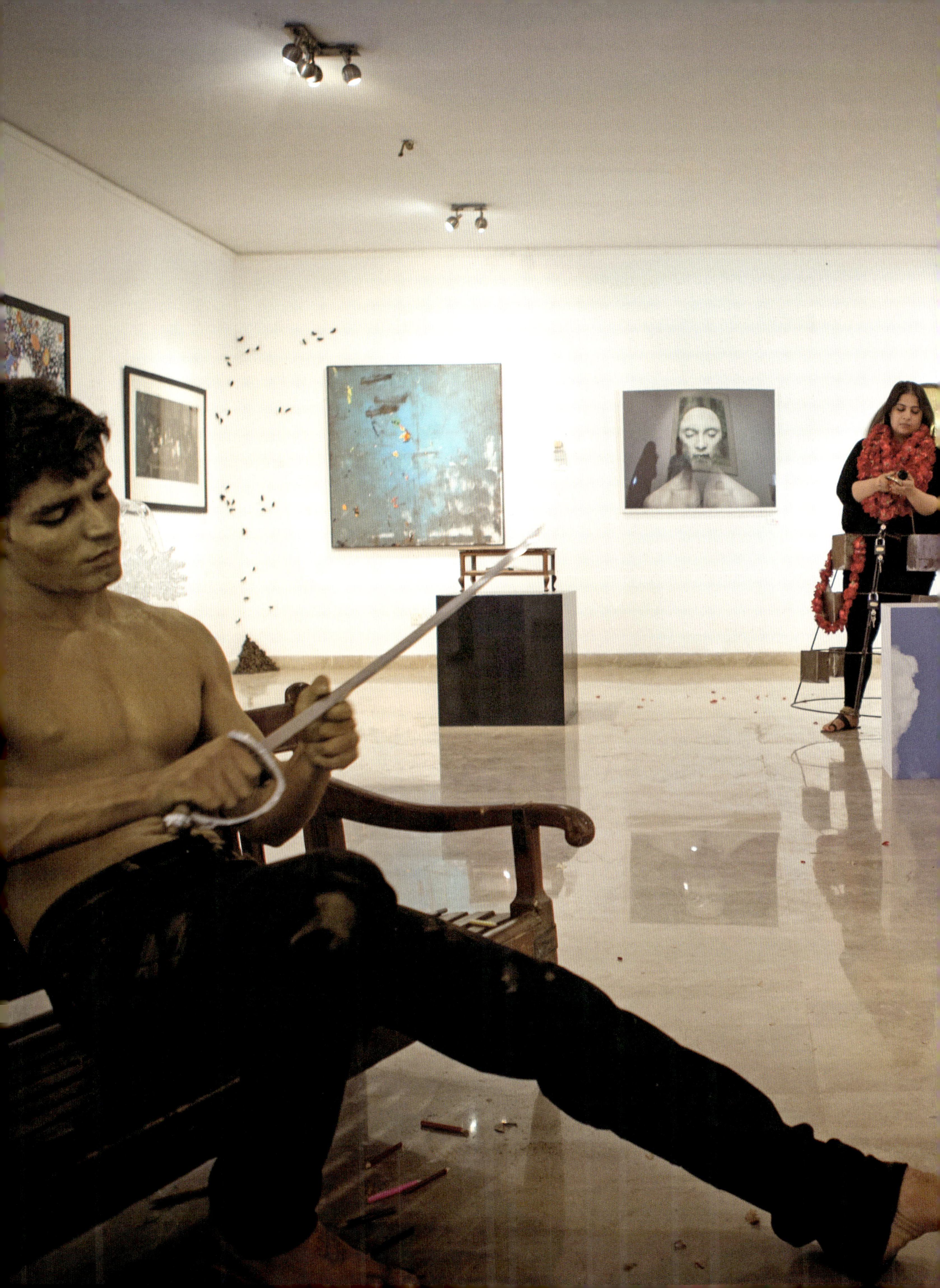

FRESH! | 2014

Curated by Raania Azam Khan Durrani, Saba Iqbal and Amin Gulgee

FRESH! was an exhibition of Pakistani artists age 30 and under that was curated by Amin with Raania Azam Khan Durrani and Saba Iqbal. Wishing to present a survey of an emerging, post-9/11 generation, the three curators reached out to art professionals and educators across Pakistan to help broadcast their open call. Hundreds of submissions poured in. After careful consideration, the curators chose 64 artists from all over the country to be part of the show, which included painting, drawing, sculpture and photography, video and performance. Strongly represented were the voices of young women. In one room blinked a neon sign by Umber Majeed, a recent graduate of Beaconhouse University in Lahore, which spelt out the Urdu words: *Vo keh rahi he ke uss ko kuch kehana he*—She is saying that she has something to say. In the mezzanine hung a dress made of condoms by Malghalara Kaleem, who grew up in Malakand Division in Khyber Pakhtunkhwa. She called the work *Is It Really Protective?* Many of the works addressed political turmoil, terrorism and war. Iffat Tehseen Amjad, who is from Gujranwala, submitted a painting in which the grieving and terrified faces of women appear at the center of a red-and-white bullseye composed of the frontpages of newspapers. Also included was a digital print by Adnan Mairaj Malik, a graduate of Karachi University. It superimposed an image of the Ziarat Residency in Quetta, the final home of Pakistan's founder Muhammad Ali Jinnah, upon a hundred rupee note. The work referenced the 2013 attack by the Balochistan Liberation Army, who torched the historical building. The exhibition was accompanied by a 155-page color catalogue that included essays as well as statements by each of the artists. It was designed free of cost by PeaceNiche, the not-for-profit NGO headed by the human rights activist and social worker Sabine Mahmud. On April 24, 2015, Sabine was shot dead on her way home after hosting a debate on the Balochistan conflict at T2F, a community space she founded in Karachi.

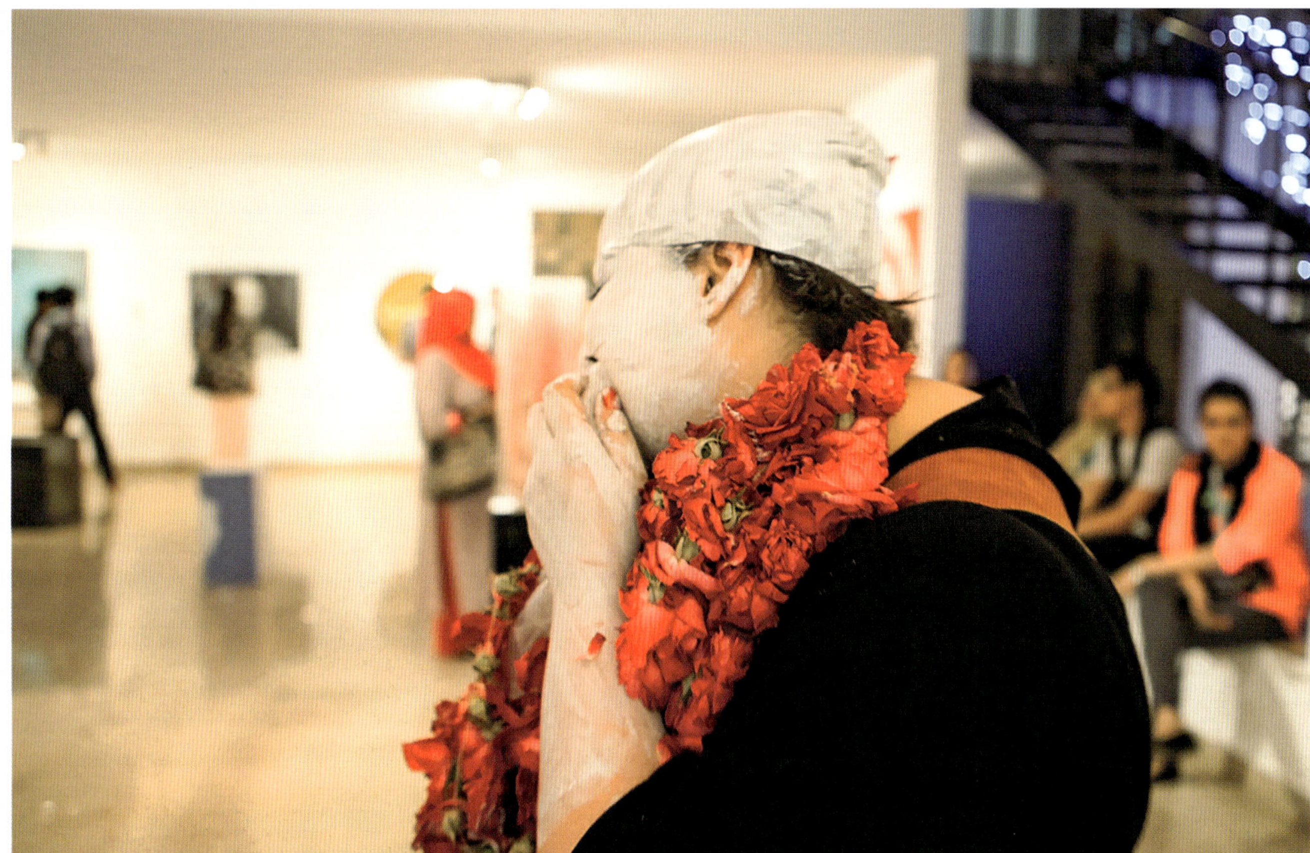

Photos by JY Photo

Dreamscape | 2014

Curated by Zameene Shah and Amin Gulgee

Together with Zarmeene Shah, Amin curated *Dreamscape* in December 2014. Including 48 artists, it was an exhibition of performance unfolding within a series of site-specific installations. As in *Riwhyti: One Night Stand*, the performances were executed together the night of the opening. In her curatorial essay, Zarmeene referenced a quote by Yoko Ono: "A dream you dream alone is only a dream. A dream you dream together is a reality." Sunil Shanker and Kashif Hussain, both actors from the National Academy of Performing Arts, climbed ropes suspended from the ceiling, their mouths shut with tape in an apparently Sisyphean struggle against censorship. Omer Wasim stencilled words in chalk in several places on the gallery floor. As was his intention, these fraught, private declarations were destroyed by the shuffling feet of curious viewers who thronged to the gallery to watch the spectacle. Unwittingly, the crowd had completed the work through this "performative" act. In a response to sectarian killings convulsing the region, Muhammad Ali and Manizhe Ali, black tears painted on their cheeks, sat as likenesses of the Mona Lisa in voluminous black skirts before a wall of 1,300 red roses knitted by Muhammad Ali over a period of a year. In *Things that Happen in Bed # 1*, Shalalae Jamil lay on a mattress on a landing of the gallery as a film she shot as a graduate student in Chicago was projected onto the ceiling above her. Positioned next to her was an A4-size piece of paper that proposed: "You are invited to watch a six-minute minute film with the artist in a bed. Please limit your exchange to a greeting and a good-bye." The work, like the show itself, challenged the relationship between the private and public, the asleep and the awake, the solitary and the collective.

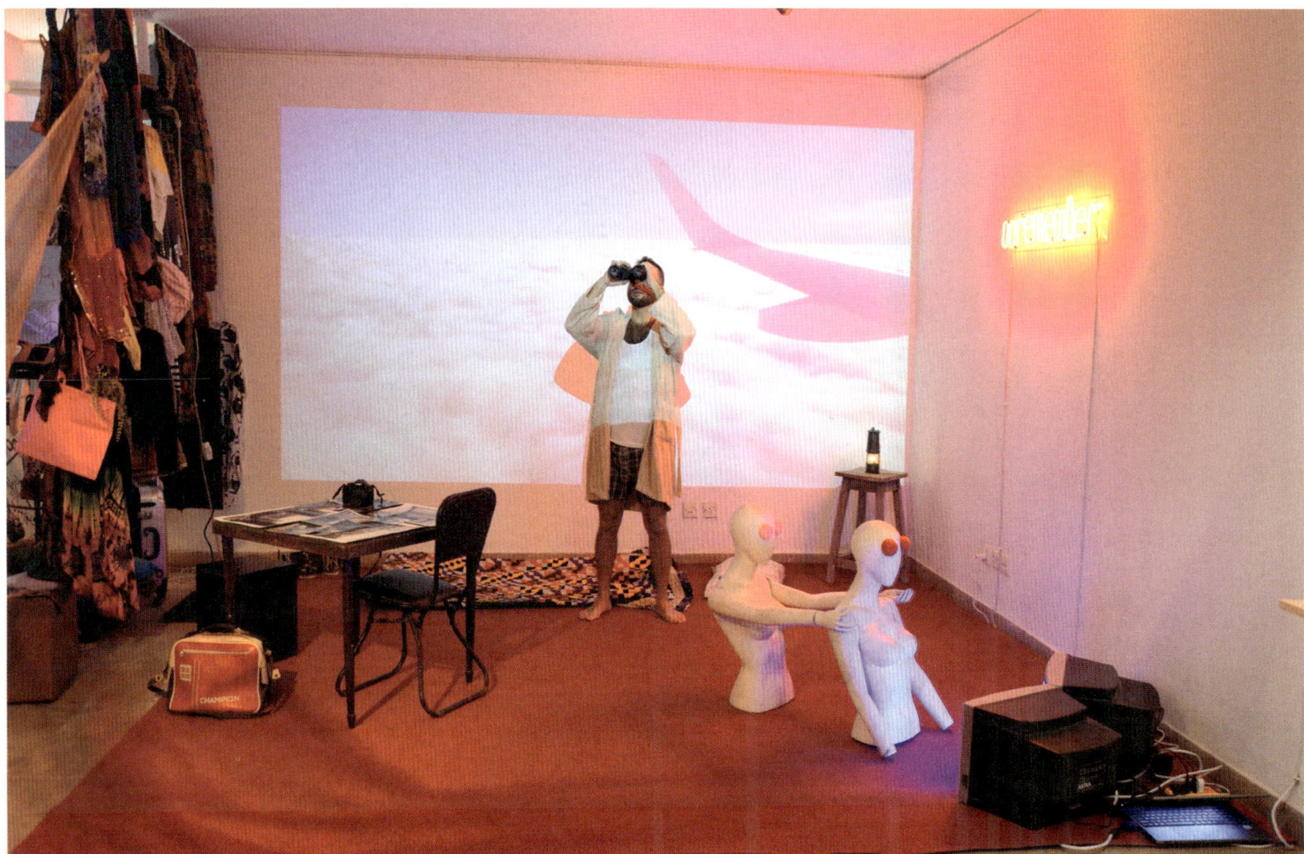

Photos by JY Photo

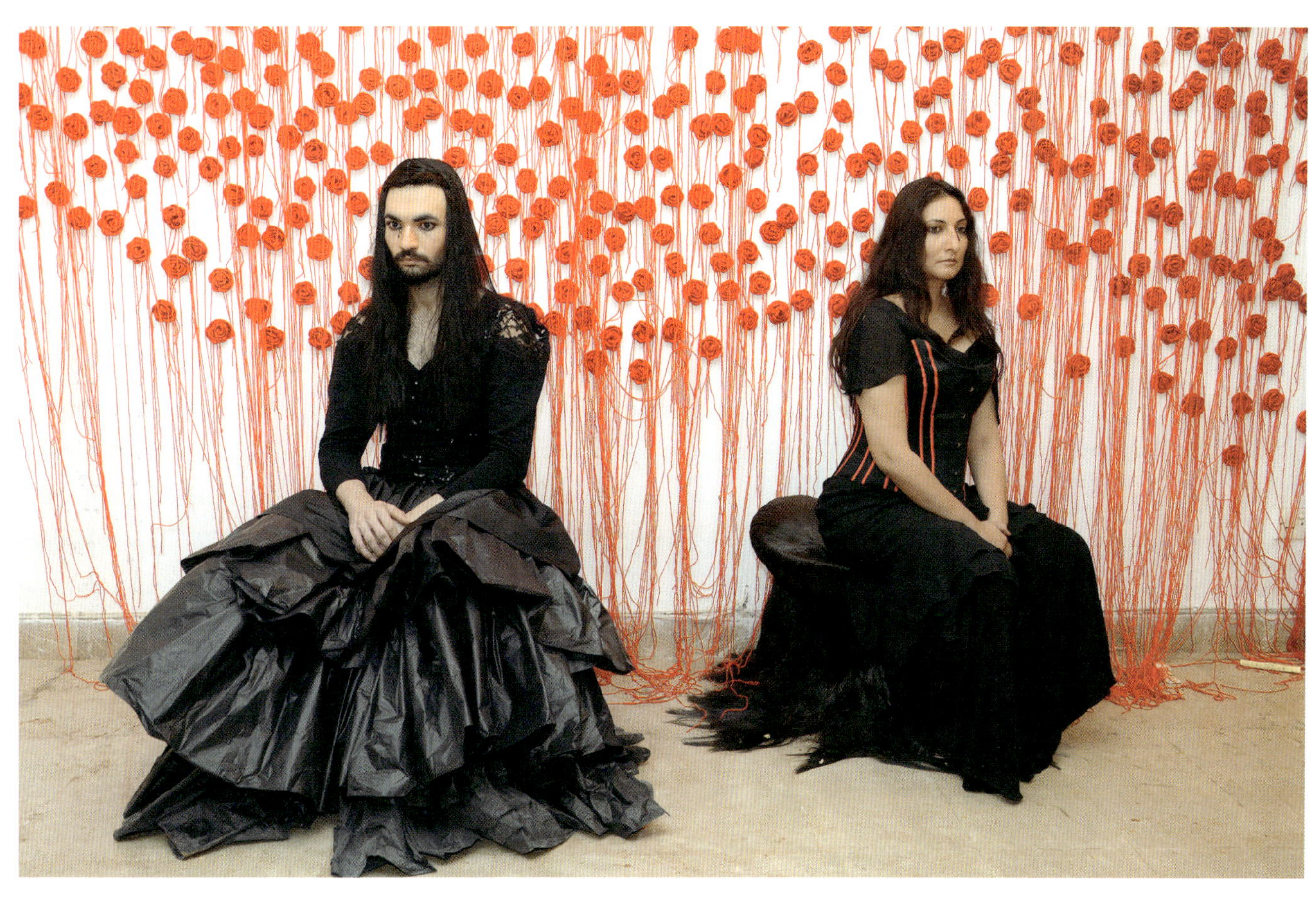

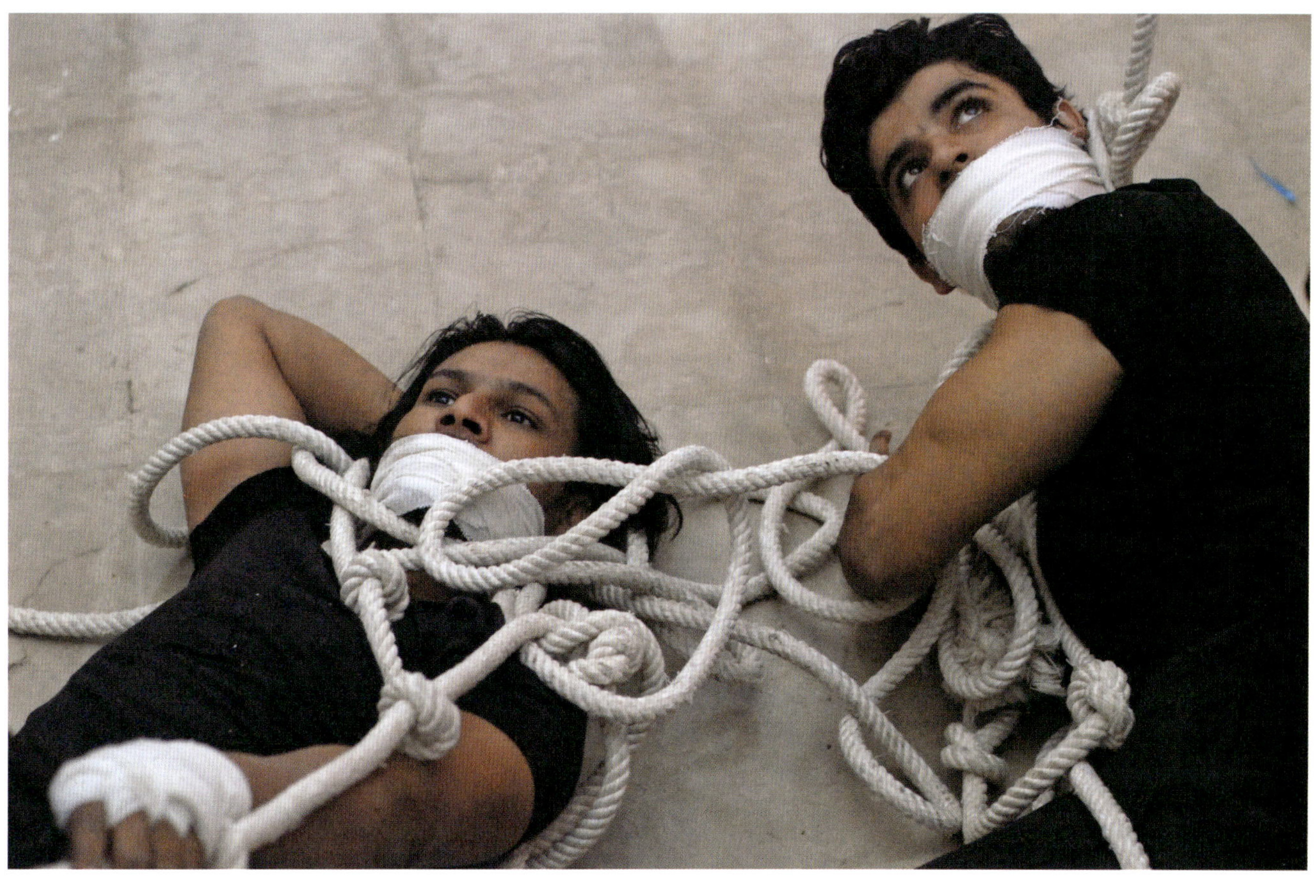

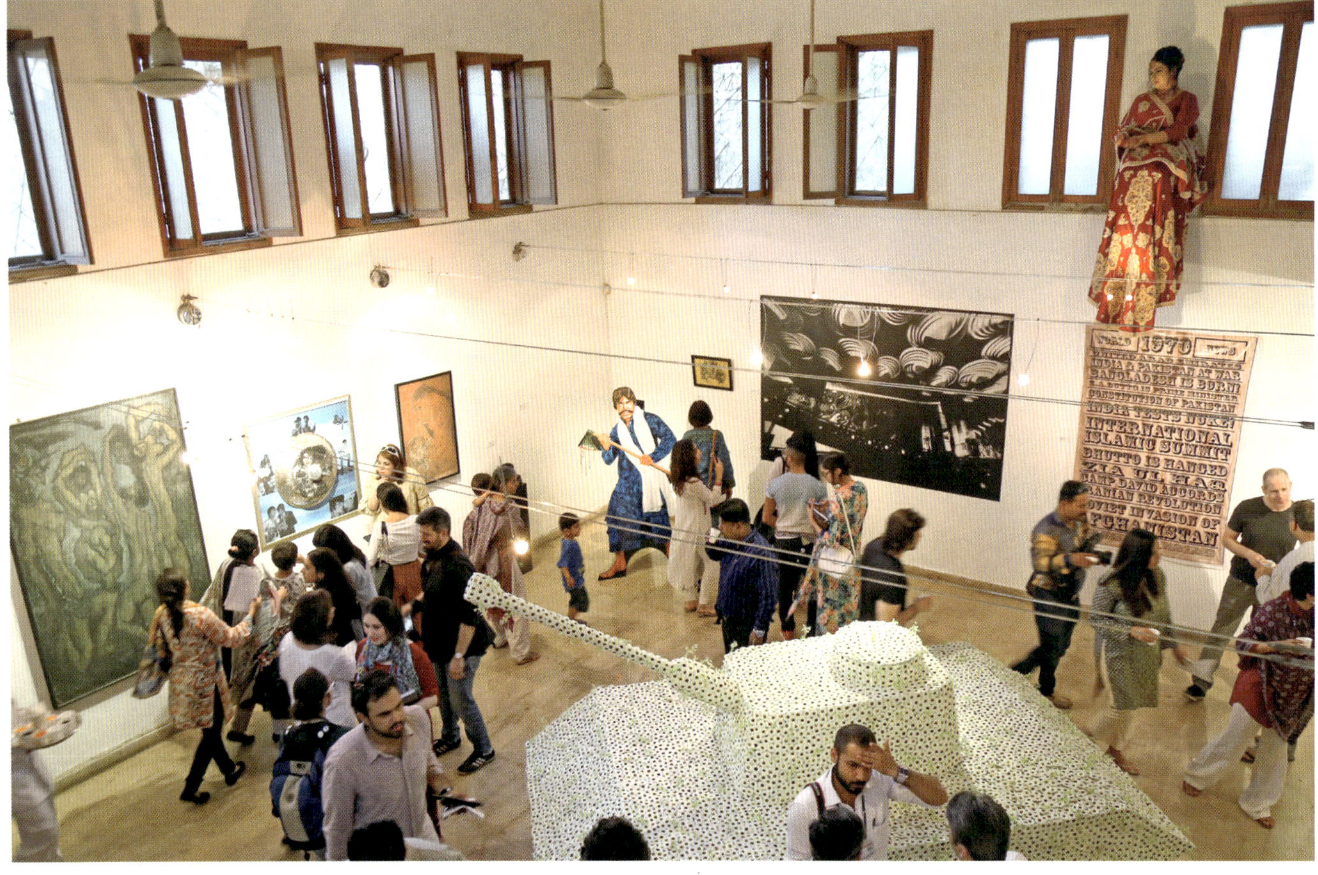

Photo by Jamal Ashiqain

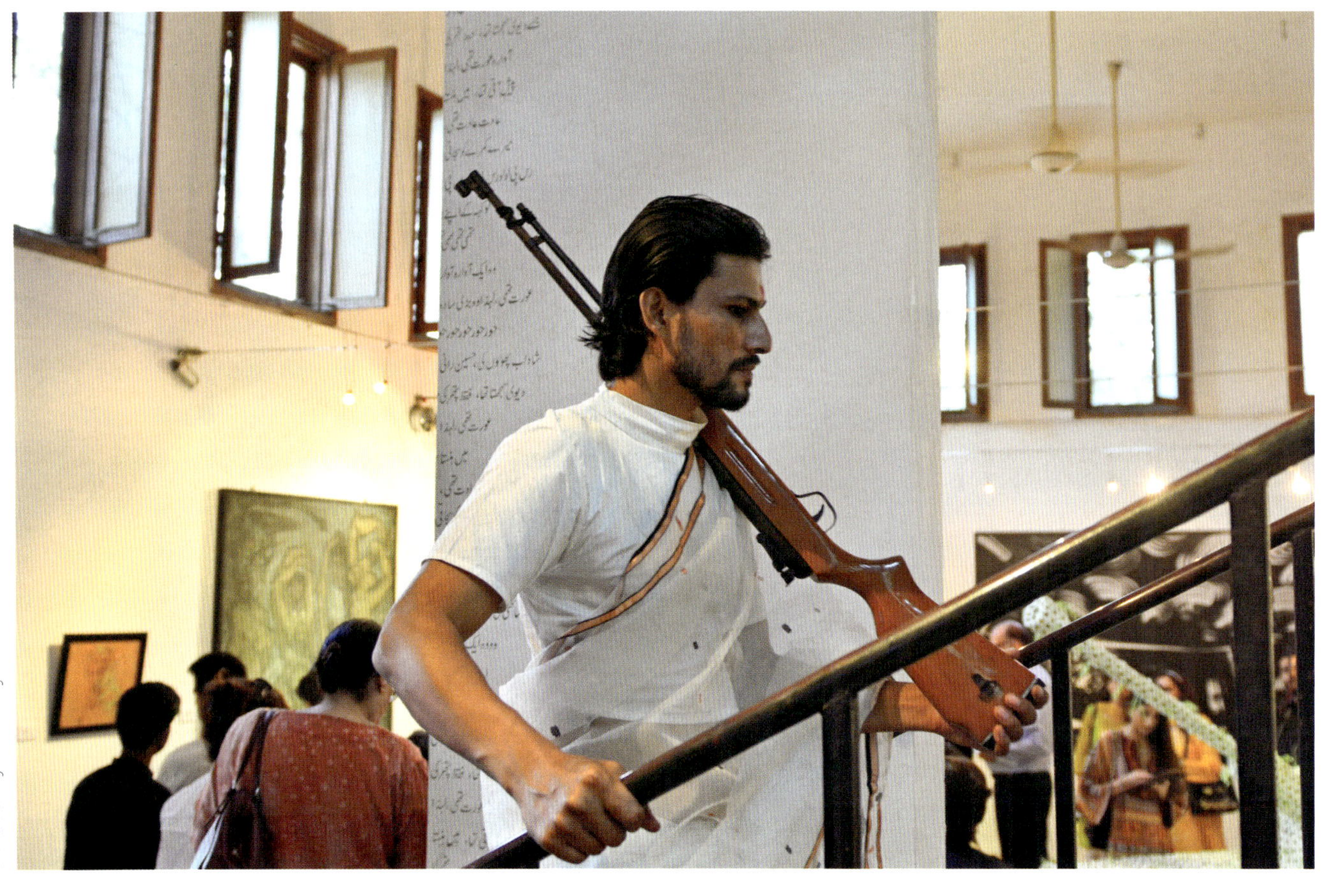

Photo by Humayun Memon

The 70s: Pakistan's Radioactive Decade | 2016

Curated by Niilofur Farrukh and Amin Gulgee

Amin and art historian Niilofur Farrukh had talked for years about organizing an exhibition on the 1970s in Pakistan at the Amin Gulgee Gallery. The tumultuous decade began with the bloody secession of Bangladesh in 1971 and ended with the religiously conservative rule of General Zia-ul-Haq, who overthrew the democratically elected leftist prime minister Zulfikar Ali Bhutto in 1977 and subsequently hanged him. For a brief few years between these tragic events, a fleeting spring of hope unleased an unprecedented outpouring of creative expression in the country. This was a period of great Pakistani television, memorable movies, emerging musical trends, flourishing dance, and revolutionary fashion. In 2015, Amin and Niilofur resolved to go forward with the project and gave it the title *The 70s: Pakistan's Radioactive Decade*, alluding not only to the nuclear ambitions of the country, but also to memories of the 1970s that remain embedded in the national psyche like the afterlife of a radioactive object. Over 50 artists agreed to participate. Some had lived the times; others knew them only through the anecdotes of their parents and grandparents. Including painting, drawing, photography, sculpture, video, installation, sound and performance, this was a cross-generational meditation on the decade. Paintings and drawings by the modernists Gulgee, Sadequain, Ahmed Pervez, Bashir Mirza and Jamil Naqsh, all of whom were productive at the time, were juxtaposed with contemporary interpretations of the period. The exhibition was followed by the book *Pakistan's Radioactive Decade: An Informal Cultural History of the 1970s*, which was edited by the two curators along with John McCarry. Published by Oxford University Press in 2019, it included essays as well as Q&As by over 50 authors that explored the decade's visual arts, architecture, theater, dance, nightlife, television, advertising, fashion, music, film, journalism and literature. By relying heavily on firsthand accounts, the editors hoped to capture the voices, and dreams, of an extraordinary but vanishing generation.

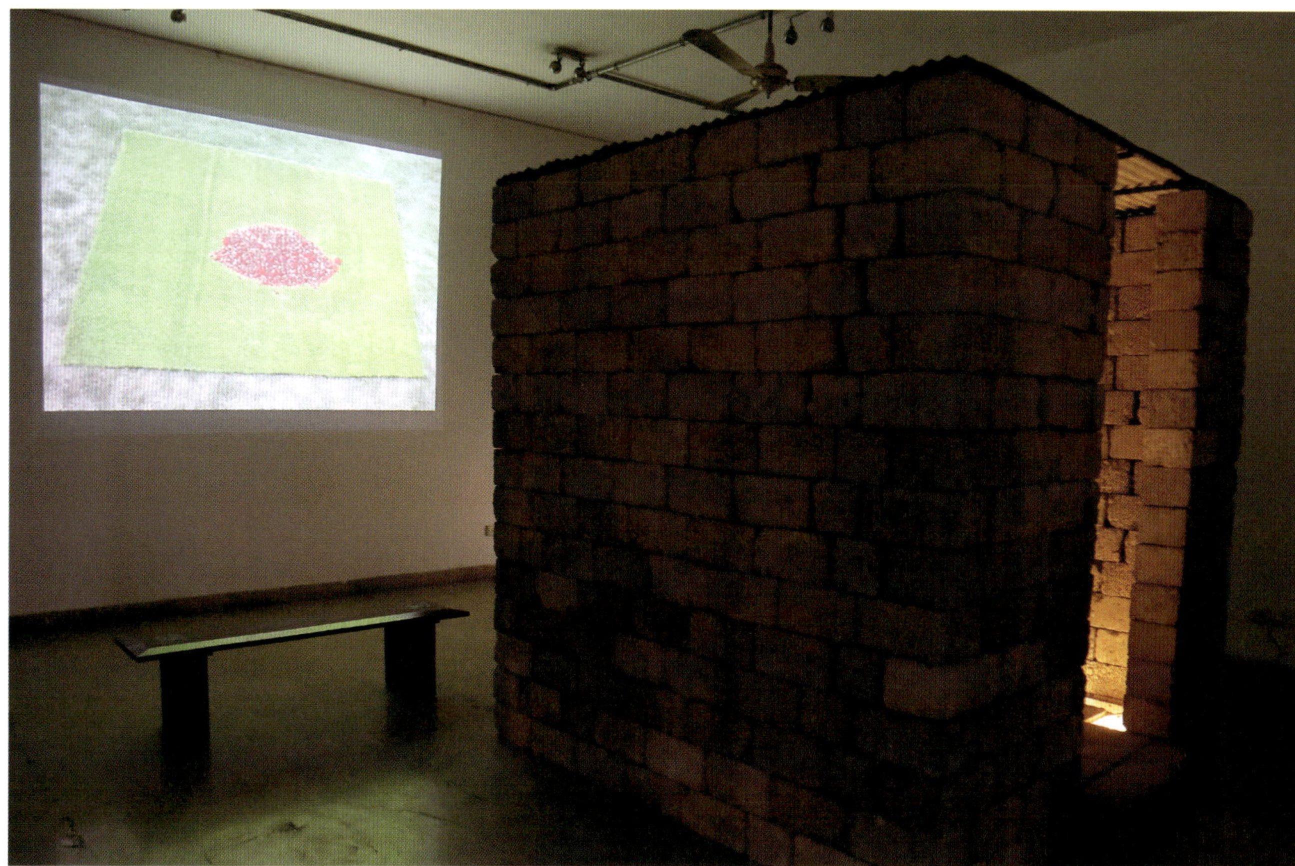

Photo by Jamal Ashiqain

Outsiders | 2018

Curated by Zeerak Ahmed, Zarmeene Shah and Amin Gulgee

When the Goethe-Institut in Karachi asked if the Amin Gulgee Gallery would be interested in hosting *Geniale Dilletanten* (Brilliant Dilettantes), a traveling exhibition that documented urban subculture in Germany in the 1980s, Amin countered with a proposal of his own: since the gallery's primary focus is on contemporary Pakistani art, why not present the German show alongside a Pakistani counterpart? The Pakistani exhibit, co-curated by Zeerak Ahmed, Zarmeene Shah and Amin was not a response to the specific content of *Geniale Dilletanten* but rather to its overarching premise. The early 1980s in West and East Germany saw an explosion in creative activity, sparked by the punk movement, that crossed boundaries and led to innovation in music, visual arts, design, fashion, literature and film. Amin, Zarmeene and Zeerak decided not to concentrate on a single decade but to identify what might be considered sub/counterculture in Pakistan from the 1970s to the present day though 17 works. The curators projected a clip from Rangeela's 1979 Urdu movie *Aurat Raj* (Women's Rule) in which the "hero," played by the leading actress Rani dressed as a man in a military-style unform, made the "heroine," portrayed by the action star Sultan Rahi, dance in drag for her. They hung photographic documentation of public works created between 2007 and 2009 by Asim Butt (1978-2010), including the image of a stop sign painted graffiti-style upon a car that had been set on fire during the riots that engulfed Karachi after the assassination of former prime minister Benazir Bhutto in 2007. On a flat-screen played a 2015 clip posted to the internet by YouTube sensation Qandeel Baloch in which she seductively lies upon a red couch and proposes marriage to cricket legend and future Pakistani prime minister Imran Khan. (In 2016, Qandeel was allegedly murdered by her brother in a so-called honor killing.) Called *Outsiders*, the German and Pakistani shows were installed as one. Viewers were encouraged to make their own connections between the two.

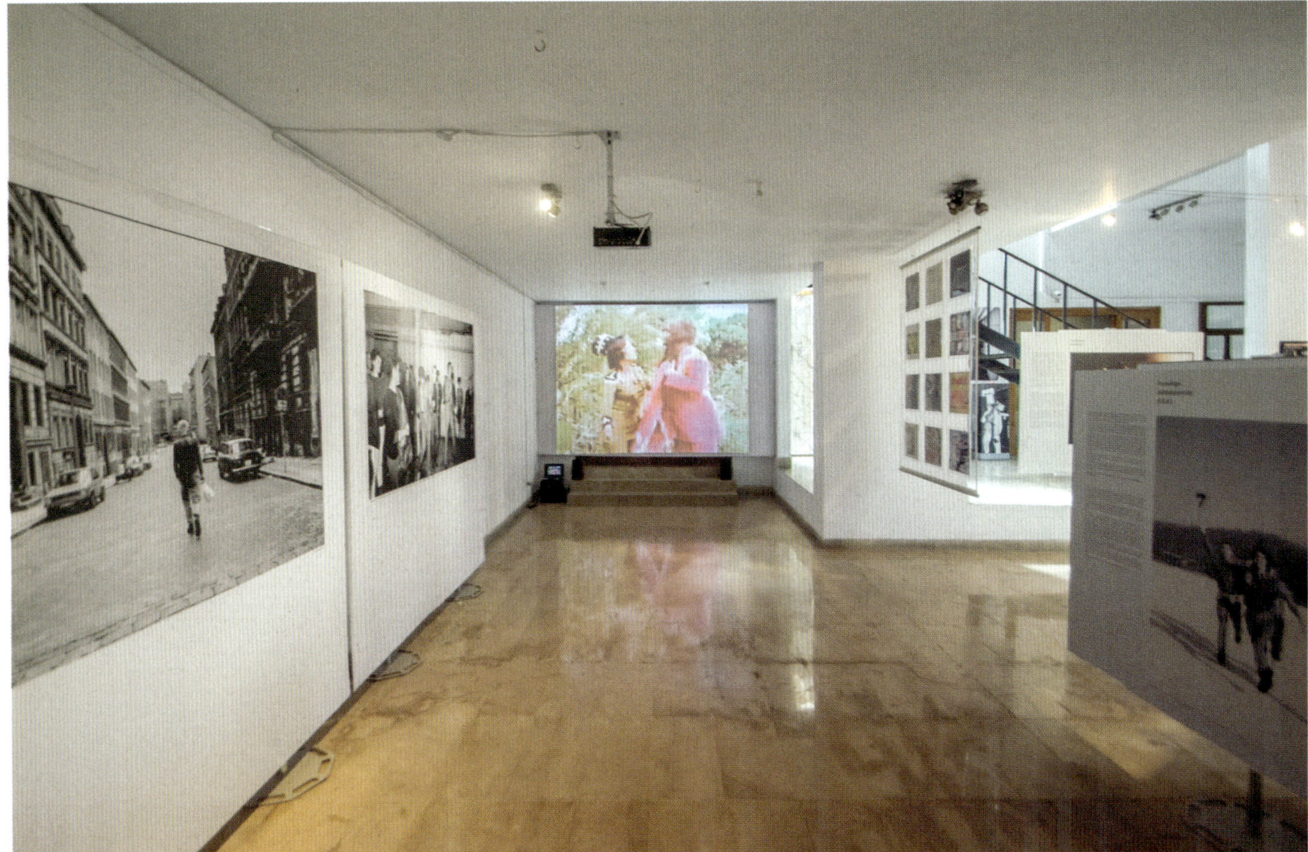

Photos by Humayun Memon

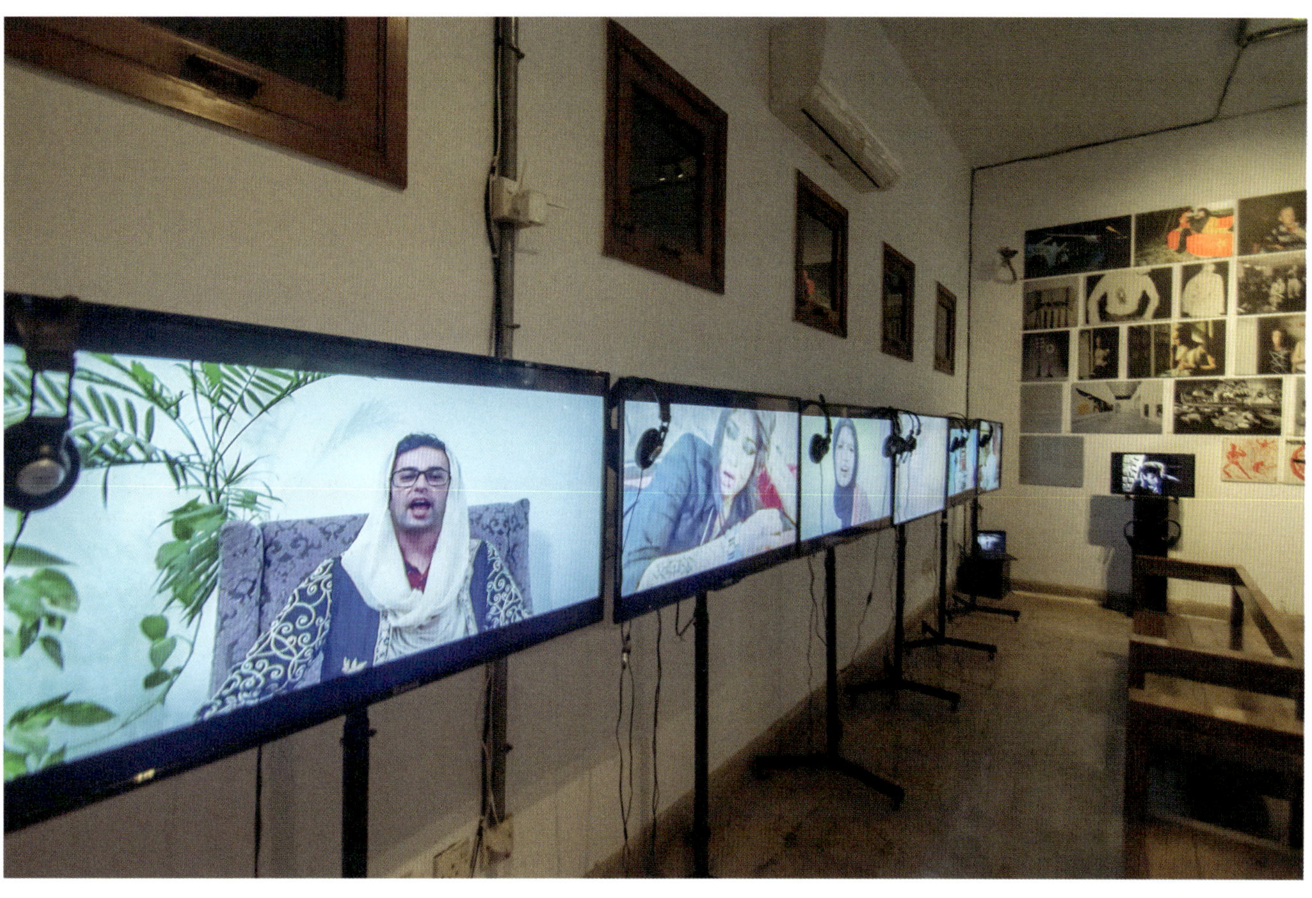

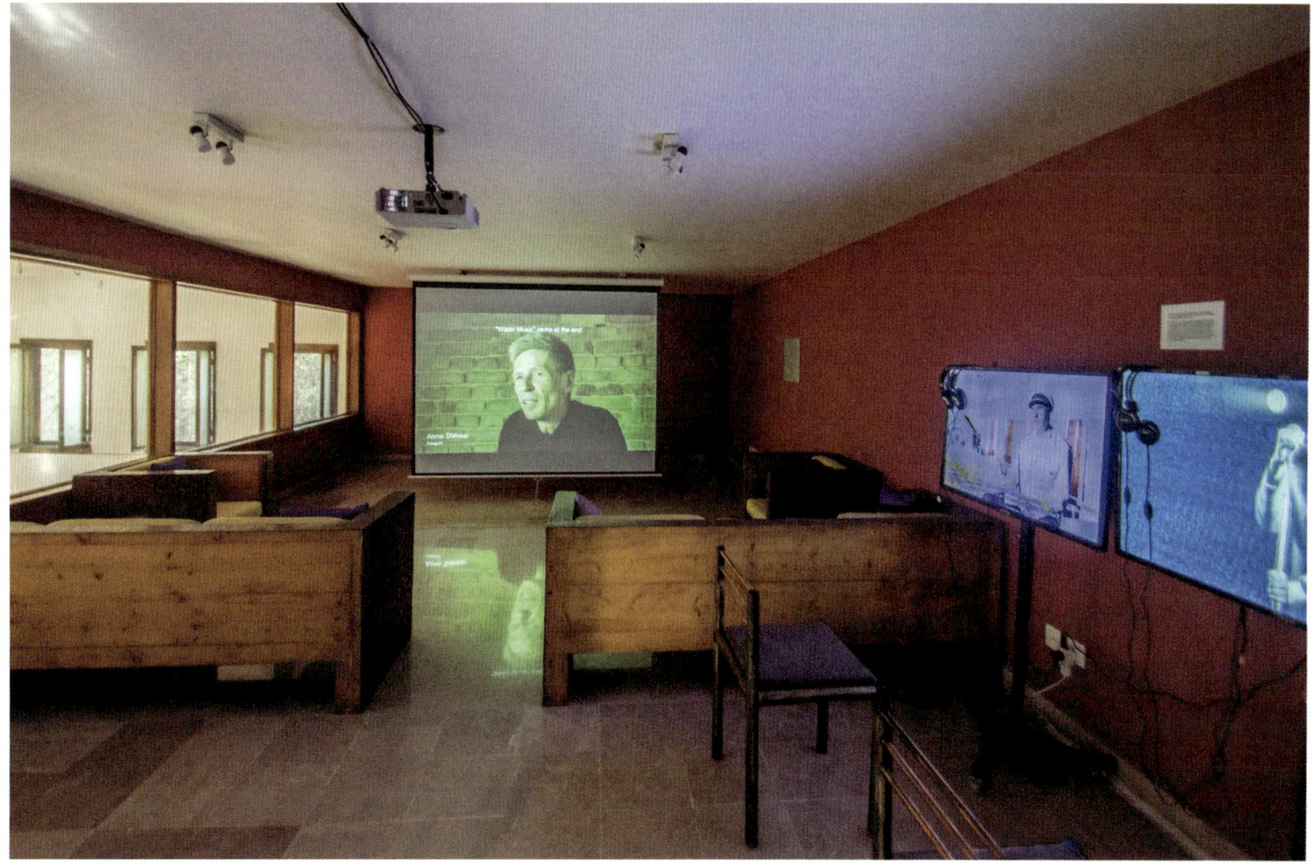
"Water Music" came at the end
Arno Dittmer

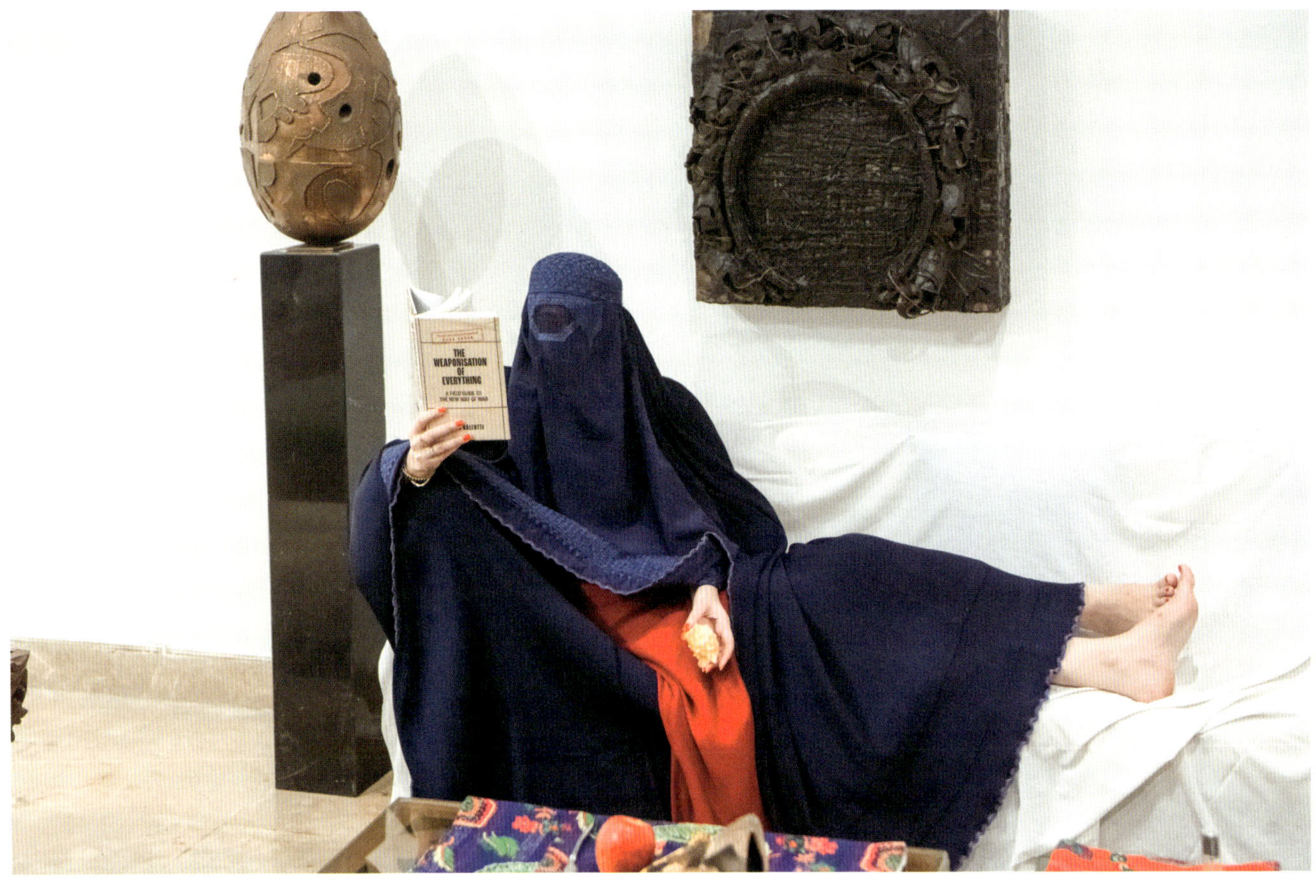

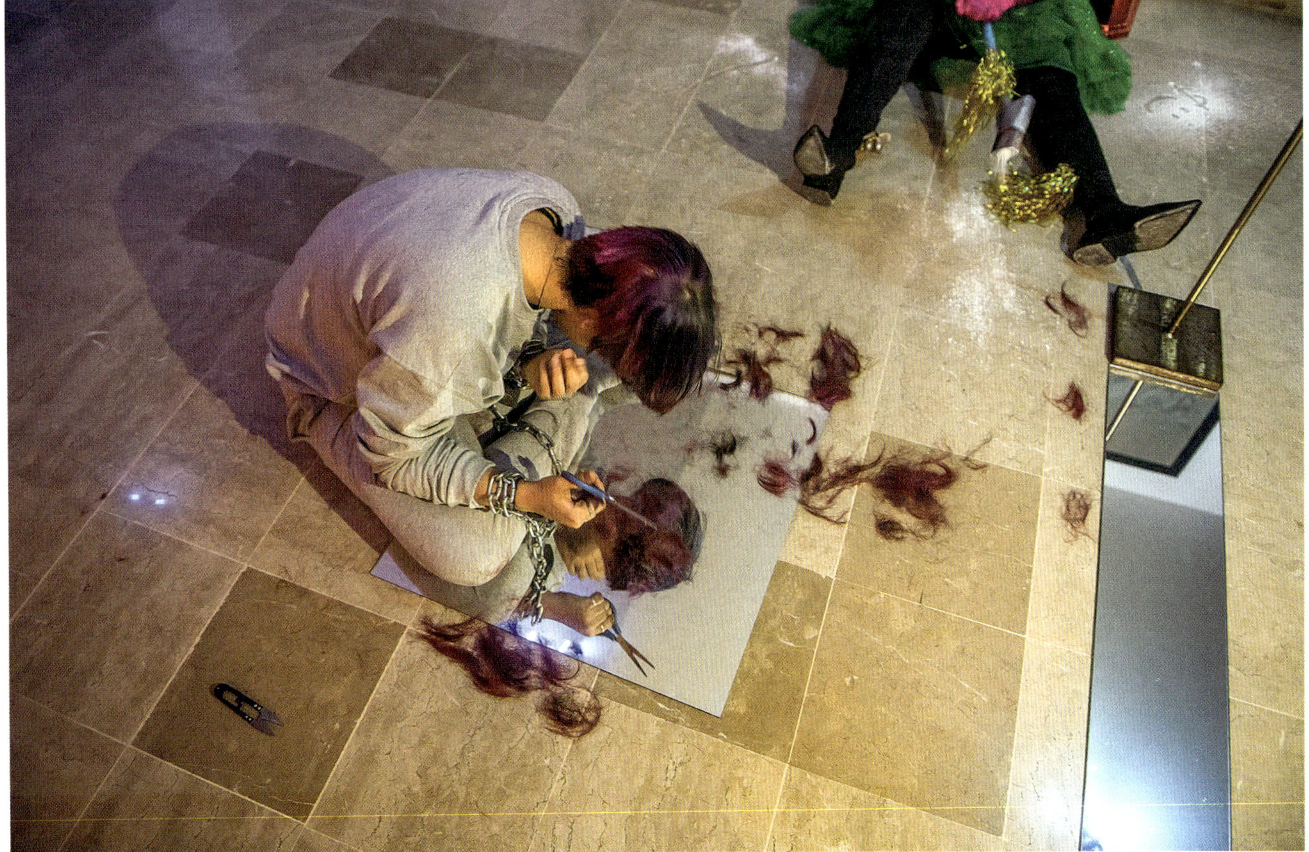

Photos by Humayun Memon

Jagah Hai | 2022

Curated by Adam Fahy-Majeed, Amin Gulgee and Sara Vaqar Pagganwala

Curated by Amin along with Adam Fahy-Majeed and Sara Vaqar Pagganwala, *Jagah Hai (Is There Space? There is Space!)* was the Amin Gulgee Gallery's first show post-COVID-19, and the gallery's third group exhibition of performance art. Unlike *Riwhyti: One Night Stand* and *Dreamscape*, which were confined to the gallery's formal exhibition spaces downstairs and their courtyards, *Jagah Hai* presented 51 works throughout Amin's gallery-cum-home. The performances played out not just below, but on the four landings of the exposed staircase that leads up through the artist-curator's living quarters to the three-tiered roof and *barsati* (rain room.) The curators issued an open invitation to the show via Instagram and Facebook, an unusual gesture in a security-conscious city like Karachi. As with all shows at the gallery, there was no charge to enter. Hundreds of people showed up, thronging Amin's wide-open space, already crowded with performers. Some of the performances addressed gender. Ayesha Toor, dressed in a sari, bound her head with various *dupatta* before burning them in the flames of torches. Yumna Ali, in androgynous gray sweats and wrapped in chains, methodically cut off her own hair. Sophia-Layla Afsar scribbled slogans, slurs and questions in Urdu that she has often heard about her trans body on strips of masking tape and pasted them onto her red dress. Other performers explored forms of storytelling historical to the region. Rahil Siddiqui presented a performance that referenced Dastangoi, an Urdu oral narrative tradition that reached its zenith in the 19th century. Dressed from the period, he sat, silent, with his legs folded beneath him on a landing before a printed verse by Mirza Ghalib (1797-1869). On the landing just above, Meher Afroz read aloud from the writings of the Urdu poet Mir Anees (1800-1874). On the main roof, surrounded by Amin's 2005 mosaic *Salaam Gaudi*, Sheema Kermani presented a work that referenced classical South Asian dance, before transitioning into contemporary movement, as she reacted to the sounds and space around her.

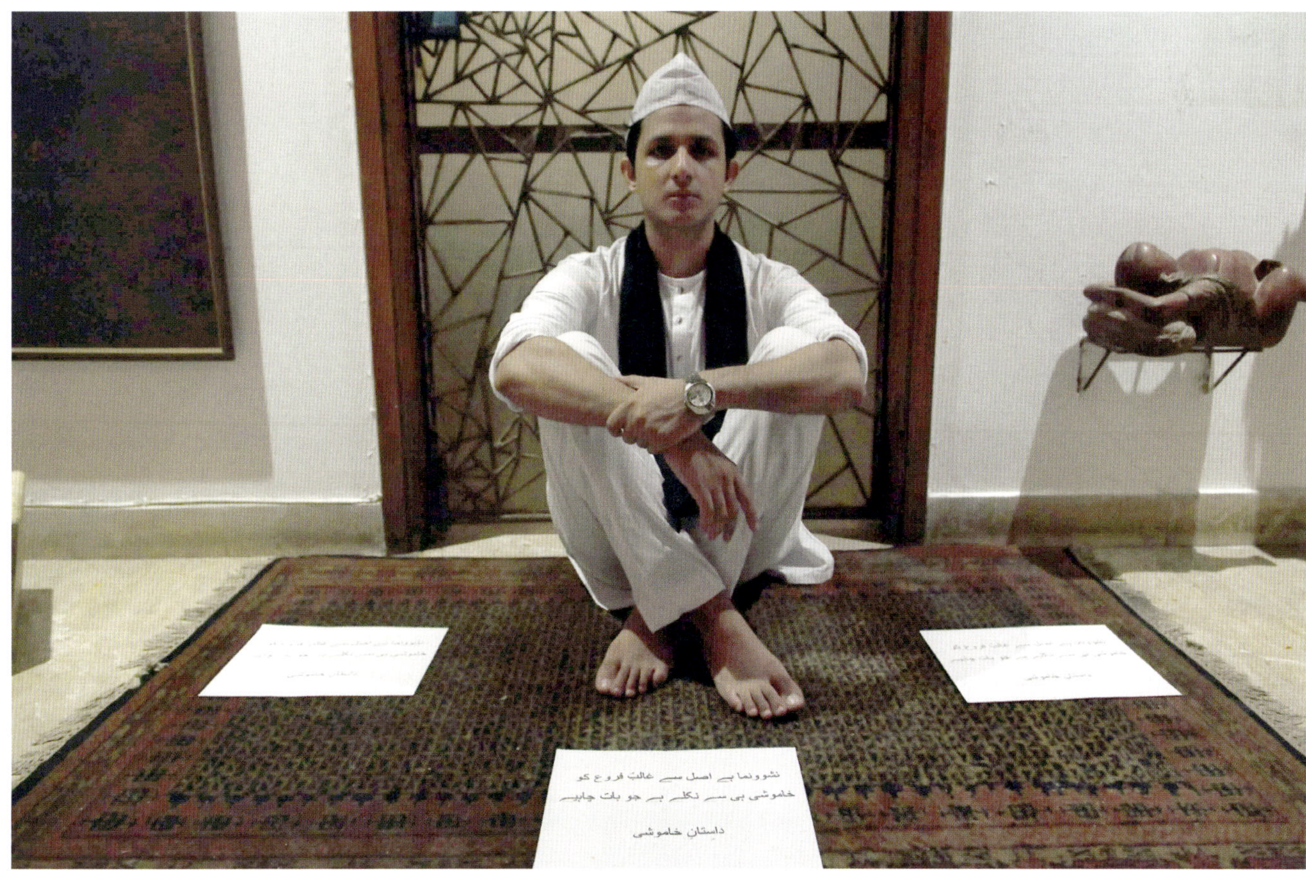

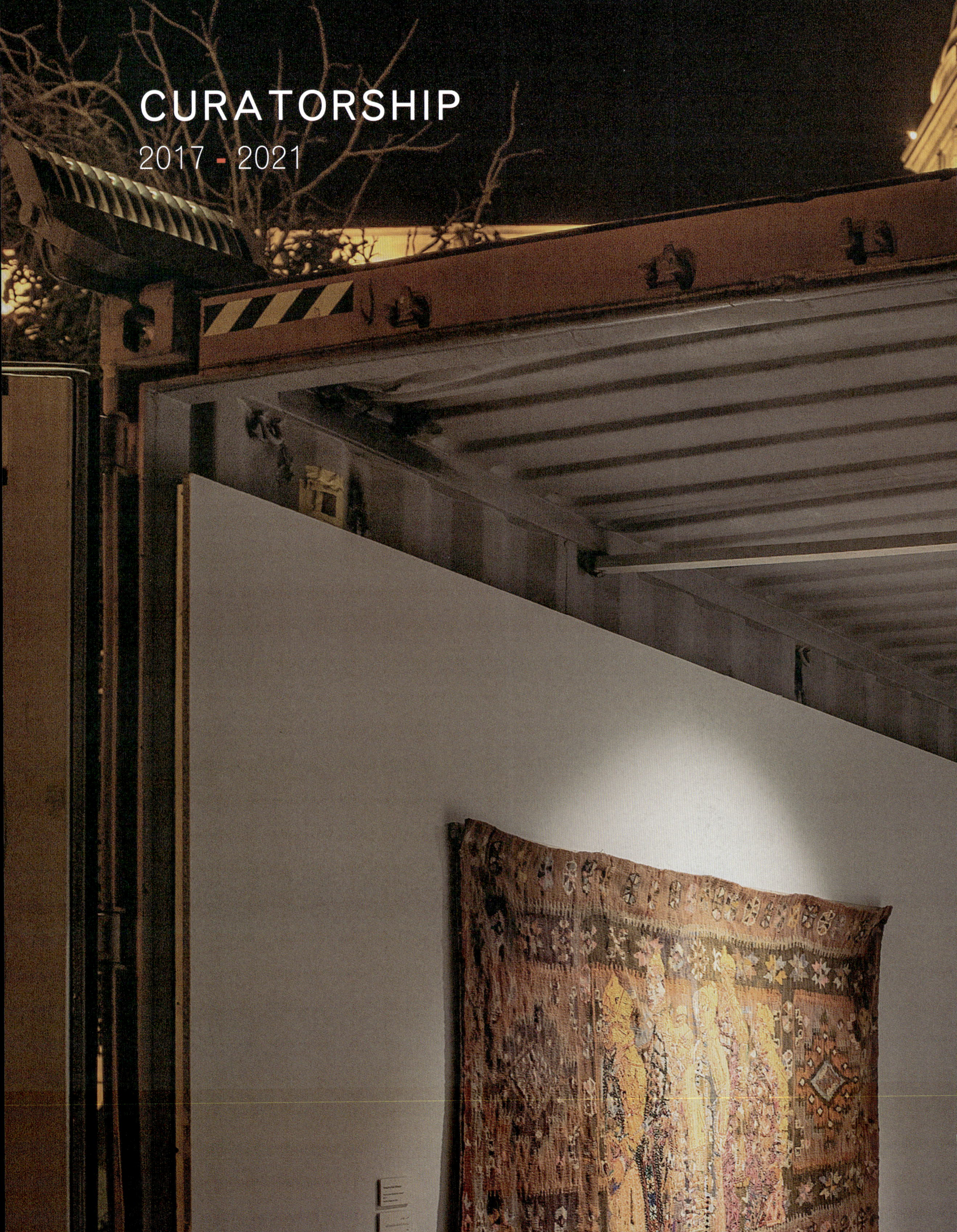
CURATORSHIP
2017 - 2021

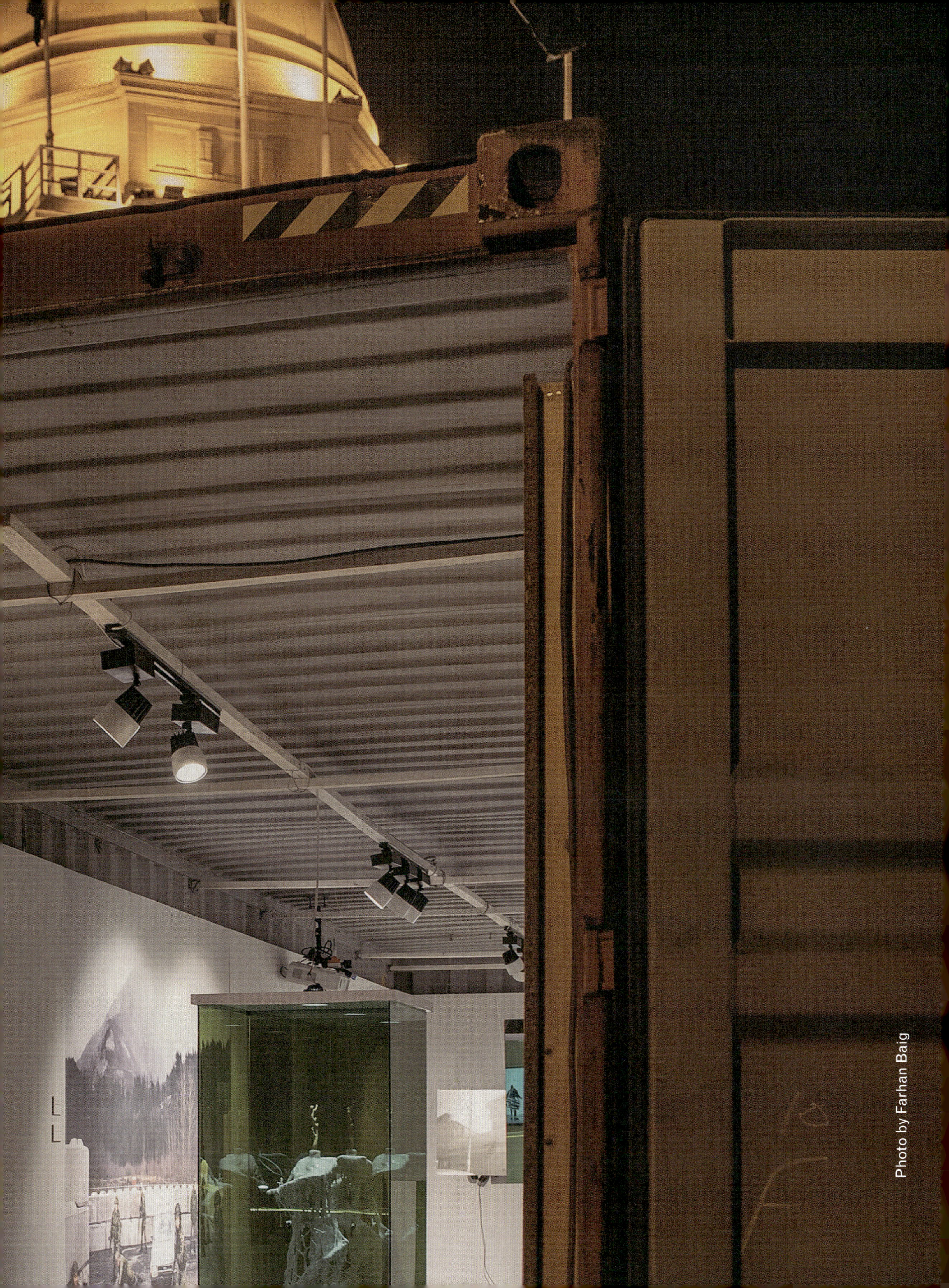

Photo by Farhan Baig

Karachi Biennale | Karachi, 2017

Chief Curator Amin Gulgee
Alliance Française Gallery, Capri Cinema, Claremont House, 63 Commissariat, Foundation of the Museum of Modern Art, Frere Hall, Indus Valley School of Art and Architecture, Karachi School of Art Gallery, NJV School, Pioneer Books, The Theosophical Society and V.M. Gallery

Amin was Chief Curator of the inaugural Karachi Biennale (KB17), Pakistan's first international art biennial. The theme was "Witness." His team included curator-at-large Zarmeene Shah; assistant curators Zeerak Ahmed, Humayun Memon, and Sara Vaqar Pagganwala; and curatorial team member Adam Fahy-Majeed. Together they worked with the 182 artists they had selected for KB17 over a period of a year. Most of the artists were Pakistani, including Shahzia Sikander, Anwar Saeed, Adeela Suleman and Hamra Abbas. Sixty international artists were also chosen, including Michelangelo Pistoletto, Yoko Ono, ORLAN and Nadia Kaabi-Linke. Amin and his team had 12 venues organized into four clusters scattered throughout the city in which to install the work. Due to the immense scale of Karachi, and the daunting prospect of traversing it, each venue was treated as a microcosm of the whole: self-contained and yet connected. Although moods and connections varied from venue to venue according to the works that were placed there, the thematic arc of KB17 remained consistent throughout. Challenging works were presented in all venues, including those located in areas unaccustomed to displays of art. The curatorial team also developed a website (www.kbcuartorial.com), which went live the night of the opening to guide the viewer though the sites. This was an expression of their belief that KB17 should be accessible to all and free of cost. (None of the venues charged admission; none of the curators received a fee.) The works selected and commissioned for KB17 bore witness in many ways. Some artists witnessed their own journeys, their memories of family and childhood, experiences of loss, their connections to the sacred, to tradition, and to their bodies and selves. For others, Karachi itself became a point of departure that led them to witness the trauma of violence, as well as the challenges presented by urban decay, the beleaguered intellectual space, barriers, migration, change, and territory. Artists also witnessed issues of gender and sexuality, capitalism and global commerce, legacies of colonialism and class divides.

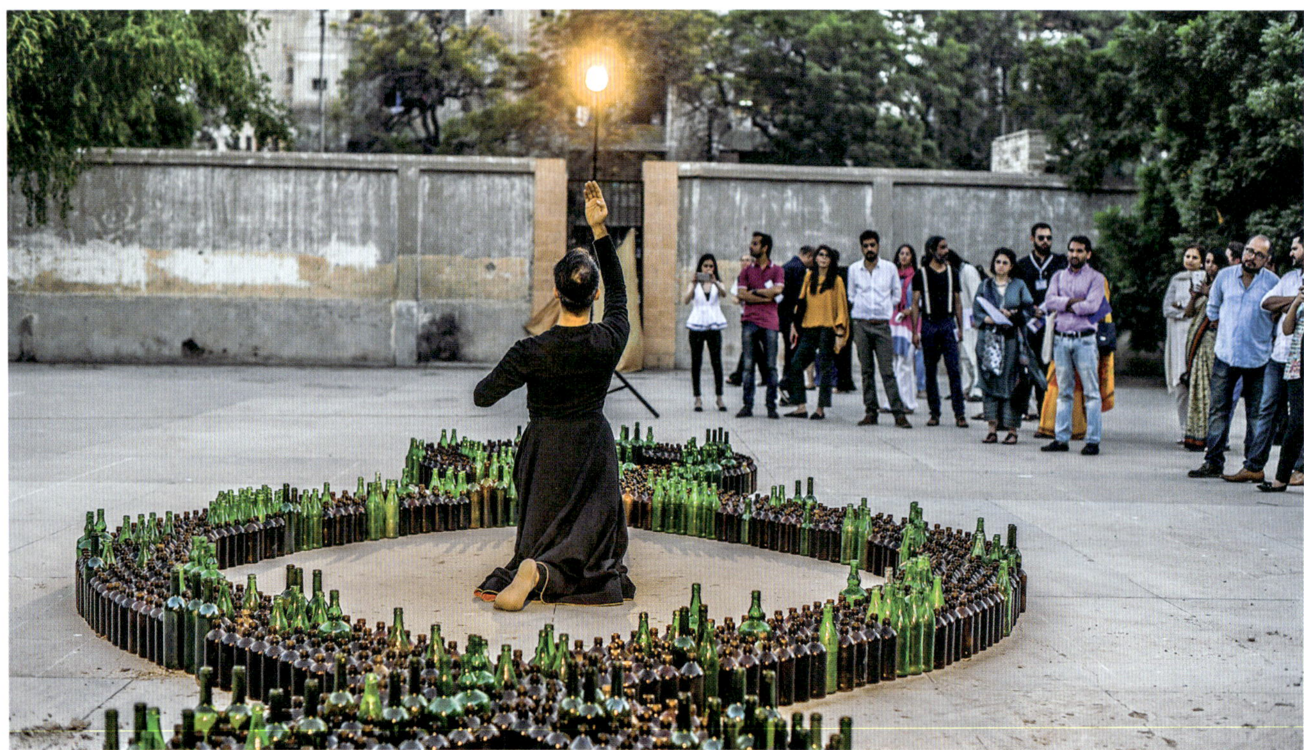

NJV School. Photos courtesy Karachi Biennale

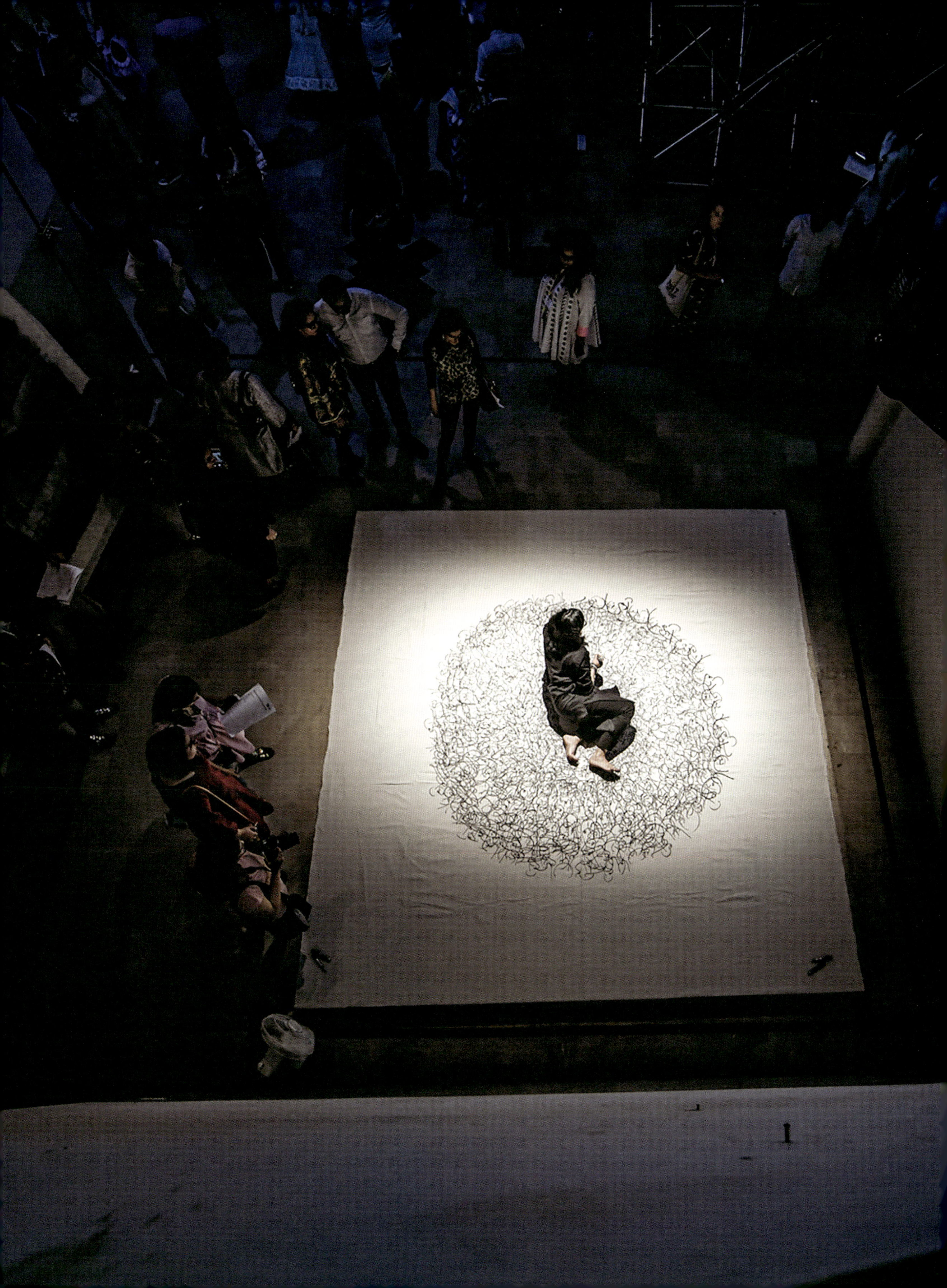

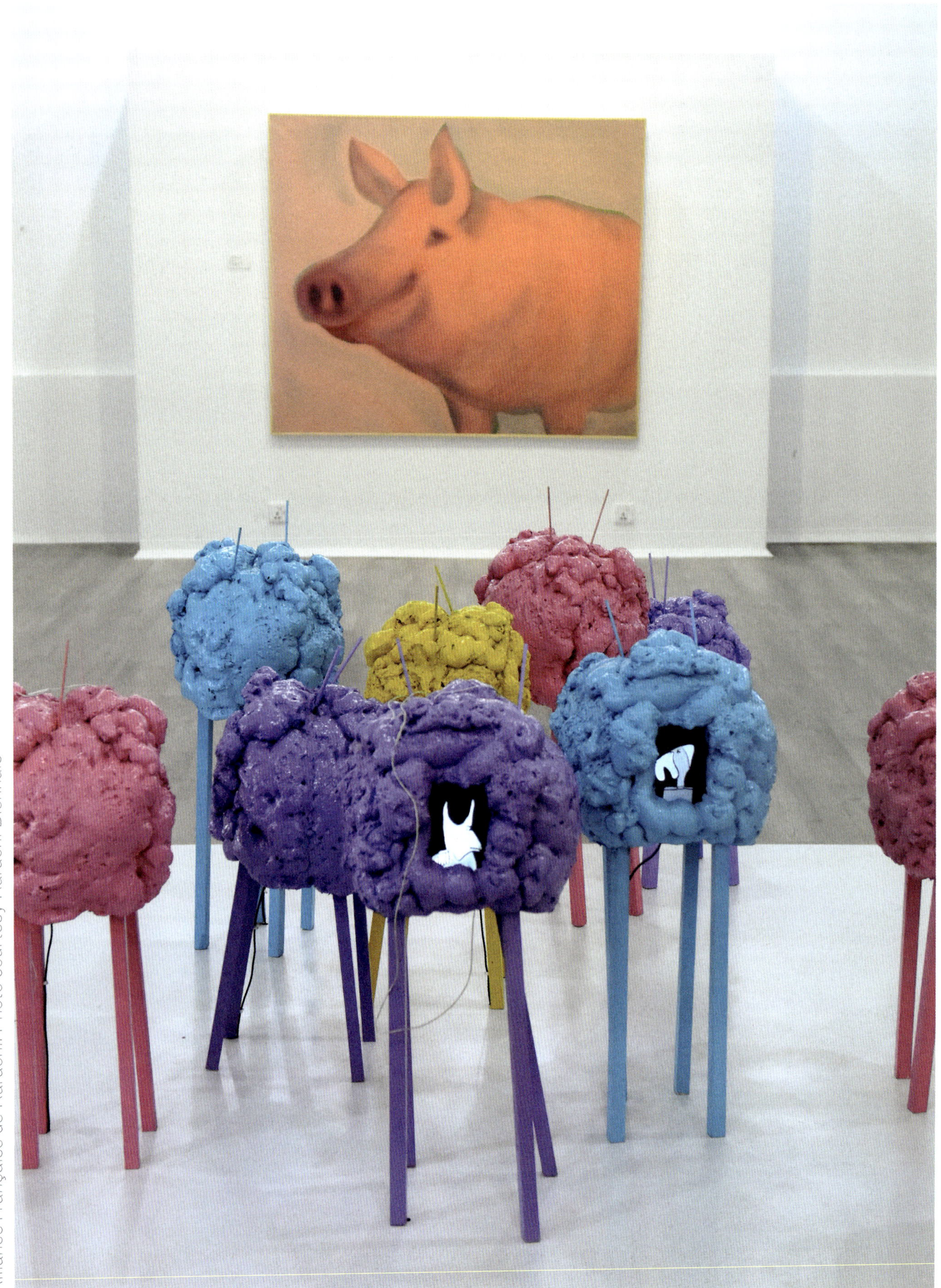

Alliance Française de Karachi. Photo courtesy Karachi Biennale

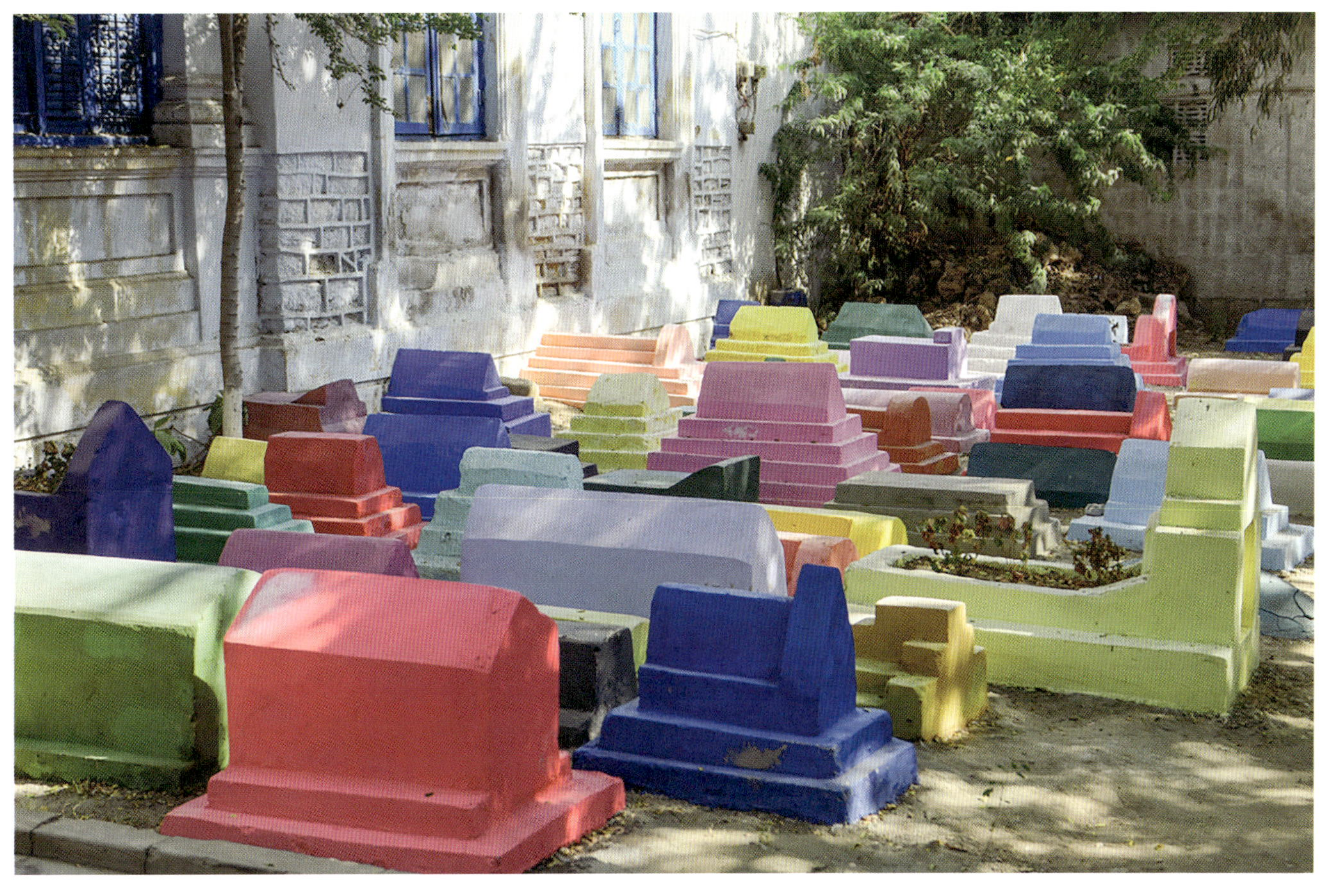

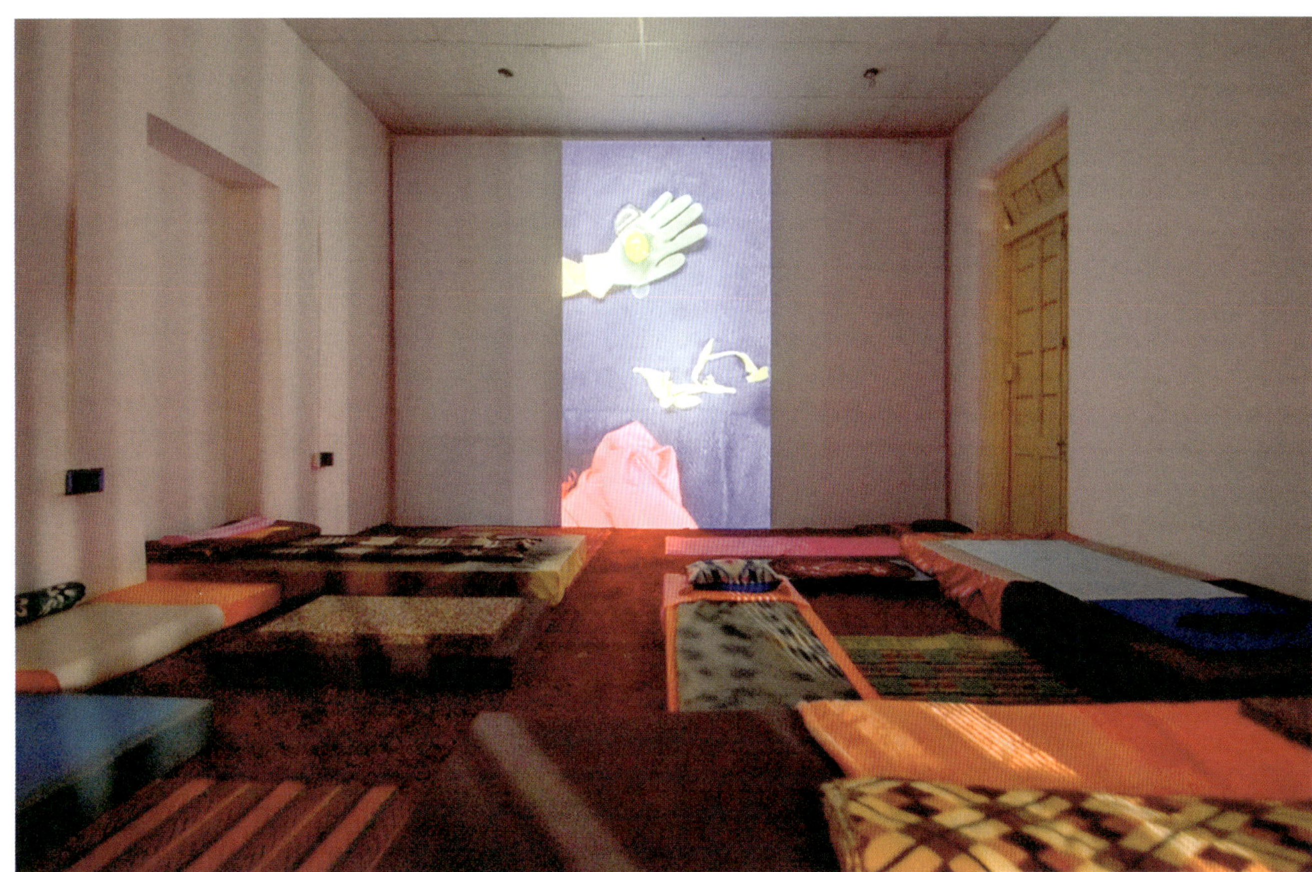

63 Commissariat. Photos courtesy Karachi Biennale

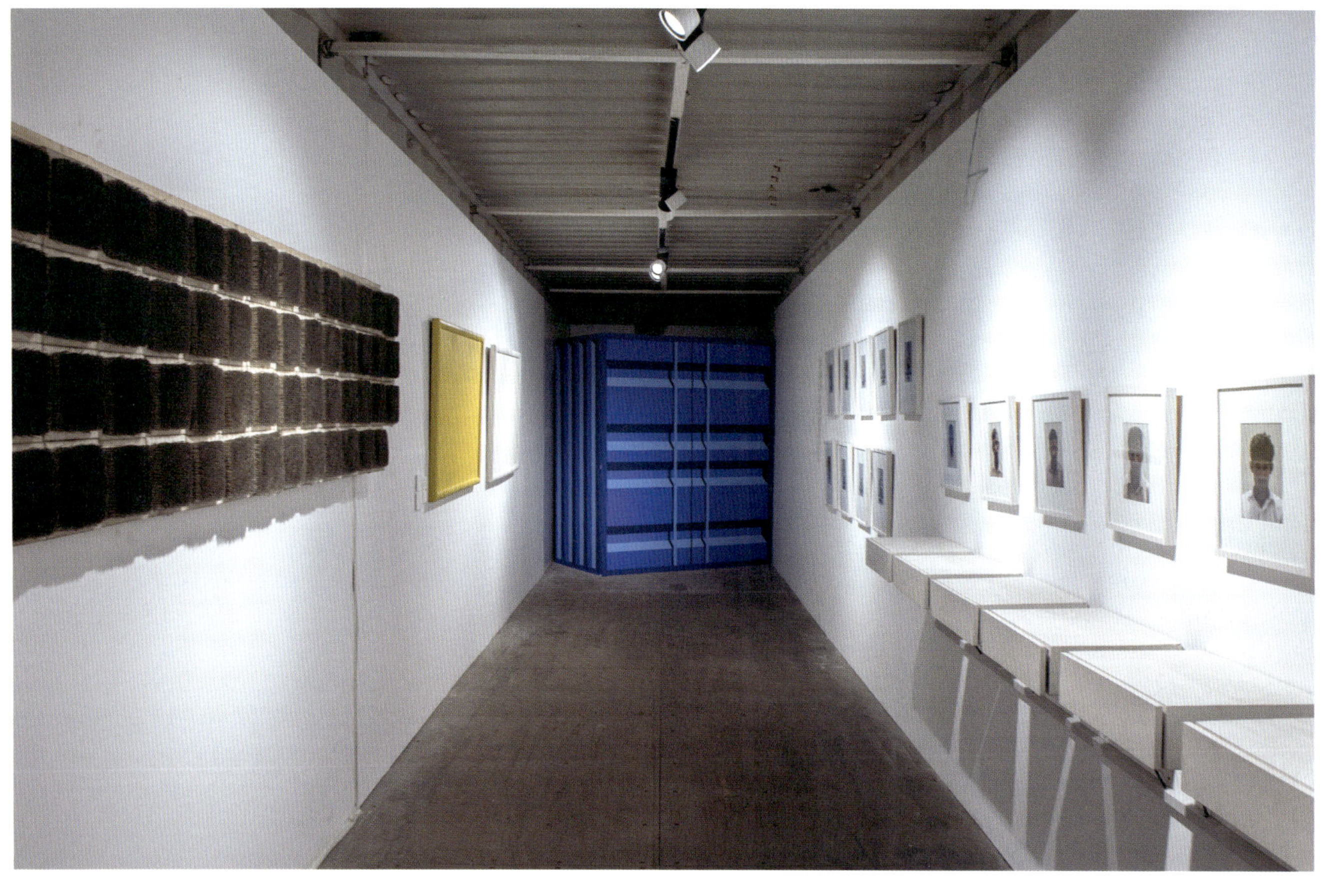

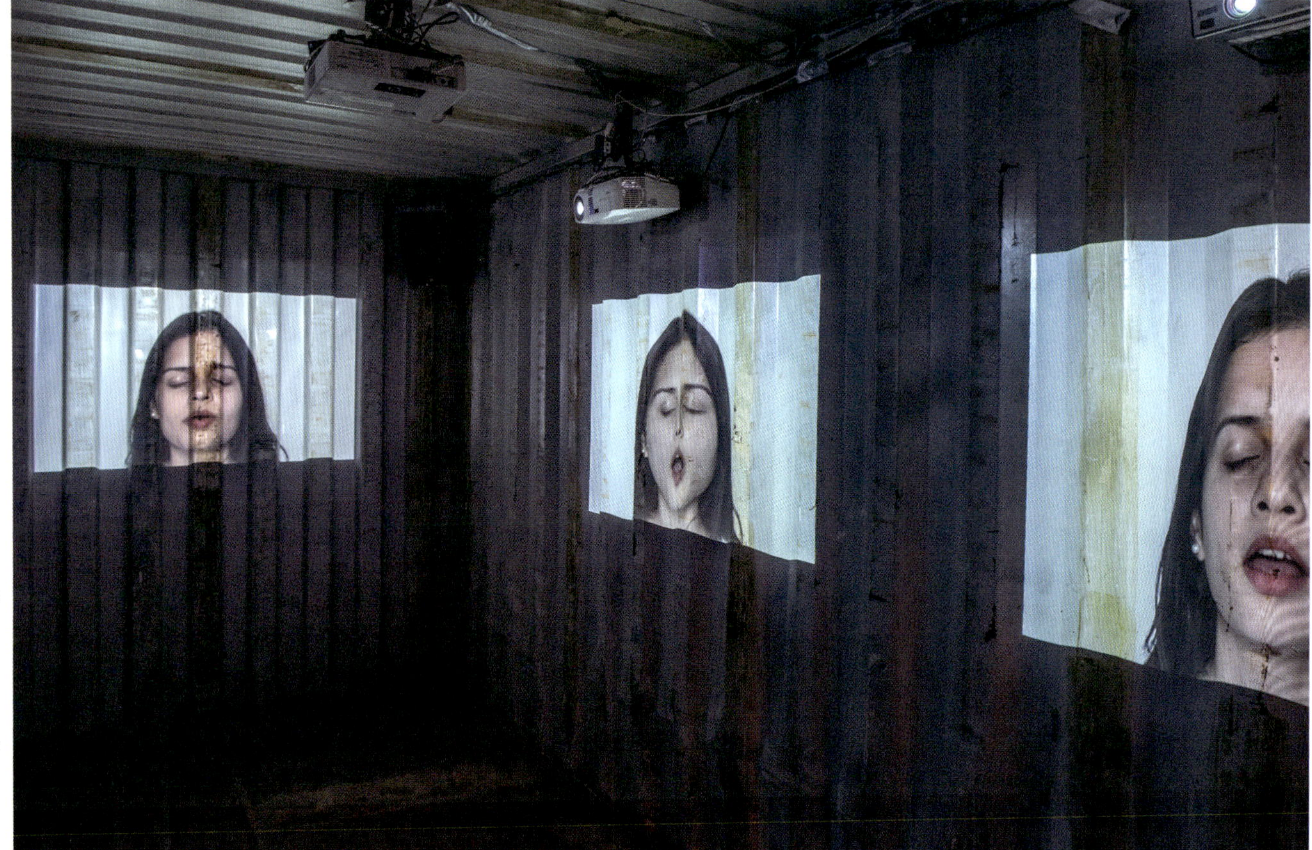

Photos by Farhan Baig

The Quantum City | Karachi, 2019

Curated by Zarmeene Shah, Sara Vaqar Pagganwala and Amin Gulgee
Karachi Port Trust

Amin, along with Zarmeene Shah and Sara Vaqar Pagganwala, curated *The Quantum City: Territory | Space | Place* for the first International Public Art Festival in Karachi. The work of 54 national and international artists was placed inside, around and on top of 11 shipping containers positioned in front of the imposing Karachi Port Trust building, which was opened to the public for the first time in over a century for the show. This squatters' maze of well-travelled, dented crates was symbiotic yet in stark contrast to the imposing sandstone edifice behind them. Shipping crates are very much linked to Karachi as it is Pakistan's main port. But they also have other associations: politicians often deliver fiery speeches from on top of containers that authorities routinely place at key intersections to block the movement of people during demonstrations. In *Portrait of a Leader*, Syed Ammad Tahir stood on a crate before a lectern fitted with a microphone and extemporaneously delivered a speech that was inspired by the oratory of former prime minister Zulfikar Ali Bhutto as well as by Charlie Chaplin's *The Great Dictator*. The 180-minute performance drew a crowd of curious passersby the night of the opening, who paused to listen to Ammad's nonsensical address. On an interior wall of another container were pasted three inkjet vinyl prints by photographer Arif Mahmood. Called *Empress Market: Past and Present,* it depicted the Karachi marketplace built by the British between 1884 and 1889 to both honor Queen Victoria and discourage lionization of rebelling native soldiers executed on the site after the failed Sepoy Mutiny of 1857–9. On the back wall of another container was projected *Dyeing Inayat Khan* by the Delhi-based Raqs Media Collective, who animated an original drawing from the early 17th century in the Mughal miniature style to suggest the threshold between life and death.

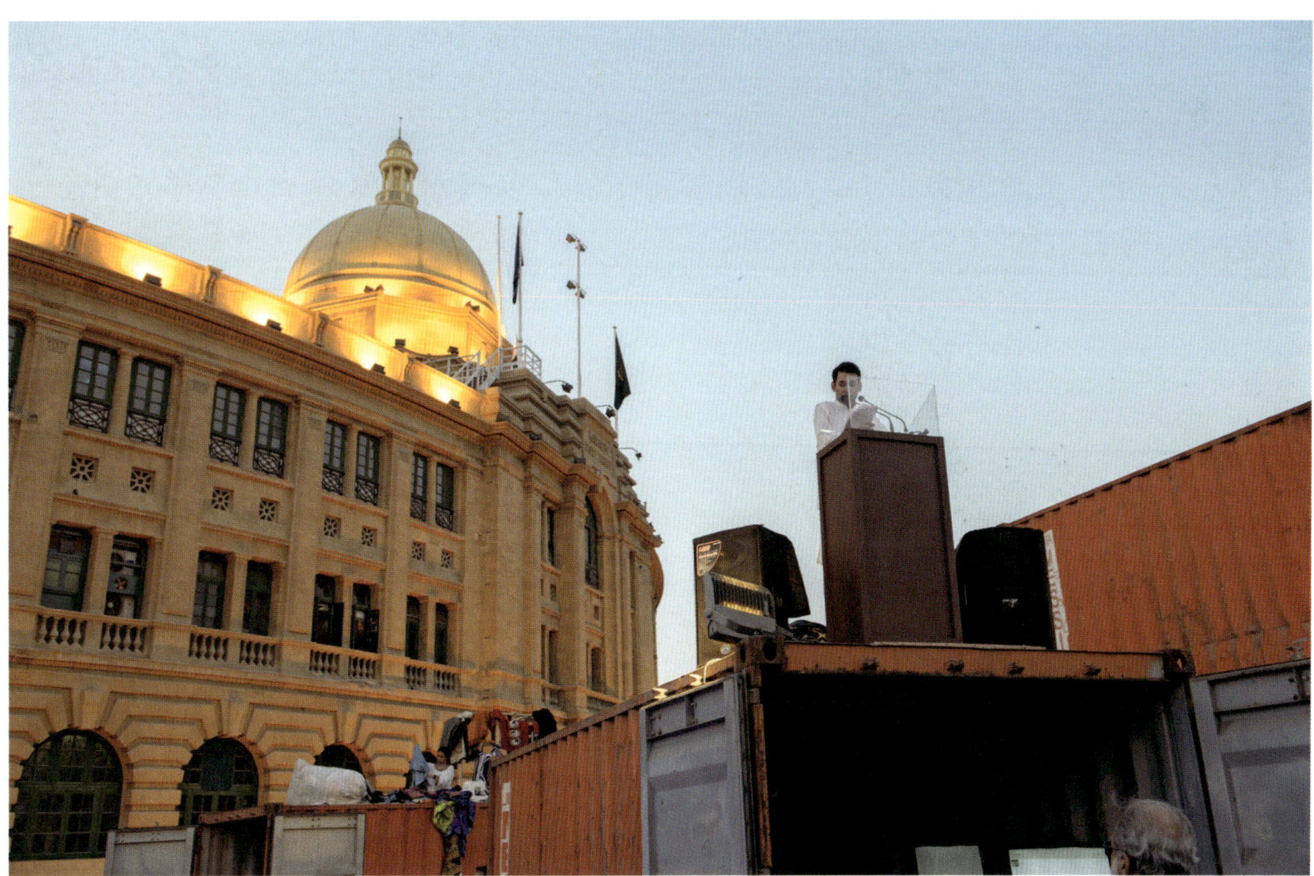

One Night Stand / Coup d'un soir | Paris, 2019

Curated by Amin Gulgee
Cité internationale des arts

One Night Stand | Coup d'un soir was Amin Gulgee's first curatorial effort outside of Pakistan. The result of his two-month residency at the Cité internationale des arts in Paris, it was a presentation of 32 simultaneous performances that included other artists in residence at the Cité as well as colleagues of Amin's based in Paris and elsewhere. Including music, video, dance, drawing and installation, the happening played out over two hours in the Cité's front courtyard, reception area, stairwell, basement corridor and auditorium. Although he later documented the evening with a 200-page catalogue in both English and French, Amin intentionally provided no guidance, either written or oral, to the audience, who had to make their way, unprepared, throughout the non-white cube, cramped with performing bodies. Wearing a futuristic costume of scrap metal and plastic, Congolese artist Precy Numbi moved robotically inside and outside the Cité for his work *Kimbalambala*. The title in Lingala refers to cars no longer fit for the road in Europe that are dumped onto the market in Africa, where they are retooled as public and private transport. Pakistani painter Amber Arifeen knelt upon a carpet of reproduced posters from 1950s French-owned Algeria. The public notices, which depicted a lone woman with her face uncovered among a group of others wearing the niqab, declared: "N'êtes-vous pas donc jolie ? Dévoilez-vous !"— Aren't you not now pretty? Unveil yourselves! Amber, wearing a hijab, knelt upon the posters like a punished schoolgirl and repeatedly wrote "devoilez" [*sic*], alluding to a 2010 French law banning women from having their faces covered in public. English performance and video artist Stephen Sheehan stood on a ledge facing the entrance of the Cité and continuously urinated inside his jeans for *We Are Giants Standing on Mountains*. The work, which was performed three years after the British people voted to leave the European Union, appeared to depict illusions of invincibility: the "mountain" he stood upon was no more than 30 cm high.

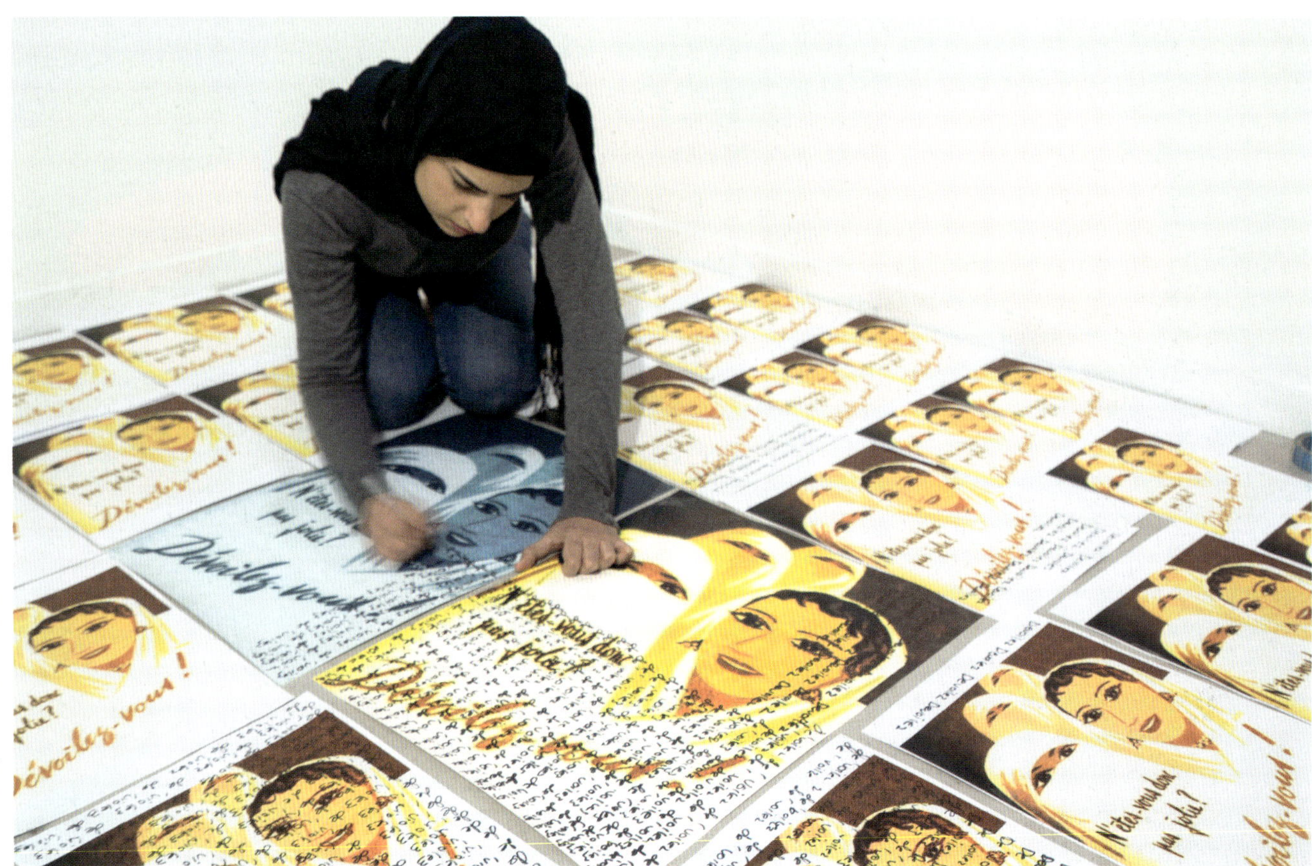

Photos by Romain Ruiz

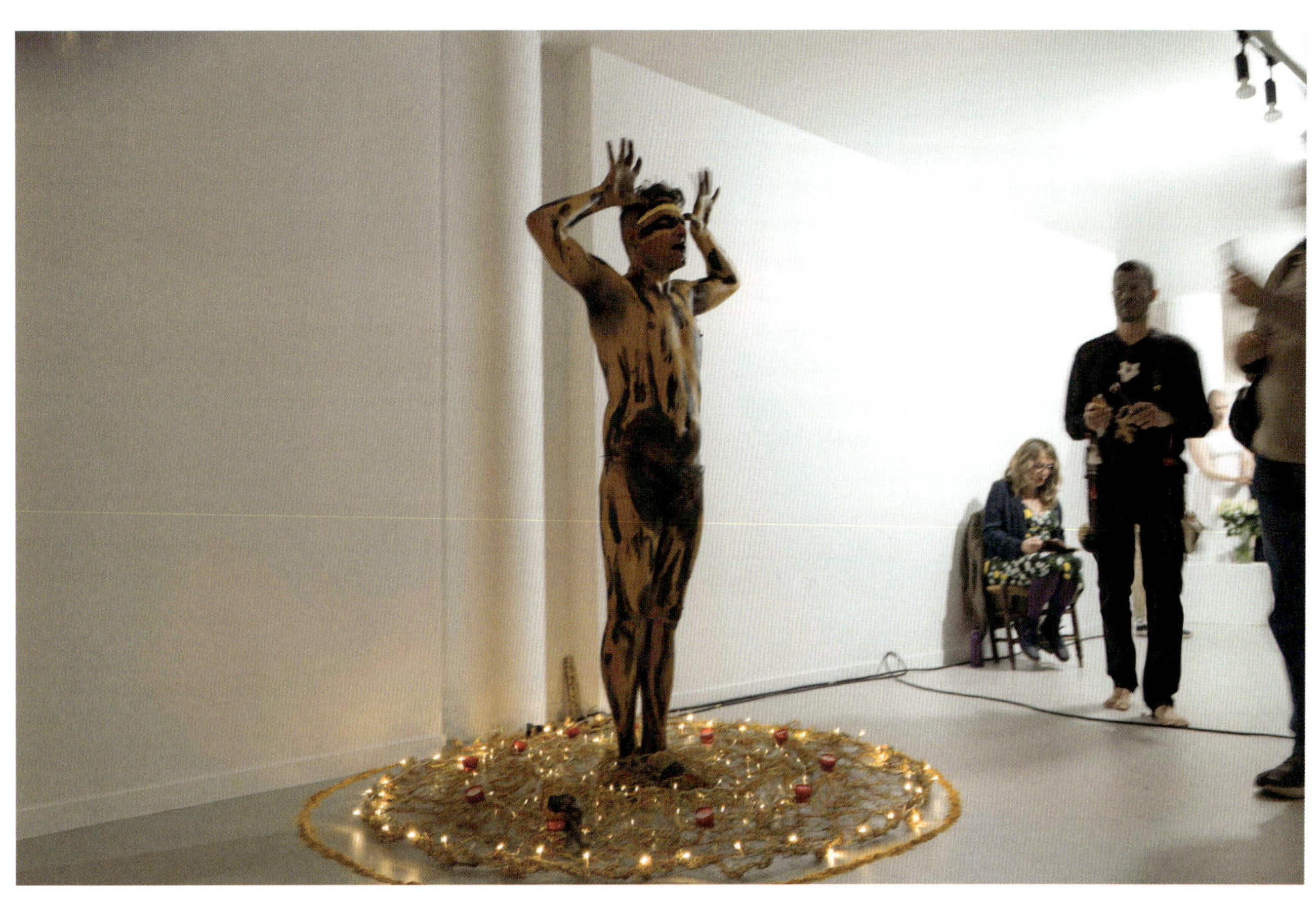

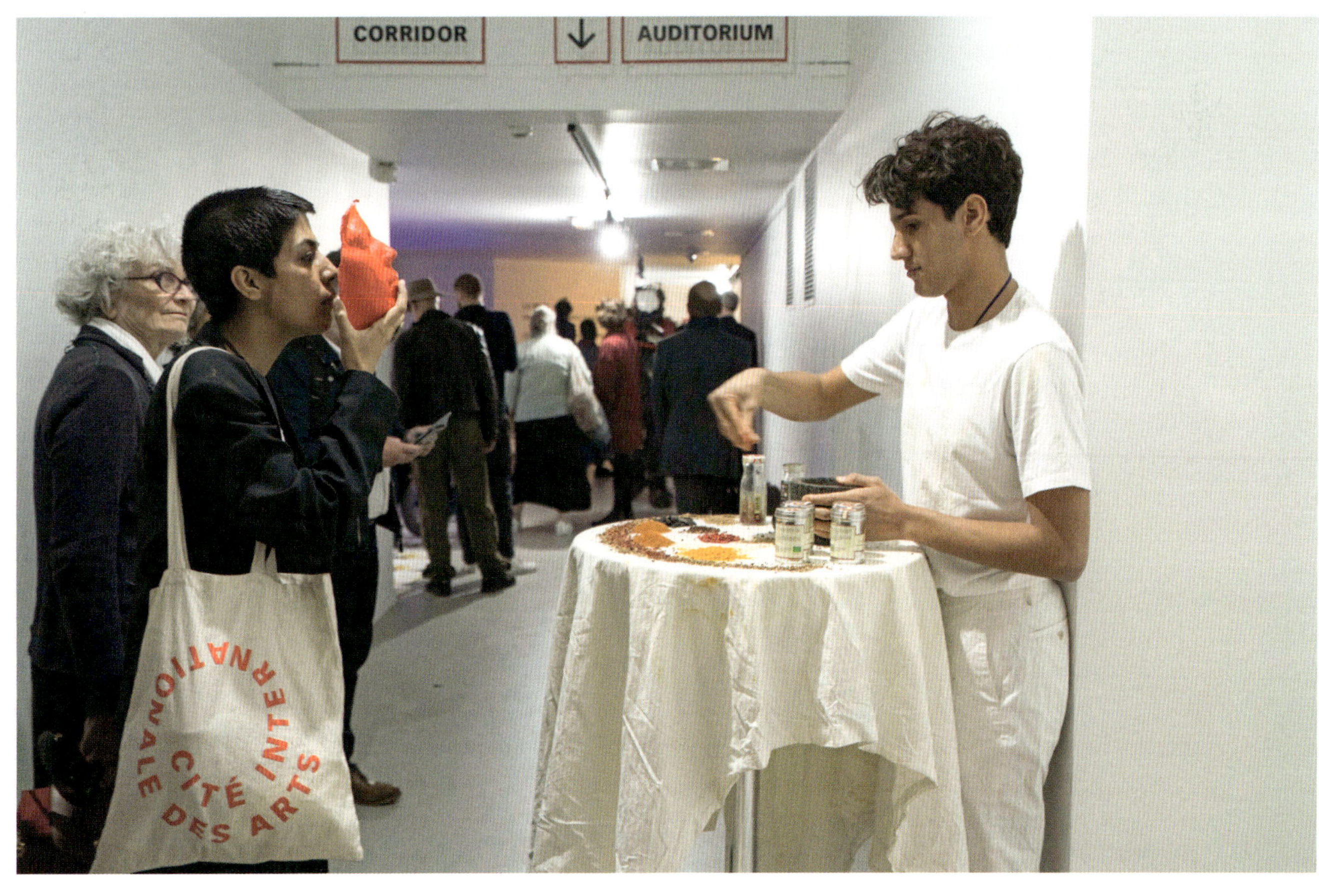
CORRIDOR
AUDITORIUM
CITÉ INTERNATIONALE DES ARTS

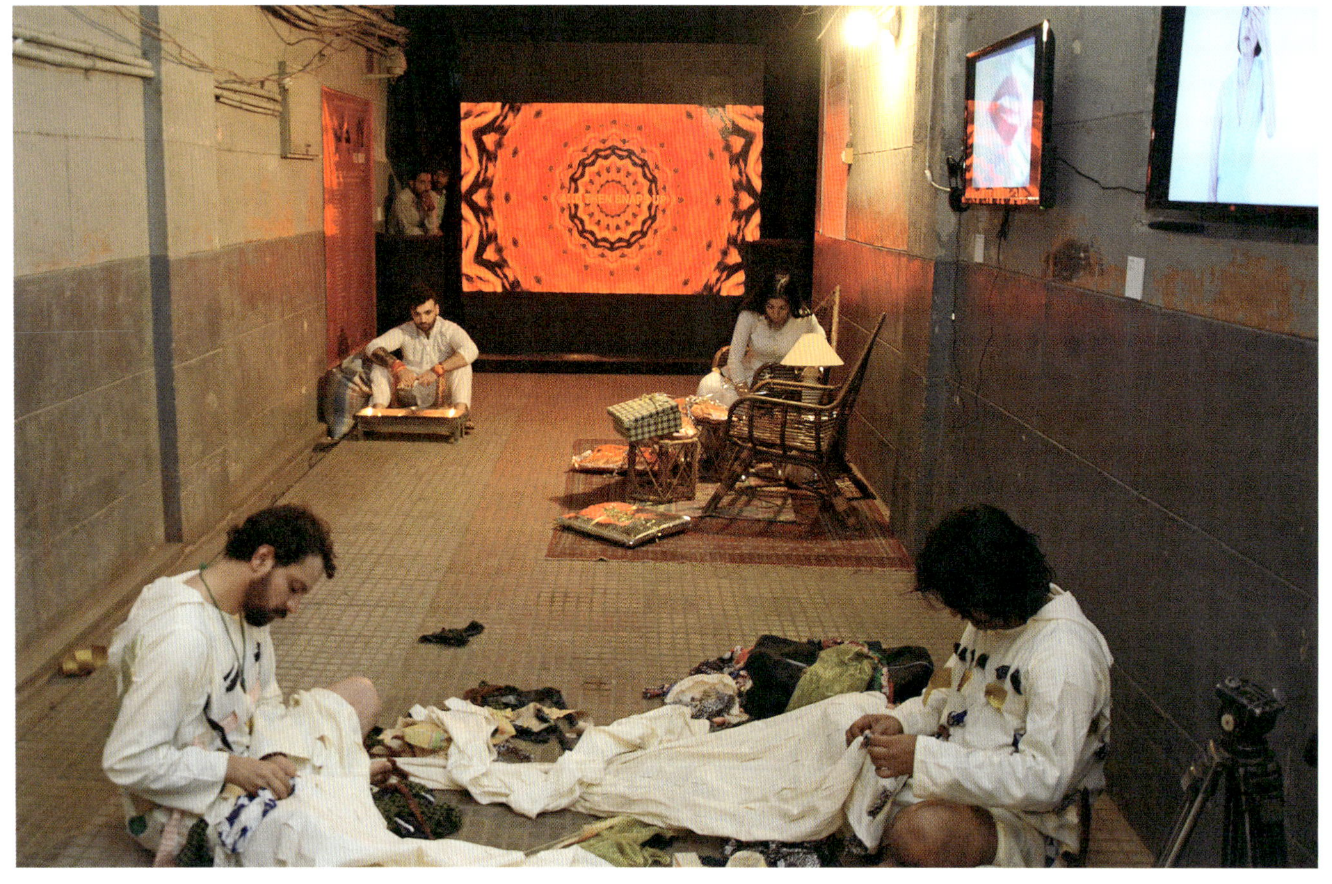

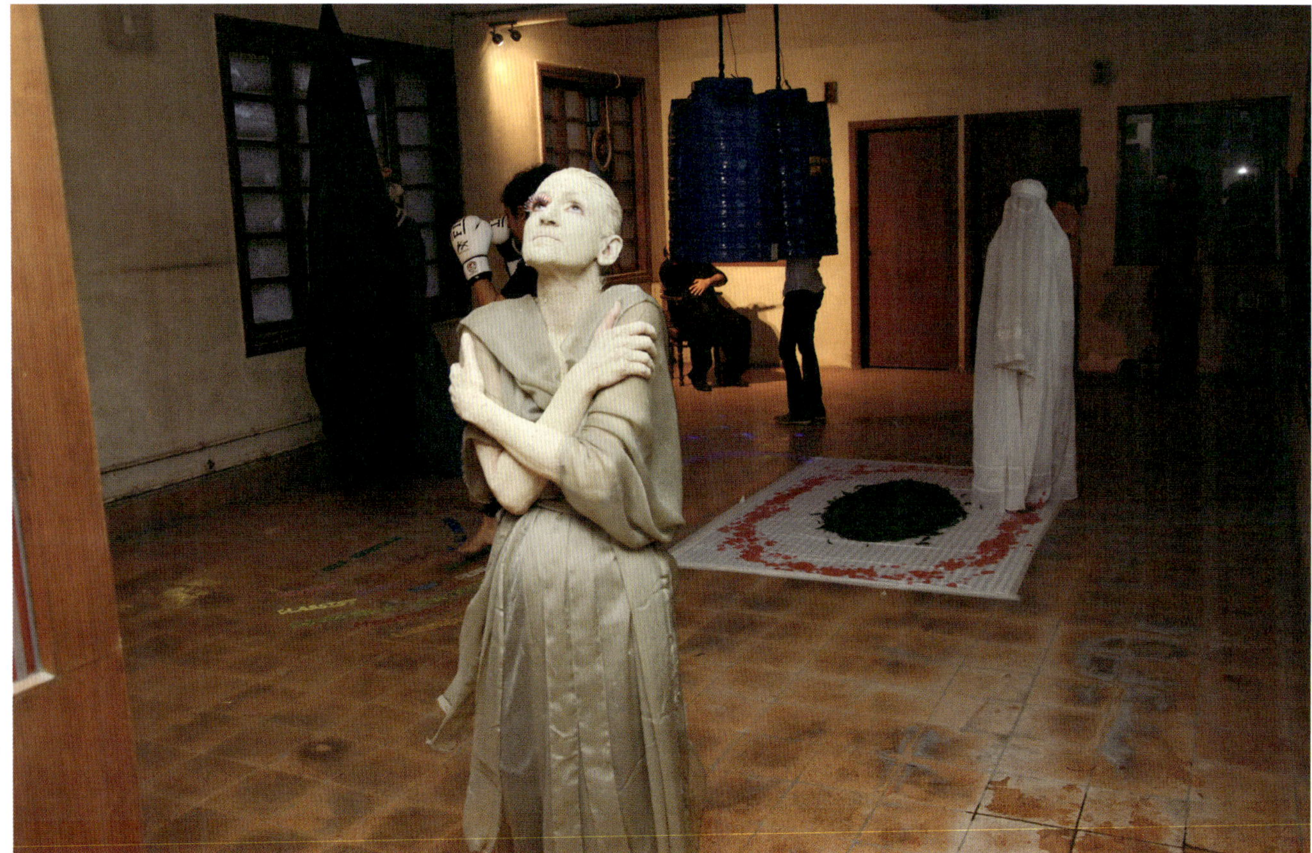

Photos by JY Photos

LAL JADOO/RED MAGIC | Karachi, 2020

Curated by Sara Vaqar Pagganwala and Amin Gulgee
Karachi House

Amin Gulgee and Sara Vaqar Pagganwala co-curated *LAL JADOO/RED MAGIC* as part of the Second International Public Art Festival in Karachi. An overview of Pakistani performance both past and present, the exhibition included 43 live works as well as 22 works recorded in photographs or video. This two-hour happening took place at Karachi House, a semi-abandoned office building on I.I. Chundrigar Road, Karachi's Wall Street. The property appealed to Amin because, as he wrote in the accompanying digital catalogue, "[it] is a surreal space straight out of a David Lynch film." Performances materialized on the sidewalk before the time-worn construction, as well as in its cavernous driveway, shadowy stairwell, stalled elevator and maze of forlorn rooms and hallways on the third floor. Included was Salima Hashmi's 1972 video *Taal Matol - Handa Hubalna* (How to Boil an Egg) from the seminal PTV sketch comedy program *Such Gup,* which used satire as a form of critique. In this skit, Salima played a high society housewife who explains in English-accented Urdu how to boil an egg. Also on view was a 305 × 198-cm inkjet vinyl print capturing Ayesha Jatoi's 2006 performance, *Clothesline*, in which the artist made her way around a fighter plane from the 1971 war installed on a roundabout in Lahore, draping it with blood-red cloth like laundry set out to dry. In a narrow alcove upstairs, a fashionably dressed Marium M. Habib alternately ripped wallpaper off the walls or stuck her head in an oven for *Critical Domesticity*. Noreen Ali sat on the stairs cooing to a dead chicken cradled in her arms. Zayed Malik, wearing a black hood and a hangman's noose around his neck, wandered phantom-like throughout the building. On March 14th, the day before the show was scheduled to open, all public events were cancelled due to the spread of COVID-19. Amin and Sara agreed that *LAL JADOO/ RED MAGIC* should be closed to the public and viewed on live feed instead.

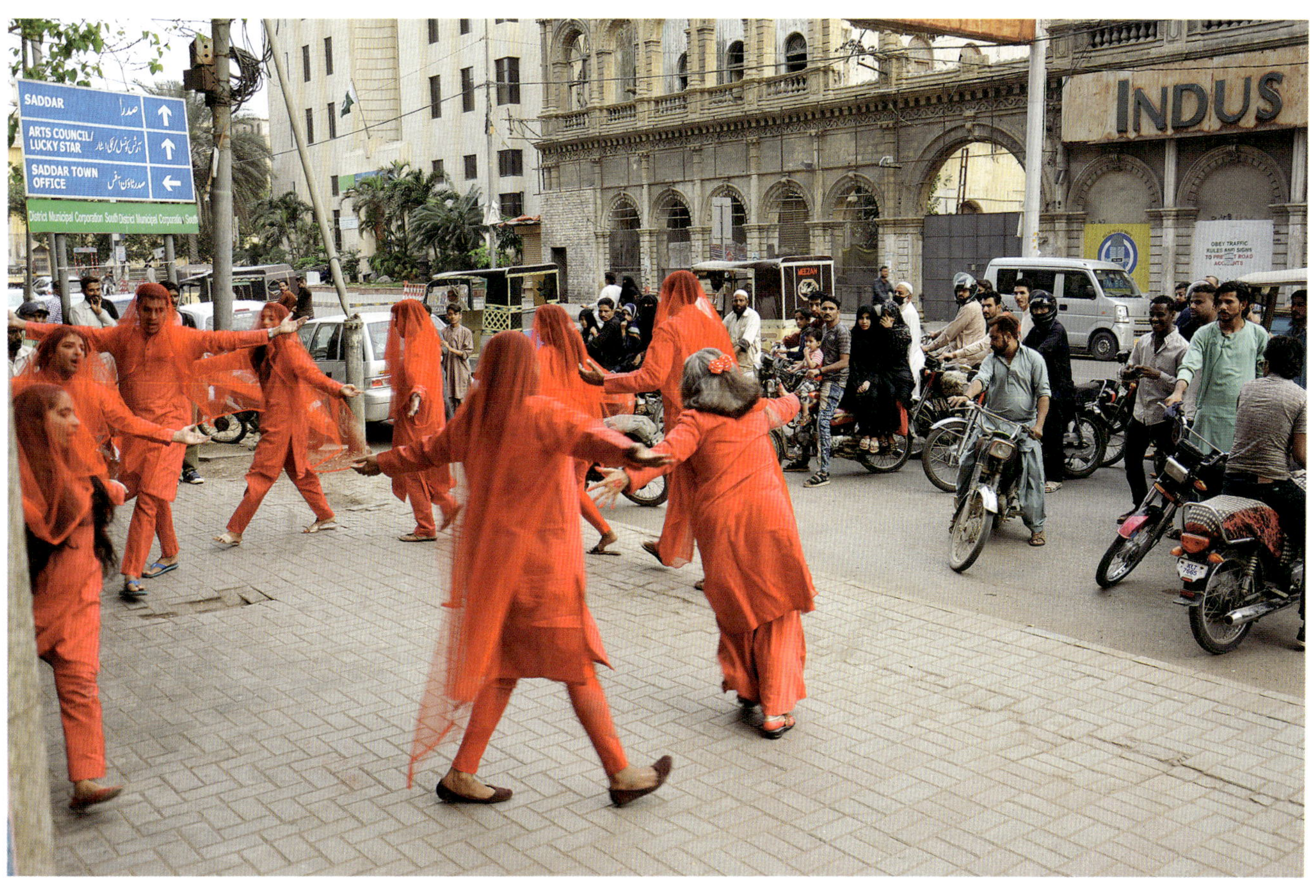

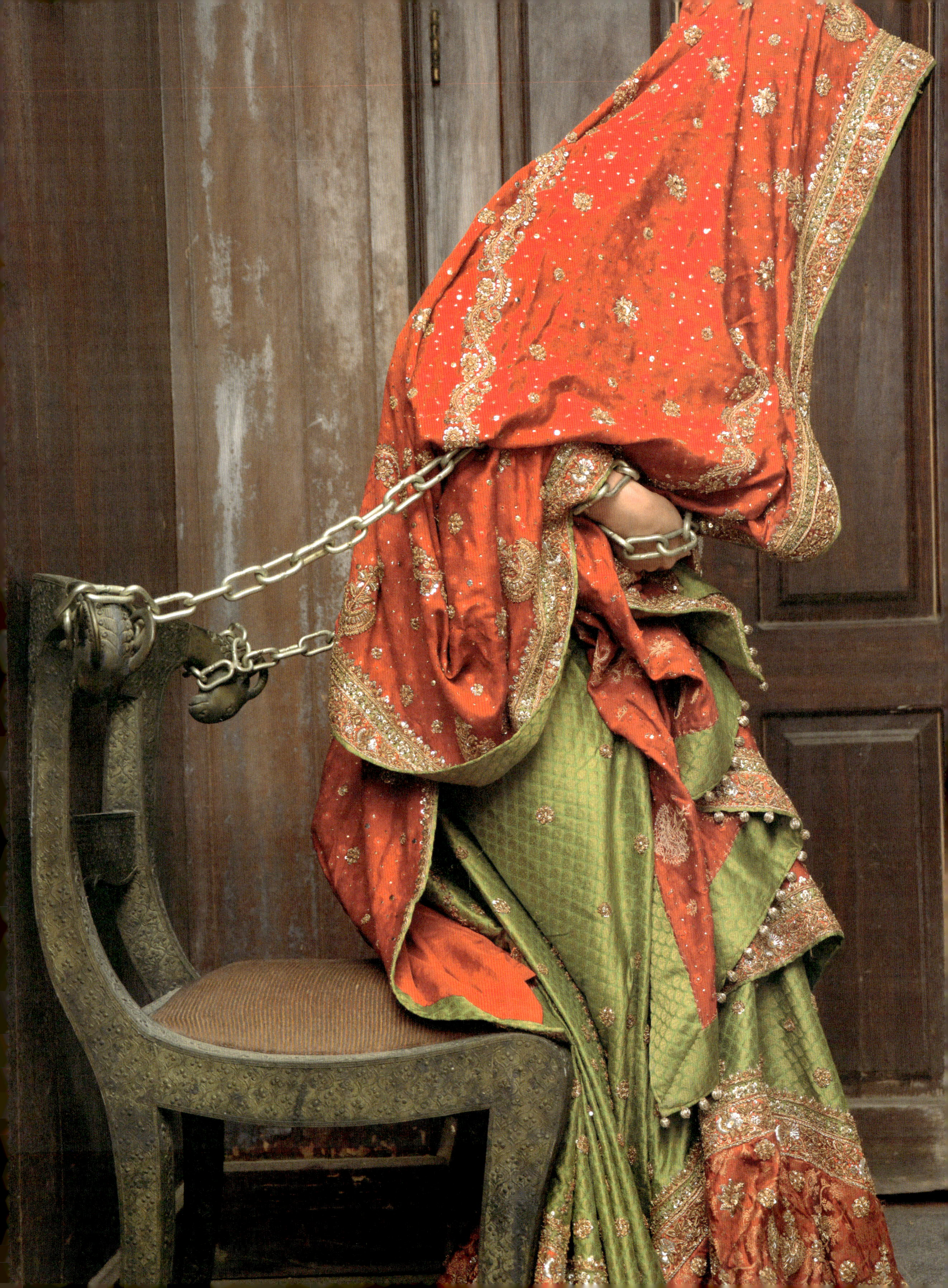

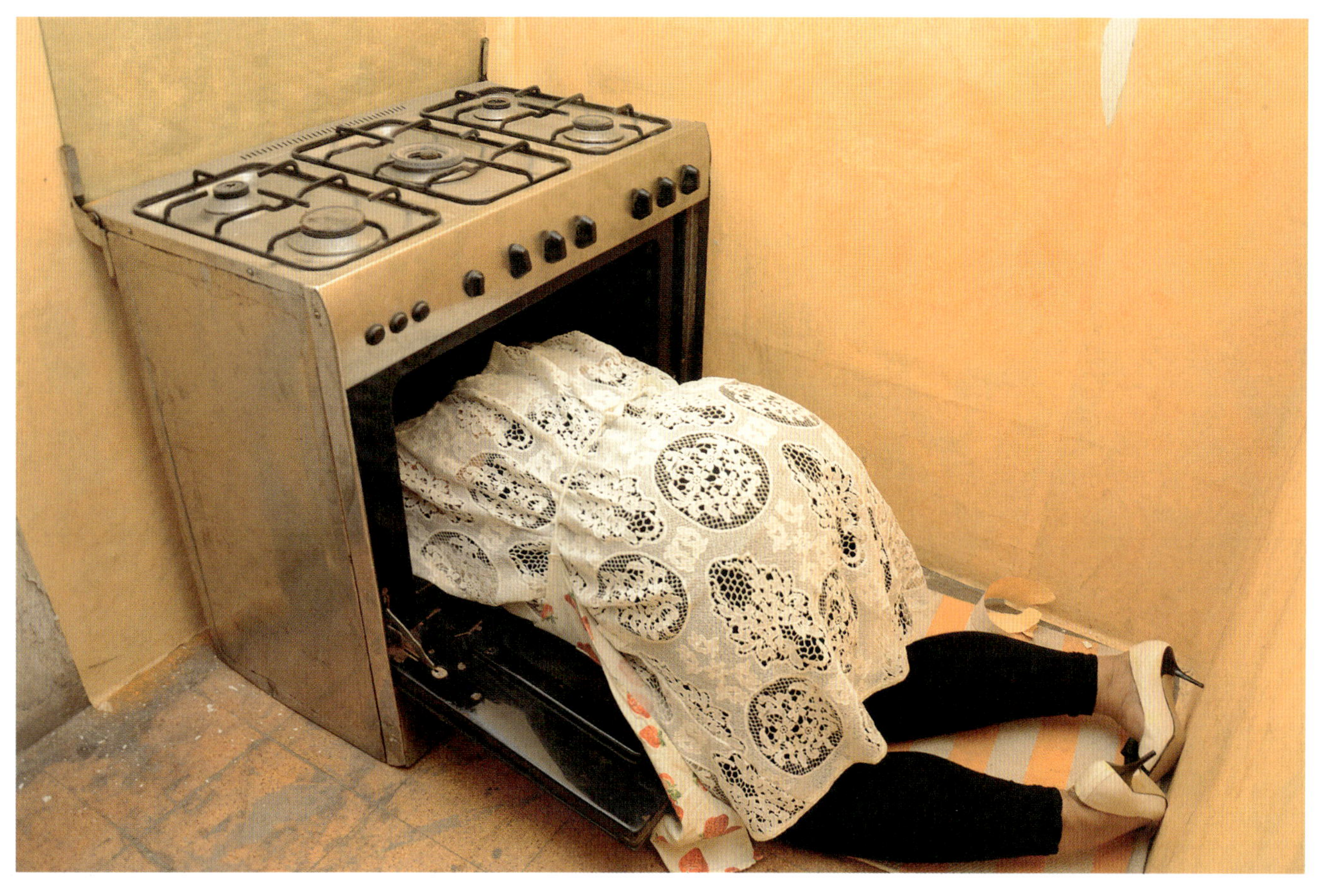

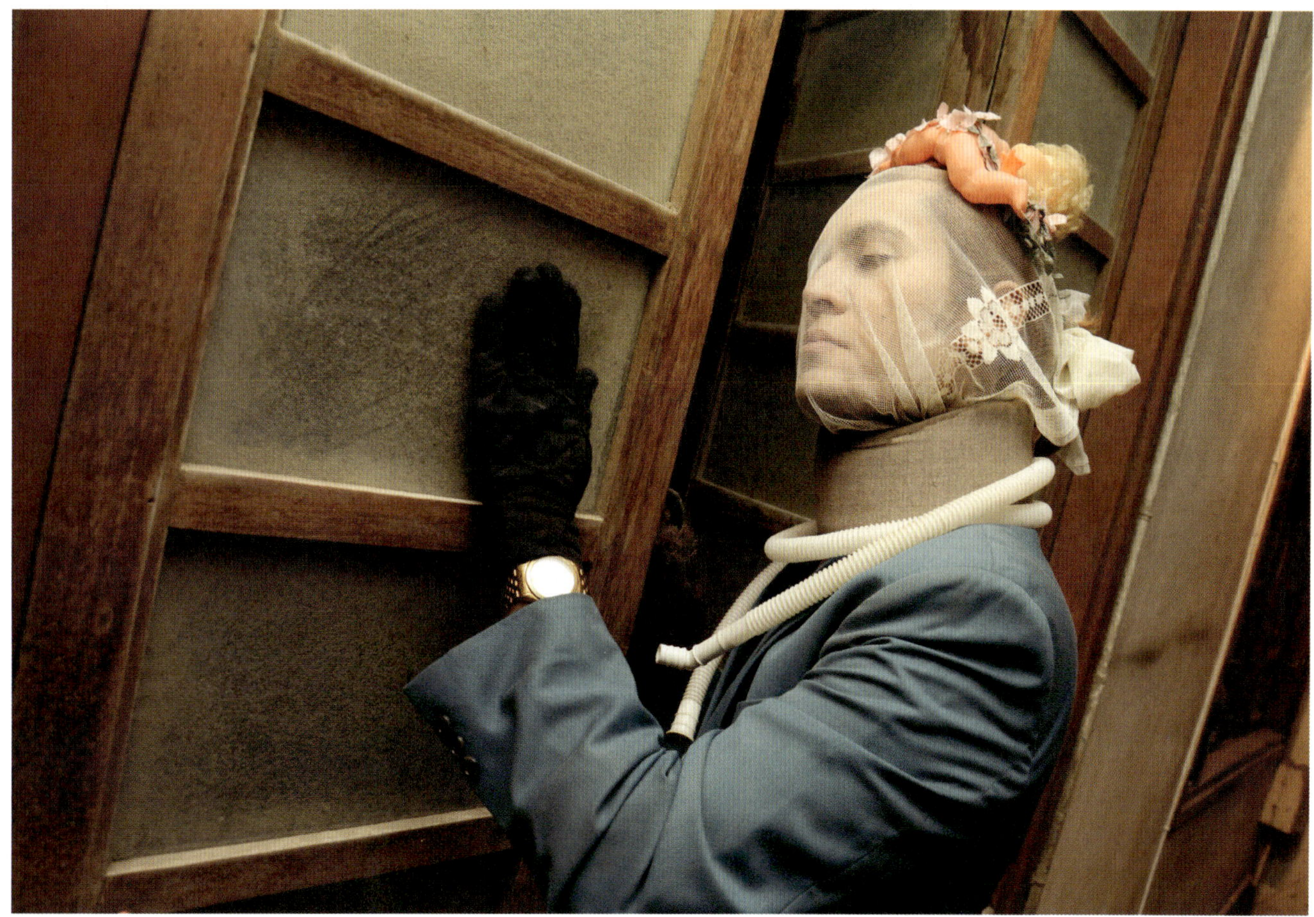

Photos by JY Photos

The Trojan Donkey | Virtual, 2020

Curated by Sara Vaqar Pagganwala, Adam Fahy-Majeed and Amin Gulgee

The Trojan Donkey was conceived at the height of the global lockdown during the COVD-19 pandemic. This online exhibition, curated by Amin, Sara Vaqar Pagganwala and Adam Fahy-Majeed, focused on performance through video. Like the Trojan Horse of lore, Sara, Adam and Amin wished to infiltrate, but only to challenge stereotypes and preconceived ideas. The horse was replaced by a donkey for the title because it was, for the curators, a symbol of Karachi: stubborn yet fleet and resilient. On April 25, 2020, from 9:18 pm to 11:13 pm (Pakistan Standard Time), the curators uploaded 80 works from 25 countries, some live, onto a dedicated Facebook page. Included was a two-channel video by Australian artist Alana Victoria Hunt which narrows in on Donald Trump's gesturing hands during his inaugural address at the US Capitol building. In ORLAN's 2018 video *Pétition contre la mort* (Petition Against Death), the French artist passionately calls for an uprising against death. Cameroonian writer Lionel Manga wanders through a marketplace in Douala reading aloud the poem *L'Acte de respirer* (The Act of Breathing) by Congolese author Sony Lab'ou Tansi (1947-1995), who died of AIDS during that pandemic. In Maha Minhaj's *Thinking About You,* the Pakistani artist fidgets on a chair, then slides to her knees, resting her head on the chair's seat, before crawling between its legs. In a world where populism is on the rise, and political poles drift further apart, platforms such as Facebook can sometimes exasperate divisions. For their part, Amin, Sara and Adam wished to use the social networking site to bring artists together in a time of shared plague and isolation. Ironically, the post-show Zoom webinar, also posted on Facebook, was hacked. The panelists from North America, Europe, Africa, Asia and Australia were forced to listen to an anonymous, five-minute outpouring of racist vitriol. In the end, this hateful intrusion only added to their discussion.

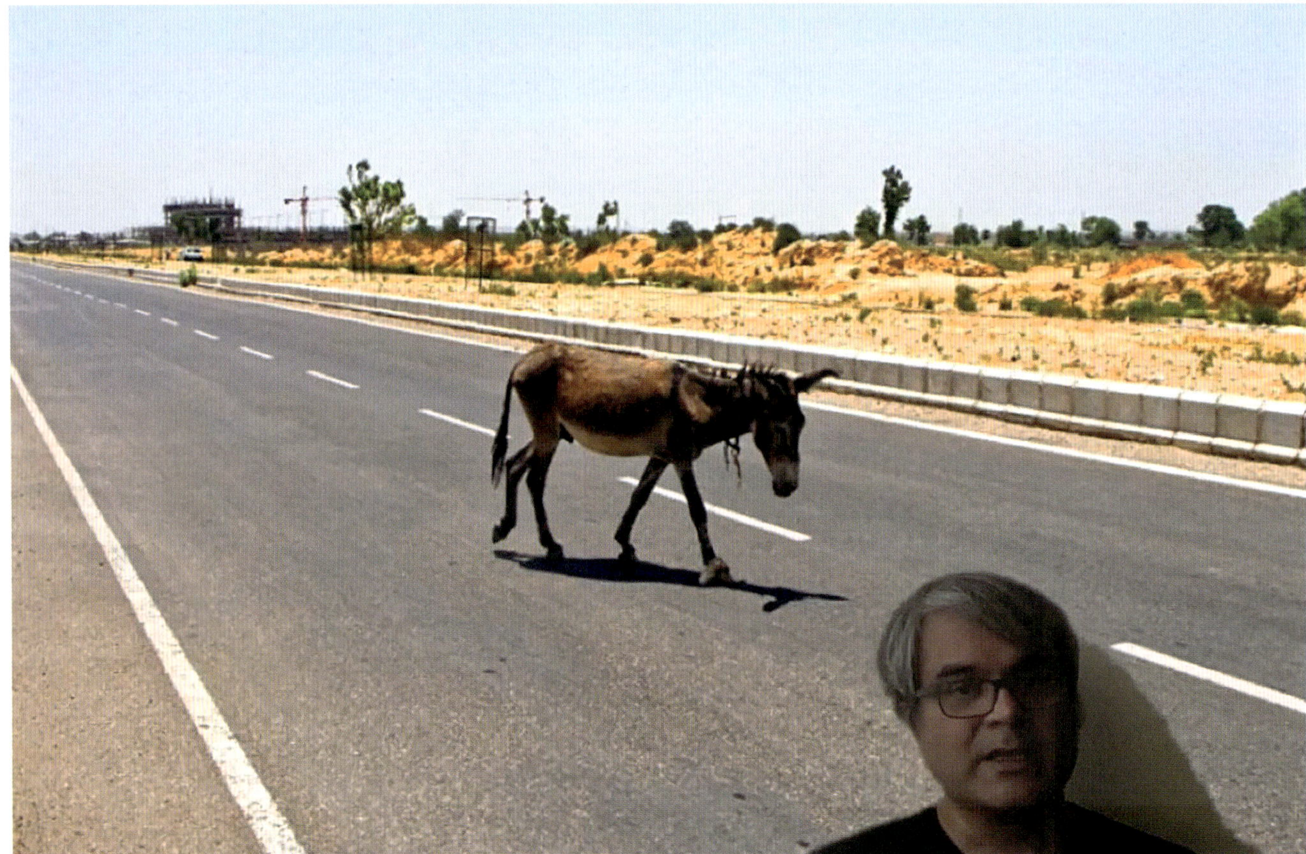

Still courtesy Raqs Media Collective

If These Walls Could Talk | Karachi, 2021

Curated by Sara Vaqar Pagganwala and Amin Gulgee
Village Restaurant

In May 2020, as the lockdown in Pakistan due to the spread of the coronavirus was eased, Amin reconnected with a friend from high school who was running the Village Restaurant in the heart of Karachi. In its heyday in the progressive mid-1970s, this eatery specializing in Pakistani barbeque was the place to see and be seen. (In 2002, it also became infamous as the site of the kidnapping of the American journalist Daniel Pearl, who was later beheaded by terrorists.) Amin and his co-curator Sara Vaqar Pagganwala felt that the restaurant, silent witness to the city, was a fitting venue for *If These Walls Could Talk.* The audience remained in their cars and watched over 77 minutes of mute video and film projected upon a wall. The 34 works from 21 countries were also glimpsed by traffic roaring down Sharah-e-Faisal, one of the city's busiest boulevards. Organized into five sections (Perspective, Conflict, Marking, Loss and Quest), these brief, global visions formed a loose narrative. Pakistani filmmaker Jamil Dehlavi offered a clip from his 1975 movie *Towers of Silence*, a surrealistic tale of a boy haunted by his mother's death. Also screened was Sebastián Díaz Morales' *Boy and Plate*, in which a boy trudges up a Patagonian hill, battling a relentless wind with a piece of plywood. He then teeters precariously on a cliff's edge, staring defiantly into the gale, which brings tears to his eyes. Gordon Cheung's *30 May 2020 Minneapolis (History Glitch)* challenged the car-bound spectators, both parked or streaming past, with an image of a burning building slowly disintegrating. The artist had appropriated a news photo of a Minneapolis police station set ablaze after the death of George Floyd for his work. In her video, Heide Hatry, a New York-based artist who grew up in Germany at the peak of the Cold War, attempts to scale a wall, then falls.

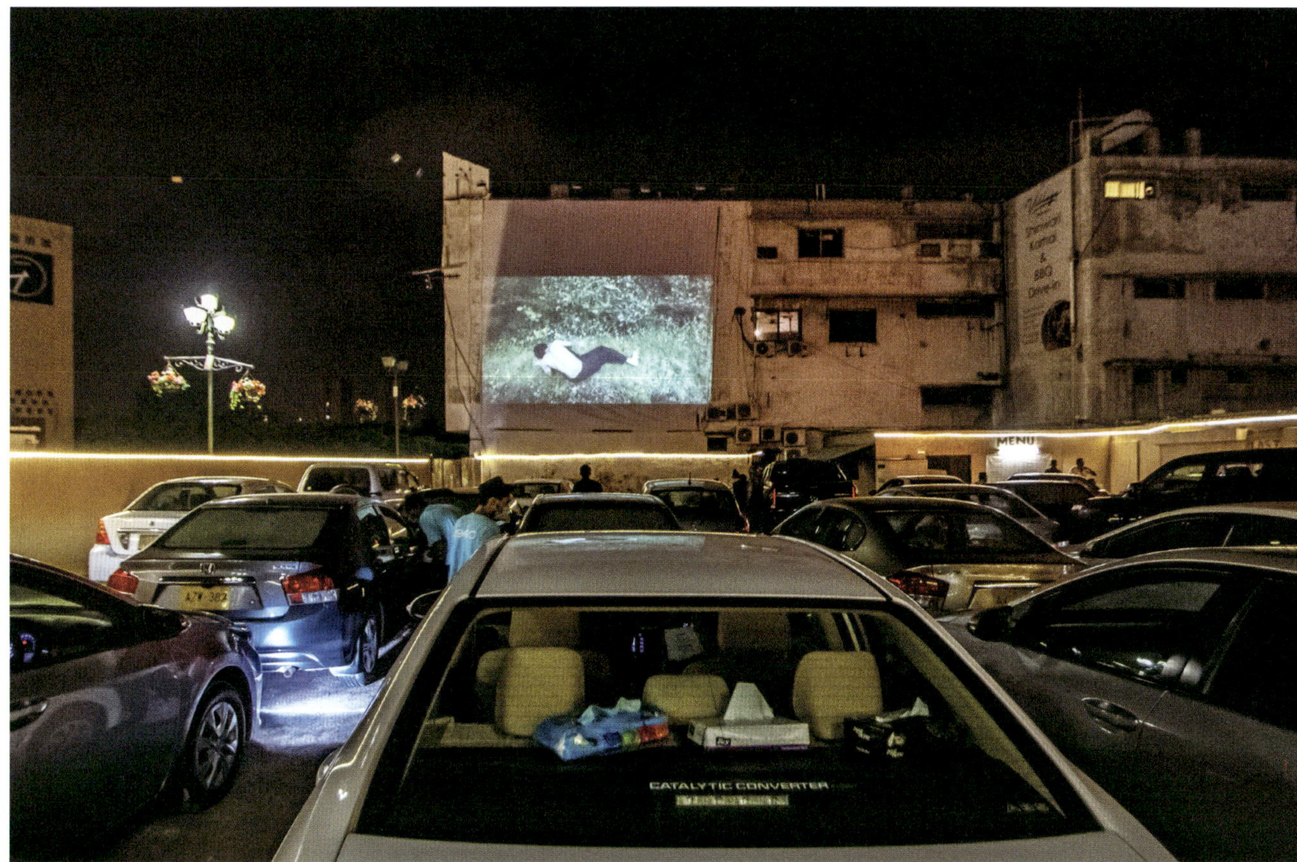

Photo by Humayun Memon

The Q Rickshaw Project | Karachi, 2022

Curated by Adam Fahy-Majeed and Amin Gulgee
Empress Market to Quaid-e-Azam Mausoleum

Amin and Adam Fahy-Majeed co-curated *The Q Rickshaw Project,* which was documented by a 10-minute, 11-second video. From 4:37 pm till 5:53 pm on January 30, 2020, nine performance works successively occurred in the backseat of Amin's *Q Rickshaw*, a tuk-tuk that he had recreated with a steel body trimmed with bells and a canopy of triangular mirror in 2015. Piloted by Anthony, Amin's assistant in his workshop, this rolling sculpture made its way through the frenetic streets of Karachi's bazaar, making nine predetermined stops, where the 14 performers (eleven women and three men) got on and off. Faryal Yazdanie presented *The Artist Is Light* with a female companion, who was dressed in a black *abaya* and *niqab*. Faryal's face was also covered by a *niqab*, but rather than a black *abaya*, she wore a white *shalwar,* her torso and arms wrapped in white bandages. As the performance progressed, Faryal continued to bind herself with the white gauze. Maham Chiragh performed *I am a trace you may not remember*. Her face and arms streaked with black, almost cartographic lines, she held a long brush, which she used to "paint" the passing road with invisible markings. As a member of the Ahmadiyya, a movement originating in Punjab in the late 19th century that is officially considered non-Muslim in Pakistan, the artist saw the gesture as an act of resistance against the erasure of her community. As the sun began to set, the shadow of the rickshaw grew longer. In the final performance, Manizhe Ali and her young daughter Zohray, decked out in brightly colored, embroidered outfits, enjoyed a picnic in the backseat of the rickshaw as it wound its way through Karachi's chaotic streets. This, for Manizhe, was their way of reclaiming the public space, which is so often denied to women in South Asia. The rickshaw picked them up at Capri Cinema, set on fire in 2012 by a mob enraged by the screening of a film rumored to be un-Islamic, then dropped them off at Mazar-e-Quaid, the mausoleum of Pakistan's founder.

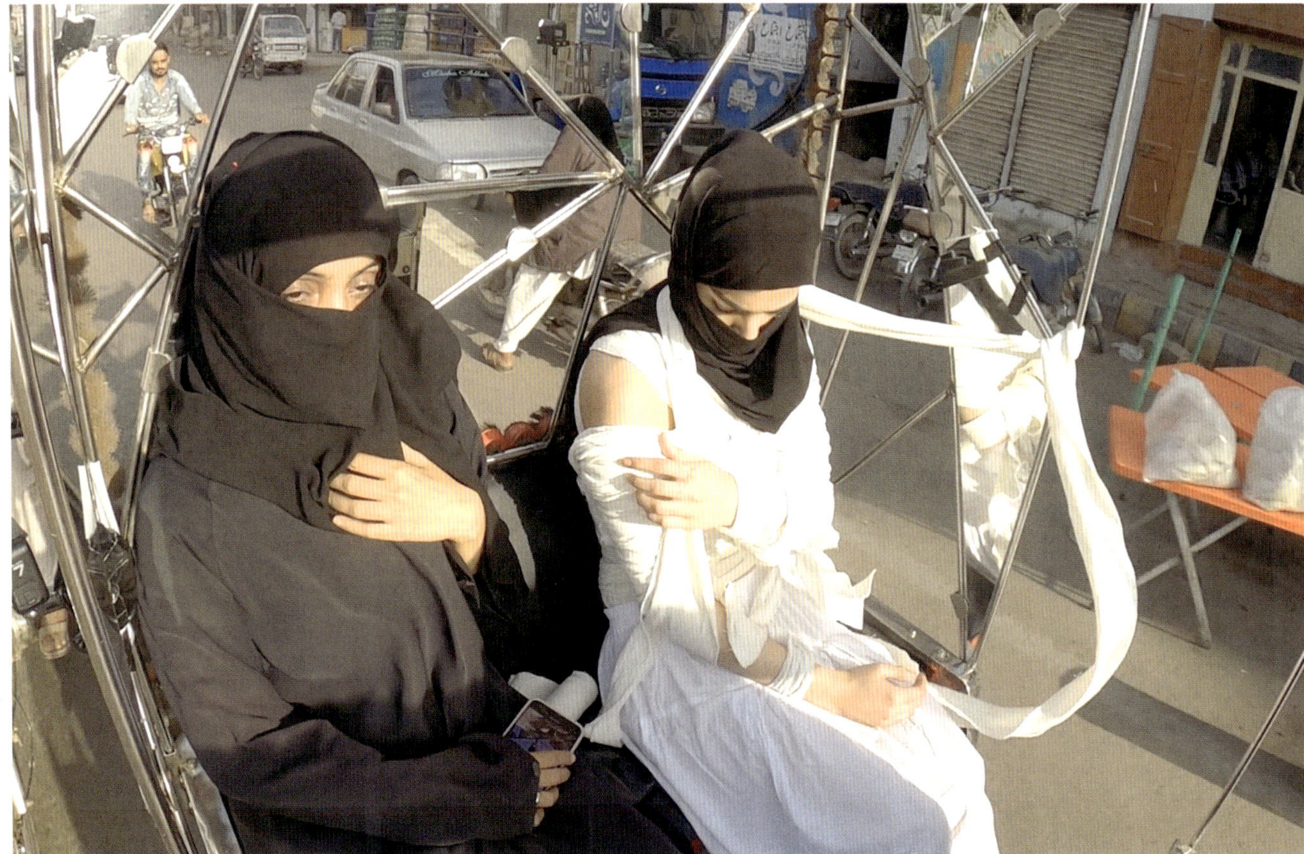

Stills courtesy Bilal Ghouri

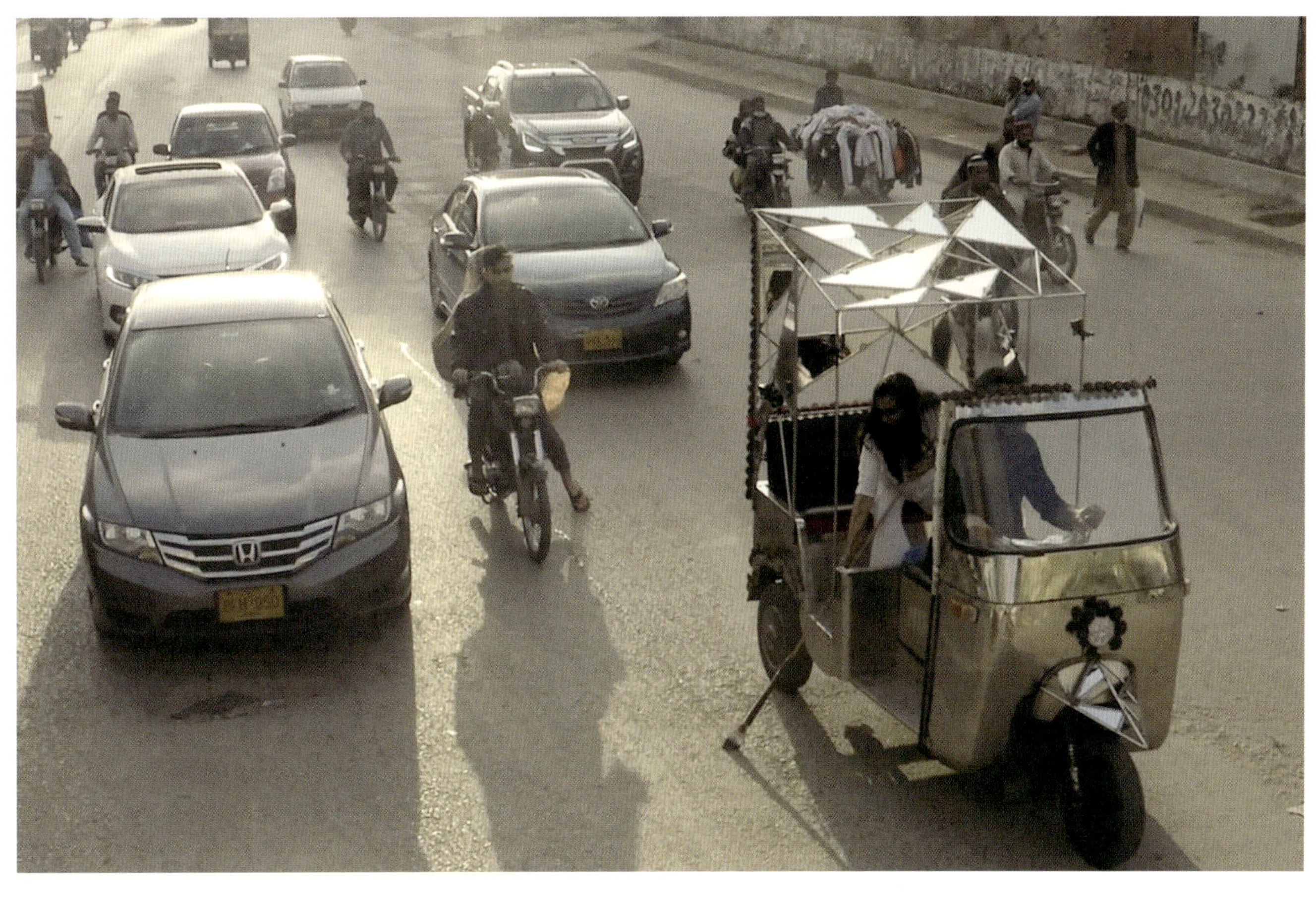

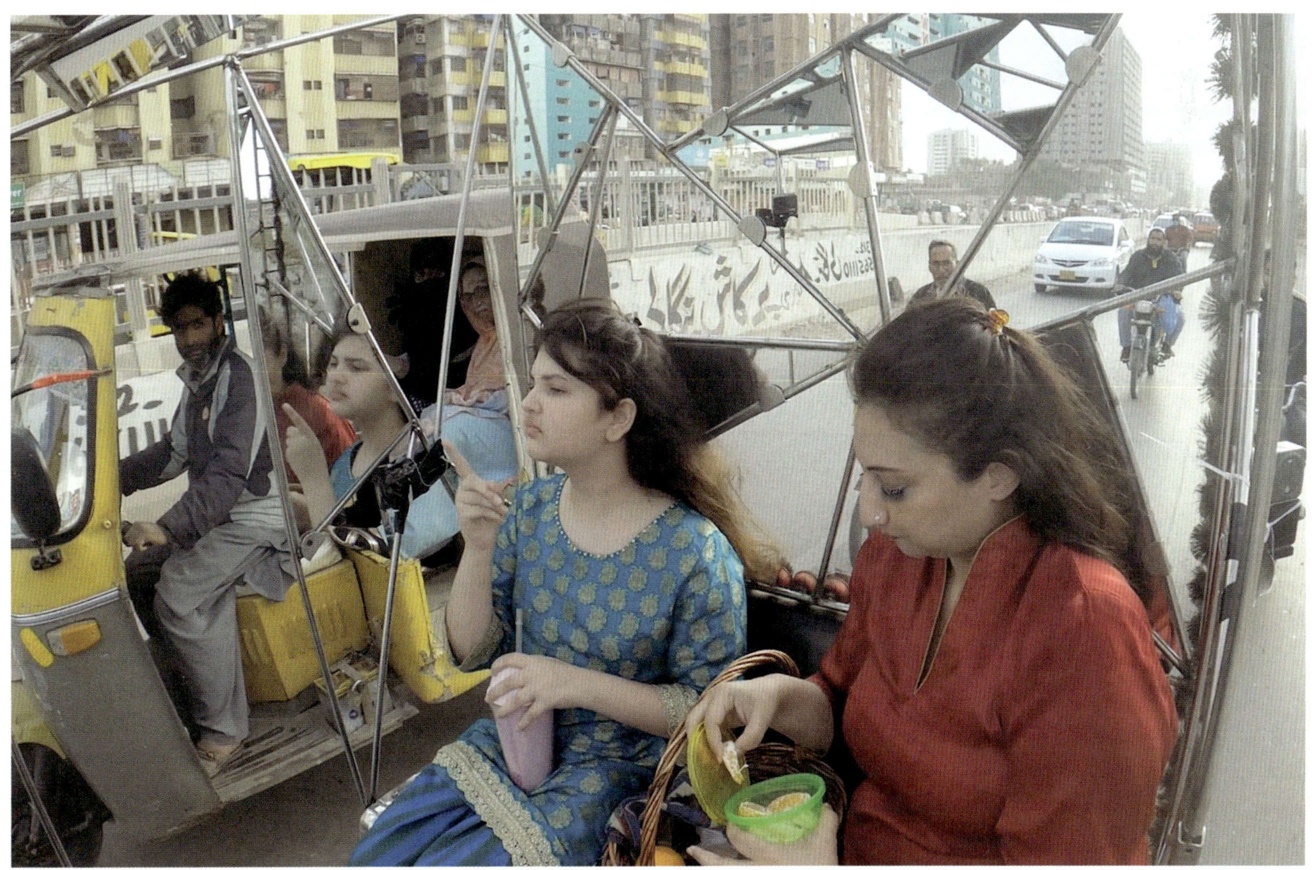

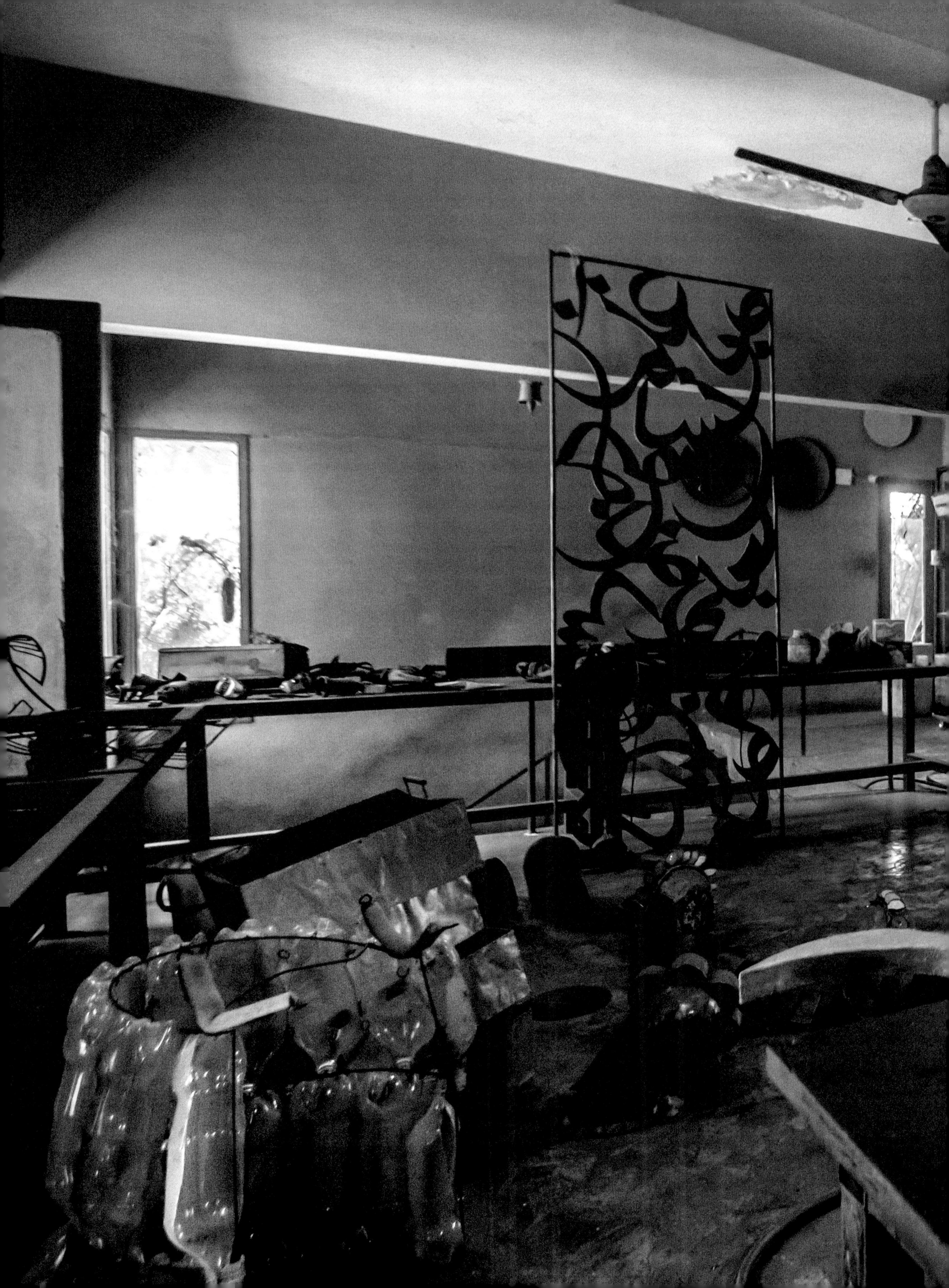

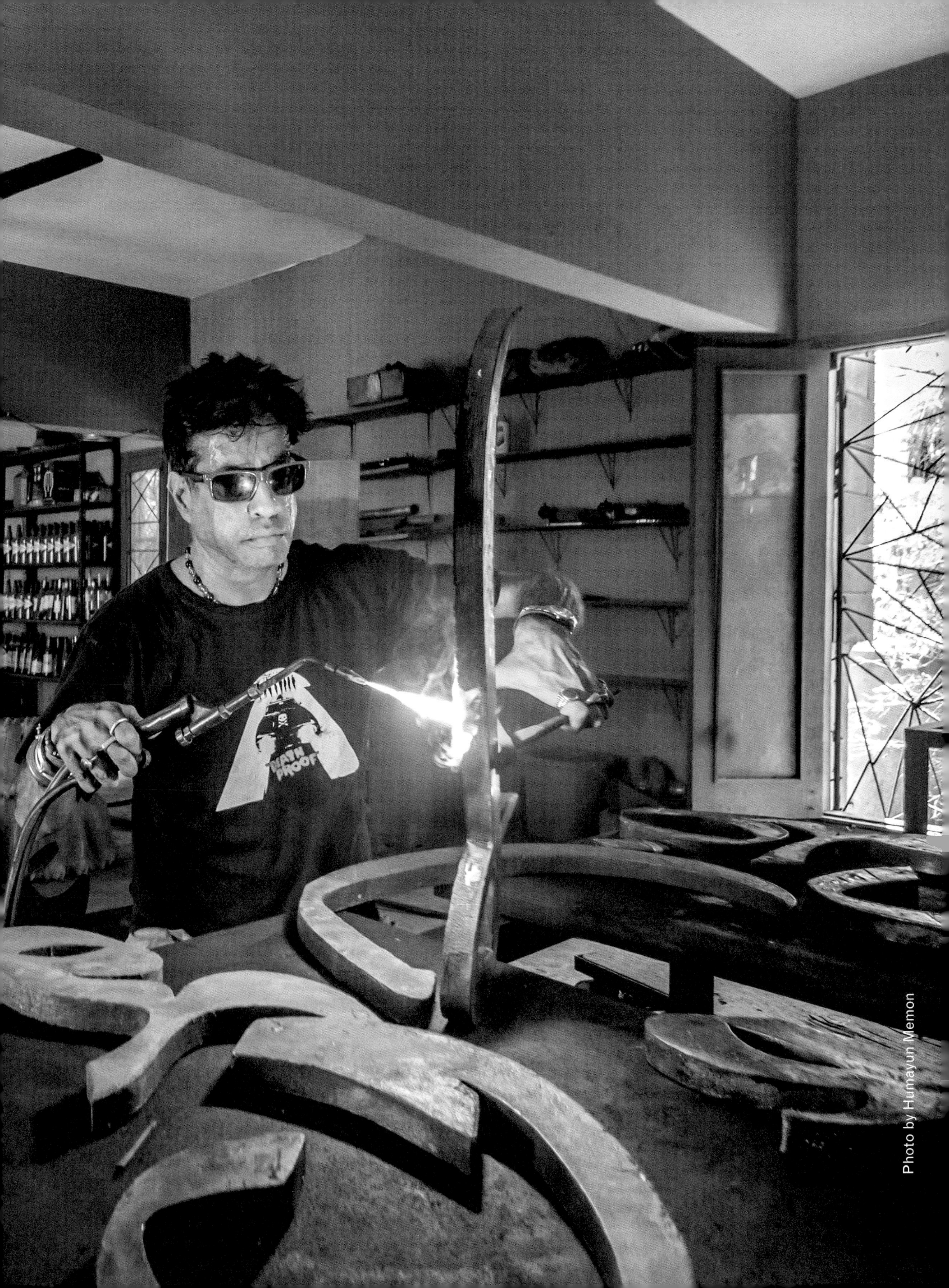

Photo by Humayun Memon

Amin Gulgee: The Universal and the Particular

Kishwar Rizvi

Amin Gulgee's sculptures are bold and complex. Hidden in the rough crevices, within the cracks of the roughly-hewn metal, in between the long sculpted fingers entwined in rope, and in the dark corners, is revealed the artist's world. His sculpture draws you in like the particles of metal dust clinging to its surface, and invites you to touch and to share its sensuality. Gulgee's work appeals to the senses of the viewer, although it would be wrong to deny its intellectual content. In this short essay I'd like to explore the formal richness of Gulgee's work and locate it within its art historical contexts. The plurality of Gulgee's sources of inspiration situates this work in the broader realm of turn of the millennium modernism. Amin Gulgee is a key representative of the exciting and challenging new artists emerging from Asia today.

Questions of identity sometimes shadow the depth of an artist's work, especially if that artist comes from outside the established centers of European and American modernism, namely London, Paris, and New York. Artists from Muslim countries, such as Pakistan, are expected to respond to both religious and nationalist ideologies, while engaging simultaneously with the wider discourses on tradition and modernity that continue to define the "developing" world. Amin Gulgee's work is without doubt a product of its cultural and historical contexts; however, his engagement with them is on his own terms. He engages with the artistic heritage of Pakistan but makes it contemporary by infusing it with new meaning through a range of formal strategies.

Gulgee's sculptural oeuvre is at once introspective and celebrative. The artist's primary dialogue is with his material, metal, that is skillfully manipulated by his crew of casters and metalworkers. Copper, his primary medium, allows Gulgee to explore a range of textures as well as tonalities. The artist creates an object "in the round," expecting the viewer to literally traverse the space surrounding the work. The pliability of copper allows the artist to compose forms that are at once mobile and intricate. The pinkish hue of the metal when it is highly polished gives the illusion that the sculpture holds within it a life as yet hidden and incomplete (fig. 1). With great subtlety, Gulgee further animates the metal and extracts from it verses in praise of God, as in the case of his calligraphic pieces, and the gestures of myriad dancers, as in his series *Touching My Face* (fig. 2).

The metal is transformed into shapes as varied as the linear and textual, as well as the figurative and gestural. Gulgee's calligraphic pieces often concentrate on a particular verse, such as the Surah Rahman that he explored in earlier works (fig. 3). More successful, however, are pieces such as *Towers II* whose tall, rectangular shapes, are formed by a series of geometric words, some of them spelling "Allah" (fig. 4). The repetition of the word and its shifting axis are in tense dialogue with the rigid verticality of the shafts forming the towers. Similarly tense and evocative is the conceptual juxtaposition between their shape, reminiscent of the Twin Towers in New York, and the calligraphy, which may be seen as a reference to the Islamic militants responsible for their destruction.

The artist is without doubt reactive to events in his world, and he may choose to confront them head on or let them sublimate toward abstraction and universals. Gulgee's work shies away from overtly political themes, although that does not make it any less political. He is more comfortable exploring personal stories – be they wrought through religion

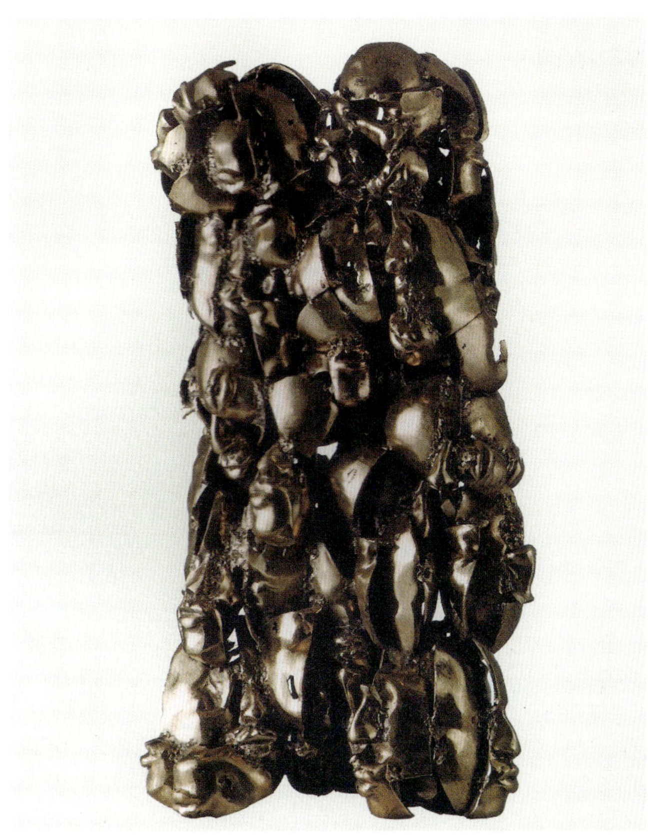

Fig. 1. *47: The Wall III*, 2007. Copper and bronze. 78.7 × 30.4 × 10 cm. Photo courtesy Galeri Petronas

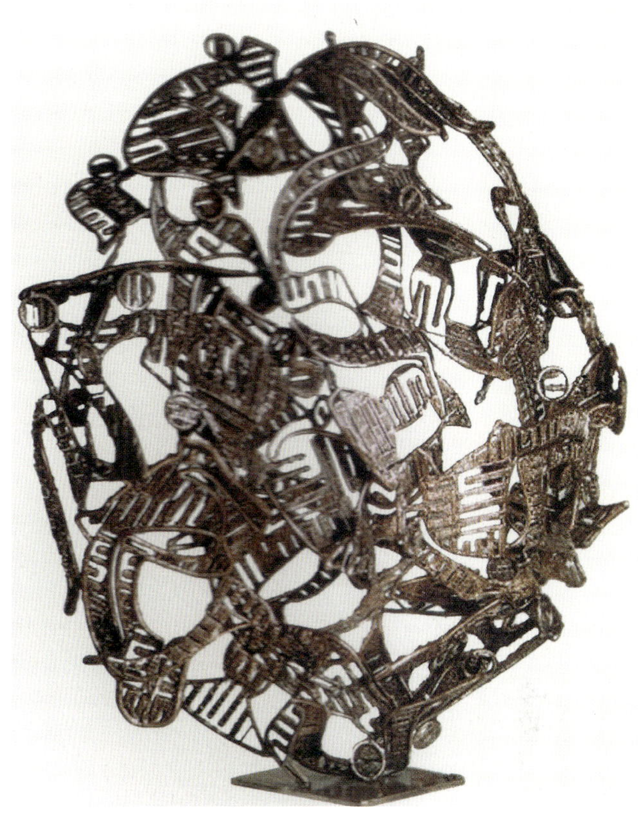

Fig. 3. *Ocean II*, 2004. Copper. 91.4 × 91.4 × 17.7 cm. Photo courtesy Galeri Petronas

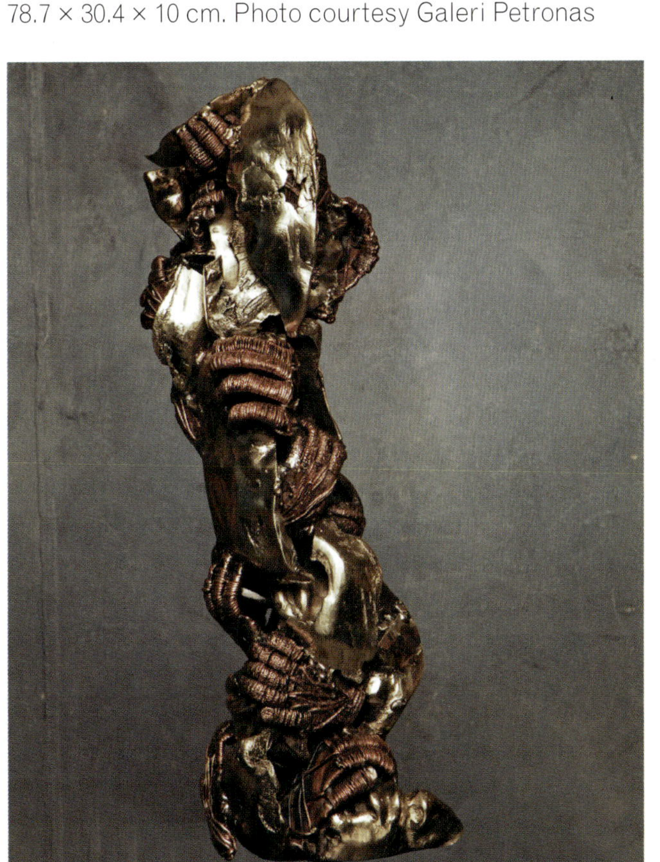

Fig. 2. *Touching My Face III*, 2006. Copper and bronze. 63.5 × 25.4 × 25.4 cm. Photo courtesy Galeri Petronas

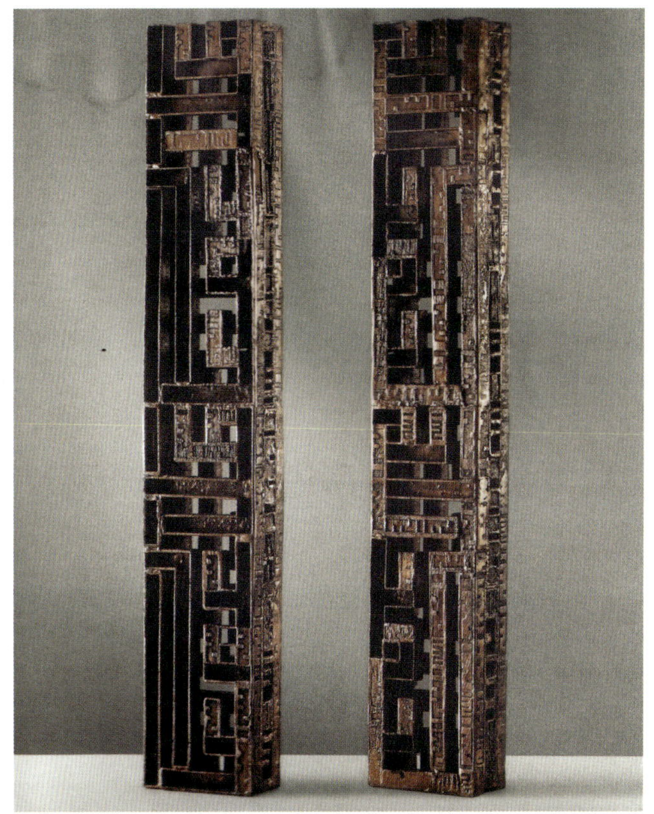

Fig. 4. *Towers II*, 2008. Copper. 109.2 × 20.3 × 12.7 cm (each work). Photo courtesy Galeri Petronas

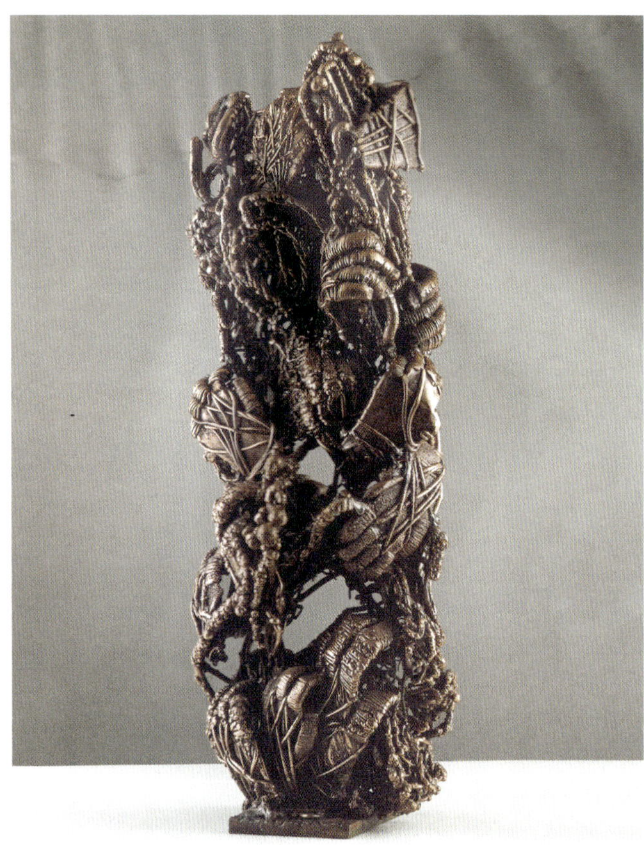

Fig. 5. *Ripping the Bird's Nest I*, 2008. Copper and bronze. 63.5 × 26.6 × 17.7 cm. Photo courtesy Galeri Petronas

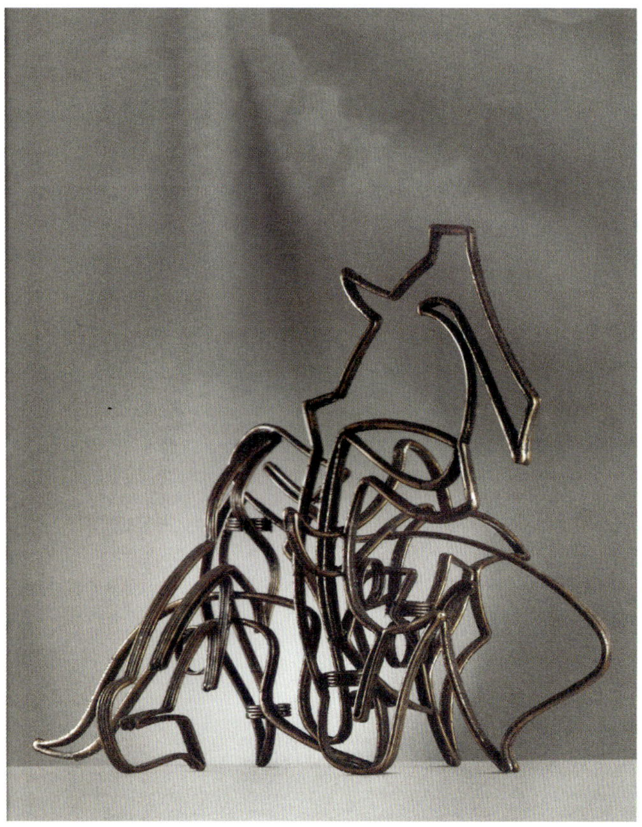

Fig. 6. *Embedded Line III*, 2008, Copper. 76.2 × 114.3 × 76.2 cm. Photo courtesy Galeri Petronas

or geography. In his figurative pieces, Gulgee draws inspiration from a wide range of iconic works, from the Buddha to Louise Bourgeois' *Spider*. The images may refer to older works of art, but the stories they narrate belong to Gulgee. The personal and intimate nature of the figurative sculptures is not surprising, given that Gulgee has used his own body as a model, for example his own face and hands in *47: The Wall III* and *Ripping the Bird's Nest I*, respectively (fig. 5). The references are nonetheless mutable and instable, as they move through the very history of art. One may wonder about the Kufic calligraphic style or whether the faces are inspired by Gandharan sculpture. What unites Gulgee's work is a sense of repose and spirituality; in them the local and personal are overlaid with the transcendent and spiritual.

In his newer pieces, Gulgee repeats themes that have permeated his work in the past twenty years. Three formal themes continue but with fundamental breaks from the past. The natural world of plants, beautifully modeled on the vegetation in his garden in Karachi; the interplay of hands and faces, that are constantly searching, yet without eyes or an obvious goal; the additive and reductive units of calligraphy, sometimes rendered geometrically and sometimes florally. The most exciting change is in the calligraphic series that appear to have moved away from literality. That is to say, Gulgee is still interested in playing with the form of the rendered text, but without the use of recognizable letters or words, as in the series *Embedded Line III* (fig. 6). This abstraction frees him from the Qur'anic verses that were his earlier subjects, allowing him to dig deeper into their meanings by abstracting their forms.

The internalisation of knowledge is most powerfully expressed in the simple form of the vertical circle, *Cosmic Chappati* (fig. 7). Knowing Gulgee's earlier work, one may place this in the category of calligraphies – however, it is now "illiterate." The circle may be understood as a cosmic form as well as a Platonic ideal. The name is playful, a reference to the humble chappati (flatbread), yet follows in the tradition defining humor as a source of gaining Divine knowledge. The universality of the circular shape is called into question by the particularities of its making, namely, the cords forming the concentric circles are unevenly rendered and often the divisions between the cords are blurred. In this profound tension, between the whole and its individual parts, in its form and its implicit meaning, Gulgee has eloquently captured the intellectual and sensual aspects of sculpture itself.

Amin Gulgee's sculpture resists simple characterisation, and in so doing, is liberated from the tendencies to define an artist by national, stylistic,

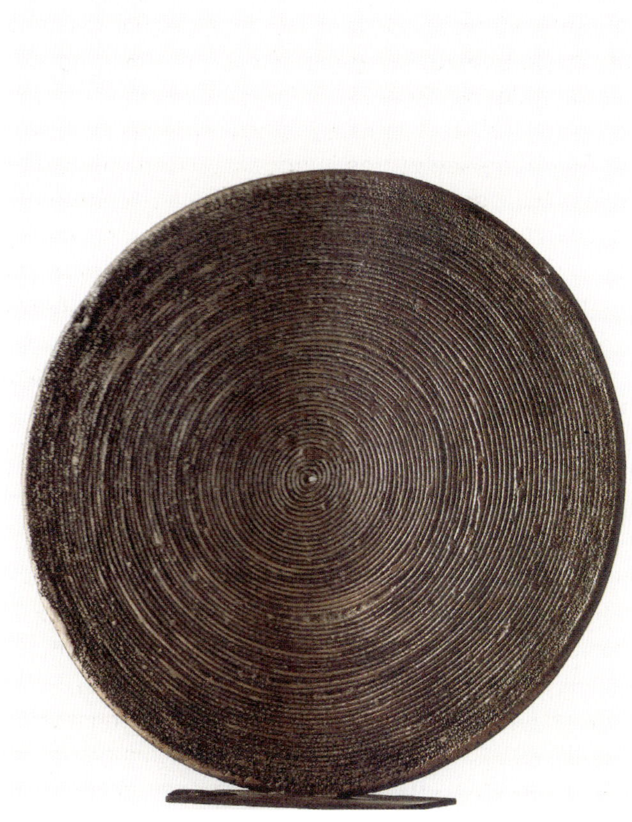

Fig. 7. *Cosmic Chapati*, 2008. Copper. 48.2 × 45.7 × 8.8 cm. Photo courtesy Galeri Petronas

or even, chronological, labels. In this resistance, he naturally invokes the most successful of contemporary works of art that are simultaneously local and universal, that respond to both tradition and modernity, and that have numerous points of reference. The forms Gulgee thus creates have multiple foci, textures and tones. They are an invitation to discover the artist's delight in his art and the passion it allows him to express.

This essay first appeared in the exhibition catalogue *Amin Gulgee: Drawing the Line*, Galeri Petronas, Kuala Lumpur, 2007.

Play Me: Conversations with Amin Gulgee

Gemma Sharpe

"The happy interaction of man and architecture," reads the headline for a 1990 article in *Dawn* on the occasion of Amin Gulgee's exhibition at the Indus Gallery in Karachi. "Amin Gulgee is full of surprises," the article opens.[1] Writing under the pseudonym Giovanni Battista, the author goes on to sketch Gulgee's extraordinary life: a joint major in art history and economics at Yale, a peripatetic itinerary "schlepping a suitcase full of crystals and copper" from Islamabad to Washington, D.C. and eventually a Brooklyn loft where he holed himself up for a month to embellish the space in a mosaic of arabesques in tile and glass. By the time the article was written however, Gulgee had moved on. He was already at work on a new mural on the roof of his Karachi home. Whereas the Brooklyn mosaics reflected their surrounding atmosphere of moribund industry and New York gothic, the Karachi rooftop was brighter, quite literally sunnier. It was also, very literally closer to home and combined local minakari-style glasswork, mirrors from Sindhi textiles, ceramics from Thatta. A large, sculpted eye at the center of the ensemble gazed out over Karachi's skyline and Gulgee's rediscovered sense of home. As Gulgee related in a 1990 interview with John McCarry in *The Leader*, at first "I didn't intend the mosaic to be so big, but then the materials began to take over. In the end, I was just their instrument. It was like the materials were using me to say something."[2]

This theme is everywhere in Gulgee's work: an intermedial and interpersonal connection between people, objects, spaces, mediums, and materials. Sometimes as play, conversation, or even as a fight. Consider for example a more recent ensemble, *Play Me* (fig. 1), performed with Sara Vaqar Pagganwala as part of the Karachi Art Summit in 2017. Both Gulgee and Pagganwala sit at a square games board in front of the National Museum in Karachi, the grid of the board echoing the latticed brutalism of the museum's architecture behind them. Amid these visual and spatial interactions however, the interaction between Gulgee and Pagganwala is unclear. The crowd appears mesmerised by a game with secret rules. At the center of all this, each piece on the board has its own mysterious quality. Look closer and see Gulgee's own face echoed in these sculptural pieces—the subject, object and maker of the game. The intersection of interaction, opponent and accomplice, playing and talking; *saying something*.

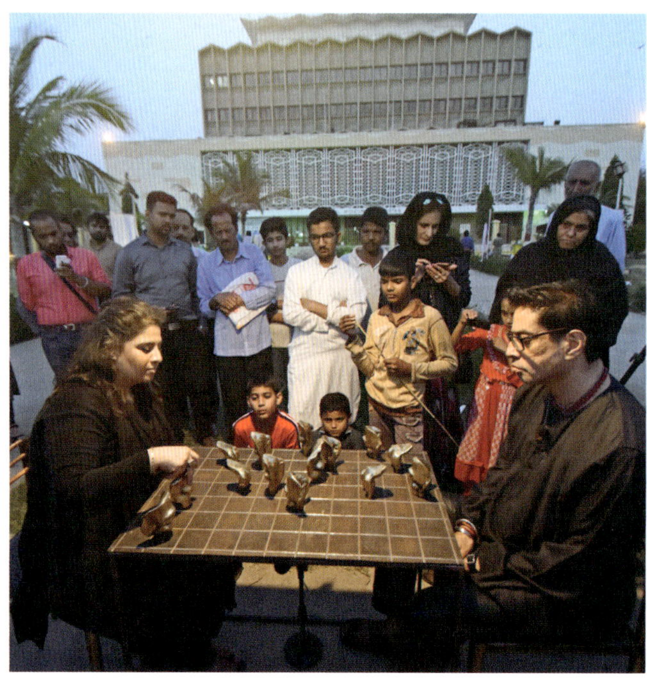

Fig. 1. *Play Me*, 2017. Performance. Karachi Art Summit, National Museum, Karachi. Photo by Humayun Memon

Gulgee plays Abramović

"*Yes, darling, you're so special. Everybody loves you. Like performance couldn't have existed without you!*" This is how Amin Gulgee might introduce himself to the great heroine of contemporary art performance, Marina Abramović. It would be the introduction of a comrade: a fellow traveller in the self-sacrificing and self-honoring practice of artist-led performance. A conversation both prickly and warm, replete with identification but also significant differences. There are striking comparisons to be made between Gulgee and Abramović as performance artists. They execute their performances with equal firmness, even severity, along with a shared tendency towards a slow and ritualized affect. The formal theme of the conversation (or silent conversation) appears in both artists' performance practices. Consider for example, the aforementioned *Play Me* by Gulgee and Abramović's iconic *The Artist is Present* performed at MoMA in 2010 or the 1977 work, *Imponderabilia* in which two naked figures stand opposite one another across a doorway, and through which museum visitors must awkwardly navigate. Both of these artist-performers also engage in a version of what Claire Bishop calls "delegated performance," wherein they bring other people's bodies into their work—to perform a professional role as models or actors, as in Gulgee's staged performances *Alchemy* (2000) and *Where's the Apple, Joshinder?* (2014), or engage in sideways tasks: the *friend* performing the role of a *wife*, the curator a *narrator*, the *photographer* a participant-guest.[3]

There is also a less colloquial, even violent tendency in both artists' performances, often directed at their own bodies. In *Rhythm 5* (1974), Abramović lay within a burning star that sucked away the oxygen from around her, causing rescuers to have to rush in. In *Rhythm 0* (1974), she provided audience members with an array of objects including pens and an axe—and the invitation to use them against her. Gulgee's 2018 performance, *Paint Me* (fig. 2), likewise saw him lying on the concrete floor of Karachi's Canvas Gallery with the invitation to audience members to paint his semi-clothed body, which lay vulnerable and exposed on a blood-red mattress. But in actuality, the comparison between these two artists only goes so far. For one thing, the roots of their performances run through very different creative soils. Abramović, for her part, emerged within a generation of artists who during the late 1960s and 1970s worked to disrupt and dismantle traditional mediums like painting and sculpture in favor of a more eclectic and less rigorously defined approach to medium. Vito Acconci's canon-shifting *Trademarks* (1970), for example, saw him biting down on parts of his own body and then inking and printing the toothy indentations, forging an intermedial space between printmaking and performance. Abramović's practice likewise turns the body into a kind of sculpture, forging a subversive alternative to that vaunted millennia-old tradition. At heart, these tactics were an attack on the sanctity of traditional mediums: painting, sculpture, the print, etc., separating them from Gulgee's performances and events in public spaces, which are less a means to dismantle any given artistic medium than to hold them side-by-side: in conversation.

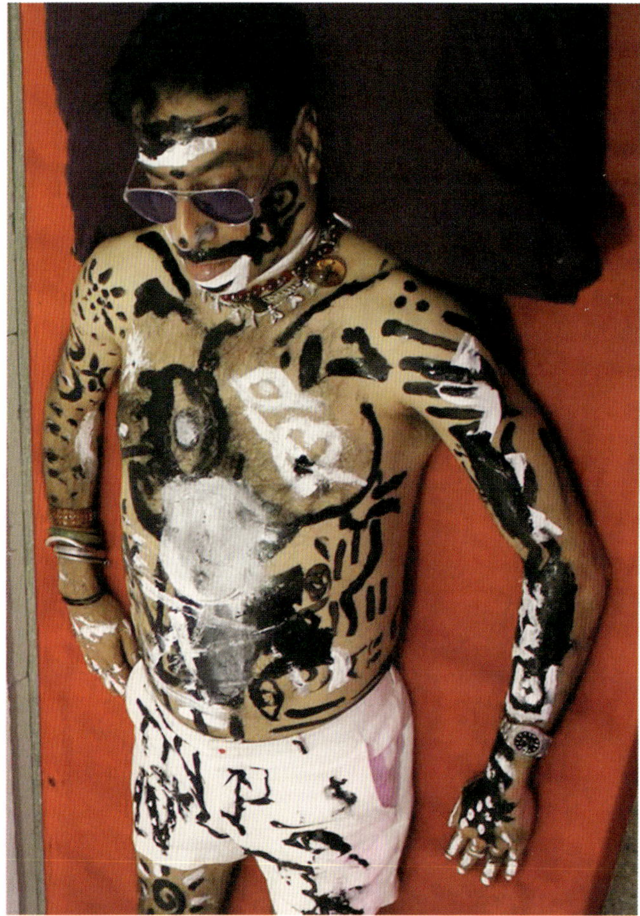

Fig. 2. *Paint Me*, 2018. Performance. *Mixed Tape [1]*, Canvas Gallery, Karachi. Photo courtesy Canvas Gallery

Moreover, to include the medium of *theater* as part of the dialogue. For the post-medium artists of Abramović's generation, theater and narrative were largely ruled out from their experiments, jettisoned along with traditional mediums for their associations with naturalism, description and literalism. By contrast, the theatrical and the narrative play a fundamental role in the logic of Gulgee's performances, reflecting an historical commingling of contemporary art performance with theater in Pakistan. Until the 1990s, contemporary art performance is rare in Pakistan, discounting anomalies including Iqbal Geoffrey's conceptual games and Ismail Gulgee's live painting events including a painting performance set to music alongside Greek artist Economos at the Karachi Arts Council in 1980.[4] Perhaps for the sake of utility but nevertheless in a way that is significant, the Gulgee-Economos performance utilized the tools of theater: stage, proscenium, a stationary watching audience.

As performances made by contemporary artists in Pakistan, including Amin Gulgee, gained more prominence over the 2000s and 2010s, a relationship to theater persisted, providing as it did a legible and productive set of tools to artists moving this practice slowly into the mainstream: Gulgee, Uzma Durrani, Shalale Jamil and Sarah Mumtaz, for example, are all artists who deploy the tools of theater, from costume and voice to an importance placed on staging, character, and a storyline (or fragment of a storyline). They follow in the footsteps of a dynamic history of theater in Pakistan, from the remnants of Shakespeare in the British colonial curriculum to the legacy of 19th century Parsee theater in Bombay and the multilingual theater of the modern period.[5] As Asma Mundrawala has outlined, conservative hostility to theater in postcolonial Pakistan meant that the form found less traction here than in post-Partition India.[6] It did however find some space to grow in Arts Councils and cultural centers and Pakistan's many "little magazines" of the 1950s and 1960s where new plays by local authors could be distributed and read in print—everything from high art to slapstick comedy. During the 1980s, another tradition emerged out of the agitations of the Zia dictatorship. Theater took to the streets in stripped down narrative interventions into the public sphere and political consciousness. At the same time, the kind of bold, classical, and romantic spectacle seen in Gulgee's performances find connection to the resplendent aesthetics of Sheema Kermani's combinations of activist theater and classical dance during the 1980s, and the radical production of plays like *Anji* performed in 1985 by the activist theater group Tehrik-e-Niswan that deployed classical and folk music and dance against the dictatorship and conventional "drawing room farces."[7] There are threads of Gulgee's performance practice growing here, not least in the productive crossover between ritual, theatrical and dance traditions. Kermani's example opens another point of contrast in Gulgee and Abramović's hypothetical conversation; that of the influence ór better *interaction* between Gulgee's performances and the fields of dance and costume, or more properly in this case, fashion.

When Gulgee returned to Karachi in 1990—and as he writes in a recent essay on the topic—the city was literally exploding—with the internecine political violence of the decade but also, and perhaps relatedly, a new energy in the arts. The subversive gestures of Kermani and others' work during the 1980s became a chaotic, heady unleashing of new experimentation. As Gulgee notes, the emerging "Zia Generation, which included me, could exhale. There was great energy in the air and the feeling that all was possible."[8] Fashion likewise bounced into life after the Zia years, carrying Gulgee along with it. Through his experimental jewelry, Gulgee joined the fashion world during the 1990s, later taking up the inherent performativity of the runway and his collaborations with designers and models to produce works like *Alchemy* (fig. 3), where theater, fashion, and dance come together in three acts. Recalling the event, which was based on the metals bronze, silver and gold, Gulgee describes his own part in the opening, bronze-themed act: "I covered my body in clay and clamped a double-sided bronze self-portrait mask weighing three kilos seventy grams onto my head and danced to a morning raga. I can still remember the weight of the headgear and hearing myself breathe beneath it. It was a transportive experience."[9]

Here then, is the fourth element: sculpture. Gulgee's performances are unthinkable without their sculptural players, which remain as sculptures in the classical sense rather than mere props. Whereas

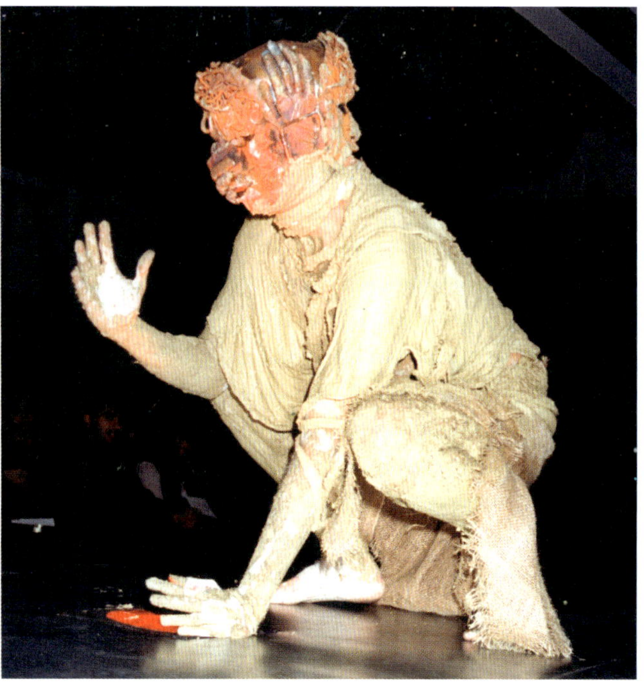

Fig. 3. *Alchemy*, 2000. Performance. ArtFest, Sheraton Hotel, Karachi. Photo by JY Photo

Marina Apa's practice thoroughly evades the world of theater, dance and for the most part fashion in order to *displace* the traditional medium of sculpture with body-as-sculpture, Gulgee takes on those forms yet maintains and embraces their respective wholeness. His point, contra Abramović, is not to smash artistic traditions but to put them *into conversation* with one another. And alongside a collaborative community of dancers, designers, models, and friends: interactions between elements that become bigger and grander than the sum of their parts.

Gulgee plays Ali Imam

I am not so angry these days
Ali Imam[10]

When the late painter Ali Imam opened the Indus Gallery in Karachi in 1971, his intervention signalled an institutional shift in the direction of independence for the city's art world. Skim through old copies of *Dawn*, *The Pakistan Times* or Pakistan's various cultural and literary magazines of the 1950s and 1960s, and a picture emerges of an art ecology played out between private spaces like homes, cafes and hotels, and official sites of diplomacy including metropolitan Arts Councils, British Council libraries, US cultural centers, and the dozens of consulates that made space available for local and international artists to show their work. While these spaces were important for artists in a fledgling art world that offered limited other options, endless ribbon cuttings and speeches from diplomats, judges, special guests and even presidents reminded them that by showing or congregating there, the city's artists were participants in a larger set of geopolitical dynamics. Imam's Indus Gallery broke through all that. It was among the first and certainly most important spaces for artists to show outside this fraught consular cosmopolitanism and to gather independently; it brought the privacy of the cafe and the drawing room into the gallery ecology and presented a space to escape from the then-dominant diplomatic circuit. Gulgee had his first major show in Karachi at the gallery in 1990 and recalls how the gallery in its early days was an intellectual hub: "every Sunday afternoon (I witnessed as a kid) there would be loud Cossack vodka fuelled discussions and fights about art and culture."[11]

"Artists came from all over the world to view exhibitions, join in the discussions and enjoy the company of the man who held it all together," Marjorie Husain recounts in her book on Imam. "Imam was available throughout the day, sometimes in his tiny study reached by climbing a rickety set of metal stairs and filled with all sorts of fascinating objet d'art. There were pages of manuscripts, miniatures, ancient brasses and antiquities from many cultures."[12] Excepting the rickety stairs and tiny meeting room, Husain's description of the Indus Gallery could work for Gulgee's gallery-residence in Clifton. Indus Gallery also established a lasting precedent for a new type of institutional space for Karachi's art world, then lacking in homegrown options. It also offered a model for the artist-centered, intimate space for community and experiment that sustains itself now in organizations like Vasl, the Sanat Initiative, and the Amin Gulgee Gallery.

The Amin Gulgee Gallery opened in 2000 and likewise presents an intermediate space between gallery and home, public and private—especially given its powerfully felt sense of personality and location within the artist's home. Coordinated by McCarry, the space offers an intimate, atelier-like environment beyond what has *now* become the dominant institution of Karachi's artworld—Ali Imam's commercial model established by the Indus. Imam's gallery was highly selective, organized around his artistic interests and sales from exhibitions, (something that the ever-notorious Iqbal Geoffrey harpooned in 1985 by burning the artworks Imam picked to go on display in front of his face). Instead, the Amin Gulgee Gallery burns down formality and exclusivity in favor of experimental, communal tumult, and an escape from the pressures of the market. Appropriately, its first major exhibition was a demonstration of works made during the first Vasl International Artists' Workshop in 2001, which has since been followed by scholarly reviews of historical moments in Pakistan to raucous one-night art events, operating somewhere between nightclub and avant-garde performance happening. The rest of the time, the gallery is filled with Gulgee's own sculptures—the sustaining objects around which this atelier learns and turns. The gallery offers a space for organic, intellectual exchange and a respite beyond the usual circuit. Moreover, a locus for local and international communities, and a testament to the original definition of curating as a form of "care" for objects and cultures. It is often said that "there is no curating in Pakistan." Or not enough... Say that in front of Gulgee or Imam and both might laugh in your face:

"What are you talking about?! It's happening right *here*."

Gulgee plays Durriya Kazi

> *Studying art away from one's country makes one look at the metaphors of one's own culture.*[13]
> Durriya Kazi

There are artists who live in cities and those who are *of* their cities. Even when their careers take them far afield, it can be hard to imagine these artists being anywhere else. Karachi has a few such figures, among them Durriya Kazi and Amin Gulgee. Kazi is most closely associated with her leading role at Karachi University's Department of Visual Studies along with the so-called "Karachi Pop" movement of the 1990s that included among others, Elizabeth and Iftikhar Dadi, David Alesworth, and later students and colleagues of the movement including Adeela Suleman and Asma Mundrawala. Kazi rightly disputes the term "Karachi Pop," however, for the way it insulates the work of these artists from the public spaces and everyday material forms they engaged with; how it ties a too-tidy string around the generative messiness of this very process. Speaking in an interview with *ARTNow*, Kazi notes the colonial inheritance of this separation of high and low and "art" from the "popular" that goes into coining a term like "Karachi Pop" (with its concomitant links to American Pop Art). Moreover, the distinction doesn't actually make sense. One of the most prominent sources of inspiration for the "Karachi Pop" artists—truck art—is a form of *painting*, she notes: "Truck art re-interprets the court aesthetic through the folk art of Western regions of the sub-continent...The decoration of transport is especially fascinating, since it uses the *language and tools of fine artists, as opposed to textile and other crafts*." In the same interview, Kazi speaks of the impact of having studied away from home, in England, on her perspective on Karachi's transport and visual infrastructure. Her words recall Gulgee's experience of reconnecting with the city on returning from abroad in 1990 through his rooftop installation—a miniature museum of Pakistan's craft and folk practices beneath an open sky.

Beyond this connection, however, it might seem odd to put these two artists into dialogue beyond their shared reputation as important figures in the city's art world. There are deep formal connections to be explored, however. Sculpture is a common denominator in the work of both artists, a medium that has thrived in Karachi and that befits the city's safe distance from the cultural refinements and colonial pedagogies foisted onto artists in Lahore. Karachi by contrast, has the glint of newness and commerce, Tariq Road rubies and the Arabian sea. This glinting surface, equal parts kitsch and majestic, lends itself to a contemporary tradition of sculpture in Karachi and its related preoccupation with the jewels and junk of the world. If the history of "Karachi Pop" were open to this more capacious and fluid understanding that artists throughout the city's history—from Sadequain to Durriya Kazi and Amin Gulgee—have habitually utilized the city's visual chaos, then Gulgee moves firmly into the picture. Along with the Karachi rooftop and public sculptures, Gulgee's engagement with the mass-medium of calligraphy—both sacred and vernacular—figures into this tendency to blur the space between art and the city. As the product of many hands and a busy studio, Gulgee's sculptures are likewise porous vessels of the city's life. And returning to the format of performance, works like *Play Me* or the more recent *Q* (2020) performed at Sanat Initiative chime with the broad public coordinates and challenges of "Karachi Pop." They enter and trouble their spaces of activity in raw, enticing technicolor, reconsidering the traditional breach between art and life and becoming in many ways the performance equivalent to a speeding, jingling bus tearing up Shah-e-Faisal—purposeful, fun, dangerous: Karachi.

Gulgee plays Gulgee

> *Nothing grows under the shadow of big trees.*
> Constantin Brancusi

For Brancusi, the shadow was Auguste Rodin, for whom he worked as a studio assistant in 1907, albeit only for a few weeks. Shortly after leaving Rodin's studio and escaping that formidable shadow, Brancusi's work jumped forward while also remaining tied to the elder sculptor's precedent. For Brancusi to dismantle the plinth, Rodin and his colleagues dismantled the exclusivity of sculpture with their often irreverent and subversive works in public. For Brancusi to champion carving, Rodin jettisoned classical perfection in favor of the unfinished mark, rough surfaces, accidents and fingerprints left on the clay. In turn, Brancusi could recuperate the perfect surface as a formal conversation with the industrial, the minimal, and a leap into abstraction. A similar equation between precedence and rupture appears in the artistic "conversation" between Ismail and Amin Gulgee, especially in their shared work in calligraphy. Throughout the modernist period, calligraphy provided source material for abstract painters including Anwar Jalal Shemza, Shakir Ali and most prominently, Ismail Gulgee, who went furthest in channelling the inherent divinity of

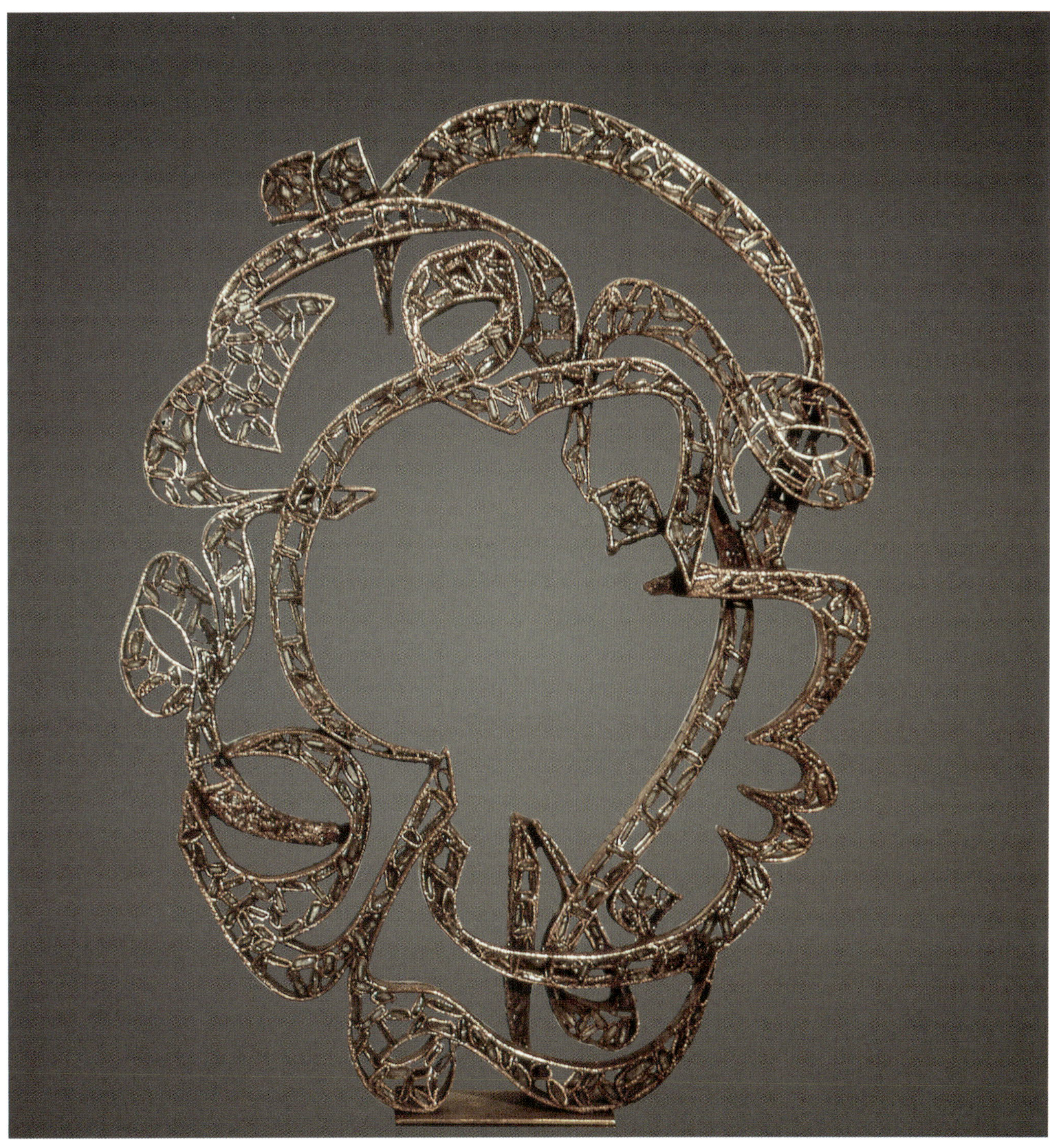

Fig. 4. *Light*, 1994. Copper and rock crystals. 66 × 50.8 × 10 cm. Photo by Tapu Javeri

the calligraphic letter into the emotional fullness of abstract painting.[14] Popular descriptors of Gulgee's painting process allude to the state of a trance, of the dervish of Sufi esoteric practice, and an unbridled and instinctive creative energy.[15] Ismail understood the rigors of calligraphy, too. Its mathematical rigors weave in and out of his paintings and sculptures, albeit often outweighed or overtaken by the power of his gesturalism.

Abstract gesture retreated from painting in Pakistan during the 1980s and especially the 1990s, however a fidelity to the rigors of *calligraphy* remained in the work of artists including the younger Gulgee. The roundel of a copper sculpture, *Light* (1994) (fig. 4) for example, compiles a Nastaliq web of Arabic letters that adhere to the proportions and grammar of that script. It also reproduces the mode of looking (or trying to look) that as Islamic scholar Gülru Necipoğlu argues is inherent to Islamic decorative art. In contrast with Western modes of creating space in artworks, namely Renaissance perspective, Islamic art, from the calligraphic tilework of the Alhambra to Persian miniatures, forces our eye to dash and scatter across the surface rather than enter it unhindered, as in Western perspective. It is not that Islamic art produces an "irrational" gaze, but an unfixed, probing gaze put into constant movement. As such, the "eye of the mind" in Islamic art, Necipoğlu writes, "fractured the unity of visual space by refracting it into an infinity of angles and brightly coloured abstract shapes with no single focus. This insertion of subjectivity into the visual process accentuated the disjunction between internal and external vision, an aesthetic attitude that would be reversed in Renaissance Europe where these two types of vision became coordinated by perspectivalism, with its 'neutral' gaze that separated subject and object."[16] This way of looking appears again and again in Amin Gulgee's sculptures, fostered by the replacement of pure calligraphic *abstraction* with a rigorous attention to the legibility of the script. The eye skitters around and behind the looping form of *Light*, engaging various cognitive and visual tasks—material decipherment of a sculptural object, the related comprehension of depth and space in the room, the task of reading text and then registering the changing effects of light *itself*.

This is a very different experience to looking at Ismail Gulgee's calligraphic paintings, which ask for a more emotive, imaginative and internal—*a modernist*—way of looking at the calligraphic form. In the younger artist's sculpture by contrast, a more scientific relationship to calligraphy emerges. Also, a more contemporary one, as the father-to-son equation of similarity and difference shifts from a modernist expression of self, intuition, and divine inspiration into a more exacting, conceptual and even guarded treatment of the form. However, looking again at *Light*, as with so many of Amin Gulgee's sculptures and installations, the abundance of jeweling and surface decoration recalls the lush surfaces of Ismail Gulgee's early abstract paintings of the 1970s and especially of his jewel-like mosaics made from cut stone. The decorative and beautiful have an ambivalent role in histories of modern art. They have been deemed frivolous and feminine, and in spaces like the subcontinent (recalling Kazi's words), reminiscent of low or othered forms like craft and courtly arts, decorative textiles or traditional miniature paintings, for example. It is striking how much both Ismail and Amin Gulgee in their own time and their own distinct ways have pushed against these haughty discriminations and embraced the lustrous, sparkling joy of beauty. They make us into magpies before the glitter and sheen of their precious metals and stones. Against a deepening derision against beauty in contemporary art, Amin Gulgee carries forward the baton for beauty, decoration and raw pleasure from the past into what might otherwise be a rather dreary present.

Like the baton passed from Kermani or Imam to Gulgee, the one from Gulgee to Gulgee is of similarity and difference and once again, a passage from the struggles of the 1980s into the dynamism of the 1990s. The dominant narrative of post-Zia art history in Pakistan is of artists running screaming from Zia's instrumentalization of calligraphy, landscape, and even oil painting, and into the new and liberating worlds of video, installation, and the miniature; then into the bosom of the "global contemporary." This narrative of spectacular breakthroughs and decisive ruptures overlooks an entire generation of artists who passed rather than hurled a baton from the past and into the present—artists like Durriya Kazi, Naazish Ataullah, Unver Shafi, Anwar Saeed, Afshar Malik, Samina Mansuri, Moeen Faruqi, Salima Hashmi, Lala Rukh, and Amin Gulgee.[17] Yet their work was fundamental to rescuing tools from the past and carrying them forward. In the work of the printmakers, Islamic ornament combined with irreligious allegories to inspire, among others, the neo-miniature movement during the 1990s. In the work of the painters, exhausted forms of abstraction gave way to figurative games, sustaining the health of canvas painting into the future. In the work of the sculptors, the smooth detachment of their modernist precursors transformed into playful assemblages of the divine and the everyday and directed into the world rather than the inner self. This often-forgotten generation unpicked the knots of a defunct chapter in the development of art in Pakistan. Their combined practices offering alternatives and continuities from the immediate past and new options for the future. New games, new conversations. Even *more* happy interactions.

Notes:

1. Giovanni Battista, "Amin Gulgee's mosaics: the happy interaction of man and architecture," *Dawn*, September 25, 1990.
2. John McCarry, "Amin Gulgee", *The Leader*, September 20, 1990.
3. Claire Bishop, "Delegated Performance: Outsourcing Authenticity," *October* 140 (2012): 91–112.
4. Akbar Naqvi, "Gulgee and Economos at the Arts Council," *Pakistan Times,* March 14, 1980, Ali Imam Archive, Indus Valley School of Art and Architecture and FOMMA, Karachi.
5. For a history of Parsi theater see Kathryn Hansen, "Making Women Visible: Gender and Race Cross-Dressing in the Parsi Theatre," *Theatre Journal* 51, no. 2 (1999): 127–47. On performance in Pakistan, John McCarry, "Has Performance Art Come out of the Fringes and Become Mainstream?," *Herald Magazine*, December 3, 2018, https://herald.dawn.com/news/1398731.
6. Asma Mundrawala, "Theatre Chronicles: Framing Theatre Narratives in Pakistan's Sociopolitical Context," in *Mapping South Asia through Contemporary Theatre: Essays on the Theatres of India, Pakistan, Bangladesh, Nepal and Sri Lanka*, Ashis Sengupta (ed.), Studies in International Performance (London: Palgrave Macmillan UK, 2014), 103–34.
7. Mundrawala, 117.
8. Amin Gulgee, "Let's Go Outside," in *Outsiders: Urban Subcultures in Germany and Pakistan*, exhibition catalogue (Karachi: Amin Gulgee Gallery, 2018), 41.
9. Amin Gulgee, "A Performative Life," in *Healing II*, exhibition catalogue (Karachi: Amin Gulgee Gallery, 2020), np.
10. From Imam's interview with M. Luftullah Khan (1988), quoted in Marjorie Husain, *Ali Imam: Man of the Arts* (Karachi: Foundation for Museum of Modern Art (FOMMA), 2003), 86.
11. Amin Gulgee, by email, July 25, 2021.
12. Husain, 74.
13. "In Conversation with Durriya Kazi," *ArtNow Pakistan,* nd, http://www.artnowpakistan.com/in-conversation-with-durriya-kazi/. See also Durriya Kazi, "Stepping over the Fence," in Naiza H. Khan (ed.), *The Rising Tide: New Directions in Art from Pakistan*, 1990-2010 (Karachi: Mohatta Palace Museum, 2008), 22–6.
14. See Iftikhar Dadi, "Ibrahim El Salahi and Calligraphic Modernism in a Comparative Perspective," *South Atlantic Quarterly* 109, no. 3 (2010): 555–76.
15. See for example, Marjorie Husain, "The Dervish of Paint," in *Gulgee* (Lahore: Ferozsons, 2000), 40–42.
16. Gülru Necipoğlu and Mohammad al-Asad, *The Topkapi Scroll—Geometry and Ornament in Islamic Architecture* (Santa Monica, CA: Oxford University Press, 1996), 210.
17. Many of these artists appear along with Gulgee himself in the recent exhibition *Outsiders* curated by the artist with Zarmeene Shah and Zeerak Ahmed at the Amin Gulgee Gallery in 2018—an important act of curatorial recovery and reexamination. *Outsiders: Urban Subcultures in Germany and Pakistan*, exhibition catalogue (Karachi: Amin Gulgee Gallery, 2018).

Structure and Form in Amin Gulgee's Sculptures

Simone Wille

The sculptural work of Amin Gulgee offers a variety of formal and structural details which allow for connections to be made with his studies in art and art history, in general, but more so with his fascination for the art and architecture that is closer to his native home. While working towards a BA in art history at Yale University in the United States, he was exposed to a range of mainly Western art histories, which led him to closely investigate the concept of Mughal gardens for his thesis in 1987. The Mughal garden—as an architectural expression—with its modular structures, its earthly and terrestrial connotations, therefore offers a way to understand some formal aspects of Amin Gulgee's sculptural works that can be seen as foundational to his versatile artistic practice.

The Mughal garden as an architectural expression with the concept of the *Chahar Bagh* or *Char Bagh*—a cross-axial, four-part garden—was adopted by the Mughals and applied throughout South Asia. It can be seen as an element for the structural planning of cities and palaces but also as a political statement.[1] The modular aspect of this concept serves as a basic element with which Amin Gulgee approaches his sculptural works. At the heart of this concept are straight lines and the curve, which are repeated in combinations that offer divisions and orientations, but most of all they offer a balanced structure. Works that date from between 2003 and 2011—*Char Bagh*, *Steps*, *Entrance*, *Jawab*, *Habitat*, *Metropolis* or *Towers*—are therefore informed by a system that relies on a balance of connected geometric units. These units form spaces or modules that appear as pairs, each one symmetrically answering each other. While *Jawab* and *Char Bagh* take up this concept literally,

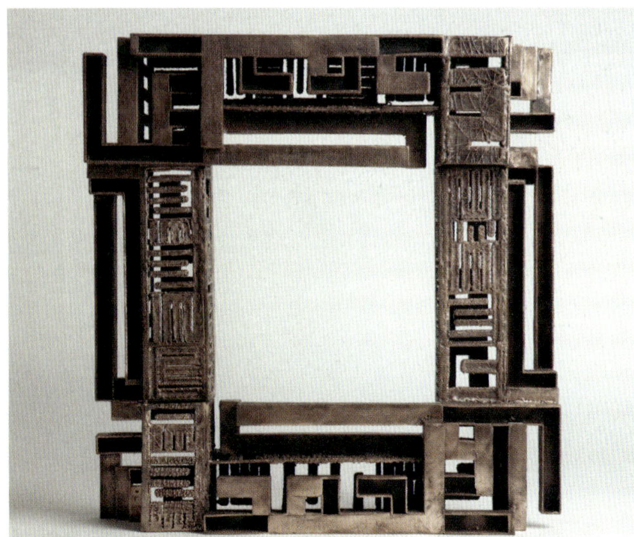

Fig. 1. *Entrance*, 2011. Copper. 71 × 71 × 17.7 cm. Photo by Shamyl Khuhro

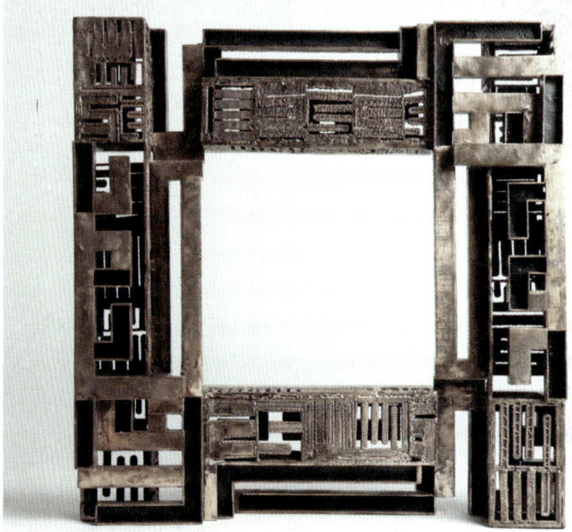

Fig. 2. *Jawab*, 2011. Copper. 71 × 71 × 17.7 cm. Photo by Shamyl Khuhro

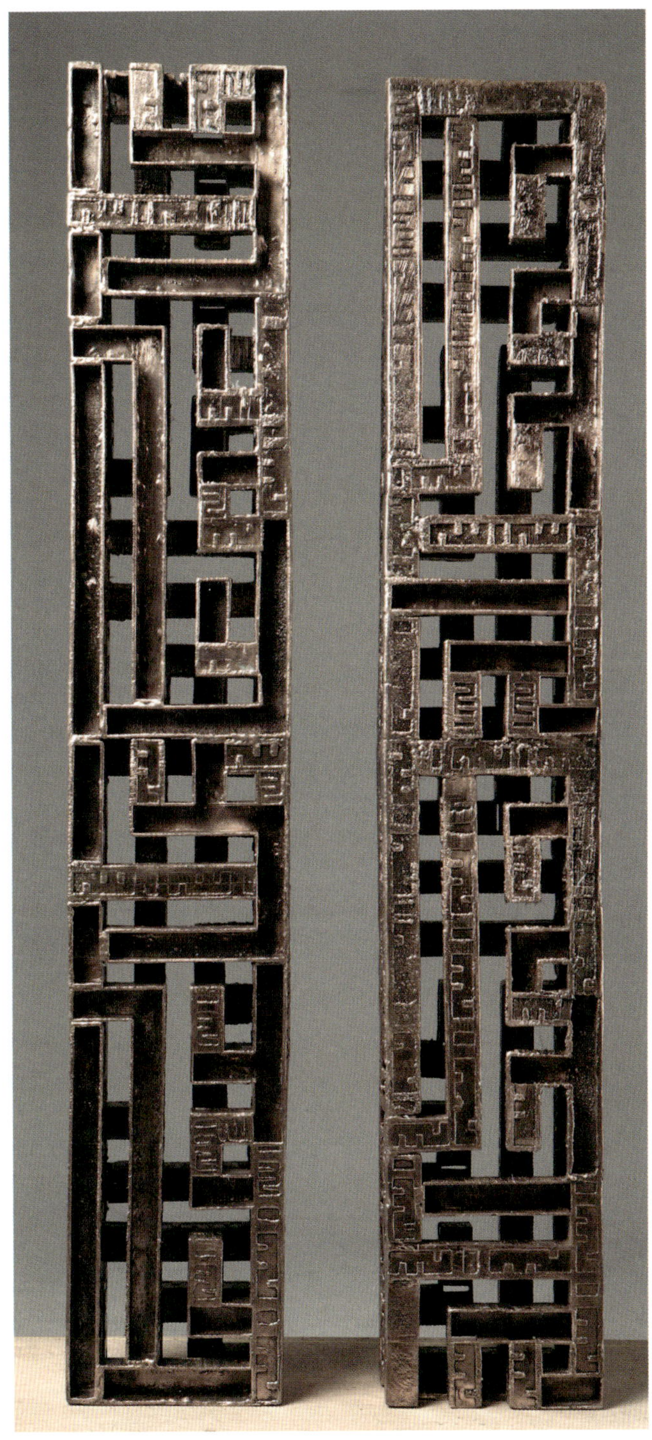

Fig. 3. *Towers*, 2008. Copper. 109.2 × 20.3 × 12.7 cm (each work). Photo by Tapu Javeri

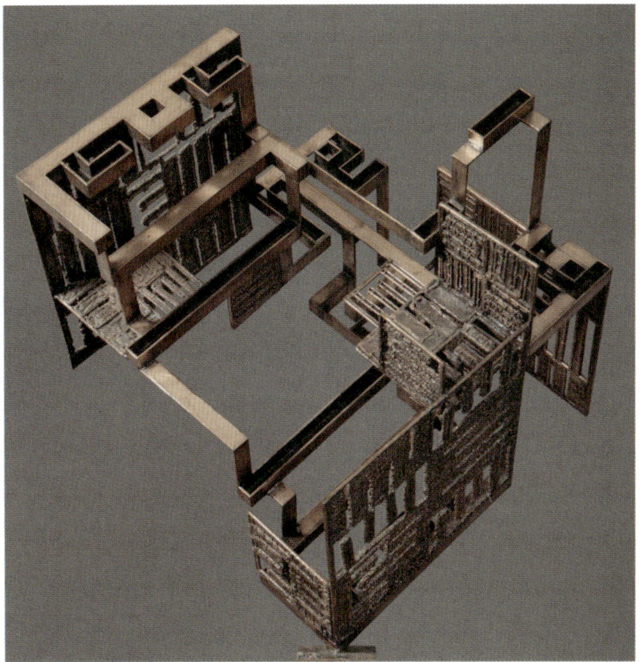

Fig. 4. *Habitat III*, 2007. Copper. 76.2 × 76.2 × 55.8 cm. Photo by Tapu Javeri

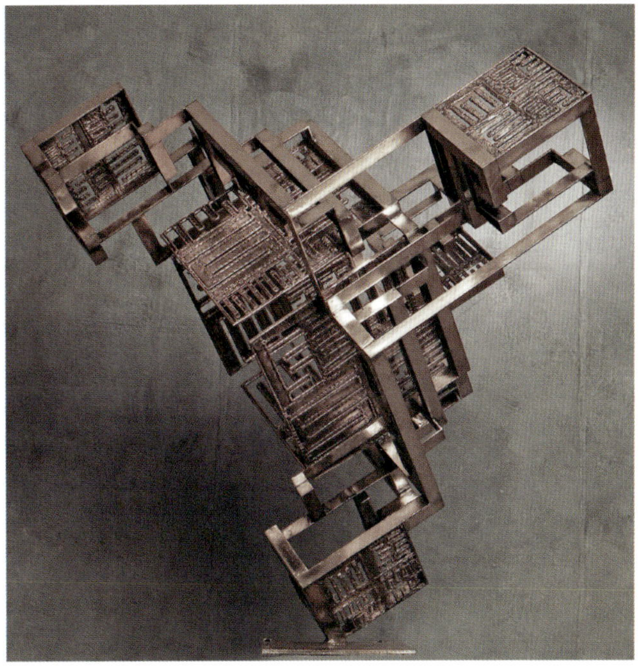

Fig. 5. *Metropolis II*, 2006. Copper. 106.6 × 106.6 × 106.6 cm. Photo by Tapu Javeri

Entrance, *Habitat*, *Metropolis* and *Towers* respond to it conceptually. *Jawab* or *qarina*—the former being the Urdu and the latter the Arabic term—which translates as "answer," "counter-image," or "companion," is an architectural but also artistic composition applied by the Mughals in such a way so that elements are arranged in mirror image along a central axis. Ebba Koch elaborates on this concept in her important analysis of Mughal gardens and Shahjahani architecture in particular emphasizing how the Arabic word *qarina* "expresses the notion of pairing and counterparts, but of integration too, thus it fits conceptually into the ideas of universal harmony that played a great role in the imperial ideology of Shah Jahan."[2]

The geometric structures that inform Amin Gulgee's works *Entrance* (fig. 1), *Jawab* (fig. 2) and *Towers* (fig. 3), are therefore perfect examples of this ordering principle. These works are carefully welded and shaped so that each geometric unit creates a harmonious counterpart. The balance and the energy of the overall composition is contained within a closed space defined by a rectangular or square frame. This leads to an absolute balance and harmony of the object. The architectural quality of Gulgee's sculptural works is enhanced in *Habitat III* (fig. 4) and *Metropolis II* (fig. 5), where the logic of the directions into which the geometric units are taken, seemingly comes at the expense of harmony and balance. Take *Metropolis II*: the way the artist carefully positions this seemingly multidirectional structure on a wooden pedestal, thereby displaying it in a state of suspension, arouses a certain lightness, which is reinforced by the varying light reflections on the copper. The spaces that were so carefully created as pairs in the works *Entrance, Jawab* and *Towers* are now made more complicated and expanded into space. This breaking out of the frame can be viewed as a response to Karachi's contemporary urban topography. Here, I am thinking of the dense network of bustling neighborhoods that are defined by the city's living spaces with its network of exterior and interior windows and doors but also the city's centrifugal energy connected to rapid growth and development in the aftermath of the Second World War.

In Amin Gulgee's sculptural reflections, the metropolis and its habitats are being structured on the basis of past architectural principles that rely on balance and harmony. Some of these qualities are seen as the foundation from where he comfortably sets out to build his performative work in a space where negotiation and translation processes are being conceptualized. Some of these works, such as *Paradise Lost* (2014), *Where's the Apple, Joshinder?* (2014), *Washed Upon the Shore* (2016), in both their physical and conceptual forms, challenge these structural qualities but at the same time are deeply immersed in them.

Notes:

1. Ebba Koch has elaborated on the concept of the Mughal garden in "The Mughal Waterfront Garden," in Attilio Petruccioli (ed.), *Gardens in the Time of the Great Muslim Empires: Theory and Design* (Leiden; New York: E.J. Brill, 1997), 140–160 (reproduced in Ebba Koch, *Mughal Art and Imperial Ideology: Collected Studies*, New Delhi: Oxford University Press, 2001, pp. 183-202) and "Mughal Palace Gardens from Babur to Shah Jahan (1526–1648)," Muqarnas 14, 1997, 143–65 (reproduced in Koch, *Mughal Art and Imperial Ideology*, 203–28).
2. Ebba Koch, *The Complete Taj Mahal and the Riverfront Gardens of Agra* (New York: Thames and Hudson, 2006), 104.

Roaming in the Arena of Witnessings and Absences: Intuition, Communion and Eros in the Work of Amin Gulgee

Robert Sagerman

Amin Gulgee's oeuvre is characterized, perhaps above all else, by eclecticism. Which is to say that, in a very meaningful sense, his oeuvre brooks no characterization whatsoever. One might prefer to simplify matters and say that somewhere near the center of Gulgee's creative practice throughout the years lies metal working in copper and bronze, but this would be a privileging of one among many media and modalities through which Gulgee has traversed. Insistence on the freedom to explore and discover, and resistance to categorization and simple, rational elucidation, are themes to which Gulgee has artfully returned time and again in his statements, oral and written. He has jealously guarded this most valued open terrain with the same vigilance with which he attends to the privacy of his studio, a space set apart in which to improvise, to unselfconsciously plumb the depths of his creative impulses. For this reason, one must tread lightly when attempting to draw out themes or interpreting ongoing motifs from within Gulgee's vast body of work.

Yet within this very resistance to characterization some important threads do emerge. In his studio, Gulgee engages in a type of communion. To make contact with an internal impulse toward that which is personally meaningful and to transmute this found, sensed meaning into material manifestation requires of Gulgee that he make contact with things that are, on the one hand, archetypal and enduring, and, on the other, ineluctably immediate and of the particular, fleeting, exquisitely fragile moment. Gulgee is deeply mindful of—and indeed, rigorously educated in—the artistic, cultural and religious traditions that constitute his received milieu. These come to constitute an underlying structure within which he can comfortably move because he, at the same time, creates in a manner that subordinates structure and tradition to the immediacy that alone, paradoxically, may enliven and reinvigorate them. One may think of his approach to the Quranic verse (96:5) with which he has so often worked, in Naskhi script, over the years. "God has taught man what he did not know." In particular, it is Gulgee's conscious move to abstract the letter forms over time that creates out of that which is literally traditional something that is reinvented as personal. Tradition is simultaneously set aside and upheld. It is through this very practice, by means of a somewhat precarious, intuitively calibrated equilibrium, that Gulgee may learn what he did not know.

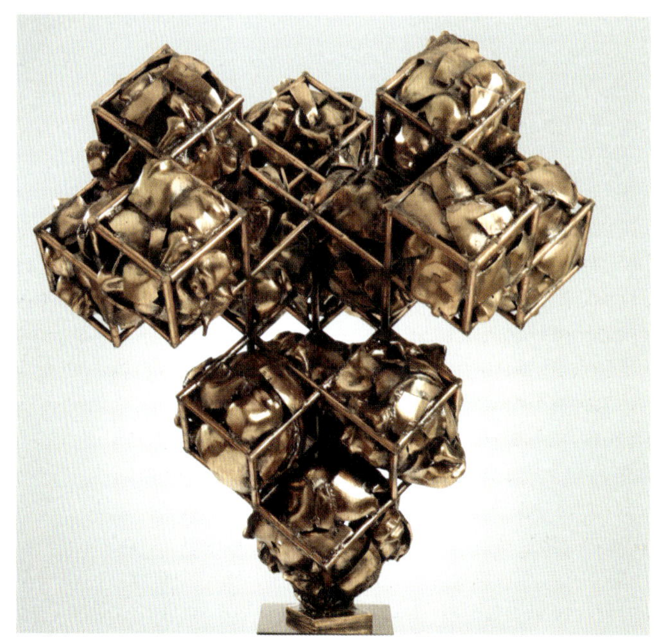

Fig. 1. *Me In the Matrix II*, 2014. Copper and bronze. 91.4 × 91.4 × 91.4 cm. Photo by Shamyl Khuhro

The impulse to breathe life, through an inner communion, into received tradition in order to summon forth personal meaning in the form of ever-unanticipated revelation shares much with what may be said, in cross-cultural terms, about the mystical project. And indeed, Gulgee has on occasion tipped his hand enough to acknowledge a powerful debt to the Sufi mystical tradition.[1] Mystics of any tradition walk a delicate line between strict, rote adherence to received orthodoxy and the unique imperative to locate within this orthodoxy the hidden keys that may, in any particular moment, initiate the experiential encounter with the transcendent. Indeed, this balance, perhaps above all else, defines mysticism.

Many of Gulgee's works visually express this type of equipoise, a dynamic contrast between an over-arching structure, beautifully impassive, and intimately personal expression. One may think, for instance, of his sculptures *Me in the Matrix II* (fig. 1), in which fragmented faces find uneasy, ambivalent containment within a strict cubic geometry, the whole finding its balance upon a base so small as to defy expectations, or of *47: The Wall* (2007) (fig. 2), in which, with what Gulgee describes as a type of violence, casts of his own face are mangled and reassembled in copper in a grid-like configuration, comprising a wall that Gulgee associates with the tearing asunder of Pakistan and India in the 1947 Partition. An exploration of selfhood and identity now is intended to operate within a further context, a literal deconstruction of self, placed within its historical milieu, fraught with the possibility of hard-won insight, a theme to which we shall return.

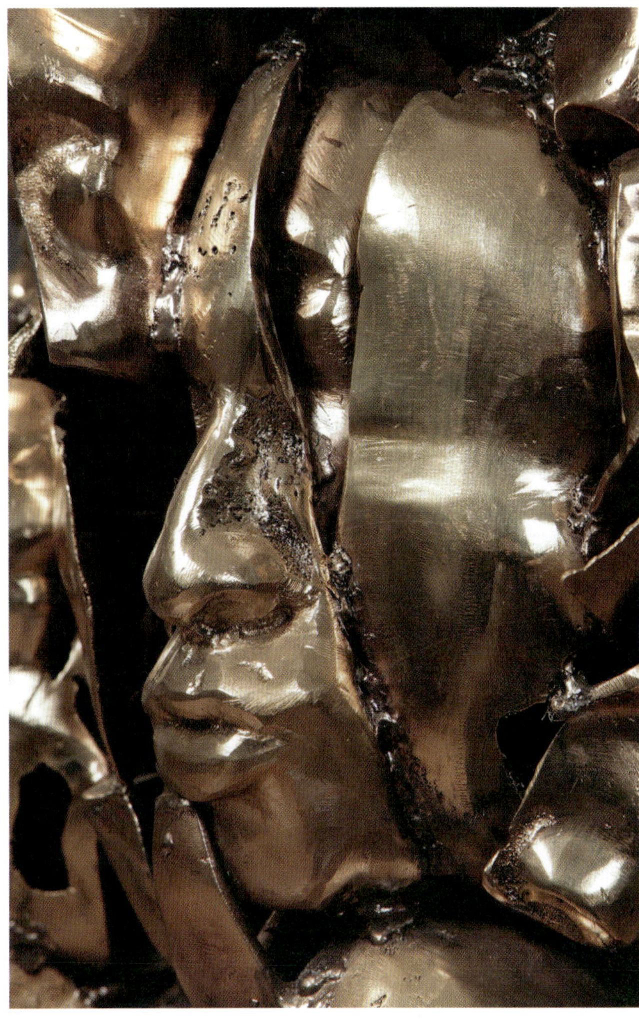

Fig. 2. *47: The Wall*, 2007. Detail. Photo by Shamyl Khuhro

Just as many of Gulgee's sculptures literally embody a delicate balancing upon their minimally sized bases, so often do they as well balance positive and negative space in lattice-like filigrees. The importance of the spaces between in Gulgee's numerous calligraphic pieces can likewise hardly be overstated. These apertures operate formally to counterpose substance against lightness, to engage space and to play with cast shadows, but they as well index immateriality itself, speaking to a transcendence of the terrestrial. We shall see how Gulgee carries forward this motif to its furthest extreme in his later work. For the moment, much more is to be found in the interplay of positive and negative space in Gulgee's somewhat earlier sculptures. One may think of *Ripping the Bird's Nest IV* (2014) (fig. 3), in which a dense network of copper tendrils enmeshes a multiplicity of human hands that, as per the piece's title, do violence to that which contains them. Openings of negative space form the very subject of the piece, irruptions of dematerialization that are infused with the weight of the immediate moment by the visceral nature of the action described. Again, the piece conveys the sense of a deconstruction in process, immateriality being that which encroaches upon the very stuff of the sculpture itself. One might ruefully imagine but an empty space above a scattering of hands on the ground with the piece's ultimate denouement. And yet, contexts within contexts, in the piece's equipoise of containment and destruction a pathos is suggested. As in *47: The Wall*, there is again here a rootedness in the real-world conduct of human beings toward themselves and to the world that contains them, evoking notions of adherence to an ethical imperative the likes of which marks out a spiritual path.

In Gulgee's *Amber Moon* (fig. 4) and *Green Moon* (fig. 5) (both 2015), the negative spaces found within a half-spherical, almost honeycomb-type structure, one that evokes the moon's pitted surface, receive a further level of attention, as they now contain translucent hues of inlaid tinted glass.

Just as the negative and positive spaces are again set in a balanced opposition to one another, so too now are the warm hues of the one piece set against the cool of the other in their installation, hanging together as they do in Gulgee's 2015 Karachi exhibition, *Washed Upon the Shore*. Likewise, front and back are set against one another; the two pieces each comprise half of a shell-like sphere, concavity set against convexity. One may think of them as two opposing parts of a whole to be reconciled, a dynamic of tension and energy, of vitality. And indeed, elsewhere in this same exhibition there was to be found a *Third Moon* (fig. 6), one that is unpaired, static, devoid of the enlivenment of navigated oppositions, lacking in vibrant color or negative spaces, and mounted on the wall in a manner that hides its concave back. It offers, for its own part, a type of starkness, its copper and silver leaf looking blasted and burned, beautifully detached in its frozen barrenness.

In a certain way, the holding in suspense of presence and absence, substance and emptiness, in the manner evoked by Gulgee may open the door to a unique and rarefied experiential state, one which stands as a hallmark of mystical practice. This fragile dynamic of presence and absence is part and parcel of the divine's simultaneous immanence and transcendence. From the standpoint of mystical consciousness, the divine both infuses the mundane world and remains entirely, undefinably other. The medieval Sufi mystic Ibn Arabi speaks of this through an unusual metaphor

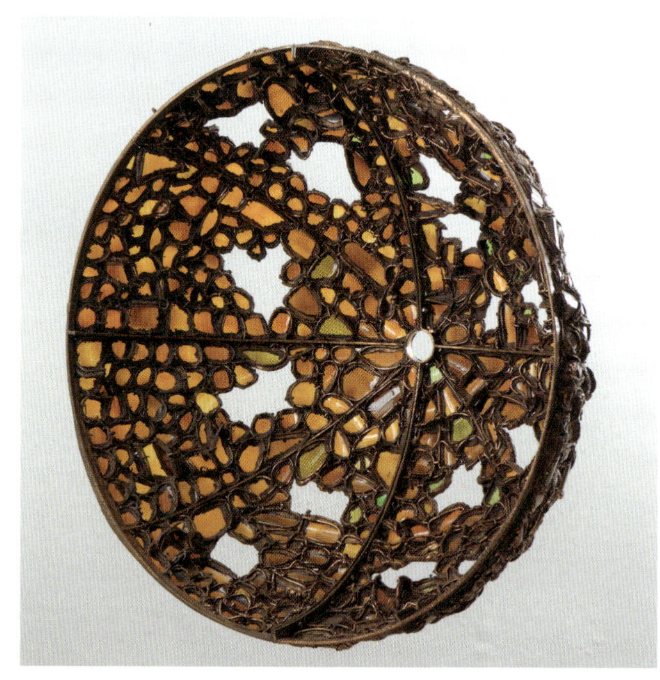

Fig. 4. *Amber Moon*, 2015. Copper and glass. 122 × 122 × 63.5 cm. Photo by Humayun Memon

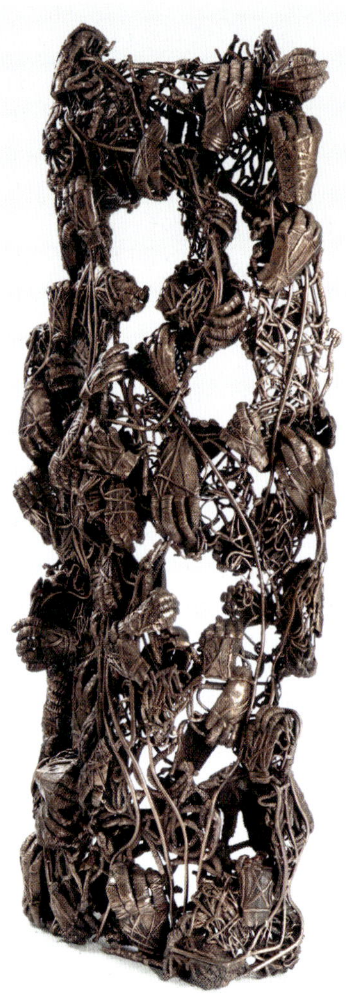

Fig. 3. *Ripping the Bird's Nest IV*, 2013. Copper. 154.9 × 83.8 × 30.4 cm. Photo by Humayun Memon

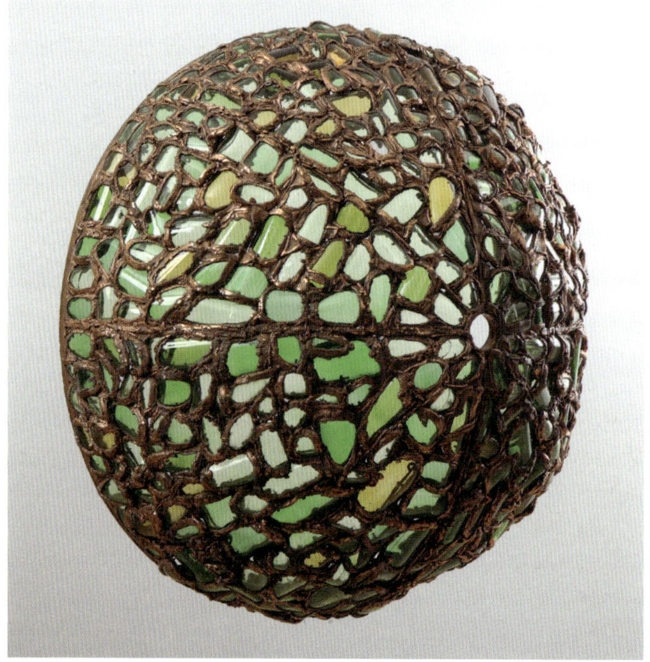

Fig. 5. *Amber Moon*, 2015. Copper and glass. 122 × 122 × 63.5 cm. Photo by Humayun Memon

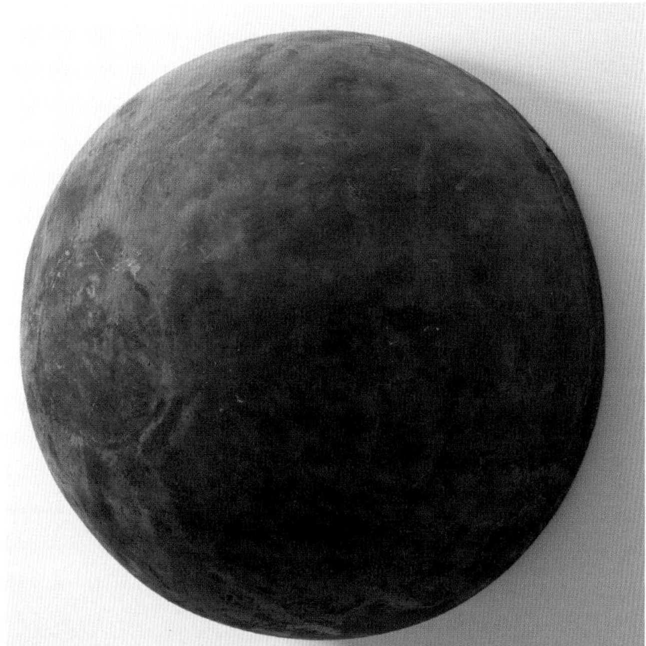

Fig. 6. *Third Moon*, 2015. Copper and silver leaf. 106.6 × 106.6 × 63.5 cm. Photo by Humayun Memon

associated, appropriately enough, with vision: "Ontologically speaking, one eye sees Being and the other perceives nothingness. Through the two eyes working together, man perceives that he himself and the cosmos are He/not He."[2] Ibn Arabi asserts that coming into a relationship with the divine requires that one embrace an openness to paradox, a mode of being that harnesses conventional thinking but does not limit one's self thereby. The divine may then be brought into immediate relation with the material. The mystical state requires the infusion of the divine into the material and vice versa, a transit beyond normal states of rationality and conventional modes of relating to the world. The result, as reflected in the quotation above, is the realized identification of self, world and transcendence. Perhaps in this lies the intent behind Gulgee's recurring recourse to the Quranic verse invoking divinely granted knowledge. At the same time, even the assertion of self-identification with the divine elicited by Ibn Arabi must be set aside in the service of a yet further openness to realization; just as Being and nothingness coincide, so too the contradiction of every assertion must be held in suspense within the mind. He writes, "You are not He and you are He."[3] Accustomed modalities of understanding and relation must fall by the wayside. To acquaint one's self with Gulgee's sense of his artistic practice is to see the extent to which he embraces a similar perspective. "My journey is an attempt to let go and tap into a source that I do not fully understand. This is an electric process that channels energy and dances," Gulgee wrote in 2011.[4] In a similar spirit again, Ibn Arabi writes, centuries earlier, "Vision happens in perplexity and incapacity, so vision is not-vision... Incapacity to attain comprehension is itself comprehension."[5]

In spiritual practice, the drive toward the experienced communion with the transcendent is typically enacted within the context of ritual, the fabric of tradition giving way to the revelation that may rend it apart. In a parallel fashion, Gulgee is most emphatic about the role that repetition plays in his creative process. Repetition is the mechanism by which he naturally works through things. Such a method of production sets the stage, for Gulgee, for the moment in which unexpected insight assumes a visual form, constituting a break or a rupture. One may look to Gulgee's chapati series to observe this interplay. The sensuously repetitive winding of concentric copper coils into circles that Gulgee named for the traditional Pakistani flatbread are split and folded into numerous configurations; they divide space, assume austere dimensionality and are reassembled into sophisticated configurations that mark an unexpected engagement with idealized geometric form. The title of the most simplified possible of these, a single disc standing on edge, is *Cosmic Chapati* (2011) (fig. 7), a title that evokes, with a touch of humor, a universalized, sacred geometry. This sense one may carry forward into the more elaborate works to conceive of a kind of celestial dance, a music of the spheres, suggested in the title of his 2011 Kuala Lumpur exhibition, *Cosmic Mambo*, albeit again here with a touch of wryness. Gulgee's commitment to the openness of his process extends to his desire for the viewer's own open experience of the work. Visual references within the work, or a work's title, only offer suggestions. The works are to be experienced or puzzled out in much the same manner that they were for Gulgee himself. Thus, when Gulgee alludes in a work's title to something redolent of cosmic geometry, it is unsurprising that he as well covers his tracks with a modicum of irreverence. The location of meaning within the work, for Gulgee, is part of a delicate and elusive process, and no less so is this intended to be the case for the viewer. A bit of lightheartedness here belies the multivalent suggestiveness of the work. The chapati series' reference to cultural context is clear enough. But as well, in the identification of the ritually presented flatbread with sacred geometry, the latter with its numinous, idealized evocation of Neoplatonic philosophy, one may discern a parallel to the mystical significance of Christianity's identification of the Eucharistic wafer with the divine Logos. This is by no means to suggest that Gulgee

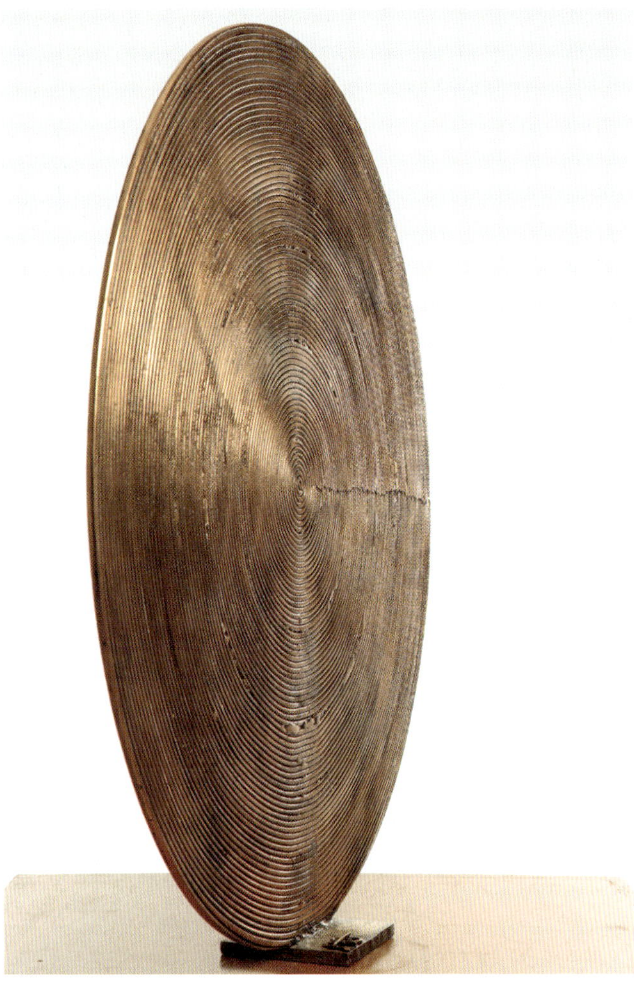

Fig. 7. *Cosmic Chapati II*, 2011. Copper. 69 × 66 × 1 cm. Photo by Shamyl Khuhro

intends such an association (although we should bear in mind that he bears the burden of a bachelor's degree in art history from Yale University); rather, as I have tried to convey, he has carefully stewarded a process of working that opens up the possibility for the revelatory recasting of archetypes, for the transubstantiation (to invoke the term associated with the Eucharist) of artwork into moment of communion.

Nowhere is this more the case than in Gulgee's multimedia project *7*. For simplicity's sake, I shall concentrate only on aspects of its sweeping realization in two venues simultaneously in Rome, 2018. I begin with Gulgee's utilization of the exterior space of the Galleria d'Arte Moderna (fig. 8). There, he has demarcated a quadrilateral arrangement that emulates the traditional Mughal Char-Bagh garden. Gulgee notes the Central Asian association of this arrangement with that of four mythological rivers which flow perpendicularly to one another, a cosmic tree that is to make contact with the heavens being located at their point of intersection. In a fashion not unrelated to the preceding discussion concerning the chapatis, Gulgee observes how this next instance of sacred geometry finds an echo in the Christian cross.[6] Archetypes resonate through innumerable cultural contexts, across millennia, and Gulgee moves freely within and among these associations. In this regard, we would do well to also note the significance of the number seven, which in the first instance recalls what we have noted about the resonance, in the Neoplatonic tradition, of numbers generally. Being perfected qualities, they were associated with the transcendent, perhaps most emphatically by the Near Eastern philosopher Iamblichus, and so played their part in this tradition's contemplative project toward a philosophically oriented *unio mystica*. The medieval Sufi Ibn Arabi, among others, was intent upon harmonizing this Neoplatonic tradition with Islam, a project which for him included associating the Logos, the divine utterance or potency mentioned earlier, with each of the prophets.

The number seven in particular finds its place within a long line of tradition concerning ascent to the

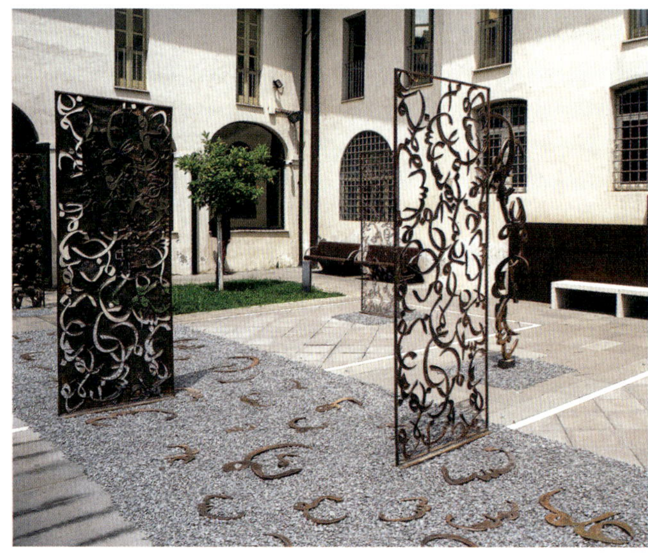

Fig. 8. *7*, 2018. Installation view. Galleria d'Arte Moderna, Rome. Photo by Fabrizio Piergiovanni

divine realm, perhaps beginning in antiquity with the person of Enoch, the seventh antediluvian patriarch of the Genesis account, whom Jewish tradition described as ascending to the seventh heaven, where he received an influx of gnosis considering the world and God himself, and where he communed with God and himself assumed an angelic or divine status. Again, Ibn Arabi, but not uniquely so, would later integrate Enoch into his own ascent narrative, and the parallels between Enoch and the doctrine concerning Muhammad's night journey and ascent to the seventh heaven are readily apparent.

We may make our way through this network of associations to a deeper understanding of Gulgee's Char-Bagh installation. For the "Lote Tree of the Limit" (Surah 53:14 and elsewhere) is likewise associated with the seventh heaven, while the four rivers that the Quran had flowing from this cosmic tree, are, in the Sufi doctrine of Ibn Arabi and in hadith, understood to signify the four kinds of divine knowledge granted to humanity. So we may see that, as with these other mystical ascent motifs, the Char-Bagh configuration suggests the linkage of knowledge of the divine with a personal inner transmutation. This archetype resounds most deeply within Gulgee's installation; the sculptures that surround the central setting of the cosmic tree of the seventh heaven, as well as the sculpted letters set into the ground, all are based upon the seven abstracted figures that Gulgee has derived from the Quranic verse concerning the divine gift of knowledge. Suggested here in a deeply personal and poignant way is a longing for the type of transformative communion that is the subject of such a deep and wending tradition.

Importantly, at the center of Gulgee's Char-Bagh installation, in the place of the cosmic tree of mystical ascent, of the seventh heaven, one finds.... an absence. Perhaps, though, this absence is more properly understood rather as an openness, not an emptiness or dearth, but an unenvisionability, charged and activated by Gulgee, like the negative spaces in the surrounding sculptures, which stand as portals to the unenvisionable, adorned with their abstracted expression of gratitude for divine knowledge. Absence is rendered as quintessential fullness, plenitude, infiniteness. It is the infinity that is part and parcel of the infinite text whose repeated citation encompasses it. The aspirant who comes into contact with this openness of absence is transformed in this place of ascent, a process that occurs through divinely imparted knowledge. The latter, naturally, transcends the ordinary, even the strictly philosophical; as Ibn Arabi puts it, "For the intellect cannot roam in the arena of witnessings and absences."[7] As to the transformation that is undergone in this place of communion, in Ibn Arabi's parlance, a "dissolving" takes place, and a subsequent "reintegration" occurs.[8] Gulgee's beautifully contemplative installation provides the setting for and perhaps commemorates such experience, placed, as ever, at the nexus of concept, aesthetic and intuition.

The endlessness of opening, activated through the infinite text's coextensivenss with the divine, is a theme discernible in Gulgee's projection piece at the Mattatoio in Rome (fig. 9). Whether in exemplars such as Ibn Arabi in Islam, Meister Eckhart in Christianity or Abraham Abulafia in Judaism, the perspective that sacred text encodes within itself the infinite pathways of the divine, and so is susceptible to infinite interpretation, spans mystical traditions.[9] Gulgee's projection piece, in point of fact, opens endless permutations of the seven figures of the Quranic verse concerning knowledge afforded by the divine. Because it cycles fluidly through the seven abstracted figures by means of an algorithm, and not by means of a recording, the combinations it presents are ever of the moment and never to be repeated. The infinity of aesthetic openings, successively offering themselves to the viewer, gives way ultimately to an experienced absence or unenvisionability, as the accumulated black forms ultimately render the entire screen black. But, as I say, the possible readings are endless, and the experience continues with subsequent white figures on the blackness. Skillfully held in suspense, opposites reverse and elide. Musical notes—seven in number—from the traditional lute-like instrument, the rubab, individually sound as each visible form manifests unenvisionability, context provided for the text.

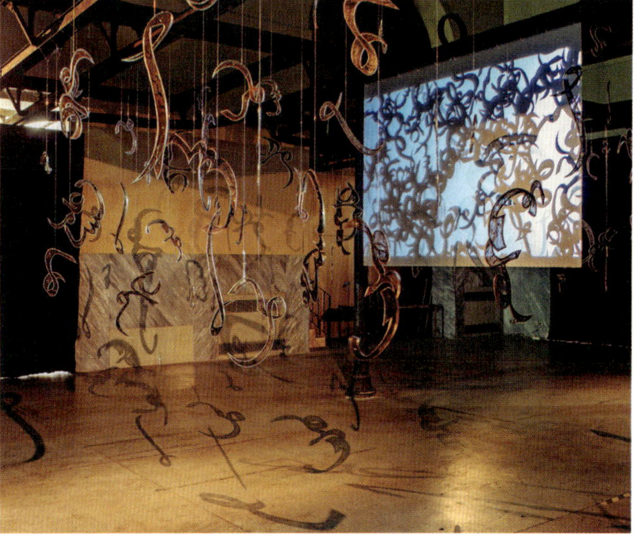

Fig. 9. *7.7*, 2018. Installation view. Mattatoio, Rome. Photo by Fabrizio Piergiovanni

The parallels here with the letter permutation meditational practice of the medieval kabbalist Abraham Abulafia are powerful. It should come as no surprise that Abulafia was deeply influenced by the Sufi Ibn Arabi, whose perspectives I have cited so many times throughout this essay. Abulafia maintained that the letters themselves of the Hebrew alphabet are to be abstracted from Scripture and subjected to combinatorial processes directed toward bringing the mystic into a connection with the letters' primeval, hylic essence, and thence into states of prophetic revelation. Letters could be endlessly permuted by the righteous adept, their combinations invoking references to Scriptural verses and to their hidden interconnections, imparting limitless, even confounding, divine insight. Writes Abulafia, "And indeed what I announce to you in the matter of the secret of the permutation is that in your uttering the permuted words, the spirit of God will rest upon you within the warming of the heart, even though you will not understand what these words teach that you will utter."[10] The inability to comprehend (at least initially) the Scriptural interpretations that arise from this deconstruction of the text into its constituent elements, and subsequent reassembly, stems from their divine origin. We have, in fact, the exact opposite of the deconstructionist perspective propounded by Derrida, for whom authorial intent is both inaccessible and unimportant in the face of the reader's infinite interpretive act.[11] For Abulafia, the disassembly of Scripture is the path to limitless interpretive possibilities, all of which, when properly undertaken, are intended by the divine Author. And again, the resonance is striking to Gulgee's process; he creates intuitively, "letting go," as we noted earlier, to "tap into a source that I do not fully understand."

A final parallel between Gulgee's *Algorithm VII* and Abulafia's practice bears noting. Writes the latter, "...the letters are signs and hints in the likeness of attributes and allegories in their essences. And they are found to be tools for man, to instruct in the way of apprehension. And for us they are in the likeness of strings of a lyre, which, from the bringing out of its voice, with the drawing of the bow in the hand upon the strings, and in the changing of this bowing from string to string, and in the permutation of the sounds that are born from it, rouses to joy and pleasure the soul of the man who seeks to rejoice. And it [the soul] will receive from its [the instrument's] delight, and great enjoyment of the soul results from this, because the joy is natural for every man."[12]

Just as Gulgee associates the permutation of his letter forms derived from the Quran with the notes of the rubab, Abulafia likens the permuted letters of the Torah to the notes of a lyre. The decontextualizing and recontextualizing of the letters through their infinite recombination utterly abstracts them, such that disassociated musical notes serve as a proper analogy. This connection is, in both cases, intertwined with the association of the letters with number; for Gulgee, the number seven presides over all, while for Abulafia the letter operations are dependent on linkages established through numerical equivalences among letter values. And again, the transcendent connection between number and music had been established by Neoplatonists such as Iamblichus (later to be absorbed within Sufism), who detected within the Pythagorean science of number Orphic mysteries concerning music.

At the same time, the above passage from Abulafia alludes to the kind of pure emotion to which music may give rise. The processes of infinite removal from context and subsequent recontextualizing, akin to the "dissolving" and "reintegration" described by Ibn Arabi, as noted earlier, creates an opening for fullest communion, which Abulafia describes in terms of joy or rapture, elsewhere characterizing it as a type of ecstasy. And for Gulgee, associations with erotic union are most certainly at work. He provides clues to this elsewhere in the exhibition. In one instance, several poets were invited to the installation to recite works of love in Italian. In another, visitors to the exhibition were invited to leave their own personal love notes as messages in bottles, these to become parts of the installation. As with the projection piece, a disassociation from context was in effect in both of these instances. The poems were recited in a language that Gulgee could not understand, while the love messages were to go unread. One gets the distinct sense that the specificity of the particular recited poem or written note is to be subsumed within a larger frame, one of encompassing eros, love. In a most remarkable parallel, Ibn Arabi treats this theme as follows:

> [N]one but God is loved in the existent things. It is He who is manifest within every beloved to the eye of every lover-and there is nothing which is not a lover. So the cosmos is all lover and beloved, and all of it goes back to Him... Poets exhaust their words writing about all these existent things without knowing, but the gnostics never hear a verse, a riddle, a panegyric, or a love poem that is not about Him, hidden beyond the veils of forms.[13]

Within this stirring final theme of an encompassing erotic union one may descry a fitting place to conclude. I have endeavored to delineate within Gulgee's incredibly varied creative output what I take to be a most central theme, that of transcendent communion, activated through a freedom of play among archetypes, one which is accompanied by profound—and profoundly moving—insight. The desire to bridge divides and to cultivate love, which, in a certain sense, is a theme which has only begun here to fully unfold, provides a lens through which to view so much of Gulgee's work. He has characterized his numerous performance pieces, for example, in terms of the enacting of ritual, establishing a deep connectedness between and among performers and viewers. Even his jewelry making Gulgee has described in terms of the physical connection that he forges, through the worn object, between himself and the wearer. All of these find their place as instantiations within a larger theme, that one which Ibn Arabi characterizes above as the mystical backdrop to all love. Gulgee has returned to sound this note time and again throughout his career, each time offering to take the viewer to the deepest wellspring of their own hearts, wherein the divine may be located.

Notes:

1. See for instance his opening statement in the exhibition catalogue, *Walking on the Moon* (Kuala Lumpur, Wei-Ling Gallery, 2015).
2. Aydogan Kars, "Two Modes of Unsaying in the Early Thirteenth Century Islamic Lands: Theorizing Apophasis through Maimonides and Ibn 'Arabī," *International Journal for Philosophy of Religion*, December 2013, Vol. 74, No. 3, 271.
3. Ibid.
4. *Cosmic Mambo*, exhibition catalogue (Kuala Lumpur, Wei-Ling Gallery, 2011), 5.
5. Aydogan Kars, "Two Modes of Unsaying in the Early Thirteenth Century Islamic Lands: Theorizing Apophasis through Maimonides and Ibn 'Arabī," *International Journal for Philosophy of Religion*, December 2013, Vol. 74, No. 3, 274.
6. *Through the Looking Glass*, exhibition catalogue (New Delhi, Nitanjali Art Gallery, 2013), 27.
7. Franz Rosenthal, "Ibn 'Arabī between 'Philosophy' and 'Mysticism': 'Sūfism and Philosophy Are Neighbors and Visit Each Other'. *fa-inna at-taṣawwuf wa-t-tafalsuf yatajāwarāni wa-yatazāwarāni*," Oriens , 1988, Vol. 31 (1988), 10.
8. James Winston Morris, "The Spiritual Ascension: Ibn 'Arabī and the Mi'rāj, Part I," *Journal of the American Oriental Society*, Oct. Dec., 1987, Vol. 107, No. 4, 639, 641–641.
9. Ian Almond, "The Meaning of Infinity in Sufi and Deconstructive Hermeneutics: When Is an Empty Text an Infinite One?" *Journal of the American Academy of Religion*, Mar., 2004, Vol. 72, No. 1 (Mar., 2004), 97–117.
10. Robert Sagerman, *The Serpent Kills or the Serpent Gives Life: The Kabbalist Abraham Abulafia's Response to Christianity* (Leiden: Brill, 2010), 135.
11. Ian Almond, "The Meaning of Infinity in Sufi and Deconstructive Hermeneutics: When Is an Empty Text an Infinite One?" *Journal of the American Academy of Religion*, Mar., 2004, Vol. 72, No. 1 (Mar., 2004), 109.
12. Robert Sagerman, *The Serpent Kills or the Serpent Gives Life: The Kabbalist Abraham Abulafia's Response to Christianity*, 116.
13. Aydogan Kars, "Two Modes of Unsaying in the Early Thirteenth Century Islamic Lands: Theorizing Apophasis through Maimonides and Ibn 'Arabī," *International Journal for Philosophy of Religion*, December 2013, Vol. 74, No. 3, 270.

Fearless

Salima Hashmi

"Fearless" is the word which springs to mind when beginning to talk about Amin Gulgee. "Fearless" on many counts and many levels. The overwhelming expressiveness which surrounds you in a rush when meeting him, leaving no space to step back to parse the elements of the encounter. The insistence on sharing every fragment of that energy which flows generously from him is one of the facets of that absence of fear.

It embraces the truthfulness which is at the root of each relationship however fleeting, however timeless. There are no transactions in these shards of time, these freewheeling encounters. In a world where defences are painstakingly constructed and put in place as soon as we gain a sense of selfhood, the fear of being vulnerable accompanies it. Amin Gulgee brushes aside this disquiet and embraces vulnerability with aplomb. That is just one aspect of his ability to transcend barriers.

The assembling of these energies steers him on his way through his artistic avatars and culminates in diverse bodies of work. As one attempts to pin down the influences that have flowed and mutated over the years one cannot ignore the artist's father figure who dominates the landscape of Amin Gulgee's early practice. In cultures such as ours, where traditions in music, performance and every kind of artisanal skill tangible and "intangible" are inscribed within the framework of family, clan, tribe and terrain, the burden on a young practitioner can be incalculable. No doubt Amin Gulgee has borne this at a profound level.

A child of privilege, he was anchored onto a pedagogical path quite removed from the artmaking world around him. What happens when head and heart are separated? There was a skirting around the problem during these years at university in the United States. One senses this was a time of inquiry and intellectual pursuit which developed both understanding and expression.

Choosing to tread a path which beckons and offers a vast realm of possibilities requires fearlessness even as the artist gingerly probes what lies within him and its metamorphosis into material richness.

Richard Sennett in *The Craftsman* speaks of how the sense of touch informs "the intelligent hand." The motions of the pen, the extension of the hand as it gestures with a flourish the first letter of the alphabet, Alif, acquire a significance beyond its calligraphic intent. Amin Gulgee builds upon this gesture, embracing the forms and signs that trace the arabesque of the written word.

In its sweep, he took in the elements of the form and made each one eloquent in its own right, free from the constraints of word and message. The form attaining its own meaning. Amin Gulgee's meanderings along these pathways have been manifold. He has investigated both adornment and solitude. The one flamboyant, the other focusing on the solitariness of the body. From the latter has emerged the passage into performances. The body is ready to receive the sum of our depredations, our unease with existence, alongside the celebration of its physicality.

By choosing to venture into a new and untried direction, Amin Gulgee was setting himself free from the trappings of the authority of tradition and burden of legacy.

The measures of "correctness" still pursued him, but were looser and less imposing. Listening to his own body initially and then carefully following its teachings, he could orchestrate the many disciples that come with other bodies. No one can accuse Amin

Gulgee of scientific thinking; he delights in intuition and the intensity of the unknown. The shift into performance implies a leap of imagination coupled with fearlessness. Performance on the surface may be seen as an alien art form in the Pakistani context, not easily accommodated by audiences. But there are interesting indigenous parallels. Not unknown in traditional societies was *swaang bharna* whereby an individual would take it upon himself (or herself) to don another personality, transforming themselves with an intensity so convincing to the members of their community that they would become the audience sharing the vehement rigor of the performance. I have witnessed just such a performance in Anarkali bazaar more than 35 years ago, in the company of Zahoorul Akhlaque. We watched in amazed silence as a man, drenched in simulated blood, with chains adorning his body, walked slowly and quietly through the bazaar. Zahoorul Akhlaque recognized the performance, which was not religious but cultural. It created a catharsis for the people who witnessed it and remains an intensely graphic memory for me. The capacity of the human body to become the vehicle for symbolic and imaginative expression is infinite and the basis for many forms including theater, film and dance.

In Amin Gulgee's oeuvre it incorporates the immediacy of location and the potential for escape from it. Both as practitioner and as curator, Amin Gulgee's storytelling is fluid, both creating and dispelling unease. Amin Gulgee explores the vastness of the Universe as the backdrop for those narratives. The striving to commandeer planetary images, which are forever elusive, forever subtle, is a formidable task. Contemplating spiritual goals, while confronting the insecurities and displacements of our existence, calls for constant negotiation and inventiveness. Thus, the presence of parallel mythologies and a restlessness abound in Amin Gulgee's work. With customary fearlessness, he looks into the Universe with the yearning that humankind has forever experienced and continues his struggle to fathom its darkness, and what lies beyond, through the physicality of the body and the materiality of what is at hand.

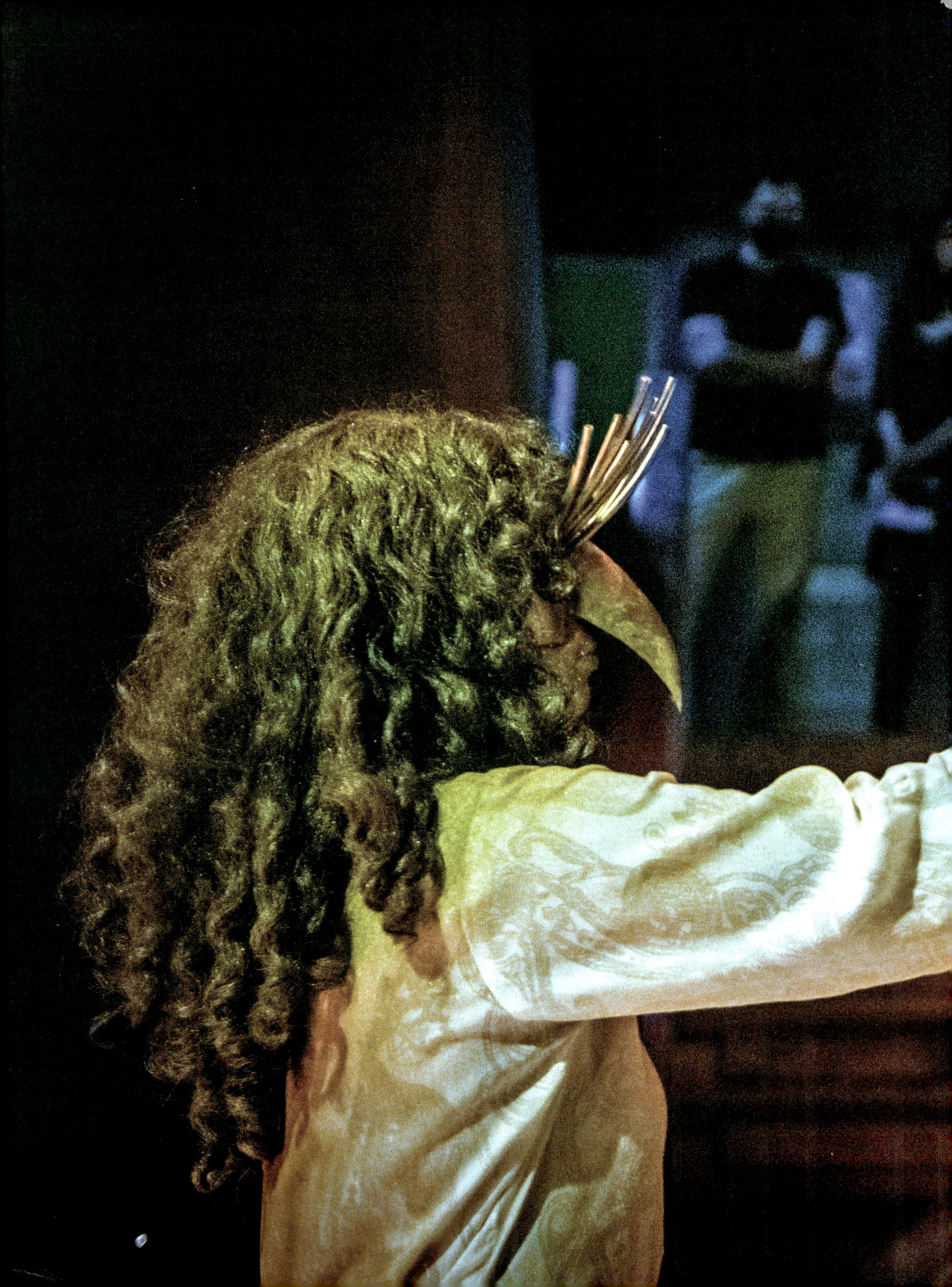

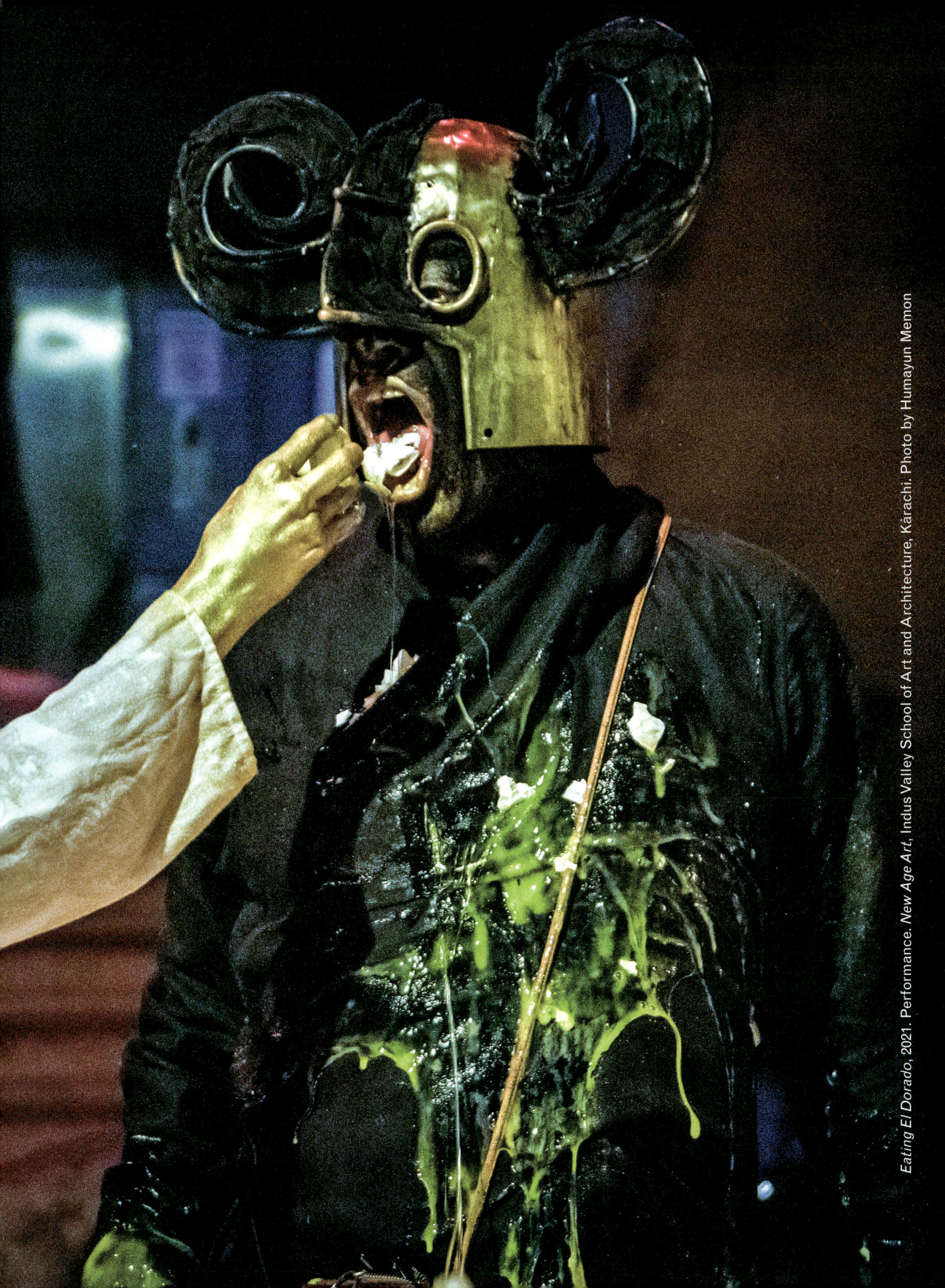

Eating El Dorado, 2021. Performance. *New Age Art*, Indus Valley School of Art and Architecture, Karachi. Photo by Humayun Memon

Contributors

Atteqa Ali is Associate Curator, Arts of Global Asia at the Newark Museum of Art. Her book-length study of socially engaged art in the extended Middle East region is entitled *Collaborative Art Praxis and Contemporary Art Experiments in the MENASA* (Palgrave Macmillan, 2020). *Play: Subversive Contemporary Art in Pakistan and the Diaspora* (Oxford University Press, 2022) examines subversive practices in Pakistani art at the turn of the millennium. She has also written for several publications, including an essay that examines fundamentalism, terrorism, and art in Pakistan for the anthology, *Contemporary Art: 1989 to Present* (Wiley Blackwell, 2013) and an essay on the impact of institutions in the UAE on contemporary art in the MENASA for the anthology, *Museums in Arabia: Transnational Practices and Regional Processes* (Routledge, 2016). She has organized several exhibitions including a project at Twelve Gates Gallery in Philadelphia entitled "Back to the Future: History and Contemporary Art in the Middle East, North Africa, and South Asia" that considered the work of artists utilizing historical references to talk about current social and political events.

Maryam Ekhtiar is currently Curator in the Department of Islamic Art at the Metropolitan Museum of Art. She began working at the museum in 2003 as a specialist in the field of 19th century Persian art and culture, calligraphy, and later Persian painting. She received her Ph.D. from the Department of Middle Eastern Studies at New York University in 1994 and has worked and taught at various museums and universities, namely the Brooklyn Museum, New York University, and Swarthmore College. Dr. Ekhtiar was a key member of the curatorial team involved in the extensive reinstallation of the MET's galleries of the Arab Lands, Turkey, Iran, Central Asia, and Later South Asia, which opened in 2011, and co-editor of the catalogue of masterpieces from the museum's collection of Islamic Art. In addition, she co-edited *Art of the Islamic World: A Resource for Educators* which was released in 2012 and has organized several exhibitions and written articles and lectured extensively in the fields of Iranian art and contemporary art from the Middle East. Her latest book, *How to Read the Art of Islamic Calligraphy*, was published by the MET in 2018. She continues to present, publish and organize exhibitions in her areas of expertise.

Oleg Grabar (1929-2011) attended the University of Paris, where he studied ancient, medieval, and modern history, before moving to the US in 1948. He completed degrees from both Harvard and the University of Paris in 1950. In 1955, he obtained a Ph.D. from Princeton University. He served on the faculty of the University of Michigan in 1954–69, before moving to Harvard University as a full professor. In 1980, Grabar became Harvard's first Aga Khan Professor of Islamic Art and Architecture. He was a founding editor of the journal Muqarnas in 1983. He became emeritus from Harvard in 1990, and then joined the School of Historical Studies at the Institute for Advanced Study, becoming emeritus there in 1998. Professor Grabar's major works include *City in the Desert: Qasr al-Hayr East* (Harvard University Press, 1978), *The Shape of the Holy* (Princeton University Press, 1996), *The Mediation of Ornament* (Princeton University Press, 1992), *The Great Mosque of Isfahan* (New York University Press, 1990), *Epic Images and Contemporary History: The Illustrations of the Great Mongol Shahnama*

(University of Chicago Press, 1980), and *The Formation of Islamic Art* (Yale University Press, 1973).

Salima Hashmi is an artist, contemporary art historian and curator. Professor Hashmi was the founding Dean of the Mariam Dawood School of Visual Art and Design at Beaconhouse National University, Lahore. She taught at the National College of Arts, Lahore, for 31 years and was also Principal of the College for four years. She has written extensively on the arts. *Unveiling the Visible: Lives and Works of Women Artists of Pakistan* was published in 2002. Her books also include *Memories, Myths, Mutations: Contemporary Art of India and Pakistan*, co-authored with Yashodhara Dalmia (Oxford University Press, 2006). She also edited *The Eye Still Seeks: Contemporary Art of Pakistan* (Penguin Books, 2014.)

Dominique Malaquais (1964-2021) was an art historian and political scientist. She worked mostly collectively, in her own name and under various pseudonyms. Her work addressed intersections between political violence, economic inequity and the making of urban cultures in the late capitalist present. She held teaching positions at Sarah Lawrence College and Columbia and Princeton Universities in the US and at Sciences Po in France. Later, she was Senior Researcher at the National Center for Scientific Research (CNRS) in Paris and taught at École des Hautes Études en Sciences Sociales. Dominique was the author of several books and numerous articles. Publications include two edited volumes—one a reflection on Africa-Asia exchanges as seen through the visual arts, literature, urbanism and spirituality (with Nicole Khouri) and the other on the archival turn in contemporary Africa-based and Diaspora arts (with Maëline Le Lay and Nadine Siegert). Among her other curatorial and research undertakings were: *Panafest Archive*, a cross-media initiative on Pan-African festivals of the 1960s and 70s (with Cédric Vincent) linked to a web documentary by the same name and *Dakar 66*, an exhibition held at Musée du Quai Branly-Jacques Chirac, Paris (with Sarah Frioux-Salgas and Cédric Vincent); *Kinshasa Chronicles*, an exhibition about Kinshasa as seen through the eyes of its youngest and most experimental arts practitioners (2018-2021 – MIAM, Sète and Cité de l'Architecture & du Patrimoine, Paris, with Androa Mindre Kolo, Fiona Meadows, Claude Allemand, Sébastien Godret, Mega Mingiedi, Jean-Christophe Lanquetin); *Yif Menga* (with Julie Peghini), a film/teaching/publication/exhibition/colloquia project on performance as politics. Dominique was Associate Editor of the Pan-African platform Chimurenga and sat on the editorial board of the arts journal *Savvy*. She was a past President of the Arts Council of the African Studies Association (ACASA).

John McCarry received his BA from Yale in East Asian Studies. His writing has appeared in *National Geographic* and *GEO* and in the Pakistani news magazines *Herald* and *Newsline*. He is the author of *County Fairs* (National Geographic Society, 1997) and co-editor, along with Niilofur Farrukh and Amin Gulgee, of *Pakistan's Radioactive Decade: An Informal Cultural History of the 1970s* (Oxford University Press, 2019). He has served as coordinator of the Amin Gulgee Gallery in Karachi since its inception in 2000.

H.M. Naqvi is an award-winning author. His debut, *Home Boy*, was hailed as a "remarkably engaging novel that delights as it disturbs" by the *New York Times*, included in *The Guardian*'s list of "Best Pakistani" and "Best 9/11" novels, and awarded the DSC Prize for South Asian Literature. His second book, *The Selected Works of Abdullah the Cossack,* was called a "delirious love letter to Karachi" by the *Wall Street Journal*. Naqvi has worked in the financial services industry and taught creative writing at Boston University and the Lahore University of Management Sciences. Over the years, he has appeared on CNN, NPR, and BBC World Service.

Kishwar Rizvi is the Robert Lehman Professor in the History of Art, Islamic Art and Architecture at Yale University. Her recent publications include *The Transnational Mosque: Architecture and Historical Memory in the Contemporary Middle East* (University of North Carolina Press, 2015), for which she was selected as a Carnegie Foundation Scholar, and *Emotion, and Subjectivity in Early Modern Muslim Empires: New Studies in Ottoman, Safavid, and Mughal Art and Aulture*, editor, (Brill, 2017). Her earlier publications include *The Safavid Dynastic Shrine: History, Religion and Architecture in Early Modern Iran* (British Institute for Persian Studies, I. B. Tauris, 2011) and the anthology, *Modernism and the Middle East: Architecture and Politics in the Twentieth Century* (University of Washington Press, 2008), which was awarded a Graham Foundation publication grant. Professor Rizvi's fieldwork includes research in several parts of the Middle East, including Turkey, Saudi Arabia, Iran, and the United Arab Emirates. Current projects include research on contemporary museums in the Gulf as well as a new book on the Safavid ruler, Shah Abbas, and global early modernity. Kishwar Rizvi teaches undergraduate introductory surveys on Islamic art and architecture, as well as seminars on art historical methods, the representations of kingship, and art and politics within a transnational context. Her courses focus on modern and contemporary architecture in the Middle East; the global Renaissance; Ottoman, Safavid and Mughal art and architecture; on the intersection between painting and poetry in Persianate art; and on the artistic, cultural, and political significance of illustrated travel literature in Europe and the Middle East from the medieval period to the present.

Robert Sagerman holds a Ph.D. in Hebrew and Judaic Studies from New York University (2008), as well as Masters Degrees in Religious Studies, Art History and Fine Art. He has written extensively on the intersection of Jewish and Christian mysticism, Sufism and art history in the Middle Ages and Renaissance. Among his published work is the monograph *The Serpent Kills and the Serpent Kills Life: The Kabbalist Abraham Abulafia's Response to Christianity* (Brill, 2010). He has worked for two decades as a fulltime artist, having had more than thirty solo exhibitions of his paintings, primarily in the US and Europe.

Zarmeene Shah is an independent curator, an academic, and writer currently based in Karachi, Pakistan. Focusing on global contemporary art with specialist knowledge of the Global South, and Pakistan in particular, Shah's research-based practice investigates ideas of power and control, geography and territory, rights and access. Since 2010, she has curated and been involved in the production of several notable and often large-scale exhibitions of contemporary art institutionally and independently, including *The Rising Tide: New Directions in Art From Pakistan* (2010), the 4th Cairo Video Festival (2011), the politically focused *Parrhesia I & II* shows (2011 & 2015), AltheaThauberger's *Pagal Pagal Pagal Pagal Filmi Dunya* (2017), and Madiha Aijaz's *Memorial for the Lost Pages* at CAG Vancouver (2020). Amongst other prominent projects and appointments, she has served as Assistant Director and Curator of the Mohatta Palace Museum (2013), and Curator-at-Large of the inaugural Karachi Biennale in 2017 (KB17). She is currently Associate Professor at the Indus Valley School of Art and Architecture, where she has previously served as Head of the Liberal Arts program, and has recently been appointed Director Graduate Studies.

Gemma Sharpe is an art historian specializing in modern and contemporary art from South Asia, Cold War histories of art, and museum and exhibition studies. Between 2010 and 2014 she lived in Karachi, Pakistan, where she was a Lecturer in Art History at the Indus Valley School of Art and Architecture and a coordinator at Vasl Artists' Association. She received her Ph.D. from the Graduate Center, City University of New York in 2019 and was a Postdoctoral Research Associate at the same institution between 2019 and 2021. She is currently a Getty/ACLS Postdoctoral Fellow in the History of Art (2022-23). She joined the Cleveland Institute of Art as Assistant Professor in Art History in 2023.

Simone Wille is an art historian, based in Vienna. From 2016 to 2021 she directed the research project *Patterns of Trans-regional Trails: The Materiality of Art Works and their Place in the Modern Era, Bombay, Paris, Prague, Lahore, ca. 1920s to early 1950s* (P29536-G26) and from 2021 to 2025 she directed the research project *South Asia in Central Europe: The Mobility of Artists and Art Works between 1947 and 1989* (V 880-G), both fully funded by the Austrian Science Fund FWF. Wille is affiliated with the University of Innsbruck where she regularly lectures on transnational developments of 19th and 20th century modernist art. Her publications include her book *Modern Art in Pakistan: History, Tradition, Place* (Routledge, 2015) and the edited volume *André Lhote and his International Students*, Zeynep Kuban, Simone Wille (Innsbruck University Press, 2020). Her research focuses on 19th and 20th century transnational modernist art; South Asian modernism; socialist communist movements; decentered, multi-site, mobile and "entangled" accounts of modernist art-trajectories and networks.

Alexi Worth received his BA from Yale and his MFA from Boston University. He has had numerous solo exhibitions at Elizabeth Harris Gallery (New York), Bill Maynes Gallery (New York) and DC Moore (New York). Recent group exhibitions include *Open Windows*, curated by Carroll Dunham at the Addison Gallery (Andover); *Private Future*, curated by Michael Cline at Mark Jancou (New York); and *In A Violet Distance*, curated by David Humphey at Zurcher Studio (New York). He has received awards from the Guggenheim Foundation, Tiffany Foundation and New England Foundation for the Arts. Worth has written for *The New Yorker*, *Artforum*, *T magazine*, *Art in America*, *ARTnews* and *Slate*. He has written catalog texts for artists such as Martha Armstrong, Carroll Dunham, David Humphrey, James Hyde, Susan Jennings, Jackie Saccoccio, George Nick, Jim Nutt and Philip Pearlstein. Worth lives in Brooklyn NY with his wife, the architect Erika Belsey, and their two boys. He is represented by DC Moore Gallery (New York).

Artist's Acknowledgements

Looking back is always difficult for me. Without the love and support of the many people who believed in me, the process of compiling this tome would have been painful. I am truly grateful to the writers who contributed to this monograph. Oleg Grabar's and Kishwar Rizvi's essays first appeared in the catalogue of *Drawing the Line*, my solo exhibition at Galeri Petronas in Kuala Lumpur in 2007. All other articles were written specifically for this project. My editor, John McCarry, and I asked individuals to comment on my trajectory. The approach and length of the piece were entirely up to them. The people invited to this party ranged from academics, curators, critics, novelists, to visual artists. I am so touched that they all showed up. I appointed John the task of writing individual texts for each one of my performances and curatorial projects since he was a witness to them.

I have been a practicing artist for over 30 years and, since I do not teach, my priority is in the making. I had hundreds of slides stored carefully in plastic jackets. I am so thankful to Hormuz Irani, who developed my website (www.gulgeeamin.com), who meticulously scanned them. (I had to explain to him what a slide was because the technology was from before his time!) Over a period of two years, Kiran Ahmad and I pored over the images, attempting to bring order to my chaos. Her clean and clear design philosophy was invaluable. We decided to cull a lot of my earlier works from the sculpture section and instead show only certain works from each series. Also, we chose only a selection of pieces for the installation and public works sections of the book. Her humor and stamina kept me breathing throughout this long birthing. I would also like to mention Bilal Ghouri, who has done many of the videos of the performances and exhibitions which appear as QR codes in this story. His invisible presence and astute eye created sensitive documentation. The images I have used are by photographers I have worked with over time. I have the greatest respect for their vision and insight. I am also indebted to Hussain Dada, who not only copyedited this monograph, but held my hand spiritually through this journey.

Lastly, I would like to acknowledge my late mother and father, Zaro and Gulgee. Without their blessing and support, John and my partnership would not have been possible in Pakistan. The last time I saw my mother was on the afternoon of December 13, 2007. Being the Aga Khan's birthday, a day special for my family, she brought over a new painting by my dad as a gift for the two of us. "*Beta* (son) look at it," she marveled. "These are the colors of life!" She accepted an offered glass of white wine and sat down on my couch. Focusing her intense gaze on me, she said, "I need you to do three things. One, give up smoking; two, do a book on your work; and three... I don't remember now, but it will come to me." I never found out what the third thing was.

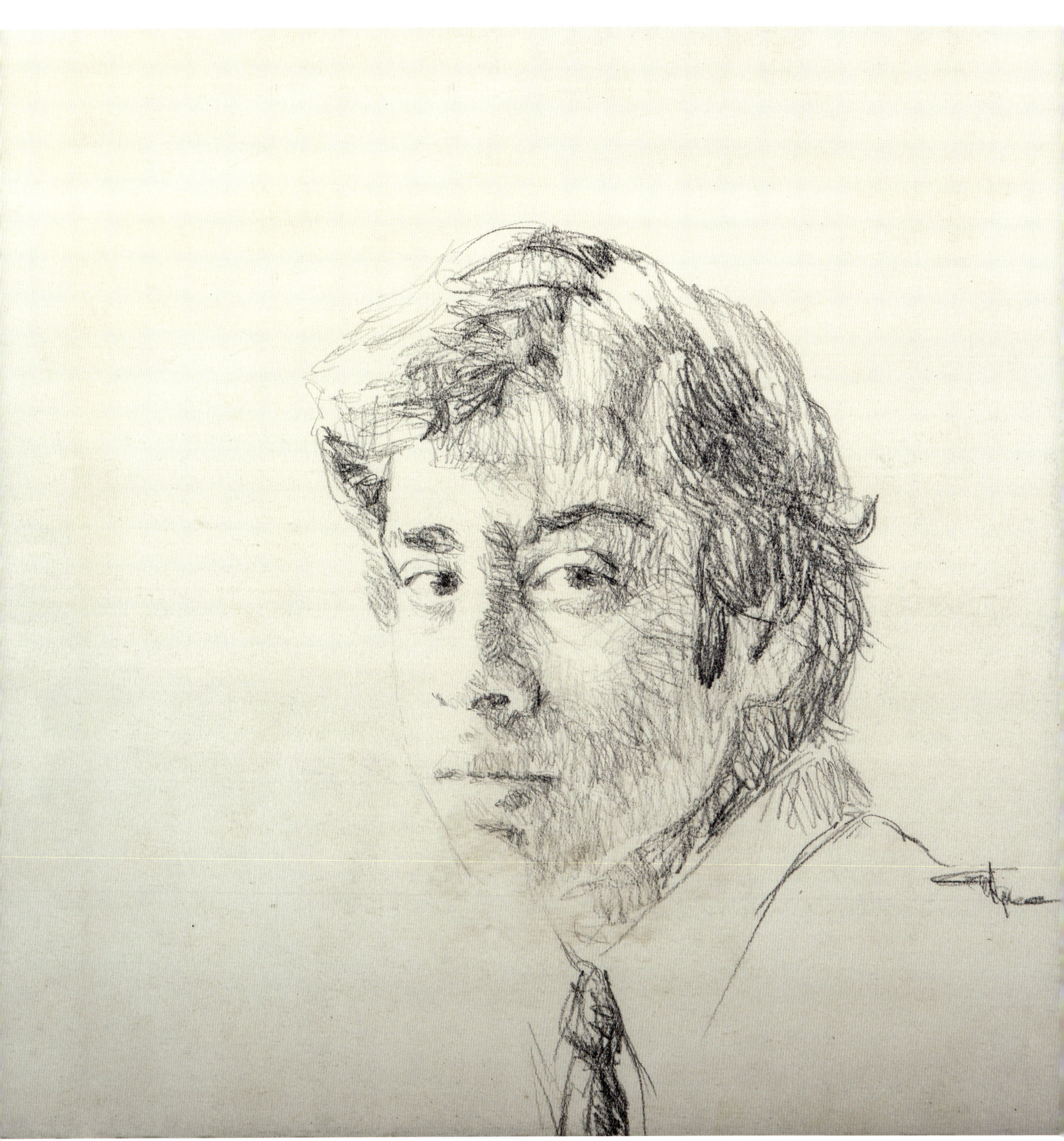

Ismail Gulgee. *Portrait of My Son*, 1982. Pencil on paper. 36.5 × 36.5 cm

Front Cover
Amin Gulgee wearing *Shattered Mask*, first performed in 2014 for *Paradise Lost*, Frere Hall, Karachi. Photograph by Humayun Memon, 2022

Back Cover
Amin Gulgee wearing *The Copper Mask*, first performed in 2000 for *Alchemy*, Sheraton Hotel, Karachi. Photograph by Humayun Memon, 2022

Design
Kiran Ahmad

Editorial Coordination
Manuela Schiavano

Editor
John McCarry

Copyediting
Hussain Dada
Noa Strada

Layout
Kiran Ahmad
Faycal Zaouali

Texts for Performance, Amin Gulgee Gallery and Curatorship by
John McCarry

Supported by
Zahid Majeed
Karim and Almas Tellis

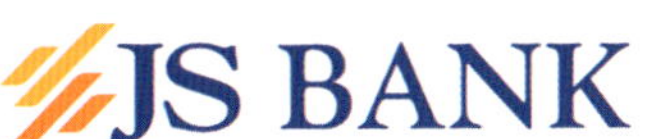

First published in Italy in 2024 by
Skira editore S.p.A.
Via Agnello 18
20121 Milano
Italy
skira-arte.com

Printed and bound in Italy. First edition

ISBN: 978-88-572-5292-6

Distributed in USA, Canada, Central & South America by ARTBOOK | D.A.P. 75 Broad Street Suite 630, New York, NY 10004, USA.
Distributed elsewhere in the world by Thames and Hudson Ltd., 181A High Holborn, London WC1V 7QX, United Kingdom.

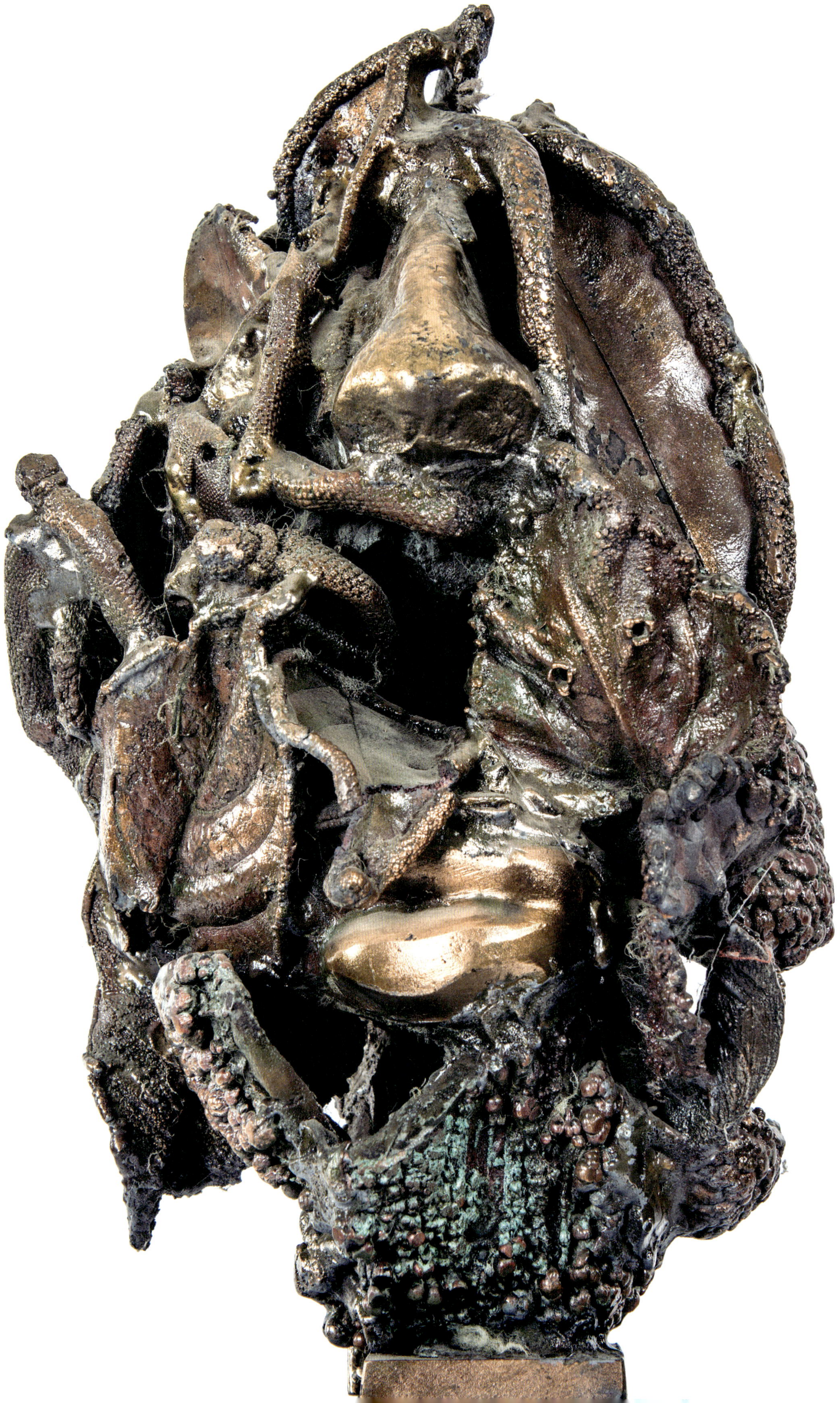

The Conversation, 2016. Detail. Photo by Humayun Memon